COOLIDGE

COOLIDGE

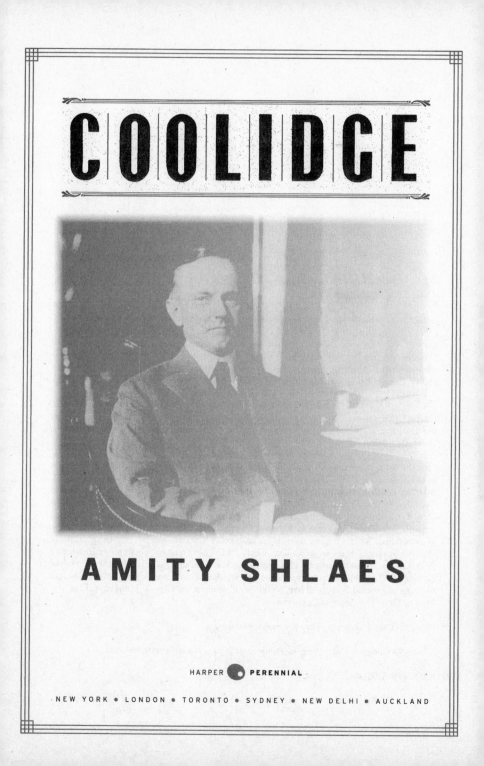

AMITY SHLAES

HARPER ● PERENNIAL

NEW YORK ● LONDON ● TORONTO ● SYDNEY ● NEW DELHI ● AUCKLAND

HARPER ● PERENNIAL

A hardcover edition of this book was published in 2013 by HarperCollins Publishers.

HarperCollins books may be purchased for educational, business, or sales promotional use. For information, please e-mail the Special Markets Department at SPsales@harpercollins.com.

Grateful acknowledgment is made for permission to reproduce the following illustrations in the photo insert: All images courtesy of the Library of Congress unless otherwise noted. BORN ON THE FOURTH OF JULY: Vermont Division for Historic Preservation, President Calvin Coolidge State Historic Site. THE OUDEN, AN EDUCATED FIRST LADY, A SON'S SENSE OF OFFICE: Calvin Coolidge Presidential Library and Museum at Forbes Library. A STRIKE TO END ALL STRIKES: Walter P. Reuther Library. THE ALLY, A NOTARY'S INAUGURATION, WONDER BOY, REST AT LAST: Corbis. SURPRISINGLY LOQUACIOUS: Jay N. "Ding" Darling Wildlife Society. TECHNOLOGY AS KEY: Getty. "I DO NOT CHOOSE TO RUN FOR PRESIDENT IN NINETEEN TWENTY-EIGHT": Photograph by Susan Strange, courtesy of the Library of Congress. A DIFFICULT DECISION: Forbes Library. A TEST OF CHARACTER AND FEDERALISM: Vermont Historical Society, Barre, Vermont. Photographer: Grover Templeton. LIKE THE MEN OF OLD: The Granger Collection.

FIRST HARPER PERENNIAL EDITION PUBLISHED 2014.

Library of Congress Cataloging-in-Publication Data is available upon request.

ISBN: 978-0-06-196759-7 (pbk.)

18 OV/RRD 10 9 8 7 6 5 4

FOR ELI, THEO, FLORA, AND HELEN
WITH RESPECT FOR THEIR PERSEVERANCE

CONTENTS

TIMELINE

1872: John Calvin Coolidge is born on July 4 at Plymouth Notch, Vermont.

1875: Abigail Grace Coolidge, a sister, is born.

1885: Death of Victoria Moor Coolidge, Coolidge's mother.

1890: Death of Coolidge's sister, Abigail. Graduation from Black River Academy.

1891: Coolidge enters Amherst College.

1895: Coolidge is graduated from Amherst College cum laude. Coolidge reads the law in Northampton, Massachusetts.

1897: Coolidge passes Massachusetts Bar and opens law practice. He is appointed to Republican City Committee.

1898: Coolidge appointed Northampton city councilman.

1900: Coolidge chosen as city solicitor, reelected in 1901.

1901: President William McKinley is assassinated. Vice-president Theodore Roosevelt becomes president of the United States.

1904: Coolidge becomes chairman of Republican City Committee. President Roosevelt elected to a new term.

1905: Coolidge marries Grace Anna Goodhue of Burlington, Vermont.

1906: Coolidges move to Massasoit Street house in Northampton. Their first son, John, is born. Coolidge is elected to lower house of Massachusetts General Court, where he serves through 1909.

1908: Coolidge's second son, Calvin, is born. Republican William Howard Taft elected president.

1910–1911: Coolidge serves as mayor of Northampton. Coolidge's father, John Coolidge, is elected to Vermont state senate.

1912–1913: Coolidge serves in state senate. Democrat Woodrow Wilson elected president, prevailing over President Taft and Bull Moose Party candidate Theodore Roosevelt.

1914–1915: Coolidge serves as president of the Massachusetts Senate.

1916–1918: Coolidge serves as lieutenant governor. U.S. enters World War I.

1919: Coolidge serves as governor of Massachusetts. Boston Police strike.

1920: Republican ticket with Warren Harding of Ohio as presidential candidate and Coolidge as vice-presidential candidate wins U.S. election.

1921–1922: Coolidge serves as U.S. vice president.

1923: At President Harding's death, Coolidge becomes U.S. president.

1924: Death of Coolidge's son, Calvin. Thomas Edison and Henry Ford visit the Coolidges at Plymouth.

1924: Republican ticket with Calvin Coolidge as presidential candidate and Charles Dawes as vice presidential candidate prevails over both Democrats and Progressive Party's Robert M. La Follette, Sr.

1925: Coolidge works on tax legislation. Summer White House located in Swampscott, Massachusetts. Coolidge delivers "Toleration and Liberalism" speech in Omaha.

1926: Key tax legislation becomes law. Coolidge spends summer in the Adirondacks at White Pine camp. Coolidge delivers historic speech on the primacy of the Constitution in Philadelphia.

1927: Flood of Mississippi. Flight of Charles Lindbergh. Coolidge makes statement: "I do not choose to run for president in 1928." Flood in Vermont. Coolidge vetoes McNary-Haugen Act, opposing government price fixing in agriculture.

1928: Coolidge vetoes McNary-Haugen legislation a second time. Coolidge and Secretary of State Frank Kellogg steward Kellogg-Briand Pact through Congress. Republican Herbert Hoover is elected thirty-first president of the United States.

1929: Coolidges retire in Northampton, Massachusetts. Stock market crash.

1930–1931: Coolidges purchase the Beeches, their final home. Coolidge pens successful newspaper column.

1932: Coolidge campaigns for President Hoover, who loses to Democrat Franklin Delano Roosevelt. Heavy unemployment.

1933: Coolidge passes away.

INTRODUCTION: THE CURSE

DEBT TAKES ITS TOLL.

To no one had this ever seemed clearer than to a sixty-one-year-old farmer named Oliver Coolidge who languished in Woodstock Common Jail in Windsor County, Vermont, in the spring of 1849. Coolidge was behind bars because he owed a neighbor, Frederick Wheeler, $24.23. He had not honored a contract because he lacked the money to honor it. Now his debt had climbed to $29.48 because the justice of the peace had ruled that he had to carry the costs of the creditor, $5, and a fine of 25 cents for the serving of papers.

Oliver Coolidge's fate was all the more troubling because some of his relations were faring well. The Coolidge name enjoyed respect throughout Windsor County, in the neighboring state of Massachusetts, and across the rest of New England. Carlos Coolidge, a distant cousin, was serving as governor of Vermont. Coolidge's older brother, Calvin, owned the family farm at Plymouth Notch, a hamlet not far from Woodstock. Oliver's rage built as he thought of his brother. Over the years Oliver had deeded land or land rights to Calvin: one of the properties involved had been called the limekiln lot.

The lot lay on a hill in Plymouth Notch. Some of those transfers Oliver had thought temporary. He had given one piece of land, he reminded Calvin in a letter, against "your promis that you would redeed at any time." But now Calvin would not give the farm back. The Calvin Coolidges had decided to keep the land "in the family." That meant the

Calvin Coolidge branch. This was especially bitter. Calvin might pass land that had been Oliver's on to his own son, Calvin Galusha Coolidge, or to a grandson.

Cases like Oliver's had always been common. Back in 1786 a Massachusetts man named Daniel Shays had led a rebellion against heavy taxes. The aggrieved followers of Shays called for a time when there would be "no more courts, nor collectors, nor sheriffs, nor lawyers." Ever since then New Englanders had quarreled over whether debt was the fault of the borrower, the lender, or those who issued the currency. They had quarreled too over the merits of punishments for debt. To sit in prison for debt, or a charge related to debt, was perverse. Vermont laws were changing so that debt alone could not justify imprisonment. A few years earlier a book about the sin of sanctimony and the grace of forgiveness, *A Christmas Carol*, had been published. Its villain was the miser Ebenezer Scrooge. The journals of New England featured *A Christmas Carol* on their Christmas list; its author, Charles Dickens, often pointed out the trap of the debtor's situation and the absurdity of debtors' prison. That same year, 1849, newspapers were serializing a new Dickens work in which one of the main characters, Mr. Micawber, landed in debtors' prison.

It was a text older than Dickens that sprang to Oliver Coolidge's mind: the Bible. To Oliver it seemed that his brother Calvin and his sister-in-law resembled Ananias and Sapphira in the Acts of the Apostles. These two had sold their land and pretended to give the entire proceeds to the apostle Peter but secretly withheld part of what they had received. For that, God had struck Ananias and Sapphira dead. The farmer blamed his brother for participating in the events that had led him to be "shut up" in jail and accused the brother of pressuring his son, Calvin Galusha, to go along with him in whatever scheme furnished the precondition for Oliver's loss of land: "You teased Galush until it was done," the farmer wrote.

That year spring came late to Vermont, with heavy snows into April. As Oliver weighed the damage of debt, the demons closed in. Lame in one leg from birth, Coolidge had never been able to farm as well as the others. The land they all farmed was rocky in any case, but his land was of poorer quality than his brothers'. Oliver and his wife, Polly, had many more children than the rest and though many were grown and some had died, there were others still to care for. His family had seen, as he wrote in one letter from the prison, "mutch sickness."

On Central Street outside the jail, the traffic of carriages and trades-men moved all day long. From behind the walls and the stone fence, the farmer sent out despairing letters in his idiosyncratic spelling to one family member after another. To his niece Sally, Oliver grieved that "my health is not good, I have the rumities in my back so that it troubles me to get to and from my bed." To his brother he expressed anguish for his wife, Polly, at home. In the past Polly had "labored hard early & late to make her family comfortable and still labours hard." On April 29, 1849, Coolidge sat down to rhyme out in quatrains all that was wrong with the world. He scratched out a curse upon his brother Calvin's head:

> *But if still you will reject him*
> *And his council set at nought*
> *O how you will fear and tremble*
> *When to judgement you are brought*
> *O has God your soul for saken*
> *Has he past your spirit by*
> *Has that holy spirit left you*
> *In your sins to sink an die.*

There was something irrevocable about the curse. It seemed too late, as well, to right a life like Oliver Coolidge's. His debts might never be paid. Death loomed. There was nothing left to do but succumb.

Yet Oliver did not succumb. He persevered and was released from the prison. His story took an unexpected turn: the aging farmer and his wife, Polly, then traveled west; Oliver spent time in Columbia County, Wisconsin. Oliver, Polly, and their children began new lives. Polly somehow traveled even farther, to Minnesota, where she was buried. Instead of dying out in Windsor County, Vermont, the Oliver Coolidges and other migrants like them populated the Midwest.

There have been times when the American people, like Oliver Coolidge, lost heart, feeling themselves locked in a prison of their own making. There have been times when debt pinned down the United States as it once pinned down Oliver. One such moment came after World War I, when the national debt hit $27 billion, a level nine times higher than what it had been just a few years before. Income tax rates were high. Jobs were becoming scarce. Angry veterans roamed the streets of cit-ies, furious that they could not pay prices for food or clothing that were double what they had been before the war. The country did seem lost, if not cursed. Yet within a few years the panic passed and the trouble eased. The curse became blessing. The reversal was in good measure due to the perseverance of one man. That man was in fact the heir to the contentious limekiln lot, the great-grandson of Oliver's brother Calvin: Calvin Coolidge, the thirtieth president of the United States.

Born in 1872, almost a quarter century after Oliver left Vermont, Calvin Coolidge, the president, never lost his land as Oliver did. In the bookkeepers' ledgers at Plymouth Notch, the president's father, like his grandfather and great-grandfather, fell on the precious creditor side of the line. Yet from the start in the hamlet to his death in 1933, Calvin Coolidge did confront challenges. The acres he inherited were so poor that the men in the Midwest laughed when they recalled it, more rock and hill than dirt. When Coolidge reached high school age his family sent him to school in Ludlow, twelve miles from Plymouth, and often he walked. Death visited Coolidge constantly; he lost his mother, probably to tuberculosis, the winter he was twelve; the ground was so frozen she could not be interred for weeks. Several years later, Coolidge's companion and only sibling, Abigail, died suddenly and of mysterious causes. Young Coolidge himself was always so sickly that both his father and he worried that he might never complete his education. He was deeply shy and found it agonizing to meet even the adults who entered his parents' front rooms.

Adulthood brought more trials. Indeed, to an improbable extent, the chapters of Coolidge's life after childhood are chapters of near failure upon near failure. Coolidge almost didn't leave the village, almost didn't make it at college, almost didn't get a job, almost didn't find a wife, almost disappointed as a state senator, almost stumbled as Massachusetts governor, almost failed to win a place on the Republican presidential ticket in 1920, and almost failed in Washington once he arrived there as vice president in 1921. As president, Coolidge almost failed to win the backing of his party, almost gave in to grief after the sudden death of his sixteen-year-old son, Calvin, Jr., almost capitulated to a recalcitrant Congress and unruly foreign leaders. Surveying the travails of the thirtieth president, some writers have suggested that those personal defeats are the essence of the Coolidge story. They err. Coolidge's is not a story of "Yes, but." It is a story of "But yes." For at every stage, Coolidge did push forward, and so triumph.

Coolidge himself identified perseverance as the key to that triumph. "If I had permitted my failures, or what seemed to me at the time a lack of success, to discourage me," he wrote in his autobiography, "I cannot see any way in which I would have ever made progress." Students of Coolidge so associate Coolidge with perseverance that they often attribute to him a paragraph that he did not write: "Nothing in this world can take the place of persistence. Talent will not; nothing is more common than unsuccessful men with talent. Genius will not; unrewarded genius is almost a proverb. Education will not; the world is full of educated derelicts. Persistence and determination are omnipotent." Those words in fact were printed as filler in newspapers from as early as 1910, often without an author, but they sound so much like Coolidge that people assume he wrote them.

Perhaps the greatest persevering of Calvin Coolidge, the one for which the red-haired president is known best, was his persevering in the very area that plagued Oliver: debt. In his personal life, Coolidge brought saving to a high art. Coolidge was so parsimonious that he did not buy a house in Massachusetts even after he became governor, so careful that the Coolidges owned no car until after he achieved the presidency, so strict about money that his son John never forgot it. Thrifty to the point of harshness, Coolidge rarely relented when it came to money.

Upon learning that Coolidge had become president, acquaintances approached Calvin, Jr., his son, who happened to be working in a tobacco field in Hatfield, Massachusetts. The others told Calvin, Jr., that they would not work anymore if their fathers were president. "If your father were my father, you would," the boy replied. It was as president that Coolidge's saving proved so exceptional. Coolidge hacked away at the federal budget with a discipline tragically missing in his well-intentioned predecessor, Warren G. Harding. Coolidge vetoed fifty bills and turned down new spending, even for projects such as farm subsidies and construction of rural postal roads that would have immensely benefited the region from which he hailed.

The Coolidge budget was fundamentally different from our modern budgets in that military costs, veterans' funding, and the national debt made up more than half of outlays. But the pressure to expand programs was as strong as it is today. Coolidge's budget vigilance was so steadfast it lent itself to caricature; some artists depicted the thirtieth president as a Victorian throwback. The doyenne of the Washington social scene,

Alice Roosevelt Longworth, repeated a line until it became famous: Coolidge looked as though he had been weaned on a pickle. A contemporary paper, the London *Sunday Chronicle*, even published a parody of *A Christmas Carol* with Coolidge in the part of Scrooge.

Yet if Coolidge was a Scrooge, he was a Scrooge who begat plenty. Coolidge served for sixty-seven months, finishing out Harding's term after Harding died in early August 1923 and remaining until early March 1929. Under Coolidge, the federal debt fell. Under Coolidge, the top income tax rate came down by half, to 25 percent. Under Coolidge, the federal budget was always in surplus. Under Coolidge, unemployment was 5 percent or even 3 percent. Under Coolidge, Americans wired their homes for electricity and bought their first cars or household appliances on credit. Under Coolidge, the economy grew strongly, even as the federal government shrank. Under Coolidge, the rates of patent applications and patents granted increased dramatically. Under Coolidge, there came no federal antilynching law, but lynchings themselves became less frequent and Ku Klux Klan membership dropped by millions. Under Coolidge, a man from a town without a railroad station, Americans moved from the road into the air.

Under Coolidge, religious faith found its modern context: the first great White House Christmas tree was lit, an ingenious use for the new technology, electricity. Under Coolidge, the number of local telephone calls went up by a quarter. In Silent Cal's time, Americans learned to chatter. Under Coolidge, wages rose and interest rates came down so that the poor might borrow more easily. Under Coolidge, the rich came to pay a greater share of the income tax.

How did the curse become a blessing? In World War I, government policy had been so dramatic that it was like a great pendulum, swinging wildly back and forth and intimidating those in its path. Coolidge reached out his hand and stilled the pendulum. Or, to put his achievement more simply, Coolidge kept government out of the way of commerce. When in 1929 the thirtieth president climbed onto a train at Union Station to head back home to Massachusetts after his sixty-seven months in office, the federal government was smaller than when he had become president in 1923.

Somehow, the extent of the Coolidge achievement is not known. Coolidge figures infrequently in the great national conversation about presidents; when he does win mention, it is often as a caricature of

Puritanism, Silent Cal, or as a placeholder between Roosevelts. My preceding book was called *The Forgotten Man: A New History of the Great Depression*; in researching that book on the 1930s, I discovered I was writing the prequel, the story of a forgotten president from the 1920s. Getting to know Coolidge, I puzzled out the reasons for his obscurity. Our great presidential heroes have often been war leaders, generals, and commanders. That seems natural to us. The big personalities of some presidents have drawn attention, hostile or friendly: Lyndon Johnson, Franklin Roosevelt. There are plenty of personal events in Coolidge's life, many of them sad ones, but he was principally a man of work. Indeed, Coolidge was a rare kind of hero: a minimalist president, an economic general of budgeting and tax cuts. Economic heroism is subtler than other forms of heroism, harder to appreciate.

The overlooking of Coolidge is in any case a shame, for full knowledge of this president enriches the study of all presidents. Without seeing Coolidge in the ranks, we cannot entirely appreciate the office. In different ways, many ranging far from economics, Coolidge emulated, resembled, or inspired many other presidents. Like John Adams, another plainspoken lawyer from Massachusetts, Coolidge endured dark days as vice president, and at times shared Adams's appraisal of the vice presidency as "the most insignificant office that ever the invention of man contrived." Like Adams and George Washington, Coolidge was uncomfortable in high society. Like Adams and Washington, Coolidge was comfortable with that discomfort. Like Abraham Lincoln, Coolidge frustrated others with his slowness to respond, but acted decisively when he did move. Like Lincoln too, Coolidge lost a son while in office; like Lincoln, he pushed ahead and achieved much despite that loss. Like Grover Cleveland, Coolidge resisted the expansion of government and perfected the use of obscure legislative devices like the pocket veto in the service of that cause. Like Theodore Roosevelt, Coolidge ended a period of corruption and poured great energy into improving the reputation and quality of government service.

Like Woodrow Wilson, he deemed international law the best approach to prevent war, and poured his heart into campaigning for such a treaty. Like Warren Harding, Coolidge understood the value of predictability in government: that a predictable tax policy and predictable policy toward debt were the bases for strong commerce. Like John Kennedy, he looked to the skies and new technology to lift the spirits of the men below. Like Lyndon Johnson, Coolidge was a former vice president who masterfully completed legislative work left unfinished after the untimely death of his predecessor. Like Gerald Ford, Coolidge healed a country with civility after a period of scandal involving his predecessor. Like Ronald Reagan, who did appreciate him, Coolidge understood that a government that was too large could infringe upon freedom. Like Reagan too, Coolidge took a controversial stand against a powerful public-sector union at a key moment in U.S. history, in his case the Boston police—a move that opened a new and calmer era of less union unrest and increased employment. Like George H. W. Bush, Coolidge understood the great importance of civility and character in the presidency, that a man lived not for himself but for service. Like George W. Bush, Coolidge saw that individual freedom and religious faith can go hand in hand, and saw that many Americans believed that too. Like Washington again, Coolidge saw danger in a lengthy incumbency in the office of the president. It was Washington whom Coolidge emulated in his deliberate decision not to seek reelection in 1928.

Our ignorance of Coolidge hurts more than our understanding of the presidency; it diminishes our understanding of his era, and our past. The education in rhetoric, religion, classics, and geometry Coolidge received at his quirky independent school, Black River Academy, and at Amherst College reminds us how our schools have changed since then. Coolidge and the poet Robert Frost never knew much about each other; Coolidge was a Republican, Frost a Grover Cleveland Democrat. But the lives of the pair crossed in odd ways, including at Coolidge's college, Amherst. And Frost's themes—independence, responsibility, character, property rights—also preoccupied Coolidge. There was some of Coolidge as well in the work of Will Rogers, the superstar columnist of the era. Rogers liked the president so much he wrote a column to help Coolidge find work after the presidency. Without knowing Coolidge, Americans cannot know the 1920s.

To be sure, there were areas where Coolidge fell short, as a man or president. He was not always patient. His intuitive sympathy for free markets notwithstanding, Coolidge never fully grasped the damage of his party's pro-tariff plank. He spoke out against intolerance and bigotry, but did too little to stop them. He thought so well of other statesmen that he never foresaw the extent to which Benito Mussolini, Adolf Hitler, or Japanese leaders would take advantage of international disarmament agreements and use those agreements as cover to arm for war. He likewise never entirely foresaw the extent to which succeeding presidents and Congress would diverge from precedent when it came to economic policy. The thirtieth president therefore never imagined the consequences of such a divergence: a depression as lengthy and severe as the one the United States experienced over the ensuing decade.

But there are many fields in which Coolidge surpassed other men and other presidents and set a standard. Most presidents place faith in action; the modern presidency is perpetual motion. Coolidge made virtue of inaction. "Give administration a chance to catch up with legislation," he told his colleagues in the Massachusetts Senate. "It is much more important to kill bad bills than to pass good ones," he wrote to his father as early as 1910. Congress always says, "Do." Coolidge replied, "Do not do," or, at least, "Do less." Whereas other presidents made themselves omnipresent, Coolidge held back. At the time, and subsequently, many have deemed the Coolidge method laziness. Upon examination, however, the inaction reflects strength. In politics as in business, it is often harder, after all, not to do, to delegate, than to do. Coolidge is our great refrainer.

What compelled Coolidge to persevere and enabled him to succeed? The traditions of Vermont and its "hardy self-contained people," as he described them, always inspired him. Respect for the written law animated him, but he also cherished the spiritual and what we call natural law: "Men do not make laws. They do but discover them," he told Massachusetts state senators in 1914. His wife, Grace, one of the most beautiful first ladies, gave him the confidence to move forward. A ferocious discipline in work proved crucial as well. As documented in White House appointment books, whereas other presidents met sporadically with budget advisers, Coolidge met faithfully and weekly with his Budget Bureau director, General Herbert Mayhew Lord. An intuitive understanding of the struggles of small business aided Coolidge. Though he was not, like Margaret Thatcher, born over a storefront, Coolidge was born beside one. A keen sense of timing also helped him: Coolidge, a shrewd politician, knew when to fight and when to wait. A thorough understanding of the devices of government, and a willingness to use them, also proved key. Also crucial was the Coolidge willingness to be unpopular, which he displayed while still governor of Massachusetts, when he stared down the striking Boston police, or when, as president, he turned down his own people, farmers, by repeatedly vetoing subsidies for them.

Always, a philosophy of service inspired Coolidge. He served his family, to whom he was intensely loyal; he served the law and the people. He was among the most selfless of presidents, ranking individual above political constituency and office above individual. Once, on a walk with the president, Senator Selden Spencer of Missouri tried to cheer Coolidge by pointing to the White House and asking, in a joking tone, who might live there. "Nobody," Coolidge replied, "they just come and go."

Much later, in 1969, Richard Nixon spoke of a "silent majority" of Americans who thought progressives went too far; that phrase came not from Nixon but from the past. The advertising executive Bruce Barton wrote in 1919 that "it sometimes seems as if this great silent majority had no spokesman. But Coolidge belongs with that crowd, he lives like them, he works like them, and understands." The teacher who identified the primacy of service for Coolidge was a professor who instructed him in his final years at Amherst College, Charles Edward Garman. Garman, a philosopher, also inspired Coolidge's friend and ambassador to Mexico, Dwight Morrow. Garman spoke of life as a great river journey. The professor told his students that, as Coolidge paraphrased it, "if they would go along with events and have the courage and industry to hold to the main stream without being washed ashore they would some day be men of power." Garman's image of the river, of water, and of his own task as pilot navigating amid the waves defined Coolidge's life.

There is little evidence that Coolidge ever learned much about Oliver Coolidge beyond the name, or that he was aware that the limekiln lot property itself he inherited, along with a mare colt and a heifer calf, had once been part of a family squabble. "I never knew what had become of the descendants of Oliver," Coolidge wrote a cousin, Ada Taintor, who inquired from Minnesota in January 1920. But genealogy always preoccupied Coolidge. Late December 1925, for example, a period crucial for his proposed tax legislation, found Coolidge distractedly writing to the town clerk of Wallingford, Vermont, to inquire about the precise birth and death dates of another ancestor, his great-grandfather Israel Brewer, Calvin Galusha's father-in-law, and the dates when Brewer had paid taxes. The old limekiln lot itself, hardly good for farming and of value mostly only for wood and maple sugar, remained present all through the life of the thirtieth president. As a boy he worked the plot with his father. From his boardinghouse at college, he wrote home to ask if it was throwing off any revenue he might use for necessary expenses. Yet later, the president's sons, John and Calvin, played on the land; Calvin, Jr., liked to collect spruce gum. After the death of Calvin, Jr., at age sixteen, it was up the road to the old limekiln lot that his mother, Grace, went to dig up a young spruce as a memorial to him. She replanted the spruce on the White House grounds so that the president might see it from the windows.

When Henry Ford visited Plymouth, his hosts, the president and his father, gave the automaker a sap bucket from their sugar equipment. In his final days, Coolidge's father leased the lot to a tenant and wrote friendly copy to describe "nice sugar" made by the tenant from the sap collected there. The Coolidge sympathy for tariffs, including tariffs on Canadian maple sugar, grew out of experience; the Canadian product competed with the small harvest of his lot. Toward the end of his presidency, Coolidge journeyed west, partly to call on regions crucial to the Republican Party but also to trace the trail that his forebears, men like Oliver, had blazed. He shipped headstones from Vermont to Wisconsin for the graves of the parents of his grandmother Sarah Almeda Brewer Coolidge, Israel Brewer, and Israel's wife, Sally. Vermont, Coolidge believed, should honor those who had left her and try to understand why they had done so.

Indeed, all his life, and at every station on the great figurative river, Coolidge never ceased to probe the same questions of debt, money, commerce, growth, and prosperity that had so affected Oliver, puzzling over in his mind what might be the right balance. Coolidge's inquiries into political economy were so intense and so fruitful that it is, again, hard to understand why they are not better known. From time to time historians—more than economists—try to blame Coolidge for the Great Depression and therefore downgrade his policies. A market correction was due in 1929. Coolidge himself anticipated that drop. In fact, he fretted over its possible consequences. The country would endure trouble, he knew, yet he remained convinced that arbitrary interventions, experiments, would only prolong the downturn. But the contention that Coolidge can be blamed for the extended double-digit unemployment of the 1930s is a stretch. Many of the events that converted the 1929 break in the Dow Jones Industrial Average from a serious market crash into the decade-long Great Depression took place after Coolidge's presidency or in places far away.

Perhaps the deepest reason for Coolidge's recent obscurity is that the thirtieth president spoke a different economic language from ours. He did not say "money supply"; he said "credit." He did not say "the federal government"; he said "the national government." He did not say "private sector"; he said "commerce." He did not say "savings"; he said "thrift" or "economy." Indeed, he especially cherished the word "economy" because it came from the Greek for "household." To Coolidge the national household resembled the family household, and to her displeasure he monitored the White House housekeeper with the same vigilance that he monitored the departments of the federal government. Our modern economic lexicon and the theories behind it cannot capture Coolidge's achievements or those of his predecessor, Warren Harding.

It is hard for modern students of economics to know what to make of a government that treated economic weakness by raising interest rates 300 basis points, cutting tax rates, and halving the federal government, so much at odds is that prescription with the antidotes to recession our own experts tend to recommend. It is harder still for modern economists to concede that that recipe, the policy recipe for the early 1920s advocated by many men of both political parties, yielded growth on a scale to which we can only aspire today. As early as the 1930s, Coolidge's reputation and way of thinking began their decline. Collectives and not individuals became fashionable. Sensing such shifts, Coolidge at the end of his life spoke anxiously about the "importance of the obvious." Perseverance, property rights, contracts, civility to one's opponents, silence, smaller government, trust, certainty, restraint, respect for faith, federalism, economy, and thrift: these Coolidge ideals intrigue us today as well. After all, many citizens today do feel cursed by debt, their own or their government's. Knowing the details of his life may well help Americans now turn a curse to a blessing or, at the very least, find the heart to continue their own persevering.

ONE

SNOWBOUND

Plymouth

THEY WERE THE ONES who stayed.

They told themselves this as they trudged past the houses up the road to the old lot in the spring snow. The lot itself was a challenge. Farming there was especially difficult because the soil was too rocky; the hill curved up too steeply. For a period the family had burned lime there, but the railroad had not chosen to come to Plymouth and no one could get the lime out. Now, in the 1870s, they found themselves returning to the limekiln lot for humbler, simpler harvests: wood or sugar. The logs could be sold by the cord. The lot lay above their farm, to the west, and sugar maples were plentiful there. In April, they tapped the trees. Their family fashioned the wooden buckets themselves, sometimes branding the bottom with their name in capital letters. They carried the buckets of sap to a sugarhouse, where it was heated and made into syrup. Each year eight hundred to two thousand pounds of maple syrup and hard sugar were produced this way. They liked the trees, which grew up with them, like siblings or children. Others, even relatives, had deemed such harvests paltry. Those others had headed west to the Great Plains, where your prosperity unfurled before you, flat and vast, like a yellow carpet.

But not John and Victoria Coolidge. If the land tested them, they liked that about it. The spring sugaring was only one part of an annual cycle of ingenuity, well established by the time John, of the fourth generation of Coolidges in Plymouth, became an adult, in the 1860s. After the sugaring came other challenges, which one could lay out in a list beside the names of the months: Mend fences. Shear sheep. Weave. Raise horses or puppies. Get the cows to pasture. Plant hay. Get hay in. Even the level fields below the lot were tough to cultivate. Later, in fact, a study would show that not one acre of the land in Plymouth, a town of farmers, was truly arable. Still, the rhythm of the cycle kept them going. By autumn, they were slaughtering animals. The last to be slaughtered was a cow. There was always milking, summer or winter. But without a railroad, milk was like lime: hard to turn into money. Milk spoiled. To sell a calf or a peacock, they had to take it twelve miles by cart to Ludlow, where the depot was.

Because nothing was ever quite sure, it was best to have a hand in everything. John Coolidge kept the small store at the center of the village. He also served as insurance agent, sheriff, tax collector, notary, everything a man could be in a town. John's wife—her full name was Victoria Josephine Moor Coolidge—gardened and sewed. His mother, Sarah, taught Sunday school, delivered babies, and did the weaving. His father, Calvin Galusha, had experimented with peacocks and horses. In 1863, Galusha put out to stud Young Arabian, a fifteen-hand bay with "all the action and command of limb that a cat or greyhound is master of," for a fee of $10. Through his mother Calvin Galusha claimed a trace of Indian blood, and in him there seemed to be the ingenuity of the Native Americans and the Puritans combined.

The stage on which they lived their lives was small: their house, five rooms behind the store; the 1842 church, with a pew for which Calvin Coolidge, John Coolidge's grandfather, had paid $31; a stone schoolhouse; and a few other farms. Beyond the store, a few dozen rods away, about two or three hundred feet, lay the house of Calvin Galusha and his wife. Beyond that were the lakes, the river, and the twelve-mile trip down the steep hill to Ludlow. In the old days there had been cabins; now the houses in Plymouth, Plymouth Union, and other hamlets in the area were mostly white clapboard, with red barns. While the weather was still warm, John Coolidge and Calvin Galusha traveled about the county or the state, often on official business but always keeping an eye out for new ways to gain a livelihood. There had been a gold rush in the area back in 1859, with several hundred miners converging on the town that June, claiming to find four to eight dollars' worth a day. Disappointment had followed excitement. "Gold is found upon the farm of Mr. Amos Pollard near Plymouth Pond," the paper in Ludlow, Massachusetts, had written. "The metal is so diffused that it costs more to get it than it comes to." Granite too had been found here in Plymouth, enough for fence posts but nowhere near the amounts that could be mined in other parts of the state, such as Barre, Vermont, which called itself the "Granite Center of the World." Windsor County had always suffered bad luck: long ago the state capital had started out in the town of Windsor but had relocated to Montpelier, depriving the area of much commerce. Death came too often, so often that there were two hearses stored in the town, one on wheels for summer and one on blades for winter. John Coolidge's brother, Julius Caesar Coolidge, had died around the time he had married. Others had wasted away from tuberculosis, or consumption; the cold long winters there seemed particularly hospitable to the illness, which was known as the "New England disease." Victoria seemed susceptible.

To explain their life to themselves, villagers like the Coolidges turned to the classics: the plays of William Shakespeare, other old English texts, and the Greeks and Romans. They saw analogies in the stories of rebels after whom they were named: Oliver Cromwell, John Calvin, or Julius Caesar. It was to Julius Caesar that Mark Antony had "thrice presented . . . a kingly crown, which he did thrice refuse." In Plymouth at town meetings citizens also invoked Cincinnatus, who left his plow to serve in Rome as dictator, settled a dispute among warring tribes, then returned to his plow once the crisis was past rather than settling into dictatorship. There were also, of course, analogies to the American Revolution; it was a matter of lively debate in Vermont whether Brutus had been justified in his assassination of Caesar, or whether Ethan Allen had been right in playing off New York, the new Congress, and Canada against one another.

Church and church meetings filled any time that remained in their days. And the Bible was the villagers' basic text; it reached everywhere, even into their cooking. The Coolidge family recipe collection contained instructions for "Scripture Cake":

One cup of butter. Judges 5:25
Three and one half cups flour. I Kings 4:22
Two cups sugar. Jeremiah 6:20
Two cups raisins. I Samuel 30:12
One cup of water. Genesis 24:17
Two cups figs. I Samuel 30:12
Two cups almonds. Genesis 43:11
Six eggs. Isaiah 10:14
One tablespoonful honey. Exodus 16:31
A pinch of salt. Leviticus 2:13.
Spices to taste. I Kings 10:2
Two tablespoonfuls baking pow. I Cor. 5:6
Follow Solomon's advice for making good boys (Proverb 23:14),
and you will have good cake.
Bake in a loaf and ice.

The autumn made town meetings, churchgoing, even socializing, harder. And snowfall could shut Plymouth Notch off suddenly and entirely, making the steep hill road impassable. Such isolation could come in a matter of hours, as in a poem by John Greenleaf Whittier, "Snow-Bound." "A fenceless drift what once was road," as Whittier had put it. The only way out was to build a new road, an ice road, laboriously, by packing snow over so that a sleigh might slide across the hard surface. Keeping the house warm was another challenge. In the bedroom there was soapstone to be heated on the stove; it warmed the bed for hours at night in the winter. In Whittier's own New England village, Haverhill, Massachusetts, the sun was so weak it gave off, at noon, "a sadder light than waning moon." In such a place, "ere the early bedtime came,"

> *The white drift piled the window frame*
> *And through the glass the clothes line posts*
> *Looked in like tall and sheeted ghosts.*

There was a kind of comfort in the snowbound period; it was the only time the Coolidges had a moment to take stock of their accomplishments. They belonged to no one else; they succeeded because they lived economically. John Coolidge wrote down everything in small notebooks: the taxes to be paid, the taxes to be levied, what might be collected, what might be spent on a trip to Ludlow or Boston. The Coolidges believed that others might succeed as well if they managed similar thrift. The terrifying price of not living within one's means had long been evident, both to them and to others, and could be heard in the family lore they repeated to one another when they told the old stories. The second name of John's father, Galusha, could be heard in some of those stories. Jonas Galusha had been a famous Vermonter who had come to prominence as a captain fighting against General John Burgoyne during the Revolutionary War. When Daniel Shays, the farmer rebelling against debt, had fled north, Galusha had been charged with repulsing the refugees and driving them back south. From 1781, Galusha had served as sheriff of Bennington County, a job where he had come to know the consequences of debt as few know them. Debt collection and cruel laws made enforcement "onerous and perplexing to the last degree," as a later historian put it.

In the Vermont records is the notation of the state's obligation of 10 pounds, 4 shillings, and 6 pence to Galusha for fulfilling the sentence of the Supreme Court of the state by cutting off the ear of one Abel Geer and branding his forehead with the letter "C," probably for "counterfeiter." Such experiences were not easy to forget: debt preoccupied Galusha, an upright dignitary, all his days. Later Galusha went on to serve as judge and governor, holding the latter post for multiple terms. In those final years, he wrote explicitly that he disliked the debt collection process. The reality, Jonas Galusha saw, was that "more money is spent in the collection of such debts than is saved by the collection."

Another Coolidge cousin, Carlos Coolidge, had also served as governor of the state for two years, and in that period too there had been legislation to deal with debt. Nowadays that was not possible: repeated terms for an incumbent offended Vermonters' sense of independence from their own government, so they rotated governors, one year's service each, from the two sides of the Green Mountains. The tradition of one year service would be known as the "Mountain Rule." If a man could stay within his means, if he could stay healthy, this life of independence was the highest choice of all. Some who had left had come back or longed to. In the Plymouth Notch cemetery was the grave of Barton Billings, son of another family daughter, Calvin Galusha's sister Sally. Billings had died in Kansas, and his epitaph read: "Carry me back to old Vermont, where the rills trickle down the hills, there is where I want to lie when I die."

Still, John and Victoria could not help seeing, the majority of the Vermonters who left did not want to come back. Over the years Calvin Galusha, Sarah, and John found themselves lonelier than they imagined. Nor were the Plymouth citizens alone in leaving. In the 1850s alone, 50,000 more had departed Vermont, mostly heading west, than had come in. A factor they had never imagined, the Erie Canal, had made that western migration possible. Talents like the Rutland-born blacksmith John Deere had abandoned Vermont and founded great companies out west.

Indeed, one could argue that it was their own line, John, Calvin Galusha, and Calvin before him, that was breaking tradition by not leaving. A move was not necessarily cowardice; sometimes one moved on to build a better life. Their Coolidge ancestors had left Cottenham, England, and come over in the time of John Winthrop, perhaps even in the same fleet with the *Arbella*. On that voyage, Winthrop had delivered a sermon about living as a model: "Wee shall be as a citty upon a hill, the eies of all people are upon us." Winthrop's City on a Hill was called the Massachusetts Bay Colony, a place where the settlers must improve upon what others had built at home. The Coolidges had made their own city across the river from Boston, in Watertown, where they had fast established a reputation for ingenuity and thrift. Trade with Boston was important, but the Charles River was in the way.

The Coolidge ancestors had worked out a solution: one had built the first bridge across the Charles River by stringing eight-foot baskets across the span, then fortifying it with wood and stone. The settlers of Watertown were not content with an ocean to separate them from old England; they sought political separation. In 1631, the inhabitants of Watertown objected to a levy for public defense imposed from above by their English governors. They, still Englishmen, were being taxed without consent. The result was that free men in the colony were permitted to have representation, elect a governor, and choose a deputy to a general court. Coolidges created and attended some of the first town meetings, helping to establish what would become a familiar form of government in New England.

A Coolidge forefather had signed the Dedham Covenant, which explicitly posited as its goal to keep out those who did not fit: "That we shall by all means labor to keep off from us all such as are contrary minded, and receive only such unto us as may be probably of one heart with us." The reasoning was simple: create virtue and lead by example. Testing virtue—inviting too many different thinkers into your midst—was, in their view, too dangerous. There were still numerous Coolidges all around Boston, many wealthy and distinguished. A few were also descended from Thomas Jefferson.

That first John Coolidge in Plymouth, Vermont, a Revolutionary War soldier, had taken a farm in the town, then known as Saltash, and shortly acquired plots of land for his children. By renaming the town Plymouth the Coolidges and the other settlers signaled to the world now that they were endeavoring to make a yet another "citty upon a hill." The old name under the New Hampshire charter, Saltash, was set aside.

Their new "citty" was really a chain of hamlets: Plymouth Notch, Plymouth Union, Plymouth Kingdom, and others with settlements that had been given less obvious names—Frog City, for example. The Coolidges had become local, married locals, and fallen into the history of those contentious people, invariably taking sides in local conflicts, bloody or pecuniary—the battle of Vermonters versus New Yorkers or debtors versus creditors.

Every July, Calvin Galusha, his son, John, Victoria, and the others marked a number of anniversaries. One was the anniversary of the Declaration of Independence of the thirteen colonies. But there was also the anniversary of the first Battle of Bull Run in the Civil War, to which the state had given many men; Vermont, after all, had been the first state to call for the abolition of slavery in its constitution. Another John Coolidge, a doctor who had served at Antietam, was buried in the little cemetery as well. John and Victoria might remember July 1609, when Samuel de Champlain had discovered the great body of water, Lake Champlain, that now defined their state's border. In July 1777, the Republic of Vermont had made its own declaration of independence at Windsor, a few miles away, announcing that inhabitants of the Green Mountains would "form a government best suited to secure their property, wellbeing and happiness." It had been July 1782 when Ethan Allen, pounding his cane and ranting against the clergy, had finished dictating a book after leading the Green Mountain Boys in battle against their great enemy, New York. All those events and their facts jostled against one another in Vermonters' minds; some preferred the Ethan Allen story to the Civil War or the Revolutionary account.

In July 1872, in the midst of all these anniversaries, the first child of the couple who stayed was born. They named him John Calvin Coolidge, after his father and grandfather, after all the other Johns and Calvins who had gone before. The anniversary that the child's birthday happened to fall on was that of the Declaration of Independence, which the village marked with festivals and an annual game: the men of Plymouth Notch stole an old cannon; the men of Plymouth Union stole it back.

Within months of his son's birth, John Coolidge went to the state capital, Montpelier, to serve as a state legislator, another quest that seemed necessary; if one wanted to ensure that prosperity would be possible in the future of Vermont, one must participate in framing that future. Victoria was young and delicate. Though Plymouth was still a hamlet, the store was its center, and the traffic there wore on the young mother. "I hope you will end your public life this year and then we will retire to some quiet place. I do not care for even the honor of being the representative's wife," Victoria wrote John. But John enjoyed the honor. He was working on soldiers' legislation and told his mother he wanted to prepare so well he could give a speech on the topic. He joined the state committee on reform schools and served on it for the next few years.

Victoria drew consolation from the landscape, sunsets, flowers, and, always, books and reading. One of the first toys the Coolidges gave their new son was a set of blocks with the alphabet on one face and Roman numbers on the other. In 1875, Victoria had a daughter, Abigail Gratia Coolidge, to join Calvin. The education of Calvin and Abbie started with scripture. There was no regular minister at the church; traveling preachers passed through. But Coolidge's grandmother Sarah taught them the Bible by the chapter.

From the start, the entire Coolidge clan focused on training this new son to take his place as a citizen in the Vermont community. When Calvin was three, his grandfather took him up to Montpelier to visit his father the lawmaker and placed the boy in the governor's chair, hewn from the timbers of the USS *Constitution*, known as "Old Ironsides," one of the United States' first ships, authorized by the Naval Act of 1794. The Vermont State House was a grand structure; the governor's chair sat in a large Greek classical office with pedimented windows. On that trip the boy spied a stuffed catamount in the state museum, and that too made an impression upon him.

Soon enough, the children came to know firsthand the challenges of rural life. When Coolidge was just learning to read, his grandfather

Calvin Galusha became ill. The ailing man had his grandson read from the Gospel of John: "And the light shineth in darkness; and the darkness comprehended it not. There was a man sent from God, whose name was John." When he died, Calvin Galusha left Calvin a mare colt and a heifer. He also deeded him "the use and yeald of a certain piece of land" on his farm, forty acres to be passed along as "absolute property" of his grandson's children. That was the limekiln lot. The language the grandfather had chosen rendered the bequest even less valuable: one could hardly borrow against something that could not be given up. The purpose of such an inheritance, the whole family knew, was not merely to pass something on; it was to tie his grandson to the land. Coolidge's grandmother read to him from the Bible, but also from *The Green Mountain Boys*, a book about Ethan Allen: "All that may be sir, but those who know Ethan Allen will laugh at the very idea of there being found a man in New England who can outdo him in feats of either strength or courage." There were also law books lying around the house, along with other texts.

George Washington, who had led his great-great-grandfather's army, loomed large. One of the volumes in the Coolidge house was *Washington and His Generals*. In it the boy read not only of the wars but also of Washington's time as president. Washington had "made his government steady and respected abroad." But he had also served reluctantly; after two terms the first president had seen it unfit to stay on; he had after all, the book said, "pined for the rest of a quiet home."

The adults in Plymouth worked to pass on to the children the skills for the eternal combat with the landscape. Calvin's father could build a cabinet; Calvin also made his own. His grandmother wove fabric, and the women made patchwork quilts; Calvin, at age ten, stitched a quilt top of Tumbling Blocks, a dauntingly sophisticated pattern. His father got the hay in; Calvin raked. His mother tended the lilac bed. The boy could whittle and knew every tree, the mountain ash, the plum, and the lilac bush around his house. The boy's father noted with relief that Coolidge was diligent at sugaring and much later told a reporter proudly that Coolidge could get "more sap out of a maple tree than the other boys around here."

Around the time the children began school, Victoria weakened. Her family often found her abed with an unmentioned illness—consumption, probably. She stayed home from prayer sessions. Religious groups came to her; itinerant ministers stayed at the house. She kept busy with her hands and knit a counterpane for Calvin and his future bride, an emblem of her hope for her son. That left Coolidge and his sister with their father and grandparents, to follow them about and observe the town. Even when small, the boy saw politics firsthand: at town meetings, it was his father who worked or spoke; Calvin sold apples and popcorn at the meetings, as his father had before him. The villagers noticed early that Calvin was always quiet; when someone played the violin, he would not dance, but was always observant. Though by party Plymouth Notch was Republican, it was also intensely democratic; one of the town elders was a Democrat and served as moderator. Some of the documents said, "To act on the following documents, viz.," the old Latin abbreviation for *videlicet*, which meant "that is to say." But the elder always read, "to act on the following questions, vizley" and so was known, with great affection, as Old Vizley. The smallest unit of government was the school district, and much of what went on in Plymouth focused on that: the room and board for teachers were subject to bid, and the family with the lowest bid got the contract. The amount, Coolidge later remembered, tended to hang around $1.25 for two weeks in winter and 50 cents for the same period in summer. It was during his childhood that Plymouth first gave women the chance to vote on school issues.

As the boy soon learned, the political life of Plymouth ran on its own annual cycle. Town officers were chosen at a March meeting, where the town also set the tax rates. There was also bonded debt to manage due to road construction and costs incurred during the Civil War and by the freshet of 1869, one of the many floods that plagued Vermont. Come September there was another meeting, a freemen's meeting, where the town elected its delegates to the state government, as well as to Congress, and presidential electors. At an annual district meeting at the schoolhouse, villagers chose the school officers, such as Calvin's father, and set the rate of the school tax. Everything happened on a small scale of pennies and dollars: collection of a snow tax, payment for care of an indigent. But the town felt itself the basis of all that was above it: the county authorities and state authorities in Montpelier.

The records John Coolidge kept show the painstaking effort of town leaders to budget and manage a small amount of cash. The town paid Coolidge's father $11.40 for superintending the schools; $1 to someone else, unnamed in a town report, for a day's labor; 50 cents to someone else for a half day of work on a road in winter; $104 to a woman, May A.

Sawyer, for keeping a poor or sick man, "C.J.," for one year. That year the town also paid $1 for a pair of shoes for a child. In all, Plymouth's expenses in that year were $3,182. One year the other men of the town wanted to raise a large amount of money with a new tax. John Coolidge abstained from voting, saying that "he did not wish to place so large a burden on those who were less able, and so was leaving them to make their own decision," Coolidge later remembered.

At the store too, the boy could observe the clockwork that was commerce. His father paid $40 a year rent for the store and turned over $10,000 a year in goods. That left room for fat profits. But John and Victoria would not charge high prices to their neighbors; that might turn away business. It was better to operate on narrow margins and hope to sustain volume and trust. John paid his blacksmith $1 a day to run the blacksmith shop. In the store he had to set prices and decide whether to haggle. In the end he took only $100 or so a month profit out of the store business. That was enough to pay for a maidservant around the house and some other expenses, but not enough to live richly. Many people who came to the store borrowed small sums to buy items on credit. Remarkably few did not pay the money back.

The railroad that had come to so many Vermont towns chose yet again not to come to Plymouth in the 1870s and 1880s. John Coolidge rode a wagon to another town to catch the train to Boston for business; he rode the night train to avoid the cost of a hotel. Even the school Calvin attended betrayed the fragility of the Vermont economy. One year all three teachers who taught there wrote "No," one in capitals, on a questionnaire asking "Is the school house in good condition?" The school year began in May and ended in February; the roads were too muddy and the sugaring was too demanding for pupils to take time to go to school in spring. Coolidge did well enough at his studies; he even pulled pranks, as his grandfather Calvin Galusha had in his time. He not only liked practical jokes but saw that others liked them.

But more serious thoughts also ran through the boy's head. His mother read the Romantics, and the style impressed the boy: "From scenes like these, old Scotia's grandeur springs." The town of Plymouth Notch was contemptuous of snobbery: when a maidservant needed a ride in the wagon, the children of the employer would give up their places and stay home. One of the things the Coolidges had fled when they had left Boston was the sanctimony of the Massachusetts Bay Colony. One of the Coolidge children, probably Calvin, penned a romantic short story that reflected both the popularity of Henry Wadsworth Longfellow and Plymouth's skepticism at Puritan sanctimony:

> *Many years before the faithful echo of the Lake has answered the crash of timber as some tall giant of the forest fell beneath the pitiless axe of the white settler, a pale-faced maiden had her home beside the murmuring waters. She had been a Puritan but the stern magistrates had banished her from the cold comfort of their fireside because from natural sympathy for suffering she had shown kindness to one of the detested sect of Quakers.*

A shadow hung over their lives: the melancholy Victoria was becoming sicker. One March, on her thirty-ninth birthday, Calvin and Abbie were called to their mother's bedside. Within an hour she died. "The greatest sorrow" that can come to a boy had come to him, as he later wrote. He took a strand of her hair and preserved it in a locket. From that point on, their grandmother Coolidge, sometimes called Aunt Mede, stepped in, helping to raise both children.

The death hit the boy hard. He grew taller, thin and quiet. People wondered whether he too might be susceptible to consumption; they agreed that his small features and pale looks recalled his mother and fitted the general stereotype of the consumptive. People noticed him walking back and forth along the way to the cemetery. That was how he might be all his life. After all, the simple school in Plymouth was enough, in those days, to qualify both the children as teachers; Abbie even taught one semester in a neighboring town.

But even in the period of grief, curiosity stirred in Calvin. John Coolidge and Aunt Mede thought to send the children where they themselves had studied, Black River Academy in Ludlow. On the morning of the first trip to school, it was icy, which meant a fast ride but a cold one. Coolidge and his father climbed into the sleigh while it was still dark. A calf happened to ride with them, going to market in Boston; John admonished his son that the animal would reach the great city now, but the boy would have to wait for years to be ready. Yet Calvin was in good spirits. As they rounded the hill, the light of day struck them. Much later, the boy would recall the ride as magic: "I was perfectly certain that I was travelling out of the darkness into the light."

One of the first places the boy inspected in Ludlow was the railroad depot. The depot overlooked a mill; in that town there was noise, not only Central Vermont Railway trains heading back and forth but the noise of the mill and the bells from all the churches. For amusement he would visit the railroad yard, formidable in its scale and noise. It was there that Calvin got a sense of what Plymouth was missing. He wrote of his inspection of a shipment from Canada, "saw a fir tree 24 foot in circumference it was a monster." The train made everything possible. Marvelously, he found, he could travel by himself to see relatives. Aunt Sarah Pollard lived at a nearby station in Proctorsville. She was his mother's sister, so it was almost like going home to his mother; his uncle Don ran his own store, and Coolidge could work there, shelving or delivering. Oranges and lemons were making it to that part of the world now, and some fruits were even going to Plymouth, but there was a larger selection in Ludlow. For a time he even worked a job at the Ludlow Toy Manufacturing Company making miniature doll prams or wagons with bright vermilion wheels. The boy put his wages in the Ludlow Savings Bank.

The school itself was its own illumination, and there were others like it all over New England. The school, Black River Academy, Baptist in background, enjoyed great independence; its head could shape its curriculum and had time to get to know the children. Secondary school was not compulsory: parents contracted with schools and paid them. The schools did not always have dormitories. Coolidge would board with friends or acquaintances and attend the school. After a few terms he might return home to Plymouth, as his father and grandmother had, to farm or run the store.

At first it seemed that he wanted to; being on his own was hard. Rooming with friends and hired hands selected by his father was not like life in Plymouth. When his grandmother wrote to him in the spring of 1887, Calvin replied with alacrity, telling her that hers was the first letter to arrive from Plymouth Notch: "I rec. your letter today and was very glad to get it for it was the first one I had rec. from home since I left there almost three weeks ago." The letter featured an ambivalent tone that family members would shortly come to recognize as typical of Calvin: "I am in first rate health and I am having a good time but I wish I was at home for there I could have a better time but having a good time is not everything to think about in this world. I am going to stay to the reunion so tell papa he can come down for me Friday night late or wait until Sat." Calvin hoped to convince his father to send Abbie to join him. In February, 1887, he wrote Abbie, another of his wavering commentaries, "I suppose you are having a good time fact is I know you are having a better time than you will ever have down here though you do not probably see it in that light." At home he was qualified to teach school to elementary pupils, but here at Black River Academy he had, at least at first, trouble keeping up. Most of the pupils at the academy had other obligations; some of them stayed home for one term a year to work. Some, such as Ida May Fuller from Rutland, seemed destined for clerical work. Another classmate, Albert Asa Sargent, came from Ludlow itself. Yet another, Ernest Willard Gibson, came from Londonderry. The pupils from out of town boarded with families in Ludlow. Calvin's roommate was not a pupil at all but a man in his late twenties, a clerk known to his host family, the Boyntons.

Even in that small group, Calvin did not shine. In his first term, he took algebra, grammar, and civil government. His grade average was 83.8. The boy required coaching in several subjects, but especially in an area that would plague him for the next decade: math. He studied, but that did not always help. "I do not expect to pass in algebra," he wrote Abbie in an 1887 letter. He would squeak by with a 71.

Still, over the course of the years in Ludlow, life smoothed over for the red-haired boy. He moved in with other boys his own age from the school, dwelling for a time with another boy from Plymouth, Herbert Moore. Alone, he turned to the library: "he didn't play ball or skate nor did he hunt, swim or fish, or go in for any sports, except that he walked every day," Moore recalled. Instead, he read his way through the library— "every book in it," Herb said.

Little glints of the boy's humorous confidence began to shine through. A classmate recalled later that Calvin used to come to his room in the evening for help with math problems. "I remember one night as he came in he said to the housekeeper: 'Well, I've come down to help Henry do his algebra again.' He said it so solemnly that she asked me afterward if I was falling behind in my algebra." He wrote his father to ask whether his sister might join him in Ludlow. Abbie, a cheerful girl, the opposite of Calvin, did go to study at Black River toward the end of Calvin's career there. She arrived in February 1888, just before a blizzard. Tough where Calvin was hesitant, she wanted to teach again, and directed her father without hesitation. "I hope you can get me a school, and I think you can if you try I don't care where it is," she wrote to her father. Calvin's grades moved up from the low eighties to the low nineties. He moved up to a higher track with more classes, even though that track was more expensive: $7.20 a term instead of the $6 a term for the standard course. He gained an affection for the orations of Cicero and saw that he might use oratory in his own life. His own equivocations continued, whether they referred to humans or the animals he knew: "I do not think she [a cow] is gaining much so I guess she will die but hope she will not." But Cicero did not equivocate, and Calvin began to learn from him.

At home, the rural economy still tested the family. John was wondering how to make better money from dairying. Sheep farming had enjoyed a boom and then fallen back. If a business did survive, it seemed to the Coolidges, that was in part because tariffs protected it. John's work in law enforcement was wearying. A feud that began while he was still at home and continued through Calvin's years at Black River Academy was typical. Over the years a cousin, Warren Taylor, had worked a farm with his father south of Plymouth Union. Taylor had married a woman from Sherburne. To avoid the tax collector, Taylor moved to Sherburne each year in March at tax collection time. In 1884, the selectmen of Plymouth ordered the tax assessor to go to Sherburne and assess Taylor's property there as well. Then Coolidge, the bailiff, was ordered to arrest Taylor and take him to Woodstock Common Jail. But Taylor could not be found.

The schoolboy followed the reports his father gave of each stage of the drama. Taylor paid but then sued, contesting the assessments. In 1887, the county court decided for the town, and John was assigned to collect $269.63, which included back taxes and penalties. In 1889, John Coolidge would arrest Taylor and take him to Woodstock Common Jail, the same one where Oliver had sat four decades before, albeit updated with brick and an addition. Taylor would spend the night in the prison, which he described as a "stone house with an iron bedstead for a couch," among "thieves and ruffians." After his release, Taylor would take John Coolidge to court for improper arrest. William Stickney, an old classmate of John Coolidge who lived in Ludlow, was engaged to represent John. It was an unpleasant business, and one had to ask what it was about the place that put people like Taylor into the straits they were in.

Now, toward the end of the decade, President Grover Cleveland and Congress pulled down the tariff wall as a farmer might pull down an old wall on his property. Cleveland, a Democrat, was a true free-market and hard-money man. Cleveland's consistency inspired many, including an old New Englander, William Prescott Frost, who, transplanted to the West Coast, campaigned for Cleveland with his young son Robert, later to become a poet. Cleveland's change benefited those who used wool to manufacture clothing and other goods, because now, without a tariff, good foreign wool was cheaper. But in the part of Vermont where Coolidge lived, and in Ludlow, the effect of Cleveland's move was to give an unassailable advantage to Australian merino over Vermont merino. The farmers joked about it: they said the lower tariff policy had so decimated the wool farmers that "a Democrat couldn't look a sheep in the face."

In 1888 Coolidge turned sixteen and gave his attention to a national election, that between Cleveland and Benjamin Harrison, for the first time. One question of the contest was protectionism; another was the durability of prosperity: villagers such as Coolidge's father did not always know whether they could comfortably pay that $7.20 a semester for their children's schooling. Calvin became so interested that the contest even penetrated his dreams: "dreamed C carried Ind by some over 4000 and NY by 30." In fact, the election proved wonderfully intricate. Cleveland won the popular vote, but Harrison triumphed in the electoral college, taking the presidency. That was all right with Vermont, which had given Harrison almost three times as many votes as Cleveland.

The spring of Calvin's final year at Black River Academy took a sudden and dark turn. His sister, Abbie, became ill with a fever and terrible pains in her stomach. At first the doctor thought the illness would pass; Calvin was the more delicate one, everyone believed. But Abbie did not get better. Three doctors were brought in, but she died within a few days in March 1890. Years later, the doctors would guess that it was appendicitis that had killed her, but at the time it was just another of those mysteries borne away with the winter hearse. John gave his son an obituary, which Calvin delivered to the newspaper in Ludlow. In April, Coolidge wrote to John, "It is lonesome here without Abbie."

After wavering and despite the death, Calvin began to look forward again. He was finishing well at the academy. A principal who had recently arrived, George Sherman, thought Calvin was college material. Sherman took care to help the boy prepare for his college exams. Sherman was plotting the boy's application to his own college in Massachusetts, a morning's train ride south from Ludlow. Calvin too was considering how his life might be at Amherst and how to soften the isolation of entry.

For graduation, in May 1890, Calvin wrote and memorized a speech about the power of oratory; he noted that it was Cicero's voice, "the force of Cicero's oratory," that had helped drown out dictators and "made even Caesar tremble." The speech was also about the advances Great Britain had enjoyed after free traders had won their case there: "What mighty changes have been wrought in England's political system within the last fifty years by the indomitable energy of such orators as Vincent, Cobden, Bright and scores of others, who traversed the kingdom advocating the repeal of the Corn Laws and other measures which were once deemed Utopian and hopeless." There was an inconsistency between his praise for the free-trade Britons and the pro-tariff rule in his region. It was actually an inconsistency typical of New England, which liked to see old England's markets open even when some of its own were closed. *The Vermont Tribune* lavished praise on him: "Calvin Coolidge gave an historical resume of the influence of oratory in the formation of public opinion and in the great movement of history."

But with school ending, the question pressed: what might Calvin do now back in Plymouth Notch and without Abbie? It was the isolation that troubled them all again. Yet again, John Coolidge was trying a new venture. Without a train or, yet, refrigeration, it was hard to commercialize the milk of Plymouth Notch. He and the nearby farmers therefore thought they would try their hand at making cheese. Cheese, after all, could be preserved and could withstand slow transport. Breaking the old rule of do-it-yourself, they imported a cheese expert from Shrewsbury, Eugene Aldrich.

By early summer, the new factory was buying thousands of pounds of milk from surrounding farms. The cheese factory was an intrusion upon the life of the Coolidges. The cheesemaker, Aldrich, even moved in with the family for a time. The wagons of milk went past the Coolidges' door; the smell of it permeated Plymouth Notch. The village did not mind, though; this stink was the stink of commerce.

But the cheese factory was still a modest venture. Plymouth did not feature a big lake or river for easy transport, as did the towns on Lake Champlain. In 1877 and 1878, a merchant and quarry owner on Isle La

Motte in northern Lake Champlain made money shipping ice to New York, where the Hudson had not frozen over in two warm years. But such opportunities did not seem to come to Plymouth. The prospects for a railroad to the town were still dim. And with each year that passed, it became clearer that whatever the Coolidges did in rural Plymouth would have to be on a small scale. The Great Plains were unrelenting in their competition with old New England. In the past year alone, as Calvin had finished school, six new states had been admitted to the union: North Dakota, South Dakota, Montana, Washington, Idaho, and Wyoming. Looking around themselves and at the factory, and at the neighbors with whom they sometimes quarreled, the Coolidges came to a cautious decision: they would follow the advice of the principal. Calvin would go down to Amherst College to sit the entrance exam in September. He was often sickly. But it was clear that something with books, maybe medicine or the law, would suit him more than keeping store or farming. If he became a doctor, he could come back to Plymouth; if he became a lawyer, he could practice in Ludlow. It was evident that he wanted to move into the greater world. John and his mother, Sarah, took comfort in the thought that Amherst was not really so far away, just down the Connecticut River Valley, in an area where Coolidges had been before. But everyone understood. Calvin was the heir to the family that stayed. Now he was leaving too.

TWO

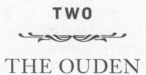

THE OUDEN

Amherst

NO FRESHMAN IN THE history of Amherst College seemed less likely to succeed than John Calvin Coolidge, class of 1895. The thin country redhead did not speak. He boarded at Trott's on South Pleasant Street, ten minutes from the college, farther away than most students. His roommate was not another freshman, as was common, but an upperclassman, a champion in the hammer throw. The Protestant college in the Connecticut Valley attracted students from all over the country, boys with far more social experience and ambition than he. The others moved along the streets and into and out of the school buildings or chapel fast; they stopped to talk, but not to him. The school newspaper, *The Amherst Student*, spilled the names of undergraduates liberally all over its pages, but not his.

It was only because of a loophole and a recession that the young man had even made it to Amherst at all. He had botched his first entrance exam, in September 1890, when he had arrived at the college town with a cold and come down sick in the middle of the tests. It had been bronchitis severe enough to scare them all. The same *Vermont Tribune* that had reported his graduation oratory had mentioned now that J. Calvin Coolidge was "gaining slowly." Eventually, he had returned to Black

River Academy for a short period of tutoring and review. From there he wrote to his father, "I have not the training of a man from a school like St. Jonsbury [sic], Saxton's River, or Phillips Exeter, but I hope I have the ability yet to secure it." His old headmaster, George Sherman, chagrined and aiming to boost the reputation of Black River Academy, pondered how to regroup. Sherman recalled that a school farther north than Plymouth, St. Johnsbury Academy, maintained a special arrangement with Amherst. When students completed satisfactory work at St. Johnsbury, they were automatically admitted to the Massachusetts college. The headmaster at St. Johnsbury, Charles Putney, was operating in the midst of a downturn. The Fairbanks family, which had endowed St. Johnsbury, was dying off; several faculty members had volunteered to return part of their salaries to the school rather than put it farther in the red. Dividends from the railroad stocks that had supported the school had been suspended.

Putney made an exception to precedent and allowed Calvin to come and try to qualify for his certificate in one term. John Coolidge shipped Calvin up to St. Johnsbury for a crash course in Latin, algebra, Greek, and elocution. Perhaps the alacrity with which John had agreed surprised Calvin, but John himself had been preoccupied; over the spring of 1891, he was courting the schoolteacher Carrie Brown, and a neighbor. Calvin, a normally erratic speller who became worse when anxious, had written his father in determination, "I believe I can get a certificate." St. Johnsbury and Putney had indeed given him one.

He had begun to count on going to Amherst and thought not only of the academic but of the social side. "Dick Lane thinks he and I had better go down to Amherst some time this spring to see about getting me into a society there. The societies are a great factor at Amherst and of course I want to join if I can," Coolidge wrote his father. There were so many fraternities that getting in might not be hard. The year Coolidge entered, 285 out of 352 students enrolled were affiliated with one of nine fraternities, the largest being "Deke," Delta Kappa Epsilon, the granddaddy fraternity of New England. His father had indeed married Carrie, thus setting to rest any concern his son might have at leaving him alone. Calvin instantly took to Carrie; missing mother and sister so long, he was glad to have Carrie and considered her a new mother.

The college that he encountered in his first few weeks of the fall of 1891 was worthy. Amherst had been founded not in the name of wealth or sport or Greek fraternities but to educate poor students to be ministers. It had been a splinter of a splinter: men who had deemed Harvard University too impious had founded Williams College, safe in the wilderness of western Massachusetts; Williams President Zephaniah Swift Moore, dissatisfied, had moved over to Amherst from North Adams, and students had followed him. From its beginning in the 1820s, Amherst had been small but mighty. "The infant college is an infant Hercules," an astonished writer named Ralph Waldo Emerson had written in his diary after passing through. "Never was so much striving, outstretching, and advancing in a literary cause as is exhibited here." The students, he said, "write, speak, and study in a sort of fury, which, I think, promises a harvest of attainments."

Amherst welcomed all Christians but tended to the Congregationalist, like St. Johnsbury, where Coolidge had worshipped at "the North Congo," the North Congregational Church. The fervor of the professors also recalled his grandmother Sarah Brewer, a Baptist. Christianity was, one president had said, "top stone and cornerstone" of Amherst, a fitting image in a region known for its granite and marble.

The quality of the education was seen as high enough to create leaders. "Terras irradient" was the Amherst motto: "Let them illuminate the earth." Amherst men might become senators, preachers, or diplomats. The Amherst campus was its own City upon a Hill, situated to exploit a view of purple mountains. The steeples there were like those of Vermont: steeples of independence. The town itself, like St. Johnsbury and Ludlow before it, was showing Calvin how the world worked; the Fairbanks' factory in St. Johnsbury had made great scales, purchased the world over, by customers as far away as Russia. In Amherst there were bicycles everywhere, whereas a few years before, there had been only horses.

Here in Amherst were names and achievements to aspire to. Among Amherst graduates was Henry Ward Beecher, who had preached abolition so successfully in Brooklyn. Even junior professors at Amherst were extraordinary: Charles Garman, who taught philosophy, had been described by none other than William James as "the greatest teacher" of all the colleges. Another Amherst star was a young librarian named Melvil Dewey, who had come up with a new classification of knowledge. During one Sunday sermon, staring at the pulpit, Dewey had come up with a way to organize books: "while I lookt stedfastly at [it] without hearing a word," Dewey later wrote, "my mind absorbd in the vital problem, the solution flasht over so that I jumpt in my seat and came very near shouting 'Eureka!' It was to get absolute simplicity by using the simplest known symbols, the arabic numerals as decimals, with ordinary significance of nought, to number a classification of all human knowledge in print."

Coolidge learned quickly that there were Amherst dynasties, not always wealthy but respected, chains of alumni with names such as Stearns or Dickinson. The bells of Stearns steeple, which chimed in the key of E, had been given by the father of an Amherst man who had died at Williamsburg in the Civil War. A Boston merchant, Frank Stearns, was class of 1878; he had married the daughter of an officer who had brought back a cannon from the Civil War; Stearns was also the name of an Amherst president. Stearns had his own department store in Boston. A Dickinson had founded Amherst, and another Dickinson had ferociously guarded the college's virtue; Edward Dickinson, the son of the founder, Samuel, and father of Emily, made it clear that Amherst would sacrifice all rather than become impure. Laying the cornerstone of the Barrett Gymnasium in 1859, Dickinson, a Whig politician, had warned that if the structure were "desecrated to any purpose of immorality," it should be destroyed: "Would that a fire consume it or an earthquake throw it down."

Austin Dickinson, Edward's son, was the school treasurer; the poems of his late sister Emily were praised in the press. The Dickinsons were royalty and broke rules, their own or the college's, with impunity; Austin was an indifferent bookkeeper, and there was gossip about an old affair he was said to have conducted with the wife of the astronomy professor, David Todd, class of 1875. Henry P. Field, class of 1880, was the son of a professor, Thomas P. Field, class of 1834, and a loyal alumnus. He was also the Dickinson family lawyer, based in Northampton, the county seat. Field, a bachelor and secretary to his class, stayed at the Lord Jeffery Inn whenever he visited other alumni. Field's law partner was John C. Hammond, class of 1865. Both men, Calvin noticed, were Republicans. Herbert Pratt, a member of his class, was from a family that had made a fortune in kerosene and given the school the Pratt Gymnasium and Pratt Field, completed in the spring of 1891, just months before Calvin's arrival. For such people, doors seemed to fly open.

But for him the doors shut one by one. Fraternity recruitment came. Charles Andrews, a young man he met, pledged Phi Delta Theta. Dwight

Morrow, a boy from a family with even fewer resources than his own, found a new home at Beta Theta Pi, which maintained a gaudy house with a prominent porch on the corner of College Street and Boltwood Avenue. "He was master of the situation," Coolidge would say later of Morrow's response to it all. Boy after boy found some kind of affiliation. Coolidge looked on, helpless.

Athletics likewise did not seem possible, and that too hurt because physical fitness was a near obsession at Amherst. Coolidge lacked the talent that would win someone a name on the field; he was not an especially fast runner, he was not especially comfortable with a ball, and he was certainly not comfortable dancing. He could not make a team. He experienced the well-known shock of arriving at a school and finding oneself to be not steps but leagues behind the serious athletes. One of the humiliations of college was that students' physical shortcomings were quantified—and meticulously. Amherst had its own health guru, another dynasty man, Edward Hitchcock, the son of a geologist and Amherst university president. He taught physical culture—what we today would call health studies—to the freshmen. Hitchcock was also a pioneer in anthropometry, the study of the physical measures of men. Not only did "Doc," as he was known to the students, record the height and weight of each Amherst freshman, he also measured them up and down and tested them for strength of lungs, arms, and legs. He carefully recorded additional physical characteristics of decades of Amherst students and took extra care to study students who stood out.

A fellow freshman in Coolidge's year, H. W. Lane, held Hitchcock's attention: "Mr H. W. Lane of this class makes the most remarkable record of strength tests in our books," Hitchcock wrote. Ernest Hardy of Northampton, the county seat, weighed in the heaviest, at 191 pounds. Coolidge weighed only 119.5 pounds, below the class average, despite a height that was slightly more than average, 68.9 inches. Other physical characteristics were also recorded, such as hair color: Coolidge was one of five "auburns" counted in the class.

If Coolidge could not be Greek, at least he could read Greek, along with Latin. But even in academics the reception was less warm than he had hoped. With newspapers being the only input from the outside world, the professors and clergy were giants at a campus like Amherst. In 1890, professors' salaries were $2,500, more than twenty times tuition. The step up from laborer to professor was immense, for the average wage earner in 1890 earned $425 a year. When a young Scottish American, Alexander Meiklejohn, just Coolidge's age, began his first job as an assistant professor teaching philosophy at Brown, in 1897, he would receive a salary almost equivalent to that of his six brothers combined. A "prexy," or university president, earned even more than the professors. The giants did not seem to pay much attention to Coolidge. They read lectures aloud; the first-year students' work, just as at the academies, was to memorize, recite, or stay silent. Coolidge found his assignments both unsatisfying and tiring. There was a word, he learned, for a man who was left out without a fraternity: they called such a man an ouden, from the Greek for "nothing." Some of the oudens at Amherst were oudens on principle: Harlan Stone, a year older, rejected fraternities as "a rather artificial way of forming friendships." But most in the band of outsiders were never invited, boys too quiet or too much the hayseed to make the cut.

"I am in a pleasant place and like very much," Calvin wrote to his father, John, on October 15 of his freshman year, in a kind of shorthand. "but suppose I shall like better as become better acquainted, I don't seem to get acquainted very fast however."

He was back where he had been at the beginning at Black River Academy: on the margin. There was nothing to do but press on and wait for Christmas. As he trudged around, Coolidge found that he often thought of home. In November, he wrote home to his grandmother, starting out bravely, "This term is almost done it is 11 weeks since I left home; I never was away as long before but to be gone one week is just about the same as 11 only a repetition of the same thing. We get very good advantages here for quite a broad education." Shortly, though, he segued to that beloved topic of the homesick, food: "I suppose you will have the bed set out in the kitchen for me when I come to stay with you and I can have some coffee with cream in it I have not drunk a cup of coffee as I remember since I came here. . . . I don't like their potatoes here." When he went home at Christmas, he had not yet received his first grades. Amherst graded on a scale of 2 to 5. Calvin, perhaps suspecting that his grades would be far worse than 4 or 5, decided he did not want to go back to college. As much as his father would have liked him to stay home, he saw that school was worthwhile in Calvin's case. There was also the principle of finishing what one started. His father sent him back.

Returning to Amherst in January 1892 was even harder than starting in September, perhaps harder even than sitting down to take the exams while he was sick in 1890. "I hate to think I must stay here 12 weeks before I can go home again," he wrote to Plymouth Notch. "I think I must be very home-sick my hand trembles so I can't write so any one can read it. It is just seven o'clock I wonder if you are most home there is some snow here but it has stopped snowing now." His life seemed to be going in the wrong direction: "Each time I get home I hate to go away worse than before and I don't feel so well here now." The grades for the first semester were indeed disappointing 2s, just passing, which "seem pretty low don't they?" as he wrote to his father January 14.

With no exit, though, he gradually pulled himself together. There were bright points if you looked for them. Coolidge's work in mathematics was good enough for him to move up a level. Though he was not chosen to speak at the freshman dinner, his recitations in class didn't go too badly. Politics somehow afforded distraction from loneliness. The local Republicans were beginning to catch his eye. He saw that they and other parties advertised; even college boys hung out signs reading "Womens' Rights and Free Cider" or "Free Silver and Non Compulsory Church"—an appealing idea at a school where chapel was mandatory. His stepmother kindly sent him graham crackers and jelly, which he shared with his roommate, Alfred Turner; together he and Turner even decorated, putting up a curtain at the door to insulate their room. There was even the possibility, but just that, of a fraternity membership; a senior, Charles Stebbins, asked if he would join a new fraternity, Phi Gamma Delta, which was establishing a chapter. Coolidge, timid, offered one of his ambivalent answers: "I don't know but I would." The possibility faded. Still, he determined that he would loyally follow Amherst sports and began to report scores and stories of games back to his father. Somehow the dread second half of freshman year finished. He had not succeeded, but he had not failed; five or six men left the college, but he was not one of them.

Though Coolidge was an ouden at school, he was somebody at home, and that summer Plymouth welcomed him back and did its part to cheer up its native son. Dell Ward, an old friend, was there waiting for him; the two plotted to steal the old cannon back from Plymouth Union, where it had been for the year, and succeeded, at 3:00 A.M., in moving the weapon and its carriage up the hill to their own village. His fellow villagers invited him to speak, another boost, and Coolidge took the challenge of oratory seriously, preparing a rousing speech: "Roll on America! Roll on, bearing rich blessings with o'erflowering hand through the endless ages of all eternity." The cannon he carefully dismantled and hid under his grandmother Moor's bed.

Back in the autumn, he found Trott's discombobulated, with twenty-six boarders, often strangers, eating at different times; he still sometimes had to eat alone. He decided to move to shift his meal place. It didn't hurt matters that the price was cheaper: $3.50 a week instead of $3.75. The proprietors of the new place were black: "They are coons," he wrote in the language of the day. He wrote also, in regard to football, that "our best man of last year" was now playing football for Harvard, advantaging Harvard. "He is a negro by the name of Lewis." This was William Lewis, who was now studying law at Harvard. Calvin was endeavoring to talk more of "we" and "us" to try to find ways into the community.

But the community was not ready for him. Beyond Turner, his roommate, and a few others, it was still hard to make contact. He noticed a lack of resilience in himself. Other students, such as Dwight Morrow, seemed to be able to turn circumstances to their own favor in a way Calvin could not. When he compared his Amherst progress with theirs, he fell short. Coolidge wrote home asking for money: there was scarcely a letter to Plymouth, in fact, that did not contain some kind of request for cash: "I think I forgot to mention in my last letter the gymnasium uniform that I have to get, each man is measured the first of the term and they send off and get the uniforms made, they are eleven dollars."

Morrow, by contrast, had taken on the task of finding cash himself, in part by borrowing from his soldier brother, in part through tutoring in math, and, eventually, by winning cash prizes. What money Morrow took from his father he considered not a gift but rather a loan, borrowed "off Papa." Coolidge's own arm had healed well enough from a boyhood break, and he stood, as Hitchcock had noted, slightly above average height. Morrow was decisively short; one of his arms bent oddly, the result of a fall from an apple tree when he was twelve. Another student, Mortimer Schiff, handed down shirts to Morrow, but the shirts bore Schiff's monogram, "MLS." Morrow's mother asked what the letters stood for. "Morrow's Little Shirts," her son told her blithely. Morrow had a way of turning disadvantage to advantage, of pushing on, so that people admired his humor and pluck. Even in politics, Morrow seemed to move ahead fast. It was Morrow, not Coolidge, who went onto the board of the new Republican Club.

His sophomore year, Coolidge took Greek, rhetoric, German, and analytic geometry. He had not yet conquered the undergraduate challenge of managing time and sleep. William Tyler, his Greek teacher, was famous; that was the last year he would teach "Demosthenes on the Crown." Coolidge wrote home drily that if Demosthenes' speeches were the best to be found, the world had not made much progress in rhetoric in the two millennia since he had spoken. He sometimes could not stay awake in the class. An anonymous classmate published a rhyme in *The Olio*, the yearbook:

> *The class in Greek was going on*
> *Old Ty a lecture read.*
> *And in the row in front there shone*
> *Fair Coolidge's golden head.*
> *His pate was bent upon the seat*
> *in front of him; his hair*
> *Old Tyler's feeble gaze did meet*
> *With fierce and ruddy glare*
> *O'ercome by mystic sense of dread*
> *Old Ty his talk did lull—*
> *"Coolidge, I wish you'd raise your head*
> *I can't talk through your skull!"*

Though he may have slept, Coolidge was coming to value his teacher's lectures and discovered a new blessing; these courses, heavy in logic, focused him. He was beginning to plan instead of merely to react: he posted a paper on the wall to remind himself when homework was due. Perhaps too the subject matter compelled him. Like Coolidge, Demosthenes had started out sickly. He had even spoken with a lisp. He had become a great orator notwithstanding. Demosthenes' rebellion against the kings paralleled the rebellion of Calvin's own forefathers against England.

In the fall of 1892, politics were also heating up, and that cheered him on. He knew his father supported Benjamin Harrison, who had endorsed a strong tariff that included protection for wool. This time he was able to take in the national questions, along with the Vermont ones. After a boom, prices for steel were coming down. Carnegie Steel in Pennsylvania had cut wages significantly, by 20 to 40 percent. The

Amalgamated Association of Iron and Steel Workers struck at Carnegie Steel's Homestead Plant over wages; then the strike broadened. This wage issue was a new one: before such big factories had been established, workers hadn't been able to compare salaries easily. The companies, led by Henry Clay Frick, the chairman of Carnegie Steel, saw the outcome at Homestead as crucial: if they could not cut wages when they needed to, they believed, they would not survive, especially if the 1890 tariff was repealed. By the summer of 1892, eighty thousand men west of the Allegheny had laid down their tools. With the aid of the state militia, the steel company broke the strike, but only after Alexander Berkman, an anarchist, found his way into Frick's office, shot him three times, and stabbed him for good measure. Frick survived, but the horrifying event shocked all. Coolidge doubtless followed the story, even from Plymouth Notch. After the Homestead strike was settled—the company won a bitter victory—the papers carried stories of Berkman's trial and conviction, as well as his association with a flamboyant woman anarchist, Emma Goldman. Depending on whom you talked to, that was the problem of either Harrison's predecessor, Grover Cleveland, or Harrison himself.

Harrison was a big spender; under him, the federal budget had reached a billion dollars for the first time. Harrison also supported tariffs. Cleveland campaigned against the Sherman Silver Purchase Act, passed in 1890, blaming it for instability; by expanding the money base beyond gold, he alleged, the Harrison administration had set the stage for a panic. Americans were choosing to redeem their new silver money for gold, which in turn was reducing the gold supply and forcing a contraction upon the economy. At Yale, which Amherst played against in football, there was a professor, William Graham Sumner, who was laying out the argument against protectionism. But Cleveland was living it.

In addition, the political experts noted, Cleveland was a champion of the so-called pocket veto, refusing to sign a bill until Congress adjourned, at which point it died. A regular veto could be overridden, but not a pocket veto. With a pocket veto, the executive enjoyed the additional advantage that he might veto without the usual enumeration of his objections. It took an aggressive, even bloody-minded, president to reject Congress's work in that way. Cleveland had vetoed more than four hundred bills, many of them individual favors, such as pensions to veterans.

The professors at Amherst cast their vote—for stability, the gold standard, free trade, and Cleveland. *The New York Times* reported that "[of] the thirty-three professors constituting the Faculty of Amherst college, seven are for Harrison and twenty-three for Cleveland." The Amherst fans included Edward Dickinson; David Todd; John Bates Clark, who would become famous for his economic theories; George Olds, a new math professor from Rochester who was already a favorite of the students; and Anson Morse, the college's expert in politics. Some of the professors felt strongly enough to write a public letter supporting Cleveland and send it to the *Times*. "We remember his tariff message, his pension vetoes, and his letter against free silver as conspicuous instances of disregarding personal considerations for the public good," they wrote.

Harrison lost to Cleveland, a shock to the student body of Amherst, which was more Republican than its teachers. On November 17, 1892, Coolidge wrote to his grandmother to report, "The democrats have a celebration here this evening and I shall go out to see some of it." Coolidge's letters home were fast shifting from accounts of homesickness to discursive analyses of politics. After the election he wrote to John about the fickleness of the voter, "The result of the election was as much a surprise to the Democrats here as to the Republicans, and nobody seems able to account for it satisfactorily yet. I do not think it much use to blame Chairman Carter [Thomas Henry Carter, the chairman of the Republican National Committee] or the tariff or the Homestead affair, the reason seems to be in the never satisfied mind of the American and in the ever desire to shift in hope of something better and in the vague idea of the working and farming classes that somebody is getting all the money while they get all the work."

AS THE YEARS PASSED, the student's confidence grew. The oudens formed their own society. The first of Coolidge's new friends was John Percy Deering from Saco, Maine, another rural New England Republican and a prominent football player. In early 1893, Coolidge moved with Deering and another man into Morse's boardinghouse, closer to campus. A second new friend was Ernest Hardy of Northampton, the county seat, the boy who, Dr. Hitchcock had noted, was the largest in the class. He was an ouden, most likely, out of economy. Together Hardy and Coolidge were a noticeable pair, the heavy and the thin. It was to Hardy's town, Northampton, that Coolidge went on errands; Hardy introduced him around. Coolidge found a cobbler on Gothic Street he liked, James Lucey, an Irishman with a growing family who had arrived from County Kerry in 1880. Lucey had bought a home but was still paying off the mortgage. Coolidge noticed how hard Lucey worked. Like Coolidge's father, Lucey derived pride from crafting his work and told Calvin that the best way to secure a good future was to deliver quality.

As an undergraduate Coolidge also attended lectures by traveling experts, sometimes about religion and often about economics. Such excursions into the real world fortified the oudens, reminding them that college joy was ephemeral in any case. To boys such as Hardy and Deering "town"—the municipality—meant more than "gown": campus life. Deering later recalled in a newspaper interview that during the holidays they "used to visit each other and work on each other's place. It's always more fun for a boy to work on someone else's place, you know." On and off Deering and Hardy ate with the brothers of the fraternity Beta Theta Pi. Shortly, Deering and Hardy were approached about entering Beta Theta Pi. Hardy said "yes," but Deering asked whether Coolidge might join as well. The Beta Theta Pi brothers, however, including Dwight Morrow, did not want to include Coolidge. Morrow made it explicit that he was unwilling to take the oddball. Deering refused to join without Calvin. The two stayed proud oudens.

In 1893, an incident at the college called to mind why one might be ambivalent about joining other boys in fraternity-style fun. After the annual freshman dinner, some students in the class had fallen into "the meshes of the law" and "were forced to give up a small quantity of plunder in the shape of porcelain and gilt letters which they had taken from the store windows," *The Amherst Student* reported. Such activity was not unusual. There was a tradition at Amherst of the sophomores preventing the freshmen class from having their picture taken; several years later the sophomores would break up a photo session of freshmen so violently that the photographer sued for damages; he was represented by the firm of the two Amherst grads in Northampton, Hammond and Field. Coolidge did not join in the small-time looting; he already deemed himself as much town as gown. As the son of a shop owner, he could see, too, that that year, merchants could ill afford extra costs. Banks were failing all over the country. National Cordage, the most actively traded stock at the time, went into receivership. The supply of gold the Treasury held dropped below $100 million for the first time since 1879. In Massachusetts employment figures were added up for industrial plants.

In April 1893, the plants employed 320,000. By September, that number was 248,000, a drop of more than 20 percent. Students could see with their own eyes that people were losing jobs and walking away from their homes rather than paying their mortgages. In Boston, R. H. Stearns, the department store run by Frank Stearns, the devoted Amherst alumnus, was hosting a fire sale on black clothing: "When we planned to alter our store we intended to very much enlarge our black goods department and so gave much larger importation orders than usual. Now that we are compelled to give up the changes for the present, we are left with this large stock." At Amherst and other colleges, currency crowded out all other topics. William Graham Sumner of Yale was lecturing that this crisis was not a bank or a market crisis at all but a currency crisis actually caused, in good measure, by the very step meant to mitigate it, the 1890 Silver Act.

Now that the terms of the gold standard had been fiddled with, the market sensed more fiddling to come. Later, in a book, Sumner would codify his analysis: "The constant apprehension was, so long as then-existing legislation remained in force, that the unit of existing monetary relations would be changed. Such an apprehension is the surest ground for panic which can be offered. The panic which resulted when this fear became more specific was not a bank panic, nor a crisis in which the banks had any responsibility." President Cleveland, of the same view as Sumner, recommended repeal of the Silver Act, thereby sending a signal that the United States would stick to the gold standard. Some perceived repeal as the salvation of the economy, others as a blow to commerce; in the farmland the Silver Act repeal was considered a disaster.

That year Calvin became eligible to vote; in the late summer of 1893, he took an oath of citizenship in Plymouth; his interest in politics grew yet more. as did his loyalty to the Republicans. He noticed that, while out of the presidency and in the midst of a sharp downturn, Republicans were winning gubernatorial contests in Iowa and New York. "Republicans are wearing a smile this morning," he wrote his father after the elections that autumn of 1893. Coolidge was also beginning to take an interest in the Republican parties of Massachusetts and the state of Maine, where Hardy and Deering were active.

Politics inspired Coolidge to begin to speak publicly. The boardinghouse meals were his start. The ready audience at table afforded him an opportunity to perfect his delivery of jokes. He found he could hold a room's attention, if only for a minute. A story from that period that Deering later told about Coolidge stands out. One of the places he and Coolidge boarded was the house of a dog fancier, who gave them twenty-one meals a week—too often potato salad, Deering later remembered. One morning their host served sausages for breakfast. Coolidge pounded his table with fork and knife. The diners fell silent as he called the head of the house into the room. He demanded that the owner produce every dog he owned in the dining room before he would eat.

Coolidge's new boardinghouse skills gave him the confidence to test himself in more formal debates. That same autumn of 1893, he couched his usual request for money in terms of recent accomplishments: "In view of the fact that yesterday I put a debate said to be the best heard on the floor of the chapel this term, in view of the fact that my name was read as one of the first ten in French, in view of the fact that I passed in Natural philosophy with a fair mark whereas many failed, and lastly in view of the fact that the purchase clause of Sherman Bill has been repealed thus relieved the cause of financial panic, can you send me $25. the forepart of next week?"

By the second half of junior year, he was even getting good enough to go up against the big names of the college. In January 1894, he reported one of his first opportunities to debate more formally, and against none other than Herbert Pratt, the fraternity favorite and child of the Pratt dynasty. Pratt was a great football player; he had joined the toniest fraternity, Alpha Delta Phi. Yet it was Calvin who prevailed. To his father Calvin wrote, "I had a debate yesterday as to whether a Presidential or a Parliamentary form of government is the better; I had the parliamentary side which is not particularly popular in as much as it is really to show England's government is better than ours, and I spoke against Pratt of Brooklyn who is a very good debater and a general favorite being captain of our foot ball team. But the parliamentary side won by a large majority when the question was decided." In this period Coolidge also followed, through *The Amherst Student*, the progress of other debaters. The spring of 1894 also brought the annual Hardy Prize debate, one of the big Amherst contests. The question in 1894 was "Should the State of New York extend the suffrage to woman?" The debaters drew sides, according to *The Amherst Student*. On the negative side was a senior just about to graduate, Harlan Fiske Stone, who took second place.

In February 1894, there came startling news from Boston: Morrison

Swift, an angry veteran, had marshaled hundreds of the unemployed to demonstrate at the State House for a public works program, a new idea. At Amherst young people were also hearing about the tariff and a new federal levy of a sort that had not been seen since the Civil War period, the income tax. The two revenue vehicles had been paired in legislation, the former being the Republicans' preferred device for collecting federal revenue. Democrats opposed the tariff, reasonably enough, on grounds that it tended to work by hurting the poor and consumers—a sound assessment, since consumption of goods subject to tariffs such as sugar and coffee took up a greater portion of the little man's budget. The second vehicle, the income tax, was put forward by a new voice, William Jennings Bryan, a lawmaker from Nebraska who edited the *Omaha World-Herald*. William L. Wilson, a Democratic congressman from West Virginia, was among those shepherding the legislation through. The new income tax, a 2 percent levy, was designed to fall on those who earned over $4,000 a year, far more than, for example, the earnings of Coolidge's father. Wilson argued that it was not a class tax but rather "an effort, an honest effort to balance the weight of taxation in this country." Republicans and classical liberals and even New Englanders certainly ought to be for the tax, Wilson said, for another reason: it was simple. One of the great New Englanders, William Graham Sumner, had described an income tax as a "simple form of taxation" that was preferable to other kinds of taxes. Said Wilson: "New England taught that doctrine to the South and West and therefore has no right to come up today and complain because her own teaching has been used against her."

But Coolidge saw that others would not concede William Wilson's points. Justin Morrill, a senator from Coolidge's own Vermont, thought Wilson had it backward on the question of budgets and the faith in the U.S. fiscal house. Income taxes were to be avoided because they were a symptom of fiscal weakness, "the resort only of nations which are always wrestling with financial deficits." "Surely," Morrill went on, "we cannot afford to decorate the annals of our Republic with a vile copy of this foreign excrescence." He sought to reveal the income tax for what it was: an unapologetic blow against the rich of New England, whose citizens would bear a full two-thirds of the burden. Yet a third group of income tax opponents made a more fundamental case: that the income tax was unconstitutional. The Constitution stated that Congress had the power to tax, but only "without apportionment among the several states, and without regard to any census or enumeration." Many lawmakers took this to mean that states must be taxed evenly, regardless of their population.

Young Coolidge was not sold on the income tax either. In tones softer than Morrill's but still definite, he objected in a February 1894 letter to his father, "I do not like an income tax, it taxes the land and the crops at the same time, it is too expensive to collect." The college junior theorized that "no man's income is permanent enough to admit of taxation, it will easily be a source of corruption."

Coolidge's political awakening took place at a time when the United States was first waking up to new questions itself. One was the income tax, which would indeed become law in 1894; but another was the question of whether a factory worker as contrasted with, say, a farmer was due something different from government. Before industrialization, there had been no one unemployed in the modern sense: a farmer could be underemployed, and he could be broke, but he was not out of work in the definitive way that a factory hand is when the gates of a factory close. But now people were not finding work.

In March 1894, Coxey's Army, a band led by an Ohio man named Jacob Coxey, started as five hundred unemployed and then grew, headed toward Washington, D.C., passing through Homestead, Pennsylvania, at one point. In the spring of 1894, as well, employees of the Palace Car Company went on strike in Illinois after Pullman reduced their wages. But it was hard to compare past and present; there were not even always good numbers. In 1893 and 1894, quantifying joblessness was still a young science. Charles Dow, the editor of a new paper, *The Wall Street Journal*, had begun to compile yet another product, his first market average; the Dow Jones Industrial Average. In the same years Dow Jones made and marketed the ticker, an electric machine that spat out stock prices for banks and offices. The Dow data that moved on the ticker were originally made up of nine railroads and two industrial stocks.

The Pullman Palace cars, private cars for rail lines, represented all Americans' dreams. They were the mode of travel to which everyone aspired, but now the prospect that workers would ever get near to riding one was dimming. Pullman workers were especially outraged because Pullman, also their landlord, did not cut rents in his company town or prices in the company store commensurately with the wage cuts. The strike spread throughout the industry so that hundreds of thousands of workers and dozens of states were involved; transport ground to a stop.

In the summer of 1894, before Coolidge's senior year, President Grover Cleveland called in U.S. marshals and 12,000 U.S. troops on the argument that the strike was interrupting the U.S. mails, a federal responsibility. In the case of Pullman, the violence was worse than at Homestead. The strikers' opponents cited the new Sherman Antitrust Act, which prohibited restraint of trade. They argued, successfully, that the workers themselves were a combination restraining trade. Progressives who believed in both organized labor and trust busting found the use of the latter to hurt the former perverse. Eugene V. Debs, the leader of the strikers, went to jail for six months; Judge William Woods sent Debs to jail in Woodstock—not Woodstock, Vermont, but Woodstock, Illinois, far out in McHenry County, near the Wisconsin border.

The price to both sides in lost hours, lost dignity, and lost profits was enormous. Many smaller companies, including one called American Steel and Wire Company, saw their workers go on strike. American Steel and Wire fired its workers for striking, among them a young man just Coolidge's age named Leon Frank Czolgosz. So did many other companies. Others did not fire their workers but instead cut their wages. At Fairbanks Scales in St. Johnsbury, where Coolidge had crammed, directors had ordered a 10 percent reduction in wages for some workers; others were working shortened hours. But the international market stabilized business at Fairbanks; when the economy was slow at home, sometimes overseas orders made up for the shortage. But there were no strikes in St. Johnsbury. The lessons of Pullman, Homestead, and Fairbanks were hard to absorb or clarify. Could a company never cut wages in a downturn? Was cutting wages wrong?

The missing jobs had something to do with the missing money, and everyone had his own idea about what had gone awry, or how to fix it. Jacob Coxey himself made money the center of the story; he even named his infant son, who was along on the trip, "Legal Tender Coxey." Those were the same years when William Jennings Bryan of Nebraska was warning that capital was exploiting the worker and that hard money—the gold standard—would strangle farming. The undergraduate Coolidge kept his own books rigidly and noticed when others were lax. The loose management of Amherst's treasurer, Austin Dickinson, did not escape him, though he saw that it allowed students some flexibility. "My tuition is due first of March and can be paid any time," he wrote home in spring 1894. Nonetheless, Coolidge still found himself coming up perpetually short. As at Black River Academy, his college letters home were peppered with requests for money. He himself was tiring of that and on the lookout for a way to reverse the flow.

He was in fact already finding a professional skill that might one day earn him a living: speaking. When the outside world matters, students turn to peers who know how to talk about that world. The men at Amherst could see that Coolidge was such a peer. The experience of living politics in the town meeting meant he knew more than men who had only heard about it secondhand, from the papers. That esteem in turn gave him the confidence to speak on nonpolitical topics, or even mix politics with humor. Coolidge's fellows suddenly saw in him something like what they saw in Dwight Morrow—that rare ability to turn potential humiliation into good cheer. The junior class at Amherst celebrated each year by donning plug hats (big top hats), grabbing canes, and then racing one another down Pratt Field. The last seven to make it across the line were obliged to buy the other seventy-odd dinner at Hitchcock Hall. Coolidge came in among those last, mired in dirt. Perhaps he stayed behind intentionally, for the losers got to give a speech.

Coolidge entitled his talk "Why I Got Stuck." Turning his pockets inside out for his classmates to demonstrate the effect of the dinner price on his resources, he hammed it up as if he were horsing around with Wilders, Coolidges, and Browns back in Plymouth. The material of the speech is no longer available, but later those who attended remembered phrases. "You wouldn't expect a plow horse to make time on the race track or a follower of the plow to be a Mercury." He also quoted the Bible: "The Good Book says that the first shall be last and the last shall be first." A classmate, Jay Stocking, later said the others had not expected much: "Opinion was divided as to whether he would rise and say he was unprepared or whether he would content himself with saying that he stood for the affirmative." Instead, when Coolidge spoke, "The class had the surprise of its life. He spoke cogently, fluently and with a good sense of humor and won his case hands down. It was as if a new and gifted man had joined the class."

Arriving back at college for his final year in September 1894, he made an effort to decorate his rooms and enlisted Carrie in Plymouth to help him and make, as he wrote in a detailed note, "five pillows, two 20 × 20, two 16 × 16, and one 12 × 12." The ruffles, he noticed precisely, were to be "4, 3½ and 3 inches," according to size. She sent them. His grades were improving. E. B. Andrews, the president of Brown, came to Amherst for a meeting of college presidents and took the opportunity to lecture undergraduates on the merits of the bimetallism Cleveland was abandoning. All that made an impression on Coolidge, who ordered a copy of Andrews's two-volume *History of the United States* from Charles Scribner's Sons; the bill for the book was $2.67.

For the first time in his life, Coolidge now felt the pull of Boston, "the hub," as the city was known. Some students, he knew, went there for graduate school, like Lewis, the black football star, who was studying law in Cambridge. The law school at Harvard was growing fast. Coolidge luxuriated in the thought he might have some choice about where to live; his college curriculum reinforced that sense of freedom. Having picked his way gingerly through Amherst's requirements of Greek and algebra, he could now devote himself to topics that interested him. He might take more Italian, which he enjoyed, and drop German, which he didn't. He could read history, politics, and philosophy.

Two teachers especially helped Coolidge to formulate his ideas in those final years and, more importantly, revealed the principles behind them. The first was Anson Morse. Morse, a scholar of political alignment and particularly the development of modern political parties, offered exactly what Coolidge had longed for: political context. His course started with Europe, marching through the emperors and reforms, and so inspired Calvin that he was moved to come up with some improbable comparisons. Hearing of the attack by the reformer Charles Parkhurst, Amherst class of 1866, upon Tammany Hall, Coolidge wrote his father, "Dr. Parkhurst has done great work in purifying the city and smashing the ring. I look upon him as a modern Savanarola [*sic*]. I am proud of him as an Amherst man." Morse could not only mention the principle of liberty but trace it for you: "We saw the British Empire rise until it ruled the seas."

Morse explained Coolidge's own past to him. George Washington's greatness, according to Morse, had simultaneously been his weakness: he had not understood the partisan spirit and had been taken aback when new political parties did not side with him. Morse saw that political turnover checked corruption and drew the consequence: "The term of power for every party must therefore be limited." Morse tracked the Whig decline around the time that Carlos Coolidge, and for that matter William Dickinson, had attended the Whig Convention in 1852 and taught step by step the rise of the Republican Party in the place of the Whigs. "Our course in history is very interesting this term, they say we have the best course of any college in New England," Calvin wrote his father. Morse admired Andrew Jackson for his success at garnering popular support and strengthening the executive office, yet on balance ranked Jackson lower than other presidents. He, like Sumner at Yale, was beginning to ask whether Jackson's flamboyant legacy had merely caused turmoil in the future. Morse liked to point out that presidents' health could affect history as much as any policy. William Harrison's triumph over Martin Van Buren, he said, had actually been a "fruitless victory," since Harrison had died soon after inauguration. The vice presidential candidate the party had chosen, John Tyler, who had become president when Harrison died, had, as Morse put it, "shattered their legislative program."

A second professor to catch his attention was Charles Garman, who had so impressed William James. Garman taught his own private blend of psychology, philosophy, politics, and ethics. A product of strict Congregationalism, Garman too came from up north; he had been born in Limington, Maine, the son of a minister, and had graduated from Amherst in 1872. Still young, dark, and suffering from a mysterious throat condition, Garman was a mystifier, a charmer of young men, with an edge of hocus pocus; a favorite topic of his was automatic writing, a practice in which the writer purported to be transcribing a message from the spiritual realm as a medium. Everything he did was special and different; his course began in spring of junior year and ended only with graduation. His habit was to teach in an overheated room bundled in coats and shawls, concerned about the cold. Unlike other professors, who insisted upon knowledge and memorization, Garman ran a seminar. He talked; then the students talked back and he listened. For most of the students it was a revolutionary experience; Garman's classroom felt not like a classroom at all but like a debate. Stepping over the threshold, they could feel the calendar move forward half a century. Garman produced pamphlets that were themselves mysteries, bearing a special announcement at the front: "This pamphlet though printed is not published; it is in every respect private property. It has been only loaned to the students in the psychology division on two conditions. First, that it be carefully preserved and promptly returned when called in; Second that the student to whom it is loaned does not in any case let it come into the hands of any person not a member of the psychology division."

It only boosted Garman's popularity that he was waging a very public contest with the president of Amherst, the pious, rigid Merrill Gates. Gates and Garman both taught philosophy; Garman, however, was more popular. President Gates asked to sit in on a single Garman class; Garman countered that Gates must attend the whole course if he was to judge it. Garman, another Amherst alumnus, went over the head of Gates to write to the trustees about the future of his employment. Coolidge's junior year, the spring of 1894, found the professor brashly negotiating with the University of Michigan to teach there instead. The battle was all the more exciting because of the imbalance of credentials: Garman, with only an MA after his name, was the David, locked in combat with a Goliath of a president who was PhD, LLD, and LHD. In June, when Coolidge headed home for his final college summer, Garman flashily tendered his resignation. To Gates's humiliation, the trustees backed Garman, even going so far as to award him an honorary degree of doctor of divinity. Garman agreed to stay, which meant that Coolidge would be able to study under him senior year.

The boys followed the drama blow by blow. Though earlier he had praised Gates to his father, Coolidge's notes home now suggested he sided with Garman; Coolidge wrote John that "I understand the trustees are getting unsatisfied with him, I am not looking for his removal very soon but think it will come in time if he does not change his policy." Partly it was because Garman, unlike Gates, did not preach at him; he, like the other boys, was grateful for that. But there was also the pleasure of the group: to be in Garman's class was to be admitted to a brotherhood all by itself. He, Morrow, and the others would remember it forever. In Garman's classroom, Coolidge realized he had made it into at least one fraternity, and an important one, the fraternity of Garman men. He could see that the others, Pratt, Andrews, and Morrow were continuing to reappraise him.

The substance of Garman's teaching was different from that of other philosophers. Sumner of Yale laid out an elegant algebra to explain the challenge of the progressive impulse. "A," he said, might want to help "X," the man at the bottom. And "B" might want to as well. But there might be a problem if "A" and "B" banded together and coerced "C" into funding their project for "X." "C," the taxpayer, the man who paid and prayed, was what Sumner called a forgotten man. Garman was murkier than Sumner but offered a version of the same idea: the group was less important than the individual, Garman said, because there was really no such thing as group happiness. It was even a mistake to speak of sacrificing individuals for "the happiness of the community." The community was composed of individuals.

Garman didn't see much value in industrialization, either. Like the author Thomas Hardy, whose recent controversial novel, *Tess of the d'Urbervilles*, was popular in Great Britain, Garman deemed industrialization dehumanizing: you could not make a machine of a laborer but made "a devil of him first." There were many Amherst grads who would have found that last view especially quaint. Arthur Vining Davis, class of 1888, had joined the Pittsburgh Reduction Company, a new company with a patent to use electrolyte reduction to extract aluminum from bauxite. Selling the aluminum was hard; people didn't know what to do with it. But Davis and the others had found a banker, Thomas Mellon, to help them; the year Coolidge had finished high school, Davis had tried to convince a pot maker in Erie to buy a kettle he had fashioned of aluminum. Next he tried housewives themselves. He had found an angel in Mellon, who could influence both local and national politics. Lawmakers had introduced lines into the 1890 tariff that protected his new aluminum business from foreign competitors. The future of aluminum seemed unlimited; there would be nothing dehumanizing about aluminum if it helped housewives or served other purposes.

Yet the young men, Coolidge among them, found enormous inspiration in Garman. His emphasis on the individual, rather than the group, went against the Europeans, including the Marxists, who cast everything in the context of classes and groups. In April 1894, as Coolidge was just beginning Garman's class, workers in Lowell, Massachusetts, won a victory over employers who had tried to cut their wages; after a walkout, the employers agreed to keep the wages the same. Garman told the boys that every strike was "hopeless in the long run."

Also interesting was Garman's emphasis on property. "The right of property is exactly the doctrine of the state," Garman's stenographic notes show him saying in 1893. His definition of property was not, however, a completely free-market one. He drew a distinction between two kinds of jobs: those that represented simply "furnishing employment" and those that represented service, which was higher. "But why should not all employment be in the line of service, of public improvements instead of useless work for some rich man? Is there any excuse for this at all? Not an iota, and I want you to preach this belief when you get out of college." Indeed, one ought to be willing to work without pay. "The most satisfied men in history are not those who have received the largest pay, but those who have rendered the greatest service to their age, often entirely without pay. What is the financial compensation Christ received?" Property, however, included an obligation to serve others. In other words, Garman, as unusual as he was, was teaching in the Amherst tradition. Ordained or not, his students would serve all their lives just as ministers once had. Service could mean going back to the village. Garman was also echoing Emerson, who had written a summary of the superiority of returning home many years before, and of his contempt for high-society men like those who dominated the fraternities at Amherst:

> If the finest genius studies at one of our colleges, and is not installed in an office within one year afterward in the cities or suburbs of Boston or New York, it seems to his friends and to himself that he is right in being disheartened, and in complaining for the rest of his life. A sturdy lad from New Hampshire or Vermont, who in turn tries all the professions, who teams it, farms it, peddles, keeps a school, preaches, edits a newspaper, goes to Congress, buys a township, and so forth, in successive years, and always, like a cat, falls on his feet, is worth a hundred of these city dolls.

Such discussions made explicit the conflict about returning that had been stirring in Calvin for years. On some days, the undergraduate was suddenly drawn again to Plymouth: "I have been thinking what I should do when I get out of College," he wrote home in tones entirely different from those heard in his plaints of freshman year. "Would you like to have me start in the store and live in Plymouth and live for Plymouth?" Better to dwell in one's own "citty on a hill" than to be a "city doll."

But on other days the senior was certain it was better to dwell just about anywhere else than in a village that was miles from nowhere. For the first time Coolidge put the question of staying directly, even sharply, to his father: "Would you prefer to have me enter some profession and go away and leave my community as almost every man of your generation who had ability did *except my father*?" In the old days it had been his father who had reported to him on the world. Now the son reported to his father: "I see [Oliver Wendell] Holmes is dead. . . . The Autocrat of the Breakfast Table on whom the years sat so lightly and who had only just declared that he was 85 years young. No one but Gladstone is left of those great men who were born in 1809. . . . The nineteenth century is slipping away. We are to live in the scientific age of the 20th century and must prepare for it now. There are millions who can only be hands and only a few who can be heads." Perhaps Calvin could be one of those heads.

The greatest of Garman's gifts was that he offered the students an image that allayed their concerns about failing, sinking, when they first plunged into the water of postcollege life. They sensed they might graduate into trouble: whether the president was Cleveland or Harrison, men were not always finding work; things seemed to be picking up, but there were many men idle. A career was like a body of water, a river. To prevail in the end, one need not captain the ship at first. All that was required to move a career forward was to stay with events and stay with the mainstream, avoiding crosscurrents. Sometimes the way forward would not be discernible; but the great trend was in the end "perfectly definite." If one started that way and hung in there, the waters would move one forward; chance would play a role and eventually one could become "a man of power." Garman believed that the very process of choosing was the crucial first step. To hear such ideas, to get a chance to discuss them, was marvelously comforting to the seniors as graduation approached.

Older and slightly larger—he had gained pounds and a few millimeters of height in college—Coolidge in that last year of college suddenly felt braver. His rooms were better, his friends were better, and he sensed that other men might like him. "I am confident I have gained a power of grappling with problems that will stand by me all my life," he wrote his grandmother. Morrow, Coolidge, Pratt, Deering, Harlan Stone from the year before, Professor Garman, George Olds, the wonderful math teacher—they were all united by the senior experience of the class of 1895. Buoyed, Coolidge undertook a number of projects as a senior. The first was to set about winning a name for himself in the class by running for class office. At Amherst, there were numerous officers for each class. Herbert Pratt ran for secretary, and Dwight Morrow would win the slot of class orator. Coolidge selected as his target the second orator's office, Grove Orator; he cast off his shyness and campaigned as if he were his father. "I put more work into that than Alfred did into the Freemen's Meeting," he wrote his father, the Alfred being Alfred Moore, a town treasurer in Plymouth. Listening to Coolidge, the other men heard what they had missed before: wisdom passed down from John and Calvin Galusha before him: "One should never trouble about getting a better job. But one should do one's present job in such a manner as to qualify for a better job when it comes along." The same autumn, the lucky autumn of his senior year, Coolidge published a short story in the October 1894 *Amherst Literary Monthly* that ranged far from both his debating and his humorous styles. The story, "Margaret's Mist," told of the maiden Margaret, who, betrayed by her fiancé, leaped to her death in Ausable Chasm, in New York. It was a romantic tale in the style his mother and he had favored: "the black water closing over her buried the sorrowing maiden forever beneath its bosom."

Even the economy that awaited them beyond college might be picking up. In late October 1894, he debated Charles Burnett on the topic of "Do the United States owe more to England or to Holland?" The pro-Dutch side might have advanced the facility of the Dutch in creating markets, their religious tolerance, and their expertise in commerce. The pro-English side argued for the purity of the Pilgrims and assailed the Dutch tendency to glorify and reinforce social class. The case that commerce was more Dutch than Anglo-Saxon was becoming harder to make in any event, as great brands were now being established by Americans descended from Puritans as well as Dutchmen.

The machine of commerce seemed more powerful than any ethnicity. What mattered was how innovative a merchant or manufacturer was, whether he could invent better machinery or improve a market. R. H. Stearns in Boston again provided an example. Stearns was an aggressive advertiser. That same autumn Stearns helped the newspaper that carried his advertising, *The Boston Globe*, with a letter testifying to the power of the *Globe*'s platform. Sunday night the paper carried a Stearns ad for 124 pairs of blankets, marked down to $1.90 owing to imperfections from their usual retail price of $4. By 10:41 the next morning, the company reported: "ALL SOLD." To console those who came too late, it sold blankets of the next best grade at the same price for the remainder of the day. As proud as Boston was of its commerce, it was also proud of its stock exchange; that year Clarence Barron, a young editor, published an entire volume on the stock market, *The Boston Stock Exchange*, making the case that when it came to finance, the "hub" truly was one.

Coolidge used some of the material from his debates to enter an essay contest sponsored by the Sons of the American Revolution. Coolidge submitted a piece on the concept of liberty as it existed in Great Britain before American independence. His point was a simple one: the American Revolution had not been about moving past Great Britain, it had been about the colonists reminding the corrupt Great Britain under King George III what its own freedoms were about. American liberty was English liberty, an idea popular among English-Americans but not so obvious to the Irish-Americans who were now populating the Bay State. Coolidge singled out important events: the confirmation of the Magna Carta by King Edward I; the Glorious Revolution that had driven out King James II. Of the Revolutionary War, Coolidge wrote, "Nor was it at first so much for gaining new liberties as for preserving the old."

It would be a long while before he knew the results of the essay contest, but in the meantime came another victory: he won the Grove Orator slot. Taking the job of graduation day speaker seriously, he put effort into the composition of his speech. He was writing more cleanly and less affectedly. In old speeches he had used the word "I" frequently and written long sentences; now he tried to cut himself out and shorten the sentences. Garman's message of selflessness was already penetrating.

Recognition usually comes when it is no longer necessary, and that was the case in Coolidge's senior year. It turned out that Phi Gamma Delta, the fraternity that had talked to him years before, might actually establish a chapter at Amherst. This time, Coolidge and Deering were both tapped. Coolidge did not hesitate. In fact, he was proud. "The fraternity, which I joined, rec'd congratulations quite as much as did I," he wrote to his father. Now he needed a dress suit, which cost $55, as well as a pin: "College men are always proud to wear a society, greek letter pin and are very seldom seen without it." He promptly leaped into Greek activities, attending dinners.

The fraternity was worth it, just as investing in a suit was; he sensed now that speaking was a great part of his life and that he might eventually earn money through it. Dwight Morrow went to Northampton to see the girls at Smith; Coolidge, however, was drawn there for errands and speeches. Phi Gamma Delta held a regional dinner at the Norwood Hotel there; a Yale senior complimented Coolidge on an impromptu toast he had made. "There is nothing in the world gives me so much pleasure as to feel I have made a good speech and nothing gives me more pain than to feel I have made a poor one," he wrote, triumphant. "I think I must stand very well in college now."

So close to graduation, Coolidge sent home letters that were a mix of high and low, private life and politics. One dated February 3, 1895, was typical: Coolidge first made a little joke about his own currency short-age and President Cleveland's: "I have paid out about $5,00 of the money you sent me before for current expenses so I have some by me though I have lent some which will be returned in a day or so I expect. There! That is my currency bill and I hope you will give it more approval than Congress gives Cleveland's ideas of currency." Then he tried out the idea of practicing law: "If I could read and digest the principle [*sic*] works of Burke, Hamilton and Webster, I should get a very strong hold on legal and political ideas, and then if I could add to it some actual experience of my own I should have a wisdom that at least would insure me a liv-ing if it did not give me power to direct great measures for the welfare of communities or states." Finally he appeared to lose heart: "I am only trying to get some discipline now. I never earned any money and I do not know as I ever made any happiness but I hope these may come later. I am almost ready to think of coming home again. . . ."

A trip home for his last spring break to the Vermont mud shifted his mood yet again. He could see his father struggling with his springtime work as road commissioner. "The heavy rains must have cost the Town considerable," he wrote sympathetically. "I hope you will be able to fix up the roads so every body will not be whining about them. Almost every sluice in Town needs to be repaired." In Vermont there was always some unexpected disruption: the summer after freshman year, lightning had struck his father's barns, burning them. Coolidge spelled out his ambivalence yet again for his patient father: "I have not decided yet that I want to leave Plymouth, not because I like the place to live in, I do not, not because I could do more good there, there are larger fields, but because I may owe some debt to the place."

The ensuing months found him and his father discussing not whether or not his trade would be law but the details of his legal education. There were two ways one could qualify to practice. One was law school. Several members of the class of 1894 attended school; Harlan Stone, a year out already, had enrolled at Columbia University in New York. Dwight Morrow was considering law school too. But there was another possibil-ity, the old way, for country lawyers: to read law while at a law firm, like an apprentice, and then sit the bar exam. That was less expensive. It was also what two lawyers the Coolidges knew, John Garibaldi Sargent and

William Stickney, had done. Sargent, an older graduate of Black River Academy, had attended Tufts and then read the law in Ludlow. Now "Garry," as he was called, practiced law with Stickney, who was climbing in Vermont politics. Sargent was the model of a gentleman—an enormous man, six foot four, who would build a library and a much-admired vegetable garden. To live like Garry or Stickney would be to live closer to what Jefferson, Garman, and Emerson described, closer to Cincinnatus. Coolidge, still eager to spend a few more years on a campus, gruffly informed his father that Stickney and Sargent's way wasn't the only one. John might try to educate himself on the merits of law school: "If you want to find something about law schools see French of Woodstock. . . . I do not think you will find the answer in "Men of Vermont" [an old book]. I should like very much to impress upon you that my life will be in the twentieth century." But again, typically, even as he postured, he vacillated: "But still a law office may be the best place to get discipline." He was nervous before his Grove Oration.

Yet the speech was a triumph. Calvin summed up the college experience, including its triviality, as a four-year period that "begins with a cane rush where the undergraduates use Anglo-Saxon, and ends with a diploma where the faculty use Latin, if it does not end before by a communication from the President in just plain English." The speech was also a quiet declaration of victory, a celebration of Calvin's own ability to make others laugh over a whole speech. "The mantle of truth falls upon the Grove orator on condition he wear it wrong side out," he declaimed. He promised in the speech to share with them "the only true side of college life on the inside." The fact that he was the orator proved to himself that he was finally there—at the inside, within college life. Harlan Stone later recalled that he had been "impressed by the humor, quiet dignity and penetrating philosophy." His grade point average was scarcely stellar at 78.71 but was ten points above where he had started freshman year. His graduation was noted in *The Caledonian*, the newspaper of St. Johnsbury, along with that of another St. Johnsbury alum, William Boardman. Coolidge also caught the attention of the alumni who were present for the graduation days, including John Hammond, the Northampton lawyer.

Students ran an annual survey to profile the seniors, asking them about religion, marriage plans, career plans, and so on. There was also a poll as to who was the brightest in the class; Dwight Morrow won hands down, but "Cooley," as the others sometimes called him, also received some votes. He was a long way from the oblivion of freshman year. Their responses to such questions were another chance for the seniors to try to demonstrate their wit. Coolidge did not forgo the opportunity. Under the question, "Are you engaged?" he wrote, "Severally." But he also delivered more serious responses. Under "politics," he listed himself as Republican. Asked their denominational preference, most other young men identified themselves as Congregational or Presbyterian. There was one Catholic in the class list and there were two Unitarians. "Presbyterian," Morrow wrote.

For denominational preference, however, Coolidge wrote "None," as did several others, including Ernest Hardy, his Northampton friend. As primitive as that response may sound, it did not mean that Coolidge was atheist or agnostic; it meant that he was unwilling to cede the independence, however slight that ceding, that affiliating with any denomination would entail. Others, when asked their work plans, listed "Law," "Business," "Travel," or "Undecided." Morrow wrote "Law"; Coolidge wrote "Undecided." When it came to the question of his plans for the following year, Coolidge simply replied "Nothing." This was the puerile dare to the world: don't ask me too early, or I shan't tell. It was also a play on "ouden," his own reminder to his peers of how far the rejected freshman had come. As the days of packing up approached, Coolidge made it clear to his father that the advantages lay with law school: "As a matter of fact the best law offices will not take in a man to do office work, such as the ordinary student does in the country office, unless he has been to a law school."

But the preference for the academic study of law at Columbia or Harvard was not the main point of the letter. That main point came in the quirky syntax of the final line: "P.s. I have not decided to study law." This time the ambiguity in a piece of Coolidge correspondence reflected maturity, not weakness. What this line said was that Garman was right: the decision itself mattered most, more than, say, the merits of either reading the law at a firm, attending law school, or working at the counter at the Notch. The quiet Vermonter who had seemed so unlikely to succeed now had good prospect of doing so. Suddenly Coolidge knew that he could undertake, even master, tasks that were unbearably difficult as long as the choice to undertake them was his own.

THREE

DETERMINATION

Northampton

THE NEW FORBES LIBRARY sat up on a hill, more fortress than book house. Its exterior was daunting pink granite taken from the Milford area of New Hampshire, alternating with pieces of red Longmeadow sandstone that had been hauled to Northampton. Each piece of slate on the roof was specially tied to girders that had just been laid a few months before by the Berlin Iron Bridge Company of Berlin, Connecticut; the roof was already renowned for its fireproof aspects. Inside, surrounded by the rock and thousands of books, amid the hissing of the new steam pipes, sat a twenty-three-year-old, Calvin Coolidge. He was reading the law after all.

The decision had been made for the simplest of reasons: economy. Tuition at Harvard Law that year was $150, and the university catalog estimated additional expenses of up to $471. That kind of outlay might have suited the Boston Coolidges, one of whose sons, Archibald Cary Coolidge, was a Harvard history instructor, and another, a renowned mathematician named Julian Coolidge, a Harvard graduate in Calvin's year, 1895, summa cum laude. But in the end it just hadn't sat with this Coolidge, necessarily, or with his father, struggling as John did with the cheese factory. Dwight Morrow was already signed up to clerk at a family firm, Scandrett and Barnett, in Pennsylvania. Coolidge had traveled to Saco, Maine, to see Percy Deering. From there the graduate had written to an acquaintance of his father's in Montpelier, former Vermont governor William P. Dillingham, who had a law office. It had been his last ambivalent letter about the law school choice. "If I could get into a good office, I am thinking of reading there some time," he wrote to Dillingham. "Is there a vacancy in your firm? . . . I should be pleased to go up to the city to talk with you or you can advise me by mail as to the terms you would take, if you ever bother with students." But meanwhile, Coolidge's friend Ernest Hardy had signed up to read law at the office of the attorney Richard Irwin here in Northampton. Thanks to Hardy, Coolidge secured an interview at Hammond and Field, another firm of Amherst men in the county seat. Hammond recalled having heard Coolidge in his Grove Oration. Hammond and Field offered Coolidge and another man, Edward Shaw, desks in their shop.

The task of mastering the law daunted, but a more inspiring symbol than Charles Forbes, the judge who had endowed this great library, would have been hard to find. Forbes had died only fifteen years before and was still a legend around the town, a cautious attorney who had assisted Daniel Webster and structured the will of the founder of Smith College, Sophia Smith. Thrift, above all, had yielded the fortune that paid for the library: an abstainer from alcohol and a bachelor, he had spent little on clothing and had carried the same gingham umbrella decade in, decade out, in order not to waste pennies on raingear. Again to save, he had dwelled in a small apartment above an office, rather than in a proper house. Investing cannily, especially in railroads, he had left a legacy of $252,000, despite the fact that his law practice had not exceeded $2,000 per annum. As Coolidge studied, in the library or at Hammond and Field, he set for himself two goals. One was the career goal: he would do as Garman had recommended and dip into the river of life, into a career, by qualifying as an attorney, a process that normally required three years. Maybe he could qualify in two. He set a second, private, goal as well: to find a wife.

Coolidge's determination resembled that of his father and grandfather, when, as young men, they had plowed or heaved rocks from the hillside in Plymouth. But right away, even in these first nights at the library, he could see that the prospects of reward for hard work here were far greater. By day, Northampton buzzed with energy, a new building going up everywhere one looked. In the dusk, lights made the streets of Northampton bright, so that the day was longer there than in the countryside. His delicate lungs liked the steam heat systems, which warmed rooms without covering them in coal dust. There was commerce here in Northampton, and there was also something more precious: access. The Boston and Maine Railroad had just given Northampton a new connection to the state capital by opening North Station in Boston. Trolley track would soon be laid that connected Northampton to the nearby towns of Holyoke and Amherst.

Along with a node in the network of commerce, Northampton was a node in the network of ideas. Educational ventures of many varieties had been founded there: A well-known author, statesman and philosopher, George Bancroft, had created an experimental school for children on Round Hill. Alexander Graham Bell had helped to establish what had become a nationally known school for the deaf, the Clarke School for the Deaf. There was a young college for women, Smith College. As if that were not enough, there were new institutions for self-education rather than education by teachers, reading rooms, and libraries like the one Forbes had established in the spirit of the great Andrew Carnegie. Towns like this were paradise to a young man from the farm hills. In fact, Northampton was even called "Paradise." The singer Jenny Lind had given it that nickname years before when she had visited. Lind had liked the trees and the green, but Northampton was also a paradise for commerce. Here a dictum of George Bancroft, the philosopher who had started the school, seemed to hold:

"Commerce defies every wind, outrides every tempest, invades every zone."

Serving commerce was also the work of Coolidge's new law office, which stood at the corner of Main and King streets, in a bank building at the heart of Northampton. Reading the law meant what it said, reading, and sitting in the swivel chair at his new black walnut desk, Coolidge plowed through James Kent's *Commentaries on American Law*. Kent began with international law, limning the advantage of written law among nations: "The most useful and practical part of the law of nations is, no doubt, instituted or positive law, founded on usage, consent, and agreement." However, one could not exclude, Kent wrote, the importance of "natural jurisprudence," which came from God. Beyond Kent, Coolidge read William Blackstone's *Commentaries on the Law of England*.

Blackstone had held that the job of the formal law "is to protect individuals in the enjoyment of those absolute rights which were vested in them by the immutable laws of nature." He had published his commentaries before the American Revolution, but in towns like Northampton, they were still the basis for working attorneys. Before Blackstone, Coolidge remembered, there had been Demosthenes, the stutterer, whom he had already studied. The great orator pronounced, "Every law is a discovery, a gift from the gods." That was a different approach from that being developed at Harvard Law School. It was different from, but not the opposite of, the image of the law put forward by Oliver Wendell Holmes, Jr., the son of the "autocrat" whose death Coolidge had noted. In *The Common Law*, a widely regarded treatise published the decade before, Holmes had emphasized cases, experience, and judges, not universal truths. But whether Coolidge sided with Holmes of Harvard or Stickney and Sargent of Windsor County, he could see something clearly already: this material was first-rate. New England's soil might be wanting, but her legal tradition was rich, something you could mine forever like the granite of the walls around him in the library. This law was not merely worthy of replication; it was worthy of export. When Northampton's capital and Northampton's connections combined with New England's law, there was no limit to what might be achieved.

The senior lawyers here took their share of cases involving the sort of petty battles and small feuds that preoccupied John Coolidge. That summer the Amherst College treasurer, Austin Dickinson, had died suddenly and the firm was representing Austin's sister, Lavinia Dickinson, in a dispute with his mistress, Mabel Todd, over a small patch of Amherst property. But the growth in Hampshire County meant most of Hammond and Field's work focused on more important quarrels. The pair represented trolley companies and railroads. Many cases related to larger principles such as property rights. The firm was also representing a man who, in excavating his land, had caused a cave-in on a neighbor's property; that was the very issue that had been preoccupying lawyers across the country throughout the period of industrialization. The most infamous example of it had been one of the great disasters of the era, the Johnstown Flood, which had taken place the year before Coolidge graduated from Black River Academy. Wealthy men, including Andrew Mellon, Henry Frick, and Andrew Carnegie, had purchased an artificial lake dug near Johnstown. Their workers had shored up its dam, but surveyors in Johnstown, downriver, warned that the engineering was insufficient to prevent a flood. The river flooded in 1889, killing two thousand people. But the fact that the club was incorporated had shielded the members from personal responsibility.

Coolidge would have welcomed an opportunity to chat with his bosses about principle and case, but just as he had feared when deliberating whether to read law, the employers would not look up. So the silent clerk set his own patterns. The court also sat on Main Street, in another new fireproof structure, situated on the same grounds that Daniel Shays's men had trodden when they came to stop the judges from sanctioning foreclosures. There were three civil and two criminal terms a year, and Coolidge made it his business to attend. Coolidge boarded at 162 King Street, across from the Boston and Maine Railroad yard, with a couple in their seventies, Charles and Rhoda Lavake. The Lavakes' daughter, who stopped by, noticed that he sometimes spread out and worked in the living room, with insufficient regard for what the others were doing. Soon he had a traffic pattern: the Lavakes' to Hammond and Field, Hammond and Field to the courthouse or the library. Sometimes he visited with James Lucey, the shoemaker, one street off his path, and got to know Lucey's friends, who were Irish and mostly Democrats. The issue of alcohol filled the newspapers; Lucey was a member of a temperance society. Lucey talked to him about clients and politics and offered up simple rules: Remember people. Help them. Using your office to help voters was not, in their eyes, always corruption; it could be plain old good service. Calvin also stopped at the barber's; his college hairstyle, side part and curl, was too long for meetings with clients.

Within days, Coolidge discerned another reason his new bosses passed by his desk without stopping. Both men were seeking political office. Field was running for mayor and was, Coolidge discovered, already an alderman; Hammond was going after the district attorney's slot. The pair always knew the latest about Amherst College. Field and Hammond, who sat on any number of local boards and committees, knew even more about Northampton. In July, Hammond had been chosen chairman of the board of trustees of a new hospital for consumptives.

Through his employers' campaigns that fall of 1895, Coolidge came to discern that spectacular growth brought with it its own challenges: crime, police work, and budgeting were three big ones. He also learned more about the exciting national movement starting up in the cities that he had noticed at Amherst: progressivism. Progressives preached reform in all towns, but everyone seemed to have a different idea of what reform was needed. What was it precisely? "Reform is Puritanism," the mayor of Boston, Edwin Upton Curtis, was telling his colleagues. Curtis's focus was Boston's police force, which was ridiculously decentralized. Police work was also the big issue in New York: the city's population was exploding, and so was its crime rate. A new police commissioner for the city had been appointed at a salary of $5,000 a year, a level Coolidge only dreamed of: he was Theodore Roosevelt, a young man from New York's Dutch aristocracy. "I want to see a police force here that is the finest in the world," he said. He was working on making admission to the police force more meritocratic and less subject to the wills of various political powers, whether "American, German or Irish," as he divided them. Under Roosevelt, policemen were trained, for the first time, to carry a pistol. Like the politicians of Northampton, Roosevelt was contending with the temperance controversy; in New York there were three competing impulses, Roosevelt said: "a strong sentiment in favor of honesty in politics," "a strong sentiment in favor of opening saloons on Sunday," and "a strong sentiment of keeping the saloons closed."

Hammond and Field had their own ideas of how young cities might handle such challenges. Field joined with a reformer named George Washington Cable and fixed up some rooms at the old Methodist church to create a space for the education of immigrants that they called the Home Culture Club. The idea was that the immigrants might there, at meetings, have a chance to learn history, civics, and English. With the immigrant population of Northampton growing fast, it was of course also a way to get to know future voters. In New York, Roosevelt was doing something similar, working with Jacob Riis, a social worker, to improve the spirits of young people so that they did not all become "toughs," as Roosevelt termed them; one such reform measure was the establishment of boxing clubs in the city. Watching those leaders, Coolidge could also see that Northampton was no poor jumping-off point for politics, either. Indeed, a Northampton man had once been governor of the state; Caleb Strong, who had read law in Northampton and become one of the Constitution's framers, had served for a total of eleven years at the beginning of the 1800s. As governor, Strong had proved feisty; deeming foreign policy to be the province of the states, not Washington, he had refused to send the Massachusetts militia against the British in the controversial War of 1812.

COOLIDGE'S COLLEGE FRIENDS HAD also now plunged into Garman's river, though not always happily. Dwight Morrow was languishing in his clerkship at a family firm, trying to organize his life so that he could attend Columbia Law School. Morrow tried his hand at politics for the first time, canvassing for his brother-in-law Richard, who sought a spot on a school board. But Morrow wrote to Charles Burnett, another classmate, "I have had my first contact with the great unwashed American sovereign and to say that I am discouraged and disgusted with city political methods is putting it mild." Morrow's nostalgia for Amherst only grew. "Life," he wrote that same classmate, "does not have any knight errantry left to it now." He wondered in his letters whether it might be a better idea to go back to New York. Maybe it was better to be a city doll after all.

Even in well-lit Northampton, there were dark moments for Calvin. In those first months he longed for some affirmation of his industry, some evidence that he would succeed in this endeavor. The Sons and Daughters had awarded him the silver medal for his essay on the principles fought for in the American Revolution. But his father had simply teased him, saying that the medal would "buy no bread and butter." At Thanksgiving, several months into the law, he teased back by writing to ask about the revenue from the wood on the limekiln lot. What if his father bought it from him? "I think I ought to have about one dollar a cord." Still, unlike some of his peers, he was not longing for Amherst. He liked both the law office and politics; case work suited his temperament better than school. Even the Berkshires of Massachusetts did not feel as strange as they might have. After all, Coolidges had dwelled in the area before; he did not feel he had migrated but felt he had "reverted" to Massachusetts. Dillingham, the esteemed Vermont lawyer, had finally replied with an offer to Coolidge to read law at his office in Montpelier. Coolidge now wrote him a politic refusal on Hammond and Field letterhead: "I had noted some little delay, but knew you too well to think it came from anything like discourtesy on your part. You see I am settled for the moment. I should perhaps prefer Vermont; but I could not better my place anywhere else out of the shadow of the green hills."

Thinking of Garman again, he kept studying. He now applied to his own case the advice he had given Dwight Morrow: one should not seek a promotion; one should do the best job in one's own work until others noticed. That notice finally began to come around Christmas, when Hammond and Field, both of whom had won their election races, began to loosen up and look around. Henry Field was surprised to see his clerk's name in the *Hampshire Gazette*: "It has been announced that J. Calvin Coolidge, a law student in Hammond & Field's office, has been awarded both the silver and the gold medal by the organization of the Sons and Daughters of the Revolution." The gold medal had come on top of the silver, earned earlier in the year. Field took the paper over to the quiet clerk to ask whether it was his name in the news. Yes, he replied, it was. Where was the medal? Coolidge slid open a drawer in the desk. There it lay. Had he told his father? No, Coolidge replied. But his father did find out and apparently even reproached him that he had not heard sooner. Coolidge wrote back and first needled him a bit: "I am quite sure you merely said that it would 'buy no bread and butter' at the announcement of the silver medal and so I had no reason from that to suppose you were interested in my winning medals." Then, however, the son went on to describe his prize in detail: "It is round like a coin weighs about nine ounces and is worth about $150." He signed the letter "Your affte son, J. Calvin Coolidge." The medal was embossed "J. Calvin Coolidge." But the young lawyer was in the process of ridding himself of that "John," and soon after he would become, simply, Calvin Coolidge. At some point, someone, probably Calvin, would rub out the "John" altogether. He was beginning to show who he was.

Mrs. Lavake died; Coolidge changed rooms more than once, scarcely noticing. The law was becoming his home, the cases his substitute for furniture, or friends. Hammond's spot as district attorney gave him a wonderful window into criminal law. And now Mabel Todd of Amherst, the astronomy professor's wife, was contesting Austin Dickinson's will in Hampshire County Court. On November 16, 1896, just after the elections, Hammond and Field filed a bill of complaint alleging that the Todds were taking Dickinson property by "misrepresentation and fraud." Field was also representing Susan Dickinson, Austin's widow, in another case. It involved graft by one of Austin's employees, Edward Baxter Marsh, at the Treasurer's Office. Marsh had used college funds to buy stocks. There was no evidence that Austin had known of it, but the case reflected poorly on Dickinson's stewardship.

Sometimes, very briefly, Coolidge did get away from work. He rowed, albeit rarely, and sometimes tried a little golf; the others found playing with him wearying because he treated the task as work. In the summer of 1896, he finally made it home to Plymouth. Again, his village magnanimously gave him a stage to debate on. At the Democratic National Convention in Chicago, William Jennings Bryan had warned that the East was killing the heartland with its gold standard; the farmer, he said, must not be crucified on a "cross of gold." The villagers, farmers but still mostly Republicans, were divided on the issue. They asked Coolidge to debate the gold topic. It was a pleasure to perform before his family. Just as in college, being home reminded him that he was making progress. Back in Northampton, he began to find friends. From time to time he dropped in at the S. E. Bridgeman Bookstore, where he befriended Robert Weir, a clerk and the grandson of a temperance activist. John Lyman, Coolidge's new landlord on Center Street, was also a "dry." Coolidge noticed Mabel Maynard, the daughter of a neighbor, Henry Maynard, and several years younger than himself. Mabel had red hair, like Coolidge himself and like Abbie. She was an accomplished musician, sang in public, and was at the center of the Republican political crowd in Northampton. Coolidge seemed to gravitate toward lively women with skills, rather than homebodies.

As he learned the law, the silent clerk began to speak, if only tersely, and his colleagues began to see a utility in his manner; his terseness appealed to clients. Like the friends at boardinghouses years before, they now began to set him up, so that his silent act would have greater effect. A selectman named Orville Prouty from the neighboring town of Hadley came to ask about whether he could move the body of a man killed while rowing on a lake. Prouty explained the problem to the slim man at the desk, who happened to be Coolidge. "Can move body," was Coolidge's three-word reply. Reports are that Prouty then asked, "Are you sure?" only to receive a four-word reply, "Yes, can move body." Prouty asked the boss, Hammond, how to react to the short understudy. Hammond replied: "I've found out when he says a thing is so, it is." The client soon saw that Hammond and Coolidge were correct. He was ready to come back with more business.

The 1896 presidential election pulled them all in; the clerk looked for ways to help his employers and his party. William McKinley, the Republican candidate, was a gold-standard man; the GOP, he said, needed to defend the standard. A former mayor of Northampton, John O'Donnell, had written a letter in the *East Hampshire Gazette* defending bimetallism. Coolidge penned a breathy, floral rebuttal to O'Connell for the Republicans to the *Hampshire Gazette* but also began to think about his own career. Northampton was made up of seven boards; for each board there were an alderman and a city councilman. The Republican City Committee selected the candidates. Coolidge joined the Republican Committee for Ward 2 in 1897, a year in which Field was running for election again. The issues were services such as streetlights and plumbing; towns needed to spend more, and more rationally. Field wanted to create a Board of Public Works for the young city and add a policeman, who would be Northampton's eighth. Field and Hammond both won.

In 1897, Coolidge finally found better rooms, this time because of a friend. Robert Weir had become the steward of the Clarke School for the Deaf and been given a house at 40 Round Hill Road as part of his compensation; he in turn made Coolidge his tenant. Though it was a year earlier than planned, Coolidge thought he would see if he could pass the bar exam. The county committee that oversaw the bar exam included Hammond, so Hammond withdrew to let the two other judges, William Bassett and William Strickland, evaluate his clerk.

Coolidge badly wanted some kind of victory. His Amherst peers were heading in various directions. Herbert Pratt was working in the family oil business and even donned blue overalls for a stint at the Queens County Oil Company; that year he had married Florence Gibb, whose family, like his, summered in Islip, Long Island. Dwight Morrow was studying law at Columbia and had an on-and-off girlfriend, Elizabeth Cutter, a Smith alumna.

Around his twenty-fifth birthday, July 4, 1897, the clerk finally had something to show: he had qualified with Bassett and Strickland, a year earlier than expected. Hardy too had qualified, as had the other clerk at Hammond and Field, Edward Shaw. His first goal was as good as accomplished. His family could see that "John" was really gone: his new business cards and other official documents now read "Calvin Coolidge."

Staying at Hammond and Field was not an option; the attorneys had let him know that. Coolidge therefore played down his achievement, warning his father that the next years would be hard: "Apparently there is no course for me but to open a law office in Northampton at a cost of about $700 and the probability of not making a living for a long time.

What do you think about it? I suppose this is what you contemplated when you sent me back to college five years ago and when you sent me down here two years ago—rather than let me try to live in Plymouth." He would need money, and he sent the usual peremptory orders to his father: "My books will cost $400." Back and forth went the letters from Plymouth to Northampton. Coolidge's uncertainty in turn made his father and stepmother anxious. In August 1897, Carrie wrote to send him a $3,000 life insurance policy, one of a number taken out in Calvin's name over the years. She also wrote to inquire, "Your father wants to know if there are any new developments in your business prospects."

Calvin considered practicing law elsewhere, including in Lee, Massachusetts, in the Berkshires. But Lee, which lacked streetlights, was no longer enough for Coolidge, now a Northampton "city doll." "It is just about like Ludlow," he wrote his father of Lee. "There is not a steam pipe in the town. Office rent $100, not lighted or heated. . . . The things I care for in life were not there. I know coal stoves are not very good for me." The great rail depot at Ludlow that had so impressed him as a boy now seemed tiny next to what was going up in Northampton and Boston. In another letter, Calvin laid out his image of his own independence: "I wish to furnish my office myself. I shall make my expenses as reasonable as possibilities permit. You will have to peace out my income until I can make it meet my expenses as you do now. An overcoat will be all I need for a year"—he wrote "peace," not piece, probably unconsciously, but it reads like a bid for his father's support. After throwing out a few names of possible employers, John, in one letter, finally suggested that Calvin work it all out by himself. "I cannot advise you in regard to best place for you to locate. Everything being equal I think Mass. preferable." Then he added a line to cheer his son on: "At first no doubt it will be a struggle to live but perseverance and fidelity will bring success."

As he settled himself in the fall of 1897, Coolidge chattered on about investments, perhaps in part to distract himself from the daunting thought that he would probably be hanging out his shingle alone. He tried to get his father to invest in a railroad between Northampton and Amherst, even working out the math for him: if the population between the towns rode back and forth once a week and there were 12,000 people in Northampton, 4,700 in Amherst, and 1,700 in Hadley, he reckoned an investment of $150,000 total would earn between 8 and 9 percent. A distant cousin, the engineer M. A. Coolidge, had worked on a rail line from

Amherst to Sunderland; the new line would take one "from Amherst House [a fine hotel in Amherst] and set him down at the Mansion House [in Northampton] quicker than steam."

By February 1898, it was settled: Calvin would stay in Paradise. He opened an office of his own in the Masonic Building on Main Street. It was just a few steps from Hammond and Field, but still it was his own. An ad in the Northampton City Directory listed him as "Calvin Coolidge, Law Office and Justice of the Peace"; the listing came under those of another attorney and the Northampton Paper Box Co. The office rent was $200 a year, double what he would have paid in Lee. He inherited some money from the Moors, his maternal grandparents, after his grandmother Abigail died in 1892, and that gave him a little breathing room. The cases he took were the common fare of the small-town lawyer: writs, deeds, rent collection.

That spring the United States was readying for war with Spain; President McKinley signed a declaration of war in April. Coolidge, who was very busy, could scarcely look up. When he did, he saw that Roosevelt, the municipal reformer and now assistant secretary of the navy, was heading for the front, believing that a man who took the position that one should fight for free Cuba ought to demonstrate his goodwill by fighting: "he should pay with his body." The Second Massachusetts Infantry, headquartered in Springfield, mustered in for war on May 10.

It was a brutal war with disconcerting collateral damage, and when a man from the town of Amherst fell, killed by a falling mango tree at the Battle of El Caney, it took eight mules and ten Cubans to exhume him and transport him to a ship back to the United States. The man was Walter Mason Dickinson, a distant cousin of the Dickinsons at the college. Roosevelt won at San Juan Hill and became a hero, but the war itself was not popular at home. "Send Second Home! Emphatic Demand of People in Massachusetts," read a headline in *The Boston Globe* on August 12, 1898. The regiment was mustered out by November, just around the time of the election. Coolidge could see that the war of liberation that the Cubans had thought they were waging had not turned out to be quite that. The U.S. Congress passed the Platt Amendment, formulated by Secretary of State Elihu Root, which stipulated that the United States would remain in Cuba until Cuba was ready for freedom.

In the fall of 1898, Coolidge sought his first serious political office, a seat on the city council. "Running for offices can be divided into two kinds of activity," wrote Quintus Tullius Cicero, the younger brother of the more famous Marcus, "securing support of your friends and winning over the general public." Coolidge found that what had applied in the day of Cicero applied in his as well: not only Mr. Lucey or Hammond and Field were important, though they were; finding new voters along the streets of Ward 2 was necessary as well. He managed well enough to win the slot.

The most important thing in Coolidge's life, though, was to make money through the law and end his requests to his father. Clients seemed to like him. In a trade where talent bills by the hour, the long-winded often fared well. But clients resented the extra charges. Coolidge's taciturnity, as in the case of the man on the lake, proved an advantage. So did his intuitive tendency to settle rather than litigate. In September 1898, the *Amherst Record* reported that Coolidge was representing the estate of William Kellogg, an Amherst man; Coolidge received $184.91 for the work, inclusive of expenses. Some days, he envied day laborers, writing his father, "There must be a good deal of satisfaction in knowing on Saturday night where you can earn twelve dollars the next week, and that the town will pay you. In the practice of law one never can have that feeling."

When the law failed him, at least once, he tried investment, with Hammond as his guide. Transport, which was always improving, still fascinated him. Through Hammond, and on his own, he had learned about trolleys and rails. Having personally experienced the great difference transport could make, he was thinking of investing in the trolleys. Hammond and Field represented the New York, New Haven and Hartford Railroad Company. The railroads were consolidating, and the antitrust crowd was focusing on railroads as an evil target. Coolidge was trying to offer the perspective of the railway's innovators and investors to a professor who, he sensed, might not yet have been exposed to that perspective.

To get a look at the inside of banking, he became counsel for and vice president of a new bank, the Nonotuck Savings Bank. He sent his father a birthday present, a signal of his hopes of earnings to come. Late in 1899, the city council selected Coolidge to be city solicitor, a job that did pay $600, a useful addition to the revenues from the practice. Like Round Hill itself, the curve of his rise was not steep, but visible.

As he left his rooms and came back, Coolidge found he was often bumping into Alfred Pearce Dennis, a young teacher at Smith College. Dennis too lodged on Round Hill, but in better rooms. Dennis, like most people, was initially fascinated by Coolidge's silence. They ate together at Rahar's, a new inn on Old South Street, where Hardy boarded. Liquor was legal in Northampton, and Rahar's advertised "foreign and domestic liquors and cigars," as well as "purest beer imported." There Coolidge found himself in another discussion about gold; Mrs. Rahar, the inn-keeper, demanded that she be paid with a gold coin; the men delighted in complying with her request. The new trolley circuit was up; passengers might ride a splendid thirty-two-mile circuit over two hours and a half. The entire circuit, from Northampton to Hadley and Amherst, cost seventy cents.

Coolidge's infatuation with commerce was not something all his friends, including Alfred Pearce Dennis, could share. One night, Coolidge and Dennis tested out the electric road. They rode a car that traveled the tracks up to Mountain Park, an amusement park, to observe the horses and the roller coasters. As they rode together on the roller coaster, Dennis later recalled, there were five minutes of silence, during which he dreamed of one of the Smith girls who had graduated the day before, "clothed in filmy white raiment." When Coolidge finally did speak up, it was to talk not about women but about the nuts and bolts of the railway: "I have been counting up the amount of material such as labor and crossties, rails, poles, copper wire, to say nothing of rolling equipment that have gone into the line. Some of our folks think we ought to strike for a nickel fare to Mountain Park." It was good politics to agree with a strike, he said, but he was not sure that it made sense. "Just as a matter of fairness," he told Dennis, the railroad was entitled "to a chance to make a living just the same as you and I." Dennis was dumbfounded; here was a man who seemed to miss the joy of Northampton, or another paradise, altogether.

Getting to know Coolidge as they walked up and down the streets, Dennis began to notice that Coolidge spoke well, omitting powerful curse words and even "the feebler New England diaconal oaths such as 'by heck' and 'by cracky' from his speech." He also decided, after a while, that Coolidge's silence was a form of affection. "It made him easy and comfortable to get along with. . . . But with him quietness was never assumed: it was as natural as breathing. And the queer part of it was that he was always seeking out companionship even though he did not want to talk." In the end, Dennis said, Coolidge's silence "had rather a charm for me." One might "sit with him on a three hour train from Northampton to Boston and really enjoy his companionship though he never said a word." Others, including his old law bosses, were beginning to feel the same way. Coolidge grew on them. And his aptitude for brevity continued to win notice. Now, in addition to being an advantage for private clients, the Coolidge style was an advantage for the general public. Whereas another city solicitor summed up a year's work of eleven cases in four printed pages, Coolidge used two pages to cover fifteen cases. Readers knew that shorter was harder and appreciated his work.

The year 1900 was a good one for companies and the nation generally. In the fall, around the time of the election, two brothers with a bicycle business were making improbable advances in flight with man-carrying gliders in Kitty Hawk, North Carolina. That fall of 1900, Calvin was not the only Coolidge who was seeking public office. His father's old friend William Stickney, a Black River Academy man, won the Vermont race for governor. John was to get a new post. Coolidge was by now enough of a political hand to want to advise his father, whether on dress for the inauguration or posts he might seek. He sent his father a picture of a Prince Albert coat as a sartorial suggestion; John bought the clothes and also received the honorary title of "Colonel" from his old friend.

The Vermont outcome was clear in September because Vermont held its elections early. But afterward, Coolidge waged his own more difficult campaign in the city council as city solicitor. He prevailed, winning a second term. He followed the Republicans in the wider races in the area, especially Winthrop Murray Crane, the candidate for governor of Massachusetts. Crane was related to Stephen Crane, who had sold currency paper to Paul Revere himself. Zenas Crane, Murray Crane's father, had established the current business, printing stock certificates and notepaper, in an era of poets and books, which had made him wealthy. But the son had made his mark as well. Years before, when he had been a young man like Coolidge, Crane had won for his company an enormous coup, the contract to print the U.S. dollar. Now Crane's presses at his "government mill" printed dollars for the rest of the country.

Crane differed from many of the other politicians. Perhaps because his own company employed many new immigrants, he understood the value they brought to the state. The new money would not be so easy to print without the skilled workers and Italians and Irish who worked at Crane. Crane was different from the Boston crowd that had created the Immigration Restriction League, which consisted of both Democrats and Republicans. Crane, whose paper company depended on a government contract, was a strong tariff man.

Crane's style was also unusual. The sandy-haired manufacturer's son read but was not bookish. He had a twinkle in his eye, and built a tight circle, and within that circle he and his advisers enjoyed themselves. When William M. Butler, an attorney in his entourage, moved into a Boston house next to another Crane ally, George Lyman, Crane suggested opening a door between the two houses, so that the two might meet without Boston formality and in privacy. In public though, Crane turned taciturn and became famous for skipping speeches. Other politicians talked. Crane gave few speeches. He was an operator, a power behind the scenes. It was said that he never wrote when speaking could do and never talked when a nod would suffice. The letters he did write often ended, "But I'll talk to you about it when I see you." Without speeches, Crane still proved a stellar vote getter: that year he beat Robert T. Paine, the father of a man who had cofounded the anti-immigration league, to win the governor's job by more than 20 percentage points. Governor Crane was a model of what Coolidge might become.

Despite such inspiration, Coolidge sometimes flagged. Money was still too tight, and he felt too close to the bankruptcy cases he was now representing. "I was duly reelected to the office of city solicitor," he wrote to his father in early 1901. "There were a couple of Irishmen after the job. They made me some trouble but they did not secure votes enough. I have business enough to get a fair living but there is no money in the practice of law." He was even, again, a little sour: "You are fortunate that you are not still having me to support." Sometimes his victories were mere accidents. The Democratic candidates had quarreled, leaving Coolidge with a plurality and victory. That confirmed what Garman had told him: if one avoided being sidelined, sometimes one moved forward. Representing the city of Northampton put him on the other side of the property debate, just as being tax collector had shown his father the other side of the revenue equation. He was often in court, despite his inclinations, and did not always win. The city claimed some land along a highway as its own; a private party claimed that the land belonged to him. Coolidge, representing the city, felt "I should have won these cases on the claim that the land in question already belonged to the highway." The jurymen, his fellow Yankees, sided with the private party.

And for all the progress he had made in the law, there was at first not much progress to show with women. Percy Deering's sister, Rose Deering, had caught his eye; she attended Smith. But early hope of something there had fizzled; by May 1901, he was letting her know that he forgave her rejection: "My dear Miss Deering:—There is nothing to pardon, you always do all I could wish. . . . It is very dear of you to let me come, I shall not forget. I am so tired."

He may have been tired of romance, but he resolved not to tire in his work: elections. After all, the city solicitor races were an example of Garman's theory of staying in the mainstream. Sometimes he won only because Democrats quarreled, but he did win. He also studied how politicians comported themselves and in all kinds of situations. How did the ship of state move? How did you turn it when a storm hit? Vice President Roosevelt provided a compelling answer when President McKinley was shot by an anarchist, Leon Czolgosz, a worker who had been laid off at his factory around the time of the Pullman strikes. Roosevelt was on Isle La Motte on Lake Champlain, as McKinley declined. But then the news turned dark, and Roosevelt traveled to Buffalo. By the time he arrived by the New York Central, McKinley was dead.

Stability was the dominant concern of the New Yorker. The number of hours between an old president's death and a new one's swearing in had to be short. Roosevelt himself chose the venue for the swearing in, the Delaware Avenue home of his friend and adviser Ansley Wilcox; its pillars evoked the White House and Monticello. Before the swearing in, he attended church, but at the swearing in there was no Bible, probably because everyone had moved with such dispatch. Observers could see that Roosevelt stepped with great care in these crucial hours: the Rough Rider was not rough now but rather decorous. In the name of continuity, he reappointed the key figures of McKinley's cabinet. In a very small way, Coolidge was pulled into the politics of the transition; he was assigned to give a eulogy for the president in Northampton. Coolidge spoke of McKinley's service and his devotion to his work. The young attorney could see that the sad events were an example of Garman's theory of chance: something had happened. Fate had intervened. Because Roosevelt had been in the water, now he was president.

But Roosevelt did not stay decorous long. By temperament Roosevelt was neither judge nor solicitor but prosecutor. In fact, he treated the White House as a prosecutor's office. In McKinley's time the Sherman Antitrust Act had not been used aggressively; Roosevelt, however, found it a useful tool. Roosevelt moved against the Northern Securities Company and J. P. Morgan aggressively, asking for the great company's dissolution. Astonished, J. P. Morgan asked TR if his other companies would be assailed. "Not unless we find out," said Roosevelt, "that they have done something we regard as wrong."

In an area where voters had an obvious stake, coal for heating, Roosevelt moved especially aggressively. All of New England lived with one preoccupation: how to heat in winter. Coal workers had organized a new kind of union, not like the Carpenters' Union, whose Northampton chapter, number 351, met at 38 Main Street on the first and third Wednesdays of every month. This new union, the United Mine Workers, struck in May and at first received little notice. But it stayed on strike, and with each day that passed a heatless winter became more probable. Normally companies and workers settled these things with each other, but President Roosevelt was in a mind to intervene. In September, he visited Massachusetts, where he happened to endure an accident while riding with Murray Crane. Their landau was struck by a trolley car while en route to Lenox from Pittsfield. A Secret Service man was killed, but Crane escaped unhurt and Roosevelt merely injured a leg. That underscored Roosevelt's authority: once again, as on San Juan Hill, he had laughed at death.

By October, some schools could not open owing to lack of heat. The price of coal had risen from $20 to $30 a ton. There was a fear of what Roosevelt himself termed "coal famine." Grover Cleveland, the stalwart noninterventionist, wrote to propose a solution to Roosevelt: that coal production somehow be started again for a short period to allay the emergency, "leaving the parties to quarrel." George Baer, the president of the Philadelphia and Reading Coal and Iron Company, on the other side, warned that mining was "not a religious sentiment or academic proposition," and noted that "God in his Infinite Wisdom had given control of the property interests of the country" into the right hands.

But President Roosevelt reacted differently from Cleveland or McKinley before him. First, he threatened a military solution: to send 10,000 troops to run the mines, operators and miners be damned.

From his wheelchair—the wound he had suffered in Pittsfield was now infected—he put himself forward as arbiter, inviting the United Mine Workers and the companies in to try to persuade them to find a settlement. His leg injury had emerged as a serious matter; infected, the leg refused to heal. The accident had sealed a bond between Roosevelt and Crane, to whom he now turned for support in this approach. The president also warned the country of the price if he did not succeed: "untold misery," Roosevelt wrote Crane in Boston, "with the certainty of riots which might develop into social war."

In the end, Crane, who had earlier negotiated a rough conflict between the Teamsters and employers in his state, did help President Roosevelt find a settlement with the coal men. Many of the companies were not pleased with the way Washington had forced them down to equal footing with the miners. But the part of the story that interested a man like Coolidge was that Crane had participated in negotiating a national settlement. His own prospects for rising to Crane's level were now beginning to seem real. Coolidge's career was bumping upward; he was even able to turn down a well-paying and well-respected job, that of county clerk, because he saw greater opportunities at the bar; it felt good to say no to $2,300 a year.

Still, the wife he hoped for was missing. He might have taken an interest in the administration of Cable's Home Culture Clubs, but he remained a boarder himself. Men from Amherst had found spouses—Dwight Morrow had married Elizabeth Cutter, the Smith graduate, in 1903, and Harlan Stone had been married since 1899. The truth was that Coolidge was already settling into the easy life of the political bachelor: party meetings, working, and resting in his rooms. There were women in Northampton, at Smith College, which was itself a sort of showcase for educated women. There were the female teachers of the Clarke School for the Deaf, some of whom lived in Baker Hall, a redbrick dormitory. Each time a hole wore in his sock, he put the sock aside to be darned. But he did not darn them, and the pile grew. It was as though he were living behind glass; the girls were on the other side, and he could see but not reach them. Perhaps the right girl would know to break through herself and get to him, first.

Finally, she did. One morning Calvin planted his hat on his head and began shaving. A peal of laughter coming through his Round Hill window startled his ear. The laughter, Coolidge's housemate, Weir, told

him later, was from a teacher at the Clarke School, one of Miss Caroline
Yale's recruits. The teacher lived just across the way and had spied him
while watering the flowers on the lawn outside her dormitory. Soon she
sent him a pot of flowers, and he sent her his calling card. Their first date
was at a political rally at Northampton City Hall.

The name of the laughing teacher was Grace Anna Goodhue. She
had come to Northampton from Burlington, where she had graduated
from the University of Vermont. Six and a half years younger than
Calvin, Grace was graceful, like her name, dark-haired, and enthusiastic. At Vermont she had sung in the glee club. She was one of the young
women who had helped to found the University of Vermont chapter of
Pi Beta Phi and participated avidly in the alumnae activities. She made
friends everywhere. The breezes that crossed the green at the University
of Vermont were more meritocratic and freer than the sometimes stuffy
air that overhung Amherst.

Dennis, Coolidge's partner on the trolley ride, called her a "creature
of spirit, fire and dew." Other men also found Grace stunning, and were
stunned to find that she favored the quiet lawyer. Coolidge's acquaintances noted that the Coolidge and the teacher listed on page 267 of the
1904 Northampton Directory were opposites, so stark as to make the
relationship unlikely. Grace's father, Andrew, was a Grover Cleveland
Democrat, whereas the John Coolidges were Republicans. Grace's house
on Maple Street in Burlington had steam and electricity, whereas the
Colonel still scratched out his notes by kerosene light. Calvin hung away
from the church, unaffiliated and uncertain, while as a girl Grace had
already known her mind, dropping the Methodist Church and determinedly leading her parents to the Congregationalists. He retreated into
law books; she loved theater. He disliked sports and lacked skill in them.
She could dance—not perfectly but adequately—skate, and play baseball. Whereas Coolidge was fair, she was dark; later, other women would
comment on her lustrous complexion, a shade of olive that suited both
pastels and strong colors, even the deep red or plum velvets that were
popular in the era. He appreciated handiwork but didn't do much of it:
Grace knitted, sewed, and crocheted all the time—indeed, she was so
handy it was said that she had learned to sew before she learned to walk.

Instead of putting them off, their differences drew them together.
There were also some similarities beneath the surface. The two were both
Vermonters who had traveled down the Connecticut to Northampton.

The Goodhues were descended from Puritans as well; William Goodhue had emigrated from England in 1636, and, as was the case in Calvin's family, had made his way to Vermont via Massachusetts. One of Grace's ancestors had represented Massachusetts in the U.S. Senate shortly after Vermont had reluctantly become a state. Grace's father, an electrical engineer, had owned a machine shop on Maple Street. He had also, like John, done his time as a public bureaucrat.

Captain Goodhue, as he was known, had served as inspector of the steamboats on Lake Champlain from 1888 to 1920. Grace's name was not so different from his sister's, Abigail Gratia. To Calvin, getting to know Grace felt like getting to know someone he already knew. Weir told a joke about the match: Miss Goodhue had taught the deaf to hear; now she might be able to teach the mute to speak.

And speak now he did, both in person and in letters on stationery bearing his name, in curlicue Art Nouveau lettering. The tone was both romantic and peremptory. "My dear Miss Goodhue:—As I am not quite certain what you decided about the Colonial Reception, I think I will tell you that you may expect me to call for you about a quarter before eight Tuesday evening," he wrote on June 6, 1904. "Now I shall not be happy if you do not go." And then: "My dear Miss Goodhue, The mosquitoes, have you recovered from them yet?"

Suddenly he was going to events or places he had skipped before. He took her up to Mount Tom and bought her a keepsake, a little plate. For her, he agreed to ice-skate, though he had always preferred the more for-giving snow sport of "sliding" (sledding); the fleet Grace left him behind on the ice. Around the time Grace and Calvin got to know each other, Northampton marked its 250th anniversary. The commercial town born of Jonathan Edwards's Puritanism and idealism saw no contradiction in sermonizing at parties. The celebrations included a loud parade a full two miles long and choral performances of "To Thee O Country" and "Auld Lang Syne" by Smith girls. The great novelty was the illumina-tion of the town, made possible by the recent arrival of electricity. The little courthouse fountain Coolidge often passed now lit up. Rahar's Inn, where Coolidge liked to dine, featured a flashy electric sign reading "Down where the Wurzburger flows." Murray Crane had served as gov-ernor for several years, but now John Lewis Bates, a Boston Republican, held the post. Bates delivered a fire-and-brimstone speech entitled "Is It All Evil?" In one room at a Daughters of the American Revolution event

Calvin and Grace attended, two elegant chairs stood invitingly ready. Calvin and Grace, both descendants of revolutionaries, sat in them. An usher ordered them up, remonstrating that the chairs were reserved for Governor Bates and his wife.

The governor might have seemed like royalty, but the newspapers knew he was mired in a difficult controversy. One of the oddities of Massachusetts at the time was that the governor, rather than the mayor of Boston, appointed the Boston police commissioner. Bates's appointees at the police department were contested by the policemen, many of whom believed the state and commissioner discriminated against the Irish population of the city. That was the sort of issue even Northampton politicians confronted. They not only had to hire police, they had to promote them and keep them happy.

But for now Coolidge's focus was not municipal policy; it was Miss Goodhue. Catching some of the city's festive spirit, he invited her to a meal a week after the Northampton anniversary: "Miss Boyden has promised to make us a nice old fashioned strawberry shortcake and have it ready to serve Tuesday evening about six o'clock, after we have eaten the appropriate courses leading to it. I don't just dare to turn you loose on a whole meal of short cake! . . . Besides I shall be very glad to see you, so you must not let anything interfere when I call for you." It appears that the cake date was a success; within a few days he was writing again: "You made Tuesday evening so pleasant for me that I am wondering when I may come back." By July, just after his birthday, things had gotten more intimate: "How like yourself your letters are—and you, you are like the morning in my own Green Hills and I am afraid I shall not get to Vermont."

That summer of 1904 the beguiling teacher returned to Vermont for a holiday. He discovered that even from long distance, she cheered him. Carrie Coolidge was ill, and now he had a friend to share his concerns with, even to take advice from: "I know I ought to go home to see my mother, she is not very well this summer. Perhaps I will since you recommend it." His golf practice was covered in those letters, but with none of the grimness that had come through earlier: "I am very busy at the golf club. I can hit the ball now and do not have as much trouble losing it."

Work and politics took his attention as well. George Hoar, the old senator, died that September, and Bates named Crane to replace Hoar in Washington. "He will not be an orator as Hoar was or a scholar in politics as his colleague Mr. Lodge," commented *Congregationalist and Christian World* in describing Crane, "but he will bring things to pass." The new chairman of the Republican Party of Northampton—Coolidge— noticed that taciturnity had lifted Crane to the national stage.

Tariffs to protect New England businesses were the focus of Crane's work; the more pro-tariff men in Washington, the safer New England factories would be. James Burton Reynolds, a Dartmouth man and political figure in Massachusetts, would shortly go to Washington as assistant secretary of the Treasury; Reynolds's duty was also to ensure that New England was protected. Reynolds would hang a picture of the first customhouse in Yorktown, Virginia, on the wall of his office. At a time when tariffs were the greatest source of revenue for the federal government, Reynolds's job was a mighty one. In 1907 the federal budget was less than $1 billion; his office alone collected $350 million in tariffs.

In the autumn of 1904, Roosevelt, the incumbent, stood a good chance of beating the Democrat Alton Brooks Parker, and he let the country know that he knew it. Coolidge's confidence in his own campaign seemed to parallel that of Roosevelt in his. "My dear Miss Goodhue," he wrote, "It is very nice of you to promise to show me places of interest about here, those that keep people from church. I'll confess I am not very familiar with them but you—you can show me. . . . I have half a bushel of butternuts and tomorrow when you are reading this or when you are sitting with as much dignity as you can in the deacon's pew I shall be eating and eating. Canst crack the butternut?" And also: "My Dear Miss Goodhue, How is it you are always so ready when I ask you for anything?"

By the end of September, the tone became more intimate: "Since I left you on Wednesday evening I have been thinking of what a delicious merry looking bundle you were. And now I will tell you something. I want to see you again. That's really true. . . . Will you come to the golf club Saturday afternoon. . . . Will you listen for the telephone?" And in October, he was courting her in the familiar language of contract: "A source of regret to me that I did not remind you that you owed me a note—in fact several and I find you are slow in replying. Well if you are you have so many other credits I am sure I am your debtor—bankrupt. If you will come in and see me some day perhaps I will make your will— you may bring Miss Willoughby for a witness."

As the autumn progressed, President Roosevelt's rhetoric became ever surer; thousands of college students cheered him at Madison Square Garden; it was clear that his victory was ensured. Coolidge's confidence in his campaign for Grace also mounted: "You must come—my bowling party is not complete without you." He sought, above all, more time from Grace, that she might consider his virtues from every angle. "Sometimes I think," he wrote on November 6, 1904, "the best part of having you with me is after you are gone. For it is only when I am alone again that I realize how much pleasure you really made for me and remember that I express so little of it to you at parting. . . . if *you* gave me much practice I *might* learn to do a *little* better."

Two days after Coolidge's suit for more time, the nation gave Theodore Roosevelt the time he sought with 56.4 percent of the vote. It felt good, TR would allow, to win "in my own right." In 1904, the country seemed to think it was good that Roosevelt had won, too. In March 1905, the Dow Jones Industrial Average approached the 80 mark for the first time, and Roosevelt was inaugurated, promising that he would not run again; this full term, plus the time he had served after McKinley's death, was enough. One of the first things Roosevelt did, on March 17, was to preside over the wedding of his niece, Eleanor Roosevelt, and her fifth cousin once removed, Franklin Delano Roosevelt. The ebullient Teddy overwhelmed the young Roosevelts and so starred at their event that they were overshadowed. But such behavior was not unusual for Theodore, as his daughter, Alice, would comment later: "He wanted to be the bride at every wedding, the corpse at every funeral, and the baby at every christening." People noticed that the Roosevelts took over the White House and also that they kept wonderful pets there: when Archie, their son, was sick, the attendant even took the pony Algonquin up in the elevator to visit him.

Roosevelt warned that big business, especially railroads, was taking away from the rest. Of that Coolidge was not so sure. His own work was still largely the work of representing individual businesses in town. Business was going well now, and he could see that laws themselves could sometimes hinder commerce. Business needed freedom to pursue its own course. A transfer student at Amherst, Bruce Barton, the son of a minister from Illinois, was making a similar discovery in the same years. Barton was doing fine at Amherst but felt himself "too poor to be particularly happy." Unlike Coolidge before him, Barton ambitiously sought off-campus work. He noted that college men "averse to intimate contact with irate old men and bulldogs" didn't like working as door-to-door salesmen. But Barton gave it a try, vending aluminum pans to housewives. The dream of Coolidge's classmates in the Mellon venture had taken hold: people were taking to the new product. Davis's efforts were paying off, yet men like Roosevelt might merely regard aluminum as a trust to be dismantled.

In Northampton, the population of immigrants was swelling, and that was true in other towns as well. What might be the best future for those souls? Coolidge believed that education was the best start. That year Coolidge's Home Culture Club achieved a coup when Andrew Carnegie, its great donor, paid a visit. With Carnegie money, Cable had purchased a pillared mansion on Northampton's Gothic Street, just a few doors down from James Lucey. Carnegie was Judge Forbes writ large, the emblem of what private charity could do. To Coolidge, who had made himself a lawyer in a library, it all made sense; in 1905, he became the Home Culture Club's secretary.

What was the future of the kind of laborer who went to the Home Culture Club? Was it all right for unions to organize him? The Supreme Court apparently didn't think so; in late spring 1905, the justices reviewed *Lochner v. New York*, a case of a baker in Utica who would not follow the state's laws when it came to his contracts with his workers, allowing them to work more than the state-mandated maximum of ten hours per day and sixty hours per week. The Court found that Joseph Lochner and his employees had been within their rights when they had signed their contracts. The employer and employee in their relations were not to be intruded upon. The state law, the Supreme Court held, impinged upon a right to be found in the Fourteenth Amendment, the write to "life, liberty and property." The decision was written by Rufus Peckham, a justice who had himself read law in New York State.

But not everyone agreed. "The working class and the employing class have nothing in common," read the manifesto of a new group of radical workers founded that same month of June 1905 in Chicago. The Industrial Workers of the World saw trouble ahead: "There can be no peace so long as hunger and want are found among millions of working people and the few, who make up the employing class, have all the good things of life." In the court itself the finding was only 5–4, and Justice Holmes dissented. At Harvard Law School, Felix Frankfurter had just been named editor of the *Harvard Law Review*. He snapped awake at the separate dissent by Justice Holmes. Holmes's view was that the majority justices were putting their politics above the law; "The Fourteenth Amendment does not enact Mr. Herbert Spencer's Social Statics," he said cuttingly.

Still, the differences among political men and women did not seem to matter as much as the economic growth, which was considerable. The cities were growing. "The most distinctive characteristic of our American cities is their newness," an illustrator, Frederick Knab, wrote in a book published that decade celebrating Northampton. The railroads were growing, and there were other, newer forms of transport. Some of the changes were harder for the older generations to take. Young men had always disturbed the peace of Northampton, but now they were doing so with a new and infuriating intrusion: the automobile. One Sunday evening in May 1905, a young man who gave his name as William S. McClintock drove a car on a joyride on Northampton's Elm Street. Coolidge's old boss John Hammond witnessed the ride. He made a furious report to the city on the heedless joyrider. McClintock poured salt on Hammond's wound when he responded to Hammond's inquiry with a curt reply: "None of your business." Coolidge represented McClintock, who paid a $50 fine. Nor were the new cars the whole story. People were constantly experimenting with flight. That October, Wilbur Wright would make the Wrights' longest controlled flight to date, 24.2 miles in thirty-eight minutes at Huffman Prairie Flying Field near Dayton, Ohio.

Calvin took Grace to see his father and his grandmother in Plymouth. He showed her all the beauties of his Green Mountains and the corners of his town. The houses were more primitive than those of Burlington, where Mrs. Goodhue had long since retired the kerosene lamps to the top shelf. But Grace liked Plymouth, and both the Colonel and Aunt Mede liked Grace. "That's a likely girl," the grandmother said, high praise from Plymouth. Coolidge returned so merry that even newspaper editors noted it, reporting that the lawyer in the Masonic Block had had an "excellent" vacation.

Shortly after, the pair were off to Burlington. Grace and Calvin were quietly forming their own view of how a marriage might work. They both believed, as Grace later put it in the women's magazines, that "a household must have a head" and someone else should run the house and darn the socks waiting in the bags and the drawers. They were both concerned about the cost of home owning. A couple of years prior, *Ladies' Home Journal* had published a special section on buying one's own home. The forced saving of a mortgage was presented in the magazine as a virtue. "Bless me how we did economize. . . . The lifetime of a garment extended far beyond the allotted span for such things," a Virginian wrote in the magazine. A Missouri homeowner revealed that the mortgage had trained his family to save: "So deeply was the habit of saving rooted with us, we have continued to save to some extent and now . . . have bought and paid for several other houses." That forced saving sounded as though it might suit Grace and Calvin. Calvin was setting aside money for his marriage even as he penned the letters.

Coolidge attempted to look at it all practically. The fact that Grace was a talent with a needle did not elude him; he would tease her about darning all those socks. But he did not really require the kind of house-keeper his grandmother was, nor even seek one. He did not even want the abstract wife he had been hoping for in the lonely days at the Lavakes'. What he wanted was this particular girl. He appeared in the Goodhues' Maple Street parlor in Burlington, and Mr. Goodhue inquired as to why he had come: "Up here on some law business, Mr. Coolidge?"

"Come to see about marrying Grace," Calvin replied. Captain Goodhue was taken aback, but he warmed to Calvin; he could see that he was somebody real, a professional man. It was evident both to Goodhue and to others that Coolidge was, as Garman might put it, in the swim of life. If there was a paradise for the determined, Coolidge was glimpsing it. He had made the law his trade just as he had planned those days in Forbes. Lemira Goodhue proved harder to charm than her husband. Grace's mother didn't like the idea of the marriage and, after finally relenting, still tried to postpone the wedding. She insisted that Grace wait to marry until she taught a year or learned to bake bread. They would buy bread, Calvin snapped back.

For a while, they were back in Northampton, Calvin at work, planning a run for the school committee. It would be a tight race: his Democratic opponent, John J. Kennedy, was someone he liked. "Calvin, I think I've got you beaten," teased Kennedy when they met. "Either way, they'll get a good man," Coolidge shot back. There was no point, he was learning, in making enemies. His engagement, now finally seemingly real, distracted him. The schoolchildren at the Clarke School favored Grace; it was hard to find someone who did not. They made a habit of peeping around the door when her beau came to visit at the school. One pupil remembered that Coolidge always placed his hat on the floor upon entering Grace's classroom. Mrs. Goodhue finally relented and said that the wedding could take place in 1905, but only, at the very earliest, that November.

The wedding took place in October. The Coolidges brought a counterpane knotted by his mother for the couple to take away with them. In the last hours before the ceremony at her parents' house, Grace had a few doubts and wrote to her friend Ivah Gale about the forthcoming event. She was especially concerned about how the marriage would come between her and others she loved so much. "It isn't without a great big sigh and a bigger little pain down in my heart that I begin this my last letter before the scene is changed. That might surprise my mother, who claims I have not feelings, because I don't talk about them. . . . I am sure that you and Calvin are going to like one another very much. . . . Mother isn't very strong and she feels a little bit hard because I am going so hurriedly and sometimes he says things which strike in pretty deeply. . . . Well it is almost over, anyhow and time will effect a cure, I think."

Still, when the hour came she was ready in a dress of pearl gray silk etamine. Fifteen guests, including Calvin's father, Aunt Mede, and his aunt Mrs. Pollard of Proctorsville, assembled on Maple Street. It rained, but Calvin scarcely noticed. Grace's hair was up in a pompadour, hardly comfortable but certainly the fashion. Calvin wore a Prince Albert, a double-breasted frock coat of the sort he had recommended to his father, and a derby hat, something like what he had worn when she had first espied him through the Round Hill window. The ceremony was performed by a distinguished minister Grace chose, Edward Hungerford of the Congregational Church in Burlington. Coolidge placed a gold chain around his bride's neck and set out with her. They traveled by train from Burlington to Montreal, but it could have been an automobile or even a glider in the sky, like the Wright Brothers'. For now Coolidge was flying. Miss Goodhue was his.

FOUR

THE ROOSEVELT WAY

Boston

ESCAPE WAS ON THE couple's mind as they headed north from Burlington to their honeymoon destination of Montreal. There the pair could walk, eat, or take in a show as Mr. and Mrs. Coolidge at last. But after a few days, the Coolidges found themselves restless. Determination alone had sufficed for Coolidge at the start, but it would not propel him all the way up the river of life that Garman had described. Within a few weeks the school committee election would come, and this time the competition looked tight. His opponent, John Kennedy, was Irish American, and if he won, he would be the first Irish American to hold a major office in Northampton, evidence of the new power of the immigrant group. The cross tides that Garman had warned about would sideline Coolidge if he did not understand the party well. Those moving ahead fastest took advantage of the progressive current. He might ride with the progressives, work with them as Murray Crane did. Or, perhaps better still, he might emulate their captain, the U.S. president, Theodore Roosevelt.

There was no escaping Roosevelt in any case, not even on a honeymoon. The presidency was Roosevelt's, not the other way around: Roosevelt found the office to be a wonderful tool, a "bully pulpit," as he would call it, and he used the office with energy. In Washington Roosevelt reigned omnipresent. But news of the twenty-sixth president also stretched across and up and down the continent, penetrating bookstands, cafés, and hotel lobbies from Boston to Seattle, from Mexico City to Montreal. Updates on the Roosevelt administration's Russo-Japanese Treaty made it to Canada; so did the report that the White House thought it was time to change the rules of college football. Then there was Roosevelt's decision to regulate prices charged by the continent's most important industry, railroads. Every time the president reiterated his commitment not to run for a third term, telegraph machines clattered. So irritated were the editors of the *Montreal Gazette* that they penned an ironic note of gratitude that the U.S. president sat a good five hundred miles down from the Canadian border: "Only the fact that the President is unable to leave the United States during his term of office enables the north pole to retain its seclusion."

There was much to imitate in the man. Roosevelt had overcome childhood illness to become a powerhouse who seemed nearly unearthly in his physical strength and power of recuperation. Coolidge was still hostage to his fragile lungs; even trips to the country laid him low for hours. Roosevelt had served in war, heroically, whereas Coolidge had not. Roosevelt commanded a room's attention the instant he entered, whereas Coolidge had to earn it. Roosevelt might be a Harvard man, but he lacked the deep snobbery of the old Republicans, like the stuffy Senator Henry Cabot Lodge. His brand of progressivism, too, made good sense to Coolidge. Roosevelt had a record of advancing other principles Coolidge treasured: sound budgeting instead of political waste and patronage; rigorous civil service, health care, and school reform; progressive management to benefit all and make the country more prosperous. Roosevelt understood immigrants and won some of them over— precisely Coolidge's task in the wards of Northampton for that fall's school committee contest. Roosevelt managed and placated the trade unions to preclude painful coal strikes. Roosevelt wanted to honor old laws, such as the Sherman Antitrust Act, and use them to pursue offenders. He also understood the importance of the American ideal.

Beneath it all there was the question of character. You might not know if you agreed with every Roosevelt policy, but it was clear Roosevelt had a splendid character. As *The New York Times* commented while the Coolidges were honeymooning, Roosevelt's decision not to run "made him free to act as he thought was right." Coolidge too hoped that in his political career he would always position himself to follow his conscience. It helped Roosevelt to have Edith, his wife, by his side. Now Coolidge had Grace. He was ready to move past party jobs to serious elections.

Coolidge determined that he and Grace could skip Niagara Falls and Quebec City, which had been penciled in on the honeymoon itinerary, and head home to dig in. Grace understood. She too was eager to start their real life. It felt good to return to Northampton. After all, they were coming back to a town that was already theirs. Grace's good friend Caroline Yale ran one of the city's great institutions, the Clarke School for the Deaf, which had brought her to Northampton in the first place. After ten years, the Republican Party of Northampton was like family to Coolidge, starting with his old attorney employers and branching out to many town friends and constituents, such as James Lucey. Grace saw that their life would be work but easier because they were a team. She imagined horses in a double harness. Coolidge appreciated her energy; Grace was more like his grandmother Aunt Mede than his melancholy mother. He saw that Grace might be the one to pull him along.

Coolidge turned his attention to the school committee race. The city solicitor's post was handed out by the city council, but this time, he had to run among the wards. Grace, thinking of her parents, thought she might go up to Burlington for Christmas; her mother was still smarting from her wedding. Only if he won, Coolidge teased her, sensing that he would lose. Within weeks, he did lose to Kennedy, albeit by less than a hundred votes. That was all right. A neighbor told him he had voted for Kennedy for the school post because Kennedy, at least, had children. Coolidge came back with good humor: "Might give me time."

Financially, the loss was a blessing. Coolidge needed a little extra time too to earn money for his new family. If he were to continue in politics, both Coolidges knew, they needed to save, and they intended to have fun doing so. The white clapboard Norwood Hotel evoked fond memories for Coolidge; it was where his fraternity chapter had celebrated its birth with other chapters in his triumphant senior year. It also had a Clarke connection for Grace. In fact, it had once belonged to the founder of the school for the deaf. Lunch in the enormous dining room was served to boarders and travelers for 50 cents. It was also cheap because the hotel was struggling financially. Calvin and Grace camped out there temporarily, pleased with themselves at finding such a friendly bargain; soon the hotel closed. The proprietor put the linen and silver up for sale. That in turn provided an opportunity to forage for household items. The Coolidges merrily picked up sheets, pillowcases, and even table linen, all labeled in indelible ink, "Norwood Hotel."

The next move for many couples in their position was the purchase of a house. Homes in Massachusetts towns in the area ranged in price from $2,000 to $5,000, about what a young lawyer could earn in a year if he was lucky. National banks did not write mortgages, but local home building associations did, as did builders themselves. The general perception was that buying a home was a good thing to do. "A man is not really a true man until he owns his own home," preached Russell Conwell, the charismatic founder of Temple University, in a speech he had been delivering across the nation since 1890. The advertising sections of the newspapers of western Massachusetts greeted the honeymoon couple all that fall and winter with offers of credit. "Easily owned—Single and Double Houses," read one advertisement in the *Springfield Republican* of October 18, 1905. "It's like finding money, to buy a home on our easy payment plan," read the top line of another advertisement for home loans. The forced saving for a mortgage might move them forward, just as the couples described in *Ladies' Home Journal*.

They rented. Coolidge did not like to be beholden to bankers or anyone else, for that matter. Independence was his way of protecting his freedom to do what was right. The same impulse caused him to hesitate before joining clubs. Henry Field had a pew in the Edwards Church, and Grace was a member, but Coolidge only went along. His decision infuriated his colleagues in politics; after all, the more clubs one joined, the more friends one had at election time. But Coolidge found another way to connect with fellow citizens: he deposited savings with a variety of institutions. Each additional banker who held some of his money was an additional pair of eyes that would follow him, and likely to be an additional vote.

The first rental by the unbeholden pair was that of a house of a Smith classics professor, J. Everett Brady, who had gone on sick leave. The structure—dark, shingle-style, with a gambrel roof—had several porches, an advantage for Coolidge, who liked to sit outside. Despite their commitment to frugality, the Coolidges enjoyed one luxury: the maid who had served the Bradys stayed with them. Wherever he went

Coolidge took a bookshelf with him, a small golden oak with five shelves and a sateen cover to protect the volumes. Among the books were a history of England, Dante, the Bible, Omar Khayyam's *Rubaiyat*, Tennyson, Milton, and Longfellow, as well as dictionaries in five languages and grammars to go with them. John Greenleaf Whittier, the author of the poem "Snow-Bound," was there. So was George Ade, a Hoosier humorist; Ade specialized in capturing the reaction of the farmer new to the city to political life there. Ade's *Fables in Slang* was an assembly of short, quirky regional anecdotes, but also a kind of little man's back talk to great officials.

The mixture of the heavy old ornate writing with straightforward modern prose betrayed a mixture within Coolidge. In politics, he had to be clear, like Ade, understand the region, entertain it, reward it, but not lecture to it. That he could translate Italian meant little to the people he encountered in the shops or at Rahar's, which he patronized. But in his own time, he appreciated the old authors, especially Dante: "In the middle of the journey of our life, I found myself in a dark wood." Dante captured the questing of his own first decades and his own "dark woods," the moments when the familiar landscape suddenly turned strange.

In early 1906, so very soon after the wedding, the old pattern of sorrow accompanying joy repeated. Coolidge's beloved grandmother, Sarah Almeda Brewer Coolidge, died. From Northampton, Calvin and Grace traveled up into the deep snows to attend her funeral, taking the train to Ludlow and then hiring a horse and sleigh for the ride to Plymouth. Grace, looking around, thought of Sarah Coolidge's great magnanimity, of all the years she had gone out as a midwife.

Soon Grace would be expecting her own child, and the need to earn a living pushed out thoughts of his grandmother. He busied himself both helping and getting to know clients and new voters and showing that he could deliver for the town even without holding office. The Home Culture Club received a grant of a stupendous amount, $8,500, from Andrew Carnegie, to construct a greenhouse and maintain a model garden for city workers; Coolidge was on the committee that publicly and gratefully accepted the money. He represented not only estates but also people in trouble, among them the workers of Northampton who served Smith College. Among these clients was a twelve-year-old, Mary Whalen, the daughter of a washerwoman, who was accused of stealing gold jewelry from the girls' rooms in the dormitories.

Such cases were welcome reminders of the needs of voters. Coolidge thought a good deal about campaign style in this period. It was important not only to be clear but also to let people know he valued them, to greet them on the street, to help out when he could. There was nothing wrong with doing an individual voter a service when possible; that was what politics was for. Via his wife and Miss Yale, Coolidge heard that Kennedy was doing a good job. Why not praise him? Coolidge had ladled out his share of mockery, especially in college, but could see now that attack politics yielded poor results. The best way to win was to stick to the issues and forgo any personal attacks or name-calling. Civility would be his rule from now on. He would try it out in his next campaign, for the office of state representative in Boston.

But for now, the couple enjoyed themselves. Their baby was due at the end of summer. It was a magical time for both of them. When the time of the birth grew near, the Coolidges rented, for the longer term, half of a two-family house on Massasoit Street, six houses down from Elm Street. The rent was $27 a month; Coolidge furnished the 2,100 square feet with his savings. There was electricity and a sewer line; trolleys were coming. About two weeks later, their son John was born, on the evening of September 7. The scent of clematis came through the window; to Coolidge and Grace it seemed like a benediction.

To report the news, Calvin sent his father a letter with a typically deadpan opening: "We seem to be getting along well at our house. Grace had an easy time of it and seems well and strong. She had no fever and the baby came after she was in bed about an hour—though she had little pains all day." As the letter went on, the new father betrayed more of his enthusiasm: "Little John is as strong and smart as can be. He has blue eyes and red eyebrows. Grace calls his hair red. He weighed about eight pounds and measures about 20 inches. They say he looks just like me. His little hands are just like yours. I wish you could see him." To his stepmother, Carrie, who was traveling back from Michigan, Coolidge was even more enthusiastic: "Can't you come back here from Albany and see your grandson? He came Sept 7th just as the clocks were striking six. The boy is real white and was born hungry. . . . I told Grace I should call a girl Carrie because you had no little girl." The baby, the wife, and the stepmother all made his family marvelously whole, whole as it had not been since his own mother's death.

Within a week, even as the baby's nurse sat in his kitchen, the

Hampshire Gazette was chattering on about the possibility that Calvin would accept the Republican nomination as a candidate for his first statewide office, state representative: "Calvin Coolidge has shed the most light on the situation by saying he would consider the nomination," commented the paper charitably. The salary would be $750 a year, plus mileage; it was only a half-year job, through June. The *Gazette* went on to flatter him by announcing, without accuracy, "Mr. Coolidge has acquired considerable real estate since he was came to Northampton and is now one of the large taxpayers." In late October, Coolidge introduced a Republican speaker with a set of folksy New England remarks. "The frost may be on the pumpkin, but it does not seem to be in City Hall." He spoke out for bipartisanship and electoral freedom: "It is axiomatic that popular government cannot long exist without a free ballot." After a point, he digressed to take a stab at Henry Cabot Lodge, who had recently told voters that it was a choice between the Republican Party and the "Cossacks," his way of assailing progressives in the Democratic Party. Coolidge sought to include where Lodge had excluded, to show that the progressive Republicans were men of democracy. In the Republican Party of western Massachusetts, Coolidge told his fellows, "we call in every kind, 'barbarian, Scythian, bond or free' you are welcome one and all, we care not at what shrine you worship or how you eat your pie. That includes what Senator Lodge calls Cossacks." The language was frothy, but it revealed a feature of Coolidge that others would repeatedly note in the future: he was an independent man who shied away from clubs, but he felt no shame in demonstrating loyalty to a political party, the Republicans. Indeed, he suspected vanity in the Republicans who frequently diverged from the party position in the name of demonstrating their own independence. Loyalty was not always weakness. Sometimes it was efficiency, as in the case when men rowed together on the Connecticut River.

Like all parents, Coolidge was finding that his family life gave him new insight into his work. The Republican Party in that period was obsessed with hygiene and clean food. In 1906, a young writer, Upton Sinclair, had published *The Jungle*, an exposé of the brutality and filth of the meatpacking industry. The story of dead rats shoveled into sausage machines and guts sold as "potted ham" had stirred so much outrage that Congress had pushed through a bill to regulate food and drugs. Theodore Roosevelt, reportedly sickened by reading an advance copy of *The Jungle*, had sent agents to study the stockyard of Chicago; they found substance in Sinclair's allegations. That year, he signed the Pure Food and Drug Act, which established federal food and drug regulations.

But Coolidge, whatever his party was doing, retained his conviction that much was up to the customer. When it came to medicines, the old rule of "Let the buyer beware" seemed good enough to him. In fact, he teased his new wife about that. One day he returned home to discover that Grace had bought a book titled *Our Family Physician* for the then-high price of $8.00. Grace and he did not discuss the purchase. But here his boardinghouse side came out; he couldn't resist a prank with an edge. A few weeks later she opened the book to see a note: "Don't see any recipe here for curing suckers! Calvin Coolidge." But their home was a pleasant one. Soon they would add a tiger kitten, shipped especially from Vermont; they named him Bounder.

There were other issues beyond food in the campaign. Railroad and trolley companies were dueling to dominate Northampton; in the Berkshires and the Connecticut Valley, the rails had triggered a construction boom. In Washington, Congress had obeyed the president and passed a new law, the Hepburn Act, that gave the Interstate Commerce Commission more authority to set railway freight prices. A number of railmen signaled that they could live with the new law, which they thought the ICC would enforce liberally. In November, Coolidge won his election to the lower house of the General Court, the state legislature in Boston. That meant a long separation from Grace: half a year away, at least on weekdays. Thinking it over, Coolidge realized that his father too had gone to the legislature soon after his own birth. He was finally going to Boston, all these years after his father had warned him that the calf would get there first. Just after New Year's, he took the train, arriving at North Station.

The capital still could intimidate. The State House on Beacon Hill was a glorious structure, its cornerstone having been laid by Samuel Adams, the governor, who had arrived to deliver it with fifteen white horses. Its thirty-five-foot dome shone gold, having been freshly gilded in twenty-three-carat paint the autumn before at a price of $4,758.79, a sign that in autumn 1906, Massachusetts was feeling extravagant. Oliver Wendell Holmes had originally called not Boston but specifically the State House "the hub of the solar system." The dome had been gold since the 1870s, when the commonwealth, perhaps out of respect for President Ulysses S. Grant and Congress's new commitment to the gold standard, had ordered the gilding. Everyone knew that whatever the quality of the top paint, underneath lay the honest copper of Revere Copper Company, which had covered the dome with that metal back at the turn of the century. Inside, the state's glorious history did the blazing. Framed by Ionic columns in Nurses Hall were new mural paintings of the Boston Tea Party and Revere's ride. Busts of John Adams, Daniel Webster, and John Hancock were everywhere, all asking silently, as another visitor noted, "What have you done?"

There were also Coolidges everywhere, themselves also eminences. Louis Arthur Coolidge, who belonged to Roosevelt's "kitchen cabinet," was a renowned journalist and adviser to Lodge. William Coolidge was a railroad lawyer. The clerk of the Senate was Henry D. Coolidge, who had served in that job while Coolidge had been a schoolboy in Ludlow.

But by now Coolidge was harder to frighten. Starting slowly was his routine, almost a theatrical act. Hammond, Field, Irwin, and the other western Massachusetts Republicans collaborated in that act. After all, they had seen it succeed before in the person of the quirky, silent New Englander who had made it to the governor's spot, Murray Crane. Richard Irwin, Coolidge's Amherst friend Hardy's partner, wrote an introduction to the speaker of the House, John N. Cole. In the Civil War, General Grant had always been underestimated. One colleague had commented, upon meeting Grant, that he looked like a singed cat. Now Irwin suggested that Coolidge fell into the same category.

Dear John,

This will introduce the new member-elect from my town, Calvin Coolidge. Like the singed cat, he is better than he looks. He wishes to talk with you about committees. Anything you can do for him will be appreciated.

The singed cat dwelled at the Adams House on Washington Street, a dumpy structure favored by members of the Western Massachusetts Club, the crowd of lawmakers who crossed the Connecticut to come to Boston. Coolidge's room, number 60, at the center of the building and without bathroom or water, looked out on a narrow inner courtyard. He rented the room for a dollar a day, a bed and three-quarters wooden couch where he perused the *Manual for the Use of the General Court* in the evenings. In the front it contained the U.S. Constitution with all its grandeur and peculiarities. Article I, Section 3 of that document reminded readers of the important role of a state legislature: to pick U.S. senators. Here the job of the U.S. vice president was described: "the vice president of the United States shall be president of the senate, but shall have no vote, unless they be equally divided." Interestingly, in Massachusetts, however, a president of the Senate was chosen differently, for Chapter I, Section II, Article VII read, "The senate shall choose its own president." The president of the Senate in Massachusetts had more power than a U.S. vice president, for the state constitution stipulated: "the president may vote on all questions."

As the legislating began, Coolidge started to feel his way forward. State spending was growing, he learned with interest, in part because the executive, the governor, had trouble stopping it; the Ways and Means Committee of his chamber was in revolt, calling for more formal budgeting. Cole assigned Coolidge to two committees: the Committee on Constitutional Amendments and the Committee on Mercantile Affairs.

Soon enough, he fell into a routine. He smoked cigars, drank rarely, and traveled home to his new baby and Grace on the weekends. Mondays at 7:50 A.M. he was back on the train, arriving at North Station by 10:50. That meant he could spend Sundays at home. Northampton gave him direction. Until he mastered the big issues, he could concentrate on legislating to help the town and his friends there. His first bills reflected more loyalty than quality. Hammond's fury at joyriders had not abated: Coolidge introduced House Bill 41, a plan to ban licenses for vehicles with "a speed capacity of more than twenty miles an hour when running over a level macadam roadway." Coolidge worked on his delivery, pointing out that automobiles appeared dangerous; one in nine drivers in the state had landed in court in the past year. That did not stop the *Springfield Republican* from pointing out the essential absurdity of his plan, noting that the freshman lawmaker was "at a loss to explain just how he would have the cars arranged mechanically so as to comply with the bill."

More logical was his defense of "wet" cities' rights to keep the revenues from their liquor taxes; Coolidge went before the Committee on the Liquor Law to speak against a brazen effort by the state to keep half the revenues from local liquor licenses for itself. The legislature, like nearly every legislature in the land, was preoccupied with health regulations; Coolidge stuck to commerce. The same week that the Joint Committee on Public Health debated labeling of patent medicines, he pushed through a bill that would make easier the sale of property of agricultural societies, the kind that John operated with the cheese factory. The point was to be sure that co-ops could compete in commerce and be bought and sold by private companies.

Another great progressive preoccupation was trust busting, and Coolidge contrived, with some effort, to bust some trusts of his own in an improbable industry: theater. The big-city bookers played hardball with small-town theaters like those of Northampton. If the Academy of Music Theatre was to get Sarah Bernhardt, as it had in 1906 for *Phèdre*, it might have to take or forgo other bookings, according to the big agents' will. Coolidge tried out a small bill to limit the agents' and syndicates' power. His first major piece of legislation was a broader antimonopoly bill for articles of common use, which included gasoline and ice. The leader in the case was a small Springfield company, Hisgen Brothers, which had built up an oil business; Standard Oil had been trying to buy it out or drive it out on and off since 1898. Hisgen sought legislation to control the "disreputable dealings" of big companies. Coolidge supported Hisgen. His classmate Herbert Pratt's father, a big executive at Standard Oil, was on the other side. The bill died somewhere between House and Senate, but Coolidge resolved to continue the fight against large companies. From the point of view of western Massachusetts lawmakers, after all, such fights were of small towns against big cities.

Of course, as he took his black briefcase and walked down from the State House across Boston Common, Coolidge also began to see that there were some progressive ideas he could not endorse. The city of Cambridge, for instance, wanted to invest public money in a subway system; Coolidge was one of those who objected, as the *Springfield Republican* reported: "Mr. Coolidge of Northampton gave legal and business reasons why it was best to follow the state's policy of requiring companies to build the underground conduits themselves."

As disciplined as he was, Coolidge could not force out personal troubles all the time. It was cold that year in Massachusetts; one morning at the end of January, the temperature dropped to -11 degrees. Later winter and early spring were the times of year when people succumbed to illness—his grandmother, and his mother. In mid-February came word that Garman had died of blood poisoning that had started in his throat; the mysterious disease had caught up with him after all. A flurry of correspondence started among the wistful Amherst crowd. They had advanced and were in the stream, just as Garman had instructed, but wondered how they might fare without their navigator. An old student of Garman now taught philosophy at Amherst: William Jesse Newlin, class of 1899. And shortly there came reports that another family member, his stepmother, was faring poorly.

"I am a good deal disturbed about mother," he wrote home on February 26. "Are you sure you are doing all that can be done to help her? . . . I should think she ought to have a trained nurse. . . . Everything that is possible ought to be done to stop her suffering." Grace's self-sufficiency remained Coolidge's great comfort. She continued to find friends in Northampton; her flutelike voice was recognizable when hymns were sung at the Edwards Church. She kept in touch with sisters from her sorority, Pi Beta Phi. Like Calvin, she won her peers' respect by making herself useful, starting at the bottom, opening the Massasoit Street home to member meetings.

The Boston and Maine Railroad line that Coolidge rode to the state capital was another big topic in Boston. Another line, the New Haven Railroad, had plans to purchase it. Both companies, but especially the New Haven, were already powerhouses in the economy. New Englanders were by now accustomed to railroads serving as cash cows. J. P. Morgan had gained control early in the century, but to many shareholders, that did not seem to matter. What mattered was the stability of the railroads. Evidence suggested that the rails would succeed, if only they had enough capital. After all, traffic grew every year; earnings from the New Haven's operations stood at nearly $18 million for the fiscal year that ended in June 1907; in 1901, its earnings had been only $12 million. The little trolley lines Coolidge had inspected and studied would have their best shot at survival if they could hook into the great Boston and Maine or the New Haven. Trains were everywhere, the seemingly unstoppable future.

But the very scale of the railroads made the progressives' blood boil. Here was a target worth taking down. Anything this big must be wrong. The possibility of getting the House of Morgan, that emblem of capitalism, and Morgan's appointed executive at the New Haven, Charles Mellen, was too good to bypass. The progressives' leader on the railroads in Boston was Harvard Law alumnus and attorney Louis Brandeis.

But Roosevelt's Hepburn Act, along with an earlier law, the Elkins Act of 1903, was evidence of Roosevelt's commitment to rail regulation. Brandeis argued that those were not enough: the state of Massachusetts must also constrain the powerhouses and prevent mergers among them. Among Brandeis's disciples was a young Amherst alumnus, Joseph Eastman; Eastman worked for the Public Franchise League, an antimonopoly watchdog group.

The Dow Jones Transportation Average had been dropping all fall and winter from over 130 in the summer and fall of 1906. In the first half of the year, as Brandeis intensified his probes of the railroad companies, looking to see if the companies were violating the Sherman Antitrust Act of 1890, the transportation average hit a new low of 100. The Dow Jones Industrial Average, a more general index, likewise sank sickeningly during 1907. Perhaps commerce as George Bancroft had described could not outride this storm, the storm of progressivism. Legislators, anxious to curtail the damage, tried to block Brandeis. After all, many shareholders didn't see J. P. Morgan as the demon Brandeis did; they thought, rather, that Morgan's presence guaranteed a higher share price. Brandeis wanted to take the railroads apart and make them small; he saw size itself as an evil. Much later, his papers would even be published under the title *The Curse of Bigness*. House speaker John Cole hurriedly put forward a measure to fight back, allowing the New Haven to own Boston and Maine stock until July 1, 1908.

Challenges such as the attack on railroad trusts made the critics wonder whether they had taken Roosevelt seriously enough. Back when the Hepburn Act had passed, Samuel McCall, a Republican from Massachusetts, had been one of seven in the House to vote against it. What if the regulator picked prices that hurt the companies more than he intended? McCall warned that Americans passed laws too casually, with an "easy optimism" that overlooked the effects of the laws. He hadn't liked strengthening the ICC either; he told colleagues he preferred "the natural and beneficent liberty of the courts to the cast iron regulations of a commission." E. H. Harriman of Union Pacific had seemed to exaggerate when he called the act an "anti-railroad conspiracy." Harriman had even alleged that the law had the intentional purpose of promoting the water projects Roosevelt favored, especially the Panama Canal. "I am not opposed to the canal, but the attack on railroads apparently is to create a sentiment in favor of some other method of transportation." Now people wondered whether McCall and Harriman were correct. The blow Roosevelt had struck to reduce the power of the railroads might be crippling them instead. The Hepburn Act might be deterring trade by making cross-country trips uncompetitive. From 1905 to 1907, overall U.S. exports to China dropped by half and those to Japan more than 20 percent. "The railroad campaign for the trade of the east was at an end," a trade scholar, Edwin Clapp, would later summarize.

COOLIDGE WAS NOT SURE yet what to make of the railroad fight. He kept clear of Charles Mellen, J. P. Morgan's man at the New Haven Railroad. But he understood the railroads' argument that their survival was at issue. After all, Plymouth was struggling precisely because it had no railroad. If capital like Morgan's aimed to link everything up, there should be more of it, not less. He concentrated on keeping his Hisgen bill alive and protecting local merchants. Even at the very end of the session, it looked as though passage might be possible; still, when the bill failed just hours before the recess, he was not disappointed. Getting that close was achievement enough. Thinking of 1908 already, he carefully approached the preoccupied speaker, John Cole, who failed to remember him despite the witty "singed cat" letter. Coolidge had seen that Speaker Cole planned to visit Northampton after the legislative session and offered to put Cole up at his house. The speaker replied that he would be glad to stay on Massasoit Street, and did pay the promised visit.

In September 1907, making good on Roosevelt's many threats, the federal government, represented by a star progressive, Frank B. Kellogg of Minnesota, showed up in court to prosecute Standard Oil, having already framed a full six thousand indictments. Coolidge could read all about the case in the Northampton papers and talk about it with colleagues. By now he had qualified not only as an attorney but also as a justice of the peace and a notary public; that meant that he met more voters. The Coolidges were not in Plymouth as often as they liked, and had to content themselves with sending reports by mail. "John creeps up on his knees and goes upstairs and runs all over the house," Coolidge wrote his father. His stepmother, whom he routinely referred to as "mother," was ill again. He told his father that he hoped he and Grace would make it to Plymouth the following summer, in 1908, saving, in typical Calvin fashion, a bit of news for the end of the sentence: "—with another baby."

The law practice provided some stability to Coolidge and his family that fall of 1907, which brought a genuine panic. Shares in the United Copper Company went from $62 to $15 within two days after one investor tried to corner the company's stock. The contagion spread to New York's Knickerbocker Trust Company, a major bank; on one day, October 22, depositors withdrew $8 million in three hours. Morgan had been the progressives' enemy all spring, yet in the end it was to Morgan that Roosevelt's Treasury secretary, George Cortelyou, turned for help. Morgan led other bankers and firms in rescuing banks and struggling trusts, the most spectacular buyout being that of Tennessee Coal and Iron Company by Morgan's U.S. Steel. The Clearing House, the club of banks, did its part by supplying liquidity. The trouble was wider than a single commodity speculator, metal, or bank; money had been too tight. Yet together, the Clearing House and Morgan rescued both the banking and monetary systems and the corporations. The irony was that the scapegoat had become the savior.

Coolidge's victory in the fall of 1907 came by a narrower margin than the previous year's, but he resolved that that did not matter: what mattered was that he had won, that he was still in Garman's stream. He was gaining recognition and solidifying his presence in Boston. In December, around the time he returned to Boston, Roosevelt delivered a speech that seemed to overlook what had just happened at the banks. The trouble with money, Roosevelt suggested, was that people were hoarding it rather than placing it in banks. He also assailed businessmen. "In any large body of men," he said in his annual presidential message, "there are certain to be some who are dishonest." Their example, he said, was "a very evil thing for the community." What did that mean? That Charles Mellen, whose management of the railroad had left much to be desired, required more punishment? That Morgan himself was not off the hook? Most people knew that there had been errors at the railroad, but they also thought that the merger Roosevelt had sought to stop was a good idea. Brandeis too struck again. He published a sensational pamphlet attacking the New Haven and its investments. Brandeis argued that the New Haven had hurt itself, unwisely draining its own cash by acquiring the Boston and Maine. Its dividends would have to come down. That those points contradicted the general thrust of his original antitrust case, that railroads were so mighty that they must be constrained, Brandeis did not seem to notice. The normally phlegmatic *Wall Street Journal* was now roused to a fury: "Probably never before has so audacious an attack been made on the credit of an American railroad of recognized financial stability as that contained in the pamphlet of L. D. Brandeis, an attorney of Boston, who is generally supposed to be acting on behalf of certain Boston and Maine stockholders." Even Brandeis knew that passage. Passenger ticket rates, the paper noted, had decreased 8 percent since 1901; in other words, there was not much evidence of price gouging. It was possible that Brandeis's prediction of failures was a self-fulfilling prophecy: any company so targeted would become weak if it were not already. *The Boston Globe* alleged that Brandeis's antimerger obsession would result in seeing "the state destroyed, the republic gasping its last breath and humankind swept away from the starry watches of the night."

A well-known market player, Thomas Lawson, went one further, issuing stock advice on the basis of his ability to predict the impact of Roosevelt's speeches. Some might sound portentous but be mere fury, and money could be made off that. "Tomorrow comes his first thunderbolt," announced Lawson in an advertisement he placed in *The New York Times* at the end of January. "Let the American people loosen up their ear drums, for in the vernacular, it is a syrenated corker. It doesn't do a thing to the System and the frenzied financier but shake them as a tiger does a blood-stained meatbag." Lawson's conclusion: "Buy stocks on tomorrow's message."

The Union Pacific, Harriman's western railroad, held Coolidge's attention, in part because its story paralleled that of the familiar New Haven like a second track. The Union Pacific had acquired the Southern Pacific several years before; it was Harriman's empire. All the claims of the Roosevelt skeptics seemed vindicated; the Roosevelt administration was suing to break the company apart again, arguing that the Union Pacific had in its acquisition violated the old 1890 Sherman Act, representing restraint of trade.

The advances with which Coolidge personally had to content himself were small. His son was getting ready to walk. Coolidge was back for a second year as a representative in Boston. The visit from Cole had paid off: Cole had assigned him to better committees, judiciary and banking. And Coolidge found that he liked fighting for Northampton; more than ever, he sided with town over gown. In February 1908, he argued that the state should reimburse towns for the transport of paupers to the state hospital at Tewksbury. That same month, the General Assembly debated the question of whether college towns, which received no real estate taxes from their colleges, ought to be compensated by the state government for the revenue they forwent.

Coolidge himself boldly assailed the exemption; after all, what Smith or Amherst did was not really for the town but for the whole world. The Amherst motto was not "Let them illuminate Amherst," after all; it was "Terras irradient," "Let them illuminate the earth." Smith College was a bigger financial institution than the town of Northampton itself. Why should James Lucey or the other citizens of Northampton have to pay when Smith did not? The Northampton team pointed out that Marquis Fayette Dickinson, a trustee of Amherst College, had received $1,700 from Amherst to defend its tax-exempt status in Boston; that alone was an abuse. Why was Amherst paying lobbyists instead of tax to the town of Amherst? In that session Coolidge also took care to serve the trade unions of western Massachusetts. Samuel Gompers and the American Federation of Labor were fighting judges' injunctions to halt strikes or union activity. Coolidge backed a bill that was both prolabor and progressive: the legislation barred injunctions that stopped one worker from attempting to induce another worker to strike. The *Northampton Herald* commended him: "Mr. Coolidge is entitled to the thanks of the wage laborers of his district for his manly defense of their interests."

Again money problems distracted him. The veteran clerk of the Senate, Henry D. Coolidge, was voted a salary of $3,500. But the salary of a representative like Coolidge was still $750. Almost two decades into his career, the money was still mostly flowing from Plymouth to Northampton, instead of the reverse. In April 1908, Coolidge missed committee meetings, and when he finally did return, his fellow lawmakers teased him. "No, I just had a boy born," he said. He was back in Boston less than a week after the birth but still preoccupied with his family. Coolidge's stepmother, Carrie, was still sick, and he took her to a hospital in Brookline, Massachusetts, for surgery. "She is under the care of one of New England's most celebrated surgeons," *The Vermont Tribune* approvingly reported. To his father, Coolidge wrote from the hospital on April 21 of his stepmother: "Mother continues to improve. . . . John Grace and the baby are in fine shape. John would like some apples so he claims, he says apple, apple, apple. Mother is as bright as can be. . . . I think she will be well again." By May, his stepmother was truly on the mend, and Coolidge was back in Northampton. He worried that his first son might become spoiled. "John is well but he is pretty bad," wrote Coolidge to his father on May 13. "He is very fond of the baby and keeps saying baby, baby. He pats him on the head and kisses him. . . . We have not named him yet." Eventually they settled on the name both had known all along was the right one: Calvin, Jr.

On May 21, 1908, after noting that Union Pacific Railroad had declared a dividend of 2.5 percent, Coolidge took the opportunity to give his parent a minilecture on the puzzling movements of copper and railroad stocks. It reflected his own ambivalence: was he an investor or a regulator? And if he was a regulator, what were the right regulations?

When the session of 1908 ended, Coolidge decided he would not run again that year, in part to spend time with the new baby and John, in part to scare up some cash. The Coolidges could also take stock of the Grand Old Party from the outside for a change. Theodore Roosevelt stuck to his word and did not run again, pointedly asking that he be referred to as Colonel Roosevelt, and not President Roosevelt. After William Taft beat Bryan, Roosevelt vowed to stay out of politics: Elihu Root, his old secretary of state, warned that that would not be easy. "No thirsty sinner," he told TR, "ever took a pledge which was harder for him to keep than it will be for you to maintain this position."

But Roosevelt determinedly signaled his commitment by heading off to Africa to hunt. By leaving the stage, he was helping the credibility of the entire progressive movement, which clearly had much more to accomplish. A national income tax was coming. Despite the critical assistance of J. P. Morgan in the Panic of 1907, many argued that some kind of government chartered central bank was necessary. A generational turnover was also occurring. The makeup of the Supreme Court was likely to change; shortly Melville Fuller, the great chief justice, would retire. So would Laurenus Clark Seelye, the head of Smith College since its founding. Many Amherst friends thought the college needed new blood; without Garman, there was no charismatic teacher. New spots at Amherst, in the courts, in the government—all looked to be filled by progressives.

FOR BOTH GRACE AND Calvin, 1909 provided a break, a chance to settle in. The Nonotuck Savings Bank had survived the crash, as had all the other banks regulated at the state level in Massachusetts. In Janu-

ary, the same issue of *The Bankers Magazine* that reported the details
of the Knickerbocker Trust Company reorganization announced that
Coolidge had been elected second vice president at a meeting in which
the bank had declared a semiannual dividend of 3.5 percent. Perhaps the
economy would now find a way around Roosevelt's machinations; E. H.
Harriman, the great railroad executive, seemed to suggest that when he
fitted his yacht *Sultana* for a trip down to inspect the Panama Canal.
Business took Coolidge to Phoenix, Arizona, his first trip out west. The
Union Pacific was engaged in a war with other railroads in the South-
west, seeing who could build trains and rails the fastest. The only limit
to the region's growth seemed to be the problem of water. Coolidge liked
the people's enthusiasm. Arizona was not yet a state, but he could see its
possibilities. The trip suggested to Coolidge that whatever momentary
troubles preoccupied the country, the American venture generally was
strong and would succeed.

Early in 1909, Coolidge represented Thomas Hisgen, the petroleum
dealer who was battling Standard Oil, before his old colleagues at the
Committee on the Judiciary in Boston. Coolidge challenged them to
acknowledge the reality: that small businesses were being hurt by larger
ones. He took his colleagues to task: "You forbid a labor union to injure
a man's business, but a giant corporation can do exactly the same thing."
He railed that "Havoc, spoil and ruin follow these aggregations of capital." At home, temperance, as usual, divided the town. Here Coolidge
was pragmatic, rather than idealistic. He took work as general counsel for the Springfield Brewing Company. That too involved a Boston
connection: James Curley, a legendary Democrat from Boston, was its
president.

Still, lawyering did not compensate for the fun of the political chase.
The mayor of Northampton, a Democrat, was retiring, and Coolidge
considered running for the office. Idle now after his time in the state
legislature, he suddenly had a sense that he could achieve something
greater, if only by becoming a probate judge, like Henry Field, who
had just been named to that post by the governor. He worried about his
father and Carrie, about his own family, and wondered whether he could
afford time away from them. By autumn, he was running for the mayor's
office after all. The post paid only $800—just $50 more than the representative's job—and he was not sure he could win it.

Each campaign proved a novelty, for each time, the electorate was different. The 1910 Census would show that 41 percent of adult males in Massachusetts were foreign-born, Irish immigrants being the largest group, a great change from 1890 or even 1900. Coolidge admired the immigrants' bravery and went out of his way to help them. He understood their interest in religious instruction, having attended Black River Academy, a Baptist school. Father Daley, the priest of a church in nearby Haydenville, wanted a space to build a mission in the Leeds part of Northampton; Coolidge helped arrange it. Harry Emerson Bicknell, Calvin's opponent, was in business and well liked in the town. Bicknell spoke at the Edwards Church, where Coolidge and Grace went, and argued the dry side of the Prohibition controversy. It was clear that Bicknell might win if he shook every voter's hand.

Coolidge could shake hands too. In these races, he became famous for his style of asking for aid. "I want your help, I need your help, I appreciate your help," he told voters. In the still rural community, he enjoyed the advantage of a man raised on a farm: he knew where the tobacco fields were and what they produced well; he knew when a farmer was watering the milk and when he was giving a customer extra. That knowledge impressed the farmers. They teased Coolidge and allowed him to tease them back. Republicans also counted on the fact that Northampton was a "license" town—it had, in the past, sold liquor when other towns were dry. Companies such as Rahar's would depend on Coolidge's victory for their livelihood. Northampton was a small-city; the total votes cast ran in the thousands, not tens of thousands. Coolidge's Republican allies assumed that his connections with Rahar, the innkeeper, would help in the Irish wards. It was Rahar who had helped him get the Springfield Brewing Company work in the first place. The proliquor tactics of the GOP were too much for some observers. "Rum flowed like water," alleged the *Northampton Herald* in criticizing the campaign effort. Its headline was "Rottenest Campaign Ever Carried Out in This City."

Coolidge did win this 1909 contest, but only by 107 votes. "My dear Harry," wrote Coolidge, "My most serious regret at the election is that you cannot share the entire pleasure of the result with me." That characteristic, the Coolidge habit of staying friendly, was beginning to win notice. "There is one thing we like about Coolidge," said the *Hampshire Gazette*. "He does not say anything about the other candidate." And now the furious *Herald* backed off: "The *Herald* did not support Mr. Coolidge in his candidacy. The *Herald* thought honestly that it would be better for the interest of the city if the candidacy of Harry Bicknell were to prevail. . . . but not for a single moment now in all the year to elapse . . . is the Herald going to be unmindful of the fact that the votes of a majority of the free voters in Northampton gave Calvin Coolidge Victory."

To his father, Coolidge transmitted the details. "At least 400 Democrats voted for me," he reported on December 10, 1909. "Their leaders can't see why they did it. I know why. They knew I had done fine things for them bless their honest Irish hearts." The Coolidges' friendships had paid off. "The nearer I got to my house or office, the better I did, and it was the opposite way with the other fellow." Grace was thrilled. Calvin could stay home the following year. She loved music, and the post of mayor came with three seats at the Academy. But it was sobering for both to think of yet another year of financial struggle. "I have got to have an overcoat, a business suit, an evening suit, and a cutaway suit. Grace has got to have a suit, a dress, an evening dress, an evening wrap, a dress hat and a street hat," Coolidge wrote his father, "total about $300."

There was a grimness to such accounts, and a kind of trade-off between home and job that would become familiar. If he could not balance his own household books, Coolidge determined, he would balance Northampton's. For years, a plan for a new city hall had been ready because some people had voiced concern that the old structure would catch fire. Coolidge saw the theoretical merits of the project but determined that he would prevent the building from going up on his watch. The tiresome liquor issue never went away. Northampton had its own rules on liquor, passed in the context of state legislation. Now the progressives in the state legislature were pushing the issue again, putting forward a tighter bill from Boston with mandates that would cramp Northampton vendors' ability to sell. It would be easier, under the "bar and bottle" bill of Boston, as it was called, to challenge business licenses. Under the old law, inns had been able to procure two licenses, one to sell liquor for consumption on their premises, another to sell it for consumption at home, often on Saturday night. The law forbade the sale of both licenses to the same entity. It all represented Boston's "bad faith" toward the west of the state, Coolidge charged. It was not really a moral issue; it was just more regulation that people would get around in any case if they wanted to drink. His interests and those of the barkeepers were allied on this, for the license revenues flowed to the town. If the law changed, he joked pointedly, the police chief would not get the fire engine he sought but rather have to stick to buggy and horses.

The mayor's job suited him; he found executive oversight less enervating than negotiation. His frustration turned to contentment when, after hours spent combing Northampton's finances, he found ways to save. Revenues were up, and he was able to reduce rates even as he reduced the debt chargeable to revenues. The city had received $45,000 for the sale of town land to Holyoke; that he invested. He saw that teachers were needed and raised teachers' pay. Grace, for her part, was finding her way deeper into the community. The church, just under a mile down Elm Street, was proving important to her. The year Calvin became mayor, her fellow Pi Beta Phis elected her president of their western Massachusetts alumnae group, which included nine chapters in eleven towns. That spring of 1910, Coolidge attended the Amherst reunion and saw Dwight Morrow, who reported to others how impressed he was with his classmate's success.

But Coolidge was not sure he would be reelected that year—or should be. Money remained a factor. But he was also unsure about politics. Theodore Roosevelt, tiring of his jungle safaris, was back, suddenly making big speeches. In late August, he called for a new Progressive movement to promote what he termed a "square deal." Roosevelt cited Lincoln to make the case for more support for organized labor's battles: "Labor is prior to, and independent of, capital," Lincoln had said. Roosevelt was making it clear that he would also fight for labor, "equalize opportunity, destroy privilege." That the Republicans tolerated their old hero's return so well reflected their anxiety that the Democrats were going to succeed in snatching away the progressive label. If it came to a contest, Teddy would be a better warrior than the affable, reflective Taft. When it came to votes, the Democrats were winning, especially among new immigrants. The overall trend in the Republican state of Massachusetts was Democratic. Coolidge wagered that Democrats would make big inroads in Northampton come fall. The challenge weighed on him. By the time he was ready for high posts, his party might be out of office.

At this juncture Coolidge's father provided perspective. So many years after his service in the Vermont lower chamber, John Coolidge was making a comeback: he had been nominated by the Republican Party as the candidate for state senator. That meant they both might serve at the same time. On September 6, 1910, Coolidge wrote to congratulate him: "When this reaches you I suppose you will be duly chosen a Senator for Vermont." Coolidge proffered some advice for his father: "You will not find any one at Montpelier who is better qualified to legislate than you are. You need not hesitate to give the other members your views on any subject that arises." Then came another thought that was uniquely Coolidge: "It is much more important to kill bad bills than to pass good ones." He was, like McCall, beginning to see the extent of the damage that bad legislation could do.

Vermont elections fell early, that same month, before the ice set in. His father won, and to the tiring Coolidges of Northampton, that victory almost sufficed. To celebrate, Calvin and Grace took their sons to visit his father, the senator, in Montpelier. John Coolidge's assigned seat in the Vermont State House was number 13, way off on the side of the Senate chamber, to the far right of the president; he was one of thirty senators, ten fewer than in Boston. He lived at one of the Vermont equivalents of the Adams House, Montpelier House, and listed himself in the 1910 directory as Baptist. If John was sitting in the Senate, he was "sitting in the seats of the mighty," as Grace Coolidge put it, and little John ought to see it as he had seen his father and the stuffed catamount on the wall in Montpelier.

There were so many parallels between their lives. His father's service record was impressive: he had served as a school director for nine years, a justice of the peace for sixteen, and a constable and tax collector for thirty-three. Calvin was a director at the Nonotuck Savings Bank; John was vice president of the Ludlow Savings Bank and Trust. Colonel John was a member of both the highways and the bridges committees, which gave him plenty to talk about with Calvin. Grace, who appreciated the continuity between father and son, wrote a report to Carrie Coolidge: "If I leave it to Calvin and his Father to give you an account of the trip to Montpelier they will never do justice to the matter." Though they had had trouble getting out—a pipe had burst, causing a kitchen flood—they had made a 1:13 P.M. train, which arrived at seven. That was no shorter than the rail ride Calvin and his mother and grandfather had taken back in 1874, when it had taken five hours to get from Woodstock to Montpelier. This time the grandfather, the legislator, was at the station to meet the reelected mayor and his family. The next morning, "John went to the state house with his father and grandfather," Grace wrote to Carrie in Plymouth. They phoned the Goodhues and asked them to come over. John sat in the lieutenant governor's chair and called the senate to order with a mallet. Grace herself had a mission, to get help for a deaf girl; "Went to see the Gov.," she reported. Her letter was that of a happy family in tune with itself. To Carrie she concluded, "We all wished so many, many times that you were there."

Coolidge's prophecy about the Democratic trend proved true: for the first time in his memory, both Northampton's aldermen and a second chamber, the common council, went Democratic. Coolidge himself had won, and with a slightly larger victory than before. In his victory speech, he tried to be cautious. "We have had a victory, that is all," he told the people in Northampton. But that Coolidge had prevailed where the party had lost caught the attention of Republicans across the state.

Even as he commenced his second year as mayor, Coolidge was feeling that it was time to return to Boston; he was ready for statewide work but would probably first have to serve in the Senate. In the fall of 1911, he campaigned all over Hampshire County, even in Amherst. He won, which meant another half year of weekdays in Boston. To sit in the Senate was an elevation. Now he was no longer Coolidge of Northampton but Coolidge of the Connecticut River Valley. His territory included not only Hampshire but also Berkshire and Hampden counties. He represented both Amherst and Springfield, where the Crane factories were. In his first term he chaired the Committee on Agriculture and the Committee on Legal Affairs. He was assigned seat number 3, close to the Senate president, Levi Greenwood.

The Boston of 1912, however, was different from the one of 1907 or 1908. It was lonesome at the Adams House in 1912, for with Crane finishing up a term in Washington, the old Western Massachusetts Club that had met there was disbanded. The salary for Coolidge's job was $1,000, not much even for a half year, the Senate term.

Coolidge, always tentative around cars, found that he was now surrounded by them. Though he never became completely comfortable, he was beginning to make his own version of peace with them. "It was as good as a show to watch him cross Tremont Street," a reporter later wrote. "The traffic was thick, of course, and sometimes Coolidge came to the street before the traffic cop was out in the morning. He always stopped, glanced, birdlike, up and down the street, measured the distance to the nearest car, and if he thought he could make it, started across. If that car brushed his coattails, he would not run. He had faith in his calculation."

In politics that year, he found himself dodging not cars, but progressives. Edward Filene, the merchant, had established a futuristic project, called Boston 1915, to make Boston a modern, progressive city, and had engaged the muckraker Lincoln Steffens to help him. The idea was that the Back Bay aristocracy, the middle class, and the reformers would all cooperate to cast Boston into the future. Politically, the progressives knew their support was necessary to win elections and delighted in playing the two old parties off against one another. On the national level, it seemed, everyone was vying for the progressive label. One of the cases the progressives made was that antitrust law would stabilize the country by giving small businesses a chance. At Christmas, a member of Congress from Minnesota, Charles Lindbergh, had charged on the House floor that J. P. Morgan was responsible for past and future instability. "We know that a few men control by stockholdings and a community of interest, practically all the important industries," he said.

Incorporating progressive thought was on the minds of Amherst men, who were hunting for a new university president. Some sought another minister or theologian; men of the cloth had always headed the school. Some wanted secular leadership. The division was also over what kind of man a college should produce. In a letter to Henry Field, Coolidge's old employer, Morrow tried to summarize what their hero, Garman, would have planned. Perhaps this time a preacher was not best: "Professor Garman shortly before his death put it about right when he said that during the first period of Amherst's history it had been its main function to train ministers; that during the second period which is about ending it had been its main function to train professional men other than ministers; that during its next period it would probably be its principal function to give an all-round training to men who would take a large part in the business affairs of the nation."

The demand for progressive leadership was so strong that even Roosevelt was tempted now to leap back into the fray. After all, he was still enormously popular. What's more, Taft's Progressivism did not satisfy TR as sufficient. To the surprise of Taft and many Republicans, the former president began to stake out positions as if he were running for office. "I believe in the protective tariff," he thundered in Fargo, North Dakota, that year. Roosevelt's cockiness piqued other Republicans. One was Warren Harding, the proprietor of a newspaper in Marion, Ohio. Roosevelt, Harding thought, resembled Aaron Burr in the magnitude of his egotism, with "the same towering ambitions." Dwight Morrow understood the importance of Roosevelt's dynamism and how it trumped Taft's moderation. "I believe," he wrote Charles Burnett, the classmate who had once debated Coolidge on the merits of Dutch culture over English, "that if Roosevelt should be nominated he will be elected. . . . Roosevelt, after a month's rest, will make one of his astounding turns and will outdo Burke as a conservative." Wherever politics were going, Morrow wanted to be involved now too. "Dwight absolutely absorbed in politics," Mrs. Morrow wrote in her diary. "He has spoken seven times today." Morrow put his own name forward to represent the district at the 1912 GOP National Convention and managed to draw Taft to New Jersey to campaign.

The emerging Democrat in 1912 was Woodrow Wilson, the governor of that state. Wilson's arguments against tariffs to protect big companies were so obvious and clear that they were hard to resist; tariffs, he said, were like a disease that plagued the Republican Party. Franklin Roosevelt, Theodore's young cousin, had surprised some people by publicly aligning with Wilson and the Democratic Party. Everyone was bidding for the name "progressive." In Massachusetts the legislature, for example, had recently enacted a reduction in the working hours at factories. The new fifty-four-hour-week plan was intended to help the workers. But employers promptly cut workers' wages, arguing they could not afford to pay the same for fewer hours. That in turn infuriated the workers.

From Sagamore Hill, Roosevelt's Long Island home, emanated periodic smoke signals, the evidence of the fire of frustration that burned in Roosevelt over Taft. In a speech in Columbus, Ohio, he criticized the courts for their retrograde decisions; perhaps, he said, judges ought to be fired, or recalled, if the government wished: "We cannot permanently go on dancing in fetters." It was clear now that he might seek the Republican nomination, the long-denied third term, after all. At that Coolidge bridled; even if judges were corrupt, this process, recall, could be corrupt as well. Roosevelt was putting himself above tradition and law. Coolidge lined up with eighteen other senators to block a primary reform that would have made it easier for Roosevelt to bypass Taft and capture the nomination.

As Coolidge commuted back and forth from Northampton to Boston, he and Grace began to imagine ahead to a life beyond the train. Maybe Coolidge could advance to the top of state government with the full-time, all-year job of governor; maybe he could be a senator or a congressman after all. But when it came to the substance, Coolidge was ambivalent; he still considered himself a progressive. That spring he voted for women's suffrage, the state income tax, a minimum wage for female workers, and salary increases for teachers, thereby preempting territory before Democrats or other new candidates might get to it. At Amherst, his old friends were favoring a charismatic educator open to progressive experiments, Alexander Meiklejohn, to serve as the next president. Meiklejohn would be something new for the boys; he, like Roosevelt, felt that college sports needed some new rules. And unlike preceding presidents, he was a philosopher, not a theologian. That itself was modern, especially for a college like Amherst. The trustees were proud of their choice and planned a grand festival for Meiklejohn's inauguration. Amherst was making itself over again. "Ye have not passed this way heretofore," commented the *Amherst Graduates' Quarterly*.

But he could not remain undecided forever. And as it happened that February an event forced him to confront the issue of progressivism as never before. Workers at the American Woolen Company in Lawrence announced a strike. They were protesting the wage reduction that had followed the new progressive law. The leaders this time were a new radical union, the International Workers of the World, known by their initials, IWW, or simply by their nickname, the Wobblies. At Ayer Mill, workers broke down an iron gate; bobbins and larger objects were hurled in every direction, and 11,000 workers found themselves idle. It was another difficult case; the workers, many of them Italian and Irish, were poor and lived crowded in wooden structures. In Lawrence, seventeen people crowded into a five-room dwelling. There were street battles; a striker was killed, and the authorities blamed fellow strikers, arresting Joseph Ettor, an Italian-American labor activist who had come up from New York City. Ettor was charged with murder. He and other IWW leaders were committed to a new tool, the general strike: that workers bring a whole town down in order to change corporations' policy. Police shot at protesters on Common Street in Lawrence. The IWW leaders, Bill Haywood, William Trautman, and others, set up in a hotel and called for donations to support the strike, and they poured in; the IWW collected $5,250 in a single day. The Wobblies' goal was to strengthen industrial workers' rights around the world. From all over New England bluestockings converged upon Lawrence to help the striking workers. Some sought to take the children of strikers to stay with sympathetic families in other towns; the police took the children to the Lawrence poor farm. One of the activists was a Smith alumna, Vida Scudder, who had joined the Socialist Party and now taught at Wellesley College; Scudder lectured Lawrence workers in early March.

The president of the Senate appointed Coolidge chairman of a special committee to negotiate the strike, an honor and an opportunity to retrace Murray Crane's footsteps as labor go-between. Women led the strike, and that alone made it compelling; later it would be called the Bread and Roses Strike, after a poem that had appeared in a progressive periodical, *The American Magazine*. All women wanted, they said, was decent conditions and higher wages so that they might live—bread and roses. Some inhabitants of Lawrence supported the workers, but many, especially older families, were appalled at the disruption of their town. Five thousand citizens joined a new group, the Lawrence Citizens' Association, which painted what was going on in Lawrence as outside meddling. The group also published a pamphlet that sought desperately to remind the country that Lawrence was not all Wobbly: "Lawrence as It Really Is: Not as Syndicalists, Anarchists, Socialists, Suffragists, Pseudo Philanthropists and Muckraking Yellow Journalists Have Painted It."

Coolidge worked hard, cajoling workers to pull together a committee of strikers to negotiate with a committee of company treasurers. After all, each day that the strike went on reduced the ability of the owners to pay in the future. The fight drew not only local but also national attention; in Washington the first lady sat in the first row at hearings when activists described how the police had taken the children from their mothers and caregivers their mothers had chosen. Somehow, by March, Coolidge reported that he had sealed a strike deal. The young senator helped to arrange a wage increase over what had been planned for the workers in exchange for a return to the bobbins and weaving machines. He walked away from it all unsure, struck not by the case for or against the strike but by the violence and the cynicism of the strikers; Bread and Roses did not feel, just as the paper said, like Lawrence at all; it felt like something from outside. There was nothing quaint about it; in the end the strikers and the progressives had hurt themselves. Exasperated, he wrote his stepmother, "The leaders there are socialists and anarchists, and they do not want anybody to work for wages. The trouble is not about the amount of wages; it is a small attempt to destroy all authority, whether of any church or government."

It turned out that someone else was thinking along the same lines: President Taft himself. Tiring of the progressive onslaught, he spoke out. Law could not make growth, he said. "Votes are not bread, constitutional amendments are not work, referendums do not pay rent or furnish houses, recalls do not furnish clothing, initiatives do not supply employment or relieve inequalities of condition or of opportunity." Roosevelt might favor redistribution, but he, Taft, did not. If Roosevelt was marching back onto the political stage, that was all right. Taft told interviewers that there is "no part left but that of a conservative, which I am going to play." The Republicans duly nominated the conservative, Taft.

To the shock of Coolidge's party, Roosevelt did not give up. Instead, on August 7, at a convention of a new Progressive Party in Chicago, TR, the great bull moose, allowed himself to be nominated as a candidate for a third party. The premier flyer produced by the new Progressives was called "A Contract with the People" and called for women's suffrage and limits on campaign contributions, which were dear to the railroad-oriented Massachusetts men. Roosevelt also sought farm relief, direct election of senators, referenda at the state level, and other reforms to move the country over the spectrum from republic to democracy. If Roosevelt's reforms could be summed up, they amounted to more power for the president and the people and less for the intermediaries, the politicians in between. Most Republicans could not believe their ears. They had suspected Roosevelt might run, but hearing that suspicion confirmed, they were shocked anew. The Roosevelt campaign represented not merely a betrayal of Roosevelt's friend Taft but also a threat to the Republican chance of victory.

Resigned to it all, late that August, Taft headed up to Massachusetts to golf at the Myopia Hunt Club course. The rest of the party, however, decided it was not resigned; it was furious. Defeat would come, either at the hands of Roosevelt or, more likely, because the split would give the victory to Wilson. Lawrence, despite Coolidge's earlier settlement, was far from peaceful. Joseph Ettor, accused of being an accessory to murder, was in prison without an indictment, and Lawrence rumbled with rage. The contrast between the golfing president and the angry workers, only a few miles apart, stunned observers. On October 15, 1912, came news that shook the country: a mad gunman had shot Roosevelt, the Progressive Party candidate, in Milwaukee, a bullet passing through the fifty pages of a speech in TR's pocket and lodging in his chest. Roosevelt, true to his "bull moose" reputation, spoke anyhow. "Bull Moose" was his party's nickname now, too.

Against such a hero's challenge, the only thing the rest of the Republicans could do was make their best showing. The Progressive Party was no threat to Coolidge personally. "They started to run a Bull Moose against me," Coolidge wrote his father, "but something must have happened to him—he did not run. But this is a most uncertain election." Still, the lawmaker from Northampton poured days and nights into helping his party. At an October 18 Republican rally in the Masonic Hall in Northampton, Coolidge argued that Roosevelt's concept of judicial recall pushed democracy too far; when it came to senior judges, no influence should weigh on them. Professionalism mattered over party. Governor Eugene Foss, a Democrat, had made many judicial appointments, including naming Richard Irwin, Coolidge's friend, Hardy's old boss, and a Republican, to the bench. That was an example of how judges should be chosen. Stopping Roosevelt was imperative, Coolidge told the voters; it was the most important election since the Civil War. Even Murray Crane broke his silence and delivered a speech in defense of the embattled Taft; observers counted it as his third speech ever. At a gathering for young Republicans that October, Crane stood up to say, "I am glad to be here. I want to tell you we can carry Massachusetts for Mr. Taft and Mr. Joseph Walker. I thank you."

But Republicans did not carry Massachusetts in 1912, or the nation either. The presidential victory went to Wilson, who duly prevailed over the split Republicans. Coolidge, who had taken all seven wards of Northampton, could not help wondering at Roosevelt's actions and whether they demonstrated the qualities that had first drawn him and others to Roosevelt. In a letter, he sketched out his analysis for his father: "I was sorry Taft could not win but am glad TR made so poor a showing." Just a few days later, the question of character came up. Days before Christmas, Charles Mellen, the head of the New Haven Railroad, was indicted by a federal jury on charges that the company had violated the Sherman Antitrust Act. The New Haven was now viewed as a fraud for shareholders. J. P. Morgan, who had been so grand in the U.S. constellation in 1907, was brought down into the dark, cornered by his challengers in a congressional hearing. Samuel Untermyer, the counsel to the investigating Senate Committee on Banking and Currency, wanted to know what Morgan had sought out in a borrower to whom he gave credit. The first thing in life, Morgan told the room, was character. To destroy someone's reputation for character was to destroy his credit, which in turn hurt commerce. Character, he said, was "the fundamental basis of business." Character was all.

MR. UNTERMYER: Before money or property?
MR. MORGAN: Before money or anything else. Money cannot buy it.

That left Coolidge and others to wonder whose character was the true kind, that of the honest businessman or of the righteous reformer. Both could not be true character. Coolidge had another chance to consider it all when he won the coveted chairmanship of the state Senate's railroad committee. That winter of 1912–1913, the New Haven's great rival, the New York Central, was within a whisker of finishing a splendid upgrade of Grand Central Terminal, all equipped for electrified trains; its ceiling would have 2,500 stars, sixty-three of which would twinkle with electricity, a heavenly reminder of the station's modernity and the primacy of the New York Central line. How could New England come back? The mayor of Boston, John F. Fitzgerald, known as "Honey Fitz," warned that in a new world, the one of ocean traffic and travel, Boston was slipping behind. Whereas 25 million tons of cargo left the piers of New York in a year, only 5 million now left Boston in the same period.

The seriousness of his task as railroad committee chair forced Coolidge, for the first time, to systematically trace the arc of federal and state policy back to the hopeful days early in the century. The premise of Brandeis's undertaking back then, the reason for it all, had been that railroads were so strong they required checking. Now they really did seem weak. Brandeis had gone after Morgan as a titan. The titan had been felled, not by Brandeis but by his own health; Morgan died that spring in Rome, leaving his son, Jack Morgan, to fend off the attackers. In the old days, the railroads had subsidized passenger ticket prices by making their profits in freight haulage. Now that the ICC was putting downward pressure on freight prices, the railroads could not marshal the resources they needed to make capital investments. Trolleys and trains needed the cash that fare increases would give, yet even the mention of a possible fare rise gave groups like Joseph Eastman's Public Franchise League a fresh pretext to assail the railroads again.

Consolidation seemed the only way to help the trolley lines in western Massachusetts, which ran chronically short of cash. Coolidge, from Plymouth, Vermont, knew all too well the tax of isolation that small towns suffered when circumstances left them outside a network. Northampton, even now, had a population of only 10,000; it might yet become another Ludlow, shut out, sidetracked. He knew too that a sanctimonious defense of independence was sometimes self-destructive. Hill town lawmakers such as Coolidge were therefore pushing hard for a merger of local lines with the New Haven; in fact, that might be the only salvation for the electric roads. Worcester, Springfield, and Berkshire street railways would help the western counties keep up if they could only join the New Haven. Brandeis's protégé, Joseph Eastman, was coming to the Senate chamber to argue the opposite: that the little lines needed independence to survive.

But Eastman had never known what it was like to be twelve miles from nowhere.

Coolidge battled for his western trolleys and also for the great railroads; sometimes he advocated that Massachusetts spend to help the railroads, so embattled had they become. Suddenly he felt that the cause was urgent. After all, in the period when Brandeis had distracted the railroads and idled them, other means of transport had been taking the railroads' place. The Panama Canal would soon be ready to open. And Henry Ford was perfecting a new kind of assembly, along a line, so that even more cars could be produced faster at his plants. A Tin Lizzie, as the Model T Ford was now nicknamed, could be assembled every ninety-three minutes. For the first time it seemed that the car might really compete with rails. "Real Economy: Brought About by the Use of Trucks," read one *Boston Globe* headline that spring; it quoted one auto man, P. C. Chrysler of the Garford Agency, who promised that "the driver of a horse truck may be eligible for a position at the wheel of a motor vehicle" and that "within a very few days."

The energy the young legislator poured into the railroads won notice. "Senator Calvin Coolidge, the Senate chairman for the railroad committee, went home last night with the first unfurrowed brow he has worn for a long time," *The Boston Journal* commented in May after

Coolidge had completed a draft of another railroad bill that consolidated not the rails so much as their regulation. Fellow lawmakers began to talk about Coolidge's future. Like a good poker player, he knew more and was moving faster. The others saw too what Coolidge himself did not yet see: that he was becoming more conservative. Conservatives needed young politicians to fight their battles more than ever. For progressive principles were no longer mere talk or state law; they were becoming permanent law. That year in Washington would see passage of both a law to establish a national income tax and a law creating a new central bank system, the Federal Reserve System.

There was another group waiting to support him: Amherst alumni. Men of Coolidge's generation were now just coming into their own, and the older men were there in the background to help whenever possible. Joseph Eastman was winning praise for his muckraking and exposing the financial weakness of the New Haven Railroad. Harlan Stone was now not just professor but dean at Columbia Law School. Arthur Vining Davis, the president of the Aluminum Company of America, was holding up well under grilling by the House Ways and Means Committee over the extent of his company's holdings. Dwight Morrow was finding himself being courted by the House of Morgan itself. The Amherst men sorted through them all to discern who was worthy.

The Amherst men tested Coolidge with a question on regulation. Alumni and officials in the town of Amherst were concerned that a bill pending in the General Court regarding sewage systems for the town would place unduly heavy financial burdens on the college. The college treasurer asked Coolidge to monitor the bill's progress; he also alerted Frank Stearns, the alumnus who headed the Boston department store, that he had put a query in with Senator Coolidge. Stearns was a Boston eminence; his nickname, because of his store's fame with lady shoppers, was "Lord Lingerie." He was also a reliable Amherst alumnus; he hired Amherst men and helped them. An emissary from Stearns, another Amherst man, Arthur Wellman, went to see Coolidge and transmitted an annoying report: "I have interviewed Senator Coolidge, who seemed to have entirely forgotten the matter and apparently had never read the bill." Rather than leap on the project apologetically, Coolidge told Wellman briefly that when the bill got to the Senate, he could probably do little for him. A prominent man like Stearns was not accustomed to short replies. But Coolidge's distance, instead of putting him off, somehow piqued his interest. And Stearns soon saw that the bill, when it became law, did not contain the kind of language that would hurt Amherst. Stearns got behind Coolidge.

That fall of 1913, Levi Greenwood, the Senate president, unexpectedly lost his bid for reelection. As others celebrated their victories, Coolidge focused on the open Senate president slot. Before his fellow lawmakers could regroup, he canceled a family trip to Plymouth and by phone and in person collected enough votes from colleagues to win the president's seat for himself.

"Coolidge came to town last Wednesday and showed his fellow Republicans that while some were talking through their hats he could lay down 16 of the 22 Republican votes in the upper branch of the legislature, and the other candidates and near candidates stumbled all over themselves to get out of the way of the steam roller," commented *The Boston Sunday Globe* on November 16, 1913. "It was nothing short of wonderful the way he walked right into the ring and took the prize almost before the public could realize that there was a contest," wrote the editors of his own *Springfield Republican*. He alerted his father in great pride: "I shall be the next president of the Senate. This office has been held by some great men and never by a fool. Looking after this kept me from going to Plymouth." After all those years of watching Senate presidents operate, he was eager for a chance to try his hand at the job; he too might break ties or create them, killing legislation under Massachusetts rules. For a moment he succumbed to the luxury of recalling those who had mocked his ambitions back in the day, especially a cousin, Warren Taylor, who had made fun of him in his father's time as tax collector. "I suppose it would have not looked so foolish to Warren Taylor when he saw us go by in the buckboard to the Academy if he had seen you were carrying me to the president's chair of the Massachusetts senate." The inauguration was in January. Coolidge insisted that his father come.

It buoyed the Coolidges and everyone else that business seemed to be picking up. Enough growth meant that whatever the Progressives did, productive or not, would matter less. It seemed Bancroft had been right about commerce prevailing after all, even over the "tempest" of the progressive movement. If a company figured out how to make a product better, industrial unions' demands, especially, might not matter; the workers would get the raises they sought automatically because they produced more goods. That winter Henry Ford came east to New

York to announce a plan that amazed everyone. Ford's car company was succeeding so well that he intended to give $10 million back to workers. The plan was to double their wages to $5 a day. Workers who earned more could spend more; that in turn would move the economy forward. Dwight Morrow in those weeks was thinking over whether he should join J. P. Morgan, the most controversial and exciting institution in the world of finance. Like Coolidge, he knew his next step was a momentous one, and, like Coolidge, he now hesitated. After all, the magazines he read and liked routinely targeted Morgan. He would become a target himself. Yet there was much about Morgan that he admired; he knew the men, some of whom rode with him on the train in the morning from Englewood. Clearly the House of Morgan thought he had character.

Morrow's temperamental inclination was to ride to the rescue of underdogs, especially those he himself had neglected before. That was what had happened with Coolidge, whom he was now beginning to see promise in. While Morrow and his wife were in Bermuda, he happened to pick up a newspaper showing the old J. P. Morgan as a vulture eating the entrails of New Haven Railroad shareholders. It struck him as wrong; the House of Morgan was trying, if not successfully, to save the railroad. Perhaps in its way the great financial house was the underdog. Fury at the humiliation of his potential company made the decision for him. After a lengthy discussion with his wife, after 2:00 A.M. he went down the stairs of the hotel and posted a letter saying he would join Morgan. That was a job of service that he would gladly accept. "If I am going in, I am glad to go in when the brickbats are flying." Soon it would be official, and he would be Morrow of Morgan and 23 Wall Street. His family was elated. But not Morrow, who, after the adrenaline of acceptance, felt a sense of foreboding.

The president-elect of the Massachusetts Senate, Coolidge, shared that sense. Coolidge was noticing the fateful pattern to his life: every time things went well, something happened to humble him and darken his prospects. Abbie's death during his senior year of school and his grandmother's, so close to his wedding, were examples. His Senate victory of winter 1913 was no different. Even as he prepared for his triumphant arrival in Boston as Senate president, Calvin, Jr., his five-year-old son, fell ill with pneumonia and was moved to the hospital. The fluid collected in his chest, and doctors drew it out with a needle. In one letter to John Coolidge, there was tentative news of improvement: "We think he is better, unless it gets into his other lung we think he will get well but he is very sick still." Calvin underwent surgery; a tube was placed in his chest. Grace stayed with Calvin each day. Concern for their son overwhelmed them. In a rare moment of desperation, Coolidge told the doctor, "I am a poor man but I could command considerable money if you need it." Passing the hospital, an acquaintance saw Coolidge and his son John standing at the window outside, looking up at Calvin's room in hope.

This time, Calvin's crisis passed. The boy went home with a nurse on December 23.

Just a few days later, the Senate met. And on January 7, 1914, at 11:05 A.M., the new president, Calvin Coolidge, rose to speak. The clerk who called the session to order was Henry D. Coolidge. It had been such a difficult few years, between the parties and also within the Republican Party. So Coolidge first moved to heal by unifying: "The commonwealth is one. . . . The welfare of the weakest and the welfare of the most powerful are inseparably bound together." They must remember that they were not from just anywhere. They were from the Commonwealth of Massachusetts, the hub of the world. The state had led the progressive movement; it could show the way in the future. "Have faith in Massachusetts," he told the crowd. "In some unimportant detail some other States may surpass her, but in the general results, there is no place on earth where the people secure, in a larger measure, the blessings of organized government." The states, he suggested, not the federal government, were the natural place to solve problems. He went on to give the assembled another precept: "Do the day's work. If it be to protect the rights of the weak, whoever objects, do it. If it be to help a powerful corporation better serve the people, whatever the opposition, do that." Rather than make the fatal choice between progressive and old guard, a good lawmaker would act on the merits of each individual case and judge by himself. Coolidge said, "Expect to be called a stand patter. But don't be a stand patter. Expect to be called a demagogue, but don't be a demagogue." He did offer some reservations about the progressives' practice, particularly their emphasis on producing so many laws: "Don't hurry to legislate. Give administration a chance to catch up with legislation." Some of the ideas of the progressives, especially their plans to strengthen unions, simply might not be necessary. For every step on behalf of the worker the bluestocking ladies or the unions took, a factory with a new piece of machinery might take two. "Large profits mean large pay rolls." With the Ford announcement of doubled pay still reverberating in the air, Coolidge was only articulating the obvious. He tried out another line that reflected a conviction growing inside him: "it may be that the fostering and protection of large aggregations of wealth are the only foundation upon which to build the prosperity of the whole people." In a contest, the progress of business would obviate the strikes. Above all, though, he emphasized service and humility. Laws were not to be invented by politicians or judges, or, most important, righteous prosecutors. Echoing Demosthenes, whom he had studied all those days back at Amherst, he said, "Men do not make laws. They do but discover them." Laws must rest, he said, "on the eternal foundations of righteousness."

The Coolidge who uttered those lines sounded different from the legislative Coolidge his colleagues had come to know in Adams House or the General Court. The lawmaker from western Massachusetts with the deadpan style was taking his party in a new direction. He still endorsed some of the progressives' plans. He would work with progressives, even if he was called a hypocrite. But he was not necessarily always going to be a progressive. Others absorbed all those nuances and seemed ready to follow Coolidge. The crowd was enormous: Grace stood for two hours, while John got a seat to the left of his father.

Taken aback by the mood of awe in the room, Coolidge's father wrote Carrie in the unpunctuated shorthand of Plymouth: "Inaugeration is over. Calvin done fine he is praised by the most prominent men of the State." The celebration was all so much that it made his father skeptical: "You would be surprised to see the power Calvin seems to have. I hope he makes no mistakes."

But Coolidge knew it was time for risk, not caution. He was becoming the man of power about whom Garman had written. Coolidge had ridden the waters of politics so long, managing to stay in the mainstream. Now it was Coolidge's turn to pilot.

FIVE

WAR

Boston

ONE EVENING IN AUGUST 1914, the passengers dancing on the luxury ship *Kronprinzessin Cecilie* noticed something strange. The moon had been on the starboard side of the ship when their evening, one of the last before reaching Plymouth, England, began. But now, suddenly, the moon stood at port. The evening star too had somehow moved from window to window. It was only when the guests reached the smoking room of the North German Lloyd liner and heard from the captain that they understood: the ship had turned around and was racing back to North America. War was breaking out in Europe. The *Kronprinzessin* flew under a German flag; she carried $13 million in gold bullion and silver in her cargo.

A better target for French or British cruisers could scarcely be imagined. Alarmed, the passengers, a mix that included English, American, and German, watched as the crew covered the ship's lights, shut down her radio, and headed full speed into the dark North Atlantic. Just two years before, after all, the same black North Atlantic waters had brought disaster to another ship, the *Titanic*. They beseeched the captain, Charles Polack, to blow the horn, but he would not heed them. After a few hours, the reality sank in: the threat of torpedoes was far greater than that of running into an iceberg. Soon afterward, the inhabitants of Mount Desert Island, Maine, woke to a strange sight: the great liner *Kronprinzessin* anchored like a giantess near the smaller yachts in the resort harbor.

Nor was the *Kronprinzessin* alone. Up and down the New England coast, ships were arriving unscheduled, like great birds migrating in the wrong season. In Boston, which Coolidge visited that week for the mundane purpose of dedicating a new wing to the Bulfinch State House, the *Arabic* of the White Star Line suddenly materialized. No one knew if French or German battleships would follow the fleeing liners. Boston received reports that in Portland, Maine, an employee at the observatory had heard the boom of heavy guns, perhaps the sound of the German cruiser *Dresden* and the French cruiser *Descartes* engaging in battle right there in the Gulf of Maine. This last rumor proved to be unfounded, but other disconcerting stories were true.

Coolidge had expected to pilot, but not in the waters of war. The price and provenance of marble were what he and other officials had had on their minds at the dedication of the State House; the owners of quarries in western Massachusetts, his own area, were furious because the contract for white marble had gone to a company in Vermont. The State House addition cost $750,000, a disconcerting amount at a time when Massachusetts appeared to be slowing down; the spending would be hard to justify in Northampton, when the Nonotuck Silk Company in the Leeds section, short of orders, was cutting its workers back to a three-day week.

Such details mattered less than the disruption that a European war might bring to a port city like Boston, to a state like Massachusetts. No one knew what to make of it all. Back home in western Massachusetts, Coolidge also found confusion. Just a mile and a half from Massasoit Street, a radio hobbyist named Deane Lewis was puzzling over hundreds of messages he was now intercepting as European ships called out to one another in the early hours of war. Business owners were going to newspapers to warn that the sea war would damage already slowing production. "The production of our plant is naturally dependent upon the supply of crude rubber," the proprietor of a rubber company in Chicopee Falls wrote, warning that "as this supply comes almost wholly from London and as shipping is necessarily going to be, for a while at least, seriously hindered the supply of crude rubber will necessarily become short." As one country after another declared war, the extent of it shocked.

Over the course of the coming weeks, more news came in, much of it also hard to believe. The sense of dislocation in the Connecticut River Valley was no match for what was reported on Wall Street, where Dwight Morrow at J. P. Morgan was observing something he too had never expected: government authorities were shutting down the stock market. After a run on gold had caused a run on stocks, panic set in as Europeans withdrew holdings to take them to Europe. Now Morrow was sending even more gold to Europe: the USS *Tennessee*, a battleship, had received papers of immunity from Germany and Great Britain and was now carrying $8 million in gold to Americans in England who needed to buy their way home.

President Woodrow Wilson for his part did not know what to say. Wilson had not campaigned on war in 1912, but now he had to take the lead on U.S. policy in Europe's conflict. The disruption also caught Republican leaders off guard. Theodore Roosevelt was deeply mired in a libel lawsuit involving New York State politics. The senior statesman from Massachusetts, Senator Lodge, was himself caught in Europe and had to think first not of policy but of family. Lodge's grandchildren were stranded in Dieppe, France; the senator dispatched his son-in-law, Massachusetts Congressman Augustus Gardner, to collect them before the advance of the Germans. Gardner, the papers were reporting, took his own petrol in cans for the drive and escaped with the children and their mother onto a ship at Le Havre. In the tumult Lodge had missed the opportunity to personally make a final stand against legislation he deeply opposed: on September 2, the Senate endorsed a new antitrust law, creating a new entity to manage business nationally: the Federal Trade Commission. The Republican Party was already dangerously off balance from the torpedo blow of Roosevelt's third-party candidacy; the word of real torpedoes made the political situation even more unpredictable.

Coolidge found himself torn. The crowning achievement of his first term as Massachusetts Senate president had been killing a tax on stocks at the last minute by masterfully exercising the Senate president's privilege to create a tie vote. War might mean he would have to set aside his concerns about progressivism. His party leaders assigned him the job of Resolutions Committee chair, which meant he would be an author of the party platform for the autumn of 1914. The platform mattered not only because of the war news, but because the state would soon hold a convention to review the commonwealth's constitution; the platform document could set the tone and direction.

Upon reflection, Coolidge concluded that the Republican Party of the state of Massachusetts was itself like a ship, unbalanced by war news and before that the blow of the bull moose. The ship had to be centered, it needed a new keel, and at all costs. That meant first pulling in the progressives, so that they were on deck instead of outside taking shots. It meant pulling *all* factions of the party together. Balance was all: wherever there was dispute, or costs, he must nonetheless seek the islands of agreement, the middle ground. If there was to be a war, then finding that middle ground, sacrificing principles for the duration, would be even more important. Spending would be especially important, however much Coolidge personally deplored it. In wars, Washington took the lead, but it was the job of Massachusetts to make a contribution, to show that the state could lead too, and even to get out in front of President Wilson. Two competing forces had to be weighed: the need to help the state and the need to protect individuals from an overreaching government, whether state or federal. Reading the reports of the trenches that France was digging, of Paul von Hindenburg's first great success at the Battle of Tannenberg, Coolidge and his fellow Republicans thought back to the Civil War. They all recalled how Copperhead Democrats had nearly destroyed the Union when they had failed to side with the president, Abraham Lincoln. In a time of war, unity among all governing parties would be crucial. Coolidge's Republican Party would aid Wilson in the war as the Democrats ought to have aided Lincoln.

Since Coolidge's boyhood he had been drawn to Lincoln. The Great Emancipator had become a country lawyer, just as Coolidge would. Lincoln had moved slowly, as Coolidge and the Republicans had to. Lincoln had unified. No one had matched his ability to deal with practical affairs of his time. Lincoln had often found the middle ground; he had easily sacrificed the limelight to the cause. Coolidge had been present earlier that year in Boston, when William Lewis of Amherst, the assistant attorney general, had warned Republicans at an evening smoker that they were forgetting the principles upon which the Republican Party had been founded. Lewis had identified the right hero. Other Republicans agreed. It seemed symbolic that the one innovation Lincoln had registered for patent had been a design to stabilize boats by lifting them over shoals, the result of his trips on flatboats down the Ohio and Mississippi. To reorient, especially in a time of war, Coolidge and other Republicans had to look past Taft or Roosevelt, maybe all the way past, to their own evening star. To succeed now, the Republicans had to show they were still the Party of Lincoln. The only problem was that Coolidge himself did not know whether he personally could manage all these compromises, whether he was the right leader for this period.

For now, though, Coolidge would go along. After all, in any case, these thoughts were still theory; the United States was not yet even fighting a war. On August 20, President Wilson made a formal and stiff case for U.S. neutrality. He even suggested that it was unpatriotic to oppose neutrality: "Every man who really loves America will act and speak in the true spirit of neutrality, which is the spirit of impartiality and fairness and friendliness to all concerned." In Wilson's view, the best role for the United States to assume was that of the city on a hill. But within days of Wilson's careful speech, news came to contradict him. The Germans were not merely marching through neutral Belgium; they were killing and destroying whole towns as they went.

On one day, August 22, tens of thousands of Frenchmen died trying to fend off the Germans east of Paris. Belgians were surveying the ashes of the 300,000 books burned by the Germans at the library of the University of Louvain. In London, a businessman, Herbert Hoover, was setting up a station at the Savoy with five hundred volunteers and was planning a great relief action for Belgium. Samuel Untermyer, the same progressive firebrand who had challenged J. P. Morgan in the Washington hearings, was not busting trusts that week; he was in London, running a rescue operation in his hotel and trying to hail down ships leaving the continent in the hope that they would stop and pick up U.S. citizens before they crossed the Atlantic. Congressman Gardner was calling for a new movement of preparedness: that U.S. youths be ready and trained to fight. It was only a matter of time before Colonel Roosevelt weighed in.

Coolidge began his stabilizing work immediately. On August 13, he addressed a crowd of three hundred farmers in agricultural Hatfield, informing them of a rather large appropriation he had gained for the agricultural college in the town of Amherst. When a Republican congressman, the Berkshires' Allen Towner Treadway, hosted a giant meeting for the statewide party at his Red Lion Inn in Stockbridge, Coolidge was there to speak of funding for road construction that the party had secured. He sounded the familiar themes, such as the necessity of tariffs, and pointed out that the General Court had increased appropriations for highway construction for Berkshire, Hampshire, and Hampden counties. In that period the party platform was completed; Coolidge and his colleagues threw in just about every progressive item they could think of, except the vote for women, which, Coolidge had discovered, didn't seem to have much support that year among the party's constituents. The senator also, however, included some lines that gave a first inkling of the state party's position on war. The Republican platform called for "the defense of those two citadels of freedom, representative democracy and independent courts." It demanded "justice everywhere." Then Coolidge was off to campaign for reelection.

Coolidge was by now a veteran campaigner; voters knew and liked his style. His silence was now established lore, part of the campaign. In her living room, Grace hung a sampler with an epigraph to remind visitors:

> *A wise old owl lived in an oak*
> *The more he saw, the less he spoke*
> *The less he spoke, the more he heard*
> *Why can't we be like that old bird?*

That October, Coolidge appeared as much as he could, talking to voters directly. He always fought for what was important for his constituents; that fall, it was trolley connections and lines to link more people. Though he was attacking Democratic tariff levels now, he still did not attack individual Democrats, in the Senate or in western Massachusetts. The muddle of policy actually mattered less than a sense of calm and evidence that he was willing to serve. Across the state and across the Republican Party, his followers counted on him.

Coolidge did not disappoint. On November 3, the Democratic candidate for governor, David Walsh, won reelection, but only narrowly. The lieutenant governor slot went Democratic as well. Coolidge, however, trounced his opponent, the Progressive Ralph Staab. With the Grand Old Party's platform so progressive itself, Staab had no case. "I was elected by about 2800," Coolidge wrote to his stepmother. In his exhaustion, though, the senator-elect reversed his digits: he had beaten Staab by a margin of 8,200; Coolidge's 15,326 votes were more than

double what Staab had won. Forgetting the bull moose episode would
be easier with numbers like those. "Senator Coolidge is the best vote
getter in the state," commented the *Hampshire Gazette* smugly, "and he
will be heard from later." The gratitude toward him was outsize: the
strategists concluded that he had helped the GOP gain votes where it
otherwise might not have. Other Republicans noticed that Democrats
also liked him. All seven of the Democrats in the Senate voted for him
as Senate president. In choosing Coolidge, they ignored James Timilty,
who was Democratic Party city chairman. Coolidge had unified again.
Meanwhile, the war news poured in. The Edwards Church, Grace's
church, hosted a Belgian, Lalla Vandervelde, who detailed the hardships
of the German occupation. The conditions the Belgian described hor-
rified the Northamptonites. German Zeppelins had raided England.
Germany had announced a submarine blockade of Great Britain in early
February.

The supposition of the cruise line North German Lloyd was still
that the neutral United States was the best place to keep its ships during
wartime. But in the United States, as the reports of German aggression mounted, people were not so sure. Around election time two navy
torpedo destroyers had carefully escorted the *Kronprinzessin* down from
Maine to President Roads, the Boston Harbor; a court had determined
that it was not safe to keep her in Maine because of the ice. Though her
captain, Charles Polack, had not wanted her to cross the three-mile line
into international waters for a moment, she had needed to travel as far as
ten miles out to find water deep enough for the passage to Boston. The
Kronprinzessin was now in custody of the U.S. marshal for Massachusetts;
the Guaranty Trust Company of New York was suing her for damages
alleged by her failure to deliver the gold that had been shipped on her.

Not far from Boston's harbors, at the State House, Coolidge prepared
an opening address for the 1915 Senate, the second such address. He had
to treat war, remind his colleagues of the concept of service, deliver his
message about overlegislating, and do all of it in a new way, for to repeat
his "Have Faith in Massachusetts" exhortation of 1914 would have been
to serve up dull fare. As much as he sought unity, Coolidge could not
help himself: he wanted to warn against unwarranted spending. The
State House itself, with the new additions going up, reminded everyone
of the government's extravagance. In Boston and Northampton, he pondered and came up with a new kind of speech: one whose length made

his point. The remarks he delivered that day contained only forty-four words, powerful in their combination of form and message:

> *Honorable Senators: My sincerest thanks I offer you. Conserve the firm foundations of our institutions. Do your work with the spirit of a soldier in the public service. Be loyal to the Commonwealth and to yourselves. And be brief; above all things, be brief.*

"In brief, Calvin Coolidge approximates our idea of the ideal orator," applauded the *Globe*. Coolidge's skills as a legislator were also winning appreciation. Coolidge, people noticed, always undersold and usually delivered more than he had promised. Though they could see that he was becoming more conservative, his colleagues also saw that he reasoned out every issue and made his own decision. Edward Filene, the merchant, and Louis Brandeis had pushed for the ability of savings banks to sell insurance policies. The pair saw the private insurance companies as price gougers. There was a small state appropriation in support of such policies; the private insurance companies pushed to kill it, viewing government aid as unfair competition. It was not clear that Coolidge knew what he thought about state subsidy of insurance. But it was clear that he believed that insurance was important, that his mastery of Senate procedure was only growing, and that he was not above playing a few tricks, especially in the case of voice votes.

One day when the future of that subsidy was to be decided, Judd Dewey, the unpaid lawyer for the savings bank life insurance project, called on Coolidge to lay out its value. Coolidge, typically, said nothing, except, at the end: "What you say sounds reasonable." Dewey left the office concerned; it was already late, and if action for his side was to be taken, it would have to be soon.

"What did Mr. Coolidge say?" asked a senator who saw Dewey leaving the office. "He didn't say anything," answered Dewey, "except 'it sounds reasonable.'" "My God," said the senator, "did he say that? Then you're all right." Within half an hour, the vote came, and the president of the Senate uttered his usual line: "Those in favor say 'Aye.'" There was no response. A loud outburst of "nays" went up when Coolidge asked for those opposed. His response was remembered forever by those who supported the new legislation. With no change in facial expression, he announced, "The yeas have it, and the bill is ordered to a third hearing."

Over the winter, the country struggled to form an opinion about the war. At Amherst, President Meiklejohn thought it best simply to air the issue and staged lectures for representatives of both sides. Thomas Hall of Union Theological Seminary made the case for Germany; for Great Britain, Maurice Low, a newspaperman. Much of what transpired on the financial level left Americans baffled. Forces like laws of physics were at work—they could see but could not always discern which laws or why. The gold that had fled the United States to pay for the European war suddenly poured back in, and the stock market reopened—at a higher level than many expected. European money was following the *Kronprinzessin* and making the United States its haven. The recession was quickly turning into a boom as Europeans placed orders for the war. The Aluminum Company of America, for example, received stunningly large orders from Great Britain: 72 million pounds total over two years, starting in 1915. The Aluminum Company was the sole U.S. producer; suddenly Arthur Davis, the Amherst man, was a true titan.

Led by Congressman Gardner and others, the Republicans of Massachusetts now were boiling down their war policy to one word: preparedness. If the United States was not going to enter the war, at least it must train young men. In Washington Gardner, with the enormous help of his father-in-law, Lodge, was pushing for an investigation of whether the United States was spending the $250 million a year it allocated to the army and navy correctly. That gave Lodge an opportunity to goad Wilson. The state militia of Massachusetts was known as the best in the country; the War Department in Washington was already equipping it, sending machine guns and escort wagons to the state armory at Framingham. But lawmakers in the state still wanted to inquire further. They were already introducing resolutions that Massachusetts investigate her own preparedness. The paper carefully laid out which citizens of the Bay State would qualify for military service in the event of U.S. involvement: every male between the ages of eighteen and forty-five except government officials, clergy, doctors, lighthouse keepers, government staff, train conductors, Quakers, and Shakers.

Producing leaders was also on the minds of Amherst alumni. At the college, President Meiklejohn led discussions about the war. But the Amherst men were also looking for political leaders among their own. They had Robert Lansing, class of 1886, who was working on foreign affairs in Washington. But Frank Stearns's eye kept coming back to

Coolidge. The quiet Senate president embodied the principle Stearns tried to follow at his department store: giving the customer more than he expected. The more he saw, the more Stearns liked the whole Coolidge package, of which Grace was a large part. She had her own network now in Northampton; she made friends with neighbors easily and was well liked at her church. The very thought of dressing her in R. H. Stearns finery pleased him; Grace was a natural beauty. Coolidge had the capacity to spread Amherst's name across the United States.

Stearns's father had always said the trick to good business was to acquire quality goods and then shout—advertise. Now Stearns was ready to do the same. He drew up an elaborate plan for a dinner of dozens of alumni and men of influence at the Algonquin Club. He hosted meticulously: he sent Grace flowers and provided seating charts for Morrow, who was coming up from New York, to give him a chance to make his own suggestions. Stearns also distributed reprints of the 1914 "Have Faith in Massachusetts" speech prior to the event. He even invited Coolidge's father.

Several events distracted Coolidge from those flattering dinner preparations. Among them was the sinking of the *Lusitania*, an English ship, by a German submarine; more than a thousand people died in the waters off the coast of Ireland. That was "murder on the high seas," said Theodore Roosevelt, and Republicans had to admit that he was right. The war was permanently altering the U.S. political constellation. An Amherst alumnus, Edwin Grosvenor, was already warning that the *Lusitania* would be a turning point for the United States just as the sinking of the *Maine* had been for the Spanish-American War. The alumni newspaper published a sorrowful poem that sought to capture Amherst's chagrin at the shift: "Can we forget a nation's word once forfeited?" William Jennings Bryan was transmitting placating notes to the Germans after the outrage; Wilson, stiffening, wrote to the Germans demanding that they cease such attacks.

The Amherst dinner at the Algonquin in Boston bowled Coolidge over. Suddenly he could see the value of gown along with town. The group assembled honored not only him but also his family, reading aloud, with pleasure, the example of Coolidge brevity supplied by his father in his RSVP: "Gentlemen: Can't come. Thank you, John Coolidge." "I am sure you would have been proud of the character of the men who came to honor me," Coolidge wrote to his father. Morrow attended with

Meiklejohn. At Amherst, Meiklejohn was making all sorts of changes, even planning to hire a young poet, Robert Frost. In *North of Boston*, a new collection, Frost grappled with the same issues that had long preoccupied the Coolidges and indeed many New Englanders: the obligation to hired men, the rigidity of property rights. "Good fences make good neighbors," Frost wrote, as Calvin Galusha might have.

The next step was to ready Coolidge for a run at the lieutenant governor's office with Samuel McCall, who was already making the case for more defense outlays. Stearns was more than ready to organize it all and became more explicit as the days went by and Coolidge did not signal his readiness to run. "I can shout pretty loud and pretty persistently when I am interested," he wrote Coolidge pointedly. But Coolidge allowed crucial weeks to pass while he remained uncommitted. The job of raising the Amherst flag was being taken care of by Lansing, whom Wilson was naming secretary of state to replace the departing William Jennings Bryan. After all, as Coolidge wrote Stearns crossly and accurately, declaring himself a candidate during a Senate session would drastically reduce his efficacy as president; he would suddenly become a mere partisan angler for office.

In the lieutenant governor race Coolidge would confront a substantial primary opponent, Guy Ham, a Boston lawyer of the Theodore Roosevelt style. Ham was already on the ground, "talking through the state," as *The Springfield Union* put it. Even Stearns admitted that Ham as an orator was a "spell-binder." Coolidge had never campaigned statewide; the Senate president, after all, was chosen by peers. A statewide campaign meant traveling to every county, an exhausting process for someone who had already served in politics well over a decade. "I have been in office about as long as I feel I want," he wrote to his stepmother, Carrie.

He was still finding it hard to overcome his ambivalence about the policy. Even though the United States was not in the war, war contracts were already generous and the war had put everyone, especially his colleagues, into a spending mood. Some of his important work in the Senate that year had been defensive, blocking legislation by colleagues and the Democratic governor. He could claim success for that year: the legislature of 1915 had enacted 668 acts, down from 796 the year before. There were only 147 resolutions, down from 160 the year before. The lieutenant governor position, though higher, gave Coolidge little of the sway over legislation he had enjoyed as Senate president; in Massachusetts a lieutenant governor operated behind the scenes, on committees, and as the governor's watchdog. He would have responsibility without authority in a time of spending that he deplored.

At Gallipoli, both the Allies and the Turks were losing men by the thousands. Preparedness was now a national campaign in the United States; its leaders were Leonard Wood, a veteran officer from the Spanish-American War and a natural successor to Roosevelt, and Roosevelt himself. General Wood was building a camp on Lake Champlain in Plattsburg, New York, to train officers. Four Amherst undergraduates had already enrolled. The federal government lacked cash; the Massachusetts militia would have to start the arming, and Coolidge supported that. Late in June, finding writing easier than talking, he handed Stearns a note—"I am a candidate for lieutenant governor"—and headed back to Northampton.

Still grumpy, he thought it all over on Massasoit Street, where he happened to be alone. It was the week of his forty-third birthday. Grace's Pi Beta Phi sisters had booked ten charter train cars for a transcontinental train trip to Berkeley, California, culminating in a national convention at which Grace would be elected president of Alpha province. She was enjoying herself enormously. Lawmakers and the governor of Massachusetts were also heading west on a trip, to the Panama Pacific Exposition; it was important for the state to remind others that it should not be bypassed. The Massachusetts Art Commission had approved, and the state had paid for, the construction of a replica of the Bulfinch State House, not full-size but still large enough, with its own version of the Doric Hall, for visitors to get the feel of the dignity of the commonwealth. There was also a Massachusetts Beacon, overlooking San Francisco Bay. They had talked about Coolidge joining Grace out west. But in the end he didn't want to be associated with the extravagance. "See Massachusetts first," he told someone. Those who knew him well recognized that it was Coolidge's way of saying that he was in the lieutenant governor race for real.

The 1916 campaign itself proved easier than he had imagined, in part because of a change, the availability of automobiles. By early September, he had already been to the other end of the state, speaking in Martha's Vineyard. Stearns was everywhere. "I don't know why he has been interested in my success but he has been very much so," Coolidge wrote to his father of Stearns. "He is a great worker." Coolidge easily beat Ham in the September primaries, and that cheered him on. "I suppose you have heard of the success of our friend Calvin Coolidge in the Primaries," Stearns wrote Morrow in jubilation. Incredibly, Coolidge had lost Ham's town, Boston, by only 300 votes. Coolidge might not know whether the people wanted him, but the people did.

Back in Northampton the Sunday after the primary, Coolidge was still dizzy with victory and preoccupied. He left the church with an umbrella, deep in his own thoughts, and a Ford Runabout hit him as he crossed Main Street. He found he was able to stand; the driver took him home. He was enough of a celebrity to receive inquiries about the accident but refused to disclose the name of the driver. That afternoon, he took the train back to Boston to plot the general election race with the gubernatorial candidate, Samuel McCall, a party veteran and former congressman. Coolidge's own tactic was simple, and he stuck to it: backing up McCall as he backed up the party. If McCall was for women's suffrage, Coolidge was for it. If McCall was for preparedness for a war, Coolidge was for it. If McCall was with Roosevelt, so was he. If McCall was for more state spending, he was for that too. They knew it was especially important to showcase McCall, a Bostonian, in western Massachusetts. Coolidge saw to it that Northampton firemen mustered for a display and that 150 of them materialized to hear McCall; in the town of Amherst, McCall spoke to 450 students on the drill grounds of the state agricultural college.

In Turners Falls, Senator John Haigis, the man to whom Coolidge had ceded the San Francisco junket slot, was waiting to welcome them with a band and a crowd of five hundred. Coolidge spared McCall the nitty-gritty defense work of the Massachusetts GOP so that McCall might inspire voters with lofty thoughts and plans. Coolidge and McCall covered ten towns in Middlesex County in one day. He had promised to see Massachusetts first, and he was making good on the promise.

If Coolidge was there for McCall, Stearns was there for him. The Stearns gift began with his help in explaining the taciturn Calvin to those who had not encountered him before. This damage control often had to take the form of apology. On October 15, Stearns wrote to Mrs. Arthur Lowe of Fitchburg, "I hope I did not leave a wrong impression of Mr. Coolidge. I have come to know him intimately. He is very far indeed from being 'cold.' He is reserved, but full of enthusiasm." After the primaries Stearns dictated another set of fund-raising letters, including one to Morrow.

The results lifted the Republican Party like nothing since the days before Roosevelt: McCall and Coolidge won. For the first time since 1909, the Republicans also controlled both chambers of the legislature. At the victory party, Coolidge told the crowd that they had succeeded: once again the party was united and, as the papers put it, "fit to govern." But the big story was Coolidge's margin. It was 50,000, ten times that of McCall over the Democratic Walsh. It was evident that Coolidge had carried McCall, or even the whole ticket, and not the other way around.

The result made clear that Stearns had been right: Coolidge was on the path to the governorship and more, if only the others would back him. To prepare, Coolidge found himself a partner, a Northampton lawyer with a profile like his own: Ralph Hemenway had attended Amherst, though he did not graduate, and then read the law like Coolidge. Coolidge offered to create a partnership, the understanding being that Coolidge would use the office but the law work would go to Hemenway. The door on the second floor of the Masonic Building now read in gold letters CALVIN COOLIDGE—LAW OFFICE.

The lieutenant governor's position was a largely ceremonial one, but Coolidge was determined to make the most of it. It was a kind of holding box for the governor's office, in which he was expected to spend two or three years. His job was to preside over the executive council of eight elected officials. This body was supposed to be a counterweight to the executive; the council oversaw commissions, and the governor's appointments required its advice and consent. Coolidge did not speak much at all the departments he visited. Observers noticed his ability to hear people out; later he would to be called "an eloquent listener." One of Coolidge's jobs, chairman of the Committee on Warrants of the executive council, was to oversee the spending of public money. Watching the rush to spend, he could now see more than ever before that the mechanism was broken. At both levels of government there was a problem: neither the state nor the federal government possessed a real budget plan overseen by executives. The money spent was usually approved in individual legislation so that even a governor, or the U.S. president, did not have much control. The new income tax made the damage worse. A new machine was there to raise the money, but no machine was there to control how it was spent. By the end of fiscal year 1915, the staff at the Bureau of

Internal Revenue in Washington had reached over 4,700. Congressmen were having trouble even understanding the new income tax forms. Yet his own party was about to repeat Washington's error and introduce an income tax of its own in Massachusetts. The constitutional convention was starting soon; George Churchill, a professor at Amherst, would be a delegate. Churchill and others thought the executive ought to have less power, and the legislature more. It was hard to know. While Coolidge did not have much time for some of the issues of the convention, he saw a powerful need for change. One idea lawmakers put forward was a veto of individual items for the governor; that would enable the governor to cut back on spending as a householder might.

Grace joined Calvin at the inauguration and was a guest at a special lunch in the State House Hall of Flags that followed. Governor Stickney of Vermont, Colonel Coolidge, and others came as well. Stearns was there smoothing over, making life easier, as a sort of second father to Calvin. Mrs. Stearns had already firmed up her friendship with Grace and was often a hostess to her. Amherst men were always there to cheer Coolidge on. He found he had time for speeches, and Stearns encouraged him. Stump speaking was well and good, but the best medium for Coolidge was the book. Stearns, so shrewd at marketing after his family's retail experience, thought Coolidge's speeches warranted showcasing, and by one of the great publishers such as Boston's iconic Houghton Mifflin.

The Stearnses also sought to get the Coolidges accustomed to living the life of a leading family in the state. At the fancy restaurant on Tremont Street, La Touraine, where Stearns had long dined, the Coolidges now dined as well. Swampscott, where the Stearnses vacationed, became a destination for the Coolidges, as was Marblehead, where there was another Stearns family home. Even his sons, town boys accustomed to Rahar's, were stunned at the plenty. At one point the boys were sitting alone in a restaurant and each was served an entire chicken; afterward they could not contain their excitement in reporting the bounty to their parents. An astute reporter would shortly note that the New Englander's face was changing; he was now "spare but not gaunt: tiny pads of fat upholster his jowls." The reporter, William Allen White, observed what all were beginning to understand: Coolidge was prospering.

In February 1916, Amherst alumni, triumphant over Coolidge's victories and prospects, hosted their own giant dinner of more than a thousand in Boston at the Copley Plaza. The entire faculty of Amherst and the Glee Club came by special train. Mrs. McCall; Mrs. Whitman, the wife of New York's governor, Charles Whitman, class of 1890; and Mrs. Meiklejohn sat in the balcony. Grace was there as well, seated as a guest of Mrs. Stearns in a box. Governor Whitman used the opportunity to make a clear pronouncement: "I am in favor of universal military training." Coolidge endorsed preparedness too but went on to talk of other topics. He memorialized his party's progress by quoting from a poem about persistence by Josiah Gilbert Holland, a biographer of Lincoln. His voice was still so nasal that it caught others off guard; others observed Grace containing her laughter. But the words made sense to Coolidge and his fellow alumni, men who had known each other on the day they all arrived at college: "Heaven is not reached at a single bound/ But we build the ladder by which we rise/From the lowly earth to the vaulted skies/And we mount to its summit round by round." Now more removed from the daily horse trading of the Senate, Coolidge could also be frank about his strengthening conviction in regard to business: the measure of success was not merchandise, to be sure. But, he told his peers, those who held that the economic system was fundamentally flawed were wrong. One who built a factory, Coolidge said, was also building a temple, and to him was due "reverence and praise."

The casualties mounted at Verdun, thousands a day, and Americans trembled internally at the news. On March 2, 1916, *The Amherst Student*, the undergraduates' newspaper, suggested that it was time for Amherst to form its own battalion; other colleges had already done so. The Alumni Council formed a Committee on Military Training to prepare undergraduates. In April 1916, Coolidge traveled to Amherst's College Hall to preside over a meeting on preparedness, during which an army captain and a private spoke to the undergraduates. Fifty-five men, Amherst undergrads and alumni, were shortly accepted for summer training camps.

At night now, instead of worrying about his own rent on Massasoit Street, Coolidge worried about the effects of all the new policies, including some he was involved in promulgating. Joseph Eastman would be up for reappointment on the state public service commission next year, and he would be asked to testify on the progressive's competence. On May 28, 1916, Governor McCall signed a state income tax into law, 1.5 percent on incomes above $2,000. In addition, the state levied a 6 percent tax on income from intangible assets: stocks or bonds. The day the

Globe carried the news of the tax in its business section, the front page was dedicated to a review of the Harvard Regiment of the army passing a reviewing stand at the State House. A total of 45,000 people marched in the parade. The income tax was just one of those sacrifices, like the tax on oleomargarine, that came with war. Every sacrifice seemed necessary for the war now, especially since U.S. soldiers were not in Europe. And every request was now couched in those terms of sacrifice. As usual, Coolidge was at pains not to take gifts or money.

That spring the Coolidges did accept one gift from the Stearnses: an invitation to travel together to Washington. Once again, Stearns planned carefully: the four stayed at the Shoreham Hotel, which had been owned by former vice president Levi Morton, a Republican and native son of Vermont. Shoreham, Morton's birthplace, stood in fact only about sixty miles or so from Plymouth Notch. The Shoreham was located on Fifteenth and H streets; it was a prestigious hotel where political figures from left to right—from Big Bill Haywood, the labor agitator, to Attorney General James McReynolds—could be seen. Coolidge had his first serious meeting with Henry Cabot Lodge, but what took place went unrecorded. Stearns made sure Coolidge took in a vista that included the White House and the Washington Monument. Coolidge gave a typically restrained comment: "That is a view that would rouse the emotions of any man."

The intensity of Stearns's affection was sometimes hard for Calvin to weather. Stearns demanded not only political time but also personal time, including meals and meetings. "I am away so much that I do not have the time at home I hoped," Coolidge wrote his stepmother. Stearns so admired Coolidge that he wrote Dwight Morrow to ask what he thought about giving an honorary degree to the lieutenant governor; Morrow thought it was too early. Mrs. Morrow, on her first encounter, deemed Coolidge limited. "I don't see how that sulky red-haired little man ever won that pretty charming woman," she told her husband. But she and Morrow also noticed that Coolidge paid attention to her children; he asked Anne, her daughter, about a bandage on her finger.

Some politicians, Lodge included, did not understand the idea of Calvin Coolidge either. Lodge did know a Coolidge, Louis Coolidge, who had served for years as his private secretary, and in the middle of his sixth decade he was not ready to get to know another. On June 7, the Massachusetts Republicans journeyed to Chicago for the party convention. The likely nominee was Charles Evans Hughes of New York, a Supreme Court justice. Somewhere second was John Weeks, a senator from Massachusetts. But when Lodge heard Coolidge's name mentioned, he laughed outright: "My God, Coolidge"—it was risible. Apparently, the Washington visit had not had the impression Stearns hoped for. The others, though, were less contemptuous. Judge Field called on Murray Crane at his hotel, one senior Massachusetts man to another. "I see your friend Frank Stearns is in town," Field said. "Yes, I saw him," Crane came back. "Do you know who his candidate for president is?" "Hughes, I imagine." "Judge, you have a poor imagination," answered Crane. "He's for Calvin Coolidge."

It was half a joke to both men, but with each day, a little more real. In August 1916, Coolidge served as acting governor for a month while McCall took a holiday. Seventeen guns, the Massachusetts governor's salute, were fired in his honor as Coolidge inspected the Coast Artillery Corps at Fort Warren and Fort Andrews in the Boston Harbor. A few weeks later he spoke at the home of Augustus Gardner, the lawmaker who had retrieved the children in France. Again, his job was to defend spending. The Democrats were blocking more outlays for homes for the mentally ill. Coolidge backed the administration's plans: there must be "no parsimony in the care of our unfortunates," he said. Such statements did not come easily, but he believed that this was the kind of piloting the party needed.

After all, the Republicans were not popular in the growing western states. Hughes lost to Wilson that fall, despite the fact that all the Republicans rallied behind him, including Roosevelt. Even the outcome in Massachusetts was close. Yet Coolidge won again that fall with 288,000 votes, more than his governor, Senator Lodge, or the presidential candidate, Hughes. The *Springfield Republican* trumpeted its news to the world: "Mr. Coolidge rose unvexed on the highest crest of the Republican wave." Everyone expected now that Coolidge would be governor next—only the timing was unknown, dependent on when McCall would be ready to move on.

Coolidge's political future was more certain, but his economics were not. Coolidge and others, especially Stearns, could see that prices were still rising, but none of them was sure why. Their old argument of blaming the Democrats' Underwood Tariff was weaker than ever. Even with the income tax, the state did not have enough revenue to pay everyone.

The Boston Police were an example. The policemen worked all the time, sixty, seventy, eighty or more hours a week. Their pay had not been raised since 1913. The radical IWW union was still making trouble. There was violence in many of the immigrant neighborhoods, especially the North End. On the first day of the year, a bomb hidden in a wicker suitcase at the State House had failed to go off only due to a flawed fuse. On December 6, 1916, the Wobblies held a rally in North Square. A riot ensued and policemen from Salutation Station and Hanover Street Station arrived.

The balancing act he had committed to became even harder the next year, 1917. The German kaiser turned more aggressive, declaring that submarines and ships would make unconditional war on the sea once more. That was a direct challenge again to the port cities. On March 19, 1917, Coolidge's fellow legislators voted to allot a million dollars for defense, a huge amount for the state, for the protection of the commonwealth and the federal government. It was an amount that would sink the state budget. The only, but great, consolation was that the outlay gave the opportunity to declare war before Washington did.

But barely. On April 2, Wilson delivered his war message; Congress voted to declare war within days. By May, Congress had passed the Selective Service Act, which brought in conscription.

The news fell like a bombshell among the young men of Massachusetts. Meiklejohn asked Amherst students to wait to hear from the government, but many didn't. By the college commencement of June 1917, only thirty-five members of the senior class remained. Soon a Yankee Division, the 26th Infantry, would assemble 28,000 soldiers from New England. Foster Stearns, Frank's son, presented to the new Amherst Battalion two flags, one of the commonwealth and one of the United States, in honor of his grandfather, who had served in the 21st Regiment Massachusetts Voluntary Army in the Civil War.

Eyeing the 1918 outlays for his state, Coolidge could see that the numbers were over $30 million, three times what the state had spent a decade before. The declaration of war meant that the United States had to borrow on a scale unimagined, even more than it had in the first years of the war. William McAdoo, the Treasury secretary, created Liberty Loans, bonds to sell the country to fund the war. McAdoo tried to figure out how much he needed to raise. But in the end he made an unscientific guess, which he later described: "I had formed a tentative conclusion as to the amount of the first loan. It ought to be, I thought, three billion dollars. I can hardly tell you how I arrived at the sum of three billions. . . . I am sure that the deciding influence in my mind was not a mass of statistics, but what is commonly called a 'hunch'—a feeling or impression rather than a logical demonstration." The bonds were gold-backed; the government would give the bearer the preset amount of gold due him under the gold standard instead of greenbacks, if he liked. Interest on the bonds was tax-free, which seemed an increasingly valuable advantage as tax rates continued to go up, and improbably quickly. McAdoo was not only Treasury secretary but also Wilson's son-in-law: he had married Eleanor Wilson in 1914. That meant that whatever he did, right or wrong, was not likely to be easily questioned.

When the time came for Coolidge to campaign in the fall, the whole landscape was military. Authorities had commandeered the German ships; the United States had renamed the old *Kronprinzessin Cecilie* the *Mount Vernon*; the old *Vaterland* of the Hamburg America Line was now the *Leviathan*. *Kronprinzessin Cecilie* was now serving as a homely transport ship, carrying soldiers overseas and back. Morrow was supervising war savings programs for New Jersey now, including a stamp issue where the minimum purchase price was only 25 cents. McAdoo's Treasury was exhorting New England to contribute more to the second Liberty Bond loan campaign: as of late October, New England, whose maximum quota was $500 million, was raising almost that much, outbuying other regions. Massachusetts was beaten only by Connecticut in its own region. Senator Lodge was mounting charge after charge against the president. Lodge's choice for U.S. field commander, General Wood, was not only the leader of the preparedness movement and the great ally of Theodore Roosevelt but also someone Massachusetts could claim as its own: Wood had attended Harvard Medical School. But the secretary of war, Newton Baker, chose another man to head the expeditionary force in Europe, Major General John Pershing.

In his fall campaign of 1917, the last, he hoped, for lieutenant governor, Coolidge studied the railroads and trolleys, which were becoming collateral damage of the war. Rails were in use nonstop. But despite greater traffic, they struggled for cash flow. Two separate events were squeezing the rail companies. The rate rules that the ICC had been imposing since the passage of the Hepburn Act had indeed kept rates that railroads might charge lower. But companies were finding their costs were higher, as well as their taxes. Meanwhile, workers were demanding pay increases to keep pace with their own costs. The railroads could not keep up with the demands of war. To serve the war effort, Wilson was contemplating nationalizing the railroads. Local trolleys, which had been denied the chance to link up with the great railroads several years before, were now paying the price. Coolidge was finding that it was easier to raise money for highway improvements, such as pavement, than for rail. And it was hard to know whether Northampton or the other towns would still seem like paradise after the war.

Coolidge joined fellow party members in spelling out Massachusetts' contribution: that Massachusetts had equipped its own troops before the declaration of war to help the cause. "While Washington was yet dumb, Massachusetts spoke," he said. He also listed the labor agreements that had been concluded in the name of industrial peace: Gloucester fishermen, shoemakers in Lynn, and railroad employees all had given up something in order to ensure they did not interrupt food or service delivery. "The production and distribution of food and fuel have been advanced. The maintenance of industrial peace has been promoted." The nature of the sacrifice could be expressed well in terms of ships: "Massachusetts has decided that the path of the *Mayflower* shall not be closed. She had decided to sail the seas." Everyone in Boston seemed to be working extra. The police had spent a full 20,000 man-hours helping out with defense-related projects, though their budget contained no extra funds for that. As for Washington, Wilson, Coolidge said, was now "clothed in dictatorial powers"—that was as it had to be, but Coolidge told voters that the dictatorship could "not be continued in time of peace." At Christmas 1917, the Wilson administration did nationalize the railroads, after all.

All the first half of the next year, 1918, the war pounded at them. July 1918 brought news that the plane of Roosevelt's son Quentin, who had trained at Plattsburgh, had been downed in France. Coolidge's race for governor, when it finally came that summer and fall, was not a regular race. If he had signed on to spending, he had done so less than others. There was widespread illness in the cities that year; the Coolidges tried to keep their sons in the country as much as possible. Coolidge wrote to his father that he was running for governor and offered to send Calvin up to Vermont, even by stagecoach. As he prepared his speeches, influenza struck the soldiers at Camp Devens; soon as many as one in four was down with the illness, which hit Amherst as well. The Stearnses' son,

Foster, was wounded at Saint-Mihiel. And the Germans finally had their chance to take revenge for the commandeering of the *Kronprinzessin*: a torpedo struck the U.S. Army transport *Mount Vernon* off the coast of France; thirty-five men who were locked in the fire room were killed, including seven New Englanders. Remarkably, the ship made it back to a French port on her own steam. As the election drew close, Coolidge's mood improved; he was going to win, and he knew it. His father had obliged his campaign team, helping a hired photographer collect photos of Plymouth for the paper. Coolidge's father received a note of thanks signed "Calvin Coolidge"; the joke was that the handwriting was a child's; Calvin, Jr., aged ten, not the candidate, had signed. Coolidge understood all too well that it was only luck that his sons were too young to serve; John Weeks, the Senate candidate, did have a son in uniform.

Stearns's strategy now was to sell Coolidge the man, rather than the party. In this he had support from all over the field; even Roosevelt wrote in with an endorsement, calling Coolidge "a high-minded public servant" who understood he must base his work on a "jealous insistence upon the rights of all." Stearns funded a small biography of Coolidge, and items like the Plymouth pictures. The strategy was not very costly. Later he figured that he personally had spent $6,000 plus food on the campaign—substantial but together with the other donors' outlays not enormous, given the amounts their opponent, Richard Long, a wealthy shoe manufacturer, was laying out. What's more, much of that $6,000 had been spent not on advertisement or transport but on the biography.

Coolidge's gubernatorial victory coincided with that of the country to the week: the election was November 5, and the armistice came on November 11. Coolidge beat his opponent, Long, but only by a narrow margin; Walsh, the Democratic candidate for senator, beat out Coolidge's party ally John Weeks. "It was 2:30 before the election was sure so I telegraphed Stickneys office in the morning to notify you I was elected by 17,000," he wrote his father. Then he admonished, "That is enough." Stearns was aching to move the Coolidges to an appropriate house, "if possible on Beacon Hill, but not on the Back Bay," as he wrote to Morrow. But Coolidge had already made up his mind not to undertake such an expense. Stearns saw the potential for Grace as a hostess, but the Coolidges decided to keep the family at home on Massasoit Street.

A mishap marred Coolidge's inauguration: the seventeen cannons to mark the event were fired too soon. It seemed appropriate, a signal the new governor had to get to work early, for there was so much to undertake. At the same time they had elected him, voters had endorsed a plan to consolidate the departments of the commonwealth government, more than a hundred all told, to twenty; soon the legislature would pass a law detailing the plan for enforcement of that, but it would be up to him, the governor, to make the cuts. That would mean laying off friends and political constituencies crucial to his election campaigns. Both rail-roads and street rails could not make ends meet; even if railroads were denationalized, it was hard to know when they might ever make a profit. The street railways everywhere could not raise fares without demon-strations, yet they did not have enough revenue without the fare raises. Coolidge took time in his address to comment that with the railways, "the problem is where to get the money." Massachusetts had to face real-ity: "there are only two sources, increased fares and the public treasury"; the companies were broke. Coolidge eschewed ad hominem attack. But the reality was that the very public service commission to which he had reappointed Joseph Eastman was the one keeping the trolley fares down so far the companies starved.

Looking back now, the governor-elect could see great change from the war to the careers of men he knew. The war had changed reputa-tions and created new enemies and alliances. President Meiklejohn at Amherst, for example, might teach well, but the alumni would forever remember that he had not led in the war, but followed. Harlan Stone had come in late, but had held a difficult job, judging the cases of conscien-tious objectors. Morrow had taken the lead at J. P. Morgan; his work for Liberty Bonds, in New Jersey, had elevated him. So had the fact that he had journeyed across the seas to Europe during the war. What mattered about Roosevelt now was not his rash attack on the Republican Party eight years earlier but his leadership on preparedness from the early days in Plattsburgh. The labor leader Samuel Gompers was covered with glory now, for he had left no light between himself and Wilson, telling members of the American Federation of Labor as early as January 1918 that to impede the war with actions at the factories was "treason."

There was also great damage from the war, starting with damage to principles. Freedom had been lost defending freedom; the property rights Coolidge had defended as an attorney had often been overlooked. The primacy of the states over the federal government could no longer be assured. The great progressives of Massachusetts had decamped to Washington; Brandeis now sat on the Supreme Court, and Joseph Eastman was confirmed as a commissioner at the Interstate Commerce Commission that very month. Massachusetts, too, was a fiscal disaster: the budget he would present for the following year would be $39 million, higher than what the state had spent that year. Other states were in the same boat. Percival Clement of Rutland, the new governor of Vermont, put the problem even more plainly than Coolidge in his address. "We have reached our taxing limit," Clement said on January 10. "The war is over but the expenses of it are not paid."

Reversing the spending would be difficult. The war was being taken as a progressive victory. The old way of life was changing. Some of the useful old knowledge was being lost. At dinner with Clarence Barron that year, Coolidge talked about the future of ships. You needed great pieces of wood to build a mast. "There were men trained to go into the Maine woods and check the timber to be cut to make the knees in the wooden ships. Few know that you cannot build ships as a carpenter works and the curved parts or joints annexed to the keel must be grown." How would the new keels be steadied? Coolidge asked Barron. "There are no longer the men in existence to pick that timber."

Shipyards were on all their minds, not only because of the engineering of ships, or because of returning soldiers, but also because of the revolution in Russia. Even as Barron, who headed Dow Jones's *The Wall Street Journal*, and Coolidge, the governor, dined, British battleships were cleaning up after a brutal battle with Bolsheviks at Kronstadt. The horror stories from Russia put them all in a mood to compromise with labor organizations here in the United States. Indeed, companies might have to give in again and again to forestall something like what had happened in Russia. In Seattle that February, workers mounted a general strike; only concerted countering pressure from the mayor, Ole Hanson, caused the men to stand down. No one knew what would happen in a similar situation here, but it seemed likely Coolidge might respond less forcefully than Hanson. Boston had been through so much. Early in the year a terrible molasses spill at the waterfront in Boston had killed twenty-one and injured hundreds, adding to the sense of misery in the city. Shoemakers or police, they expected his new administration to give now, in 1919, what the commonwealth had not been able to give during the war. They knew that Coolidge would continue to meet them at a middle ground as he always had, and he knew that. They knew that he, Coolidge, feared anarchy, and would use that advantage against him.

The last cost, the greatest, had come in human life. The war had taken more than 100,000 American lives. The Yankee Division alone had had nearly 12,000 casualties. Theodore Roosevelt had not recovered from the death of his son Quentin and died early in the year at Sagamore Hill, around the time Coolidge was inaugurated. One of Coolidge's first acts was to send a eulogy for Roosevelt. Another was to sign a bill covering some of the transport costs of the thousands of troops who would converge on Boston to parade. Yet another was to write the state farm bureaus to inquire whether the soldiers might find work helping in the spring and summer harvests.

An opportunity to express such thoughts presented itself to Coolidge in February when President Wilson chose Boston to land at upon his return from Europe. Wilson's goal was to solidify U.S. support for membership in the League of Nations. Senator Lodge was flamboyantly opposed, but Wilson sensed rightly that many in the Bay State supported him. A few days before the president's visit, Coolidge had issued a proclamation saying that Wilson had come "to a city and Commonwealth that have loyally supported his efforts to prosecute the war, that are eager to pay him the tributes of respect and honor that are due to the position he holds." Coolidge greeted Wilson and Navy Assistant Secretary Franklin Roosevelt in the harbor and escorted them to Mechanics Hall, where he introduced the president before a packed hall; tens of thousands had applied for tickets. Coolidge's remarks struck the assistant secretary of the navy. Roosevelt saw that Coolidge had his speech on cards but then diverged from the cards, and spoke freely. Coolidge, Roosevelt noticed, hailed Wilson as "a great leader of the world who is earnestly striving to effect an arrangement which will prevent another war." Such a statement, friendly as it was, would infuriate Senator Lodge, who was now opposing Wilson. It also revealed Coolidge's own sentiment. He did not think that sacrifice on this scale should be made easily.

But Coolidge also spoke positively, drawing a direct comparison between Wilson and the presidents who had been his own inspiration these four years. "We have welcomed the President with a reception more marked even than that which was accorded to General Washington; more united than could have been given any time during his life to President Abraham Lincoln." In that way Coolidge was also saying that whatever the future held, this past sacrifice had to be honored. He had done what was difficult for him. He, the party, and the state had found the middle ground. They had prevailed. Lincoln especially had been right: the middle ground was the most stable.

COOLIDGE SHUT OUT ANY concern about reelection because his job now, as governor, was to reward his citizens. That early April, ship after ship docked at the harbor, and with each docking it was time to greet more soldiers returning home. On April 3, there was a parade for the returning black soldiers. On April 4 it was the turn of New England's own, the 26th Division. One hundred and twenty-three policemen showed up for special duty at Commonwealth Pier to help bring the soldiers in. Special trains would carry the men arriving on this transport to Camp Devens where they would be served beans and clean up. The *Springfield Republican* sought to provide a rough arrival estimate for anxious families: "North Adams, Adams, Springfield, Greenfield and Northampton ought to begin to assume khaki-colored hue about mid afternoon tomorrow as Companies I, K, L, and M are to be the first to benefit by the furlough arrangements."

That day Coolidge rode out into the bay with other governors to greet 6,000 returning troops. The fog obscured the view, just as it had so many other times in the war. But soon enough the great ship rose before them. She had been there before. It was the old *Kronprinzessin Cecilie*. Now the *Mount Vernon*, she listed under the weight of her passengers, thousands more people than she had borne on the Atlantic that evening in 1914. The people were the soldiers, and they were waving. Amid the din of the steam whistles, Coolidge lifted the megaphone to respond to them. "I welcome you to Massachusetts," he said.

SIX

THE STRIKE

Boston

ON MONDAY, SEPTEMBER 8, 1919, Coolidge showed up at a meeting of the American Federation of Labor in Greenfield, north of Northampton. The governor offered bland remarks about the need for more production to revive the Massachusetts economy. Then he departed for Boston, without commenting on the issue preoccupying everyone in the room: a possible police strike in the state capital. The month before, the old Boston police association, known as the Social Club, had formally affiliated with the AFL as Boston Police Union Number 16,807. Now the new union was threatening to walk out if patrolmen did not get better working conditions, higher pay, and recognition of their union. The very existence of a police union that could strike broke the rules of the Boston Police Department manual. In 1918, police commissioner Stephen O'Meara had underscored that by stating, "A police officer cannot consistently belong to a union and perform his sworn duty." O'Meara had died suddenly. But now his replacement as commissioner, Edwin Curtis, was hearing the cases of the officers who had decided to unionize nonetheless.

The AFL men meeting in Greenfield expected that in coming days Coolidge would make a display of studying the Boston police case. They also expected that at some point or other Commissioner Curtis, who reported to the governor, would negotiate with the police and make concessions to avoid a strike or halt one that the police had begun. Finally, the union men expected that the governor would in the end support such a compromise.

Conciliation with organized labor seemed the only course for a governor of any big industrial state in 1919. The return to prewar routine that most politicians, including Coolidge, had in their turn expected had not come yet. In the war, peace at the workplace had been paramount to support the military effort; now peace at the workplace was paramount to prevent unrest and violence. Europe, after all, had segued straight from war to revolution. That year in Russia, Lenin and his Bolsheviks were tightening their hold. In Germany revolutionary groups like the Spartacus League were claiming not just the right to strike but also the right to confiscate property. Civil war was racking Mexico. Authorities across the United States wondered whether American workers would move next. One of the speakers following Coolidge in Greenfield was Éamon de Valera, the Irish leader who was seeking support for the Irish Republic's independence from Britain. De Valera had appeared earlier that year at Fenway Park before tens of thousands. The *Globe* had described de Valera as "electric": "He said the things which Irish-Americans feel," the reporter, A. J. Philpott, had commented. Many of the Irish of Boston, among them many police, drew more inspiration from de Valera than from Curtis or Coolidge. And Curtis and Coolidge knew it.

Any American politician deciding whether to stand up to a union had to consider what had happened in another port city, Seattle, during a general strike earlier that year. The Seattle mayor, Ole Hanson, had condemned the general strike and "domestic bolshevism" and had even managed to force the city back to work. But the mayor had endured many attacks subsequently, and even an assassination attempt. Just a week or so before this Greenfield meeting, Hanson had resigned his job as mayor, telling reporters, "I am tired out and am going fishing." Other politicians saw what Hanson had been through and began to pick their battles. A union for police was a tame concept, one of the milder ideas that had come in from Europe with the tide that bore the returning soldiers. It would not be the end of the world for a governor or a mayor to permit it.

There were other reasons for officials like Coolidge to move softly. Veterans were not all finding work. Many were in pain or disabled. Wages represented an even greater source of tension. For years, employers and the government had warned workers that wage increases would impede the war effort. That was what the AFL's Sam Gompers had meant with his "treason" statement. President Wilson himself had promised that with peace, large companies would give overdue wage increases. Now, however, the raises were being postponed yet again. With sales lagging, companies could not make good on their promises to lift wages. Nor could town governments.

Both employers and workers looked to Washington for a sign, but Wilson was busy fighting for his League of Nations, and he clearly deemed the wage question secondary. The workers waited while Wilson feuded with senators such as Massachusetts's own Henry Cabot Lodge over what seemed petty details. The acting head of the United Mine Workers, John L. Lewis, moved more belligerently than Gompers. Lewis was calling for a nationwide strike of coal men beginning November 1. The industry experts were already warning families to buy coal early.

It was difficult in turn for any official to deny the workers on the wage question because of yet another problem: prices. The cost of food at the store was double what it had been in 1913. Such increases were nothing like what any adult could remember; you had to have worked in the 1860s or 1870s to recall such a rise. The Housewives League had recently tried to explain to President Wilson that his strike problem was caused by the nationwide price problem. The women had asked the president to seek legislation to "reduce the cost of living which thru present prices of bread, meat and corn has become unbearable. This situation more than anything else is the cause of the discontent of labor." In the war the farms had fared better by selling their grain to Europe. Now, because they had their own basics, they were more protected than the city households from the price rises. That did not mean, however, that the farmers' lives were easy either. John Coolidge's cheese factory wasn't doing much better than it had been when he'd opened it during Coolidge's college years. Grace and her neighbors were now selling the Plymouth cheese from 69 Massasoit Street, the home of Therese Hills, but that was the extent of Colonel Coolidge's success in the agricultural sector.

In Boston, the would-be strikers, the police, made an especially strong case. The city and state had worked the police hard in the war; the men had spent thousands of extra hours serving by the side of the governor or other officials at events like the parades for returning soldiers. It was the police who had taken the blows when the anarchists blew up public structures; they viewed themselves as the first line of defense against chaos. The men had received a raise that year, but the raise had not covered the price rise. Some of the police were returning veterans; many had disabled relatives to care for. So many in Boston were disabled that a former congressman, Frederick Deitrick, had even formed a Boston Blind and Cripples' Union, which met every Friday at Tremont Temple, where Coolidge often spoke. The policemen's other complaint, about conditions, was also legitimate; the Boston station houses were in rotten condition. Vermin were so prevalent that they chewed through the leather on the policemen's helmets. James Storrow, a great Boston eminence, led a committee to talk to the police and was already close to an agreement with them. Most newspapers in Boston had signaled that they were ready to follow whatever Storrow recommended.

The policemen had selected as union president a leader it would be hard for Coolidge to tangle with: a veteran policeman named John McInnes. In a city where cars moved wildly and unpredictably, and where there were not yet stoplights, McInnes stood every day reliably at Devonshire and Water streets, managing traffic. McInnes was also a military veteran. He had fought in the Indian wars and had gone to Cuba with the 9th Massachusetts Infantry. Just recently McInnes had trained troops in Texas and performed intelligence work for the army.

The police were also confident because they knew that Coolidge had given in to unions before. In April, the telephone workers across New England had struck, their opponent being the U.S. Post Office, which had seized control of the phone company for the duration of the war. The telephone ladies had affiliated with the International Brotherhood of Electrical Workers. Gompers, careful about picking his battles, had advised against the strike, but the women had proceeded anyhow, and Postmaster General Albert Burleson's efforts to replace them with soldiers had backfired. The soldiers found it unchivalrous to face off with the telephone ladies. In the telephone strike, the governor had again tried to find the old middle ground: if a government had to step in, he said, why not let it be the state of Massachusetts? Massachusetts could manage the phone company for the duration of the strike. The postmaster general had given the phone operators a wage increase. In the same days, Coolidge had signed a labor bill limiting the workweek for women workers to forty-eight hours, a concession to organized labor generally.

Finally, the Boston patrolmen knew that Coolidge could scarcely spare time for a drawn-out conflict with them. That summer and fall Coolidge needed every hour he could get for a difficult task mandated by the new state constitution. The governor must cut the number of departments in the state government. This meant laying off friends and political supporters. In a state where a governor's term ran only twelve months, this was treacherous work.

Even before the police conflict, Coolidge had already been flagging, his secretary, Henry Follansbee Long, had noted. To look over the appointments in Long's diary of the past months was to find a contrast with the relaxed time of Governor McCall, who had taken whole months at a time away from office. "Governor in about 9:30 and busy all day," his secretary's book had read on July 3. There was another entry for July 7: "Governor in early with young Calvin. He busy all day seeing people and writing veto." July 8 brought the inevitable: senators paid a call to protest the veto. The veto rejected funding for roads, including some sought by the town of Amherst.

There had been breaks now and then, of course. Sometime that summer, the visit of an old friend had provided a moment's respite: Henry Field had come from Northampton to see Coolidge and inquire how he was holding up under the pressure. Coolidge then did something unexpected: he took his first boss in the state car to Watertown. Their destination was the old burial ground where the graves of John and Mary Coolidge lay. Coolidge seemed to think he could draw strength from his ancestors. Grace and his sons, especially Calvin, sustained him in difficult moments.

"I think you might find him some comfort to you while you are alone," Coolidge had written once about the boy to his father.

"Governor getting tired of seeing people. He is planning to visit institutions," Long was writing by August 26. On August 27, the reason for the retreat to institutions had become clear: Coolidge finally handed out one of the lists of names he had pulled together, mostly by himself, in isolation, for the new, reorganized state government. What mattered was not so much the names that did make the list as those that didn't. With each cutback, Coolidge made a new enemy.

On that September Monday of the AFL meeting, Coolidge arrived back in Boston to learn that Curtis had moved forward, suspending the nineteen policemen who had taken the lead in joining the union. The governor's response was just as predicted: he conferred with his attorney general. At some point in the afternoon or evening Coolidge sent a message to the AFL Convention in Greenfield. It too contained the expected content, placating: "I earnestly hope circumstances will arise which will cause the police officers to be reinstated."

By Tuesday the strike plan was gathering momentum. Once Curtis had suspended their peers, many police were ready to move. Coolidge conferred with Curtis and Mayor Andrew Peters. The three men would have to decide on the right thing to do. The matter of jurisdiction was complicated; the police reported to the commissioner, who reported to the governor; but both the mayor and the governor might call out the state guard. All of them were now turning to the rule books and statutes. Boston employed more than a thousand policemen. Over the course of that Tuesday afternoon, the officials told themselves that a few might strike, but a majority would stay on the job. Curtis assured Coolidge he could handle any trouble.

At 5:45 P.M. on Tuesday, September 9, the event that they all had discussed so often finally occurred. More than a thousand police, the majority of the force, more than Curtis had imagined, walked out of the station houses. The men carried their big, old-fashioned helmets under their arms, like props for an era on which the curtain was now closing. Crime and violence were already a problem in Boston that year, and now the policemen had left the streets unguarded. It would be quite easy for this to expand to a general strike including telephone workers and power workers, the sort that had roiled Seattle. Curtis again told Coolidge that he could handle the strike, and Coolidge held back. The adjutant general of the Massachusetts State Guard, Jesse F. Stevens, however, would stay with him that night at the Adams House; his state troops had already been instructed to be ready for a call. Coolidge also instructed a separate force, the Metropolitan Police, to go on duty, but it was just a small group of one hundred officers. Then he headed to La Touraine on Tremont Street to dine with Stearns. The president of the R. H. Stearns department store, Robert Maynard, had already applied for licenses for private guards to protect it. Henry Wyman, the attorney general, also attended the meal. Stearns and a publisher, Houghton Mifflin, were preparing a volume of Coolidge's speeches, tentatively titled "Bay State Orations." Now, however, such publicity efforts seemed frivolous; Coolidge's future would be decided by the strike.

At Harvard, President Lowell issued a call for volunteers to protect the city. The president carefully advised young men that they were not "strikebreakers" because police could not strike and promised the students that the university would schedule makeup tests for students who missed exams because of police duty. Mayor Peters, for his part, retreated to his home in Brookline, taking reports over the course of the evening.

The policemen themselves gathered at their strike headquarters at Fay Hall. McInnes walked about in plain clothes, encouraging the striking policemen, who seemed dazed at their own action. The telephone girls who had received the patrolmen's support now moved to respond; Mae Matthew, the secretary of the union, spoke up for a crowd around McInnes, saying, "The girls will back up the police and will go out, if necessary, to help them win." The girls' antic presence lightened it all. For a few hours, the city was quiet. Coolidge and the adjutant general retired to sleep.

Later that night small, rough crowds began to build around the city. In Roxbury, a streetcar conductor was shot in the leg. Ruffians went up and down Washington Street, breaking windows. At Washington and Friend streets, a cigar store, United Cigar, was looted and its windows demolished. The Adams House, where Coolidge slept, stood between West and Avery streets on Washington; Posner's, a furniture store at the corner of Avery, was sacked that night. Crowds thronged in Roxbury and at Scollay Square. On Tremont Street, the looters targeted the smaller shops, like Studio Jewelry, just down the street from R. H. Stearns. All over, small tussles broke out. "Men fought each other, not knowing why they fought," one reporter wrote.

The next day, the papers delivered more details. At one downtown shoe store, a group had entered, taking down hundreds of boxes of shoes. The young men and their friends proceeded to try them on. "Here was presented the novel spectacle of thieves sitting in the chairs of the establishment, while others of the crowd helped to fit them with the proper size shoes. They stayed as long as they liked," wrote the *Hampshire Gazette*. At Scollay Square, a seventy-year-old worker at a fruit stand, James Burns, had held off a large crowd seeking to gain entrance, with a .38-caliber revolver. In the North End, small groups terrorized girls and women; there were reports of rapes, serious injuries and even fatalities. This was not a massacre. But for the City on a Hill, the events were unusual. Riots had hit the city before, but not riots in which authorities were not there to mount a countering force, nor riots which the police had actually facilitated. As the *Globe* wrote breathlessly in a 2-cent extra published that morning, "For the first time in the memory of man, Boston was given over to lawlessness."

Coolidge's and Mayor Peters's first action that Wednesday morning was to call out units of the state guard. At the police headquarters, Curtis sat deluged with applications by security firms and other private groups to carry guns. When they were all counted, 1,052 individuals had applied for gun permits in Boston and 390 people for licenses to serve as special policemen. Police Superintendent James Crowley spoke to reporters, telling them he could not have imagined the extent of the disruption. The period of negotiation was over. As James Storrow's commission would note in a report published later, by Wednesday morning, "it was clear to the members of your committee that the situation had become a military one."

At around 2:00 P.M. Wednesday, at the State Armory in West Newton, an alarm rang; men gathered and were told to eat but had no idea what their assignment would be. At 4:00 P.M. the bugles called the men to assembly; the men's commander told them that, as one wrote, things were "nawsty" in Boston. Marched to West Newton Station, the men rode to Huntington Street in Boston, where, after various assemblies, they patrolled Roxbury, Dorchester, and Jamaica Plain, as well as policing a large electric light plant.

Curtis was already looking past the striking police, hunting for replacements. Page one of the *Globe* carried his advertisement:

> *Volunteer Police: Able Bodied Men willing to give their service in case of necessity for part of day or night for protection of persons or property in City of Boston. Apply to me at Room B, Third Floor, Chamber of Commerce Building, except Sundays. William H Pierce Supt of Police, Retired.*

Beside this ran a spate of insurance ads, all aiming to capitalize on the emergency. "Protect Yourself," read one. "Strike-Riot-Civil Commotion and Burglary R. S. Hoffman & Co." Yet another notice informed citizens of their rights and obligations: "Bystanders must assist officers." On the major streets, department stores were covering their windows, hammering up timber to cover the glass, and making barricades; men with bayonets guarded the big shops. In Ireland citizens were waging what many in Boston considered a parallel mutiny against the some 200,000 British troops then garrisoned there. To some of the Irish-American police, Curtis was the equivalent of a British general.

Coolidge, Curtis, and Peters understood now that the state guard might not be enough to stop serious violence. And if the Boston police force, the oldest in the country, succeeded in winning concessions through strikes, the police in other cities would follow with strikes of their own. *The Christian Science Monitor* reported the reaction in Washington: "As viewed here the issue in Boston goes further than a mere dispute over the recognition or non recognition of a union." A Democratic senator from Montana, Henry Myers, waxed hysterical. "Unionization of the police of every city of more than 5,000 population will follow within sixty days," he predicted. "We will have a Soviet government within two years unless some branch of the government steps in and stops this tendency." Others were calmer but still aware of the possibility of a fundamental change in American law enforcement. Authorities in the District of Columbia had asked President Wilson to rule against a police strike there.

But Wilson, who happened to be heading west on his special train to sell his League of Nations to the country, had a much bigger strike on his mind: the threatened action by the workers of the steel industry. On the topic of the Washington police, the president punted. Wilson issued a vague notice via an intermediary: "The president suggests the advisability of postponing any issue regarding the police situation until after the forthcoming industrial conference at Washington and hopes the postponement can be effected." The police of Washington were ecstatic. They did not need to use the great weapon of a strike; they could merely threaten to do so. The conference Wilson mentioned would not take place until October 6, giving them and the police of Boston more time to make their case under a national spotlight.

Complicating matters was a sudden challenge to Coolidge and Curtis, both Republicans, from Mayor Peters, a Democrat. Searching his books, Peters determined that the law gave him the leeway to take over the police force. Peters not only called out the state guard's 10th Regiment of Boston for active duty, but also announced he was taking over the entire force from Curtis. Henceforward, the mayor would make the calls. Coolidge responded by calling in his attorney general and Albert Pillsbury, a lawyer who had fought for William Lewis of Amherst in the past.

This next choice was simple: Coolidge could back up Peters, or he could back up Curtis. Backing up Peters would not be hard, but sticking with Curtis would be the most controversial move of his career. The picture of the strike in the first days did not flatter the commissioner or the governor. Curtis clearly had not prepared for the extent of the strike or the onslaught in the city. Coolidge could be blamed for that alone. "The system as a whole must be searchingly investigated later on," muttered the *Springfield Republican*. The police union had singled out Curtis as the villain: Curtis was the one who had suspended their men. They, in turn, had Gompers to back them up, and Gompers was at the height of his power. President Wilson remained in the background, providing cover for Gompers.

Either way, there was not much time for the governor to make a decision. The angry crowds were ready for more and also ready to take advantage of any confusion at the top. At 10:00 A.M. that September 10, even as *The Boston Globe* extra was being sold, small groups set out to loot more stores in Boston. When the volunteer police in their mismatched uniforms arrived to stop them, the crowds attacked the police. The police then shot into the crowds. Clothing, shoes, shirts, and men's collars lay all about the streets amid the broken glass; in many instances young boys broke the windows and scattered the goods about without even taking them. At 1:30 P.M., riots broke out at Scollay Square, so large that the replacement police were powerless.

As night fell Wednesday, the striking police were not ready to relent. President Lowell had sided with Curtis and Coolidge, but there was a guest professor at Harvard from England, Harold Laski, who believed that the policemen should enjoy, at least, the right to join the AFL. Laski would shortly argue for conciliation in *The Crimson*. Asked whether he would give in on the key issue, affiliation with the AFL, the proud McInnes said, "Nothing doing. A police union and affiliation with the American Federation of Labor is what we are striking for and what we will accept only as a settlement." Other unions in Boston were signaling they might support him. Thirty-five hundred cooks and waiters voted to strike in sympathy with the policemen. Only a group vote at the Central Labor Union office stood between Massachusetts and a general strike.

In New York, policemen and firemen were watching closely; they were preparing to press their own city government for raises that took their salaries to $2,000 a year. The New York fire commissioner commented wryly that he promised to present to the City Board of Estimate and the mayor the plea for the higher wage, which the firemen would have loved to get, "provided they remained firemen." Wilson's relentless focus on the League of Nations meant the administration was caught off guard by the strikes. Senator James Alexander Reed of Missouri, an opponent of Wilson on the League of Nations, was in Boston to speak at Symphony Hall. Woodrow Wilson's daughter Jessie, vacationing on Martha's Vineyard, wrote her father, "The police are all on strike and there has been rioting all day. I cannot wish that he [Reed] may escape a few jolts and bruises. I hope the building is stampeded." But the Symphony Hall debate was canceled, due to the strike.

Boston maintained a small second police force, the Metropolitan police, especially important now that the regular force was gone. But even the Metropolitan police could not be counted on: fifty-three officers refused to cooperate with the governor and headed right over to the union headquarters to join. They too were suspended.

More state troops were hurried in: at 9:51 P.M. on September 10, Companies E and L of the 14th Regiment departed Fall River, Massachusetts, for Boston. But these troops arrived too late. In the city that night, Wednesday, September 10, thousands were already roaming. On Broadway, amid a mob, Captain C. T. Hadley of the 10th Regiment and his C Company ordered men and boys to stop looting a store. "The crowd laughed and hooted," reported the *Hampshire Gazette*. No one expected the authorities to fire at people. In Dorchester the guards fired into the air, but Hadley's men fired at the looters. "And the looters, still laughing and jeering, fell before the shots of the troops." The crowd panicked and ran, stepping on top of one another to escape. Others came back; the city was alive with people. Rain failed to drive them all home. "Cavalrymen rode the sidewalks on newspaper row," *The Boston Globe* reported in awe. At 7:15 P.M., a young man was killed at Howard Street in the West End; it was not clear whether the troops or a citizen had done the deed. The dead man was brought to a city relief hospital, but no one could identify him. The hospital put out some information in the hope of discovering his name: the man was about twenty-six, wore a gray suit from the Continental Clothing Company, had had his appendix out, and had had some bridgework done on his teeth. A woman, shot in the arm, arrived at the hospital immediately after the dead man. The same night, September 10, a twelve-year-old boy from Whitman, Robert Lallie, died at City Hospital from wounds he had received when police had shot into a crowd of looters. On Devonshire Street, where McInnes had so recently policed traffic, people in a crowd found themselves being forced forward by bayonets. The total deaths rose to four.

Late in the evening those who wandered around saw an amazing sight, described by the *Boston Evening Transcript*:

> *The department stores were fully lighted up as broad day light and the window curtains up so that the competent appearing men who stood guard inside might have full view of the nearby street. Two guards remained all night at each of the many doors of the Jordan Marsh Company, Filene's and the RH White buildings.*

Well after midnight into early Thursday morning, September 11, many of the state guards were still patrolling, pushing back crowds; the men of A Company in the 11th Regiment who had had nothing to eat since lunch thought the night would never end. At 2:00 A.M. Thursday, their skipper, desperate, commandeered one store of a new chain, the Waldorf System, on Dudley Street. At 3:00 A.M. yet another group, the Springfield contingent of the state guard, arrived in Boston with ammunition. Within hours, men from Greenfield, Northampton, Holyoke, Great Barrington, and Worcester were there as well. They carried guns with fixed bayonets.

When Coolidge woke Thursday morning, the police were taking more volunteer officers. At Station 2, Captain Sullivan proudly reported that a number of city leaders who had volunteered to help out in the strike were assigned to his station: Mortimer Seabury, a broker; Archie Hurlburt, the proprietor of the Boston Tavern; Bernard J. Rothwell, a former president of the Chamber of Commerce; and Huntington Hardwick, a bond salesman and former athlete. The thought that citizens and soldiers were lining up on the city's side was the first great challenge to the strikers. General Francis Peabody, a brigadier in the National

Guard, and Rear Admiral Francis Bowles, who just finished, as he put it, doing "a little dusting and cleaning" for the Emergency Fleet Corporation, ran into each other on their first day as volunteers. The police, veterans and loyal as they had been, were discovering they did not have a monopoly on heroism. The strikebreakers, too, might also play the war hero card.

At the municipal court, a young man was given a year's sentence in the House of Correction for his participation in the Scollay Square riot. Then, the case was dismissed when authorities discovered the young man was fifteen years old, and he was remanded to juvenile court. The city felt strange—people who had been friends the day before were now enemies. At the courthouse, they encountered one another, strikers mixing with volunteers and lawyers. Some of the police had come to court because old cases of theirs were being heard. Several were also being arraigned on charges of drunkenness and robbery. Another topic was the cost of the battle. The damage of the night of September 9, the first night of rioting, the *Globe* estimated, amounted to around $200,000. Reporters unearthed news for their readers: the law said that Boston itself was liable for damage to the merchants, if the shopkeepers could prove they had taken reasonable precautions.

That Thursday morning, there seemed no news in the world but strikes: steel strikes, police strikes, and the likelihood of the great coal strike. The combination of such news and "the extraordinary rioting in Boston," as the *Chicago Tribune* described it, set the stock market shivering. By 11:00 A.M., Boston saw another death, bringing the toll to five; eighteen-year-old Raymond Barnes, a sailor, was in a group that ran at shooting guardsmen; the bullet hit him in the neck, "making a terrible wound," as the *Globe* wrote. The *Hampshire Gazette* reporter could scarcely believe it was happening in old Boston: at first he saw hysteria: "Hundreds of women were in the street . . . scores became hysterical and the air was filled with shrieks when Barnes was shot down." But afterward the crowd quieted down: "Dead silence followed shooting. The mob, awed by the sight of the death, seemed unable to move." The troops surged forward with bayonets; the crowd dashed for safety, except for a few, who, panicked, lay themselves flat on the ground.

On his League tour, Wilson was finding that the reporters did not want to hear about the League; they wanted to talk about labor. Even his movements were described in terms of the labor conflict and not the

League: the press called attention to the fact that the president chose to avoid stopping in Butte, Montana, where the Wobblies were supposed to be especially powerful. Wilson, anxious, then went out of his way to praise, within earshot of a reporter from *The Anaconda Standard*, a well-known tourist draw in Butte, Frank Conley's fishing lodge, and announce his regret that he could not visit it on that trip. The president dodged the labor question by telling the press that labor's problems could be solved by applying the principles of the covenant of the League of Nations: talk, don't fight.

"There is no use in talking about political democracy unless you have also industrial democracy," *The Atlanta Constitution* reported Wilson as saying in Billings on September 11. The papers' paraphrases of Wilson conveyed a president aching with the desire for conciliation. "It became known today," the *Constitution* wrote, "the president is staking all his hopes for an immediate solution to the vexed affairs of capital and labor in this country upon the conference between employer and employees he has called to meet in Washington early in October." Then Wilson's train set out for Helena, where he was to deliver another speech.

But Boston could not wait until the sixth of October. And the fact that Wilson had come down on the side of diplomacy and in favor of Gompers made Coolidge's job that much harder. Each hour of that Thursday that Coolidge waited would be another hour for rioters. That morning there were more applications for gun licenses from companies at Curtis's headquarters; over the day an additional 846 licenses would be filed. In addition, 369 applications for licenses for guards would be received. At some point on Thursday a group of businessmen visited Coolidge. They warned him that he would not be reelected if he did not compromise. The election was so close, and Coolidge had a good shot at winning. But Coolidge was firm. "It is not necessary for me to hold another office," he told them. He told the same thing to Governor Clement of Vermont, with whom he talked on the telephone.

Coolidge did not rebuke Mayor Peters again, nor did he remove Curtis. Digging around with the attorney general and Albert Pillsbury, the old ally from Amherst, Coolidge had unearthed his own statute, which gave the governor authority to call on any policemen to aid him. Curtis, a former mayor, also weighed in with considerable knowledge and experience. Coolidge, Curtis, and Pillsbury agreed: they could and would take the position that his statute trumped Peters's. And now

Coolidge's procedural mastery again demonstrated value. Exercising his own authority under the statute he had found, Coolidge made clear it was Curtis who was in charge, Curtis was the one to exercise authority; if not Curtis, then it had to be the governor. Coolidge took over for both of them and called out every last remaining man in the state guard, so that Curtis would command between five thousand and six thousand men, vastly outnumbering the striking police. All replacement policemen and guards had to follow Curtis's orders, and not those of Peters, Coolidge said: "The entire state guard of Massachusetts has been called out. Under the Constitution the governor is the commander in chief thereof, by an authority of which he could not, if he choose, divest himself. That command I must and will exercise."

Coolidge then alerted Washington. "The entire state guard of Massachusetts has been called out," he repeated to the secretary of war, Newton Baker, and the acting secretary of the navy, Franklin Roosevelt, in a telegram sent at 11:00 A.M. on September 11, around the time that Barnes was shot. "There are rumors of a very general strike. I wish you to hold yourself in readiness to render assistance from forces under your control immediately on appeal which I may be forced to make to the President. Calvin Coolidge, Governor."

If Wilson was playing the diplomat, Coolidge was now a dictator in earnest. One of the first announcements was that the guards arriving at the city were to get steel helmets, a threatening upgrade from the policemen's leather head coverings.

Even as he sent his telegrams from the State House, Coolidge could see the roughhousers and gamblers as they played on Boston Common. Tremont Street was shuttered and barricaded from the Touraine Hotel to Park Street. Through heavy curtains or around shutters and wood, he could see watchmen. The guardsmen now patrolling the city found operating difficult. The electric lights worked, which made the streets brighter, but the telephones sometimes did not; Company A of the 11th Regiment saw no point in using them, "especially since," as one member of the company later wrote, "we expected a strike of the young ladies on the switchboard, anyway." Particularly compelling were the small storekeepers who could not afford a guard. A man later recalled that small vendors who could not afford their own private guards implored Company A to spare them a guard or two. "A timid shopkeeper," one regiment soldier later recalled, "dashed out of his establishment and hailed the Captain: 'I vant a soger,'" a soldier, "'I vant a soger for mine store.'" In Jamaica Plain a young man, Henry Grote, age eighteen, was shot and killed by soldiers raiding a dice game. The tension built when word that Richard D. Reemts, a striking policeman, had been shot and killed as well. That night, that of September 11, police required pedestrians to stay three paces away from buildings. By the end of the day a total of six dead were counted. As many as a hundred people were wounded. Others were hurt, less seriously, by the various projectiles of the conflict: bricks, cobblestones, rocks. All day long that Thursday the Central Labor Union, the umbrella group for all the unions, held meetings. All day long the city waited for reports; it was from this office that a general strike order might emanate.

Bostonians were shocked at their own city. There were rumors that the next stage in a general strike was coming, that the strike would now spread to the powerhouse, which provided electricity for the city. At some point Camp Devens sent a wagon train with supplies and ammunition. Early in the year, Vermont's state legislature had voted to help Coolidge by subsidizing the return of soldiers for the Yankee Division parade. Now Vermont promised to send 20,000 rounds of ammunition and 400 riot guns, a silent tribute to Coolidge. Reporters started calling to interview experts about what might be happening and why. What had happened to Oliver Wendell Holmes's hub, the Puritans' City on a Hill?

One reporter spoke with Floyd Allport, a young Harvard professor of psychology. Allport said, as the reporter paraphrased his words, "While the public does not realize it, there is a certain percentage of the population of every large city which will loot, destroy and institute mob rule at the first sign that they may do so uninterrupted by the law." Late in the day, Coolidge followed up with a note to Police Commissioner Curtis. "Proceed in the performance of your duties," Coolidge wrote. Franklin Roosevelt wired back that the Navy Department would help if the president ordered it to do so. A naval provost was appointed to keep order at the Navy Yard, in case the sailors mutinied. A naval craft was brought over with electricians who would be ready to jump into the plant and operate it.

Overnight, the new troops showed they were serious, mounting machine guns at the old station houses. The roster of special officers appointed kept growing. That day there were 270 applications for pistol and revolver licenses, nine times more than normal. *The Christian Science Monitor* underscored that the stakes in Boston were far higher than they had seemed even on Monday or Tuesday: "As viewed here the issue in Boston goes farther than a mere dispute over the recognition or non recognition of a union." Friday felt like a turning point. The lady telephone workers had announced a formal vote on whether to endorse the police; a "yea" from them would signal the possibility of a general strike, which, one paper noted, "would paralyze the life of the city." That Friday night too, the union of the Fire Department, much beloved of the city, would also vote on whether to strike in sympathy. Storrow, angry that his compromises had not been accepted before the strike, wrote, "There has been a rumor around town, fomented by an erroneous editorial in one of the papers, that after the men struck the Citizens' Committee was still trying to reach a compromise." That was not true, he said. Of the men, he added, "of course they were wrong, but most of these men have been serving us faithfully for years." There might have been a time, he added, that some agreement could be struck, but now "it has gone by."

Again, Coolidge confronted a choice. The obvious move would be to declare victory and then give ground a bit, finding a way to reinstate the policemen on his own terms. James Timilty, Coolidge's old friend from the Irish crowd, was sending signals that there would be no general strike. The law made it clear that Coolidge might not only take over but also call the striking policemen to return, and if they failed to do so, fine or imprison them for three months. This first option was highly attractive because it conveyed authority yet spared the policemen's jobs—some would come back. The reality, that they were losing not only a job but a trade, was sinking in with the men. The second option for Coolidge was to stand firm a few more days, and then give in and negotiate with the striking police.

Coolidge chose neither. Instead he hardened, etching out, finally, a line, for himself and Curtis. The guards would stay and the police could never come back. What's more, Coolidge put this new idea in the old language, that of Garman and his textbooks, rather than the modern labor-capital lexicon of Wilson and Gompers: "The action of the police in leaving their posts of duty is not a strike. It is a desertion." "There is nothing to arbitrate," he said, "nothing to compromise. In my personal opinion there are no conditions under which the men can return to the force."

No one had expected this. "Cops Want to Work Again, Turned Down," read the *Wyoming State Tribune* of that evening. Now seven thousand troops were patrolling, and modern electric searchlights were trained on the spaces outside the department stores. There was the new sound of cavalry on Boston's narrow streets; the Yankee division veterans and the trench helmets that some of the guard wore made Boston suddenly feel like France. Now Coolidge found reinforcement from an unexpected source. The same day that he had advocated conciliation, September 11, Wilson had traveled on his train from Billings to Helena, Montana. There, later in the day, hearing about events in Boston, he had changed his tone abruptly, coming down on the Boston police like a ton of cobblestones: "I want to say this, that a strike of the policemen of a great city, leaving that city at the mercy of an army of thugs, is a crime against civilization," Wilson said at the Helena Theater. A policeman had "no right to prefer any private advantage to the public safety."

Wilson had suddenly turned feisty, though the timing of the news cycle meant that most easterners would not get the news of the shift until Friday night, or even later. Later, Wilson hardened his position further: "In my judgment," *The Christian Science Monitor* reported the president saying, "the obligation of a policeman is as sacred as the obligation of a soldier. He is a public servant. . . . I hope that that lesson will be burned in so that it will never again be forgotten."

Such presidential inconsistency earned the scorn of *The Wall Street Journal*'s editors. "The American Federation of Labor is depriving the Law of its right hand," the editors wrote on Saturday, "and Mr. Wilson, by temporizing with the unionized, while he talks valiantly to Boston is hoisting the flag of surrender." The weekend was coming, and this might spell good or ill for Coolidge. But it was clear that what he had done would receive careful consideration. At every church, a minister was preparing a sermon. At Amherst, Meiklejohn was drafting the remarks he would deliver to the students in chapel. Amherst was full again, and the fraternities were back. He was going to talk about his summer in Europe. But he would also mention the strike: "Here we are having our police strike, our railway strike, and threatened with a coal strike. They have them all and we have to learn from their experience."

As the weekend commenced, the entire American labor movement drew its collective breath. The striking Boston police, sensing that they were slipping, sought desperately to bring the debate back to what everyone had conceded were real grievances. The editors at the *Boston Labor World*, supportive of the strikers, penned an editorial making the best case for the patrolmen, and pointing out that their weekly wage of $28 a week was scarcely enough. They published it on Saturday:

> *Taking the depreciation of the dollar as officially stated a few weeks ago, this is the equivalent roughly of $15 a week in 1914. By any stretch of the imagination, could anyone, no matter how biased, claim such a figure to be fair to a married man engaged in the thankless job of protecting his fellow citizens? Leaving out all pretty theories and grandiloquent phrases about their duty to the State, can a man, single or married, even live on such a wage? No; he manages to exist, that is all.*

The paper went on, "In all fairness, Governor Coolidge, Mayor Peters, Police Commissioner Curtis, Citizens of Boston, how would you live on such a wage?" That day, the men finally voted to go back to work. But by the time they made their offer, a door was closing: Curtis collected a ruling from the attorney general that the police had vacated their posts.

On Saturday, Bostonians were still concerned enough to arm themselves; that day there were 337 pistol or revolver licenses granted and thirteen new special officers appointed. The crucial telephone ladies hesitated in the end and would not vote to join the police. In the midst of it all, as Coolidge was evaluating the situation, he received a telegram from Senator Lodge: "If I can be of any service whatever here command me." Coolidge telegraphed back, "Deeply appreciate your friendly offer of assistance. Had no doubt at any time of your hearty support."

Next it was Curtis's turn to move: the commissioner officially discharged every policeman who had walked off the job. Learning, later on Saturday, of Curtis's action, the striking policemen gathered to meet and voted $1,000 in pension from their meager funds for the widow of Richard Reemts, a policeman who had been killed early on. McInnes proudly warned that he and the other policemen were not going to bow to opposition led by "money interests." "In the homes and the hearts of the Boston Policeman's union, we are undaunted." The men left the building singing "Pack Up Your Troubles in Your Old Kit-Bag."

The men probably expected backup from Gompers, but now Gompers was elusive, as Wilson had been. His father had just died and the steel strike, his great challenge that autumn, loomed. Perhaps unaware of the blanket discharge of the Boston police, Gompers finally sent a telegram from New York parroting Wilson's old line: the right thing to do was to await a labor-management conference in October. Why not ask "the authorities who issued the order that its enforcement be deferred until after the Presidential conference"? Gompers spoke out publicly to blame Curtis but did not fully endorse or support the union. He warned Curtis that policemen, hearing that they would not be rehired, might show the city what true violence was like; they might suffer untold miseries without work. "I suppose he is willing to assume the responsibility for the consequences of his action," he muttered ominously to the press of Curtis.

Next Gompers turned his attentions to Coolidge, whom he had carefully spared from criticism. The unionization of the police was "a 'natural reflex' of the futile attempts by the policemen to improve their working conditions," he said. Curtis was doing damage, he warned, possibly "openly antagonizing the great American labor movement." In lines scripted as much for Wilson's ears as for those of Coolidge, Gompers wrote, "If the authorities give no consideration for the human side of the question or to the advice and the suggestion which I had the honor to make, then whatever betide is upon the head of the authorities responsible therefor." Yet later Saturday, Gompers drafted a telegram for Coolidge, underscoring his own commitment to law and order and blaming Curtis yet again: "While I am not a responsible public official I assure you that I am as much concerned in the maintenance of law and order as anyone possibly could be." After all, Gompers went on, "the right of the policemen to organize has been denied, a right which has heretofore never been questioned." Gompers was preparing for his father's funeral. He shipped his telegram to Coolidge late in the evening, at 11:37 P.M.

Gompers received no reply that Saturday night. The next morning, a bright one, dawned with no reply either. Curtis, unrelenting, was planning raises for junior policemen who were in the force to $1,400 effective September 18. Company A of the 10th Regiment, which had slept on blankets on the floor of the South Armory, was now stationed on the Boston Common, policing an area that included R. H. Stearns.

On Sunday morning the shopwindows were still covered with boards and the doorways with barbed wire. But the rest of the city was ready for recovery. The replacements began to conduct traffic as McInnes had.

And now, finally, Coolidge spoke back to Gompers and the country. His medium was the telegram with all its constraints, including a protocol that treated all punctuation the same, with the word "stop" or the word "comma." The legal constraints of any response from the governor to the union leader were there as well. The result was a three-hundred-word barrage. The stops and commas of the telegram punctuation gave the effect of artillery fire:

REPLYING TO YOUR TELEGRAM STOP I HAVE ALREADY REFUSED
TO REMOVE THE POLICE COMMISSIONER OF BOSTON STOP I DID
NOT APPOINT HIM STOP HE CAN ASSUME NO POSITION WHICH THE
COURTS WOULD UPHOLD EXCEPT WHAT THE PEOPLE HAVE BY THE
AUTHORITY OF THE LAW VESTED IN HIM STOP HE SPEAKS ONLY
WITH THEIR VOICE STOP THE RIGHT OF THE POLICE OF BOSTON
TO AFFILIATE HAS ALWAYS BEEN QUESTIONED COMMA NEVER
GRANTED COMMA IS NOW PROHIBITED STOP THE SUGGESTION
OF PRESIDENT WILSON TO WASHINGTON DOES NOT APPLY TO
BOSTON STOP THERE THE POLICE HAVE REMAINED ON DUTY HERE
THE POLICEMENS UNION LEFT THEIR DUTY COMMA AN ACTION
WHICH PRESIDENT WILSON CHARACTERIZED AS A CRIME AGAINST
CIVILIZATION STOP YOUR ASSERTION THAT THE COMMISSIONER
WAS WRONG CANNOT JUSTIFY THE WRONG OF LEAVING THE CITY
UNGUARDED STOP THAT FURNISHED THE OPPORTUNITY COMMA
THE CRIMINAL ELEMENT FURNISHED THE ACTION STOP THERE IS
NO RIGHT TO STRIKE AGAINST THE PUBLIC SAFETY BY ANYBODY
COMMA ANYWHERE COMMA ANY TIME STOP

Coolidge was not sure what the effect of such a burst would be. But he realized he had known what he would do all along, even before the meeting at Greenfield. On September 1 Coolidge had gone to Westfield to commemorate the 250th anniversary of the founding of the town. The event was also a welcome home for soldiers; there was a lobster for each man. The question in the room had been the same as at Greenfield: when men ought to rebel against authorities, and when they ought to stop. To find an answer, Coolidge had gone back to Shays's Rebellion. Many of the men who had lived through the rebellion were suspicious of government; they resisted the idea of the new law from above. Their hostility had focused on the new U.S. Constitution. Such a law restricted too much, the men said—better to have no law. Then at a meeting a farmer, Jonathan Smith, had risen to make another case. Smith had started by recalling the turmoil: "Last winter people took up arms, and then, if you went to speak to them, you had the musket of death presented to your breast." Coolidge quoted that line.

Sometimes a new law, however imperfect, was better than no law. "Shall we throw the Constitution overboard because it does not please us all alike?" the farmer Smith had asked. "Suppose two or three of you," Smith had gone on, "had been at pains to break up a piece of rough land and sow it with wheat. Would you let it lie waste because you could not agree what sort of a fence to make?" In some ways the year 1919 was like 1787. The time for disruption was over; in order for the next day, the next decade, to proceed well, for there to be wheat, freedom, and lobster, law must be allowed to reign now. "We come here to honor the past, and in doing so render more secure the present," Coolidge had said.

Sunday arrived and no one was sure what came next. The terrible price of the state's action against the policemen was all too visible, as visible as the men from the Blind and Cripples' Union who filed in and on Friday nights at Tremont Temple. Against the cost to the policemen one had to balance the benefit of breaking the strike, a benefit that remained as yet only theoretical. Still, Coolidge felt certain of one thing. The progressives could not be met. Conciliation would not work. As he made his rounds in the now quiet city, he went over the police strike and kept coming to the same conclusion. This time, there was no middle ground.

SEVEN

THE REIGN OF LAW

ON SUNDAY THE BELLS of the churches broke the silence, and they were tolling in his honor. All morning, men of the cloth praised Coolidge's handling of the strike. At Boston's Trinity Church, the Episcopalian minister, Alexander Mann, cited the Acts of the Apostles and spoke of how Paul had obeyed even the Roman tyrants in the name of order. "The present great peril in American society is lawlessness, which has its source in godlessness," intoned Reverend Cortland Myers at the Baptist Tremont Temple. Unitarians at Arlington Street Church heard from their minister, Edward Cummings, that a policemen's strike was as rational as a jailers' strike that let all prisoners free or a strike of the army and navy.

"This attempt by the police should be resisted by the community to the utmost," exhorted Sydney Snow, the junior pastor at King's Chapel. At the Warren Avenue Baptist Church, Reverend Frank Haggard cited Paul Revere, as well as Samuel Adams. Haggard said that "all that noble band of patriots who fought America's first battles for freedom must have stirred in their graves at the sights and sounds of Boston this past week." Boston, Haggard told his flock, had sunk low, to the level of Petrograd and the sailors' mutiny. Even the Catholic priests, whose parishioners were the families of the Irish-American policemen, chimed in with disapproval of the rioting. At St. Vincent's Church Father Patterson called the uprising a disgrace to Catholics and told of an instance on West Broadway when he had sought to help a volunteer policeman and had seen a crowd insult the volunteer. At the Gate of Heaven church, Father Burns reminded his parishioners that the Catholic Church stood for law and order. Outside Boston, in Quincy, William Jennings Bryan spoke out, taking time off from a Prohibition campaign to deliver a sermon called "Enforcement of the Law." "I wonder what would have happened in Boston during the rioting last week if prohibition had not been in force," he said.

The next morning the newspapers picked up where the churches had left off. The line in the telegram to Gompers was becoming a refrain: "No right to strike against the public safety by anyone, anywhere, anytime." Commentators likened Coolidge to Ole Hanson of Seattle, the mayor who had stared down the strikers earlier that year. The *New York Sun* framed Coolidge as a regional type: "a plain New England gentleman, whose calm determination to uphold the law and maintain order in the situation caused by the Boston police walkout has made him a national figure." Coolidge was suddenly a person to be followed. Northampton, Amherst, and Vermont rewarded him richly for it. At a banquet at the Draper Hotel in Northampton at midmonth, diners feted their own, the "governor with the steel backbone." A chemistry teacher who had been one of Dwight Morrow's brothers at Beta Theta Pi wrote Coolidge to say he admired the tough actions Coolidge had taken. Coolidge wrote back, "I knew you would." Frank Stearns and Houghton Mifflin executives were moving into a publishing frenzy, adding Coolidge's strike statement to the galleys for *Bay State Orations* and racing it all to press: as soon as October 10, voters would be able to buy Coolidge's speeches, now titled *Have Faith in Massachusetts*, for $1.50. The book also included Coolidge's statement after he vetoed a pay raise for lawmakers: "Service in the General Court is not obligatory, but optional." The papers were picking up Coolidge ideas everywhere. The *Los Angeles Times* published a cartoon showing Washington throwing down his sword at Valley Forge over the caption "What if George Washington had struck?"

Boston seemed to approve too. R. H. Stearns was returning to business. Indeed, that very Monday, the *Globe* carried an advertisement that signaled confidence. At its entrance on Tremont Street, the avenue of barbed wire, Stearns was opening a new men's section, whose wares included "hosiery, gloves, handkerchiefs and scarves for men." That, Stearns hoped, "would prove convenient for men." Across the nation, other vendors were betting that veterans would finally get back to work. The military seemed at that point to inspire business. "We'd done so well in the canteen we didn't see why we couldn't do just as well in civilian life," a young man in Missouri named Harry Truman later recalled. Truman was opening a men's clothing shop in Kansas City that fall. Enough jobs would ensure industrial peace.

In Boston the men who had been policemen a week before wandered around the city, disoriented without their uniforms. To each other they repeated versions of the statement of Edward Keller, a fellow striker who had been wounded three times while serving overseas: "I want to say that I joined the union because we could not get our grievances redressed or listened to any other way." Now that the danger of disorder was receding, all sides could indulge in reflection about the terrible waste caused by the past week's events.

On Tuesday on Tremont Street, very near where the clergymen had damned the strikers at King's Chapel over the weekend, a police horse ridden by a replacement officer from the 369th Regiment whinnied a glad greeting at a civilian. The horse, whose name was Duffy, had recognized his policeman, Frank Leddy, a striker from Station House 15, and, nearly unseating his rider, went wild with joy. His old friend offered him a bit of sugar as a crowd gathered to watch. Leddy pronounced Duffy "a damn good policeman" as the crowd listened. Afterward, the reporter observed, Duffy checked over Leddy "as a mother would her babe." The sight of the horse and the man touched the whole street. "Duffy will be Leddy's horse no matter what happens," concluded *The Boston Globe*, which wrote up the story. Coolidge himself now also tried to find jobs for the displaced men: but not as police.

Some papers were taken aback by Coolidge's sudden fame. *The New York Times* resented the fact that a policy it admired had been promulgated by a figure unfamiliar to its editors. Channeling the snide Senator Lodge, the editors delivered backhanded praise:

> *With all due respect to all local partisan ambitions, and with no special predilection for his Excellency, CALVIN COOLIDGE, who, after all comes from the savage western part of the Bay State and is an alien to the Boston Pale, it remains the truth inescapable, probably*

unpleasant, like most truths which always look like parvenus, that
Governor COOLIDGE, having sustained without shadow of
concession or failing the power and reign of law, attacked perilously by
the Boston Police strike, will be, and has to be, re-elected.

But the fact itself could not be denied: he had upstaged a sitting president. The governor had stood firm on strikers where Wilson had vacillated, indeed was still vacillating. And if Coolidge could upstage a president, he could be a president. In the minds of Stearns and a number of other Massachusetts Republicans, the image of the Coolidges at the White House, the first lady clad in R. H. Stearns finery, was already forming. In college Coolidge had observed that men succeeded in politics when they got out in front of a movement that other politicians had not yet identified. He had realized that the country was ready for an end to the strikes before Wilson. And that was not surprising, since Wilson was now pushing his League campaign the way a locomotive pushes a train up a steep gradient. Wilson had begun his tour only a few weeks before, had already spoken well over a hundred thousand words, and had appeared before some 350,000 members of the public.

Still, it was not clear that Coolidge's new national fame would endure, or that it would even translate into reelection as governor. Fame alone, especially national fame, did not guarantee votes in Lawrence, Holyoke, or, certainly, Boston. "Law and order" was well and good, but might lose him the election in the end. It did not necessarily constitute an entire campaign platform. This was still only September, and warm, in the 60s. Who knew how his positions might look when the weather turned cold and heat depended on the coal strikers? Along with the good news there was some bad. In other cities across the nation, such as Macon, Georgia, the police merely hooted in derision when their plan to unionize and strike was deplored by authorities. On Monday, the Board of Aldermen in Holyoke announced plans to raise the wages of their own patrolmen, as well as to invite Irish President de Valera to the town. On Tuesday, one week after the strike had started, Mayor Peters undercut Coolidge by placating the firemen with the raise they had demanded when threatening to march with police. The firefighters promptly announced loudly and clearly that they would not strike, that they had never intended to strike, that they were "now, as always, opposed to lawlessness," that any other claim regarding their position on strikes was "irresponsible." From Washington, D.C., came the report that 2,400 sleeping and parlor car conductors would receive a slight raise, retroactive to May, a gesture of concession clearly designed to calm the national fevers. This method of paying groups not to strike could not be sustained by either government or private companies.

Many Republicans believed that for a politician to survive he must remain progressive. That first Monday after the strike, a reporter put his finger on another uncertainty when he asked what Coolidge's record was in regard to helping the workingman. The governor, defensive, replied that he'd signed every bill for the workingman that had crossed his desk, "except the bill to raise the pay of members of the Legislature," a reference to the veto of earlier in the year. He asked his assistant, Henry Long, to compile a list of progressive legislation he had signed. The laws ranged from a plan regulating weekly pay for injured employees in case of partial incapacity to minimum wages for scrubwomen. To Coolidge's south, Dwight Morrow was coming to the same conclusion; Morrow saw "complete intellectual bankruptcy of the Republican Party of New Jersey."

The next challenge for all was the big steel strike. Elbert Gary, the chairman of the board of U.S. Steel, was refusing to meet with the unions, despite Wilson's urgings. All across the nation, governors and senators, in part emboldened by Coolidge's willingness to resist pressure from labor, were lining up behind Gary. In Ohio, Senator Warren Harding, along with two other senators, was warning that unless Wilson stopped pandering to labor, America would be "Russianized."

On September 22, the strike commenced. From Wyoming to Colorado to Pennsylvania, workers walked off the job. In Wheeling, West Virginia, eight thousand did so. Two thousand coal miners in the Johnstown area quit. Wilson announced from his train tour that he could not interfere if Gary would not meet with the unions. For the labor movement, this was a high point, and the movement seemed to be on the brink of gaining a wider membership than ever. Even Wall Street clerks were thinking of taking up arms; *The Wall Street Journal* reported that week a meeting of the clerks at Washington Irving High School where the clerks had planned to demand a six-hour day. What was clear was that there would be more violence across the country.

Coolidge found that he was becoming a symbol in this wider debate. The more trouble elsewhere, the more the letters of support and charitable donations to help the replacement officers flowed into Boston. Coolidge wrote to his father, noting that the interest in the Boston strike and his response had been indeed "quite remarkable." In its first few days the public safety defenders' fund created by Coolidge to help pay the state guardsmen raised more than $200,000. "I feel fairly sure we can protect the government," Coolidge allowed in a note to his father, but only "fairly." Boston might be calm now, but the telephone ladies and the trolley men might yet mount a general strike. "There is a possibility of the stopping of transportation," the governor wrote to one company, Walworth Manufacturing, on September 18; companies like Walworth were being asked to form a committee to prepare for the possibility that Boston might need to supply itself with food. Replacement policemen like the one who rode Duffy were all over the city; the Boston Public Library announced a special campaign to deliver books to them in their barracks. Across the nation, other vendors were betting that men would now go back to work, and business found that September was proving to be a good month. Coolidge began to have some time for family again. Grace came to Boston.

The safest thing to do was focus on the work that remained in his term, especially the state government reorganization he had agonized over with Field. Alone in his office, Coolidge crossed out names and departments; each time he did so, he knew, he was crossing out constituencies and voters. No opponent was challenging Coolidge in the Republican gubernatorial primary, but that did not mean there was no contest: to prove he had a mandate poststrike, Coolidge had to perform better than he had the year before. Murray Crane had often made the 200-mile-plus round-trip home to vote in state elections. Coolidge, though unopposed, also made his own trip of 214 miles to vote at home on September 23. Coolidge therefore missed a call from a national eminence, Bryan, who called at the State House to find the governor departed.

Coolidge beat himself, and by a healthy margin. Even in Boston, Coolidge gained 3,000 votes over the year before. This was the first sign that Coolidge might be something more than a politician who could stare down a union. He might be an electable politician who could do so. Even after the primary, the letters poured in to thank him for the strike management. In total they would number tens of thousands, nothing like what the state government had seen before.

Suddenly, everyone Coolidge knew was rallying in support of him, right down to the neighbors in Northampton or Plymouth Notch. The Vermonters, naturally suspicious of adulation, grudgingly acknowledged Coolidge's fame: papers now carried reports from those who had known him as a boy, such as Judge Wendell Stafford, who had been at St. Johnsbury with him. *Have Faith in Massachusetts*, complete with the now-famous telegram, was finally published to respectful reviews; Stearns made sure it was distributed as a campaign document. Newspapers praised Coolidge's spare style. *The Wall Street Journal* told the nation in its most direct language that Coolidge was their man. "Governor Coolidge has shown the fibre of which presidents ought to be made," the paper wrote in an October 29 editorial about the labor situation. Dwight Morrow felt his blood warm as the prospects of an Amherst man on a national stage became more real. Coolidge was almost there, he believed.

To Stearns, Morrow summed up the good in Calvin: "For the last year I have been abroad dealing with all sort of government officials. Some of them have been Socialists like Thomas, the great socialist leader in France. Some of them have been from old conservative families. . . . I have about come to the conclusion that the division of the people in the world is not really between conservative and radical, but people that are real people and people that are not. Calvin is one of the fellows who is real. He really wants to make things better not to pretend to make them better." Bruce Barton set about writing a puff piece about Coolidge for November, timed, hopefully, to launch Coolidge as not only a governor but also a candidate for president.

Word was that the president's nonstop exertions had caused Wilson to fall ill; the reports came that he was heading back to Washington. Coolidge too felt himself going under: just after the primary he took to his bed with acute bronchitis. He was not even sure he could make a party convention. On September 26, Coolidge wrote to his father in his typical unpunctuated style, "There is no change in the situation here, my soldiers still on guard a new police force organizing." With each day that passed it became clearer that his government reorganization would hurt the very people who were crucial to his gubernatorial election. Charles Baxter of Medford, for example, was campaigning hard for Coolidge; he was planning the speaking drive for the GOP in the state that fall. Baxter was expecting to be rewarded with sinecures and places for himself and other men, and Coolidge did not know if his reorganization could accommodate that. "People applaud me a great deal but I am not sure they will vote for me," he added in his note to his father. "This was a service that had to be done and I have been glad to do it. The result won't matter to me but it will matter a great deal to the rest of America." He was warning John that the battles were not all over. More negative press would come.

Oswald Garrison Villard, the owner and editor of *The Nation*, was now targeting Coolidge's performance during the strike, making the case that Coolidge had been AWOL for much of it. Coolidge, still defensive, asked his attorney general to prepare an entire brief to prove that he was on alert during the whole course of the strike. Coolidge's opponent was Richard Long, the businessman who had eaten into the Republican vote in the gubernatorial election of the preceding year. Long's principal argument was that Coolidge had been unprepared for the disaster of the strike. Long fired off his own telegram assailing Coolidge as Coolidge had assailed Gompers. "You are to blame for failure to consider settlement with them," Long wrote to Coolidge. "A broad-minded governor," wrote the Democratic candidate, "would have been able to satisfy them and at the same time protect the dignity and honor of Boston and Massachusetts."

Later in October, Richard Long grew bolder, traveling to Greenfield, the very town where Coolidge had talked to the AFL before the strike, to allege his incompetence: "Where was Gov. Coolidge on the night of the police strike? He was in seclusion far from the scene of the trouble, safely beyond the reach of those interested in the serious situation, hiding away on the western side of the Connecticut River. If he had been any part of a man he would have stayed in Boston, this great hero, and protected the people of the city." That hurt, because Coolidge did wonder if he should have acted sooner.

Coolidge did not know who would vote for him in the general election. He thought about the Irish Americans, many of whom were registering to vote for the first time. They might not only turn against Coolidge but take other immigrants with them as well. The Massachusetts Democrats offered the additional lure of promises of spending and a prounion law for Massachusetts; Long promised voters a five-day week with six days' pay, a proposal that had credibility, coming as it did from a shoe manufacturer and not a mere politician. Long also backed a neat plan to raise the rate on the graduated income tax and use the extra revenue to give servicemen a $360 bonus.

Over the course of October, several unexpected events, however, gave further advantage to Coolidge and his Republicans. One was an emerging tragedy: Wilson, who had fallen ill around the same time as Coolidge, was not recovering easily. The nervous exhaustion announced on the western trip was now clearly something far more serious; the president was still in seclusion in Washington. The conference that Gompers had so looked forward to and that Wilson had promised would resolve all was also bogging down, and over the same point. Employers would give a lot, but they refused to deal with outside representatives of workers. Coolidge could see that the vice president, Thomas Marshall of Indiana, was stuck in an awkward position. Marshall was permitted no access to the president but could sense the trouble; the secretary of state, Robert Lansing, actually visited the president's secretary to remind him that the Constitution said that in the case of a president's "Inability to discharge the Powers and Duties of the said Office, the Same shall devolve to the Vice President." The gossips said that Mrs. Wilson was running the executive office while Wilson lay stricken. Republican Senator Albert Fall of New Mexico told others, "We have a petticoat government!" Lansing began to call cabinet meetings in Wilson's absence.

Another factor turning out to benefit Republicans, especially conservative Republicans, was the coal strike. It looked as if there would be a great coal strike along with the steel action, and that during the elections, hearths and grates would be cold. John L. Lewis planned to take hundreds of thousands of workers out that fall. The unions had misjudged the situation; instead of sympathizing with the coal men, voters sided against them. All governors and senators who were taking a stand against such broad actions or radical groups were rising in stature. Illinois Governor Frank Lowden, who called a threatened coal strike "a strike against the American public," was being mentioned as a presidential candidate. Lowden, like Coolidge, had bypassed his mayor; in Lowden's instance he had ordered out state troops to halt a meeting of the People's Council, a left-wing group accused of being pro-German. Recently the Seventeenth Amendment had become law, meaning that voters instead of state legislatures would pick senators. This was the nation's blow to the boys' club of the Senate. Now many Americans also wanted a governor, rather than a senator, as their president. But some of the names put forward were not governors', Herbert Hoover's, for example. From his impromptu rescue effort at the Savoy, Hoover had gone on to feed starving Belgium and then after that to serve as U.S. food administrator at the war's end; in other words, he was the world's most successful rescuer. Yet another name the Republicans mentioned was that of General Leonard Wood. Wood was the Theodore Roosevelt proxy, having led the preparedness campaign.

As the Massachusetts election date neared, yet another good omen for Coolidge emerged: *The Boston Post*, a Democratic paper, criticized Coolidge's opponent Long for basing his campaign on "prejudice, selfishness and disorder." Coolidge immediately wrote home to his father in satisfaction, "It is a great event to come down here and make a great Democratic paper support me, greater than being chosen Governor." On October 27, the birthday of President Roosevelt, Coolidge refined his argument for law: "We are facing an issue that knows no party. It is not new. That issue is the supremacy of the Law. On this issue America has never made but one decision." Even some of the Irish vote might go for the governor. The Catholic Irish were furious at President Wilson for his failure to include a free Ireland in his case for determination; this to them was more important than the hurt to their fellow Irish Americans in the strike. The next day, October 28, the Wilson administration's weakness was again revealed when Congress overrode Wilson's Volstead Act veto, providing enforcement power for Prohibition. It was now generally well known that Wilson was physically incapacitated; Vice President Marshall was in an agony of indecision. If he tried to enforce the Constitution, he might end up disrupting the country more and make himself look like a usurper in the process.

In the last hours before the gubernatorial election, Democratic leaders told an audience at a Democratic rally that "Calvin Coolidge is morally responsible for the loss of life in Boston in the early days of the police strike." Coolidge confined himself to one counterblow, delivered at his own rally: "When this campaign is over it will be a rash man who will again attempt to further his selfish interests by dragging a great party name in the mire and seeking to gain the honor of office by trafficking with disorder." Otherwise he remained calm. "Campaign looks all right," he wrote in a letter to his stepmother. "Am just going home to vote." It had been relatively warm in the daytime in Hampshire County that October, as high as 70 degrees on November 1. But in the period before the election, just as hundreds of thousands of coal men really did go out on strike, daytime temperature dropped into the 40s. Suddenly, the importance of a coal shortage seemed real. Republicans decided that Democrats had made this election a referendum on the steel and coal strikes, but that their own party might win the referendum. The conservatives in the Grand Old Party told themselves that progressives were becoming desperate because Coolidge, the antistrike candidate, was going to trounce them.

He did. Coolidge took the state by 125,000 votes over Richard Long, a landslide compared with his slim 17,000 margin of the year before. Holyoke, Lowell, Fall River, and New Bedford, all towns with significant blue-collar populations, went for Coolidge. The news was not merely that Coolidge had won but also that the kind of victory that he had achieved was a template for the Republican Party in the 1920 election. The fact that Coolidge fared well in places like Wards 4 and 5 of Holyoke, an area that was home to many Poles and Irish, showed he could still win support from immigrants or their children. Many in the Italian community in Springfield voted for Coolidge, while the Irish of Ward 2 went for Long. Long took the labor hotbed, Lawrence, but only barely. Coolidge increased his share in Lynn, the city divided over the police union. Every county but Suffolk, which contained Boston, voted for Coolidge, and even in Suffolk County Coolidge narrowed the margin by which he was defeated. Only 5,000 votes separated Coolidge from victory in Boston.

If the applause had pealed after the strike statement, now it thundered. For not only had Coolidge shown you could stand up against the radical workmen, he had confirmed that you could do so and still win an election. He had demonstrated that even with many new immigrants in the country, Republicans could still win, and even take votes from the opposition. "Coolidge Helped by Angry Democrats," crooned *The New York Times*, now smitten, on the day after the election. "You have upheld American ideals," wrote Governor Milliken of Maine. Even President Wilson from his sickbed wired congratulations for a "victory for law and order." Such congratulations from a president to a candidate of the opposite party were unprecedented, the pundits said. It made Coolidge like Herbert Hoover, the great administrator, a candidate who clearly might appeal to both parties.

Governor James Goodrich of Indiana, another conservative, telegraphed that Coolidge's was "a victory for Americanism." Even the Boston shoemakers' trade group and the Portuguese Civic League of

East Boston sent their good wishes. "Thank god for Coolidge and the hard-headed people of Massachusetts," exclaimed the *St. Paul Pioneer Press*. In New Jersey a man wanted to start a new American party, with Coolidge as presidential and Ole Hanson as vice presidential candidate. "Massachusetts has spoken," intoned Lodge. "It is the verdict of the United States speaking through the people of Massachusetts." Gompers and Lewis, intimidated, now began to push hard to end the coal strike. It was clear now that the following November might bring an end to eight years of Democratic rule. The *Boston Herald* that week printed a cartoon with the caption "The Pilot Who Weathered the Storm." It featured Coolidge at the helm of a ship named *Law and Order* in storm water labeled "ANARCHY."

Coolidge took advantage of the cover of victory to announce his controversial "Big List," the new names for his slimmed-down government. The papers first noted how many of the old officials had been dropped—those on the old state board of labor, those on the civil service commission, the head of the immigration bureau, and the chairman of the highway commission. In their place, bound to infuriate, were fewer departments and new names to head them. Coolidge issued a carefully worded explanation for his choices. He was acting, he claimed, in the best reform tradition, selecting the old and young, the western and the Boston man, and "Catholics, Protestants and Hebrews impartially."

Among the outraged was Baxter, one of the state politicians who had campaigned for Coolidge just days before. In the new lineup Baxter had received a position in the new Metropolitan District Commission paying $1,000, far less, perhaps, than he had expected. Baxter was especially furious that Coolidge had not appointed his law partners and other friends for whom Baxter had apparently sought help. Baxter refused the post that was offered to him and declared war on Coolidge: "We are living under a regime of a royal governor, and the right of petition is about destroyed in Massachusetts." Baxter correctly noted the weakness in Coolidge's habit of thinking things over alone under pressure or with just a few good friends: "He shut himself away from everybody except Winthrop Murray Crane and William Butler and he is as far away from the public as he was from the Boston police force at the time of the strike." Baxter went on to mock the boom for Coolidge as simply ridiculous. Dividing party leaders that way was hardly good when Coolidge needed their support. Nor were professional Republicans like

Baxter the only protesters. Women were an especially important group to politicians that year; the Nineteenth Amendment had not cleared all the states yet but was likely to in time for women to vote in the 1920 presidential election. Now women's groups were protesting because their candidate for assistant commissioner of labor, Mabel Gillespie, had lost out, and Coolidge instead had appointed a woman who had sat on the minimum wage commission. Critics would later say that he had not risen on his own merit, but had ridden the Republican escalator; here he was, destroying that escalator and thereby jeopardizing the chances that it would carry him farther, to the Republican National Convention. But these allegations could not slow Coolidge now. Indeed, the state's executive council, the body with which he had worked in those years as lieutenant governor, confirmed Coolidge's contentious list within a week of its delivery, voting unanimously in support of the governor in all cases except one, that of the chairman of the Department of Public Utilities.

Indeed, what led the newspapers was not the list but the talk of a Coolidge on another list, the national Republican ticket. The country was eager for the presidential election now, in part because Wilson's illness had already plunged the country into an interregnum. Vice President Thomas Marshall remained in limbo. Weeks of not knowing about Wilson's health were tiring the vice president. On November 23, Marshall was giving a speech in Atlanta at the Auditorium to the Order of the Moose when someone passed him a message that Wilson had died. Marshall conveyed the sad report to a crowd of a thousand, which broke into tumult; someone went to the organ and started to play "Nearer, My God, to Thee." But the news of Wilson's death was a hoax.

Toward the end of November, the Republican Club of Massachusetts formally launched Coolidge as its presidential candidate. *Collier's* published Barton's profile, a lengthy and adulatory portrait of Coolidge as a New England character. Coolidge spoke "plain words," Barton wrote. Coolidge to him seemed "cut from granite," an exaggeration that overlooked the slight softening in Coolidge's face that William Allen White had observed. Other Americans were joiners, but not Coolidge. "At any rate, he belongs to nothing," Barton concluded, making Coolidge sound not eccentric but independent. Barton told the old story from Coolidge's Amherst days that in student surveys during senior year, others had favored Dwight Morrow, the golden boy of the class of 1895, but Morrow himself had favored Coolidge.

Barton sketched the place in U.S. politics where Coolidge belonged. "The great majority of Americans," continued Barton, "are neither radicals nor reactionaries. They are middle-of-the-road folks who own their own homes and work hard and would like to have the government get back to its old habits of meddling with their lives as little as possible." Then Barton introduced a phrase that he hoped might resonate: "silent majority." Wrote Barton, "It sometimes seems as if this great silent majority had no spokesman. But Coolidge belongs with that crowd, he lives like them, he works like them, and understands." Coolidge acknowledged the help in such ventures that all the press drummed up by his friends had supplied. When he read the *Collier's* article, which appeared on November 22, gratitude overwhelmed Coolidge. He fancied himself a writer, but Barton's skill in this area surpassed that of others. "You were able to do so much more than I had any idea was possible."

In Washington, Wilson continued to fare poorly. Mid-November brought a blow that slammed the already ailing president. After fifty-five days of debate, the Senate refused to ratify his Treaty of Versailles, the first treaty in the history of the Senate to have been voted down. The presidential candidates were already pushing forward. Warren Harding of Ohio, a U.S. senator as loquacious as Coolidge was quiet, had jumped into the race. Harding had his own way of talking long-windedly, using a funny verb to describe his own circumlocutions: he bloviated, he said. Many found Harding vague. William Gibbs McAdoo, who hoped to succeed his father-in-law, Wilson, described Harding's speeches as "an army of pompous phrases moving over the landscape in search of an idea." General Leonard Wood was also pressing his candidacy; voters who wanted a return of Roosevelt wanted Wood, and their number put Wood in the lead. The doctor warrior was second only to General Pershing in fame; ever since Wilson had overlooked Wood in choosing a commander in Europe, the Roosevelt loyalists had been looking for revenge. On the national scene, others were rising. Herbert Hoover moved from strength to strength; *The New Republic* praised him.

But if Massachusetts acted in time, it might get in a name of its own. Triumphant over his treaty victory, Lodge returned to Massachusetts, and met with Coolidge for lunch at the Union Club. For years there had been so many other Coolidges in Lodge's world. They were his aide Louis Coolidge, the historian and journalist who had served him for years in the Senate; William Coolidge, the railroad lawyer and Louis's brother; and Archibald Cary Coolidge, the director of the Harvard University Library. Now, finally, Lodge was recognizing Calvin Coolidge, and told the governor that he would offer Coolidge's name at the Republican Convention as a presidential candidate. As Lodge, seventy, explained to Coolidge, who would turn forty-eight the next summer, "I am far too old. A man who takes the Presidency should be at least ten years younger than I am and it would be better if he were twenty years younger." This friendly arithmetic was the benediction Stearns and the other Amherst men had been waiting for. Stearns circulated *Have Faith in Massachusetts* all over the country and made his long-awaited trip to Washington to publicize his candidate. The merchant proudly confirmed to the press that Massachusetts would deliver a pledged delegation for Coolidge at the party convention, with Lodge and Crane there as delegates at large to back Coolidge.

Thanksgiving found Coolidge finally back home on Massasoit Street, thinking again of his family. That autumn John sent Coolidge's sons gifts of $1 each, but it was hard to know what to send back to Carrie, who was herself faring worse. Still, Calvin and Grace finally allowed themselves some celebration. Their son John was good at mechanics. Coolidge took particular joy in the enterprise of his son Calvin. The son told his father that he was saving money for a bike and getting up at 5:45 A.M. to "peddle papers." Everything seemed possible in the coming year, and worth aiming for. In South Dakota, a state Republican convention was the first to endorse a national ticket, and it named him second after General Wood as vice presidential candidate. Coolidge wrote back that he would not consider the vice presidential slot. At the State House in Boston, Governor Clement, who was visiting, promised Coolidge that Vermont was behind him all the way.

It was tradition in the commonwealth that the governor proclaim Thanksgiving each autumn. Penning his proclamation that November at the executive chamber, Coolidge made an effort to remind them all that the difficult twelve months behind Massachusetts and the country had also enjoyed some blessings. "The people have had a year of peace," he had written simply. "Law and order" might provide the basis for a splendid new era. The headline that *The Boston Globe* put on the Thanksgiving address summed up not only the outlook for the state, but also Coolidge's own: "For present attainment, for future hope."

EIGHT

NORMALCY

Boston and Washington

ONE DAY IN JANUARY 1920, reporters gathered on the corner of Pennsylvania Avenue in Washington, D.C., for the opening of the Coolidge for President office. Six rooms on the parlor floor of the Raleigh Hotel were given over to stenographers and clerks who shipped out to the nation copies of *Have Faith in Massachusetts*, which Stearns and Houghton Mifflin had upgraded with a preface by Nicholas Murray Butler, the president of Columbia University. Stearns could congratulate himself. The man who had agreed to head the Coolidge campaign, James B. Reynolds, could not have been more qualified. Reynolds had overseen tariff collection at the Treasury under Theodore Roosevelt and had, until just that month, served as secretary to the Republican National Committee.

Frederick Gillett, the speaker of the U.S. House of Representatives had also signed up to back Coolidge, providing an alluring aura of Capitol Hill authority. Gillett represented Westfield, the town where Coolidge had spoken about the importance of law, on Labor Day four months before. This wasn't all: Coolidge for President had already established an outpost, an office in Chicago, led by a woman, Jean Bennett. Mrs. Bennett would make Coolidge's presence felt in the city the Republicans had just chosen as their convention site. Her hiring also signaled the campaign's appreciation of the new group of voters, Coolidge for President was seeking pledges from delegates to the convention. Stearns and Reynolds—Stearns beaming, Reynolds exuding the appropriate political cunning—both gave interviews to the *Globe*.

Two actors, though, were missing from the warm scene at the Raleigh. The first was Henry Cabot Lodge, who ranked higher than Gillett. No Massachusetts candidacy could be serious without the benediction of the Senate leader. The second missing man was the candidate himself, Coolidge.

Indeed, it was only a matter of days before Coolidge brought down the curtain on the Washington campaigners' show. "I have not been and I am not a candidate for President," the press reported the governor as saying. And within a week the Washington office found itself ruefully shutting down, though, as a *Globe* columnist reported, "it took some time to convince Mr. Stearns that an open campaign in behalf of Governor Coolidge should be abandoned."

It seemed perverse to stamp on the brakes just as the enterprise gathered momentum, but Coolidge did stamp. He feared first of all that he might be entering the campaign too early. As much renown as he had garnered for his reelection and handling of the strike, he was not an established national candidate. Therefore his best shot at the nomination would be at the convention itself, if a deadlock among established figures such as General Wood provided a sudden opening. Money was a second reason to slow down. The progressives were scrutinizing all the campaigns for heavy spending. If Coolidge for President shut down now, and Coolidge entered the race in June, he would receive far fewer donations than General Wood, upon whose head frustrated fans of Theodore Roosevelt were pouring cash. The third reason for the sudden halt was the most important: Coolidge was not sure what he believed, and not sure that the party knew what it believed either.

The old Massachusetts mottoes of unity, tariffs, and progressivism had sufficed during the war. But they would not necessarily do so in peacetime. The League of Nations, Lodge's great whipping boy, had evoked strong passions in voters last year, but that did not mean it could elect a president this year. "Law and order," or "the reign of law," as Coolidge sometimes referred to it, certainly represented a good addition to the program. Public opinion was now so solidly behind the authorities on matters like strikes that it was hard to remember what life had been like last summer. The old policemen of Boston had long since withdrawn. In February, John McInnes resigned from the police union, declaring his union "well and truly beaten" and saying he lacked the time to give to his "regular trade of bricklaying." Across the nation, the strikers from the coal mines and the steel mills were finally giving up too. Still, law and order couldn't be the only new plan the party offered. Around Christmas, the U.S. attorney general had deported the most notorious radicals to Russia in a ship, the *Buford*; the photos and drawings of the ship had shocked many Americans. Deportion seemed a nasty, fearful act, unworthy of the United States.

And law and order alone could not address the great challenge of 1920: missing commerce. Jobs remained scarce, as Herbert Hoover, one of the likely candidates, was pointing out from California. Strikers might be relenting for now, but the problem they pointed to, high prices, was real. The progressives had been correct on that. Until the prices stabilized, the labor unions would surely strike again. Indeed, any solution to the price problem might serve as the basis for larger reform. Echoing Theodore Roosevelt, General Wood was saying that "relations between capital and labor, between those who work and those who direct must be on the basis of a square deal."

Taxes, both the income tax and an excess-profits tax, were squeezing business, and Wood was making the case against the excess-profits levy. Then there was the challenge of public debt. The federal government and states had borrowed beyond imagination in the war, yet seemed unready to stop: The very week that the Coolidge for President office opened in Washington, the Massachusetts General Court endorsed an act to authorize the towns of Braintree and Belmont to borrow more money than they already had for school buildings, and codified the taxability of retirement allowances of former state employees to make them pay for such expansions. During the war the federal government had controlled food prices, freight rates, rail traffic, and petrol. It had hired and hired some more. Now Washington seemed unwilling to let those workers go. Hiram Johnson, a progressive Republican senator from California, was calling for the abolition of "250,000 useless jobs created at Washington during the war." Even a federal government that wanted to trim itself down—and the Wilson administration did—found the task hard. A number of the candidates were pointing out that the country lacked a great unifying budget law; instead departments approached Congress individually. An executive, whether Wilson or a Republican, also lacked the staff to evaluate spending plans and enjoyed little oversight over what was spent. Congress was working on a budget law that would give more authority to the president or Treasury when it came to managing the government's funds, but no one knew how President Wilson, ill as he was, would respond. Senator Harding of Ohio, the one known for his flowing phrases, was campaigning on the promise that he would bring in a budget system.

There were other problems for which a good candidate would have to offer a remedy. The Treasury and Federal Reserve banks had manipulated interest rates, and authorities had also managed gold imports and exports. Now the controls were coming off and the Federal Reserve Banks were doing more, raising interest rates. Coolidge still routinely blamed merchants for price gouging, but here another Harding, William Proctor Gould Harding, the head of the Federal Reserve, had a different view. William Harding was telling the country that the high prices came from another source: too much bank credit, and too much money. The country, he said, had been "living in a fool's paradise since the close of the war." Simeon Fess of Ohio, a Republican leader, was saying that the situation now was "as bad as it was in the greenback period following the civil war."

Coolidge talked the price piece of the economic puzzle over with Bruce Barton, the advertising man, who came to call that winter. The governor pulled out an old document from the selectmen of Belchertown, not far from Northampton. During the Revolutionary War, the selectmen had tried to regulate prices to keep them down. That was similar to all the rules and laws written recently to check prices during the war. But the price rule in Belchertown had not worked in the days of the nation's founding. People had found another way to charge each other extra for goods. Price controls didn't work now, either. In addition to respect for the reign of law, by which he meant the laws of the Commonwealth of Massachusetts, Coolidge was now asking for respect for an older sort of law, the law of markets. "Isn't it a strange thing," he asked Barton, "that in every period of social unrest men have the notion that they can pass a law and suspend the operations of economic law?"

It was with Morrow that Coolidge took up another bit of the mystery, trade. The way Coolidge saw it, the way his party saw it, the way

Garman had taught, a tariff was the only thing that protected business at home from competition. Under a tariff, a company might charge higher prices and that in turn would enable it to pay higher wages, so there might be at least a chance of industrial peace. You had to support your industries. Each tariff helped factories employ veterans, taking the pressure off employers. Yet men Coolidge respected, not only Morrow but also Clarence Barron, had come back from Europe mad for free trade, and impatient with those who did not share their passion. Indeed, Barron was about to publish a book, which he titled *The Audacious War*, in which he would argue that the Great War had been "caused by tariffs." Tariffs had put off Germans and made them susceptible to the kaiser's crazed arguments.

Morrow, not one to let an opportunity go to waste, determined to wage a one-man campaign to educate his friend away from the party's tariff doctrine. On March 9 Morrow shipped Coolidge four volumes of William Graham Sumner, the philosopher at Yale, to read. "Throughout these volumes, you will notice the strong predilection of Sumner for free trade," Morrow wrote pointedly to Calvin, hoping that Sumner would be able to pull Coolidge's blinkers off.

Coolidge wrote back the next day, March 10, mentioning that "I have read most of the four volumes of Sumner," the governor's own way of telling his friend he had not only already heard of Sumner, but read him. Coolidge rated Sumner "on the whole sound." But Coolidge was not ready to sign on to Sumner's philosophy: "I do not think that human existence is quite so much on the basis of dollars and cents as he puts it. . . . He nowhere enunciates the principle of service." The conversation was a continuation of their old conversation at school: Morrow had offered Sumner's approach and Coolidge countered as Garman might have: "If I am poor and need the assistance of a protective tariff, why does not the law of service require others to furnish it for me?" The experienced politician in Coolidge talked back to Morrow. J. P. Morgan might say what it liked, but in the Bay State all those years, he too had studied the tariff. "My observation of protection is that it has been successful in practice," Coolidge wrote.

What might Sumner say about the struggles of the Massachusetts shoe companies that had to compete with shoes from abroad? The companies needed the protection, given their other troubles. On April 16, the papers reported that the payroll money of those companies, Slater and Morrill, in South Braintree, Massachusetts, had been stolen. In the incident, one man, an Italian American, had been killed, another wounded. The wounded man, paymaster Frederick Parmenter, died in Quincy Hospital.

The country was expecting a revival, but instead the economy worsened before Americans' eyes. Debt plagued many companies. Even Henry Ford was struggling under a giant burden of debt. Frederick Gillett told Amherst alumni at the Hotel Commodore in New York that February that "the present is one of the most critical times in the whole history of our country." The federal war debt was $21 billion alone and the entire federal debt more like $25 billion; ten times the debt before the war. State and federal taxes both had escalated in recent years. Senator Borah had once said he could not imagine the top rate on the income tax going over 20 percent; now the top rate was over 70 percent.

As Clarence Barron was noting, when a man bought or sold stock, that sale was taxed as income and taxed at rates that went all the way up into the 70s, if he earned enough. Money was therefore flooding into municipal bonds—news that pleased mayors and governors but might not create the maximum number of jobs possible. The tax-free status of those bonds was just too big a draw relative to what was lost to tax on investments. Jules S. Bache, a Wall Street banker, warned of a "strike of capital" if the income taxes were not reduced and the treatment of capital gains was not altered. Governor William Harding of the Federal Reserve Board put it another way, calling for "the liquifaction of frozen loans." The insufferable supertax on the top rates of the income tax needed to be removed. Bache also lambasted the excess-profits tax. The railroads were finally released from national control in the spring of 1920 merely to be dumped into the recession. The railroads began to sue the government for damages.

As Coolidge considered these debates, he walked around Boston with his security guard, Edward Horrigan, or smoked cigars in silence with Stearns. Early March found Coolidge still thinking that his candidacy would unfold, if it ever did, near to or before the convention. "The political situation has not changed any," he wrote his father. "The nomination will be made at the convention and not before it assembles."

The Massachusetts Republicans tried to gauge the depth of Coolidge's popularity. Letters by the hundreds still arrived for him each week. Most were from strangers, but others were from people who wanted to reestablish some old connection with him, or were friends of friends. Coolidge found he had a special following among those jurists who had read the law, as he or Ernest Hardy had. One was Wallace McCamant of Oregon, where Hardy had relocated and was now practicing law. McCamant was a graduate of Lafayette College in Pennsylvania who had also moved west and learned the law in an office. States such as Oregon were requiring that law students attend college and placing more emphasis on formal education. McCamant had led a successful campaign in his state to ensure that although the state now required college for law school entry, young students could satisfy the college requirement with proof of equivalent education. Practical education had to fight back.

Young people from all over found inspiration in *Have Faith in Massachusetts*. One fan, a college student named Whittaker Chambers, would later climb a fire escape at Madison Square Garden to hear Coolidge speak after discovering that the doors to the hall had been locked. There was also mail from the mysterious western Coolidges. One letter was from Ada Coolidge Taintor of Minneapolis, Minnesota, a descendant of Oliver, the great-granduncle who had left Plymouth under circumstances Coolidge had not heard much about. "I never knew what became of the descendants of Oliver," wrote Calvin back to her. "He was an uncle of my grandfather and a son of John, if he was really 'senior' as you have designated him."

Like George Bancroft, Coolidge took comfort in the idea that commerce could bypass all obstacles, fly out of the recession, or fly beyond the trade laws. The automobile, or even the airplane, might replace the railroad and obviate the mistakes policy makers had made in regard to rails. Every day there was some news about airplanes. Major Rudolph Schroeder, who held the national record for flying at the highest altitude, was now talking publicly about testing a new avenue across the country, a ten-hour flight at 30,000 feet from San Francisco to New York. Schroeder explained that the high altitude offered an advantage, for at that height "trade winds blow from 200 to 260 an hour." A New York hotel owner, Raymond Orteig, was offering a prize of $25,000 to the first aviator who could make a flight from Paris. But optimism about future technology scarcely amounted to a clear program. And Coolidge remained too preoccupied to think farther. Carrie was clearly dying from cancer, and he and Grace had to travel up to Plymouth.

The month of May brought a clarifying event. Two candidates, Senator Harding of Ohio and Senator Irvine Lenroot of Wisconsin, descended on Boston to campaign. The candidates joined Coolidge for an event at the Home Market Club, the official club of protectionism in Boston. Lenroot proved strong: conscious of being in Lodge's home territory, he detailed the provisions Republicans should attach to any international peace treaty produced by President Wilson or a successor.

Coolidge was tired—he had just returned from Plymouth. When his turn to speak came, he stepped up—and tripped over his own ideas. All the inconsistencies that had bedeviled him that spring came out in this speech. First Coolidge cited George Washington, who had believed in "punishing those who charge excessive prices," an old GOP line that fitted especially ill with his growing sympathy for free markets. Coolidge also allowed—throwing a bone to free marketeers—that action by government such as price fixing was wrong; "profiteering is not a cause but an effect of high prices." Production had to be increased, he went on—that was all right, but he did not make clear how. He rehearsed the old law-and-order theme. "I do not object to healthy unrest," he said, but "when it goes beyond that," the United States needed to "cure the unrest," whatever that meant. He told the listeners that tariff laws would need to be changed, but fudged on how, and then again, threw out an unconvincing line or two on markets: "We need to escape as soon as possible from the exercising of arbitrary powers and come back to the sound economic law of supply and demand."

Harding went at the same matters more deftly. He defended the free market more robustly and assailed "the false economics which lure economic control to utter chaos. The world," Harding said, "needs to be reminded that all human ills are not curable by legislation." Rather than shouting or demanding discipline, Harding appealed to common sense. It was daunting to see how Harding's gracious humor could melt even the stiff Boston crowd. "If I lived in Massachusetts I should be for Governor Coolidge for President," he jovially allowed. "Coming from Ohio, I am for Harding." Harding's rhetorical style was often criticized, but this time the alliteration soothed rather than distracted:

> *America's present need is not heroics, but healing; not nostrums, but normalcy; not revolution, but restoration; not agitation, but adjustment; not surgery, but serenity; not the dramatic, but the*

*dispassionate; not experiment, but equipoise; not submergence in
internationality, but sustainment in triumphant nationality. It is
one thing to battle successfully against world domination by military
autocracy, because the infinite God never intended such a program,
but it is quite another thing to revise human nature and suspend the
fundamental laws of life and all of life's acquirements.*

One word from the speech hung in the air: "normalcy." By normalcy, Harding did not mean that people should all be normal. He
meant that the environment should be normal and relatively predictable.
The old progressive swings in policy disrupted too much. A currency
that changed value was a problem. Extreme Red-baiting was wrong; now
that the war was over, it was time for compassion. Harding had taken a
sentiment felt by everyone—that there had been too much upheaval—
and broadened it into a plan. Sometimes the country felt normal now;
but if it could get all the way back to normalcy then commerce could do
the rest of the work. Then the knotty issues of money, prices, and even
tariffs could be sorted out.

Several days later, Carrie finally did pass away. Coolidge went up to
Vermont. Disconcertingly, this family loss came just at the same time
as the Massachusetts primary. In Massachusetts, Wood took nearly
70 percent of the vote, doing especially well in country towns. Early
returns showed Hoover and Hiram Johnson after him, Coolidge in fifth
place. Coolidge's allies still hoped for their candidate and drew consolation from one thing: they had been right to shut down the fancy office.
In Washington, hearings over campaign spending were embarrassing
the other candidates and even sidelining one of the likeliest names,
Lowden of Illinois. On June 1, two GOP delegates testified before a
Senate committee that that they had each received the equivalent of a
laborer's annual salary, $2,500, from the Lowden campaign. Overall, the
Missouri Lowden campaign manager had given out $32,000 to create
sentiment for Lowden in Missouri. Senator Reed of Missouri asked one
recipient what the campaign man, Jacob Babler, had said when he pushed
the money across the table. "He simply said 'here's a check for $2,500,'
and I asked him what it was for," the man said. "Mr. Babler told me to
take it and use it for whatever I saw fit." The same reports carried talk
of trouble in Ohio, whether from the old Mark Hanna crowd or those
around Harding; Robert Wolfe, a publisher, explained that many in the

state worried about Harding's tight crowd, especially Harry Daugherty, Senator Harding's campaign manager. They seemed to trade favors too often. Voters had no tolerance for corruption; if they were to vote for Republicans, it was because they wanted to vote the war-spoils party out of office. The issues would be what to do with navy ships such as the *Mount Vernon*, the former *Kronprinzessin*, which was now patrolling the seas carrying refugees and German prisoners of war.

As the weeks passed, there was more criticism. The Senate investigation of campaign expenses had left several of Coolidge's competitors looking spendthrift or worse; a scandal was growing about the purchase of delegates by campaigns. Wood had received close to a million dollars. The papers were reckoning that he had spent about $5,000 apiece of donors' money for his delegates. Lowden, it emerged, had spent about $415,000, one-fourth of what Wood had spent; $196,000 alone had gone to printing documents for his candidacy. Some papers were saying that Coolidge's tiny donation receipts of $68,345 might work to his advantage. Money had not been sent to other states to collect delegates, Reynolds, the manager of the short-lived campaign, testified. "His campaign has been conducted on a high plane," wrote *The Boston Post*. Harding's budget was also relatively small: $113,109 was reported. There was yet a final factor, Coolidge knew, that worked in his favor: the Republican delegates resented the senators' control of the convention; they wanted to pick their own man. "It's about time the other Republicans be heard from. I mean the governors from the great states," R. Livingston Beeckman, the governor of Rhode Island, told a group of delegates and reporters. "All the wisdom is not concentrated in the U.S. Senate."

The Boston Globe had not given up on its campaign for Coolidge and, toward the end of the month, wrote a friendly feature on Grace's homemaking. The aim was to highlight the Coolidges as savers. Silent Cal and his wife, the paper noted, paid $32 rent, recently boosted from $27; his telephone was a party line. The Coolidges lit the area around their hearth with a small tube of a gas heater. Mrs. Coolidge answered her own doorbell. Keeping his head down, Coolidge, tense, busied himself finishing out the legislative session. "You cannot realize what a burden they are," he wrote his father of the laws and lawmakers he had to steward. His father supplied the usual steadying report: "Your letter of the 6th inst. also one from each of the boys in hand. We have had a cold rain and I fear a frost to-night if it clears off. I am glad you sent thanks to those contributing flowers at time of funeral. It would have pleased Carrie much. . . . I am about as usual." He would have liked to have his father there, to help him sort out all his questions, but John stayed in Vermont.

On a warm day the week before the convention, Coolidge took a walk to clear his head, going three miles to Massachusetts Avenue and back, stopping at the Algonquin Club, where Stearns had first feted him what seemed a lifetime before. "Things are shifting very rapidly," he wrote to his father, "and I think in my favor but no one can tell what will happen there." He was still hoping his father would come down to sit with him in Boston during the convention. "Gov. Coolidge's friends believe that his chance for the nomination lies in the possibility that he may be agreed on as a compromise candidate in case a deadlock arises," wrote the *Globe*.

On June 6, the Coolidge for President contingent joined the rest of the Massachusetts delegation and rolled away on a special train toward Chicago. The Coolidge supporters and the Boston Roosevelt Club had created a new booklet, slim enough to fit into a gentleman's pocket, to circulate among the delegates. Called *Law and Order*, it was bound in imitation black leather and, thanks to Stearns's foresight, featured each delegate's name embossed on the cover. One of the quotations selected was from a Lincoln Day Speech by Coolidge, a line about the importance of Lincoln's mother: "About his cradle all was poor and mean save only the source of all great men, the love of a wonderful woman. When she faded away in his tender years, from her deathbed in humble poverty she dowered her son with greatness." Coolidge's friends said what they had always said: the fact that the convention would begin without a sure candidate gave Coolidge a shot. Coolidge's allies expected Murray Crane to lead Massachusetts in putting forward a fellow westerner. But the delegation was not united behind Coolidge, and Coolidge therefore had not shown up at South Station to wave: it would have made him look desperate.

The cause of the split was Lodge, who had refused to pick a candidate in the end. A poll of the delegates from the Bay State indicated that seven would go to Wood, campaign peccadilloes or no, and twenty-eight to Coolidge, far more than the indications of the spring had suggested. Lodge's disaffection was now out in the open. The senator's concern clearly was winning on the League; sometimes he pushed another candidate, General Wood. Riding out to Chicago, the news-man Clarence Barron spent time with William Coolidge, the railroad lawyer and brother of Lodge's ally Louis Coolidge. Coolidge touched on the concern that his distant cousin, the governor, might become indeed collateral damage in the Republican quarrels at Chicago. The governor, William Coolidge allowed, was indeed something of an Abraham Lincoln type. "He might be the hardest man to nominate and the easiest to elect," William Coolidge told Barron. Murray Crane's allies hoped he would strike back, but they could see now that Crane was ill and that the leader of the western Massachusetts faction might be incapacitated at the crucial moment. "You know there is no chance for me except when it may appear none of the leaders can get it. Then if it all my chance will come," Coolidge wrote his father as his friends traveled west.

The reports from Chicago were not auspicious. Lodge poisoned the well by opening what was now clearly his convention with an overly lengthy attack on Wilson's League of Nations. H. L. Mencken wonder-ingly described the speech as "bosh," but bosh "delivered with an air somehow dignified by the manner of its emission." Others were harsher: Lodge's speech was too hostile to be respectable and was quickly dubbed a "Hymn of Hate." No matter; Lodge had successfully moved the focus of the convention to war. Claiming his post as permanent chairman, Lodge then presided over the early rounds of the nominations, sup-porting Wood. When he wasn't doing damage from the dais, Lodge was making mischief in backroom meetings. The moment the topic of Coolidge came up in a discussion with Henry Stoddard of the *New York Evening Mail*, Lodge offered an annihilating response: "Nominate a man who lives in a two-family house? Never!" Stearns's plans, his publi-cations, all suddenly seemed naive.

Other candidates were constantly being proposed: Governor Lowden, General Wood. But not Coolidge. Crane, whom Coolidge had counted on to push back, seemed confused and spoke inaudibly. The *Chicago Tribune* complained that listening to Crane made one wish he would "shout his whispers through the electric resonator." On June 11, Coolidge wrote his father the cheeriest letter he could come up with: "Before this reaches you the nomination will probably be made. Just now Johnson is out of it. Balloting just beginning. Probably Wood or Lowden cannot win but may. If not my chance seems best."

Coolidge's name was finally presented to the convention at 2:00 P.M. on June 11; the nominator, Frederick Gillett, quoted Coolidge's old line from the telegram to Gompers to spontaneous but brief applause. A former musical comedy star, Alexandra Carlisle Pfeiffer, seconded Coolidge. Grace was in Boston, and the two sat at the Adams House to receive returns, which Henry Long delivered with an explanation. After the fourth ballot, the name Coolidge was still alive but with only twenty-five votes. Lowden and Wood, who had started with hundreds of votes each, were now losing delegates with each round.

This was the moment that Coolidge, Stearns, and the others had identified as their last shot. The leaders of the convention retreated to the ninth floor of the Blackstone Hotel to haggle. But Crane was absent. The other men learned that a fainting spell was keeping him away. The hours passed and the Republicans haggled into the night. At 2:00 A.M., Senator Harding, who, unlike Coolidge, had traveled to Chicago, was summoned from his hotel. At the Blackstone he was invited to swear to his colleagues he knew of no personal liabilities that would prevent his candidacy. Harding swore.

Coolidge's small team fought to the end. Morrow converted his hotel room into a lobbying office. He was so enthusiastic that he followed the delegates around; there was even a photo of Morrow pursuing a delegate wearing only a small towel around his waist. Soon the floor of his room was thick with cigarette stubs. Coolidge followed it all by reading occasional wires to the governor's office at the State House. But while Morrow of J. P. Morgan was wealthy, he commanded little political currency. The kingmakers were people like Lodge and the senator from Indiana James Watson. Asked explicitly about Coolidge, Watson dismissed the idea. "The speaker of the house is from Massachusetts and the leader of the senate is from Massachusetts, and that's enough," Watson told a *Boston Globe* reporter. The leaders were conferring in "the smoke filled room," a United Press reporter wrote. The phrase captured what was going on at the convention: notwithstanding decades of progressive changes to allow voters more say in the selection of lawmakers, notwithstanding the recent Seventeenth Amendment to the Constitution, party leaders were making the calls yet again. The men finally emerged from the room to announce their compromise. On June 12, on the tenth ballot, it was all over; Harding, a senator, had been chosen by his fellow senators.

Upon learning of the Harding choice, Coolidge took his hat and disappeared from the Adams House onto the Boston Common. The convention appeared over: the vice president had already been settled. The plan of the men gathered at the Blackstone, Congress, and Auditorium hotels was to select Lenroot of Wisconsin, who had made a good impression at the Home Market Club of Boston, for the slot. Lenroot made sense in all sorts of ways as a complement to Harding: he was a semiradical who would pull in the progressives under the Republican umbrella but whose own patriotic war record sufficed to defuse those who attacked him. Senator Medill McCormick climbed onto the platform to nominate Lenroot. The midwesterners found Harding too conservative and wanted Lenroot, experienced yet more progressive, to balance the ticket.

At this point, though those in Boston could not know it, something in the hall changed. Lenroot was not getting through. Lenroot might be a progressive, but the method of his selection was retrograde. Another name was ringing; "Coolidge, Coolidge, Coolidge," the delegates began to shout, even though his own Bay State delegation was still not sure whether he was their man. Finally Wallace McCamant of Oregon, the lawyer, rose to nominate Coolidge. Coolidge, he said, was a man "whose name traveled all across the country last fall when he stood for law and order and for the safety of the republic." McCamant's action surprised even those colleagues from the Senate who had been concerned about a Harding-Lenroot ticket. "He never at any time mentioned to me about what he intended to do with reference to Coolidge, and I have since been told that he never mentioned it to anybody else," remembered James Watson of Indiana much later. The crowd at Chicago, grim over the smoke-filled room and the wheeling and dealing from which it had been excluded, lightened up on the realization that it might determine the outcome.

Fifteen states seconded McCamant's Coolidge nomination. The cheering drowned the other names out to such an extent that some of those attending were displeased. It was as though "a cow kicked over a lamp," the *Globe* reported, referring to the original Chicago fire. "The flames bursting out in every delegation ran around the galleries as if on the wings of a gale, and Senator McCormick was left standing on the burning deck whence all but him had fled." Impressed, the reporter opined that the Coolidge fire was "the first real, wholly unpremeditated stampede that ever took place at a national convention." Commented

George Pepper, a Pennsylvania senator, "Some humble delegates had defied the Olympian thunder and stampeded the convention for Coolidge." Commentators observed that the nominator had come from the West and that the enthusiasm that had been lacking for Harding was there for Coolidge, as a stampede occurred and everyone waved flags. "For Once Delegates Have Own Way," trumpeted the *Chicago Tribune*. The newspaper noted approvingly that the delegates had picked Coolidge "without any management visible in the process."

In the Adams House rooms, the phone rang around 8:00 P.M. Coolidge was back and answered it. When he put the phone down, Grace asked about the call. "Nominated for vice president," he said. "You don't mean it," she said. "Indeed I do," he replied. "You are not going to accept it, are you?" "I suppose I shall have to," the governor replied.

Still, the disappointment of the Coolidge team at their second-place showing was enormous. Stearns was furious, histrionic even, and would stay that way for many months. "Those who were at Chicago do not hesitate to say that you were crucified by your own people," he would write Coolidge a full year later. Stearns and the others kept underscoring that Coolidge's qualifications had been as strong as those of many of the other candidates. Lodge and Crane both had let down their man—Lodge out of indirection and vanity, Crane more because of the indecision and weakness of old age. "Many of us feel however," wrote Morrow, "that if Senator Lodge had stood by him in Massachusetts he would have had a very real chance." Vice President Marshall, who did not lack a sense of humor, sent a telegram to Coolidge on news of the nomination that was only half a joke: "Please accept my sincerest sympathy."

Coolidge himself tried to take the second-place outcome philosophically. "I am sure Senator Harding is a good man, and an old friend of mine," he wrote his father. "I hope you will not mind." "I am some surprised and pleased to hear of your nomination for Vice President and hope you and Mr. Stearns are not greatly disappointed," his father wrote in a letter that crossed Coolidge's in the mail.

He and Harding, after all, had in common their relief that the machinations were over. Now they could concentrate on policy. Harding returned home to Ohio in triumph to be greeted by a crowd of 50,000, and settled down on his front porch to base a campaign there. In his homecoming speech Harding returned to the theme that had resonated: normalcy. Then Harding, himself an editor, commented on the word's reception: "I have noticed that word caused considerable news editors to change it to 'normality.' I have looked for 'normality' in my dictionary and I did not find it there. 'Normalcy' however I did find, and it is a good word." By normalcy, he reiterated, he meant "a regular steady order of things." Not that the old order would come back, "But we must have normal order." Coolidge would soon begin to chime in with his own version of the phrase: "old times."

July brought the Democratic nominations for the presidential race. Thomas Marshall, the kindly Democratic vice president who had ribbed Coolidge, had had a difficult spring. His foster child had died, leaving his wife and him in a state of mourning they found hard to escape. Now he entered his name for the presidential slot but found little support. James Cox, the newspaperman from Ohio, won the Democratic nomination for the presidential slot in July. The Democrats had won the war, and the plan of Cox's team was to collect votes as a reward for that victory. Franklin Roosevelt was chosen as his vice president. Cox set out on a speaking tour that would not stop until his election and would give 238 speeches on that tour alone. Coolidge had Barton, and Harding had his adviser from advertising, Albert Lasker, a man who had successfully marketed Lucky Strike cigarettes to women, to craft their thoughts. Cox campaigned on independence and integrity. He also spoke out for organized labor, arguing that the GOP's hostility to unions was downright ungrateful. At last Gompers had found a new ally. "A good clean fair man" was how Gompers characterized Cox on July 6. Cox went at the labor theme. "What of the millions of men, women, and children of all creeds, religious and otherwise, who stood in the ranks as firm as soldiers overseas, undivided by things they once quarreled about?" he asked. The GOP was cruel to attack labor now, he said: "Why the sneer at labor, with the veiled charge that it was a mere slacker?"

How to respond? Fewer strikes meant more workdays and greater prosperity. But Coolidge was more aware now than before that worker frustration was warranted. "Have you harvested the fruits of your labor, the price of your victories?" a flyer for an anarchists' meeting found in the pocket of Bartolomeo Vanzetti, one of the men arrested in the South Braintree case, had asked. The rise in prices had made people desperate and fostered the general assumption that all money was a gamble, up for grabs. Another result of the lottery mood was a business scandal Coolidge had to oversee. Hundreds had invested their money in new, untested firms that promised credulous Bostonians unprecedented earnings. The Securities Exchange Company, one of the small firms that had promised extravagant returns, was enduring a run. Critics were now beginning to say that its founder, Charles Ponzi, had invested nothing, merely recycling money to new investors. Coolidge directed his attorney general to order an inquiry. The ripple effect was hurting banks, and individuals were losing what they had thought were true fortunes. Investigation was the job of the state authorities in Massachusetts; states regulated stocks and bonds. Ponzi was arrested and sat in East Cambridge jail. The state treasurer, Fred Burrell, was mixed up in the scheme; $125,000 of the state's funds had been in Hanover Trust Company, a bank that had closed its doors. Burrell had been working as an advertising agent on the side. As governor, Coolidge issued a warning to banks not to buy advertising from the state treasurer.

Coolidge understood his job as vice presidential candidate as supporting Harding; it was a replay of the years he had backed up Governor McCall. But the more he thought Harding's plan over, the more comfortable he was with it. In normalcy, Harding had come up with a concept that made sense for the party and the country. And the crowds now gathering around him seemed in their turn to support his own endorsements. At Northampton, a sea of boater hats greeted Coolidge the day he formally received his nomination; photographers that summer followed Coolidge and his family around, demanding photo poses almost nonstop. He and his son Calvin, both in white shirts, arranged themselves carefully in the Massasoit Street yard before a soapbox car so that reporters could snap an image of the Coolidges at home. Images of Coolidge wearing his grandfather's old blue wool haying smock also proliferated.

Coolidge and Grace traveled out to Marion with other Republicans to call on the candidate at his home. The Hardings' lifestyle differed so much from the Coolidges'. Mrs. Harding had run the newspaper in Marion with Harding, and now she ran his preparations for office with him; she referred to "Warren Harding" when she spoke to third parties as if her husband were a brand, not a man. The Hardings hung close to their friends and advisers, who were in turn more talkative than a candidate's advisers would be in New England. They spoke often and on the record, and moved the campaign focus away from the League of Nations and the wartime bitterness. The Harding advisers had under-

stood early that even "law and order" was too bitter a motto to emphasize exclusively. "I find the underlying thing in the minds of the people is
the demand for a change in the Administration," Harry Daugherty, the
attorney who was close to Harding, told the people around the porch.

Even in the good mood of the general campaign, however, the mut-
tering about the Harding crowd continued. People wondered whether
Harding was hiring too many friends—not just near allies, such as
Daugherty, but old acquaintances, such as Colonel Charles Forbes, a
recipient of the Croix de Guerre in France who had served state govern-
ments and Wilson and ran a construction firm in Tacoma, Washington.
Forbes had helped ensure that the Washington State delegation went for
Harding.

But on balance, the Coolidges were pleased with their visit. The
Hardings received them warmly. To share his luck with Coolidge,
Harding hunted for a four-leaf clover on his well-trodden lawn, found
one, and pinned it onto Coolidge's lapel. They could feel the comfort
of being part of something larger. Now the authorities at the Federal
Reserve banks were raising interest rates, so that those rates, like the
prices, were higher than what adults had known before: the discount
rate, the rate banks charged other banks, was 7 percent at the Federal
Reserve Bank of New York. Many prices were coming down: "Women's
ingrain silk stockings at prices unprecedented this year," read a *Boston
Herald* advertisement for R. H. Stearns. Wall Streeters believed that this
tightening would reduce prices permanently. But others were uncertain.
Symptomatic of the general confusion was an editorial in a Lincoln,
Nebraska, paper *The Daily Star.* The paper roasted Harding for failing to
tighten interest rates enough: "Through Senator Harding's action, wild
speculation was permitted to continue while production was retarded,"
commented the editors. "The youngest follower of economics will see
this action merely aggravates the situation." Farm prices were dropping
in 1920, suggesting deflation, so this allegation, that interest rates might
yet be too low, was an odd one for a paper to make. It was even odder
when the reader realized that the Lincoln paper had mistaken the head
of the Federal Reserve, W. P. G. Harding, for the presidential candidate.

The first great test of the Harding-Coolidge ticket came in
September, when Maine held its early vote. Coolidge went to Portland
and gave a speech emphasizing that to oppose Wilson's League was not
necessarily to be isolationist: "Ever since this nation was established,

it has never been isolated. Not isolated but independent, free, rendering service to all mankind." Franklin Roosevelt, the Democrats' vice presidential candidate, pointedly vacationed in Eastport and not at the family place in Campobello, New Brunswick, over the border, in the days before the Maine ballot. On September 11, a Saturday, during the anniversary of the strike, Coolidge gave a speech in Manchester, New Hampshire. Coolidge stressed the necessity of withdrawing the special powers Congress had given government before the war. "The independence of the Congress" too, he said, "must be preserved." Under Wilson, the executive branch had grown too large. The navy secretary, Josephus Daniels, snapped back that Coolidge was inconsistent or worse. "The first half of his speech was to declare for American participation in world affairs and it was essentially sound," Daniels noted, "but he made a lame and impotent conclusion by approving Harding's toothless Hague tribunal." He went on to say, "But by reason of the straddle policy of his party Governor Coolidge had to repudiate his splendid recital of American duty to the world, as well as to itself." Roosevelt was sharper than Daniels even, countering on the day of the Maine election. Republicans like Coolidge, Roosevelt said, backed a Congress that would "have the president's office a chief clerkship for the carrying out of its policies."

In New England, Coolidge knew, the best way to come back after such a putdown was to prove oneself even humbler than the opponent suggested. Coolidge therefore lectured on thrift. Speaking to the National Association of Life Underwriters, he announced that he had not bought a suit of clothes in eighteen months or a pair of shoes in two years. Once supply and demand could function freely again, Coolidge said, industries such as the woolen industry of Massachusetts would also function. At home, as well, the Coolidges struggled with finance. Someone had given them a police dog. Coolidge wanted his father to take it but John demurred. "A dog is no joke," Coolidge wrote. "They cost money."

Whether because of thrift or pride, the Republican victory that year in Maine proved historic; Harding carried more than 65,000 votes. The Republicans made gains even in cities such as Portland relative to their performance in 1916. The GOP women had come out in force. "All records broken in size of total vote and plurality," commented *The Boston Globe*. Coolidge was even blunter in the telegram he sent Harding on September 14: "Judge nothing can prevent your election." After

Maine, Coolidge and Harding went back to their lecture circuit. Yet again, Coolidge found Harding's themes easy to support: less injurious meddling from abroad, less meddling in business. Wilson had indeed vetoed the federal budget system legislation put forward by Republicans, but that just meant the Grand Old Party would put through a second version. Indeed, on the budget, the habitually jovial Harding hit hard. Washington was conducting a "financial orgy" that only a budget could halt, Harding said in Wheeling, West Virginia. A budget was worthy because then "there would be set up in Washington an establishment"— reporting to the president—"which would have full and complete knowledge of every activity." There had to be a way to reduce the national debt without "undue taxation." Government had drawn "the very life blood from the channels of business to keep itself alive." In this bloviating, one could hear the common sense. Harding was placing faith in the restorative power of commerce.

Just a few days after the Maine vote came an event that tested such faith. As the bells of New York's Trinity Church rang for the lunch break, an anarchist's bomb in a horse-drawn cart exploded, hitting the epicenter of capitalism, J. P. Morgan headquarters. Just three minutes before, circulars signed "Fighting Anarchists of America" had been found by a letter carrier at Cedar Street and Broadway. The explosion was caused by a powerful "TNT bomb, reinforced with iron slugs," as the police reported the next day. The impact was so great that one slug landed on the eighteenth floor of 61 Broadway. It was a far greater explosion than any of the individual bombs that had gone off in 1920 or the year before. Morrow, inside, sustained cuts to his head and hand as the windows blew out. The dome on the structure, the pride of J. P. Morgan, shattered. The walls were pockmarked from the stones that had hit them. Fifteen people were killed instantly. Others lay dying on the street. Every window at Bankers Trust across the street was also damaged. The precious tickers, machines that spit out the stock prices were hit, in both their glass tops and their wooden frames. It all seemed a horrible setback. Everyone knew that Attorney General A. Mitchell Palmer would now have a pretext to launch a campaign to renew the deportation raids and revive his hateful sedition law. Officers were called in to guard the million dollars in gold that the Federal Reserve kept under the ground.

But those present in the Morgan office at the bombing noticed something else. One ticker, Clarence Barron's ticker from Dow Jones, still clattered. The glass bell over the machine was smashed, and shards had embedded themselves in its slender wood frame, but the apparatus continued to spew news of the explosion and then, all afternoon, the details of its consequences. The sputtering little machine sent a signal that the whole nation heard. Commerce would not be stopped.

In October, Coolidge could feel himself growing into his new role; he looked forward to Washington. The same Wall Street that was recovering from the bombing was now betting seven to one that Harding would prevail over Cox. "We will carry all of the West," Elmer Dover, a Republican national committeeman, wrote to Harding. Looking over the northwest, Charles Forbes, who was seeking a spot on the shipping board, sent an equally confident message to Marion: "You will make a sweeping victory."

Toward the end of the campaign, as if to mark the finality of Coolidge's departure from Massachusetts, his great mentor, Murray Crane, died. A crowd came together at Crane's house on Sugar Hill in Dalton to pay its respects; Coolidge sat with Lodge in Crane's drawing room. The death confirmed what Coolidge already knew: that Crane had failed at the convention because he was sick. "Had he been his old self at Chicago I feel the result there would have been different. . . . He was a great man," Coolidge wrote his father. At the funeral there were no cross words, but when Lodge commenced posing for pictures, Coolidge found himself unwilling to join him and finally snapped, "I came to bury my friend. It's no time for photographs."

On November 1, Coolidge wrote his father a preelection report. It featured the usual mixture of relief, concern, and sharp Coolidge humor about the economy. The difficult inflation puzzle still plagued him, but he was cheerier now. "Came home yesterday. Boys are well. Your dog is growing well. She has bitten the ice man, the milk man, and the grocer man. It is good to have some way to get even with them for the high prices they charge for everything. In the morning Mr. Stearns will try to find out how to telephone returns to you."

The return numbers were so strong that not even Lodge could sniff at them. On Harding's fifty-fifth birthday, Harding, Coolidge, and normalcy took more than 60 percent of the vote. James Cox's Democrats won only 34 percent. In the electoral college, the GOP collected 404 votes to 127 for the Democrats. Not everyone understood the extent to which Coolidge deserved credit for the outcome. The Germans, for example, remained steadfast in their fealty to the idea of Archibald Coolidge as victor, with the *Berliner Tageblatt*, still confused, writing that "through the victory of the Republican ticket Archibald Cary Coolidge has been elected vice president of the United States."

In fact Calvin Coolidge had made a difference. Tennessee, where Coolidge had briefly traveled, rewarded him and voted for a Republican over a Democrat in the presidential election for the first time since 1868. Coolidge's actions during the police strike were often cited as the reason for the GOP success. "The people not only beat Gompers and Cox. They were at particular pains to rub it in," gloated *The Wall Street Journal*. When it came to the Senate, the Democrats had prevailed in the South but nowhere else. The Republicans picked up ten seats; crucially, they gained in western states such as Nevada, Idaho, and California. The Republican majority in the upper chamber was now 59 to 37, which meant that from his seat as president of the Senate, the new vice president, Coolidge, would be likely to see the passage of many laws he endorsed. The tariff proved an especially big seller in places such as Utah, where tariff advocate Reed Smoot had won 56.6 percent of the vote. As for the House of Representatives, the Grand Old Party now held nine out of ten seats outside the South. With a total of 302 seats, it had almost 70 percent of the House, a historic record. The result was a shift in the official policy of the Grand Old Party. It was not so much the progressive party as the party of low taxes, tariffs, less central government, and stability.

In December, the Coolidges traveled out to Ohio a second time, this time in snow, to visit the Hardings. They found there were still crowds of hundreds bidding for the president-elect's attention; William Jennings Bryan was set to arrive shortly. Someone mentioned a plan for a vice presidential residence in Washington; Coolidge promptly nixed it—as "inappropriate" in a time of budget cutting. The Coolidges found the Hardings marvelously receptive. Harding invited Coolidge to sit in on cabinet meetings, marking a shift for a president-elect. Harding was a unifier, Coolidge said. The vice president–elect did not find himself favoring the word "normalcy," but he described their shared agenda another way. It was time to end the confusion, to recognize the cost of operating "in this time of uncertainty," as he told *The New York Times*.

Back east in Plymouth, Massachusetts, just before Christmas, Coolidge made another try at expressing where the country might go.

Excavators there had been digging up the original rock where the pilgrims landed, in time for the tercentenary of the year of the landing, 1620. A crowd of hundreds assembled there, among whom were local children and mill hand immigrants, "still faulty in their English," as the papers reported. The vice president–elect, Mrs. Coolidge, and Senator Lodge stood before the citizens. Coolidge pointed out to the crowd that there was nothing noble about the pilgrims' blood at the time they voyaged. It was their deeds that distinguished them for later Americans. They had been "oblivious to rank, yet men trace to them their lineage as to a royal house." It would be futile, Coolidge said, "to search among recorded maps an history for their origin. They sailed up out of the infinite." The way the pilgrims had lived, by example, provided value for others; in fact, "no like body ever cast so great an influence on human history." Preserving that tradition, Coolidge was saying, seemed a primary endeavor, if only because it benefited so many others, regardless of background. Coolidge's second point was made by the ring of the telephone: the Rock's anniversary was being celebrated with a connection from Massachusetts to the West Coast and the governor of California. Daniel Webster had prophesied, a century before, that Plymouth would be heard "to the murmurs of the Pacific seas." Now Coolidge used the public phone call to make good on that promise. Governor Stephens did not pick up, but his secretary and Coolidge conversed before the crowd. "I wish you to say to Governor Stephens that Massachusetts and Plymouth greet California and the Golden Gate."

As he thought about the prospects for change, Coolidge felt his hopes lift again. The party platform suited Harding's intentions, and his own. On the need for the new budget system, the document was especially clear: "The universal demand for an executive budget is a recognition of the incontrovertible fact that leadership and sincere assistance on the part of the executive departments are essential to effective economy and constructive retrenchment." Harding was already thinking about how to win party support for tax changes. Coolidge could see that Harding was selecting friends from Ohio for key cabinet jobs: Daugherty for attorney general, for example. But the president-elect was also naming great powerhouses to advise him: Herbert Hoover, who was universally respected, went to the Commerce Department, Charles Evans Hughes to the post of secretary of state. Also notable was the appointment of Andrew Mellon, the Pittsburgh magnate, as Treasury secretary. After the convention, the limits on giving had come off; Mellon had raised $400,000 in Allegheny County. Interviewed, Barron told the press that "the finance success associated with the name of Mellon in Pittsburgh is a good augury."

Coolidge had been accustomed to the citizens of Massachusetts, who had respected him by keeping their distance; now huge crowds came to see him wherever he went. In Atlanta, where thousands greeted him, someone stole his overcoat while he was inspecting a YMCA building. Fending off the praise and the flattery was also a challenge. Theodore Roosevelt's sister Corinne Roosevelt Robinson, still grieving over TR's death, invited Coolidge to speak at the Women's Roosevelt Memorial Foundation, telling Coolidge, "I would rather have you as the speaker of this meeting than anyone else for your works seem to me to be a reincarnation of both Abraham Lincoln and Theodore Roosevelt." Coolidge did not know how to respond and asked Morrow whether he should accept. The new administration needed to move quickly in all areas. As soon as the election returns were in, Coolidge embarked on a crash course in every area of administration, turning to anyone, regardless of status, to gain the most accurate and succinct information. His distant cousin Archibald, a Harvard professor and leading expert on treaties and international law relating to war, knew better than almost anyone else the legal background regarding the neutrality of Belgium. But the same cousin, Coolidge also suspected, might exploit the opportunity of an informational query to trap the vice president–elect into listening to hours of lectures. To gain the benefit of Archibald's knowledge without paying a prohibitive cost in time, Coolidge crafted his own single-paragraph summary of the law as it had been before the war and sent it over to Cambridge: "The great powers of Europe made a treaty for the neutralization of Belgium under which they agreed not to violate Belgian territory by invasion." But the vice president–elect also helpfully advised his cousin as to the form of the response he expected: "You are familiar with European subjects which I am not so that I wish to ask you if the following statement would be correct. Perhaps you can indicate by writing 'yes' or 'no' on it and returning it to me." Even so, the Harvard cousin could not resist shipping back a response of several paragraphs to the State House.

In the interregnum, Coolidge and Grace retreated with Frank Stearns and his wife, Emily, to Asheville, North Carolina, for a brief rest, but even there, at the Grove Park Inn, hundreds of people came to greet Coolidge. Nor did the letters, the books, and the advice fail to penetrate. From Morrow there came a biography of Alexander Hamilton, a tariff history of the United States by F. W. Taussig, and other documents on tariffs, mostly skeptical. Morrow had not given up on converting Coolidge.

Beyond briefings and learning, there were other challenges to consider. An austere, budget-cutting administration had to serve as a model of thrift. While the Coolidges were in Asheville, Congress, confronting the greatest national debt in its memory, opted to conduct hearings about whether the outlays for the war had been warranted. The lawmakers were so angry and so insistent in their pressuring of the officer who oversaw the supply management of the American Expeditionary Force, Brigadier General Charles G. Dawes, on the price of French horses that the general exploded, shouting, "Hell and Maria! I will tell you this, that we would have paid horse prices for sheep if they could have hauled artillery." But Dawes was on the defensive.

Fortunately, the Hardings did seem ready enough to budget, both publicly and privately, as Florence Harding reminded them in her direct way. Grace wrote Florence Harding again to inquire about dressing for the inaugural ball. This gave Mrs. Harding her first opportunity to pull rank. The inaugural ball had been canceled for austerity's sake, she informed Grace. So they would not need to get fancy dresses. "It does simplify for us, doesn't it?" she added.

Whatever the dress code, both Coolidges, in fact the whole family, still looked forward to inauguration day. The vice president–elect carefully crafted a train itinerary down to the inauguration for his father, who was staying with the boys in Northampton. Solicitously, he arranged that the Colonel change trains in New Haven rather than in New York, where the transfer was more difficult and the crowds greater. "You will leave here Thurs March 3 am at 8-20, reach New Haven at 10-41." After switching cars there, Colonel Coolidge was to ride to Washington and arrive at 8:45 P.M. with the boys.

Service was on Coolidge's mind as he carefully drafted the vice president's address. It had to set the stage for Harding and facilitate his legislation. The Hardings and Coolidges rode to the inauguration in matching Packard Twin Sixes, the first time a first and second couple had traveled by car. The crowds noticed the grace with which Harding turned to his partner in the vehicle, Woodrow Wilson, inclining his top hat in kindness toward the frozen face of the retiring president. Coolidge was led into the Senate chamber to be sworn in. For some members, it was their first glimpse of Coolidge. "Mr. Coolidge, a medium-sized man of auburn hair who was escorted to Vice-president Marshall's right," Henry Fountain Ashurst, a senator from Arizona, described him in his diary.

At 12:20 P.M., Vice President Marshall sent a signal throughout the chamber, and at 12:21 P.M. Coolidge was sworn in. The "I do" rang clearly in the room. Marshall introduced him, and Coolidge followed with his own speech, 434 words, the length a typical Coolidge signal, like the inaugural address in the Senate back in 1916, that he was committed to cutting back. The Constitution, he said, might be about governments and people, both plural, two groups. But beneath that lay a more important relationship established by the Constitution, without which the former meant nothing: "a new relationship between man and man." The Constitution was there, but only to back up and express what happened between men in commerce every day, between country lawyers like him or notaries and clients. Unless the trust between the individual men was right, the whole mechanism was off. Coolidge closed with humility. "I take up the duties the people have assigned me," he told the senators.

The speech did not resonate as Coolidge intended, in part because the crowd rushed off to hear the president. The enormous pressure to do right, to keep up with the crowd without being rude, made the family nervous. A newspaperman from the *Boston Daily Advertiser* asked John Coolidge, the president's older son, if he would report on the inauguration for the Sunday edition. John, cautious, demurred. Calvin, twelve, agreed, penning an article short on detail and long on goodwill:

By Calvin Coolidge Jr.

The Boston Sunday Advertiser has given me the privilege of stating how I felt at the Inauguration and what impressed me the most. I saw my father inaugurated. I felt very sorry to see Mr. Marshall go out of office.

I was very proud of my father. I liked to look at the ministers of other countries. They were dressed up in gold lace and bright colors. When I went out on the platform I saw the crowd extending way down the street. They looked very nice.

It impressed me very much to see the men of the Supreme Court.
They looked sort of business like.

Before a crowd of 100,000 Harding then gave his speech, far grander
and more ambitious than Coolidge's and of high quality. America must
not expect too much or experiment too much, he said. He warned against
change for its own sake. It was time to retrench and give up perpetual
progressivism. "No altered system will work a miracle," he said. "Any
wild experiment will only add to the confusion. Our best assurance lies
in efficient administration of our proven system." Harding might pursue
some items on the progressive agenda. But he sought no Square Deal,
such as Theodore Roosevelt had offered. What this administration
wanted was to find its way back to the Old Deal.

It might achieve that. "Owing to mechanical device," the invention
of the microphone, Harding's voice "carried perfectly, for great dis-
tances," commented *The Washington Post*. As Harding spoke, a shaft of
sunlight hit him, seeming to bless his remarks. Beneath the new president stood marines, sailors, and soldiers, each group bearing standards,
a reminder of that group asking the most of the new administration, the
millions of veterans across the country. A group of wounded soldiers
from Walter Reed sat not far away from the grass, many in wheelchairs,
missing limbs. Shortly they would be loaded onto army trucks to go back
to the hospital, a clumsy, pitiful sight. Harding stopped to promise them
that he would address their concern. "I want to assure you that a generous country will never forget the services you rendered," he said.

Then it was off to the Senate to renew his bonds with old colleagues,
men who would make it possible to turn his plans into law. That too,
Coolidge could see, was a rousing success, for the senators were delighted
at the surprise visit. Senator Lodge had already set the stage for Harding
by clearing the names of his cabinet nominees with fellow Republicans,
the majority. To general merriment, Harding read aloud the names of
his cabinet, which were approved on the spot. If any administration
could take care of the veterans' troubles and the country's as well, this
one could. When Harding read off before the Senate and Coolidge the
name of Albert Fall for his cabinet, Fall's brother senators began to cheer
loudly and joke that he must leave the Senate floor, where no private citizen was allowed to sit. "Throw him out!" they joked. Someone suggested
to Coolidge that Fall be affirmed instantly in his new post without the

formal confirmation process; the motion passed unanimously, to more clapping. It was a dazzling display for a novice to observe: Harding had so many friends. Another was Senator James Watson of Indiana, who was fond of both Hardings. "He could smoke a cigarette, or a cigar, or a pipe, he could take a nip of liquor without ever using it to excess," Watson later reflected back with affection about Harding. The new president, Watson said, personified trustworthiness: "He had one of those affidavit faces whose very appearance carries conviction." Only in Washington could Coolidge appreciate the extent of Harding's web of contacts; the Hardings' dearest friends were the McLeans; Edward McLean, conveniently, owned *The Washington Post.*

All the cabinet members but Mellon would be sworn in the next day. Edward Douglass White, Jr., Chief Justice of the United States, was instructed to swear in the new Treasury secretary at once. As it turned out, White, not being a notary, was not qualified, and Mellon would have to take his oath with the others the next day. But the signal that the Treasury must go first was the important part. The economy came first in this new era. Harding and Coolidge now had an opportunity Coolidge alone had not enjoyed. Together, the pair could do more than navigate the river. They could change its course.

NINE

❧✦❧

"A MOST INSIGNIFICANT OFFICE"

Washington, D.C.

THE COAT AND TAILS lay on the bed in suite 328 of the Willard Hotel. These were the overalls of the vice presidency, as one journalist wrote. The work itself was as clear as the hay before his father in the Vermont field. The task of the vice president was to assist the president in getting the department heads, the cabinet members, the legislators, and the press to go along when Harding implemented his "rigid yet sane economy," to back the president up in saying "no."

In a city accustomed to "yes," that was a tall order. Washington in 1921 held a higher opinion of itself than even Boston did, and found little evidence to contradict its own opinion. The architecture itself saluted the government's grandeur. Buildings in the District of Columbia stood well below the height of the Capitol dome, the result of long-standing zoning laws; the effect was to rank government above commerce. Union Station, where the Coolidges had arrived from New England, had been designed "to distinctly subordinate it to the Capitol," as one architectural journal noted. The society life felt more French than American, more prewar than postwar. Protocol demanded that the wives of senators and congressmen call formally at the homes of the cabinet officers. Each call had to be returned, and then the rounds began again. "Imagine five hundred or more women going around leaving cards with the stolid industry of mail carriers," one observer, Wilson's Treasury secretary and son-in-law, William McAdoo, wrote in wonderment. That such etiquette was demanded amid the mud, mosquitos, and infection that were the District of Columbia seemed absurd.

But if anyone could charm the United States' capital city, the Hardings could. That the first couple proved from Harding's very first hours in the presidency, with the controversy over the inaugural ball. Washington craved a ball. Yet Harding himself had promised that that year would be a year of "putting all celebration aside." His inauguration compromise was reasonably, if not perfectly, principled. No public ball took place, just as Florence Harding had informed Grace. But Edward McLean, the owner of the *Post*, and his wife, Evalyn, hosted their own private dinner. Three long tables set with a fancy gold and silver services and seating a hundred each were laid out beneath candelabras and Barberini tapestries at the McLean home on I Street. This dinner, as it turned out, was the most elaborate, the papers reported, since Washington had hosted the Prince of Wales.

Mrs. Harding was performing similar magic. She made a big demonstration of forgoing a $10,000 allowance for redecoration of the president's quarters and brought her own furniture instead. In addition, on the very day of inauguration she opened the gates of the White House to receive throngs on the grounds. "Let 'em look in if they want," she shouted to the maids when they moved to close the curtains on the spectators who pressed their noses onto the glass. "It's their White House." Yet in private she maintained an elaborate wardrobe; the tails of six quadrupeds hung upon her breast when she greeted the Coolidges at Union Station, whereas Grace sported only a modest fur collar. At the McLeans' inaugural dinner, Grace had, just as might be expected, found herself sartorially outclassed by Mrs. Harding and indeed the entire crowd, especially the hostess, Evalyn McLean, in silver brocade from Paris.

Even in these early hours, the Coolidges sensed that they might never catch up to Washington. Their hosts, the McLeans, were not merely wealthy but spectacularly so; Evalyn owned the Hope diamond and had recently worn it when attending the theater with Florence Harding. The McLeans maintained a second home in Virginia, outside the capital; Harding liked to golf there. Edward McLean's efforts had proved indispensable during the campaign period: he had assigned another newspaper he owned, *The Cincinnati Enquirer*, to endorse Harding over James Cox of nearby Dayton, Ohio.

Grace's dinner partner that first night at the inaugural dinner was General Pershing, the great hero of the war. Pershing had one son, Warren; his wife and daughters had died in a tragic fire before the war. Grace won the general over by talking about his son and hers. Coolidge found the transition less easy. In fact, as often happened at big moments, an illness came over him: this time it was a stomachache. He might be silent, but the lack of formality in the inaugural proceedings disturbed him; it was unlike the Massachusetts inaugurations. Any semblance of unity had disappeared when the crowd had raced from the Senate chamber and his own address to the East Portico. The sight of President Wilson in his last hours at the White House had also been striking. Next to Harding, who walked up and down steps with ease, Wilson seemed old: the office had done that to him. As the first evening passed, however, even Coolidge could feel himself being charmed. The owner of the Hope diamond personally walked Coolidge to his seat, mixed him up a dose of water with bicarbonate of soda, and made sure he drank it; then she got him another. The McLeans had the ability to establish instant intimacy, and told the Coolidges their story: Evalyn had endured a brutal car accident as a girl and, just a year before, had lost her son Vinson in another car accident. Ned McLean moved in a faster crowd than Bostonians were accustomed to. But in his way McLean was merely the kind of friend Coolidge was developing in Clarence Barron, a press man.

The morning after the inauguration, the Hardings demonstrated their ability to negotiate public sensibilities once again. The Calvary Baptist and First Baptist churches, the two big churches of their denomination, waited in vain for attendance by the new first couple. But the Hardings did make an all-important gesture of observing the Sabbath when, at Grasslands Country Club that morning, Harding chose not to golf along with the others. Along with Harding were senators Eugene Hale of Maine and Theodore Frelinghuysen of New Jersey; Frelinghuysen was seeking Harding's backing for a coal commission.

Later in the day, at the White House, the Hardings received crowds of friends from Marion while Harding contemplated assistant secretary appointments; he had already met with Secretary of State Hughes over tensions in Panama and Costa Rica. Giving a powerhouse like Hughes, the 1916 Republican presidential candidate, such a prominent cabinet position was itself a testament to Harding's confidence and savvy. Mrs. Harding too moved forward with confidence; she not only opened the White House but let it be known that the house would be open to the people routinely for teas and lawn parties, as well as, word came out, an Easter egg hunt for children on the South Lawn. The Hardings together boldly terminated a congressional perk. Heretofore congressmen had handed out tickets to tour the White House as favors; Mrs. Harding ruled that people could enter without tickets. An intense, anxious woman, she followed politics and opined confidently. The White House staff was already a bit afraid of her. She suffered from kidney disease and had brought her own doctor, C. E. Sawyer, to Washington. Generously Harding made Sawyer a brigadier general; a second doctor, Joel Boone, who was with the navy, served on the presidential yacht, the *Mayflower*.

The Hardings had McLean and the *Post*, but neither they nor the Republicans stopped there when it came to managing their reputation. Will Rogers, a stage, radio, and print humorist, functioned as an arbiter of American taste. Though he was an old rodeo hand, not a professor, Americans looked to him for political analysis as well. Once Rogers endorsed a politician, the country could like him; indeed, it almost had to. William Hays, the Republicans' press adviser, ensured that the necessary meeting between the new president and Rogers occurred, with Harding earning a rave review. After the meeting, Rogers wrote some notes of his visit down in his hotel room: "Didn't even get to start to introduce me before the president said 'Hello, where's your chewing gum?' So instead of me telling him anything funny, he starts in repeating things I had said in the Midnight Follies for years." Harding, Rogers thought, represented the right mix of country and power. The man made mistakes, but undid them by acknowledging them. Harding was no hayseed. "So the fellow who tells you he's right from a farm to the White House is cuckoo," he reported. "I told him I wanted to tell him the latest political jokes. He said, 'I know 'em. I appointed most of them.' So I saw I couldn't match humor with this man so I called it a day." It didn't hurt the new administration's popularity either that, despite advertised cutbacks, it was clearly offering some jobs, especially patronage jobs at the Justice Department. "Most of the job seekers who came to Washington for the inauguration and pie cutting want to see Harry M. Daugherty," noted *The Boston Globe*. Harding had already made it clear that he would force an extra session of Congress so that he might exploit the momentum of a new presidency for more support for his legislation.

The Coolidges kept up their efforts in those first weeks in Washington. Grace took her new social challenges very seriously, visiting cards and all, though, as she admitted with a laugh, most of her time in dining rooms theretofore had been spent on the floor, laying out track for the boys' miniature trains. Washingtonians noted approvingly that Grace "kept her wits at the end of her tongue." From the kind Mrs. Marshall, her predecessor, she learned she had to preside over a luncheon for Senate wives in the Senate Office Building on Tuesdays. That Grace deemed unfair: she must "at once become the presiding officer of the advanced class." On Wednesdays, the wife of the vice president received guests in her drawing room; the open house was announced not by invitation but in the society section of the newspaper.

That meant the crowds piled in; one day, Mrs. Coolidge learned that a bellboy was out on the street, shouting, "This way to Mrs. Coolidge's apartment." Many hundreds of people materialized and, as Grace wrote to her sorority sisters, they treated access to her open houses as a kind of right: "A few draw a chair right up to the tea table and proceed to make a 'square meal.'" In a letter to Foster Stearns, the Stearnses' son, Grace did say what was on the tip of her tongue: "I'll never dare to be 'at home' again for fear somebody will be crushed to death." Coolidge suggested that if the Hardings could have lawn parties, they, the Coolidges, should have sidewalk parties.

Another day during the inaugural rush, Mrs. Coolidge showed up at her suite to find reporters in the bedroom inspecting her dresses, which were laid out on the bed. Mrs. Stearns had pulled them out to show inquiring reporters. The journalists looked over her shoes, which were, fortunately, from Lynn, not Paris. The press noted everything about them: that Grace favored heels between one and two inches high and that the linings were printed with her name, "Mrs. Calvin Coolidge."

Humor, the Coolidges thought, might help them through. Someone commented that they had been invited to eat at the home of someone whose name was not in the *Social Register.* "No conclusion can be drawn from that," the vice president commented. "I've been in it myself only half an hour." Grace wrote Stearns gaily that Calvin in his way was becoming a "social butterfly." Coolidge told others he had to eat somewhere; he jollied along his small staff as well. When socialites pressured Coolidge, he merely went into his shell. But they did not relent. One story about that did not die. A lady seated beside Coolidge told him she had heard he was silent. She had made a bet, however, that she could get him to say more than two words over the course of the evening. "You lose," Coolidge said. Grace managed the damage from the encounter by repackaging it and circulating it as an anecdote. Perhaps Washington would come to like Coolidge in time as Massachusetts had. After all, it had known Murray Crane. Coolidge, wary of squandering physical energy, liked to leave evening gatherings at 10:00 P.M. Fortunately, his diplomatic rank as vice president meant he was free to be the first to leave.

Harding, by contrast, seemed able to work all hours. Lawmakers were staying for an extra session, which meant that the president would have a chance to pass his new agenda, especially the new budget legislation. Through violent hacking at the military budget, the Republican Congress had managed to cut the government back faster than Wilson would have liked; Wilson and the Democrats for their part had pushed up taxes, pulling in revenue. But the budget was still around $6.3 billion for 1920, and the schedule of government debt meant that in coming years many of the budgetary advances could be reversed. The aim was to retire debt, not to expand it. Harding now intended tough budget legislation with tougher review to make the tenuous surplus permanent; $6 billion was still twice as high as necessary. "We can reduce the abnormal expenditures, and we will," Harding boomed at the inauguration. Resolve alone would not suffice; Harding maintained that the federal government needed the budget office he had campaigned for.

On the Tuesday after the inauguration, Coolidge attended his first cabinet meeting. The men posed for the photographers outdoors, and Coolidge was seated to Harding's left. To Harding's right was Charles Evans Hughes, and to the right of Hughes, Mellon. Indoors, at the cabinet meeting around the mahogany table, Coolidge found himself impressed. Harding sat at one end of the table, and Coolidge at the other. The ten men who sat between them in the new chairs—the silver nameplates were not affixed yet—were powerhouses; Harding had the strength to handle big personalities. Hughes would deal with the controversial issue of Versailles and international law from the State Department. Some of his first work, in fact, was smoothing over Roosevelt's: Harding wanted to push through early an already negotiated treaty with Colombia that included a payment of $25 million to compensate for Roosevelt's orchestrated theft of the isthmus of Panama. From the Commerce Department, there was Herbert Hoover. Hoover, who sat near Coolidge, tended to glower into the distance. But Coolidge could see that Hoover was more efficient than the rest; here was someone who could beat him when it came to getting through office work. John Weeks, Coolidge's own Massachusetts ally, was also there, already digging deep in the details of war surplus goods in the job of secretary of war. Harry Daugherty was there as attorney general; Albert Fall, with his signature handlebar moustache, came from Interior.

It was Mellon who caught Coolidge's eye. The new Treasury secretary sat near Harding, at the other end of the table. Mellon was a name Coolidge had first heard before in relation to Arthur Vining Davis. Today the magnate from Pittsburgh was, after Henry Ford, the United States' most admired, and most eccentric, businessman. Mellon too felt like a newcomer; when he exited the cabinet meeting, the reporters would note, Mellon was surprised to discover the little knots of men in the anteroom and slipped away. What Coolidge saw, however, was not the awkwardness but the determination. At the end of the Wilson era, the Federal Reserve banks raised the key interest rate, the discount rate, mightily, from 4 percent to 7 percent. Two Treasury secretaries, Carter Glass and David Houston, had participated in that initiative with William Harding; the Treasury secretary sat on the board of the Federal Reserve. Those hikes had been painful, but lower prices had followed. Mellon was likely to sustain the policy of tight credit. Yet there was one area where the work had scarcely begun: income taxes, with the top rates still above 70 percent. Getting the tax code back closer to the prewar top level of 7 percent seemed an impossible task, but Mellon planned to cut as far back as he could to prewar rates. That spring Mellon would write in a circular to bankers, "The people generally must become more interested in saving the government's money than in spending it." Mellon, like Coolidge, did not like to be quoted, but reporters heard him warn that the United States had no "stallion dollar." The dollar did not automatically proliferate; growth was not automatic, as some assumed. The groundwork had to be laid for it to do so.

The other cabinet members were shouldering equally heavy loads. Selling off the navy's oil reserves made sense from both the fiscal responsibility and the efficiency points of view. The man in charge there, as interior secretary, was a westerner who understood oil and gas better than anyone else: "Petroleum Fall," the former senator Albert Fall of New Mexico. There was a new department, the Labor Department, and therefore a new cabinet member. While the Hardings' Airedale, Laddie Boy, waited outside, the meeting proceeded briskly. Harding let it be known that the cabinet might meet twice a week while undertaking the initial work of legislation. Harding inquired as to protocol of publicizing such meetings. Hughes, the senior presence, let him know that such decisions were up to him. At the same meeting Harding let his colleagues know that Senator Lodge would stay in the powerful position of Republican Senate leader.

In the Senate chamber Coolidge had his own work cut out for him. There was much to learn that differed from the rules and the protocol of the General Court. There were plenty of people around to help him, including an assistant to communicate the basics. In the House the speaker was Frederick Gillett, Amherst class of 1874, who had nominated him in Chicago. Senator William Dillingham sat before him in the Senate, the same Dillingham to whom Coolidge had addressed the tentative job application back in 1895. Dillingham had fought hard to restrict immigration in the past and plotted yet more immigration law now. Lodge loomed. The role of the president of the U.S. Senate was in many ways weaker, just as Coolidge had discerned in the old days reading at Adams House, than the role of Senate president in Massachusetts. Here in Washington the president might break a tie but not create one. What's more, Coolidge quickly realized that this time careful study of rules might be fruitless. The Senate was more clan than forum. Rules were there to be broken. Though the new amendment had become law, most of those present had been chosen by state legislatures, and the Senate remained their club. "The Senate would do anything it wanted to do whenever it wanted to do it," he would say. Small wonder John Adams had called the vice presidency "the most insignificant office."

As the weather warmed, the McLeans' estate off Wisconsin Avenue proved a crucial refuge. Mrs. McLean took it upon herself to see that Coolidge improved his golf game. The vice president had no more desire to golf now than he'd had in the days when Northampton friends had sought to lure him to the Warner Meadow Golf Club, but golf he did. Mrs. McLean noticed that he golfed in suspenders and said not a word until the seventh hole. She teased him about his suspenders; he attempted to tease back, but his tease fell a little flat. "Your dress is wet in the back," he said. "Think you ought to know it." Because the McLeans invited them, the Coolidges came back; Coolidge improved until he became, as Mrs. McLean commented, "quite a fair golfer."

In some ways it was turning out to be a good time for the Coolidge marriage. In Washington, they were together as a couple, going out, far more often than they had been in all the years of politics and small children. In Washington, Grace's beauty was appreciated. Coolidge was not frugal about Grace and even scouted the shops for dresses. Emily and Frank Stearns helped out with additional garments. Grace thoroughly enjoyed meeting all the new people, especially the eminences. She met not only Madame Marie Curie but also every sort of diplomat or European dignitary. Several she found hard to take. After Margot Asquith mocked Harding's education, someone reminded her that Harding had gone to college. "Oh, your American colleges," the Englishwoman had shrugged. "She should be called Ego, not Margot," Grace wrote. Grace sat with Coolidge during his stomachaches and hay fever.

Yet as the weeks passed, life in Washington did not become easier. Unlike Harding, Coolidge was not penetrating. The initial curiosity over Coolidge was crystallizing into incomprehension. Men in Washington were not yet ready to mock the *Social Register*. "The elections of 1920 imported into the city of conversation as one of its necessary consequences perhaps the oddest and most singular apparition this vocal and articulate settlement has over known: a politician who does not, who will not, who seemingly cannot talk. A well of silence. A center of stillness," wrote Edward Lowry, the journalist who had first noticed that for Coolidge, a coat and a pair of tails performed the same function as overalls.

Life at the Willard also proved purgatory. The rooms cost $8 a day, compared with the $32 a month for Massasoit Street. That ate into the vice president's salary of $12,000 a year. Mrs. John Henderson, the widow of one of the framers of the antislavery amendment to the Constitution, was said to want to donate a residence on 16th Street for the vice president. That would have been convenient, but her gift was only a rumor for now. There were other costs beyond the monetary in Washington. Children did not really fit in here, though their sons came back for school breaks; Grace and Calvin, Jr., popped corn on the small electric stove. The elevator man, Harry Vogel, let the boys run the elevator, sometimes for an entire evening, when their parents were out. But it did not make sense for their boys, now teenagers, to live with them in the small hotel apartment, nor did it make sense for John and Calvin to travel back and forth on the Colonial Express from Northampton to Washington.

This last reality disappointed the Coolidges especially. "It does not seem as if it would pay to have them here," Coolidge wrote his father morosely when the question of whether the boys might return again soon came up, "when they have only been away four weeks, as it would cost about $100." The Coolidges considered leaving their sons in Northampton for the next year and asking Colonel Coolidge to come down and live with them in Hampshire County. But the Colonel did not seem enthusiastic about leaving Plymouth Notch. Uncertain about his sons' future, Coolidge temporarily assigned Stearns to look after them during a Northampton school holiday and escort them to a play at the Hollis Street Theatre in Boston. The subject of the play was the life of Abraham Lincoln.

Adding insult to injury, the Coolidges, great animal lovers, found they could not have pets, either. Cats, like children, did not fit in at the Willard. One evening Grace found a tiny consolation in the form of a family of mice who had found their way into the room. The mice returned often, and Grace fed them bits from the hotel table. The other visitors might criticize her etiquette, but in the mice, "I firmly believe that I thus acquired some friends in Washington who would have pronounced me the perfect hostess." Coolidge, for his part, read. Beside his bed was a table stacked with texts on tariffs from Morrow, as well as the Constitution and other documents.

Meanwhile, Harding simply barreled forward, even calling an extraordinary session of Congress, which meant that the usual March or April finish of Congress would be delayed. Shortly Congress passed, and Harding signed, the budget law. The law featured several interesting attributes. The law unified the budget, just as promised, so that the executive could review the budget all at once before his signature made it law. Beyond that it gave the executive the power to review a budget already passed. He might, if he had the patience, then demand that departments spend less than the amount first appropriated to them. In addition the law created a research and enforcement office for the executive, a Budget Bureau. "Good for Mr. Harding," wrote *The Baltimore Sun* in approval. "Mr. Harding is a good natured man but he is showing the Republican elephant that on occasion he can use the goad as effectively as Mr. Wilson used the whip on the Democratic donkey." Harding followed that legislative coup with a coup of an appointment: the first head of the new Budget Bureau would be Charles Dawes, the flamboyant general who had snapped a Hell-and-Maria at Congress when lawmakers had questioned wartime outlays. Now Dawes committed himself with theatrical zeal to the new cause, reducing the budget.

On June 29, Harding showcased his new bureau and its new director at a large administration-wide event at Albert Fall's Department of the Interior. With Coolidge beside him on the platform, Harding himself opened the budget event, pulling the whole room in to share the drama of their negative endeavor: "Fellow workers: I do not think there has ever been a meeting like this." The war, the spending, the out-of-control budget had to stop; the scope of his project was nothing less than a total change in direction: "We want to reverse things." With enormous fanfare, Dawes then spoke, promising to make government fairer, cleaner, and, above all, less expensive. Dawes's primary challenge boiled down to a simple phrase: army surplus. The government must divest itself of all the extra goods and departments the war growth had generated. Dawes was even creating a Federal Liquidation Board, an entity whose entire purpose was to shutter government and military offices. He was already boasting that he could shave a percentage point or two off that year's budget. To dramatize his austerity, he carefully furnished his new office with secondhand furniture and his own two brooms. The new budget law was already making a difference. Harding was not just saying "no," he was inventing a whole theater of "no." The meeting was just one of a series; they would take place every six months from now on.

In the areas where Dawes confronted trouble, Harding backed up his budget deputy with a series of executive orders. Harding also used an executive order to transfer the petroleum reserves from the Navy Department to the Department of the Interior. Fall had a plan to realize great savings for the country. The war debt that hung over the country could be lightened through the sale of natural resources in Alaska, if properly handled. Then taxes need not go up. Fall saw a whole future in enterprise if only America's energy could be unlocked. "All natural resources," he preached, "should be made as easy of access as possible to the present generation."

In that active period, Harding made several other advances that earned admiration. The first was to call a naval conference to reduce the number of battleships in the world, so that the great waste of war did not repeat itself. The Washington Naval Conference, as it was formally known, instantly became the number one topic in Washington. Again, Harding had managed to reward the city while doing as he pleased; hosting such a conference, underscored, as almost nothing else could, Washington's power and élan. One of the demands of the disarmaments conference was ferocious entertaining by the White House. Over and again, Harding hosted groups of men to haggle over the details of the treaty.

Nor were the treaty participants the only White House visitors. The Hardings invited all parties in all negotiations to the White House; Harding smoked, chewed tobacco, and drank. Mrs. Harding, called "the Duchess" in her crowd, was always there, playing poker or tending drinks. "She asked me upstairs at the White House and in what had been my father's library I was shown every known gambling device and drinks galore," wrote Theodore Roosevelt's daughter, Alice, her sense of propriety finally offended. The Harding White House featured "the general atmosphere of a convivial gambling saloon," all in the era of Prohibition, she noticed.

When Harding didn't celebrate at home, he was with what was known as his golf cabinet (usually including Senator Frank Kellogg of Minnesota) or his poker cabinet. The latter group was a larger group that met in parties of eight at the White House or at the homes of friends and included Attorney General Daugherty, Secretary Fall, and sometimes General Dawes, General Pershing, Charles Forbes, and, from out of town, Harry Sinclair, the oilman. Even Mellon attended the poker cabinet sometimes. The poker cabinet averaged twice a week at the White House with another night elsewhere; the games started after dinner and went to twelve thirty but usually not much later. This was hours after Coolidge retired.

The Harding pace exhausted the White House, including the chief housekeeper, Elizabeth Jaffray, who had been there in the days of serving lobster Newburg to the Tafts. She rode about in her brougham collecting food for the Hardings and their hundreds of guests. Harding, however, seemed to enjoy it all. The only concession he sought was in the menu. Germany itself was still under suspicion, but not German food.

"Please, Mrs. Jaffray, couldn't I have sauerkraut and wiener wurst?" the president asked her often. "You know men do like that." Mrs. Jaffray was charmed. From the housekeeper with the wurst to Senator Lodge, Washington understood Harding and liked him.

June passed, July came, but Harding's special session showed no sign of ending. On the last day of the month of June, the Senate voted 60–4 to confirm William Howard Taft as chief justice of the United States. "Men do what I tell them," Coolidge had once told his father, but here, clearly, they never would. Some of the policies under way were ones he could not sanction. Jobs were finally proliferating. Yet Herbert Hoover was convening an enormous unemployment conference that seemed an invitation to expand federal spending. There was no escaping his own weakness in the Senate. Some of the lawmakers seemed to live to upstage him. Senator Oscar Underwood, a veteran lawmaker and the minority leader, chided Coolidge because he had failed to completely state an issue presented, the practice of the Senate. Because the Republicans had a large majority in the Senate, even the tiebreaking authority of his post mattered little.

In that early period, Coolidge also committed an error that would haunt him. The Harding administration did not want to support large farm subsidies—another new area the government seemed to want to enter. But some progressives among Republicans and Democrats were in favor of them. Coolidge promised the progressive George Norris that he would call on a Democrat who supported such subsidies. Then, perhaps remembering his loyalty to Harding, Coolidge decided he could not and left someone else in his chair, the unhesitating Charles Curtis, to recognize someone from the administration's side of the debate first. Norris deemed this slipup by a new Senate president an unforgivable breach of trust. Photos of action inside the Senate chamber were rare in those days. But the senators had what they sought: the equivalent of the new vice president looking shifty. Even in Massachusetts, there was some criticism.

There was an additional rub. In the Senate Coolidge might be the titular leader, but Lodge was the true ruler, "a figure apart," as the writer Edward Lowry described him, as senior senator to whom others, including Harding, always bowed. An intellectual snob, he presented himself as a poet rather than a lawmaker. Alice Roosevelt Longworth—now married to a congressman, Nicholas Longworth of Ohio—noted that Lodge had disdained even Wilson, the former president of Princeton, as not in his own league. Every senator wanted something from Lodge; an easy way to get it was to pander to him by poking fun at Coolidge. Pat Harrison of Mississippi, a leading Democrat, was particularly attentive. "One of his favorite indoor sports," wrote a colleague of Harrison, "was to rise and comment, with sarcasm tinctured with good humor, upon some reported act or utterance of Vice President Coolidge." Lodge was always there to ignore or challenge him directly, to remind him why he was in the Senate and not in the White House in the first place. He was the bane of Coolidge's existence.

Grace's Lodge was Florence Harding. The first lady's tyranny was a tyranny of the weak. She had been a single mother in her youth and had endured the ferocious snobbery of senators' wives when she had first come to Washington. That rendered her compelling. But now that she had risen to the position of first lady, she exploited her status. She took out her anger and her poor health on others, summoning mediums to talk with the dead or raging through the White House that someone had robbed her when she misplaced a necklace. Mrs. Harding told Alice Longworth she had a little book from her Senate days in which she had noted the names of those who had snubbed her. Now she could get her revenge. Toward Grace, Florence Harding evinced a mixture of friendliness and envy. Florence Harding had her own color, "Harding blue," to match her eyes. But as the other women noted, every color looked good on Grace.

Coolidge's general sense of frustration was so great that he could not always contain his anger. It came out in a series of articles he worked on in this period for *The Delineator*, a women's magazine published by the pattern publisher Butterick. Coolidge delivered the first manuscript just after his inauguration; indeed, the letter he wrote when he submitted the article was, he noted, the first he had penned on vice presidential stationery. The articles were remarkably incoherent and hostile, attacking a section of New York public school teachers as a branch of the Socialist Party; Coolidge quoted *The New York Times* as saying "the teacher's desk has been made a soapbox platform" for politics at one high school, DeWitt Clinton. "Enemies of the Republic" detailed the work of the Intercollegiate Socialist Society at various women's colleges. "Smith Seems Sane," read one headline, perhaps a reflection of the Coolidges' acquaintance with Smith and the fact that its president, L. Clarke Seelye, had hosted Coolidge's acceptance ceremony there the summer before.

The attitudes in the article reflected the times and also criticisms he and Morrow were fielding about Meiklejohn's Amherst: that Amherst was impious, that its faculty and guest lecturers featured too many progressive instructors. But the articles did not sound like Coolidge, who made a point of avoiding public statements in areas he hadn't studied: "I am not qualified to discuss educational matters," Coolidge had written once to Morrow when refusing an invitation to dine with the president of Colorado University. Writing of Coolidge's criticism of Vassar, Professor Burges Johnson of that school noted accurately, "It tends to bring about just the opposite result from that for which Mr. Coolidge has notably fought. He does not believe in government by emotion, and yet such an article containing innuendos based on insufficient evidence tends to let loose a flood of emotional antagonism to this college, and colleges in general."

As July moved forward, legislating became an outright contest of wills between the Senate and Harding, with each side pressing to outlast the other. Here the president again demonstrated stamina. Just after July 4, Coolidge's birthday, Harding went back to Capitol Hill, his old haunt as a senator, with Frelinghuysen, his golf ally, to reconnect and recruit allies. "The president's arrival was a surprise to Capitol employees," commented *The New York Times*. The gesture worked. The senators were glad to see Harding, their old brother.

Bonuses for veterans dominated all budget talks. The veterans were so numerous, and, in 1921, so many of them were still in need. Yet the general program for all that the lobbyists sought would reverse the direction of the savings campaign. Harding made his own case, arguing that the bonus would "virtually defeat the Administration's program of economy and retrenchment." The lawmakers were not ready to accede. So a few days later, Harding went back to argue against the bonus yet again. A new commitment to such a large group would be a "disaster to the Nation's finances." Lawmakers should get back to work on tax cuts and other measures. If Harding and Coolidge could fend off the senators and congressmen, the pressure from the veterans might lessen. Thirty-eight states had already created some form of bonus or pension for the veterans, and it seemed important to Harding and Coolidge to keep these responsibilities at the state level. Another principle Harding and Coolidge aimed to guard through their opposition to the larger bonus plans was insurance: here, they both believed, the appropriate role for the government was to broker or create private life insurance policies for vets; the government already had an office in that business, the War Risk Bureau.

Yet again, Harding's boldness yielded results: the Senate voted 47–20 against the great bonus. But the vote came at a cost to peace in the Senate chamber. On July 15, Grace Coolidge took her two sons to watch the proceedings on the bonus bill. It was the first time they had observed their father preside over the Senate. The boys were quiet; the reporters noticed that one read a book as the bonus debate droned on. That same day the Coolidges visited, Senator Porter McCumber of North Dakota, a Republican, began a heated debate with Senator Reed of Missouri, a Democrat. A crowd surrounded them; Coolidge pounded his gavel. In less than a minute each senator was ready to do battle. "Only the most polished finesse," the *Los Angeles Times* reporter noted, "prevented Senator McCumber and Senator Reed from engaging in a 'fistic encounter.'"

When the dust settled, Coolidge could see that Harding again had struck a masterful compromise. There was no big and permanent bonus commitment for Washington that year. But the funds would flow to those who required disability benefits and rehabilitation. The concession was the abolition of the old War Risk Bureau, with a new Veterans Bureau to replace it. Colonel Charles Forbes, his old friend, would move over from the War Risk Bureau to head the new Veterans Bureau. The bureau and other related funding represented a significant outlay: $600 million or $700 million a year instead of $300 million. It would build hospitals in fourteen regional offices to serve the vets all over the country.

Later in the summer, the Coolidges made it back home for a brief visit, only to realize how much they liked New England. "I love every stick and stone," wrote Grace. In Plymouth, Massachusetts, they hosted the president and Mrs. Harding at an extravaganza commemorating the anniversary of Plymouth Rock. It felt good, too, to be able to host some of Washington on their own turf or in their own waters. In Northampton, they found themselves turning to local projects. That summer Coolidge, using the vice presidential privilege, appointed Thomas Plummer, the boy who lived in the other half of their two-family house, to West Point; Thomas's father was the Northampton High School principal and a Democrat. The Coolidges also decided their charity would be helping the Clarke School for the Deaf. The Coolidges and Dr. Alexander Graham

Bell announced a plan to raise $500,000 for the struggling school. It was a rare move for Coolidge because it opened him to the appearance of compromise: a vice president who invited friends to give to a certain charity might appear susceptible to bribery. There Coolidge's sense of gratitude for once overcame his caution: it was Grace's charity, and he wanted to thank Grace. In that period or soon after, he picked up the patronage pen himself and signed a letter to Stearns regarding Grace's old school. "Some time ago I became a Trustee of Clarke School for the Deaf of Northampton," he wrote. He invited Stearns to join a national board of directors. "It is my privilege formally to invite and personally to urge you to accept a place," he added. "I know the value of the work of the school." The letter was typed out on his Northampton stationery, as though he were still a small-town lawyer, but the heading above the date read "Washington." But he did not send the letter.

In Washington that fall, the Coolidges again tried to advance. They had a routine now. On Sundays they sat in a pew not too near the front at the First Congregational Church. Coolidge "liked it because it was not too far forward and he could enter and leave without being overconspicuous," the minister, Jason Noble Pierce, noted. At the suggestion of Joel Boone, the navy doctor, the boys were boarding at Mercersburg Academy, a school ninety-odd miles outside Washington. In the rush of Washington, the school made sense for the boys; the distance was in any case less than that of Boston to Northampton. Calvin, Jr., was writing his first essays. In one, he wrote, "At my Grandfather's house in Plymouth, Vermont I can go to the woods anytime. Sometime I hunt for spruce gum. It grows on the side of a spruce tree and can be cut off with a knife. I like to go nutting." Another recalled his sickness as a boy: "When I was five years old I caught pnewmonia. I was taken to the hospital. I missed about two months out of the first grade, but I passed all right." Grace took dancing classes at the home of Mrs. John Henderson, the doyenne who had mooted the idea of a house back in 1920. She coaxed her sons to dance: John was willing; Calvin, Jr., less so. She found stores she liked, such as the Martha Washington candy shop, which was also favored by Evalyn McLean. Grace became a fan of the Harper Method of hairdressing and adopted a distinctive hairdo, the horseshoe marcel.

Coolidge's challenge remained supporting an administration with a temperament wilder than his own: Harding's crowd seemed constantly to find itself in little scandals. Across the country, papers were noticing that Harding and his party were particularly liberal with post office jobs. Normally only the best-qualified candidates were recommended for postmaster jobs. President Harding changed the policy by an executive order and allowed the postmaster general to select among three candidates, a shift that gave his post office cover for picking political favorites. "We all know that politics is politics and we are not finding any great fault with the Harding administration of applying the policy of 'to the victors belong the spoils,'" wrote the *Tribune* of Fairfield, Iowa, after the local post office job was handed to what it deemed an unworthy Republican. "But we would like to have the Administration come clean and not indulge in these little pleasantries about the merit system."

Soon there was even more trouble for Harding, especially in the area of the Veterans Bureau. The bureau was expanding at an alarming rate; in the Bay State alone, Forbes was building a giant government hospital, with capacity for 500 tuberculosis patients and 500 additional patients. The veterans, still unemployed, were finding they were not getting what was promised, and that the prices in the contracts for the buildings Forbes was constructing seemed inflated. The Harding recklessness drove Coolidge to an inspection of his own acts and conscience. Second thoughts about even the Clarke School overcame him. On top of his note to Stearns, which he had not sent, Coolidge now appended a note on a piece of stationery of the U.S. Senate, in which he expressed his reservations. "Do not consider this a request from me," he wrote tersely, "Probably you better say no."

As it turned out, Coolidge was assigned to represent the administration's conscience in public very soon after, at a giant convention of the American Legion at the end of October planned for Kansas City, where 83,000 citizens had given $2 million to build a memorial to the veterans and casualties of the Great War. The stakes at Kansas City would be high. Every senator who had failed to vote for the bonus bill was receiving angry mail. Senator Medill McCormick, whose wife was friendly with Alice Roosevelt Longworth, received one such blast from the American Legion's Theodore Roosevelt Post 627. "We are now frankly giving you an opportunity to take a positive open stand disregarding party and presidential orders, and show us if you are our friend or foe." Yet more veterans were claiming that the Veterans Bureau was not fulfilling its specific mandate to serve the wounded. In fact, Forbes was being brought to the convention specifically to address those concerns.

Frank Stearns and Coolidge traveled to Missouri together by train. The trip took a day and a half, and was tentative up to the last minute; a rail strike was threatening schedules of the Santa Fe line. Coolidge was such an unknown in Kansas City that the *Star* got his name slightly wrong, listing him as "Calvin F. Coolidge." But there were those among the vets who knew him, especially vets from New England; Governor Hartness of Vermont was in attendance.

Bunting and other decorations adorned Union Station in Kansas City when they arrived, a welcome organized by Harry Truman, whose haberdashery in Kansas City was struggling. It fell to Coolidge to represent the federal government before restive veterans. Like his speech before the American Federation of Labor that September day in Greenfield, this speech was difficult, aiming to please a group with which the administration profoundly disagreed. Coolidge was forthright: "Your glory lies in what you have given and may give to your country not in what your country has or may give to you." The vets liked Coolidge and invited him to stay.

Back in Washington, Daugherty was running a very popular campaign of clemency and forgiveness for citizens jailed during the Red Scare. He was preparing to commute the sentences of several dozen prisoners held in penitentiaries for war crimes, evidence of the administration's generosity. This was a Republican way of showing respect for decency, freedom of speech, and dissent. At Christmas, Debs did walk free, and Daugherty and others carefully publicized the news.

But by December there were more Harding stories. Without regard to how this looked in a time of austerity, Daugherty was also brazenly insisting that Mellon accept appointments of Harding loyalists at Treasury. The important office of assistant treasury secretary in charge of internal revenue and customs—tariffs—had gone to a key Harding man from Tacoma, Washington, Elmer Dover. Mellon, the secretary, found he had little say over the matter. Coolidge's reservations found expression in his speeches, especially when he was away from Washington. "Shall we use our power for self aggrandizement or service?" he asked that December at an address in Montpelier, his father's and grandfather's old haunt. "It has been the lack of moral fibre which has been the downfall of people in the past." In the state with the Mountain Rule, he was reinforcing the concept behind the rule, character in leadership. After the speech, Colonel Coolidge approached Earle Kinsley, a leading Republican in the state, to say, "Calvin wants to see you in his room." Kinsley asked Coolidge whether Harding would be a candidate for renomination in 1924. If not, they would nominate Coolidge. "No president can decline a renomination," Coolidge said. Then he added an ominously final-sounding plan: "I will serve my term as vice president and then return to Northampton to resume the practice of law."

Stearns too was disappointed in Daugherty, and sensed something off about the Justice Department. Prices were down. At R. H. Stearns, silk stockings with lisle tops and feet had sold for $2 in November; by Christmas the firm had dropped the price of the stockings to $1.85. Yet Attorney General Daugherty at the Justice Department was just launching a new campaign against stores for their prices. On December 22, just before Christmas, Daugherty announced a federal investigation of prices for food, fuel, and clothing. Daugherty's department would do its part to drive down prices by spotlighting "unconscionable" profiteering; it was time the Justice Department set out to "get these smart fellows." Stearns desperately sought an interview while in Washington, and failed to get one. Denied his interview, Stearns returned to Boston and exploded. Why was the administration not more solicitous of commerce? "I am sorry that I did not have a chance to talk with the Attorney General," Stearns wrote to Coolidge. "While his Secretary was very courteous and intelligent about the matter, he was buried deep in papers." Daugherty found time for Debs but not for business.

The point was a larger one, Stearns wrote. What infuriated merchants was that they had hoped for more freedom in peacetime, but here Daugherty was perpetuating wartime price management, and that was itself unbearable. "The Administration should realize that for several years merchants were rasped almost beyond their capacity to stand it." Seventy-five-cent veiling, a topic that had animated the committee the month before, preoccupied Stearns. "When they were making some of their investigations here two or three years ago, they investigated one of our neighbors and they discovered a piece of veiling which was being sold for 75 cents a yard. The store when asked what it cost, said it cost 10 cents, but it was bought in a miscellaneous lot of goods on which the store had to make desperate efforts to come out even." Perhaps, wrote Stearns of Daugherty, "he can differentiate between robbers and respectable people a little more carefully." The cynicism of the Harding crowd also struck Earle Kinsley, the Vermont Republican. A vacancy fell open in the Circuit Court of Appeals for the Second Circuit, which covered New York, Vermont, and Connecticut. The Vermont bar wanted to recommend the appointment of John Redmond of Newport, Vermont, and delegated John Sargent, the state attorney general and friend of the Coolidges, to make the case to Daugherty. It was Vermont's turn, the Vermonters felt: Vermont had never had a judge. But all that Daugherty asked was "What did the Vermont delegation do for us at Chicago?" The Veterans Bureau continued to spend and that year was set to outgrow the navy in size, with a budget of $455 million in 1923.

Grimly, Coolidge determined to focus on service. The economy was finally picking up. For the year 1920–1921, Ford had sold more than 1.25 million touring cars; this was the first twelve-month period in which sales had topped the one million mark. Dawes was moving forward in the same dramatic fashion. On February 3, 1922, Dawes went before a thousand officials, again with several brooms, to dramatize Harding's original commitment to sweep Washington clean and his own determination to continue rationalizing the still considerable inefficiency of government. This time his emphasis was not on budget numbers but on redundant purchases. With one broom, Dawes pounded the floor of DAR Hall: "There is your broom that meets navy specifications. And"—another broom—"here are brooms that don't meet those specifications that sweep just as well." The navy had sinned by buying new brooms rather than taking 350,000 army brooms that would have done fine. Dawes bragged that Mellon handled the intrusions of his inspectors well: "Secretary Mellon is a businessman. His fur didn't go up or his back arch when my coordinators came in."

Dawes was claiming that his work would lead to savings of a full $2 billion; the savings in another eighteen months would be $3.5 billion. If enough was spent on help for veterans, and the disabled were taken care of, and the economy continued its recovery, then Dawes's enterprise might be worth it, for the unrelenting pressure to create a permanent payment system for veterans, a great federal pension, might abate.

If not, the Dawes budget work was in vain: the Congress would only add back in what he cut. Lawmakers from both parties were wildly scrounging about for ways to finance a bonus; a tax increase seemed inevitable. On February 16, Stearns telegraphed his two cents on the bonus from Room 730 of the Hotel Touraine. "From any point of view believe it is a mistake," he wrote, but "if it must be then sales tax least objectionable." When Coolidge discussed taxes with Clarence Barron, he did not discuss whether there should be a tax increase; he discussed the difficulties of passing a tax increase: "How we are going to raise the taxes, I don't know." There were always other challenges. Grace maintained her rule of no politics in public. That January, however, Mrs. Harding, perhaps inadvertently, managed to position Grace to violate it. Unable to attend a meeting of the National Women's Republican Club, the first lady asked Grace to substitute. Grace found herself reading a message from Mrs. Harding that called upon women for "party loyalty, conviction and devotion." This document was, the papers commented, "the first political manifesto by the wife of an American President." It was an embarrassment for the Coolidges.

Sensing that Coolidge was in a funk, Stearns wrote to him frequently and even, in one letter, unconsciously promoted the vice president to chief executive. Writing on January 20, 1922, to let Coolidge know of some praise Coolidge had received from Wirt Humphrey of Chicago's Hamilton Club, Stearns reported that the club members "were very much pleased to meet President Coolidge." In the same letter, Stearns went on to assure Coolidge that Humphrey had heard of Vice President Coolidge and "repeated suggestions that he will be the logical candidate for President after President Harding has served his eight years." Stearns commiserated with Coolidge for his various setbacks but then reminded him, in case Coolidge had forgotten, that neither of them had sought the vice presidency for him in the first place. Later he chided Coolidge, "I came away from Washington quite a little disturbed by your statement that you were getting suspicious of everybody." He went on, "It makes me a little sick at heart that you should not get much more comfort out of your success." The only one who could destroy goodwill toward Coolidge, Stearns wrote, was Coolidge himself. "I cannot imagine any way in which even you can destroy it unless you persistently for years make folks feel that you are not interested in them. I know you are. Let them know it."

Now it was Coolidge who exploded. If expressing interest where he had none was the price of success, it might not be worth it. "Your letters all received," Coolidge shot back. "I do not think you have any comprehension of what people do to me. Even small things bother me. But that is no matter. I can't go to New York for Mr. Mott or anyone else. I have been there *eight* times." The senators noticed that he dined alone and with his face to the wall. The ladies' magazines praised Grace in order to blame Coolidge. "Heaven only knows how much the Coolidge family needs her leavening," commented the *Woman's Journal*, the periodical of the American Woman Suffrage Association, noting that Coolidge presided over the Senate "like a sphinx over Egypt."

Over the course of the spring, Coolidge's mood did not improve. That April also brought a Gridiron dinner, a ritual press event at which the newspapermen entertained the government and grilled the politicians. The dinner took place at the Coolidges' hotel home, the Willard. It was a mark of the recovery that this year the coal strikes were not even a subject at the dinner; the event's planners found the topic too old to address yet again. The same night, a fire roared through the Willard and the rooms were evacuated. When Coolidge tried, quietly, to reenter, one of the many guards asked him who he was. "The vice president," Coolidge answered and was allowed to move forward until someone asked, "Vice president of what?" When Coolidge replied that he was the vice president of the United States, the guards sent him back safely behind the barriers. They had mistaken him for the vice president of the hotel.

The price of their status, having it or lacking it, was becoming clear to all the Coolidges. Around this time, the president's son Calvin wrote a poem that captured the family ambivalence about Washington. The title he gave it used the same word Stearns had used: "Success."

Success, O magic word, Success!
How much you mean to happiness
Men seek you over e'ery land,
But scanty few have you in hand.

Men slave for you and with life pay
If they can clutch you for one day
You are the subject of their prayers
To you they give their thoughts and cares

Men say untruths for you alone
And by foul means you're called their own
Yet rest not till their dying day
Because they grasped you in such way.

Grace preserved the poem, typed on the stationery of the Willard.

Still, the spring of 1922 was the Coolidges' low point. They were now beginning to derive some comfort from the sense Coolidge was not alone in his struggles to promulgate quality policy in Washington. Mellon was struggling with plans for tax simplification and also with the Harding gang's plants in his own department. The secretary prevailed in a skirmish when a Mellon loyalist, Internal Revenue Commissioner David Blair, squeezed out several Harding supporters. One Harding man was C. C. Childs, a former Yale football star who had competed in the hammer throw at the 1912 Olympic Games. Mellon's staff suspected that Childs and a colleague had removed privileged documents from the office when they had left. Blair sent the Secret Service after them. Furious at being followed, Childs pushed a Secret Service man against a tree and punched him unconscious. There were rumors that Elmer Dover would back Childs up and bring the fired men back. But Mellon, after calling on Harding at the White House, confirmed that the men would not be reinstated.

Each hour that Mellon spent on politics was an hour away from cleaning up after the war, itself a never-ending struggle. Congress had created a debt commission to collect money it was owed from foreign governments, and put forward a plan for twenty-five-year payment, which foreign governments promptly attacked as selfish. "There once existed a ferocious creditor he was called Shylock," a French senator from Martinique, Henri Lémery, was quoted in *The New York Times* as saying. "Has America, which but yesterday we acclaimed for her generosity and idealism, fallen to the role of a Shylock?"

The great domestic legacy of the war, even beyond the debt, remained the size and waste of government. Out west, one of the navy properties was a great oil field that lay under a butte, officially Naval Petroleum Reserve No. 3 but known as Teapot Dome for the butte's funny shape. Some engineers were arguing that the surrounding private companies were tapping the oil out from under the Dome. The best thing to do might be to grant a concession to drill there; that would both allow commerce to take over the business there and reduce the United States' dependence on oil drilling in Mexico. (Clarence Barron commented often that though New England did not know it, much of its oil came from Mexico.) Granting oil concessions to private companies was like granting a great company the right to operate Muscle Shoals, the dam that had been constructed to produce nitrates during the war. It was important to do this now, Harding and Coolidge believed. If they did not then these sectors might stay forever in public hands.

But the lawmakers were suddenly querying the way Harding went about his commercialization of Teapot Dome. They were realizing that the interior secretary, Albert Fall, intended to lease the valuable Naval Petroleum Reserve No. 3 without putting the project out for bids. The transfer to Interior from Navy had already taken place with the seeming endorsement of all, including the navy secretary and the navy assistant secretary, Theodore Roosevelt, the president's son and Alice's half brother. The early word was that Fall was writing a contract with Standard Oil. By Good Friday, April 14, 1922, *The Wall Street Journal* was serving up a scoop: the Wyoming reserves, some 200 million barrels of high-grade oil, would be leased to Mammoth Oil Co., a company created by Sinclair Oil, the company of a Harding campaign donor, Harry Sinclair. Fall claimed that Sinclair was a good choice, better than the alternative, which was teaming up with a giant like Standard Oil.

Now the Progressives had the issue they had been longing for. Senator Robert La Follette of Wisconsin was moving with alacrity to spotlight the transaction and demanded an investigation of the Teapot Dome concession. The administration hoped that La Follette, who was often pooh-poohed as a mere blowhard, would not find a following for this. Yet the Senate unanimously passed La Follette's resolution while Coolidge watched from the Senate president's seat. More resolutions followed. As Miles Poindexter of Washington State put it, there were two questions hanging over big oil concessions: "Was it necessary for the government to sink wells or to have wells sunk upon its reserve in order to meet an attack upon the oil underneath its own property by which it was being drained? In the second place, are the means which have been adopted by the Government for doing that the proper ones, the best ones, to the greatest advantage of the Government, which could be obtained?" The gas price at the pump was not up especially, but the prospect of profits from gas was even more enormous than people had guessed in the spring, and the markets knew it. Oil share prices in total had risen by a billion dollars since the beginning of the year as shareholders tried to get their part of the auto boom.

In June, Coolidge took a breather from it all and went up to Amherst, where he had, so long before, speculated as a student about the corruptibility of any larger government created by an income tax. His son John was coming nearer to college age. The vice president even spent an hour at Phi Gamma Delta house. At Amherst, however, a general skepticism about the flamboyant Meiklejohn was sweeping the trustees and alumni. Meiklejohn had just spent yet another year in Europe; the faculty resented his absences, and the trustees resented his failure to raise more funds. In the background was the old war issue. "I have heard from so many sources that there can be no doubt whatever Mr. Meiklejohn threw as many obstacles as he could in the way of military training and participation in the war by undergraduates," wrote Harold M. Bixby, a St. Louis banker, adding, "He does not understand the Amherst spirit." Others were concerned with Meiklejohn's attitude toward religion; he was not against it, but seemed to be pulling the college away from faith and toward philosophy or politics. Meiklejohn was establishing classes for local workers in Holyoke and Springfield; that seemed to be pulling the college into the world in a way some of the faculty disliked. There was something disingenuous about Meiklejohn playing at conciliation with workers when union and management seemed ready to go to war.

That summer, they did go to war. In June, the administration won a key case against violent strikers: *United Mine Workers v. Coronado Coal* affirmed that strikers were liable for the damage they inflicted on companies' property. On July 1, 300,000 rail workers walked out, shutting down commerce. The strikes halted the upward trend of business; the strike was taking the recovery hostage. The administration had begun to appoint conservative judges who would be a help in the endless battles between companies and unions. A key judge was James Wilkerson, confirmed recently as a federal judge in Chicago, replacing the progressive Kenesaw Landis, who was doing double duty as a federal judge and baseball commissioner. On September 1, Attorney General Daugherty struck: the administration sought and won a temporary injunction against strikes from Wilkerson, the Harding appointee, in Chicago. It was an example of Harding at his toughest. Gompers was furious; he called the injunction a document that suspended "every constitutional guarantee of free speech, free press, and free assemblage." As for Wilkerson, he was a mere Daugherty "pet," Gompers said. But Harding stood firm: the strikers were wrong, as the injunction said, because they represented interference with interstate commerce. Writs were served across the country to union leaders; they could no longer, after eight weeks, halt work. Later in

September, Judge Wilkerson handed down a second injunction, of stronger power. There Harding, like Coolidge, saw no middle ground.

The Republican prospects for the midterm did not look good. Harding, Coolidge noted, faced a challenge in another area: the veterans. The senators had finally succumbed to the pressure and passed the bonus bill Harding had persuaded them to reject the year before. They figured, as the police had, that Harding would sign it: the midterm elections were close. His veto would certainly lose the party votes. But Harding vetoed. The least Coolidge could do was campaign loyally, and he did, discovering something surprising in the process. In Washington, Lodge still reigned, but the campaign reminded Coolidge of a funny thing: he was more popular than Lodge, who might even lose his seat. To lose Lodge would mean "a loss to Massachusetts in prestige and influence in Washington that might not be regained in a generation," the Republican Club of Massachusetts said. During the campaign they all, including Grace and Governor Cox, found themselves back together at Treadway's Red Lion Inn. At the town hall in Great Barrington, the Republican noted, the enthusiasm for Coolidge was especially strong: "Given Ovation at Rally," the *Springfield Republican* reported. Afterward, Lodge bought the papers and saw the headline. Lodge bitterly tore the paper into pieces. "I wish they would accept me as an institution or a monument this one time," he complained to a friend.

In the end Lodge did hold his seat, but only barely. And Harding's Republicans did hold on to their majorities. But the Grand Old Party leaders found the party had narrowed its lead in both houses significantly; its fifty-nine-seat majority in the Senate dropped to fifty-three. In Minnesota, the isolationist Lindbergh did not win, but Frank Kellogg, a venerable Republican who had endorsed Wilson's League of Nations, a member of the old golf cabinet, was also defeated. Emboldened, bonus fans pushed through another bonus bill, daring Harding to veto. Senator Holm Bursum of New Mexico, a fellow Republican who had taken Albert Fall's seat when Fall went to Interior, led the legislation, which created monthly payments of $72. These payments were not for the veterans of World War I, but rather for veterans of preceding wars and their widows, of whom there were in total about 200,000, all of whom were now able to vote in federal elections. Although this kind of bill did not cover the millions of World War I veterans, it was a wedge; once it passed you could pass another one like it.

The Christmas season neared. Mrs. Florence Henderson, the owner of the wonderful residence, invited Grace to a dance at her house; Grace, who had become a better dancer, was given the honor by Mrs. Henderson of leading a march with Mrs. Henderson's son, John B. Henderson. Bursum suggested that Harding would sign on Christmas Day "a Christmas present from the nation to the veterans." Vetoing this modest-seeming bill would make Harding look like Scrooge. As Harding thought over all this, Mrs. Harding was recovering from a serious bout with kidney disease. There was little time to prepare for the holiday season. The White House Christmas would be simple; each White House employee received a $5 gold coin from the Hardings.

In early January, Fall resigned, a shock to all. Fall had been so popular with Harding and his fellow senators that they did not know how to handle his downfall. The next day, not pausing, Harding vetoed the bonus bill with an unyielding statement. The Bursum bill, he noted, established a precedent of paying veterans, regardless of need, each month. "The commissioner of pensions estimates its additional cost to the Treasury to be about $108 million annually," Harding noted, an outlay that took the country in the wrong direction at a time when each dollar saved was hard won. More important, "I venture the prediction that with such a precedent established the ultimate pension outlay in the half century before us will exceed 50 billions of dollars." The country could not help any one group without helping the other groups.

The cabinet members who had sat around the mahogany table for two years now were concluding two things. The first was that Harding's personal dedication made Harding worth supporting. But the second was that the trouble around Harding now stood a realistic chance of bringing his party down in the next election. The magic they had seen in Harding in those early days had been illusion. Though Harding had seemed to succeed by making "no" sound like "yes," the reality was that he had succeeded with the Washington crowd because he did say "yes," and too often. That was his temperament, to say "yes" no matter what his mind or his party told him. Harding, winningly rueful as always, even quoted his own father at a press conference to explain his troubles. It was good that Warren had not been a girl, his father had said. He would always be in the family way—because he couldn't say no. Among the senators, especially, there began to be more discussion about Harding. What was their former colleague doing at the White

House? Why were there so many contracts given out? James Watson, who represented Indiana, drew his own rueful conclusion. "The simple fact is that my dear old friend just did not like to work.... He simply was not adapted to the place and daily shrank from its exacting and grueling toil." In his choice of people Harding might have squandered the opportunity to complete the steps necessary for normalcy. Alice Longworth, as usual, put it all the most damningly: Harding was not a bad man, she thought. But he was a slob.

That winter, there was more illness on the East Coast. A virus, the influenza—passed through Washington. Secretary of State Hughes and the British ambassador both came down with it. So did Sam Gompers. Even Harding fell ill. The same period brought the death of John B. Henderson, with whom Grace had danced at a party in December. Henderson expired at the hospital after an intestinal operation. Harding came down with the "grippe" the third week in January. While he was recovering, Mrs. Henderson, the lady with the mansion, announced she would honor her son by giving her house, now valued at $500,000, to the American people as a vice presidential residence. Congress needed merely to approve the gift.

As more news of the Veterans Bureau reached him, a fury was finally building in the president. To others, he looked weak—the recovery from the flu seemed incomplete. Forbes went to the White House, and Harding took him by the neck and shook Forbes "as a dog would a rat," as one surprised witness reported. "You double-crossing bastard!" Harding shouted. Forbes headed for Europe, and cabled his resignation. By now it was clear that Forbes had stolen not thousands of dollars but hundreds of thousands, even millions, from the hospital construction. Nicholas Murray Butler, the Columbia president, happened to visit with the Hardings around this time. The topic of the residence came up, and Mrs. Harding, forgetting perhaps that Butler had written the introduction to a book by Coolidge, responded with such a flash that it took Butler aback: "I am going to have that bill defeated. Do you think I am going to have those Coolidges living in a house like that? An apartment hotel is plenty good enough for them." The Senate Committee on Public Buildings and Grounds wrote to Mrs. Henderson to refuse the offer, noting that the maintenance would be $15,000 a year, "and it is the policy of Congress to practice the strictest economy." Mrs. Harding was also sharing her thoughts about Coolidge with others in Washington.

She was thinking they should change the Republican ticket, jettisoning the awkward Coolidge. Her cousin wrote Mrs. Harding that Governor Lowden was a good partner for Harding. "From the present viewpoint Governor Lowden would be more helpful than anyone whose name has been mentioned." The first lady also had a plan for a political makeover: a trip out west, to new territory.

The Senate was hurrying because this year it planned to leave in March; the special sessions were over. In the last days, Lodge, his ego raging, could not resist another insult to Coolidge. It was traditional for the Senate to vote a resolution of thanks to its president when the session concluded. With Lodge close by, Coolidge steered the Senate to the moment. But when the minute came for the resolution to be offered, it was not. The silence was heard throughout the hall. Then Lodge announced that he had nothing further to communicate from the chief executive. Coolidge simply called the sixty-seventh session of the Senate to a close.

It was not the slights but the scandals that gnawed at Coolidge. Of course the Coolidges would not take the residence: the general concern about scandal was too great. The Hardings might plot a new term, but meanwhile their projects were losing credibility before the nation's eyes. The Veterans Bureau was the single biggest new department of the Harding administration, its signature statement. If the bureau was siphoning off public money and spending it, then the entire government case against waste became risible. Here was wrongdoing significant enough to besmirch the administration. Normally a sound sleeper, Coolidge was suffering great bouts of insomnia. Morning came too soon, marked by a blast from Fort Myer on the other side of the Potomac. "How I hate that sunrise gun," he told Grace.

The Harding administration, and with it the whole Republican plan, was stuck. The political capital Harding was spending reducing scandal damage was leaving him too depleted for important projects. If he didn't bring taxes down more and further rationalize government, if he didn't rein in the ICC and FTC, Harding's revolution would abort. A top tax rate in the 50s or 40s was still too high for Mellon. But the evidence that Harding had tired of tax cuts was plain to see in the bond market. Long before, a decision of the Supreme Court in the case of *Pollock v. Farmers' Loan & Trust Co.* had exempted municipal bonds from taxes. When tax rates were high, the bonds had great value, which was reflected in the difference between their prices and those of taxable bonds. The spread between corporate AAA bonds and high-grade municipal bonds tended to narrow when tax cuts were likely. Every time the tax rate was cut a point, the tax-exempt status of the bonds lost value. Now the spread was widening again. The market valued the tax-exempt bonds because it knew Harding was tired. The bonds' advantage was likely to endure. Harding himself conceded as much. "My own best judgment is that for a year or more to come we had better leave the question of modified income taxes alone," he wrote to Otto Kahn of Kuhn, Loeb in April 1923.

Harding was also weakening in the area of credit and money. William Harding, the governor at the Federal Reserve, was the emblem of hard money, and Wall Street believed he had contributed to normalcy. "It was William Harding who 'stemmed the tide'" of inflation, wrote a columnist in Clarence Barron's new namesake magazine, *Barron's*. "Harding's masterful stand in forcing the speculators to unload and calling upon the banks to restrict credit to necessities only" had met with "loud cries from those whose toes had been squeezed." As a result of William Harding's strict policy, the periodical concluded, "That is all history now." Once the markets had understood that the government was serious about tightening money, interest rates came down everywhere. Yet now President Harding was shipping Governor Harding off to Boston, where he would serve in a less important post, head of the Boston Federal Reserve Bank. For the top job at the Federal Reserve, President Harding appointed another friend from Marion, Daniel Crissinger, who had been serving as comptroller of the currency. Crissinger was more likely to lead the Fed banks in loosening money and credit than William Harding might have been; the farmers noted with elation that he owned several head of cattle and hogs, in addition to holding various positions at banks and companies. Mellon was not pleased.

Such issues, however, could be momentarily set aside: Congress had recessed and the Coolidges were heading home. Grace was thrilled to return to her "refuge," as she called Northampton. Once more, she might see her friend Therese Hills and ride around in Mrs. Hills's car, which they had nicknamed "Dulcinea," with their sons. Now Grace realized that in the end it was religious faith, her churches in Washington and Northampton, that helped her find her way through and past

Washington. Before her departure from Washington a friend snapped a reflective picture of Grace in the Willard. Grace autographed it, "Not in rewards but in strength to strive the blessing lies."

From Washington might come reports of trouble. On March 14, Charles Cramer, Forbes's former general counsel at the Veterans Bureau, shot himself with a .45-caliber revolver. In late May one morning at 7:30 the White House housekeeper, Mrs. Jaffray, heard Attorney General Daugherty in a rage; he was unable to get his deputy, Jess Smith, to the phone. A White House usher had to tell the attorney general that Smith had committed suicide that morning.

But in Northampton, these reports were just distant thunder. The real preoccupations were family: Grace's father was failing, and in late April, he finally died. Coolidge canceled a speech and the Coolidges traveled up to Burlington from Boston. It was a sad but calm time for the couple, and the Coolidges finally had a chance to think about their hectic two years in John Adams's "insignificant office." That high society in Washington had not brought Coolidge into its fold was not due to his style of dress, the expression on his face, or his breaches in etiquette, Coolidge realized now. Alice Longworth slighted Coolidge because he represented a threat to the activist wing of the Republican Party and the legacy of her father, Theodore Roosevelt. Mrs. Harding, likewise, was not snubbing them out of pure nastiness; she was protecting her own husband's patronage. Society ladies of the District had often mocked the Coolidges' interest in Vermont and Massachusetts. But the ladies were mistaking federalism for provincialism. By talking about a state and its interests, you reminded Washington that the states had made the union. The Coolidges' difficulties had to do less with personal failings than with a disagreement about what they had come to Washington for in the first place.

At Amherst, the Meiklejohn drama was playing out in disquieting fashion. The trustees, led by Morrow, had polled the faculty and found that more than half supported Meiklejohn's removal. Meiklejohn, Robert Frost concluded, had taught the boys to favor thinking instead of learning. But as Frost, now no longer on the faculty, also noted, "by thinking, they meant stocking up with radical ideas, by learning, they meant stocking up with conservative ideas." It was not, in the end, merely that Meiklejohn's overspending and his appointments were so off; it was that the confidence of the school was lost. Progressives such as Meiklejohn seemed to push and push: one gave in to them only to feel them push farther. The sessions where Meiklejohn met with the trustees were difficult; like Garman, he would not leave without a fight. The Amherst board determined itself nonetheless ready to act. In a battle far more unpleasant than they had imagined, the board now finally wrestled a resignation out of Meiklejohn. The event took place in the philosophy room of the library on a hot night with students and reporters outside observing it all with field glasses.

Meiklejohn indeed did not go quietly. He refused an offer of a chair in logic and metaphysics as a professor and announced he would sever his connection with Amherst after a year's paid leave. He delivered a lecture about Christ and his revolt against the Pharisees, who supported the traditional order, a clear jab at his board. Furious at the board, students set the flag at Johnson Chapel at half-mast and tolled the bell as for a funeral. Three out of twenty-nine full professors and five of the fifteen associate professors quit with him.

The Meiklejohn case was in its way a version of the police strike: an ugly snapshot that had to be endured for what seemed a more important cause. Only this time, Coolidge and Morrow were not even sure they themselves were in the right. The drama was a recasting, after all, of the dramas of the Amherst of their young years. Meiklejohn was what Garman had been in their day, the young Turk who challenged the establishment. That scenario made them, Morrow, Coolidge, and the others, the old reactionaries, like President Gates in their time as undergraduates. At commencement, Coolidge was seated awkwardly, with Meiklejohn between him and the board chairman. Several students hissed and booed when the trustees were seated. The *New York World* described Coolidge: the vice president "glared straight ahead, his cigar long since dead," through the ceremony, and then, after the degrees were given, "hastily turned about and slipped off the dais." *The New York Times* criticized Coolidge as one of the trustees "who could not be said to be in sympathy with liberal doctrines." Walter Lippmann sneered in the *New York World* that Meiklejohn had fallen short because "he is a patriot, but not, by Calvin Coolidge standards, a 100-percenter." The owner and publisher of the magazine *The Nation*, Oswald Villard, printed part of Meiklejohn's final speech in his July 4 issue.

There was nothing Coolidge could do, or ought to say, about Meiklejohn now. He could only talk about what was on his own mind, which he did at a less awkward speech on Memorial Day in Northampton. The American spirit was not about what happened in Washington, he said. If the republic was to be maintained and improved that would "be through the efforts and character of the individual." The American spirit, by which he meant the spirit that lived between men, always survived, and "those who have scoffed at it from the days of the Stuarts and the Bourbons to the days of the Hohenzollerns have seen it rise and prevail over them." Neither Stuart nor Bourbon could compare to the American settler who had started out in New England and pioneered across the country. Coolidge plunged himself into the delicious detail of local politics, visiting the trustees of the People's Institute, the new name of the old Home Culture Club, speaking at the anniversary of a local bank, and talking to the papers about the advisability of constructing another city hall instantly or later on. Coolidge counseled postponement.

The details of the Harding travel plan filtered through to New England, eerily similar to Wilson's plans just four years before. Harding and the first lady would head west, on a 15,000-mile trip, and greet the country, ending up in frontier territory, Alaska. Accompanying Harding would be those cabinet members whose visits might please the troubled workers and farmers of the West. That included the new interior secretary who had replaced Fall, Hubert Work; Agriculture Secretary Henry Wallace, for the farmers; and Herbert Hoover, the Californian. In addition, General Sawyer, the doctor, was along, as was Dr. Boone, his deputy. Harding had wanted to bring the *Mayflower* to transport him from Alaska on the last leg, but his party was so big that the navy ship *Henderson* had to be booked.

On June 21 in St. Louis, Harding was still campaigning for his World Court, listing the "indispensable" conditions under which it might exist. But by July 1, when Harding was resting at the Old Faithful Inn in Yellowstone Park, his plan, which had seemed ready to pass a month before, now faced certain defeat in Coolidge's Senate. Harding, whose health had provided such a contrast to the outgoing president's just two years before, was now ill. Yet Harding, like Wilson, did not relent; he spoke and toured nonstop. By midmonth, when Coolidge went to Waterbury for the funeral of Senator William Dillingham, Harding arrived at McKinley Park in Alaska. The papers reported that Harding had run the locomotive himself for twenty-six miles.

At the end of July, as the Coolidges headed up to Plymouth, there was word that Harding had fallen ill again. On the trip to Seattle, Harding was ill during the night but insisted on going ashore the next day. The Coolidges tried to proceed calmly, though the knots of reporters who began to materialize made them aware that something had changed. The reporters who accompanied them inspected the Holstein cows and watched them try to get at the hollyhocks. The reporters visited John Coolidge's cheese factory and saw the 120-quart tanks of milk that arrived at the cheese factory on Fords. Coolidge, half-smoked cigar between his fingers, showed the reporters around; they inspected the town meeting place in the cellar of a little church and waved appreciatively at the wooded hills, where new spruce, valuable as timber, was growing up. When the reporters moved to depart, Coolidge came after them with a pile of letters he needed mailed from Ludlow.

By then there was regular telephone service in the day to Plymouth Notch, including long distance. But the phone lines shut down in the evening. From Plymouth, the boys were to be dispatched to summer activities—John to a military training session at Camp Devens in Middlesex County, a display by the Coolidge family of their continued fidelity to the idea of preparedness. They were sending their younger son, Calvin, to work again at a job he'd tried before, harvesting in the tobacco fields of Hatfield, outside Northampton. In that way, at least, they could help a local industry, and one that Coolidge, a great cigar smoker, was known to prize.

When their sons left, the Coolidges remained in Plymouth. Disconcerting details that suggested reason for worry about Harding kept popping up in the papers; bouquets of gladioli and asters stood outside the Hardings' five-room suite on the eighth floor of the Palace Hotel. Canaries and lovebirds were brought in to comfort the Hardings, and Dr. Boone stayed in the third bedroom of the suite. Coolidge had not seen Harding since March. Coolidge saw it in the unusual attentiveness of the reporters, whose eyes now followed him like prison guards'. He was asked what he might do "if anything happened." Nothing was going to happen, he told them. Harding was just plain exhausted, Coolidge told the papers, he had "worn himself down, very much as Mrs. Harding did, in the service of the American people." "Coolidge Sure of Harding's Recovery" was the headline he wanted, and the papers obliged. On August 2, the Harding story was still there in the papers, but Harding seemed to be improving. "Harding Gains," read a *New York Times* head-line that day. Coolidge undertook to operate with ax and mallet on an ailing maple that stood outside the sitting room of his father's house; it was the tree under which his mother had sat with her needlework.

The night of August 2, the Coolidges retired early. They were sleep-ing when there was a knock; Colonel Coolidge, not Calvin, answered, and then called up to the sleeping vice president and his wife. When he heard his father calling, Coolidge knew that something had happened; there was a tremor in his father's voice. From Bridgewater had come the news: Harding was dead.

The next moves came intuitively. Coolidge had spoken often about the country's real life taking place on the most local level, and had taught this, as if teaching a class at Amherst. Now he would live it, with the humblest of ceremonies. A telephone line was being arranged so that Coolidge might speak with the secretary of state, Hughes. Congressman Porter Dale, who happened to be campaigning in the vicinity, arrived. Coolidge, for his part, opened the U.S. Constitution to survey what Article II, Section 1 said on the presidency. All that was there was: "In case of the removal of the president from office, or of his death, resigna-tion, or inability to discharge the powers and duties of the said office, the same shall devolve on the vice president." A few lines later was the oath of office a new president needed to take. That was all.

The special phone line was up by 2:30 A.M. Coolidge prepared a state-ment of condolence and sorrow about Harding. He spoke with Hughes, who said the event must be witnessed by a notary. Unlike Justice White, who had not been able to swear Mellon into office in 1921, John Coolidge was still a notary.

The reality of the death had begun to reach the rest of the coun-try hours earlier. A reporter rang Henry Cabot Lodge to get his reac-tion when the news came out late in the evening; the old senator was not pleased to be wakened. While the reporter was making his apolo-gies, Lodge, having pieced it all together, suddenly cut through with his response: "My God! That means Coolidge is president!" The Morrows were seated at dinner with Robert Frost and others at their home in Englewood when a call came. Morrow took the call. When he returned to the table, Frost later recalled, Morrow's eyes were unseeing. "What is it, Dwight?" the others asked. Silence, for a moment. Finally, Morrow spoke: "Calvin Coolidge is president of the United States."

Coolidge may not have been the first to realize the impact of the news, but with the little inauguration ceremony, he was the first to attempt to give the transition from president to president meaning. By kerosene lamplight, before a small group that included his wife and Porter Dale, a congressman, in a small town far away from even the county seat or the state capital, a new U.S. president was sworn in by his father. With the emphasis on the Constitution, on the Bible on the table, on the notary's authority, Coolidge was saying that this time, the presidency truly would be the kind that presided over the old contract between man and man, just as he had described it in his inaugural address of 1921.

The Coolidges retired for a few short hours. At 7:20 A.M., the new president appeared on the porch in a blue serge suit, black tie, and white Panama hat to greet reporters. Before leaving Plymouth they asked the driver, Joe McInerney, to stop in the little graveyard so Calvin could visit for a moment the plain grave of his mother. It was a somber moment but also a quietly optimistic one; even the graves of Plymouth gave him strength. Florence Cilley, the proprietor of the general store, rang all the subscribers of the Southern Vermont Telephone Company on the line to Bridgewater so that they could turn out to wave the new president good-bye.

The driver headed down the steep hill to Plymouth Union, then sped up to twenty-five miles an hour, passing Lake Amherst, through the high hilly hamlets of Vermont and Belmont, whose steeple, people claimed, reached close to God. At Rutland, a crowd of two thousand waited; the chief superintendent wanted to supply a special train, but the Coolidges preferred to take the 9:35.

Soon, John at Camp Devens and Calvin at the Hatfield tobacco farm would know about the change as well. In the coming hours and days, resolve would form in the hearts of each of the members of the Coolidge family: resolve to offer service, as Coolidge had said in that Vermont speech, service above self-aggrandizement. "I want you all to love me and pray for me," Grace wrote her sorority sisters, so that she might do good work as first lady. At Camp Devens, reporters converged on John. John told the reporters that he did not feel any different from the way he had felt when his father had been Harding's vice president. John knew his father would do his best, and John hoped that, in time, that would be good enough.

Both boys, too, would receive fan mail. Calvin would receive a letter from an East Orange, New Jersey, boy congratulating him upon becoming First Boy of the Land. "I think you are mistaken in calling me the first boy of the land," Calvin wrote back, "since I have done nothing." The first boy of the land, Calvin wrote, "would be some boy who distinguished himself by his own actions." A title, an office, had to be earned.

As the train rolled, Coolidge began to write his own plan to earn the office of the presidency. He had to finish what Harding had started, to prove that the war period had been an interlude, to take the country back to a time of smaller national government. The Senate monotony, the hours at the far end of Harding's cabinet table, all made sense now, especially because his family was with him. The presidency was a job for which his whole life had prepared him. That was the message of confidence he needed to convey to a sorrowing country. As Coolidge left Vermont, he put it simply. "I believe I can swing it," he said.

TEN

~~~~~~~~~~~~~

THE BUDGET

Washington, D.C.

THE MEETINGS TOOK PLACE once a week. He scheduled them at 9:30 A.M. on Fridays, before the session with the full cabinet at eleven. That was not really enough time, especially when the cabinet meetings began at 10:30 instead of eleven. He and the budget director actually needed more minutes, not fewer, to prepare if they were going to fend off the cabinet. But for now, Coolidge kept the appointment at 9:30.

Together, the new president and his budget director cut, and then cut again. The cutting differed only in scale from the cutting John Coolidge had labored over so long by kerosene lamp, trying to match outlays with meager revenues from the school tax or the snow tax. Coolidge and Herbert Mayhew Lord, the director, were just two New Englanders, one from Plymouth, Vermont, the other from Rockland, Maine. Still, there was a sense of awe and duty to their meetings. In the president's appointment diary beside one of their early sessions, someone had written in the word "necessary." They might be plain New Englanders, but here they were, hacking back the great corpus of the government of the United States. Over the pair hung the awareness of the federal debt; the payments on the debt were manageable now, but scheduled to explode in coming years. Coolidge and Lord, in counsel with Treasury staffers, set their targets: the debt had to come down to below $20 billion from $22.35 billion. The budget itself should come down from $3.2 billion to $3 billion. The ephemeral budget surplus must become permanent. Once they had truly checked the budget growth, they might lower tax rates. Coolidge added a second budget meeting whenever he could. Even when he and Lord thought they could not cut more, they still cut.

The budget cutting sessions were one way Coolidge sought to earn the office, to put the work in the terms his son Calvin had described in the tobacco field. To Coolidge, earning the presidency meant finishing what Harding and he had started years ago, achieving normalcy. But it also meant protecting the office itself, ensuring that the troubles that had dogged Harding did not permanently damage the authority of a president. "I am going to try to do what seems best for the country, and get what satisfaction I can out of that," Coolidge told Frank Stearns, who with Mrs. Stearns early on was assigned a bedroom at the White House. "Most everything else will take care of itself."

Finishing the work of normalcy or doing what was best for the country might not be easy, though. Lord was General Lord, just as Dawes had been General Dawes, the hope being that a budget director of high military rank would command respect. But by August 1923, the old sense of war emergency was gone, and citizens were as likely to laugh at officers as to heed them, especially after the betrayals at the Veterans Bureau. Voters wanted the federal government to spend, and lawmakers were ready to help. Each dollar Coolidge and Lord saved was a dollar Congress might disburse. Every government spending scandal that emerged eroded the administration's case for economy. To convince the country that the federal government should live modestly, the administration's personnel had to live modestly. Any hint of overspending at the White House would undermine the executive case that the federal budgets must be slashed; any further construction scandals at the Veterans Bureau would strengthen the case for bonus payments, which put cash in the hands of veterans rather than officials. A scant fifteen months stood between the White House and the election, when Democrats might gain yet more strength and lure Republican progressives over to vote with them and wipe out the Grand Old Party. If, say, tax legislation was to pass, it had to pass soon, in the spring.

To succeed, Coolidge reckoned, he must be like Lincoln, a master administrator, dealing with the "practical affairs of his day," as he himself had once described the sixteenth president doing. Coolidge had to pick his battles carefully. Grace and his sons had to stand beside him. "I don't know what I would do without her," Coolidge had written to his father soon after arriving in Washington in 1921. If his family did stand with him, and if all else went well, then, Coolidge thought, he would indeed be able to "swing it."

In those first days, though, it was Theodore Roosevelt, not Lincoln, whom everyone thought of first, and the way Roosevelt had protected the presidency through his exemplary management of the transition after McKinley's assassination. Like Roosevelt, Coolidge needed to prevent any crises and keep the country calm until it had passed through bereavement and he was ready to launch policy. If he was concerned, he hid it. As Secretary Hughes said when he greeted Coolidge at Union Station, "There is nothing to do but close the ranks and go ahead."

A stream of visitors greeted Coolidge and Grace when they woke at the Willard that first Saturday morning in Washington. The newsmen hung about the hall, accosting Stearns and anyone else they could collar to see if they could elicit a tidbit of news. All of the guests, officials or press, had to be assured, whether they liked it or not, that for the moment policy would not change. That fall, just as in Roosevelt's time, a great coal strike threatened, and therefore Coolidge received Samuel Gompers for a brief meeting. Immigration was their topic, but it was the strike, of course, that was the real issue. The postmaster general, Harry New, was in for a visit even before Gompers; Coolidge told him to "continue right along in the same old way." Roosevelt had managed his transition without a great disruption in the stock market; Coolidge needed to do the same, even though Treasury Secretary Mellon was absent in Europe. The new president promised Mellon's emissary, Parker Gilbert, that not much would change, so that Gilbert was able to cable Mellon the same day that he had had "a good talk with the President" and that Coolidge was "absolutely sound" on "tax revision, soldiers' bonus, and the agricultural situation."

Other callers at the office included Jason Noble Pierce, the minister at the First Congregational Church—the church had invited Coolidge to join, and now, Coolidge announced, he would. Sometime that first day Coolidge had seen General Lord; he had also planned a second meeting, for a week later.

That morning at the Willard, Coolidge managed to shut out the mendicants for a moment and found time to do the most important thing: write out a declaration of a national day of mourning for Harding. The senators had loved Harding and had shown him that by refusing to override any of his five regular vetoes. Americans had loved Harding too. They did not know much about his past and did not care to. How he had died, from an aneurysm or a heart attack, did not matter. However Harding had transgressed, they now forgave him. "Betrayed by friendship is not a bad memorial to leave," Will Rogers wrote in his column. The funeral train rolled east day and night from San Francisco to Washington, but the trainmen found that the darkness did not diminish the crowds: a total of 3 million people showed up at the stations. Thinking of Harding, Americans like Coolidge thought of Lincoln, McKinley, and Wilson, so quiet now in his house on S Street, and reflected that the presidency carried its own curse. Those who had known Harding's good intentions, who had seen him shift, were the most distraught. Eulogizing Harding on the radio, Charles Dawes broke down at the thought of the death of his dear friend. The presidency truly was, as Pierce preached to his congregation on the first Sunday they returned, a "man-killing job."

Accompanied by Chief Justice Taft, a man Coolidge was coming to respect, and other members of the cabinet, the Coolidges traveled out to Ohio for Harding's funeral. In the sweltering Marion heat, Attorney General Daugherty fainted. Mrs. Coolidge stood by Mrs. Harding and Coolidge by Taft. "She is very nice," Taft wrote to his wife of Mrs. Coolidge, underscoring the words. There were other formalities, including one at which he hesitated. Daugherty, the attorney general, insisted that Coolidge take a second oath of office. John Coolidge's notary status was not enough to swear a president in, Daugherty said; the man who swore Coolidge in needed also to be a government official. Coolidge took the oath a second time. But he did not advertise the fact. It was that first oath that had mattered.

Meticulous continuity was also Coolidge's aim when it came to personnel. From the first hours he made it clear that he would retain Harding's cabinet. A clean sweep was tempting, but to Coolidge continuity seemed more important. His decision, for continuity, was one of the most difficult of a lifetime. The Washington Post owner Ned McLean, an emblem of the Harding crowd, pressed for a visit in those early days. On August 21, Coolidge wrote to McLean to explain his position: "I was sorry not to have you call before you went away, and trust you will come in at once on your return. What I am anxious to accomplish is the support for the policies of the administration that will carry them on to perfection. In fact, that is the only thing to which I want to give any consideration." He kept Hoover at Commerce and John Weeks at the War Department, even though his Massachusetts crowd was not the same as Coolidge's. Henry Wallace, a progressive, kept the Agriculture post. Daugherty, the attorney general, would stay, and so would Edwin Denby, the navy secretary. Hughes agreed to stay, and that was a relief. Mellon arrived in the third week of August with a resignation letter in his pocket, but he and Coolidge talked, and Mellon forgot to take the letter out. As he left, Mellon remembered and pulled out the letter. "Forget it," Coolidge said.

Even when it came to the smaller choices, Coolidge punctiliously opted to keep things as they were. The Coolidges asked Harding's doctor from Ohio, C. E. Sawyer, to stay on, despite wide rumors that the doctor would leave with Mrs. Harding, the patient who had brought him to Washington in the first place. Boone, the navy man who served as Sawyer's deputy, would stay with them in service on the *Mayflower*. The White House housekeeper, Mrs. Jaffray, would keep her post. With each employee, the Coolidges underscored the need for as little change as possible. "I would like, Mrs. Jaffray, for everything to go on just as it has in the past," Grace told the housekeeper.

At 6:15 on one of those early mornings at the Willard, Coolidge walked out to discover Edmund Starling, Harding's Secret Service man, who was reporting for service. Starling had taken only a single day to recover from his president's death and the ride on the funeral train. "Good Morning, Colonel Starling, I've been wanting to see you," Coolidge said. "I want you to stay with me during my administration." Then the pair took their first walk together, down F Street, toward the Washington Hotel. The photographers were already there—that was one distinction between the presidency and the vice presidency, the unceasing attentions—but after posing, the pair went to the Martha Washington candy shop, which Grace favored. Only once did Coolidge slip up, and only slightly, with his continuity message. The White House usher, Irwin Hoover, had served decades, as Mrs. Jaffray had; he was known universally as "Ike." Just as he had told the others, Coolidge told Hoover, "I want you yourself to keep right on as you are." But then, after describing the family desire to keep the public from the second floor, where they had crowded in with the Hardings, Coolidge had added something else: "I want things as they used to be, before." And Ike, looking at Coolidge, knew that by "before," Coolidge meant as in Wilson's day, not Harding's.

Continuity required patience. George Christian, Harding's secretary, had pushed Coolidge to move over to the executive office, and on August 13, Coolidge sat down at the big mahogany desk. But Mrs. Harding stayed in the White House residence even after the funeral in Marion. Rather than cause a fuss, Coolidge split his time, working when he could at the White House and staying with Grace at the Willard. As the days mounted, the head of the mail room at the White House perceived that the result of two presidential offices was that "in a few days complete chaos had been achieved both at the Willard and the White House executive office." Yet even when pressed again, Coolidge would not relent. "We are going to get in as soon as we can," Coolidge simply told the press at their August 21 conference with him. In this strange interregnum period, Coolidge found comfort, and even humor, in humility. One early morning in the Willard bedroom, a sound woke Coolidge. A strange young man had broken in and was going through his clothing. In the morning light, Coolidge could see that the burglar had taken a wallet, a chain, and a charm. "I wish you wouldn't take that," Coolidge said. "I don't mean the watch and chain, only the charm. Read what is engraved on the back of it." The burglar read the back: "Presented to Calvin Coolidge . . . by the Massachusetts General Court"—and stopped dead in shock. He was robbing the president. It emerged that the burglar was a hotel guest who had found himself short of cash to return home. Coolidge gave the burglar $32, what he called a "loan," and helped him to navigate around the Secret Service as he departed.

When Mrs. Harding finally departed for the McLeans' and the White House lay open, Grace, for the first time, lost her nerve. "Just now it occurred to me that I would begin my letter here in the only home I have now in Washington, take it with me as I go and finish it in that great White House on Pennsylvania Avenue," Grace wrote her Pi Beta Phi friends on the day of the move. "There is so much that even I am bewildered." The Hardings' Airedale, Laddie Boy, still patrolled the premises. Someone had placed a black ribbon in his collar. Grace described herself as "Alice in Wonderland or Babe in the Woods." It was all confusing: the White House in this period maintained a staff of eighteen to serve guests, whose entertainment was funded by the administration. But the feeding of the staff, many of whom lived in quarters in the White House, had to be covered by the salary of the president.

The Coolidges took one bedroom, but Grace also claimed a large room as a sitting room, bringing in Mary Lincoln's famous rosewood bed carved with grapevines and birds. The twin beds that had been the first couple's beds before were for Calvin and John, who, the hope was, might have more freedom than they had had at the Willard. Grace placed them in another large room that had once been Alice Roosevelt's. There were tennis courts at the White House laid in by the Roosevelts, and the boys could play there. Just recently, the tennis champ Bill Tilden had played an exhibition game for the Hardings. Here, finally, was a place where the family could have pets and pianos. Laddie Boy would go to a caretaker whom Mrs. Harding had selected. Soon, Grace told herself, they would get a new puppy. Grace found her own comfort in the ability to place a time limit on her new service, writing her old friends of the White House, "which must now become home to me for a year and a half."

In the office Coolidge found Harding's chair was decorated with a black crepe ribbon to memorialize the absent chief; he received a new chair but changed the room little, keeping a steel engraving of Lincoln that Theodore Roosevelt had left behind. Stearns was his first caller, just as he had been at the State House in Boston. Coolidge, Starling quickly saw, "was not particularly proud of being president," in the sense of being vain about it. Coolidge walked around quietly, touching things from time to time and smiling to himself; he still wore the suspenders of a Vermonter, and that made him a quaint sight in the great corridors. Nonetheless, Starling also saw, Coolidge was not afraid; he slid into the office naturally. After all, the pediments over the doors in the office were not so different from those at the governor's office in Montpelier. The foyer of the Memorial Continental Hall, where the semiannual budget meetings were held, was clad in marble from his own Vermont. Coolidge came up with his own nicknames for the White House staff and cabinet: "Ol' Colonel Starling," "Ol' Man Stearns," "Ol' Man Mellon." He talked about "my navy secretary," or "my car" or "my secretary of the Treasury," Starling noted. The White House staff already had a nickname for him too, from vice presidential days, "the Little Fellow," a reference to the fact that Coolidge was inches shorter than Harding and Starling, who stood six feet tall. But most of the time they referred to Coolidge more respectfully, as "the president." Grace was always "Mrs. Coolidge," or "the first lady." The boys were simply "John" and "Calvin."

On August 13, Coolidge had a second meeting with Lord; they were already falling into a rhythm. On August 14, the new president announced he was hiring an experienced former congressman, C. Bascom Slemp, as his secretary, the equivalent of chief of staff; Slemp was a southern Republican, a rarity, a Virginian who knew his way around the Hill. Now Coolidge was ready—more than ready—to launch his own policy campaign. He would take Harding more literally than even Harding had, to "perfection," as he told McLean.

"Coolidge demands economy in budget," blared a *New York Times* headline that appeared August 15, just so there was no doubt about what the policy might be. As one of their first steps, Lord and Coolidge sent around a stiff letter to all government departments, warning that they needed to remember to spend less—$300 million less in total—than they had asked for earlier in the year. Somehow or other, the budget estimates and spending had to drop yet further; the onus was on any department that veered in the opposite direction, and sought more, to submit a supplemental statement "showing the additional amount which you believe required, allocated to appropriate titles and setting forth the necessity therefor." Within days, just to prove they meant it—Lord, like Dawes before him, was a ham—Lord issued a demand for a cut of $6.5 million, or about one-fifth, in the budget of the District of Columbia. Nor was the District of Columbia alone. To their shock, navy officials learned around the same time that the navy would lose 20 percent of what it had asked for; even naval aviation would be disappointed. The ships the navy expected under the freshly ratified naval treaty would not all be funded. Reconditioning of the old *Mount Vernon* had already been rejected by the Shipping Board as too costly; now it seemed impossible. It was one thing to cut after the war. It was another for a government to cut perpetually in peacetime. "President to Be Own Watchdog," marveled the *Los Angeles Times*.

The extent to which the new administration would prioritize economy became clear at one of the first press conferences, one that Mellon, finally on U.S. soil, was able to attend. Coolidge, more relaxed than they had ever seen him, led his cabinet to a pose outdoors on the White House lawn before a crowd. As the cameras of Fox News and others rolled, Coolidge seated himself in the center chair, and Secretary

Hughes placed himself to the president's right, legs spread out wide. The seat to the new president's left waited open for Mellon. But Mellon was seconds slow to arrive. In that moment, the camera caught Coolidge's eagerness. The presidential eyes hunted for the Treasury secretary. The president's arm motioned. The tap of the hand was swift but unmistakable, invitation and command:

You sit right here.

Mellon wanted more tax cuts, and Coolidge wanted to go along, so long as he could square such a move with Lord's reports on the budgets. But even before Coolidge could strategize further with Mellon and Lord, he experienced firsthand the great challenge of the presidency: unexpected events. In the first half of September, disaster struck in Japan: an earthquake killed 250,000, and Coolidge appealed to Congress for relief. The Philippine Independence Commission was protesting actions of Governor General Wood, Coolidge's old opponent in the presidential race. Anthracite coal men did strike, and Coolidge, while backing up Governor Pinchot of Pennsylvania, did not intervene. In the end Pinchot made a settlement that included a wage increase. But the miners had not won the prize they had sought: owners' agreement to a closed shop in which only union miners could work.

Still, in those first few weeks and months Coolidge and Lord sustained their budgeting rhythm. The Veterans Bureau under the corrupt Forbes had grown alarmingly, consuming a full $461 million, a seventh of the budget, in the fiscal year that had just ended. Lord and Coolidge saw that the bureau planned a cut of $25 million below the year earlier, but on September 15, Lord announced that the cut should be more like $40 million or even $50 million. In addition, the pair decided to resist the commissioners of the District of Columbia, who had protested the August cuts. General Lord told the District that all provisions for new public works as well as new school sites and buildings had to be omitted.

Meanwhile, Coolidge and Mellon began planning the tax law. Twice Coolidge received the chairman of the House Budget Committee, Representative Barnaby Madden of Illinois, and he also met with the incoming chairman of the House Ways and Means Committee, Representative William Green of Iowa. Green and Senator Reed Smoot of Utah agreed: there could be a tax cut, or there could be a bonus, but not both. Congress was not scheduled to meet until December, a great blessing as Mellon needed the time to structure spring tax legislation. The less time Congress was in session, too, the less time there was to demand new laws. Yet congressmen were after him to call a special session that very autumn. Allen Treadway was still in Congress; his erstwhile pupil from Massachusetts, Coolidge, had risen far above him. Treadway called on the new president to complain that Pinchot's agreement had raised the price of coal by 70 cents a ton or more, which would make for a hard winter in New England; certainly Congress should meet to address this, and earlier than December, Treadway said. But on this Treadway found Coolidge intractable.

One by one, Coolidge's old teachers and antagonists again came through: Gompers again, Lodge, Senator William Borah of Idaho, Alice Longworth. Hoover was in—people were mentioning him as a possible name for a 1924 candidate instead of Coolidge. Frank Kellogg, the ambassador to Britain, also came. All discovered what Treadway had discovered: Coolidge bore no grudges but would not be intimidated. Borah wanted Coolidge to lead the country leftward on labor. Indeed the senator's first demand when he met with Coolidge was that he "get rid of Daugherty," the nemesis of the United Mine Workers—Coolidge refused. Borah decided to tell the press he thought that Coolidge might well be nominated in 1924 as the GOP candidate "if he makes good," a veiled threat but also something of a vote of confidence.

Secretary Hughes visited several times and wrote down his impressions: whereas he had never found Harding alone, Coolidge was often by himself with his papers and cigar. Hughes was so struck by the difference that he would write down what others had merely discussed: Harding tended to say yes when you went to his office; with Coolidge by contrast the answer was almost always no. Coolidge's nos, Hughes guessed, would stick; unlike Harding, he had the temperament for it.

"The atmosphere was as different as a New England front parlor is from a back room in a speakeasy," Alice Longworth, who was coming to like Grace, would later recall. Longworth mattered; Longworth's husband had just become the House majority leader, a key figure in the tax debate. Tentatively, the Coolidges began to establish their own traditions. They planned to bring a great Christmas tree for the people, a fir to stand at the Ellipse. Middlebury College from their own Vermont would send the fir. The tree would be illuminated in a new way, with electric lights.

Will Rogers mocked the remaining complainers in a column headlined "Will Rogers Wants to Know Why Coolidge Hasn't Settled

Everything—Has Been a Month." Then Rogers listed all the areas in which Coolidge had done nothing: "France and England are about to go to War over how much they owe each other. Why don't he come out at once for the League of Nations and stop this coming war? Babe Ruth was changing the style of bat he used. Yet the president had done nothing. Congress wanted an extra session." Rogers's plan for Coolidge was the same as Coolidge's own: "About the only way I know of for him to make himself solid, after all these colossal failures, is to not only not call Congress now, but not call them at all. I tell you if he did that he would go down in History as another Lincoln."

Once again, Coolidge had somehow won by causing others to underestimate him, to believe that someone else—a party leader, a fortuitously placed friend—had engineered his rise. At the *Boston Herald*, a writer named Frank Buxton penned an editorial titled "Who Made Calvin Coolidge?" It mocked the skeptics by tracing all their claims over the years, going all the way back to the Massachusetts Senate debate, through the police strike and the debate over whether Mr. Lucey, Frank Stearns, Murray Crane, or even Coolidge's mother was responsible. "Who made Calvin Coolidge?" Buxton asked again at the end and finally concluded, "Calvin Coolidge, of course! Give another man those same foes and friends and he might still be as far away from the White House as most sons of Vermont."

The president was set to speak in December, when Congress returned. That would be the moment to launch a tax bill. The recession was over, and revenues were pouring into the Treasury; $300 million, Mellon was reckoning, would be the annual surplus for fiscal year 1924, more than he had imagined. Instead of 58 percent, the top income tax rate would have to go down to 31 percent, a combination of a lowered 6 percent base rate and a lower "supertax," or surtax, of 25 percent. A good share of the rate cuts came at the top of the tax schedule. This was not merely to favor the rich, as many said. The tax rate cuts at the top were designed to favor enterprise. If people got to keep more of their money, they would hire others, Mellon said.

Unlike Lord and Coolidge, Mellon and Coolidge did not meet often; sometimes they communicated by correspondence. When they did meet, they scarcely spoke. Coolidge smoked his fat cigars; Mellon smoked his small black cigarettes. Many affairs preoccupied the Treasury secretary: refinancing U.S. debt; foreign loans; his two children, Ailsa and Paul;

and the recent and painful fact of his ex-wife Nora's remarriage. Still, soon both men began to feel the bond. In Mellon, Coolidge was finding the cabinet member who shared his moral outrage at expenditure. In Coolidge, Mellon was finding a skilled legislator who might help him realize an old dream. Others observed the strength of the connection. People said of the pair that they conversed in pauses.

As he got to know the Treasury secretary, Coolidge could see that he and Mellon came at the question of the budget and money differently. Coolidge believed higher taxes were wrong because they took away from men money that was their property; he believed lower rates were good precisely because they encouraged enterprise, but also because they brought less money. Low rates starved the government beast.

Mellon thought there was more to it all. He believed in what he and a few others referred to as "scientific taxation." Scientific taxation was simple, Mellon's team explained. Most people simply stuck with their arithmetic. They took the new tax rate, multiplied it by the old number of sales, and reckoned their loss. Their arithmetic did not allow for the possibility of more sales. Mellon thought lower rates could yield more revenues. The government was like any business—railroading, for example. Coolidge was well familiar with freight rate schedules, and could compare the cost of transporting hay and grain from the trans-Missouri country to the Great Lakes with the rates that covered similar products when shipped in New England. How did a business decide what price to charge for freight?

The answer was a shipping company always aimed to charge, as the railmen put it, "what the traffic will bear." If the company raised fees too high, people would not use your company or your railroad to ship their goods. And sometimes a big cut in rates brought many more customers. Such a large rate cut would therefore cost only a little revenue. Sometimes you could lower a freight rate and even get more revenue than you had at the higher freight charge. Then you not only made up what'd you lost on paper but gained extra revenue. In any case, what mattered in all such readjustments was the change on the margin. You wanted the price, the freight rate, to be just low enough that someone would ship an additional box or an additional container, rather than choosing to wait another day.

Some Americans already thought more in terms of cars than trains. So Mellon showed how the theory underlying scientific taxation applied to cars as well. Ford Motor Company had reduced the price of Model T's, yet was earning more money than it had before; it was making up on volume what it lost on price. Having laid out his examples, Mellon moved on to taxes: one might cut tax rates and get more revenue, not less. Top rates, the surtax on top of the base, or normal tax, mattered especially. Another way to envision it all was in terms of harvests and Thanksgiving, for which Coolidge was preparing a 1923 proclamation. Commerce was like plants or trees; America's "fruitfulness," as Coolidge called it, might be greater if it were less taxed.

Mellon was imagining a great virtuous circle. The money that flowed when he cut the taxes would enable him to pay off the federal debt faster. Right now, thanks to the hard work of the Federal Reserve governor, William P. G. Harding, interest rates were low. The rates, however, might not stay that way forever; Mellon had to refinance now. Lower interest rates would of course also benefit Europe, whose nations owed so much to the United States. All of these ideas, but especially the idea of growth that threw off extra tax revenues, were relatively new to Coolidge. But, he saw, even some of the progressives agreed with some of what Mellon said. Senator Bursum, the great New Mexico pension activist, actually told *The New York Times* flat out that he thought a reduction in tax rates might not force a reduction in revenue, but rather the opposite.

There was yet more to Mellon's story. Efficiency, Mellon taught, could be improved elsewhere in the tax code. Currently the code allowed full deductions for business losses; Mellon thought only a portion of the losses should be deductible; the traffic of business could bear that, in his judgment. Dividends went untaxed; Mellon wanted to treat them and some other forms of unearned income as taxable, and at a higher rate than wages. States were borrowing at rates that alarmed Mellon, enjoying the advantage of the tax protection for municipal bonds. Money that could be invested in private companies was going to those states. That protection ought to be reduced.

One way was to pass an amendment to the Constitution ending the special tax status of all new municipal bonds, so that cash in the future might flow to private-sector companies. It was important to protect the old bonds because they were contracts, but by doing this prospectively, one could divert capital back to companies. Another way to narrow the spread on bonds was to lower the income tax rate so that the value of the tax break for holders of municipal bonds or old Liberty bonds would be less. All you had to do to start that process was to signal you were serious about income tax cuts, more serious than Harding. Here Mellon was accurate and clever: ending the special municipal bond status was a goal of many of the progressives, including Bursum.

Coolidge was not sure he liked all of Mellon's ideas. But he knew he liked Mellon, who differed little, after all, from Andrew Carnegie or Judge Forbes in the way he thought about capital. Coolidge also liked the way Mellon's mind worked. Mellon, in turn, appreciated that Coolidge did not waste his time, as President Harding had. Coolidge decided he would present the Mellon Plan, as the Treasury called scientific taxation, on December 6, in the president's annual message. Rather than simply transmitting the president's message, as presidents had in the past, Coolidge would deliver the message himself. He and Mellon really would get the law next spring if the speech was good.

But to give a good speech, one had to find time to write it in the first place. That too was proving difficult, for besides senators and congressmen, or cabinet men, representatives of foreign governments also called. Coolidge deemed it the president's job to receive them but found that ambassadors especially ate up time, whether they were his own ministers or emissaries from other countries. October brought the Italian ambassador, his own ambassador to Ecuador or Bolivia, and the Hungarian ambassador. David Lloyd George, the former prime minister of Great Britain, passed through; Coolidge escaped a dinner but did have to meet him. Every session with a dignitary was a session that he could not have with Mellon or Lord. Beyond the reception of the diplomats, there were other obligations to receive people, some of which had not changed much since the days of James Garfield.

On a regular working day, the president shook hands with four hundred people at lunch and sometimes many more. On special occasions such as New Year's Day, the hands numbered in the thousands. The regular meetings with the budget director took hours; Coolidge had also committed to another set of regular meetings, press conferences. His old instinct not to join institutions, he saw, could still help him. Every group he joined promptly exploited the presidential connection in ways that were alarming and sometimes just plain corrupt. Even old friends could not resist exploiting the advantage of knowing a president. After he joined the Congregational Church in Washington, his family minister, Kenneth Welles, at the Edwards Church, could not conceal his glee at the power derived from being able to claim a president in the fold. In a letter to the president, Welles got specific on the power Coolidge's step would give him to get support from congregants: "It is going to give me a grip on some men like Fred Farrar and Judge Field which I never otherwise would have had." A group visiting in early October requested that the president come to New York to speak on November 2 at a memorial for Harding. Half testy, half amused, Coolidge challenged them: "You shall decide for me. Shall I honor President Harding by carrying on his work or shall I speak in Manhattan?"

One of the topics that would have to be addressed in the speech was immigration. Gompers and several other union leaders enthusiastically backed congressional plans to restrict immigration. Domestic workers would confront less competition and enjoy greater leverage with employers. The late Senator William Dillingham of Vermont had been shaping a new immigration law into a system of quotas for regions when he died. Coolidge was willing to go along with restrictionists. "I am convinced that our present economic and social conditions warrant a limitation of those to be admitted," he wrote. But he was not hostile to immigrants already in the United States. And he was especially concerned at the widely supported Japanese exclusion provision that many congressmen hoped to make law. The Japanese government already restricted emigration, and he felt that the Japanese would think that a U.S. ban would cause them to lose face. The Japanese government was miffed at the naval agreement; Coolidge saw no need to add insult to injury. Japan was a growing power.

Coolidge also had to convince voters that no soldiers' bonus was necessary. Even as he drafted his speech, though, Coolidge could see the case for the veterans' bonus getting stronger. The Senate was holding hearings on Charles Forbes's Veterans Bureau, and the reports of impropriety were extensive. At one hospital in Washington, Mount Alto Veterans, a dental aide was even caught stealing gold allocated for veterans' teeth. That was the same hospital where Emmett Rogers, son of one of the White House staff, was being treated. One man, the new director of the Veterans Bureau, General Frank Hines, had been paid $4,800 a year for two hours of work. As evidence of not just thousands but tens of thousands of dollars taken grew, the senators were taken aback. On October 22, Senator Ashurst noted in his diary, "A man with disheveled hair, loose lips troubled eyes and trembling hands appeared before the Committee," shouting that he was there to defend himself. It was Charles Forbes himself. Every dollar that Charles Forbes had embezzled at his Veterans Bureau was another argument for a bonus, which bypassed suspect officials.

Coolidge also had to find ways to get the country past the Harding scandals. After all, if Forbes had been such a crook, perhaps there were others in the administration like him. The senators wondered about their old, respected colleague Albert Fall at the Department of Interior. Ashurst noted in his diary that when he saw Fall, unlike Forbes, the man seemed calm. At least for now. The controversy over the western oil concessions likewise simmered on. Thomas Walsh, the Montana senator leading the investigation of Teapot Dome, was not letting up. There was no reason he should have, for more evidence kept coming to light. On the last day of October, irritatingly close to the anniversary of the armistice, the papers were carrying more incredible news: Forbes's bureau had paid nine times the appraised value for a site in Excelsior Springs, Missouri, and then built a hospital on such shabby plans that no veterans were being served there.

It was hard to know what to say about such theft to groups such as the Spanish-American War veterans, on his schedule for a meeting on November 20. Coolidge took counsel where he could, meeting with Hughes and others. On November 19, Coolidge dined with another key character in the drama, Attorney General Daugherty. Daugherty was defending the authority of Navy Secretary Denby, who was generally under fire for his support of the transfer of Teapot Dome to Interior's authority. One reason Teapot Dome stayed in the news was that Harry Sinclair was now telling the public that production could quadruple to 20,000 barrels a day over the current 5,000 level. Senator Thomas Walsh of Montana was making clear that Fall might have been bribed by Sinclair; now Sinclair was getting his reward. Walsh was going for blood.

The tension of Coolidge's big speech hung over the White House. Coolidge's walks with Starling calmed him, and he was beginning to take Starling's counsel to exercise. Farm boys, who are accustomed to being around animals, tend to walk carefully with their hands close to their sides or behind their backs: animals startle unexpectedly. Coolidge was no exception. Starling taught Coolidge to stride, using his arms, and after a few days, Coolidge did try, putting his head way up and his arms out so far that Starling had to stay a few feet behind. Starling believed he understood his new boss; the Congregationalists of Vermont were not so different from the Presbyterians from the Kentucky Hills. Both prized their independence. What others took for indecision in Coolidge, Starling judged to be just the independent man luxuriating in his freedom of choice. After his walks, Coolidge went to the mail room; if Ira Smith, the mail officer, was not there, Coolidge would park his feet on his desk and read through the incomings; when Ira was there, Coolidge looked for "mails"—he used the plural—from his father.

The first lady for her part did not need to learn how to march. Grace marched naturally, and could go miles in a day, dog and Secret Service along with her. Not only dogs but birds came to her White House; visitors found her communing with birds, cats, and dogs. She found herself conferring frequently with Dr. Boone, the junior navy doctor who had introduced her to Mercersburg, where the boys were studying. With no children of her own in the White House, Grace made other children welcome, including the Boones' daughter, Suzanne, whom she invited for a sleepover in the Lincoln Bedroom. In the morning, the Secret Service man Jim Haley, whom Coolidge called "Ol' Man Haley," played with the girl. Suzanne got Coolidge to smile.

Still, as the date of the opening of Congress and the presidential message approached, Coolidge's temper grew yet shorter. What if it didn't go well; what if the tax plan flopped? The economy of the country mixed in his head with his private economy. The presidential salary seemed enormous, at $75,000. But there were plenty of costs to being head of state, including feeding the White House staff, the task of the housekeeper Mrs. Jaffray. The president applied the same scrutiny to the household budget as he did to the federal budget. Later Mrs. Jaffray described her shock. "The president of the United States for the first time took a personal interest in the actual management of the White House." Coolidge observed that though everyone else drove cars, the housekeeper was still in her brougham, pulled by horses. He noticed that she shopped at first-class establishments, as well, whereas she could be saving. The custard pies did not please him; the corn muffins were also unsatisfactory, and Mrs. Coolidge sent to Massachusetts for a different recipe. Defensive, Mrs. Jaffray tried to point out the savings. The same Prohibition that had taken revenue from Andy Mellon's Treasury actually yielded a tiny serendipitous savings for the White House; wine, an expensive component of state dinners, need no longer be supplied. But

Coolidge did not seem entirely satisfied, and inquired into other areas. Also unlike the other presidents, this one, she noted, "liked at least the privilege of discussing the menus."

Even Grace was not immune to the president's ill humor. Around Thanksgiving, she went to Fort Myer to try riding with the assistant secretary of war. She looked wonderful in riding clothes. But when Grace came back, Coolidge forbade her to go again. "I think you'll find," he said, "you'll do well in this job if you don't try anything new." One Sunday, Dr. Boone came upon the president in his bedroom reading the speech aloud. Coolidge was worried about whether his vocal cords would be strong when he delivered the address. Others also wondered why Coolidge had opted to break with precedent and read the document aloud. The speech would be broadcast across the country, the first broadcast in which multiple commercial stations hooked up to carry a presidential address. The technology added to the glamour but also fueled the anxiety. Senator Watson of Indiana was not enthusiastic about Coolidge, but he appreciated the man's bravery. It was only eight months from the humiliating adjournment at which the senators had chosen not to thank Coolidge. "It really was a bold thing for him to appear before the two houses of Congress to deliver a message," he thought. In addition, of course, there was Coolidge's delivery: Coolidge, by Watson's terms or indeed those of other senators, was hardly a strong orator.

A packed House of Representatives was waiting when Coolidge arrived to speak on December 6 at 12:30. Mrs. Coolidge sat with Mrs. New, the wife of the postmaster general; Alice Longworth and Samuel Gompers were also in reserved seats. "His high-pitched voice reached all parts of the galleries," The New York Times noted. Coolidge set out his goals lucidly. "Our main problems are domestic problems," he said. The federal household mattered most. The budget system was working. He would maintain it. But he would also prioritize new tax law to change the tax system. Congress had to join him. Tax-exempt securities should lose their special status. It was wrong to tax earned incomes, and movie tickets, as the country now did. There needed to be a revision in the progressivity of the code.

By slowing down for the budget, Coolidge had license to supply detail, and to work out, for the public, Mellon's thinking for the first time. If you lowered tax rates, it might sound as though you were losing revenue. But lowering surtaxes, Coolidge said, "will not greatly reduce the revenue from that source, and may in the future actually increase it." To underline the seriousness of his tax message, Coolidge had taken the time to write out a note in his hand, a facsimile of which was then published in the papers, saying that "to reduce war taxes is to give every home a better chance. . . . Of all services which the Congress can render to the country I have no hesitation in declaring this one to be paramount." And the president threw a challenge to the lawmakers: "The country wants this measure to have the right of way over many others."

This speech impressed Coolidge's audience beyond anything it had expected. Some Americans focused on the level of preparation, which betrayed a man far more serious than the one depicted in a joke about the Coolidge presidency, that he was "the accident of an accident." France liked the speech; so did U.S. industry. Though he had not backed agricultural subsidy, a farm regulators' group, the National Association of Commissioners, Secretaries and Departments of Agriculture, found the speech acceptable. State bankers endorsed the Mellon Plan. Even Samuel Gompers of the AFL dutifully offered praise: "Pretty good, as a whole." Journalists began to trumpet Coolidge's possibilities in such exaggerated tones that the editors at *The Wall Street Journal* had to laugh. "It is almost pitiful if it were not so funny to observe the newspapers which a week ago were accusing Coolidge of sitting on the fence and of having no opinions of his own falling over their own feet to join the procession," the *Journal* wrote on December 8. The powerful Senator Watson of Indiana pronounced to all that "his future success was assured." Frank Stearns, energized, declared what the country already knew: Coolidge was running for office and would be the Republican candidate in 1924.

The audience at the House of Representatives noticed that Coolidge's style of delivery was different. Harding had liked to twin concepts; his speeches had rolled along, alliteration following alliteration, like a story or a steamboat upon the Mississippi. Coolidge still spoke artillery style, almost as briefly as he had in the now-famous telegram to Gompers. League of Nations—topic closed. World Court: yes. Bonus: no. Help for disabled veterans: yes. Merchant fleet: move to private ownership. Recognize Soviet Russia: not until it recognized its obligations. In all, the new president telegraphed positions on thirty-three items, including the question of lynching. Congress ought to use its power to prevent and punish lynching, Coolidge said. By the time he was done, Silent Cal had uttered seven thousand words.

The radio, the new medium, had proved Coolidge's friend. On the radio you didn't need to have a strong voice but a clear one. And Coolidge's was clear—it had wire in it, as someone would say later. The next day, the St. Louis station, KSD, telephoned the White House to ask about a small problem: "that grating noise." It had been the rustle of Coolidge's papers as he turned the page. But most impressive of all was Coolidge's boldness. It takes guts to stake your presidency on an issue, and Coolidge had done that with Mellon's tax bill.

Within days Coolidge showed his new strength in two moves. The first was to force the Grand Old Party to make Cleveland the site of the 1924 convention, a show of his new strength in the party. He also took time to place an additional demand on the party: cut back the party platform. He didn't want to repeat the error he had made as a young politician in writing the Massachusetts party plan with all the gifts to progressives. It was wrong to have a platform with too many "catch planks," specific gifts to specific groups to corral votes. Lincoln in 1860 had demanded a short platform, in fact less than two thousand words; Coolidge sought something like that. Length of texts mattered, just as it had in Massachusetts.

Next Coolidge broadcast another speech, this one only eleven and a half minutes: a eulogy for Harding that Coolidge delivered from the White House. Men came and set up a microphone in his study, which was then connected by land wire to WCAP of Washington, WEAF of New York, and WJAR of Providence, Rhode Island. This time 25 million people listened, the papers recounted with awe. The week marked a boom for radio receiving sets, as they were still known. That year only 400,000 families owned radio sets; the figure would shortly move into the millions. The medium seemed to Coolidge a marvelous accident that had just arrived for him. It obviated the kind of endless touring that had brought down Wilson and Harding.

At the Gridiron dinner a few days later, Coolidge's new status was evident. The Gridiron Club outdid itself with a special skit about the endless pilgrim commemorations, "Pilgrims of 1924." In the background, the club placed an image of the *Mayflower*, the presidential yacht for which the president's fondness was already known. Frank Stearns, John Weeks of the War Department, and even Henry Cabot Lodge played pilgrims. Hiram Johnson, Bob La Follette, and William Borah— the rebel Republicans—all appeared dressed as braves. John and Calvin also went, and the club made a point of welcoming them to the ranks of the White House sons. The club had invited presidents' living sons to the dinner; ten were able to attend, including Abram Garfield, Robert Taft, and Richard Cleveland.

That December, the Coolidges, quietly satisfied, began to plan for 1924. Coolidge sought to reduce the number of weekdays he would need to spend with visitors to the White House. He took a count and, noticing there were now six dogs in the White House, wrote his father, "I wish you would ask Aurora if she would not like two or three of them. We also have two cats. We could spare her a cat." Aurora Pierce, the housekeeper in Plymouth, did not, however, necessarily want a dog. The *Mayflower* was a yacht, but he and Grace found utility in it; it became their vehicle for garnering support for legislation in 1924. On December 15, they ignored a chilly wind—it was nothing like Lake Champlain at that season, after all—and took Senator Robert Howell of Nebraska, Senator Peter Norbeck of South Dakota, and representatives Walter Newton and William Green of Minnesota and Iowa, respectively, out on the water and down the river as far as Quantico.

Fog impeded another such trip: the agriculture secretary, Senator Watson, and John T. Adams, the chairman of the Republican National Committee, were held up at the pier with the presidential party to outwait the fog, but in the end the trip was abandoned. Some in the White House were already exhausted by the pace of it all. Slemp, riding with Dr. Boone, confessed that he could handle the clerical work of his job as secretary and he could handle the political work—but not both.

On December 18 came word that the Christmas tree, despite its special handling, had arrived in Washington with one great limb broken; the navy was contriving to fix it. The next day, Henry Ford gave an official endorsement—but it was more like a blessing—of the idea of a second Coolidge term. That left the Democrats, who had supported the idea of a Henry Ford candidacy, in an awkward position. The United States, Ford said, was "safe with Coolidge." There was one other fact that made the holiday brighter: Nicholas Longworth, just elected House majority leader at the beginning of the month, was making it clear that in 1924 he planned to push the tax legislation to a vote before the bonus vote.

The tree going up on the Ellipse, south of the White House, was the symbol of all they had achieved thus far. Perhaps the president might, after all, together with Slemp, manage the Congress and get the legislation he sought the next term. Perhaps some of the challenges might take care of themselves. Every month that a federal bonus was not passed, one state or the other passed some kind of bonus. That, to Coolidge's mind, was proper; it was the states' job, not the federal government's, to take care of citizens. By the end of 1923, nineteen states had found ways to finance the bonuses.

At 5:00 P.M. on Christmas Eve, Coolidge pulled the switch to light the thousands of lights on the Christmas tree. Many members of the cabinet were in Washington, including secretaries Hughes, Hoover, and Daugherty, but Mellon had gone home to Pittsburgh. The Coolidges celebrated alone with Mr. and Mrs. Stearns. In the Blue Room, Grace and their sons put up their own small tree and trimmed it. There were also Christmas carols; several thousand people joined the choir of the First Congregational Church to sing "O Come, All Ye Faithful" and a new tune composed by Jason Noble Pierce, "Christmas Bells." John and Grace joined them. Mrs. Coolidge gave a dance for sixty boys in the blue room, and took a turn with each.

The Coolidges were well satisfied with their first Christmas at the White House, Grace wrote to her Robins, the sorority sisters, "In no sense does it overwhelm me, rather it does inspire me and increase my energy and I am so filled with the desire to measure up to this God-given task that I can almost feel his strength poured into me." Coolidge, too, could congratulate himself that his efforts had been worthwhile; finally he had enough to take care of others. Grace's mother, Mrs. Goodhue, was already living at the Coolidges' house in Northampton. His father was turning seventy-nine that year, and Coolidge thought he might arrange for a relative, Josiah Coolidge, to work Colonel Coolidge's farm so that his father might have a bit more leisure. Coolidge would pay for that. Aurora, the housekeeper, was there to make a home for John. It had taken decades longer than he imagined, but now funds were clearly flowing from Coolidge to his father. To his father Coolidge sent a check from a life insurance policy that represented "20 years of small savings," as he told Colonel John. Father Coolidge received a check of $477.80.

Coolidge's preoccupation with money, the perceptive Starling noticed, was not necessarily hostile: it sometimes was part of affection. Behind the grouch, there was sweetness; if you spent enough time with the man, you could feel it. Sometimes the men went into the kitchen; Coolidge made sandwiches from cheese as strong as a billy goat. If one sandwich was larger than the other, Coolidge would add cheese, or shave some down, to make them even. Starling expressed his admiration for a chief executive who made his own sandwiches. "I have to furnish the cheese, too," the president muttered.

As the New Year approached, Coolidge smelled legislative victory and, rather than relenting, picked up the pace. The exhausted Slemp was dispatched on a trip to the South to recruit conservatives for the Coolidge presidential campaign of 1924. On December 30, all four Coolidges, the Stearnses, and General Lord took another ride on the *Mayflower*. Mrs. Lord was along and so was Alice Longworth, her own status slightly elevated with the rise of her husband to the position of House majority leader.

On January 1, Coolidge and his cabinet marked the opening of his first full year of the presidency by shaking 3,891 hands in four hours; Grace wore a dress of red chiffon and entertained Ailsa Mellon, Mellon's daughter, and others in the Blue Room. Coolidge's first scheduled meeting of the year was with the all-important Mellon on January 3. On January 8, the Coolidges hosted Mellon for dinner at the White House. The more he knew Mellon, the better he liked him. Mellon offered so many insights, including one relating to the time that Lord and he spent cutting and paring the budget. Members of the Mellon cabinet recalled a lesson Mellon had once given them all on sunk costs. The administration had hesitated about the case for renovating an old war plant and had turned to Mellon. Quietly, with many qualifications, he had described what he had done in a similar situation with one of *his* war plants. His advisers had thought about rebuilding, and the investment had already been $15 million or $16 million. Was it better to invest or to "wipe it off," in the accounting parlance of the time, and start over? The latter, Mellon had concluded. "I told 'em to scrap it."

Now, on taxes, Coolidge and Mellon pushed forward. The men told themselves they had the angles covered. The Treasury was readying a plan to publicize the tax problem: a National Tax Reduction Week, scheduled for early April. Mellon, cheered to have the support of such an ally, even planned to market his ideas. Mellon's deputy, David Finley, was pulling together statements by Mellon and the administration into a little book that Macmillan would publish. The regular worker did not pay the income tax, but, Mellon believed, the regular worker would benefit from the tax rate cut. Therefore he titled his book *Taxation: The People's*

Business. The book was remarkable in its clarity, and for what it did not contain: the word "tariff" appeared only once, and revenues from customs were described as "abnormally high." For General Lord that month, Coolidge scheduled six meetings, one the day following the Mellon meeting and five others at 9:30 in the morning. The semiannual budget presentation, which would come on January 21, would provide the valuable final reminder of the government's seriousness and goodwill. After that meeting, they reckoned, getting the law passed would be easier.

There were more signs that the Coolidges were beginning to feel at home in the White House. Grace's sorority sisters at Pi Beta Phi commissioned Howard Chandler Christy to paint her portrait. She posed in a sleeveless red dress with another new dog, a white collie named Rob Roy. Grace was stunning in the dress, so stunning that it gave Coolidge pause. It was one thing for his wife to be his ambassador, another for her to be glamorous; he did not like to admit it, but it irked him to have Grace so available to the world. Did the dress in the painting have to be so red? Could it not be another color? The artist told Calvin the dress had to be red; contrast was important because the red set off the white dog. If contrast was necessary, Coolidge countered, why not dye the dog red?

At Continental Memorial Hall on the twenty-first of January, Coolidge and Lord gave the case for saving their all. Standing before the crowd, Lord reminded his colleagues of their progress. A former newspaperman, he knew that stories lived in details, and he supplied them. Lovingly, Lord rehearsed the savings he had managed to elicit through some combination of coercion and cajoling from the departments. $55,747.41 in telephone and transportation bills had been saved for the District of Columbia in the preceding six months. The federal government had long wasted money paying rail freight for the 55 million pounds of paper that the Government Printing Office used annually. This year the federal government had forced a rewrite of the contracts so that payment included delivery of paper; the use of federal trucks to deliver the paper to the printing sites alone saved $25,000 annually. At Fort Bidwell Indian School, in California, a fire had destroyed the laundry. Indian reservations were a federal responsibility. Instead of buying new equipment, the officers in charge had found a surplus boiler at Mare Island, California, and taken it to the Indian School; other surplus government equipment had been shipped from Camp Lewis, Washington. The coordination had spared taxpayers the bill for new equipment.

Lord also made sure to mark the progress of the great budget cut campaign. Through their cuts they had saved more than $100 million, so that spending would be $3.053 billion, very close to the $3 billion target. The surplus, once ephemeral, was now more solid, at $300 million. It fell to the president to frame it all, to remind the audience of the change. This was the government's sixth such meeting since Harding had signed the budget law; only a short time earlier, the budget law had not existed; this was "a new kind of meeting," as Harding put it. The budget law was a success, Coolidge said. But it was only the beginning. "As for me, I am for economy," he told the crowd. It was the wrong time to fall into extravagance. Mellon and Coolidge could congratulate themselves; the law was almost in their hands. Longworth was proving wonderfully feisty. House Democrat John Nance Garner had a proposal that emphasized tax cuts for the lower group of earners on the tax schedule. Others offered pension plans and made the case, compelling to read, that veterans should come before tax cuts. But Longworth was insisting boldly on the Mellon-Coolidge plan, and feistily. "We have you beaten," he told the soldiers who wanted to put the bonus first.

Longworth spoke too soon. The floor leader had not realized how tough the veterans were or how determined the progressive Republicans. Some attacked the Mellon Plan. Congressman James Frear of Wisconsin took Mellon's idea of prospectively removing the special tax status of municipal bonds and recast it so that the tax break would be denied all municipal bonds, including the billions-worth already outstanding. That, Mellon's lawyers wrote, would be unconstitutional, retroactive confiscation. Senator James Couzens of Michigan argued that there was not enough evidence that Mellon's dramatic plan to halve the surtax of 50 percent on the rich "would be for the good of the country as a whole."

Mellon, stung, stung back. The Mellon Plan, he said, was not to help an individual millionaire; it was to make capital available for all. Now, feeling feisty himself, he made his first error: he went directly after the senator. His Treasury staff wrote to Couzens, "It is reported in the newspapers that all your capital is now in tax-exempt securities, and I have not seen any denial from you. This means, if it means anything, that you pay no income tax."

That was a slip Couzens was too clever not to exploit. By referencing Couzens's personal finances, Mellon had legitimized the discussion of all politicians' finances, especially, of course, his own. Couzens did not squander the opportunity and assailed Mellon personally: "So long as you have entered into the record of my securities, will you please tell us what your securities are; how much you own of each and how you will benefit by the reduction of the surtaxes as proposed by you?" Mellon was working on establishing an independent appeals board so that citizens might get their tax cases heard in a fairer and more systematic fashion. Progressive lawmakers, both Democrats and Republicans, began preparing additional language for the tax legislation requiring their own version of transparency: that the amounts of all filers' tax payments be put on public view at their local post office. Posting the returns of the wealthy in their communities would provide fodder for a million progressive investigations.

Democrats could write tax plans and go on the radio too, as Joseph Robinson of Arkansas, the Senate minority leader, showed with a WRC broadcast of his own critiquing the administration's plan. Perhaps Mellon's idea wouldn't work, said Robinson; after all, this was theory, it could "not be demonstrated that 25 percent is the one and only rate which will diminish investment in tax-exempt securities and commercial enterprises." He went on, "From what evidence does it appear that a maximum of 40% levied on incomes above $200,000 will not have the same effect to a greater degree?" Democrats had their own ideas about tax cuts: The Democrats preferred a surtax rate in the 40s, not the 30s or the 20s. They wanted what the papers described as an "earned income" credit applied especially favorably to farmers and small store proprietors. They wanted to repeal or reduce more of the small consumer taxes that remained. Meantime, of course, the Democrats, were working on the bonus bill, racing to vote it through before the tax law. Robinson knew how to frame ideas in the intellectual contest. The father of tax cutting was not Mellon, Robinson said, but Woodrow Wilson, now so quiet in his home in Georgetown. It was Wilson who had urged changes in the tax system back in 1920.

Very soon after this came word that Wilson had died. Calvin and Grace heard the news while in church and instantly headed over to the Wilsons' to leave their cards. Later, they rode in the funeral procession. Wilson was buried in Washington in the Cathedral Church of Saint Peter and Saint Paul. The death reminded Coolidge that he could not forget his international duties despite the ferocity of the tax fight. The bill to restrict immigration continued to enjoy more support than his tax plan. Its details depressed him. He supported slowing immigration for a while, but remained concerned about the exclusion of Japanese people and the Japanese government's response; it had always monitored emigration itself. Coolidge cared about the dignity of the immigration process; in January, he and Lord had, unusually, spent some extra cash when they ordered an appropriation of $300,000 to improve conditions in the detention quarters on Ellis Island, including adding new equipment for the nursery and kindergarten for detainees, electric wiring for the station, and 350 new beds to replace the flimsy wire-bottomed cots. The World Court was worth fighting for too, and in that campaign Coolidge might find allies among those who opposed the tax bills. After all, fellow politicians were always hunting for common areas with their opponents. While Mellon and Couzens were trading blows, coconuts arrived in the mail for the president: they were a gift from another progressive, William Jennings Bryan. Bryan wrote to ask if Coolidge would consider debt forgiveness for Europe. Coolidge could not agree to breach of contract. That seemed immoral. But he could agree that one partner might in a new contract agree to easier terms; that was what Mellon was doing with foreign debt when he could.

The Harding scandals were also finally closing in on him now. Democrats were alleging that Daugherty had known of a kickback scam that had benefited his late deputy, Jess Smith. Again, Coolidge was torn. Sometimes Daugherty overwhelmed him. But he was loath to unseat someone just because others were attacking him. Hoover and Hughes advised the president to ask the entire Harding cabinet to submit their resignations; then the president need only accept the ones he wanted to. "No, don't do that," Coolidge joked to Hughes. "It might leave me alone with Daugherty!" Hoover, the commerce secretary, thought Coolidge was too slow. "He greatly delayed the removal of Daugherty from the cabinet," he later wrote. At the end of January, Burton Wheeler of Montana, a progressive, found a way to put Coolidge on the defensive, just as Couzens had done with Mellon: he introduced a resolution that the president had to call on Daugherty to resign. Coolidge summoned both Daugherty and Senator Borah to hash it out at the White House. As Coolidge sat in silence, Daugherty and Borah railed at each other. Meanwhile, the Democrats were on the hunt for evidence of Coolidge's complicity in Teapot Dome. Coolidge sought out an Amherst man, New York congressman Bertrand Snell, a classmate of Harlan Stone, for advice.

Each day taken up with scandals was a day lost for taxes. In early February, Coolidge made a crucial decision; he would hire external investigators and separate himself as much as possible. Atlee Pomerene of Ohio, a former lieutenant governor and U.S. senator, and a Democrat, was Coolidge's choice for special prosecutor. In addition, Coolidge named Owen Roberts, an eminent Philadelphia lawyer and Republican, to the case. Fall, who had seemed fit in the autumn, was now reported too ill to testify. It was becoming clear now that the interior secretary had accepted cash via an intermediary. "Not in my time has the country been so startled by the act of a public servant as it has been by the disclosure that Secretary Fall actually took money in a satchel," wrote Morrow. "It has quite demoralized men's thinking."

The next disappointment was Nick Longworth. Instead of holding to the prescripts of the Mellon Bill, Longworth was already crafting a compromise; Coolidge and Mellon feared that the new bill veered too far away from their original plan. On the floor of the Senate, Couzens of Michigan, now sensing victory, remained on the offensive, calling for investigations of the Treasury Bureau of Internal Revenue and also of Mellon. Lawmakers were already drafting their bonus legislation. Slemp was dispatched as an emissary to the Hill to make the case, again, for the administration's rate structure. Coolidge made his own version of a pitch with a February 22 radio speech on George Washington and sacrifice.

Longworth's compromise was worse than the White House feared. Republicans teamed up with Democrats, 408–8, to pass a bill that diverged sharply from the Mellon Plan. The reduction for top earners would be smaller and for lower earners greater. The top rate would be 43.5 percent, a significant drop but nowhere near the 25 percent or 30 percent Mellon dreamed of. Under the House plan, there was enough left over, the lawmakers assured, for a bonus.

Coolidge and Mellon still hoped. There was good news to savor. The House of Representatives gave Coolidge a victory when it approved the sale of Muscle Shoals to Henry Ford. The plant had been so mismanaged in the war and after that it seemed obvious to Coolidge that selling it to Ford was a good idea. But there once again, despite the special prosecutors and the recent resignation of Navy Secretary Denby, the shadow of Teapot Dome was still long. If leasing Teapot Dome to Harry Sinclair had been a corrupt mockery of privatization, then was not the sale of Muscle Shoals to Ford the same? Governor Gifford Pinchot, who had negotiated the coal situation the prior autumn, opposed the sale. Progressives in the Senate found endless reasons to block it.

Coolidge held on by focusing on the tax project. He crammed February with Lord appointments, fitting in five for the short month. For March he scheduled a record number of meetings with Lord: seven. "Calvin is having a hard time but he has a wonderful composure," wrote Taft about the Harding scandals. Morrow thought perhaps Daugherty should resign and Coolidge should move Hughes over to take Daugherty's place. Atlee Pomerene and Owen Roberts won an injunction to stop further tapping of the naval reserves by Edward Doheny; their cleanup effort was proceeding fast enough that Teapot Dome might indeed eventually recede. Coolidge's advisers pointed out that commerce was picking up without prices doing the same. The jobs that had been absent for so long were back. Only one in twenty men lacked employment, not one in ten, or even one in five, as had been the case in some cities during the recession. The real danger now was a shortage of hands. From Mercersburg that spring, Calvin, Jr., would write to his grandfather with an offer to help with the hay crop, "as labor is scarce." The automaker Ford was powering ahead. March 1924 would see a record number of trucks and cars delivered, 206,000. The policy of tight money at the Fed and budget cuts had forced a severe downturn, they could see, but the policy had also made the downturn short.

Both Coolidges looked forward eagerly to the arrival of their sons for spring break in March. Anticipating their arrival, Grace planned four musicales. The boys liked tennis, and the White House announced it would host the drawing for international teams for the Davis Cup on March 17. Calvin, about to turn sixteen, was growing fast that year. John would graduate and was heading to Amherst. The pair had become more sophisticated. Each issue of the *Congressional Record*, complete with all of their father's failures and triumphs, was sent out to Mercersburg, and now the boys talked politics. The school trained the boys to debate, and Calvin was elected to the Mercersburg 15, a leadership group among the students. John showed Grace's ability to appreciate life hour to hour; he danced well and Grace danced him off his feet when he was at home.

Like his father, Calvin had a quick tongue; like his mother, the boy knew how to render awkward situations easier. When the boys' headmaster, Dr. Irvine, visited, he played pool with Grace, the boys, and Dr. Boone. That was a bit of a risk on the Coolidge side, since the Coolidges knew that Irvine, pious, might not approve of such an activity. To make things even more difficult, Irvine played poorly that day. It was Calvin who cheered them all by making a joke of it. "Well, Doctor," he said, "you give splendid evidence of not wasting your youth."

Coolidge himself did not hear the quip; indeed, he was away so much that the White House now had two entourages: his own and Grace's. In Mrs. Coolidge's case that crowd was Mary Randolph, the first lady's secretary, Jim Haley; the Secret Service man; and Dr. Boone. The white collie, Rob Roy, was attaching himself to the president, following him into the office when he disappeared to work. All the other animals followed Grace, who made a life of animals, music, and children when possible.

In April, after her boys left, Grace entertained again: the Pi Beta Phi sisterhood came to Washington to see the White House and praise and serenade their now eminent sister. The portrait by Christy was complete—perhaps too risqué for the president but nonetheless among the most beautiful paintings of a first lady ever made. All the staff noticed that Coolidge could behave oddly at times. Once, in a strange mood, he could not resist placing a foot on the immaculate train of his wife's dress. But everyone also noticed his affection: "She was his queen," remarked Maggie Rogers, a maid, later. With the help of Coolidge himself, Mr. Stearns, and many Washington vendors, Mrs. Coolidge went from one sartorial victory to another. At Easter, the Coolidges hosted Sarah Pollard of Proctorsville, Vermont, Coolidge's aunt, aboard the *Mayflower*; Grace wore what the paper described as a "sand-colored Poiret twill wrap with a dark brown fur collar," matching sand-colored shoes, and a soft gray scarf of tulle and matching gloves.

The pair did come together on the *Mayflower*, which was becoming a true refuge for the family. It touched the staff to see that the president found ways to relax, even to play, while out on the water. Grace knitted; Coolidge donned a special navy cap with a black visor. A navy officer detailed to the ship had purchased it for him at Brooks Brothers, a vendor whose prices Coolidge considered extravagant. Coolidge loved the cap. The navy men who manned the ship, especially Dr. Boone, saw that Coolidge was unfamiliar with nautical routine; to everyone and at every query the president replied, "Aye, aye, sir." They all laughed with their captain.

As the days passed, the scandals and investigations narrowed the prospects for the Mellon Plan. On March 28, Coolidge finally asked for Daugherty's resignation. Coolidge knew that Daugherty would not go quietly, and he didn't. Daugherty warned, legitimately, that by firing him simply because he was under attack, rather than after a conviction,

Coolidge was setting a dangerous precedent. Coolidge now faced the problem of replacing Daugherty as well. "I haven't been able to reach any decision about appointing an attorney general," he told the press at his conference on April 1. "Of course, what I am trying to do there necessarily is to get a $75,000 or $100,000 man for a salary of $12,000." Who that $100,000 man might be the reporters already had a good idea: Harlan Stone, who was now making something like that figure of $100,000 on Wall Street. Stone was quickly confirmed; the White House broadcast his appointment widely. Finally, Coolidge was moving past "continuity."

What unified Coolidge's nominations, the reporters could see, was his emphasis on integrity and honor in the nominee. Generally, Coolidge went out of his way to avoid giving office to personal friends. Stearns was often present, and very welcome, in the White House. But Coolidge never sought serious advice from Stearns, the way Wilson had with his Colonel House. Coolidge clearly valued Amherst, but handed out few spots to Amherst men. At 23 Wall Street, the telephone did not ring for Morrow, though he was, by now, one of the senior investment bankers in the world. Stearns sometimes had trouble containing his frustration at Coolidge's resistance to advice. When Coolidge did choose a man he knew, he did not always consult that man. And once appointed, a Coolidge acquaintance operated alone.

The secretary of labor, James Davis, was angling to find out what the president thought of something. Coolidge said to Starling, "You tell ol' man Davis I hired him as Secretary of Labor and if he can't do the job I'll get a new Secretary of Labor." Stone, likewise, made his own calls at the Justice Department. He shifted personnel around; removed William Burns, the head of the Bureau of Investigation; and curtailed wiretapping, one of Burns's favored tools. Stone replaced him with a name Herbert Hoover's staff had recommended, that of Burns's old lieutenant: the (unrelated) John Edgar Hoover.

Even with Daugherty gone, the tax campaign was not going well. The irony was that the more Coolidge saw of the evidence, the more he saw the logic of what Mellon proposed. "If the tax bill had been passed as it was introduced," he told reporters on May 1, "the country would have seen a large increase in business." Coolidge pointed out at his press conference that "just at the present time there is a good deal of money piling up in banks," money that was frozen, unused. It was personally painful to see Mellon, whom Coolidge was coming to admire so much, become the scapegoat of congressmen. On April 10, the normally stoic Treasury secretary emitted an uncharacteristic bleat of concern. Couzens was not merely firing at him but waging outright war. Mellon wrote to Coolidge that "all companies in which I have been interested have been sought out" by Couzens's investigators. Couzens had even gone so far as to hire a private investigator to look into Mellon's affairs, paid for by the senator himself. In the same letter, Mellon complained to Coolidge that "if the interposition of private resources be permitted to interfere with the Executive administration of government, the machinery of Government will cease to function." Coolidge defended his friend, issuing a public rebuke to the Senate, warning that it had to be held responsible for the disorder it caused with such an investigation.

The assaults on Mellon achieved their desired effect; they distracted the executive branch while the bonus legislation marched forward, indeed so quickly it caught Coolidge off guard. "My Dear Mr. Secretary," wrote Coolidge on April 24, the day after a version of the legislation passed the Senate by a vote of 67–17. "Please have an analysis made for me of the bonus bill with a statement of the effect it will have on the Treasury, and such criticism of it as may occur to your Department. This is urgent." Many lawmakers sought to frame as inhumane those who rejected the bonus plan. The papers reproduced reports that some firms were requiring employees to publicly oppose the bonus. This, Coolidge quickly clarified for the press, was "utterly un-American." There were veterans who felt entitled to a bonus, but there were others who felt such a payment was wrong and jeopardized the future. The Ex-Service Men's Anti-Bonus League argued that the American Legion had "committed the organization unequivocally in favor of a program that the conscience of the thousands of its members rejected."

The only conceivable way to win the tax battle now, Coolidge guessed, was to pour all his time into making political trades. One concession was to go along with the version of the immigration bill that contained the Japanese exclusion language he so detested. On April 19, he told reporters that he hoped for a compromise: "I am attempting to see if there is any way that that question can be solved so as to satisfy those that want to have restriction and at the same time prevent giving any affront to the Japanese Government."

The time given to these battles, however, represented even more time away from his family. John's graduation was coming up. Coolidge badly wanted to pull the family together to attend. In several letters, he tried to get his father to come down and join him in Washington or at the graduation in Mercersburg. Again, his father resisted travel. In late April, just as Coolidge had feared, the Bursum Bonus legislation was passed by both houses, well before the tax legislation was through. This version of the bonus sounded modest—it granted pensions to soldiers of old wars, going back to the war of 1812, but left room for expansion under a trick clause that offered pensions to "certain named soldiers." Coolidge vetoed the bill on May 3, the day after his twenty-fourth meeting of the year with Lord.

Reporters noticed that the president was now forgoing his morning walks to concentrate on work. Sometimes, when Coolidge worked, he could not help thinking of his sons. On May 9, he wrote a letter to his Amherst friend Frederick Allis about John's upcoming time at Amherst: "I need to find him a place to room. I think it would be a little better if he could have a room in a private house. If he is in the dormitory he will have no protection from anyone that wants to come into his room day or night." Coolidge knew Stephen Brown of Northampton through his parents; Brown was going to Amherst as well. Perhaps Allis could find a room for the boys, "a bedroom and study, with running water in the room." Maybe the boys might have the room Coolidge once had at Dr. Page's. Coolidge wrote to Dr. Brown, Stephen's father, to ask about the possibility of the boys' rooming together. On May 13, Grace took Coolidge to the circus to distract him from his concerns. The same day, and with the tax bill not yet law, the Senate sustained Coolidge's veto of that first bonus bill.

But much broader bonus legislation passed in the House and Senate around the same time. Coolidge wrote his veto, leaving only the spaces for the numbers blank. The day after writing Mr. Allis, Coolidge met with Lord and Mellon, who made a strong case against the legislation; all in all the law would cost $6 billion, double what they aimed to spend a year. Coolidge vetoed the House version of the second bill on May 15 and the Senate version two days later. The new law would cost $146 million in fiscal year 1925—not the whole of the amount of the surplus, but a good share of it. In total, over twenty years, the bill would cost $2.28 billion, as Coolidge noted in a veto statement on May 15. There were millions of veterans across the country; once they were paid, they might have to be paid again. Even a bonus bill was not free of administrative costs, he warned. In the bill, Coolidge said, we "wipe out at once all the progress five hard years have accomplished in reducing the national debt.

"We have no money to bestow upon a class of people that is not taken from the whole people," he continued; the individual was going to lose out to the group. This was the point he had been trying to make when he spoke of emulating Lincoln's party platform. The bonus bill, he and Mellon suspected, would kill off the prospect of tax reduction. The same day as Coolidge issued a veto of this second bonus bill, May 15, the House voted 306–58 and the Senate 69–9 to pass an immigration bill that contained the Japanese exclusion measure.

Upon receiving this information, the president took to his apartments with a cold, turning away visitors. Even Longworth and Madden of Illinois, who came over to the White House to discuss the bonus with Coolidge, had to content themselves with visiting Mr. Slemp. Later in the day, his veto of the costly pension bill was indeed overridden by the House. By May 19, the day the Senate followed with its override of the pension bill, Coolidge was not better. Allies he had expected to vote with him had not. Lodge had voted to override as well, in support of the bonus. The *Boston Herald*, stunned at the humiliation to Coolidge, decided to conduct a public poll in Boston, asking for voters to choose among two statements about the new soldiers' pension: "We believe Coolidge is right" and "We believe Lodge is right."

The congestion in his chest worsened. The doctors at Walter Reed Hospital encouraged him to try a new treatment. The scientists at the Chemical Warfare Service had noticed that workers who spent days with chlorine suffered from few colds. They now recommended gassing patients to reduce their colds. Secretary of War Weeks had already tried chlorine gas for his cold and found it beneficial. For forty-five minutes, Coolidge inhaled in an airtight chamber; afterward, he declared himself better. In taking the cure, he strengthened a fad: 146 members of the House of Representatives and 23 senators also tried it. On Coolidge's next trip, he brought Grace, who submitted to the treatment with him out of solidarity; both Coolidges afterward announced that their plan in the future was to "get out in the open oftener." But Coolidge did not feel like going out. Just as he recovered, Mellon's book arrived, proudly published in maroon and gold binding with gold leather. But the plan in the book would not be realized this year. If Congress overrode an immigration veto, he would suffer twice an indignity that Harding had never suffered.

The opposition was quick to crow, not only at the victory but also in mockery of Coolidge's tactic of cutting first. "If the Republicans had possessed courage they would have created a deficit and then we would not have a bonus," the Democrat Carter Glass told a ladies' luncheon in Philadelphia on May 27. The surplus "was just an invitation to the Treasury raiders." In Coolidge's place, he told the ladies, crying crocodile tears, "I would resign." The Republicans' error had been in cutting so much that they had a surplus.

The bad news kept proliferating. Coolidge had to decide whether to sign the immigration bill. He wanted to restrain immigration but was not as great a fan of quotas as Dillingham had been; Coolidge no longer spoke in the racialist tones of the unfortunate articles he had written as vice president. His position now was that he did not like to judge people by their race or creed. Longworth was finally delivering up the compromise he had worked on for the tax bill. The top rate was still high; the Congress had voted to focus its cuts closer to the bottom of the tax schedule. Therefore the law might not encourage the commerce and growth Mellon envisioned. The bill that came to the administration also contained several measures crafted to infuriate the wealthy. One was an increase in the estate tax, a jab at Mellon, who had long fumed about the damage state estate taxes had done to the estate of his late friend Henry Frick. Finally, it contained a section that represented the progressives' revenge against Mellon and Coolidge: citizens' and companies' tax returns would be open to the public. "As soon as practicable," the law read, citizens' names and their tax bills should be "made available to public inspection." No one was quite clear whether the publicity requirement applied to returns for 1923 or 1924, or whether the Supreme Court would uphold this breach of privacy or not. But most legal experts seemed clear that the "Peeping Tom Law," as it was instantly dubbed, meant that the names of taxpayers and their payments would be posted at district offices of the Bureau of Internal Revenue, if not the post offices. Adding insult to injury, the tax legislation cost more than they had planned; Coolidge and Lord would have to redouble their efforts to compensate for the loss.

"The President Should Veto the Tax Bill," prodded the *Sun* of Baltimore. There was simply "too small a reduction of surtaxes." The result would be evident when Coolidge reckoned up his own taxes. Did the 1924 act perhaps even represent an increase for someone who earned, as he did, about $75,000 a year? Under the very loosest interpretation of the diminution clause in the Constitution, no increase was allowed while a president or a judge was in office. Garrard Winston, an undersecretary at Treasury, ran the numbers for him. Under the 1921 law, a man with a net income of $75,000 would pay $13,372 in federal tax; under the new law he would pay $13,145, scarcely a difference. In addition, the new legislation decreased the amount one could deduct in capital losses, so that some people would pay more tax. The great unleashing of capital Mellon had sketched would not come.

The Wall Street Journal made matters difficult for the president by making this an issue of pride. Coolidge had to veto or be humiliated. This Senate was not making law; it was "hazing the president" through his Treasury secretary, it alleged. And there was more humiliation in other bills before him, such as the immigration law.

On May 26, he sat down at a little desk on the White House lawn, bit his lip, and signed the immigration law, appending his own special criticism of the Japanese exclusion component. For years, the gentleman's agreement under which Japan herself had monitored and restricted emigration had allowed the Japanese to save face when it came to immigration, to pretend at least that migration policy was a decision of the Japanese sovereign. Tokyo was withdrawing its ambassador from Washington; the U.S. ambassador to Japan, Cyrus Woods, was likewise retreating, though he claimed his resignation was in part due to the illness of his mother-in-law, who had been injured in the recent earthquake. Coolidge warned that the historic relationship with Japan was now disturbed, and unnecessarily so; instead of avoiding "new ground for misapprehension," Congress had created it.

The same day he signed the immigration law, Coolidge escaped the White House and took a long walk through Washington, betting that citizens would not recognize him. He wanted to try to shake off his cold through exercise. Secret Service men trailing, he crossed through business and commercial districts and even window-shopped, thinking about prices and what he had accomplished. It took a few hours for the papers to catch up with the story.

The greatest shame, he considered, was the tax bill. On Saturday, May 31, he met with both Mellon and Lord. Was the tax cut worth what it might cost the budget? Earlier they had defined "scientific taxation" as tax law that promoted growth by cutting at the top. If the bill was not sufficiently scientific—and by Mellon's terms it wasn't—wouldn't the bill cause the government to forgo revenue? Then government debts in turn could not be paid off. Interest rates would go up. Growth would be more sluggish. The people might get used to larger government. All these possibilities in turn made it likely the administration would never get the budget down to that $3 billion goal. General Lord, whose images ran to the classical, would later talk of feeling like the mythical Greek figure Tantalus, who was immobilized beneath a bunch of tempting grapes; though the grapes hung close, he was never able to reach them. The $3 billion mark was that tempting bunch of grapes for this administration. Each time Lord thought he could get there, something like the bonus bill happened and the government had to spend more, not less.

What's more, when it came to timing, Coolidge and Mellon were trapped. Coolidge had made a point of rejecting special sessions of Congress, on the simple principle that they provided opportunity for more legislation. Activists tended to like such sessions for the same reason; indeed, La Follette of Wisconsin was seeking one now. To repair the bill, however, would require such a session. Even if he did not sign this tax bill, the bonus bill would set them all back. The details of the outlays that the bonus would require were just beginning to come out; $132 million was needed for the first year. Major General Robert Davis of the War Department was estimating that 2,517 clerks would have to be hired to deliver the bonuses to the veterans. A "deficiency bill," a new law, would have to be passed to pay for the costs of the veterans' bonus. That would reduce the surplus for which he, Lord, and Mellon had worked so hard. Mellon was alleging that signature of this tax bill would send them into deficit. Everything was now moving in the wrong direction.

The president took a final weekend on the *Mayflower* to consider it all. With him came a copy of the as yet unsigned tax bill, comments by General Lord and Secretary Mellon, and planks of the Republican platform. Not only was the tax bill unsatisfying; Coolidge's demand that the platform be 2,000 words, like Lincoln's, was also going unheeded. The 1924 GOP platform, at 5,200 words, was not much shorter than the 1920 platform, and several times the length of Lincoln's platform. The president walked the deck for several hours and had the Sunday *New York Times* delivered to him by naval airplane at 10:30 on Sunday. From the *Mayflower*, no word came, but reporters heard that Coolidge had dictated something.

When Coolidge considered the tax bill, though, he saw that disappointment obscured some strong advantages. The tax bill did cut tax rates for many taxpayers. Middle earners saw their base rates come down.

Higher earners paid less income tax in total. That was, to Coolidge, a good thing. It was always good for the government to take less. Most important of all was the future: If he went along with this bill and withstood the humiliation, he and Mellon might get another shot at tax legislation. In Mellon he had found the partner that Harding could not be: the partner with whom he could finish a job.

There was something familiar about the feeling of spring in Washington to him. Over the years, the Senate had beaten him down, indeed, humiliated him in ways it had never humiliated Harding. Yet the country did not see the failure of the tax law: it saw his industry, that Coolidge had tried. It appreciated the budget sessions. Senator Lodge had gone against him yet again in the override of the pension bill, but the *Boston Herald* poll had yielded an astounding result: by a ratio of 250 to 1, Boston voters had endorsed Coolidge on the bonus. Boston understood how much the spending of the war had disrupted, and they appreciated his effort. They appreciated normalcy.

The big powers like Hearst and Ford liked the Mellon Plan, but Coolidge's popularity went beyond taxes. It was the devotion to service that struck people. His ideas and the culture were in harmony. Columbia University's Pulitzer Prizes were awarded during the veto debacles in May. One prize had gone to an autobiography that was largely about the possibilities America offered to immigrants if they assimilated, *From Immigrant to Inventor* by Michael Pupin. Assimilation was also Coolidge's emphasis. Another Pulitzer had gone to Robert Frost, the instructor at Coolidge's own Amherst, for *New Hampshire*, a collection of poems about the virtues of New England. The book included "Stopping by Woods on a Snowy Evening." Though Coolidge was not friendly with Frost and preferred the poetry of precursors such as John Greenleaf Whittier, "Stopping by Woods" and other poems by Coolidge's fellow New Englander kept touching the themes that Coolidge himself probed: honoring commitments, even at the tired end of a day. Yet another prize went to the editorial "Who Made Coolidge?" All his life, Coolidge had found favor by delivering more than others expected; now, in a more profound way that went beyond his law-and-order popularity after the strike, the American people gave him their favor. Coolidge had not won the tax battle, but he had won the battle for more time, even another term as president. The tax idea, if not the execution, had gone farther than it had under Harding, and many important forces appreciated that. The great newspaper magnate William Randolph Hearst let Clarence Barron know that he was especially impressed by the tax plan. Ford approved. Barron's support at *The Wall Street Journal* meant something, too.

On June 2, Coolidge made his great wager: if he stayed around, and ran again, he could yet prevail on taxes. He signed the stopgap tax bill for now, but accompanied it with a strong letter, a declaration of war. The bill, the letter acknowledged, would bring significant relief to voters, especially the 25 percent credit the bill gave taxpayers on the payment for the prior year's tax return. This was a relief, especially because the economy could not forever grow straight up as it had that year. But such credits, Coolidge warned, did not represent true tax reform; they were only temporary measures. It was perverse to raise estate taxes to 40 percent as the law did, to sustain the income tax with a top rate in the 40s and to sustain the tax-exempt status of municipal bonds. Money would continue to flow into tax-favored state projects but not to inventors or entrepreneurs. The publication of tax returns constituted a violation of privacy, sacrificing "without reasons the rights of the taxpayer." Much of the bill was so destructive, he said, as to jeopardize the future of the country. Coolidge channeled Mellon's memos in his statement, in places adding bits of his own: "A correction of its defects may be left to the next session of the Congress. I trust a bill less political and more economic may be passed at that time. To that end I shall bend all my energies."

"All my energies," though, meant that at that very moment, he needed to show he was not giving up. Family would have to wait again. Congress might override his veto, but that would not stop him from vetoing—within days, to make clear he meant it, he vetoed a postal salary increase bill. The sale of Muscle Shoals had stalled, and Ford was not even sure he wanted the plant on the river anymore. But the principle of making the federal budget smaller by separating parts of it to run on their own was still worthy; the post office took in so much revenue that independence was possible. "The postal service rendered the public is good," he acknowledged. He warned, however, that the precedent of an increase for the post office staff was itself troubling: "an organized effort by a great body of public employees to secure an indiscriminate increase in compensation should have the most searching scrutiny." Congress could override some vetoes, but in the future, Coolidge might emulate Grover Cleveland and use the pocket veto, which was technically more difficult but impossible to reverse.

In addition to the postal veto, another waterpower project awaited evaluation: Congress had authorized a dam across the Gila River in Arizona as part of the San Carlos Irrigation Project; the public effort was in part justified in that the dam served Indian lands. Coolidge was inclined to sign the authorization, but only if it was not a breach of federalism; study required days. The day after Coolidge signed it, Grace headed to Mercersburg to attend John's graduation. Mrs. Stearns and Dr. Boone also went. A portrait of Dr. Boone was unveiled during the celebrations, and John received a prize for his essays. Coolidge was not there.

Coolidge and colleagues were mired in the final planning for the GOP convention, which fell early, in June. La Follette of Wisconsin was making noises about a third-party run. Coolidge's only true opponent for the presidential nomination within the Grand Old Party was Hiram Johnson, a California progressive. Hoover, however, fought down Johnson on Coolidge's behalf, and Coolidge won the California primary, securing the nomination.

Still, the convention, so different from that of 1920, constituted a tribute. The president again absented himself, but this time the GOP leadership would run the event on his behalf. Lodge, who had ruled in Chicago, would be scarcely in evidence in Cleveland. The *Hampshire Gazette* was practically gleeful at the victory of western Massachusetts over Boston: "The plan is to keep Lodge out of positions of power at Cleveland. The reason is obvious. The Senate leader, representing Coolidge's home state in the Senate, has been opposing the President." In Cleveland, western Massachusetts men and Vermonters were everywhere. Mr. Lucey, the cobbler, attended, as did dozens of Vermonters wearing brown farm smocks, a tribute to the Coolidge garb, and carrying walking canes made of wood from the Coolidge farm.

In Vermont, Colonel Coolidge was able to hear his son's nomination by radio. It was a convention so confident and confident in Coolidge that it at first seemed sleepy, the result a foregone conclusion; the crowds did not show up. The boys were still at school taking some tutoring though graduation was over. Calvin, Jr., suddenly wished himself home, as his father had so often when he was at boarding school. Dr. Irvine, as strict a disciplinarian as General Lord, did not approve of homesickness. Calvin took a different view: "Some boys leave because they get homesick when they come here. Doctor Irvine says that kind of boys will run all the rest of their lives, but I think he is somewhat too broad in this statement."

Picking Coolidge was easy, but the Republicans were having a hard time settling on a vice presidential candidate. The party first offered the vice presidential slot to Frank Lowden of Illinois. Lowden turned it down, as did Senator Borah, who was woken up in the middle of the night to be felt out in regard to his interest in the Republican ticket. "For which position?" was all Borah would ask. His "no" was another way the Senate was talking back to Coolidge. Finally the party settled on Charles Dawes. The Illinois man was a strong choice, an action man to pair with the reserved Coolidge. Dawes had made his first fortune in utilities in the Midwest; he was a gifted musician and had composed a tune, "Melody in A Major," that would later be heard in a popular song. Dawes also boasted a distinguished career as a banker. It was Dawes's brother Henry, the comptroller of the currency, who was showing why the little western banks were so vulnerable; isolated in their towns, prevented from having branches by states' law, they rose and fell with the price of wheat or corn. In the war Dawes, like Hoover, had distinguished himself by rationalizing supply and distribution. Dawes, the first budget director, was the human symbol of the budgeting program; he had even published a book about the budget. As if this were not enough, Dawes had also worked in Europe on a plan to help Germany repay its debts. For a tax-and-budget candidate, Dawes made a good partner.

It was also gratifying to Coolidge that Dawes appreciated the invitation. Dawes heard the news while in his birthplace of Marietta, Ohio; the next day a crowd surrounded his house and the church rang its bells. Other people might have mocked the vice presidency, but Dawes was overjoyed; he saw this as a chance for leadership: "Just then it seemed to me the greatest office in the world." On June 7, even as the Republican Party was selecting its vice president, came the news that the German Reichstag had voted to support the Dawes Plan; it was another coup for Dawes and sealed Dawes's candidacy. Mellon had a plan to give the vice president greater powers, including supervision of some bureaus and agencies, so that the executive need cover less. This appealed to Dawes.

To find resolve, Coolidge now turned to his family. Toward the end of June, when the boys were finally coming to the White House, Coolidge tried again with his father, inviting him down for his own birthday, July 4. The Central Vermont had a new train he wanted to try that ran from Montreal to Washington: the Washingtonian. If his father could get to White River Junction, he could take the train direct to Washington, bypassing the onerous transfer in New York. His father would have to leave in the middle of the night but would arrive in Washington at 2:15 P.M. As for clothing, Coolidge promised he would take care of that when his father arrived. From Mercersburg, the boys came, after spending some days studying. Calvin was thin—he had grown again and was taller than them all. John was heading to Amherst in the fall.

The week the boys arrived, the Democratic National Convention began in Madison Square Garden in New York City. The Republicans' convention of 1920 looked tame by comparison. The great glooming presence that overshadowed the conference was the Ku Klux Klan: some Democrats wanted condemnation of the murderous group written into the party platform, but others were blocking it; in New Jersey, across the river, Democratic Klansmen held a rival rally. The Klan hung like a cancer on the party's future. That year, the convention and its shadow were nicknamed a "Klanbake." On the floor of the convention itself, there were fistfights over the Klan. Senator Walsh, the leader of the Teapot Dome Investigation, served as the convention chairman, and the challenge was proving tougher than investigations of Harding's cronies. Walsh "whacked vigorously and consistently" with his gavel, the reporters noted admiringly, but his delegates still raged wild. Governor Al Smith enjoyed the home field advantage. Smith's fellow New Yorker, Franklin Roosevelt, joined Smith under the lights, bravely reentering politics after his bout with polio. This was Roosevelt's perseverance. Roosevelt came forward to the podium and nominated Smith as the party's "Happy Warrior." The Smith supporters howled with joy, calling out so loudly that the papers wrote headlines such as "Pandemonium Breaks Loose." At one point Walsh pounded so hard that the head of his gavel flew off the base into the air; the projectile hit a man and gave him a concussion. At first McAdoo, Wilson's son-in-law, whom the Klansmen supported, seemed the most likely winner. John W. Davis, one of Dwight Morrow's partners at J. P. Morgan, was considered likely for the second spot.

On June 28, the Coolidge family marked the progress of the past year with yet another short sail on the *Mayflower*; a new radio installed on the craft would enable them to listen to the Democrats' convention. Coolidge had a speech to write for the National Education Association, and, more important, the semiannual budget meeting of the government was coming up. The Teapot Dome investigations continued: the federal grand jury indicted Albert Fall, Sinclair, and Doheny. The Coolidges now seemed removed from the investigations in both their own minds and those of the people. On June 30, John and Calvin played tennis with Dr. Boone and Dr. James Coupal. The boys played several sets. The family donned business clothes for photographers; they posed with Charles Dawes, the new vice presidential nominee, and then alone, as a family. The photos showed John, now a high school graduate, looking straight into the camera, or frowning; Calvin, Jr., smiled or peered into the distance past the camera.

Later that day came Coolidge's last chance before the summer to frame his achievements and plans, the semiannual budget meeting of the government at Memorial Continental Hall. Grace had a box there; Calvin, Jr., sat behind her. By now the president and his budget director had become an act; they marched through a show before two thousand government employees, an event that was a mixture of sermon, circus, and pep rally.

"We are often told that we are a rich country, and we are," Coolidge told the crowd. But as in the Gospel of Luke, "where more is given, more is required." The president laid down the law for those departments that would not cut. "I regret that there are still some officials who apparently feel that the estimates transmitted to the Bureau of the Budget are the estimates which they are authorized to advocate before the committees." The only lawful estimates were the president's. Finally Coolidge again stressed his theme: "I am for economy. After that I am for more economy. At this time, and under present circumstances, that is my conception of serving the people."

Many in the audience knew General Lord well, not only for his demands upon their department but also for his writings. The newspaperman crafted his reports, especially the one for that summer, to market the concept of savings. A Budget Bureau report told, for example, of the federal government's pencil policy: only one pencil at a time was now issued to government workers. Those who did not use their pencils to the end were expected to return the stub. The economy measure had worked. "Our item of expense for pencils is materially less," Lord's report boasted.

Like Will Rogers at the Ziegfeld Follies or a carnival barker out of Mark Twain, he moved about the stages, telling little stories to convey the scale of the budgeting achievement. Congress did not understand the achievement of saving $2 billion, Lord complained theatrically. The lawmakers were perfunctory, that was all. His own position reminded him, he said, of a schoolboy who had been asked by a demanding master to calculate two times thirteen. When the boy said, "Twenty-six," the teacher replied, "Very good." The boy was miffed. "Very good! Gee, it's perfect!" The same, General Lord told his officials, held for the executive branch's work. That was his way of flattering himself and also the departments. In the box, Calvin, Jr., smiled, appreciating General Lord's theatrics. The national debt was down to $21.25 billion from the $22.35 billion of the year before. The budget was in surplus. That very week Ford had announced that it had just made its ten millionth car.

In the back of all the Coolidges' minds, as they posed for photos or watched Lord, was the Democratic National Convention in New York. Each ballot that went by without a candidate for the Democrats was good for Coolidge; their indecision showed the GOP was not the only party to be divided. The Democrats had already reached a fifteenth ballot without outcome by that night, when the Coolidges got home. McAdoo came in first with 479 votes, and Al Smith came in second. The field was still wide open, and ballot after ballot was announced over the White House radio. It was Calvin, Jr., especially, who paid attention, lounging on the great sofas as he listened to the convention. Calvin seemed tired, Grace and the staff noticed.

On Wednesday July 2, the Democrats voted again and again, without reaching the two-thirds necessary to declare a candidate. By evening the party had completed its forty-second ballot with McAdoo, Wilson's Treasury secretary, leading with 503 and then 505 votes to Al Smith's 318. "Mac, Mac, Mac U Do!" the crowd shouted. John Davis, the Wall Street lawyer, was pulling up from behind. Meanwhile, in Cleveland, La Follette held his own separate convention, of the new Independent Progressive Party, in preparation for a third-party run. The Progressives' platform would include public ownership of railroads, higher taxes for the rich, and the abolition of injunctions in labor disputes of the kind Harding had used. The town of Northampton was preparing a birthday card for Coolidge; 500 citizens signed it. The state of Massachusetts went one better and sent a mammoth card with 20,000 signatures, topped by that of Governor Channing Cox. July 2, a Wednesday, also brought news that Coolidge, Lord, and Mellon had been too modest in their estimates; the federal surplus was a full $500 million, not $498 million, as he had said recently, or $300 million, as they had claimed even earlier.

At the White House, Mrs. Jaffray noticed that the boy Calvin was limping about. "What in the world is the matter, Calvin?" she asked. Just a blister, he told her. Tennis. The same day Dr. Boone materialized again to play; there was to be a foursome with the boys and Jim Haley. But when Boone arrived, Jim and John were playing singles; Calvin, Jr., was not there, and they said he was not feeling well. Boone ascended the stairs to the second-floor apartment. When he arrived, he found him in one of the twin beds; Grace had moved a piano in and was playing for him. Boone asked him whether he had any injuries. "Yup," he replied. Where? "On a toe." Boone made a note: "I found a blister, almost the size of my thumbnail on the third toe, just behind the second joint on the anterior surface." Calvin, Jr., also had a fever of 102 degrees.

Something else rang an alarm: strange streaks ran up the boy's leg, a sign of blood poisoning, infection. Boone telephoned Coupal, the senior physician for the White House. That night, Dawes went to the White House. He himself was still neck deep in negotiations with Europe and planned to leave that night for New York to see Dwight Morrow and Owen Young, both of whom were also involved in the German talks. The dinner should have been a celebration for the conclusion of the Dawes plan, but the president seemed, to Dawes, preoccupied. As Dawes walked out of the White House, he passed an open door. Calvin, Jr., was in bed with his illness, and the president was bending over him, a look of great pain on his face. Dawes, who had lost his own son, suddenly felt closer to Coolidge; Calvin's illness must not be an ordinary one. Others in Washington were now getting the word that Calvin had fallen sick so fast. It was as if "the boy had been bitten by a poisonous snake," Chief Justice Taft wrote to his wife.

Calvin's fever mounted. Boone and Coupal, overwhelmed, summoned other doctors, including a distinguished name from Temple University in Philadelphia, John Kolmer. Blood tests confirmed that the boy had an infection. Colonel Keller from Walter Reed and the other doctors conferred in the long corridor on the second floor; perhaps it was appendicitis.

Calvin's illness had all their attention now. It did not matter to them that in New York the Democrats' division—they passed fifty ballots, and then sixty—was playing out to the Republicans' advantage. Perhaps the desperate Democrats should just give up and nominate Coolidge, Will Rogers joked in a column. With each day of distance from the difficult congressional session, it was becoming clearer that Coolidge's popularity with voters was powerful enough to offset the schemes of lawmakers of either party. Sometimes Coolidge pretended to conduct official business, meeting with the new secretary of the navy. But he could not sit still long and afterward paced around the White House grounds.

The work from the navy laboratories came back: the infection was *Staphylococcus aureus*, which was bad but not as lethal as streptococcus. Coolidge had planned a lunch with Wallace McCamant of Washington State, a kind of thank-you; he had come so far from the day when McCamant had put his name to the crowd at Chicago. But at the lunch, Coolidge was distracted. His father had not come after all, and now Coolidge wrote him a letter, falling back into their old simple way of talking. "Calvin is very sick so this is not a happy day for me. He blistered his toe and infection got into his blood. The toe looks all right but the poison spread all over his system." Calvin had had "all that medical science can give" but that science had not seemed to get them very far. Coolidge could not concentrate; he remembered that his son liked animals, so he went out on the grounds and captured a small brown rabbit to show the boy in the sickroom. A smile flickered on the boy's face. In Cleveland, La Follette made the formal announcement of his run, but the Coolidges scarcely noticed. The stretcher came to remove the boy to Walter Reed. The physicians tested everywhere and found the same thing: staph. Dr. Deaver of Walter Reed chiseled at some of the bone in Calvin's leg to take cultures of it. Staph yet again. At 1:49 P.M. on July 5, Miss Randolph, Grace's secretary, sent Grace's friend Therese Hills a disquieting update: CALVIN STILL CRITICALLY ILL EVERYTHING POSSIBLE BEING DONE BEST SPECIALISTS CONSTANTLY IN CONSULTATION IT IS HOPED THAT HIS POWERS OF RESISTANCE WILL CARRY HIM THROUGH WILL KEEP YOU ADVISED.

The next day, July 6, found the rowdy Democratic convention nearing collapse. On July 7, after the eighty-first ballot, the contentious party had still not come to a candidate. The leadership took the extraordinary step of releasing delegates from their commitments to see if the vote would fall differently. Even that did not suffice to calm the room. Around lunchtime, a flag that reached from the bandstand caught fire, with policemen and firemen adding to the sense of chaos. The Democrats, many of whom had stayed up several nights straight, were becoming punch-drunk; in between the discussions over whether to choose Al Smith or John Davis, there was rampant speculation that Senator Walsh was engaged to the social activist Florence Harriman.

At Walter Reed, Calvin, Jr., faded into and out of consciousness. John had been brought over for a visit; the White House staff noted the shock on his face at his younger brother's state when he returned. CALVINS CONDITION STILL CRITICAL HE IS MAKING A WONDERFUL FIGHT PRESIDENT AND MRS COOLIDGE HOLDING OUT WELL, the telegram that day from Miss Randolph read. At points Calvin imagined that he was leading a battle and suddenly shouted, "We surrender!" Then he ordered the nurses, "Say it too. Say you surrender." "Never surrender," Joel Boone told Calvin, but he and Kolmer were becoming increasingly desperate. On the evening of July 7, Kolmer told the Coolidges that their son was fading. Both parents sat by Calvin's bed; the president held his mother's locket in Calvin's hand to let the boy know he would be joining his grandmother. Twice, when Coolidge let go, Calvin dropped it. At one point the medics decided to give Calvin oxygen; the wrong valve on the tank was opened by mistake; the tank exploded and some part of the apparatus hit Dr. Boone on his chest.

The Democratic convention was still on the radio. Colonel Coolidge listened from his special hookup in Vermont. At 10:50 that Monday night in New York, after the eighty-fourth ballot failed to produce a candidate, Chairman Walsh suddenly surprised the crowd in Madison Square Garden by calling for a pause. Something near silence filled the Garden. Then Walsh spoke into the microphone, just a few words, which Colonel Coolidge also heard. A low moan lasting many seconds filled the hall as the crowd responded to what Walsh had said. The sound of the grief as it traveled around the room, a *New York Times* writer noted, suggested the "nearness of the White House to every American home and the solicitous regard in which all people hold their president." A country exhausted by politics suddenly saw the presidency, and Coolidge, in a new light. Wrote the newspaper: "Their sorrows are his, as he frequently testifies, but in an especial sense his grief is also theirs."

All knew what came next. At the White House, the staff would ready the rooms for the funeral. The flower wagons would roll on the streets. The chimes of Epiphany Church would ring. The paperboys would call out "Extra!" The special train would leave Washington with its sorrowful cargo. The letters would pour in. Now the president was like Lincoln indeed, and in a way not even the speechwriters could have scripted. Calvin was gone.

ELEVEN

THE SIEGE AND THE SPRUCE

Washington, D.C.

WHAT JUMPED OUT WAS the number. It was $1,841,759,316.80, the total income tax revenues for the fiscal year that had ended in June. The number was too high. The year before, revenues had been $1,691,089,534.56. Nor was this the only leap. Several of the documents that were passing across his desk suggested that revenues would be higher than expected. Why? Numbers always drew Coolidge, and figuring out such a puzzle would distract him for hours.

Distract him, that was, if anything could. For if he even chanced to look up, to glance out a White House window, he would see it there, between the tennis court and the fountain: the spruce from the old limekiln lot. The tree was five feet tall, shorter in fact than Calvin had been when he died, but about the size they remembered the boy as being. On their last day in Plymouth that summer, Grace, John, Coolidge's father, and the Secret Service man Jim Haley had gone down together to the lot with a shovel to select it. Grace and the others had wrapped the spruce's roots carefully in burlap, sprinkling in extra dirt to protect them. Grace was planning to order an inscription on a bronze plaque for the spruce, in Calvin's memory. If the spruce survived. For a Vermont spruce, Washington was strange soil.

"When I look out that window I always see my boy playing tennis out there," the president told Richard Scandrett, Dwight Morrow's brother-in-law.

Coolidge knew he had changed since Calvin's death. In darker moments, he told himself that the presidency had caused the event. Working backward, he reverted to a logic as rigid as that of the preacher Jonathan Edwards. Had Coolidge not been president, Calvin would not have played tennis on the court outside. Had Calvin not played tennis, there would have been no blister. Had there been no blister, Calvin would not have died.

The process of politics held less interest for him now. But when it came to completing the work that Harding and he had begun, Coolidge found, he was more determined than before. Lincoln had not given up when his son had passed away; indeed, it had been after Willie's death that he had made the decisive move that had won the Civil War, replacing the ineffectual General McClellan and eventually settling on General Grant to lead his armies. Coolidge would not give up until he completed his own campaigns: the campaign to push the government back—back from spiritual life, back from commerce, back from new sectors in the economy— and find prosperity and peace. Protecting the space that faith enjoyed in American culture, the realm of the spiritual, seemed to him especially important. In those early days after Calvin's death he had refused many appointments, but had agreed to talk to a group of Boy Scouts in a telephone hookup. "It is hard to see how a great man can be an atheist," Coolidge had told the boys. "We need to feel that behind us is intelligence and love." Now he was preparing a speech for the dedication of a statue of a Methodist bishop, Francis Asbury. In that speech he wanted to make clear his conviction that government's power, since the days of Jonathan Edwards, had derived from religion, and not the other way around.

When it came to legislation, Coolidge again rejected the scattershot approach to lawmaking and aimed for a single goal: tax reform. These revenue figures, the high numbers, suggested that Mellon might be correct in his hypothesis. Cutting rates brought more revenue. So cutting rates even more might bring yet more cash. He determined to be audacious and seek a more dramatic reduction than even what they had put forward in the spring with the Mellon Plan. The sacrifice of Calvin's life could be offset only if something great, something that went farther than Harding or he had hoped to go in the past, was gained.

Tax reform demanded a true campaign, requiring not one but a string of victories: a surplus; a victory at the polls that November 1924; the wooing of Congress; exquisite management of the moody Senate by a new vice president, Charles Dawes, if they won; and more careful footwork by the men at the Treasury. To get Mellon his law, Coolidge needed to personally bank even more goodwill by sustaining his campaign against waste, mounting a siege of saving that would prove his administration was now virtuous enough to topple the opposition. If passage of such a tax law was possible at all, it might come, because of the oddities of budgeting and the congressional calendar, only as far ahead as 1926. That did not matter, nor did the preceding spring's tax defeats. When one spruce failed, Coolidge thought, you did not give up. You planted again, until the roots took hold.

At first both Coolidges' grief had been so great that they had not thought at all. The death of Calvin had seemed to them like the death of everything. When Coolidge had ordered a headstone for Calvin he ordered others for himself, Grace, and their son John. At Plymouth Notch, at the cemetery down the road, Grace had placed the boy's Bible on his casket to be buried with the boy in the little cemetery, near Calvin Galusha; Coolidge's mother, Victoria; and his sister, Abbie. The death of Calvin seemed to them all like the death of their family. Coolidge took John to the house to mark his height on the porch. Next to the mark, he wrote, "J.C., 1924." Then he asked John how tall Calvin had been. They guessed together where Calvin's new line should be. "C.C., 1924," Coolidge wrote. And then added, "if he had lived."

In Plymouth Notch, Grace put up an old windmill that Calvin had built and painted. Coolidge wandered around inspecting his maple trees. They decided that this time their mourning color would be white. Grace donned white dresses for the bereavement period; Coolidge and John wore summer white trousers. All of them fixed their sights not on the next presidential term but beyond it. That August, the Forbes Library in Northampton let it be known that the president had just given the library a stack of family photographs from Plymouth, the beginnings of the presidential collection that would be housed there.

In the restlessness of mourning, the Coolidges that summer had moved from Washington to Northampton to Plymouth, then back to Washington and to Plymouth again. The prospect of plunging into a political campaign seemed impossible, yet even in August Coolidge had known he did not want to give up the chance to run again. The Republican Party had been growing restless too; grief or no, the election was less than a hundred days away. It needed Coolidge to come out of mourning. The agonized Democrats in New York had in the end passed over McAdoo and selected John Davis as their candidate; Davis was reasonable enough, conservative enough to pull away votes from Coolidge. Senator Bob La Follette had been launched as a third-party candidate after his own tumultuous convention in Cleveland. Together, the Progressives and Democrats could still beat the Grand Old Party. The Democrats might win with a plurality as Wilson had in 1912.

One reason the scenario was possible was farms. Farming still employed a quarter of the population. Easterners' tariffs and the deflation that had been caused by bankers such as W. P. G. Harding at the Federal Reserve made farmers' existence tough. The farmers could not afford the prices of everyday goods when their corn or wheat sold for far less than it once had; mortgages they had taken when expansion seemed possible now proved fatal, and many were losing their farms. The farmers were caught in "economic thumbscrews," as La Follette would put it. La Follette had been born in a log cabin in Primrose, Wisconsin; his campaign would be that of the farm against the big city and big money. Intellectuals were joining the farmers behind La Follette. One was Felix Frankfurter at Harvard, who deplored, especially, the ejection of Meiklejohn from Amherst, with which Coolidge was associated. "Coolidge and Davis have nothing to offer in 1924; they have no dreams," wrote Frankfurter to the journalist Walter Lippmann. At least, Frankfurter thought, those behind La Follette were "struggling and groping for a dream." In the Midwest, many Republicans took the Coolidge candidacy as the signal that they must leave the party: Harold Ickes, a utilities reformer from Chicago, felt "inexpressible disgust" at Coolidge and signed up as La Follette's Midwest campaign manager. Those Republicans, like La Follette himself, presented progressive Wisconsin as a model for the country, an example when it came to taxation or even education.

Other Republican voters might follow the farmers and the intellectuals. The progressives might be the party's future. At Amherst, Morrow and others had made a distinctly conservative choice for the new president after the contentious Meiklejohn: George Olds, the math teacher whom Morrow and Coolidge had liked so much in the 1890s. But that did not mean Meiklejohn would go unemployed. In Wisconsin, authorities were preparing to welcome Meiklejohn: Young Robert La Follette, Jr., the son of the candidate, was already talking with Meiklejohn about serving at the top as a dean or president. The key state for the Republicans' future remained California; Harding had taken it in 1920, but this time voters in the state might turn to La Follette.

La Follette and Davis might be able to use Teapot Dome to bring Republicans down. New York Democrats mounted a large teapot image on the chassis of a seven-passenger car to drive around and sing songs against Theodore Roosevelt, the president's son, who served as navy undersecretary and so was part of the controversy. Among the singers who rode in the Teapot Car were Emily Smith, the daughter of Governor Al Smith, and Anna Eleanor Roosevelt, the daughter of Franklin Roosevelt. William McAdoo, a potential Democratic candidate, had lost out to Davis in the competition for the presidential slot on the party ticket in part because he had served as lawyer to the oil executive Edward Doheny. Coolidge, the vice president in the period of Teapot Dome, was still much closer than McAdoo to the Harding scandals. The papers had already identified a blemish: that spring, not expecting a second term as vice president, Coolidge had accepted a payment of $250 for a speech, plus $10 for expenses, for addressing veterans in Bridgeport, Connecticut. Thomas Marshall, the former vice president, rushed to his defense; Marshall, too, had given speeches for fees while vice president. Still, the payment looked bad at a time when Coolidge was promulgating policy relating to veterans.

The Republicans were also anxious because they worried about Coolidge's public speaking. "Fighting Bob" La Follette did not speak, he roared; grief muted Coolidge's already weak voice, making him, just as Lodge had always noted, a poor candidate on the stump. DeForest Phonofilm wanted to record three presidential candidates and package the recordings together to show in theaters. Coolidge's voice was so quiet that the crew had to adjust their equipment to capture it. Their apparatus was at the same settings when La Follette took his turn at the mike; La Follette blasted so hard the recording failed, and the technicians had to readjust and ask La Follette to record it all again. America was not made, La Follette said, "but in the making."

Responding through the grief, Coolidge had found that he could formulate policy. Two lawmakers from the West, Senator Charles

McNary of Oregon and Representative Gilbert Haugen of Iowa, were seeking federal subsidies to drive the prices of farm commodities up and help farmers. Coolidge, too, believed farmers needed cash, but thought the best way for them to get it was by establishing cooperatives, like the cheese factory in Plymouth, but on a larger scale. Even something like the cheese factory had limited potential, as the Coolidges knew all too well. John had even penned a funny, rueful poem about his cheese earnings:

> *A poet I do not claim to be*
> *So don't expect a rhyme from me*
> *Earning the dollar was very plain prose*
> *So every tinker in the town well knows*
> *For earn it I did what think you of that*
> *Tinkering and soldering the cheese factory vat.*

Coolidge was always seeking to translate John's message about the nature of farming into policy. "Well, farmers never have made much money," he said to R. A. Cooper of the Farm Board at one point. "I don't believe we can do much about it."

Coolidge, who had suffered the beratings of Agriculture Secretary Henry Wallace week after week in cabinet meetings, still opposed subsidies and the McNary-Haugen plans. The problem in the end, he believed, had come out of World War I. "If there had been no war, with its urge for increased production, we would by this time probably have quietly entered on a new phase of our agricultural experience, wherein we would have become an importer, rather than an exporter of most farm products," as he would put it shortly. He believed that farmers needed to look ahead: perhaps the best life was not on farms but rather in cities. Even since his arrival in Washington and his first encounters with La Follette, the number of factory jobs had risen relative to those on farms. Back in 1910 farmers had been a third of the employed population; now they were a quarter; in 1940 they might be just a sixth. "Brass tacks and common sense" was the theme the Republican Party settled on that year. In all areas he would work to prevent incursions by the government into the private sector. And above all, he would fight on savings and taxes. The prosperity his changes would yield represented his own dream, different from La Follette's but still real.

A mighty factor in that prosperity, Henry Ford himself, had been trekking around New England that August with Thomas Edison and Harvey Firestone. Ford, too, was probing the history of American growth, collecting arcana from the colonial time; recently he had purchased the colonial Wayside Inn in Massachusetts, whose innkeeper, it was said, had inspired Henry Wadsworth Longfellow to write "Paul Revere's Ride." On August 19, Ford, Edison, and Firestone had made a trip from Ludlow up to Plymouth Notch, where the Colonel, Grace, and Coolidge had hosted them. Once again, Grace had been the bridge; she had especially charmed Edison, who was partially deaf, with her clear speech and lipreading. The Coolidges had come up with what seemed to them the most appropriate gift: an old maple sap bucket, large, with J. COOLIDGE burned on the bottom.

Coolidge inscribed his own note: "Made for and used by John Coolidge an original settler in Plymouth. He died in 1822. Used also by Calvin Coolidge as a boy in the sugar lot when he was a boy at home." He then handed the bucket over. "My father had it, I've used it, and now you've got it," he said. The sugar bucket symbolized the fertility of early America: it had been quaint, it had lived within the painful limits of its self-sufficiency, but it had also yielded all the rest. Photos of Ford, Edison, and Coolidge were sent around the world, to show foreign governments and U.S. citizens that Ford was behind Coolidge.

Ford was buying up all kinds of American relics to memorialize the country's heroes. Lincoln, the single most important hero of the Republican Party, was also in Ford's mind. Ford was also in negotiations to buy up a collection of Abraham Lincoln memorabilia, including the bed in which Lincoln had died and furniture from Lincoln's life in Illinois. Osborn Oldroyd, the collector, was, however, rebuffing Ford; he wanted the government to buy the material. Two Congresses had turned down Oldroyd's request; at a time of budgeting, the price he wanted for the memorabilia of the sixteenth president, $50,000, was too high.

The GOP planners and Coolidge were also thinking about Lincoln, but in the context of their political campaign. As striking as it was, the parallel of the death of Coolidge's son and Lincoln's was hardly appropriate as a theme for a political campaign; it was the broader party hero they and Coolidge needed to evoke. The Republican leaders decided to create a Coolidge-Dawes car caravan, featuring a Ford Lincoln, that would travel thousands of miles across the country on the national road that bore the sixteenth president's name, the Lincoln Highway. The Lincoln was not a road that had been manufactured by the federal government; it had developed organically, as town after town put up money to pave a leg of it. The more they thought about it, the more splendid the Coolidge-Dawes Caravan on the Lincoln Highway seemed. It flattered and benefited the most important man to endorse the Coolidge candidacy, Henry Ford. The caravan brought to life not only Coolidge but also the story of American migration: a truck, starting out from Plymouth, featuring a photo of the Homestead on the side, would set out with other cars across the country.

Such an endeavor could get at the weakness in the allegation that the presidential candidate was from the city aristocracy and knew nothing of the farm. After all, Plymouth Notch did not differ from Primrose. And Coolidge's great-grandparents Israel and Sally Brewer had come to Wisconsin just as La Follette's family had and were buried in Hampden, Wisconsin, just one county over from Dane County, La Follette's birthplace. Herb Moore, a distant relation of Coolidge and an old Black River Academy alumnus, leaped into the role of stump speaker and told in town after town of Coolidge's rural beginnings. Moore was something of a carnival barker, but his points were good ones: not every farmer believed in easy money; the divide was there, just as it had been in Plymouth Notch itself in the old days. "Keep Cool with Coolidge" campaign cards featured pictures of electric fans. Standing on a two-wheel wooden oxcart, Colonel John would wave the caravan off. The vehicle would stop in Pennsylvania at Gettysburg, then head to Chicago, Salt Lake City, and San Francisco. The Republican Party hoped to marshal 200,000 cars to ride some portion of the long trip and advertise the Coolidge-Dawes ticket.

The Lincoln Highway Tour turned the disadvantage of Coolidge's silence into an advantage; his retreat represented not weakness but dignity. Dawes too would do his part. His budget achievements were legendary; when he appeared, puffing his characteristic low-slung pipe, it was like a train engine arriving: exciting and full of energy. That Dawes was given to outbursts, that he was "Hell and Maria" Dawes, made him the optimal complement to the withdrawn, quiet Coolidge. The campaign's advertising men, especially Edward Bernays, worked hard at presenting the team, and the Coolidges went along with the public relations effort.

It was the price of campaigning, and they were all nearly as practiced as Will Rogers by now. However, Coolidge also worried that Dawes might make *too much* news or that his father might not understand how reporters could make something of nothing. When Dawes called at Plymouth and lunched with the Coolidges and Colonel Coolidge in the little dining room reporters were thrilled; Dawes was much more likely than Coolidge to do something attention-grabbing. As it happened, Colonel Coolidge was the first to leave the room, and a full thirty reporters jumped him when he emerged to find out if he had picked up any gossip between the two candidates within. The president was concerned his father would say something unplanned; "I asked him to say nothing," he snapped at Dawes. He and Grace observed the reporters converge on the Colonel. "I don't think you need worry," Grace said. Later, Dawes did come out and asked the reporters what the senior Coolidge had said. "My hearing ain't as good as it used to be," they reported the Colonel as saying.

Back in Washington at the end of the month, the Coolidges and their son nonetheless found themselves playing host to Edward, Prince of Wales. Most of the papers reported it as a society event. The White House did not often receive such royalty, and the preparations were ferocious. The prince signaled that he would like the visit to be casual, but both Charles Hughes and Coolidge donned business suits. The Coolidges were still in mourning, so the prince arrived without other guests. When the prince arrived, he was in pinstripes; someone let Grace know that he had had the cuffs cut off his shirt because of the hot weather. "The poor prince," Grace wrote to her sorority sisters. "Some day I will again be a humble citizen, while he can never be just himself." Mrs. Coolidge tried to chat up the prince; there was no wine, of course, as Prohibition still prevailed. In the midst of the hoopla, John Coolidge had to join in the entertaining and learn to say "your royal highness," with Grace. John was taller than the prince and shy; he would rather have retreated to the Navy Yard for tennis with Dr. Boone. He was still far from past his brother's death. Ike Hoover, the usher, tried to make him laugh and put it all into perspective: "Well, he may be the Prince of Wales, but you're the Prince of Plymouth."

The usher had put his finger on something. The Prince of Wales was not in Washington to pull rank. He was there in part because he admired the United States: it was, as he had put it to his father, "a country in which nothing was impossible." The United States seemed to be moving ahead of Great Britain; the year before, the U.S. Treasury, under Mellon, had renegotiated the United Kingdom's war debt to the United States. The prince was also there as a mendicant. Great Britain was hoping to restore its old status by going back on the gold standard. First, though, it had to prove to the United States and to markets that it could pay back its loans. The recent agreements that Treasury and Dawes had arranged were tough, but the fact that they had been made would help Great Britain in its own campaign. And now the United States was negotiating with other countries. As its wealth and gold reserves grew, it might be able to afford easier terms to desperate foreign governments than it was giving Great Britain. The United States' budgeting was a virtuous circle that would benefit Europe as well.

Coolidge made up his mind to stop his wanderings and stay in Washington. As he and Grace tried to settle in, he thought more about the budget numbers. Just as he had seen his thinking change when Harding introduced the goal of normalcy, he was feeling his thinking changing now. Sustaining the budget siege was necessary, just as had been written in the calendar beside his very first official appointment with General Lord, because of that crucial need to live by example. He and Mellon still saw their work as redeeming the trust of voters lost in the war; Mellon was trying to convince those who had hoarded silver coins to bring them out and spend them again. If Congress strayed, the administration needed to distinguish itself by remaining faithful to its promise of savings. General Lord was figuring out ways to save money on the costly bonus act; he had come up with an ingenious plan to use lighter paper for the instructions for soldiers, saving $33,000.

The disconcerting extra revenue kept popping up in the Treasury numbers, just as it had in September. Mellon and Coolidge began to work on their explanation for tax reform. Scientific taxation theory actually functioned: with lower rates you get more activity and therefore more revenue. When you dropped tax rates, people kept more of their business and sometimes *did* more business. Take away the car tax, and people would buy more cars. Lower rates meant that the economy would grow even faster than the revenues grew. One could look at the economy as a fraction. On top was the numerator, the government. On the bottom was the general economy, or "commerce," as Coolidge called it. Coolidge had been focusing on the numerator, the government, making it smaller relative to commerce. But you could also get the same result by concentrating on the mysterious denominator. If commerce grew, while the government, the numerator, stayed the same, or grew less fast, the goal could be achieved, too. No one knew how much the economy would grow if rates were cut even farther than planned. The commerce, in the end, was the goal; that in turn would obviate the need for all the new legislation for the groups. If business was strong enough, the farmers might see prices go up; if trade was strong enough, soldiers could buy their own pensions. If commerce was strong enough, the endless pressure for new laws, as strong here as in Massachusetts, would relent. Here was one experiment an administration that so ostentatiously rejected government experiments, a party of normalcy, could embrace.

There was still a danger. The tax cuts could also have the opposite of the intended effect, making the government bigger. If the tax cuts yielded the full coffers Mellon promised, those coffers in turn would tempt Congress, Republican or Democratic, to spend more. Still, Coolidge now found himself enthusiastic enough that he was willing to run that risk. His experts saw yet another advantage in Mellon's scientific taxation. Tariffs were like Prohibition enforcement, one of those burdens one carried for the party. A request for a reduction in sugar tariffs had traveled with him to Plymouth; instead of making the decision he had wandered into the woods to check out his own sugar maples. If Mellon got his tax experiment right, then the tiresome question of tariffs would finally recede; soon income tax revenues would dwarf them entirely in size. On September 1, the day the papers carried the news of Mellon's surprise, Coolidge received labor leaders at the White House. Even labor would benefit if the tax rate came down; companies might pass on their savings to workers. The Dow Jones Industrial Average, which had remained stuck at 100 or less for years, might finally move past the 100-point barrier.

The election was the first hurdle Coolidge and Mellon had to get over. Senator La Follette, the Progressive presidential candidate, was doing well in California on a platform of nationalization of railways, power, light, telephone, and telegraph. In Peoria, Illinois, one of Lincoln's storied stops, La Follette went after Coolidge for corruption, charging that Coolidge "saves at the spigot and wastes at the bunghole." Coolidge might have been attentive when it came to the pennies, but tariffs were graft on a large scale; Mellon too got the tax refunds his treasury sent out when there was a surplus. Under a plan like La Follette's, as Herbert Hoover said, officeholders would proliferate, whether bureaucrats or elected officials. Together all officeholders would number 6 million; now that women could vote, their wives would join them and the government vote would be 25 percent of the electorate, Hoover said. John Davis, the Democratic candidate for president, was more conservative, but under Wilson the country had seen that Democrats too were capable of great nationalizations. If they teamed up, the Democrats and progressives could undo all that he and Harding had done. If he wanted to push the government back farther, Coolidge had at most only a few more years. The economy needed to grow so fast that all the errors of the past regarding the railroads no longer mattered, so that people could see that where the railroad enterprise had slowed, cars or aviation might take its place in the future.

To convey their respect for the future of aviation, the Coolidges and the Coolidge cabinet went down to Bolling Field on September 9 to inspect it themselves. Star aviators from all over the country had been traveling the continent in small hops to demonstrate the potential of the new means of transport. The airplanes were hours late, and it rained; Coolidge stood waiting in a black raincoat and rubbers, smoking cigars. Grace huddled in the car in a cape trimmed with fur. But no one at the event minded the wait. When the first planes landed, the *Chicago* and the *Boston II*, Coolidge went out to shake the fliers' hands and peered into the cockpits. Those mechanics were at least as interesting as the mechanics of tax cuts.

Even with a plan in place and with his weekly meetings with Lord, Coolidge sometimes lost heart. They had held John back from a summer at Camp Devens, but now John must leave for college. Without him, the reality of their loss hit the Coolidges. Suddenly the only child, John, bore the heavy weight of his parents' anxieties. The Coolidges had already arranged for John to room with Stephen Brown rather than on campus. Coolidge's fraternity had already invited John to become a member. Grace missed John, and Coolidge became anxious about him. On September 24, he dropped another line to his old friend from Amherst Frederick Allis with a request to watch over his son. "I thought you might help him in avoiding mistakes," he wrote. He also sent John a testy letter:

My dear John,

You have not told us anything about what you are doing at Amherst, as to what you are studying, where you are boarding. . . . I want you to take a book and set down in it all your expenses, so that you will know for what you are paying out your money. I am giving you a letter of introduction to Mr. Allis for you to give him. . . . When you don't know what to do about anything, you can go and ask him. . . . I have already indicated that I want you to stay in Amherst and study, and not be running to Northampton.

Coolidge was also tense because now he was beginning to lay out his tax plan; that week he took a stab at explaining it in a speech he delivered to several thousand druggists on September 24. It included not only lower taxes, he told them, but also a general commitment to less interference. If the government stayed out of the way and prices became more stable, businesses would not have to worry so much as they had in the past. "The successful merchant no longer attempts to thrive on sharp dealings but on service and mutual consideration." Contacts between government and business, he said, should be "as few as possible." Here he was seeking to show that he was more than merely the nominee of Ford Motor Company, which just a few days later would report yet more stupendous success, the production of a record 1.26 million vehicles in the first eight months of 1923. He was not for individual businesses but rather for all businesses. Harmony with foreign governments, Coolidge added, would limit the possibility of the greatest disrupter of business, war.

The Coolidge-Dawes Caravan set out from Plymouth that same week, stopping in Northampton to call on Mrs. Goodhue on Massasoit Street. Judge Field and James Lucey went out to greet it, along with Frederick Gillett, who was now running for the U.S. Senate. Lucey had decided he would run for office himself; like Coolidge, he had stocked up on cigars. Herbert Hoover had promised to campaign in California. Charles Evans Hughes, Coolidge's secretary of state, would also give speeches. Across the country, the caravan made its way, with speakers arguing the points: budgets, economy, and tax cuts. Once in a while, a question came up that provided the president a chance to speak succinctly. Black leaders had in the past been disappointed with the cold reception they received in his office, too little aware that this reception was accorded just about every interest group. Coolidge saw his work as freeing the individual rather than the group. Now a voter wrote to complain that a black man was competing for a nomination to run for Congress. Coolidge saw to it that his reply was published. He wrote, "I was amazed to receive such a letter. During the war 500,000 colored men and boys were called up under the draft not one of whom sought to evade it. A colored man is precisely as much entitled to submit his candidacy" as any other citizen. In general, though, Coolidge spoke little but sat with Lord, trimming and tending. Not everyone understood the Coolidge thrift or its connection with other concerns. The White House staff was irritated that he tipped poorly. Mrs. Jaffray favored her specialty shops and could not share Coolidge's interest in the new and cheaper supermarkets or in the economy of scale. Grace had to play the broker between her husband and her housekeeper.

"The budget idea, I may admit, is a sort of obsession with me," he told a group of Jewish philanthropists in a phone conversation from his room at the White House. "I believe in budgets. I want other people to believe in them. I have had a small one to run my own home; and besides that, I am the head of the organization that makes the greatest of all budgets, that of the United States government. Do you wonder, then, that at times I dream of balance sheets and sinking funds, and deficits, and tax rates, and all the rest?" He continued, "I regard a good budget as among the noblest monuments of virtue." When you budgeted, you could take care of your own people; that was important, too. Peter Stuyvesant, the Dutchman who had ruled the colony of New Amsterdam, had asked Jews to make what became known as "the Stuyvesant Pledge," to commit to taking care of their own ill and indigent should they stay in New Amsterdam. The colonial community had honored that pledge and had sustained the tradition through the centuries. Coolidge let the charities know he appreciated that: "I want you to know that I feel you are making good citizens, that you are strengthening the government."

The presidential campaign seemed to be going well, principally because the economy was. Farms still struggled, but those who left farms did all right. All fall the Fords were cranked out; even if they slowed now, people believed, the assembly lines would pick up later. The public debt was down below $21 billion. Interest rates stood now at 3.5 percent, down from 7 percent when Harding had taken office. Even Victory Bonds, still held by more than 12 million Americans, sold better now, at par, whereas they had sold below par at the end of the Wilson administration. At the Civil Service Commission, the officials could show that there were 544,671 federal workers, about 100,000 fewer than in 1920. Yet the expenses still exceeded the total expenses in 1915; it seemed reasonable, therefore, for the Republican Party to win the presidency again.

On October 2, barreling around Brooklyn, Theodore Roosevelt, Jr.'s campaign for governor of New York nearly caused a bad accident when a small truck heading along Wythe Avenue careened into their advance motorcycles; the motorcycles ended up on the sidewalk, but Roosevelt, like his father, proved unflappable and ably stumped for economy and Mellon's scientific taxation.

John Davis did not have a great caravan, but the Democrat campaigned by train. Davis stopped at Springfield, Illinois, to make the point that Lincoln did not belong to the GOP alone by laying a wreath at the sixteenth president's grave. Charles W. Bryan, his vice presidential candidate, campaigned by car and drove himself, a sign of a can-do temperament that reporters admired.

La Follette zeroed in on Coolidge's delay in returning the sugar schedule with lower tariffs. Coolidge was beholden to sugar, clearly. Indeed La Follette announced some arithmetic: every week Coolidge delayed cost housewives across the nation a million dollars in higher prices. "He evidently does not intend to make it until after the fourth of November," said La Follette, accurately enough, of Coolidge. "That is what the Sugar Trust wants."

James Couzens, Mellon's old adversary, also would not relent, targeting Mellon's connections to Wall Street rather than his tax return. Mellon, Couzens was out to prove, had not really left Wall Street when he came to Washington, an allegation that contained some truth: Mellon had resigned directorships but still communicated with his firms and kept up with their management. Couzens had new ammunition: an interim report from the FTC, which was still investigating Aluminum Company of America for antitrust violations. The commission report included testimony by Aluminum Company's president, Arthur Vining Davis, that seemed to confirm just what the trustbusters were alleging: that the Treasury secretary still ruled Wall Street. Arthur Davis had said that the company "really consists of A. W. Mellon and R. B. Mellon." The FTC claimed that the tariff enabled Aluminum Company to control the price of its product and that the company was violating the Sherman Antitrust Act. It said that the company had a "practically complete monopoly of the aluminum in the United States." John Davis, Coolidge's opponent, was publicly estimating that current tariffs on foreign aluminum were allowing Mellon to charge an extra 5 cents a pound.

Mellon and Arthur Vining Davis duly countered that the Aluminum Company and Mellon had not violated the law. Mellon's holdings in Aluminum Company were in fact only one-third of the company. But the tariffs made their defense weak. As long as tariffs protected them, U.S. companies were shutting out foreign companies and thereby hurting consumers by depriving them of lower prices. The "Battle of the Millionaires," as it was known, between Mellon and Couzens, stayed in the press.

In a way, the Coolidges found, their mourning protected them. Though both of them wanted Coolidge to win office, they no longer cared about the comments made by their political opponents. They were happiest with plants and children. On October 13, Grace surprised a crowd when she showed up at a Lincoln Memorial event for another planting; the local chapter of the American War Mothers charity was dedicating a new tree at the Lincoln Memorial. Grace had in mind that she would have another spruce, a bigger one, for the Christmas tree. This year the Christmas tree would be a living tree.

Children, especially, drew them both. Grace thought of John all the time; when she spoke of him heading north to their house in Northampton or to Amherst, she spoke of him heading "home." Despite her own loss, or perhaps because of it, she found it in herself at every instance to signal she welcomed children or even the prospect of them; it was to Grace that Alice Longworth ran when she learned she was pregnant, calling up the stairs of the White House "Grace, Grace, I am going to have a baby." Edward McLean now stood under the cloud of Teapot Dome; it was he who had fixed many things for the Harding ring. But neither Coolidge could forget the friendship the McLeans had shown them. Grace knew that Evalyn Mclean had lost a son of her own, Vinson, in a 1919 car accident. "I know you count, as we do, the boy who is singing his carols in heaven," Grace wrote to Evalyn. One morning, arriving at the White House, Colonel Starling found a boy pressing his face to the iron fence. "I thought I might see the president," the boy said. "I heard that he gets up early and takes a walk. I wanted to tell him how sorry I am that his little boy died." Starling took him in; the boy was so overwhelmed, Starling later recalled, that he could not speak. Starling explained to the president. And that time Coolidge nearly did break down; the president, Starling saw, "had a difficult time controlling his emotions." Later, when they walked through Lafayette Park, Coolidge told Starling, "Colonel, whenever a boy wants to see me always bring him in. Never turn one away or make him wait."

Coolidge took solace in service. The nature of the service he needed to render had changed over the years. Service as vice president had meant diplomacy, then the service of continuity; now the service was the tax legislation. But even more than before, the idea kept him going. Selden Spencer, a Missouri senator who had visited that summer, told a story about him. One day, walking with the president on the White House grounds, Spencer had pointed to the White House and made a joke: "I wonder who lives there?" "Nobody," Coolidge had replied. "They just come and go." Starling was surprised at how little attention Coolidge paid to the technicalities of the presidential election. While the parties worked themselves into a frenzy around him, Coolidge was quiet. "He was, in fact, more serene during that autumn than at any time in the years I knew him," he later wrote. The most consoling work of all for Coolidge, perhaps because he believed in it and because it distracted him, was the budget work, the meetings with Lord or Treasury. Rather than return to Massachusetts to vote, the Coolidges filled in their ballots on the White House Lawn, with Rob Roy between them; then they sent their envelopes to the Northampton city clerk.

Toward the very end of the campaign, death and illness intruded again. Henry Wallace, the agriculture secretary, underwent a routine operation to remove his gallbladder; instead of recovering, he developed an infection, and he was gone in a week, like Calvin. Coolidge opened the East Room for Wallace's memorial; secretaries Mellon, Weeks, and Wilbur, as well as Attorney General Stone, were honorary pallbearers. That October illness struck Henry Cabot Lodge too. Coolidge wrote him a note of sympathy. From Charlesgate Hospital, two days after the Wallace funeral, Lodge wrote back, "I cannot for a moment believe there is any doubt of your election," adding, "That you should have me in your in mind in the midst of the campaign and send me a word of sympathy and hope means more to me than perhaps you realize." From an old adversary, the message was touching. It also boded well. Few politicians could forecast elections as well as the senator from Nahant.

Coolidge remained quiet, but the party itself grew cheerier as the election approached. Staffers noticed that radio and film truly were working to Coolidge's advantage in the end. The big speakers, William Jennings Bryan and Robert La Follette, had built-in microphones, but that no longer benefited them; indeed, on the radio, the orators merely came off as overwrought. In late October, twenty-three stations all over the country carried Coolidge's voice when he delivered the final big speech of the campaign. In this speech, Coolidge once again sketched the burdens of past taxation as "despotic exactions." His policy, Harding's and Mellon's, by contrast, was to pay down the national debt. The most important thing now was to free the individual, for, as Coolidge said, "It is our theory that the people own the government, not that the government should own the people."

A *Literary Digest* poll of more than 2 million voters, taken at the end of October, put Coolidge well ahead of both Davis and La Follette. As they closed the campaign, Republican leaders simply underscored the same points again and again: the bottom line was that prosperity, budget economy, and tax revision benefited all. The prosperity and the budgeting were there; the tax revision was half done. The day before the polls opened, Northampton town fathers arranged a parade complete with a GOP elephant and summoned John Coolidge down from Amherst: he and Mrs. Goodhue, Grace's mother, sat in vehicles at the front, and other friends—John's roommate Stephen Brown, Grace's friend Mrs. Hills, Judge Field, and Judge Shaw, who had been Coolidge's fellow apprentice at Hammond and Field—also lined up.

On November 4, election day, the Coolidge-Dawes Caravan reached its destination of Bellingham, Washington, after traversing seventeen states. In Plymouth, Coolidge's father rode in a horse-drawn buggy to Plymouth Union to cast his vote. Coolidge closeted himself in the afternoon with General Lord, who emerged from the executive offices as surprised as Starling had been; Coolidge had insisted on spending their time together on fiscal affairs. In the evening, the Stearnses arrived, along with Chief Justice Taft and Senator Smoot; Coolidge told reporters he had stayed up to 12:45 A.M. because of the visitors and otherwise would have retired earlier.

As the president slept, the vote counters began to understand that the Republicans had won a powerful victory. La Follette polled 4.8 million votes, 16.6 percent of the electorate, an election-breaking share. But as it turned out, his Progressive Party took not so much from Coolidge as from Davis and the Democrats, who received only 8.39 million, or 28.8 percent. Coolidge received 15.72 million, or 54 percent, of the vote, less than Harding but still shockingly high given the rise of the progressives and the farm bloc. That was the absolute majority that had eluded Wilson, Taft, and Theodore Roosevelt. Coolidge won in thirty-five states, only two fewer than Harding had in 1920; he even claimed Montana, the state of La Follette's vice presidential candidate, Senator Burton Wheeler. Harding had taken the West for the GOP. Thanks to Coolidge, the party still owned it, California and all. In electoral votes, the victory was even clearer: La Follette took only his native Wisconsin, and Davis carried only twelve states.

Taking Rob Roy, the Coolidges went out on the White House lawn to greet visitors and pose. The photographers saw some of the first real smiles from the couple since summer. The Stearnses toasted them; they prepared for a visit from the Morrows, who would stay the next week. Reporters eager to catch more of the White House noticed that on Thursday, the White House staff was cleaning the giant crystal chandeliers from the East Room and hanging out heavy winter curtains. The staff was also busy with trees again, removing from the exposed terrace roofs boxwoods planted by the Roosevelts and replacing them with evergreen trees for the winter.

Elsewhere the Republican reaction to victory was even more energetic. Northampton staged a second parade, with Mrs. Goodhue again riding in a car. Changes in the Senate and House, Republicans noted, would make Coolidge's tax campaign easier: four seats had been gained, though in practice the number was smaller, owing to a contested seat. Nick Longworth was slated for promotion to House speaker and this time promised to be more aggressive with Republican lawmakers who diverged from the party line. Coolidge could now add more cabinet members with views closer to his own. He had his eye on William Jardine, the president of Kansas State Agricultural College, who also opposed direct subsidies to farmers, to be secretary of agriculture. Two figures who had dominated their days passed away. The first to go was Senator Lodge; Lodge, who had been ill all fall, suffered a stroke and then died on November 9. Next came word from Marion, in late November, of Mrs. Harding's death. William Jennings Bryan would pass the next year. It was strange to move forward without these old ghosts.

The stock market for its part responded to the election by bolting upward; by December 1, the Dow Jones Industrial Average was at 110, or 10 percent above where it had been in mid-October. The rises were so dramatic that some found them disconcerting. "What makes these things worth so much more on November 5th than they were on November the third?" asked Will Rogers of stocks. "I was old fashioned enough to think that supply and demand regulated the price of everything. Now I find November the Fourth regulates it." Rogers noted that "Coca Cola took a jump right out of the glass." Rogers wondered what it all meant. "I thought we elected Mr. Coolidge to lower our taxes and keep us at peace with the world. I didn't know that we had to drink Coca Cola."

Even while Coolidge and Mellon were still taking in the election results, new tax data strengthened their resolve. Even with its imperfections, the tax rate cut had done what Mellon had predicted: the tax rates had dropped 25 percent, yet the decrease in the amount received was less than 5 percent. It was wondrous: there might be a federal budget surplus despite the bonus costs imposed by the new bonus law, just as Senator Bursum, just defeated, had predicted long before. The stock market increase was the market's way of telling the administration that it already counted on the tax cut and counted on the economy thriving in coming years.

Yet Coolidge and Mellon had cleared only their first hurdle. Four more votes in the Senate were not enough to halt a filibuster: that would require two-thirds of the Senate. George Norris of Nebraska, Couzens of Michigan, and the defeated La Follette were more than ready to mount one. The idiosyncrasies of the congressional calendar worked against him. Congress adjourned in March, just as Coolidge was inaugurated. He could call a special session, but that would once again give lawmakers a chance to pass legislation he opposed. If he waited, more mysterious cash might flow in, and the case for a tax cut would be stronger. The success of his campaign, whether that year or in 1926, depended on meticulous work by the cabinet and in the Senate, by lawmakers and vice president Dawes; the House was likewise not so easy a partner as the triumphalist headlines suggested. That his administration be perceived as unified was also essential. One of his first thoughts was to foster unity by replicating Harding's generosity. He would invite Dawes, the new vice president, to sit in on the cabinet meetings, a gesture of hospitality

Coolidge had been grateful for from Harding. He wanted a close relationship with Dawes.

Unexpectedly, Dawes refused Coolidge's invitation. Beyond the slight of such a public refusal at the beginning of their partnership, Dawes's decision to stay away hurt another way. The big question in the Veterans Bureau and Teapot Dome scandals was how much information Coolidge himself had picked up in the cabinet meetings. When Dawes made a show of avoiding the meetings, he raised the question of whether Coolidge had been compromised by attending. The alternative was that Coolidge had been ignorant of what had gone on among men he saw at the White House, which was what William Randolph Hearst's executives believed. "Coolidge knew nothing of this," Hearst's general manager, Frederic C. Dumaine, had told Clarence Barron that year. That surmise kept Coolidge's name clear but also suggested that he was a simpleton.

It fell to Mellon to relaunch the tax reform. The secretary laid new groundwork in the annual report of the Treasury, which he transmitted on December 3, 1924. The old frozen loans were finally liquid again; railroads were back. The country could expect, Mellon said, "prosperous and healthy conditions such as succeeded the election of 1896"—but only if Americans did not think of taxation as a "socialistic experiment, or as a club to punish success." Mellon sought his cuts in the surtax rates, but also, again, an end to the special status of municipal bonds. He doubted the constitutionality of the gift tax. If estate tax rates came down, people would have an incentive to work harder and to save. Some taxes could come up: not only those on municipal bonds, but also corporate taxes. Nuisance taxes should end. A gleeful *Wall Street Journal* backed Mellon up with a quote from Samuel Gompers: "Only out of production can we grow prosperous."

As if to underscore Mellon's point and demonstrate that his theory was already working, the Treasury shipped out $137 million in refunds on 192,252 tax returns, some to firms that had won a judgment in tax adjudication, others simply rebates allowable under the tax law. Many of the court judgments related to war profits taxes; the Treasury was still cleaning up the war mess. Coolidge added focus by transmitting a legislative agenda to Congress that emphasized tax reform when it came to changes; when it came to other legislation, such as farm subsidies, Coolidge's main work would be defensive.

The principal challenge that winter and coming spring would be staying clear of the Harding administration scandals. The Supreme Court was deciding whether Mal Daugherty, the brother of the attorney general, could be compelled to testify. It all might still go wrong, just as it had last year. At the White House, especially now, modesty must remain the watchword. There was nothing the Coolidges could do but be amused by the gossip when it involved those outside the administration: it was an open secret that Alice Longworth's baby was Senator Borah's, and that kind of topic mattered because Borah and Longworth were both key to passage of the tax legislation.

But the White House was another zone, which Coolidge guarded rigorously. When divorce or some other shadow came over a White House staffer, Coolidge saw to it that the staffer was transferred out. Waste continued to preoccupy him. Coolidge's caution was antagonizing several of the White House staff, who missed the more forgiving style of life under the Hardings or the Roosevelts. Not only Mrs. Jaffray, the housekeeper, but also Ike Hoover, the usher, was taking a particular dislike to Coolidge. Others understood that Coolidge's emphasis on propriety was not weakness but wisdom, given the intensity of the progressives' scrutiny.

"The Harding administration scandals were so vivid in his mind," the veteran mail room chief, Ira Smith, noticed. The tension between the president and Mrs. Jaffray grated on even the normally tolerant Grace. Grace wanted a housekeeper who did not war with the president, who fixed his food as he liked and she prescribed. Instead, Coolidge and Mrs. Jaffray clashed over household minutiae. That coming spring, at one of the state dinners, Mrs. Jaffray would encounter President Coolidge coming up from the dinner room. "Didn't you think it was beautiful?" she asked of the set tables. "Yes, it's all right," he replied. "Did you step downstairs into the kitchens?" she asked. That was all Coolidge needed. "Yes, and I don't see we have to have six hams for dinner." There were a number of people coming, Mrs. Jaffray allowed. Well, it still seemed a lot of ham to him, the president said.

The living Christmas tree was to be a Norway spruce from New York State. Men were planting the tree in Sherman Square, behind the Treasury Building, one street over from the White House. On it workers hung a thousand lights, which Coolidge lit by a switch at dusk. For her own family, Grace got three little trees. She agreed to work at the Central Union Mission distributing clothing for the poor on Christmas Eve.

In the New Year, the first move Coolidge made—tiny but significant—was to change his calendar. Lord's permanent appointment was moved up to 9:15 A.M. instead of 9:30. That gave Coolidge more time to cut the budget, a task that became harder each year that passed; they were near $3 billion, but not there yet. Lord, creatively, would in coming weeks find three more cuts: the Weather Bureau would cease sending out postcards carrying forecasts, a tradition for nearly half a century; the newspapers nowadays carried such material free. Post office bags could be made of plain gray canvas, not the traditional white with blue stripes: savings, $50,000 a year. The government favored a distinct red tape for wrapping federal documents. Henceforth, it would dispense with red tape. Literally. The white string would do. The extra minutes also gave the president time to prepare with Lord for the cabinet meeting or to meet with lawmakers who might affect legislation, such as James Watson of Indiana, who came in on January 16, the day before a meeting scheduled with the new speaker of the House, Nicholas Longworth.

Coolidge laid out his thoughts at the annual convention of the American Association of Newspaper Editors. Whatever La Follette or Couzens might say, Coolidge wanted to make clear that he did not represent the interest groups on which the editors spilled so much ink; rather he, Coolidge, represented everyone—the whole country. He represented the potential in business for everyone. If business was to thrive, its importance needed to be recognized. "The chief business of the American people is business," he added. But there was always a counterweight to business—the integrity and idealism of the country that would not allow any interest group to prevail. "The chief ideal of the American people is idealism," he said. In fact, on balance, Coolidge would go with the newspaperman over the man of finance: "I could not truly criticize the vast importance of the counting room, but my ultimate faith I would place in the high idealism of the editorial room of the American newspaper." Public service was the business they were all in: newspaperman, businessman, or politician, Republican or Democrat.

If policy were to improve, not only words but also cabinet members, judges, and commissioners were also key. The Congress was in its lame-duck session until inauguration, and Coolidge knew some of his nominees would meet resistance if he put them forward in this period. But by the same token he could build comity if the Senate approved major appointments even in this early period. For an empty Supreme Court slot, Coolidge put forward Harlan Stone, who would move from the attorney general position. Coolidge had already prepped the Senate the month before with a dinner for Stone and senators on the *Mayflower*. Coolidge might have picked a more conservative man than Stone as his nominee, but Stone, his old Amherst peer, was likelier to win confirmation. The attorney general understood how the Senate worked. He had also helped quiet the Daugherty scandal, so the shift was also a reward. Stone boasted impeccable credentials; it would be hard for the Senate to turn down as unqualified a man who had served as the dean of Columbia University's law school for more than ten years. The unpredictability of senators such as Borah had always plagued Coolidge. "There goes Senator Borah," Coolidge once was heard to say. "And he and his horse are going in the same direction." But this time, with Stone, he felt confident. The Senate, still in session, did something provocative upon learning of Stone's nomination; the senators asked the nominee to testify at a hearing. There they interrogated him not on his qualifications for the job of justice so much as on whether he had in his capacity as attorney general been justified in investigating their colleague Burton Wheeler of Montana. *The Washington Post's* editorialists were outraged at both the newfangled demand for testimony and the line of questioning: "A Senator, acting in the equivocal capacity of counsel for another Senator under judicial investigation, is virtually saying to the Attorney General: I have the power to prevent you from becoming a member of the Supreme Court." But the senators duly confirmed Stone on February 5 in a 71–6 vote.

In mid-February, Coolidge gingerly, carefully sneaked a few more names in: William Jardine to succeed Henry Wallace at Agriculture and Frank Kellogg, the ambassador to Great Britain, for the job of secretary of state, since Hughes was departing. Jardine opposed price fixing, specifically the McNary-Haugen plan to drive up prices at home by government management of surplus product. Both Jardine and Kellogg were approved; Coolidge's homework and strategizing were paying off. Congress generally seemed to be in a good mood. Alice Roosevelt Longworth gave birth to her baby, Paulina Longworth; the House cheered Nick Longworth, who was also the new speaker.

As the inauguration date approached, Coolidge, still apprehensive, intensified his preparations. Dawes was in charge of soothing the Senate, and he certainly seemed to be thinking about the inauguration day. Indeed, the vice president–elect was complaining that the eighteen tickets allotted him for the inauguration would not suffice. In mid-February, Coolidge wrote to Dawes, who was still in Chicago, to ask him to be sure to stop by the White House so that they could review the details of the all-important day. "Whatever is decided on will suit me all right," Dawes reassured him on February 14. The vice president–elect assured Coolidge that his calendar was clear for the coming work; he had no special dates except one far ahead, to honor the midnight ride of Paul Revere and his ancestor, William Dawes, at the Old North Church tower in Boston on April 18.

Coolidge, mollified, decided to overlook Dawes's decision to stay out of cabinet meetings. Dawes's cooperation in presenting a modest, unified appearance at the inauguration mattered more. Coolidge was highly conscious of the dignity of the event, and where it might fit in history and, in the short term, fit in with his own plans for legislation that spring. In order to set an example of inaugural economy, the president ordered that much of the $60,000 sent in by private citizens be sent back. That winter, Coolidge sat in Wilson's pew at the Central Presbyterian Church to honor Wilson, who had been an elder in the church; the next day Coolidge and Mrs. Wilson dedicated a bronze memorial stone and new cornerstone at the church in Wilson's name. Starling, his Secret Service man, was beginning to see a resemblance between Wilson and Coolidge that others missed: "For both of them, life was largely a mental experience." But, Starling added, whereas in Wilson "this was obvious, in Coolidge it was not." Wilson looked like a professor and talked like a professor; Coolidge often brought his talk down to the commonplace as they walked, say, past a store: "If you ever get married, don't let your wife buy anything in there. My wife goes in there and it costs me a lot of money." But in Coolidge the simple talk was guile; Coolidge was making complex decisions in his head, just as Wilson had.

A second resemblance to other presidents troubled Starling: Coolidge was running down his health, as Wilson and Harding had. The obsessed chief executive needed a sport. Starling thought the president, who had never fished, might find angling relaxing; hunting also seemed possible. Dwight Morrow and Andrew Mellon had both tried a novel form of exercise: the electric horse. Like a merry-go-round steed, it moved up and down, with buttons to change the pace, supplying exercise when true riding was not possible. Now, with Starling's encouragement, Morrow and other friends sent Coolidge a steed of his own, 475 pounds and made of mahogany. The horse, called Thunderbolt, arrived and was moved into the presidential dressing room without the president's knowledge. Coolidge himself discovered the horse when he entered the dressing room and found Starling trotting along. The president was curious about the horse but not eager for the news of its existence to get out in that delicate time. To Coolidge's chagrin, someone, mostly likely the electricians from the Navy Yard, leaked the news of Thunderbolt's arrival. This was exactly the kind of story that hurt presidential dignity. "Coolidge Rides an Electric Hobby-Horse," read *The New York Times*' headline.

March neared. Coolidge's father agreed to come after Coolidge carefully ensured that Governor Billings of Vermont was traveling: "The main thing I want is that you should do what you like best." The Coolidges' son John too would come down for a single day from Amherst. Mrs. Goodhue was also coming and would stay for a longer period. On March 3, a day before the inauguration, Coolidge met with Dawes at 9:30 A.M. to confirm final details. First Dawes was to set the stage with a speech to the Senate, as Coolidge himself had done. Coolidge would then give the great inaugural address, the first to be carried nationally by radio. The president planned a measured speech, like Harding's but milder and more spiritual—fitting given the achievements of budget cutting that were behind them and his desire for conciliation with Congress. More economy, Coolidge wrote, was necessary. Coolidge decided to update Harding's "no new experiments" with a line of caution: "If we wish to erect new structures, we must have a definite knowledge of the old foundations."

The Coolidges had never been as comfortable as other first families in their role, but they were warming up to it. On the train down to the inauguration, John encountered John Trumbull, the new governor of Connecticut, and rode with the Trumbulls. Trumbull was an energetic, friendly man, with his own manufacturing company. Trumbull Electric Manufacturing made switches, appliances, and other electrical supplies, demand for all of which was growing. The Trumbulls' daughter, Florence, attended Mount Holyoke. In his high hat, with Grace by his side, Coolidge rode in an open car to the inauguration. Grace had worn white in summer; now she set the tone with gray, "a shade deeper and warmer than pearl," as the press described it. It became known as "Coolidge gray." The important day was proceeding well.

Until Dawes wrecked it. Instead of rising to give the friendly pro forma address to the Senate which he had led Coolidge to expect, Dawes could not resist the opportunity to deliver a 1,300-word rant against the Senate, three times as long as the 434 words Coolidge had delivered four years before. Senators were selfish, he suggested, in their decision to sustain the practice of the filibuster. Senate rules, written by senators, placed "power in the hands of individuals to an extent, at times, subversive of the fundamental principles of free representative government." Because the Senate had not changed its ways, "the rights of the Nation and of the American people have been overlooked."

A storm of commentary and anger welled back from the senators. "Dawes showed as little knowledge of the Senate's rules as he did good taste," pronounced Democratic Minority Leader Joseph T. Robinson. "It was exactly what should not have been said," concluded Thaddeus Caraway, a senator from Arkansas. Some senators put their analysis simply and analytically: "There are some features of the rules, no doubt, that should be changed but he defeated any change by the brutal and clownish way in which he went about it." Senator Ashurst remarked that "it was the most acrobatic, gymnastic speech I have ever heard in the Senate." "I have an opinion of the spectacle but do not care to express it," said Senator Norris. The effect was to render the presidential address subordinate; Dawes had stolen the show.

Dawes's damage that day was compounded by a technical problem with the microphone set up for Coolidge's speech. An irritating echo interrupted Coolidge's phrases, so that the content could scarcely be heard. "While he was going it was all right," commented *The New York Times* of Coolidge, "but whenever he paused for breath it sounded as if somebody over at one side was mocking him." Then came yet another insult. Unlike Harding, who had so carefully made the Senate feel important on inauguration day, Dawes failed to return to the Senate after the inauguration to adjourn it. Instead he rode back with Coolidge to the White House. James Reed of Missouri later recalled that the Senate never adjourned that day; "it simply broke up." The senators had looked for a cause to quarrel with the new administration; the vice president had supplied one. Dawes's decision not to sit in on cabinet meetings was now also drawing attention, yet another bit of evidence of disunity. The White House staff who greeted the Coolidges on their return found them silent.

Coolidge was disturbed because he suspected more trouble for the tax legislation, and it indeed came, but from an unexpected quarter: the Treasury. Mellon, still burning with anger at Couzens after all the battles, was feeling feisty, in part because of Coolidge's support. On March 9, the Bureau of Internal Revenue released a projectile aimed at Couzens: a retroactive tax bill of $10 million on stock sales back years before. The Treasury announced Couzens's bill not quietly but in a press release, so that Couzens could read about it in the *Chicago Tribune*. The Internal Revenue Bureau had reversed a Wilson administration ruling on capital gains that Couzens had realized and found the tax basis to be $2,500 a share, not $8,900. The move was especially blatant because of the earlier ruling by Wilson; indeed, the tax courts would later find in Couzens's favor. Whether upon Mellon, Dawes, or Coolidge, or perhaps all three, the Senate was spoiling for revenge.

The very next day, March 10, the senators got their chance. The confirmation of Charles Beecher Warren, Coolidge's candidate to replace Stone, was the subject of intense debate. Coolidge could see that the vote would be closer than he had expected and exploded when Starling repeated a rumor that Warren might not be confirmed. "Well, you're such a great Secret Service man I guess you know more than anybody else. You know everything. Maybe you can tell me just how everyone is going to vote." Starling saw that Warren, too, was concerned: when he arrived at the Willard to deliver messages for Warren, he always found the man with the "covers pulled over his head." When the time came to vote, the senators present were indeed divided at 40–40. But the tie-breaker, the vice president, was not there. Dawes, having been assured the vote would not take place in the next few hours, had gone home to the Willard for a nap. By the time Dawes was roused and had raced the fifteen blocks back in a taxicab, the vote count had changed. Warren was defeated, 41–39. President Coolidge thus suffered a humiliation that more than matched anything he had endured in the previous term: Dawes's error made him the first president since Andrew Johnson to see a cabinet confirmation killed by the Senate.

The progressives were beside themselves with merriment. Senator Norris mocked General Dawes with a spoof of the victorious ride of Philip Sheridan to Cedar Creek:

The great senatorial temple of fame—
There with the great General's name,
Be it said in letters bold and bright,
"Oh, Hell an' Maria, he has lost us the fight."

A sign was put up by someone at the Willard's entrance: DAWES SLEPT HERE. Coolidge, furious, put Warren's name up again within two days, an unusual and bold gesture that stunned the Senate. Again, Warren was promptly rejected. Coolidge also invited Warren to lunch on Saturday, March 14. Then he swore to give Warren a recess appointment. In response, Senator Joe Robinson, the minority leader, swore to keep the Senate in session for the sole aim of hindering such an event.

Coolidge's instinctive response to all such setbacks, but especially the debacle of the nomination, was to look homeward. After the defeat of Warren was final, he asked Starling to find John Garibaldi Sargent, his father's attorney and the former attorney general of Vermont. The startled Sargent, who happened to be at the Pavilion Hotel in Montpelier, found himself ordered down to Washington without knowing why. "Just get that grip packed and don't tell anybody, even your wife," Starling said to Sargent. The Senate, in shock at its own lèse-majesté in the case of Warren, confirmed Sargent's nomination quickly. Sargent was attorney general before he even had time to assemble the appropriate clothing: he had had to black his large brown shoes before his first public appearance. Coolidge, for his part, was well satisfied with it all. Now someone he could count on sat to his right in cabinet meetings. He insisted that Sargent stay at the White House.

Comforted to have a bit of Vermont with him in Washington, Coolidge marched forward, his eye out for possible legislative victories, whatever their size. He had nominated Wallace McCamant, the man who had called out his name at the Chicago convention, for a federal judgeship. Now that confirmation looked iffy as well. So in May, while the Senate was in recess, Coolidge gave McCamant a recess appointment to the Ninth Circuit Court of Appeals. It was enormously gratifying to find McCamant a seat on the federal bench after his support at the convention of 1920, just as it had been to appoint Sargent to an important post. Jardine had been confirmed in mid-February, along with Kellogg. Denby, the gullible navy secretary, was finally gone, and Coolidge had already named Curtis Wilbur in his place. It turned out that a recess appointment was possible for another contentious nominee, Thomas Woodlock. Coolidge placed Woodlock at the Interstate Commerce Commission because he had seen that Woodlock, through his years on Wall Street and as an editor of *The Wall Street Journal*, was the opposite of Joseph Eastman and Louis Brandeis. Woodlock understood that regulation could impede growth as well as facilitate it. With Longworth, Coolidge plotted the tax reform; there was no reason the legislation could not make its way through the Senate in the fall. To the public, meanwhile, he preached savings again: "Economy reaches everywhere. It carries a blessing for everybody."

Perhaps chagrined at his own contribution to the tension between the administration and the Senate, Mellon, too, was now working hard again to placate both senators and congressmen. At a speech in Richmond, Virginia, in March, Mellon made an effort to remind listeners that secretaries in the past had also supported reduction in taxes: Carter Glass and David Houston, two Democrats who had preceded Mellon at Treasury, were examples. Glass had opposed any increase in the uppermost brackets; Houston was "even more specific." Then Mellon went back to the only comforting thing in the story, the evidence: "It has been our experience that a reduction in taxation does not mean an equivalent loss in revenue." As he had in *Taxation: The People's Business*, here Mellon tried to put his case simply: "If income taxes are so excessive that a man of ability finds he must work more than three days a week for the Government and has but three days a week for himself he will become discouraged and decide that the result is not worth his effort."

And once more, the Treasury's revenue reports provided consolation. On April 24, 1925, the Bureau of Internal Revenue reported that the budget surplus would be over $100 million, compared with the earlier forecast of $68 million. Income tax receipts were down, but not by much; Coolidge's cutting work with Lord more than offset the difference. Lord, Coolidge kept rediscovering, was still working miracles with his "cheeseparing," as Coolidge called it to the press, cutting the budget back as he had cut back in the sandwich he had prepared for Starling. Mellon too knew how to find money: alcohol seized could be sold as medicine. The next fiscal year, that ending in 1926, the Treasury was willing to predict now, would see a surplus of $375 million, making tax reduction a safe venture. The surplus was much larger than they had expected. Mellon, seemingly recovered from his fit of rage, was making a new and subtle point. The timing of the tax cuts mattered, but so did the direction of Treasury policy. If people were sure cuts were coming, they anticipated them and commerce expanded in anticipation, just as had happened in the stock market after the crash. "In fixing rates, whether they be normal taxes or surtaxes or death taxes," said Mellon, "the controlling factor should be the effectiveness of the rates in producing revenue, not only for the year in which they are levied but over a long period of years." Tax changes should be infrequent and permanent when possible.

The rest of the economy was likewise supplying good news. Coal prices were stable and employment was so high that workers were scarce. Wages rose, even though union membership and certainly union strikes were down. The Dow Jones Industrial Average was now inching above 130. And, whatever Vice President Dawes and Senator Norris had yet up their sleeves, the chances of success for Coolidge were good. That June, he and Lord convened the ninth budget meeting since Harding's quirky law had been passed. Lord had introduced a new gimmick, a "Two Percent Club," for departments that trimmed their budget that much. Now he could report that the first charter member was the post office in Camden, South Carolina, and many others followed. Somehow or other, by March, $50 million had been shaved off the $62 million that remained to be cut from the budget to get to $3 billion. The director of the Veterans Bureau might take them still closer; the bureau's annual phone bill for long-distance calls had been $2,946.48 in 1922; now it was $184.65, thanks to cables sent instead.

Even what appeared to be waste could yield savings when an official concentrated, Lord said, citing the example of "seven barrels of spoiled, soused seal shoulders sent from Alaska." Someone on the General Supply Committee had managed to turn waste into value by selling those shoulders for $20 as crab bait. The continued plea for economy, Lord knew, "gets tiresome and wearisome," but staffers had to remember that Coolidge wished to save not to save money but "to save people." He, Mellon, and Lord would be able to report at the semiannual budget meeting that the federal deficit was down again, at $20.5 billion total, compared with $21.25 the year before. Everyone saw that there was a limit to cuts; could the government cut decade in and decade out? Lord would have a One Percent Club after his Two Percent Club. Then, Lord told his captive audience, he would create a Woodpecker Club, for government offices that pecked away at their expenses here or there. To Coolidge and Lord, both from the forests of New England, the name "woodpecker" meant something: they had often heard the distinctive *rat-a-tat* of the bird.

Coolidge's father, John, was not faring well. That spring he let the limekiln lot to a neighbor, Walter Lynds. Requests for business still came in, and John sought to be helpful. "Walter W Lynds makes nice sugar or syrup and can tell you the price," he wrote one inquirer from Joliet, Illinois, getting Lynds's middle initial wrong but making the point about the product well enough. To others, Colonel Coolidge announced, "I have leased my sugar lot. Walter Lynds makes good sirup." In June, Colonel Coolidge had surgery for prostate trouble, and the Coolidges decided to stay in Massachusetts so they would not be too far away from him. They settled on Swampscott, near Stearns. For years Stearns had longed to situate the Coolidges in a dwelling appropriate to their status. Now, probably because he was paying many of the costs, he finally got his wish. The Coolidges would dwell in White Court, an elegant home beside his. Several times, Coolidge visited his father in Plymouth Notch, hoping to convince him to move to Washington for the winter, but he failed.

Other concerns pressed that summer. The railroads were not making the kind of recovery that had been imagined; perhaps their overregulation had done permanent damage. The new recess appointee at the ICC, Thomas Woodlock, found many of the ICC's premises questionable, especially the idea that it might act as "an arbiter in economics." Maybe railroads did not require such strong regulation once consolidated, he felt. He judged the vocabulary of the ICC absurd. "What is a 'combination rate' which 'makes on' the Ohio River?" he would later write, summing up his challenge upon entering the commission work. "What is a 'joint through rate'? What is the name of Heaven is 'fourth section relief'?" Woodlock was especially frustrated at the fact that the ICC's activities, even under Coolidge, expanded. Coolidge also had to deal with the challenge of military spending. The number of battleships was being cut, but the head of the U.S. Army Air Service, Colonel William Mitchell, was making economy in defense nearly impossible by repeatedly warning that the lack of a giant U.S. force in the air made the country vulnerable to invasion by foreign forces.

It all combined to put Coolidge into one of the worst moods of his life. The staff steered clear. He fussed more about John. He was concerned, he wrote to his father, at John's frivolity. He hoped John might be drawn out of youth as he had been, and had just written William Newlin, Garman's former student and now an Amherst professor of philosophy, "I want my son John to have as near as possible the same course in Philosophy that I had. You will know exactly what that was because you were there about that time. He will bring this letter to you." John, for his part, told Ike Hoover, the usher, that White Court felt like a prison. The president still liked to oversee every aspect of John's day, Starling and Hoover noticed, and even picked at him. At one point while away from White Court, John wrote to his parents but addressed the letter wrongly so that it did not go directly to Swampscott. Coolidge exploded. "Your letter went to Washington. . . . it is accuracy that counts. Shots that do not make the mark are no good. You had better remember that. The world is full of people that almost succeed, the trouble is they won't work. Many men are almost President. But only 29 have been chosen. I hope you will not be an 'almost man.'" The Massachusetts State Legislature had commissioned the distinguished painter Edmund Tarbell to make a portrait of Coolidge for $3,500, and Coolidge sat for several hours a day. Stearns noticed and Clarence Barron would notice that Coolidge gave such artists a hard time; he made his face intentionally blank. When it came to family business, Coolidge also tended to the grim. He learned that his grandmother's brother, M. B. Brewer, had died and that the graves of her parents in Hampden, Wisconsin, were scarcely marked. He ordered grave markers of Vermont stone. In a bid to shed some light on his New England ways, he organized a trip for reporters to the home of John Greenleaf Whittier, the author of the poem "Snow-Bound."

Even that summer, however, there were times when Coolidge managed to relax. They were with friends: Frank and Emily Stearns finally had the time they longed for with "their" Coolidges; if Stearns could not be Colonel House to Coolidge, the Sherpa who helped him set policy, at least Stearns could be a good host, and share what he knew of the Coolidges with the White House staff. In all things, Stearns instructed Starling, "Mrs. Coolidge came first." Stearns brought Grace a lace cap from Brittany to protect her from the sun while she gardened. When a singer came to Swampscott, she played the piano so the artist could sing "My Wild Irish Rose."

If music cheered Grace, Clarence Barron, the jovial press lord, revived the president. Barron kept a home in nearby Cohasset. Coolidge sailed over on the *Mayflower* to Plymouth, a conscious replication of history, and then motored to Cohasset to visit the economic guru. Before they could talk business, Coolidge had to be polite. Barron, himself a large man, displayed a prize bull he owned, insisting Coolidge inspect it and, to Starling's amusement, "reeled off the frightening number of calves sired by his prize, and told how all of his children who grew to be cows gave such rich milk that it could pass for cream." Coolidge, who, notwithstanding the cigar habit, still boasted an excellent nose himself, could stand only a few minutes of it before walking away and muttering, "Some bull!"

But the material on commerce, the chance to get Barron's perspective, was well worth the trip. Wall Street was interested in chain stores and utilities. So were many consumers and shareholders; that summer the Great Atlantic and Pacific Tea Company, heretofore a closed corporation, would issue stock and give senior employees shares in its 12,000-odd stores. Other chains, such as J. C. Penney, had seen sales for the first five months of the year move up 19 percent. Barron was a living counterweight to the worriers and progressives. That summer of 1925, tens of thousands of members of the Ku Klux Klan marched in Washington. But Barron was concentrating on the economy. The anthracite men were warning that a coal strike might yet again threaten the country that autumn; Barron reminded Coolidge that nowadays there were plenty of substitutes for anthracite. Coolidge wondered about crime; Barron pooh-poohed it as a local problem. As Barron left his house, reporters jumped the newspaperman: what had he and the president said about the coal strike? "I said we did not discuss the coal strike," Barron later wrote in his diary. "Wall Street was not interested in the coal strike."

The perspective of Barron was so welcome because it allowed Coolidge to follow his own instincts and concentrate his mind on the legislation he deemed most important: the tax cut. When Coolidge returned in the fall, he found the House Appropriations Committee chair recommending that the surtax that came on top of the tax base ought to be reduced to 15 percent, which would mean a top income tax rate of something like 20 percent. The idea had been a dream just a few years before. Wages were up even after inflation, especially for skilled and semiskilled workers, after a sharp drop in the early 1920s. The recession of the early 1920s had been rough, but already memories of it were fading.

Back in Washington in September Coolidge had his mind on the future gain, the growth in commerce that would make the government look smaller, the denominator in the crucial fraction of government relative to the general economy. Aviation could not become a public-sector project; it had to stay in the private sector. The best way to ensure that was to prove that those who argued that the United States needed a big navy or an arsenal of airplanes were scaremongers. Coolidge summoned another friend, again without warning. This time the friend was Dwight Morrow, not Sargent. Morrow opened his newspaper one day that month to learn that he had been named to a board to decide what role aircraft had in the U.S. defense. The day after the news appeared in the paper, Morrow received one of Coolidge's classic peremptory notes:

> *My Dear Mr. Morrow;*
>   *Enclosed is a copy of a communication which you may have seen in the press. I request that you serve in the capacity indicated and I would like you to meet me at the White House on Thursday September 17, at 11:00 o'clock in the forenoon and lunch with me at 1:00. . . .*
>   *Very truly yours*

Morrow took a suite at the Wardman Hotel and sat down for eight weeks with eight others to sort out whether the army, the navy, or a new agency should defend the United States' skies, and to what extent. Morrow's commission summoned Orville Wright himself to testify, and Wright's modest demeanor did much to pour cold water on Colonel William Mitchell's flames. Morrow held hearings and produced a report noting that for a century the Great Lakes had been unguarded by the navy, yet Canada had not occupied the Midwest. Morrow's conclusion was classic Dwight and classic Coolidge: defense might well be necessary, but "to create a defense system based upon a hypothetical attack from Canada, Mexico, or another of our near neighbors would be wholly unreasonable." Morrow's coup de grâce was that he managed to so construct the report that his board endorsed it unanimously; even General Pershing was impressed.

In October 1925, Coolidge and Grace boarded the Presidential Special for a two-day trip, journeying all the way out to Omaha to explain the Coolidge perspective on the world to the American Legion. Here was a group of tens of thousands, leaders in the veterans' movement for bonuses. Coolidge now gave the response to the Ku Klux Klan that people had awaited since the Klan's summer marches. He called for tolerance, which he defined as "respect for different kinds of good." He also made it clear that while he might have signed legislation restricting immigration, he did not mean there ought to be discrimination against immigrants. Grappling for an image, he found himself, like Garman, speaking of ships, and perhaps thinking of his own family history and even the previous summer's trip to Plymouth Rock on the presidential yacht: "Whether one traces his Americanism back three centuries to the *Mayflower* or three years to the steerage is not half so important as whether his Americanism of today is real and genuine. No matter by what various crafts we came here, we are all now in the same boat." As it happened, the trip coincided with their twentieth anniversary; the papers noted that the trip must be different from the one they had made to Montreal so long before. The response to the speech, including that among blacks, was friendly. "Particularly do we want to thank you for that great word you spoke at Omaha, the bravest word spoken by any Executive in three score years. It sounds like Lincoln," said Henry Proctor, a spokesman for black Congregationalists. Other black leaders berated Coolidge for not speaking so frankly against intolerance during the election of 1924. Still, as the Baltimore *Afro-American* noted, the speech was a clear blow to the Klan: "Two years afterward [after the presidential election] and without apparent new cause, he whales the Ku Klux Klan between the eyes."

The Omaha trip behind him, Coolidge turned back, yet again, to taxes. In November, he went up to New York to deliver a speech he hoped would highlight the philosophy behind the tax drive. There was a perpetual tension between Washington and the rest of the country. That tension showed up in tax battles or debt discussion, but also in other ways, between states and Washington, or even cities and Washington. New York knew it was rich, but it did not always understand that its value was political. Taxpayers, indeed all citizens, also benefited from every check on Washington's power, including the presence of a separate financial capital to compete with the political capital. When the framers of the Constitution "made Washington the political center of the country and left New York to develop into its business center," Coolidge said, "they wrought mightily for freedom." A tax cut was a reduction in tax on capital; in other words, a blow struck for every place that was not Washington.

That same month, the time finally came for Mellon and Coolidge to launch their law. Coolidge pounded away on the new tax legislation, planning for a vote early in 1926. The president and his cabinet secretary laid out the outlines in November: income tax cuts, especially reduction of surtaxes, worth $193.5 million. Mellon was about to announce proud news: the federal debt was down to $20 billion; he had managed the refinancing with a skill worthy of Hamilton.

The pair therefore felt comfortable in offering not just their great top cuts but small cuts, like so many Christmas tree ornaments for the coming season: estate taxes and gift taxes, as well as taxes on cars, mahjongg sets, yacht use, and brokers were all coming down, as well as taxes on both cigars and cigar holders. Christmas itself offered a brief interlude from the tax campaign. The living Christmas tree, the Norway spruce, was in its second year in Washington; thousands of Washingtonians came downtown to see it and walk the White House grounds. Mellon and Hoover both went to Sherman Square to watch Coolidge flick the switch to light the tree beside the statues of General Sherman and Alexander Hamilton.

After the holiday, Coolidge aimed to turn back to work. But as so often happened when a project demanded all of Coolidge's attention, trouble intruded. Coolidge's father, John, was weakening. An invalid now, he remained in bed much of the time and, despite Coolidge's invitations, would not come to Washington. Like Sargent, John Coolidge took a dim view of mosquito-ridden Washington, especially after the death of Calvin. Coolidge had shipped his father cakes, candy, nuts, fruit, and books. But that did not seem enough, and Coolidge also sent his son John up to keep him company in Plymouth. A stroke had deprived his father of the use of a leg. On the morning of January 1, readying himself for the overwhelming New Year's reception, Coolidge momentarily sank to a low again: "I am the most powerful man in the world but great power does not mean much except great limitations. I cannot have any freedom. . . . Thousands are waiting to shake my hand today." Shortly thereafter, Coolidge wrote his father with another idea:

I would like to have a private telephone put in your house. It can
go in the sitting room and have a long cord on it that will permit it
to be taken to your bed, so that I can talk with you some times. The
number will not be given out and no one can call you up, so you will
not be annoyed with it and I will be glad to pay whatever expense is
incurred.

To that, at least, the Colonel acquiesced, and in a local paper, there was a report that John McManama, a New England Telephone employee, was now the recipient of a Havana cigar "stamped with the chief executive's name and presented to him by the father of the president." The Coolidge father and son spoke now once or twice a day.

The president was also placing other calls, some directly. The administration and the lawmakers were now nearing the end of the tax siege, the victor haggling with the defeated. This was a period of furious back-and-forth for the tax legislation; Coolidge and Mellon would not relent until their bill was law, safe from the fate of 1924. The haggling continued. Coolidge wanted corporate taxes low. The lawmakers wanted to raise them slightly. The Republicans sought that cut in the cigar tax. Senator Smoot wanted to strike the cigar tax reduction. Mellon wanted everyone to pay a little tax. The Treasury secretary found it uncivic to remove too many from the tax rolls. The Democrats mocked him; there were so many other taxes the little man still paid. Mellon wanted to keep or shorten the maturity of public debt; the Democrats wanted to increase the number of years the public debt was paid down to more than thirty. Mellon fought back. "Pay your debts while you can," he admonished. In desperation, the opponents of the legislation began to quantify the share of the tax break that the wealthy would claim. This, they were discovering, was an easy way to frame an opponent. General, across-the-board cuts of any progressive structure always favored the rich, since they had been paying more under progressivity to begin with. Senator George Norris pointed out, "Mr. Mellon himself gets a larger personal reduction than the aggregate of practically all the taxpayers in the state of Nebraska." So he did. But Mellon paid more tax than the citizens of that state as well.

Still, scientific taxation did prevail. The new tax schedule Mellon's men drew up was a beauty to behold, with its surtax rate topping out at 20 percent. The top rate, surtax plus base, was 25 percent. The hated publicity requirement in the tax code was stripped out, so that tax returns were again private. Estate taxes came down. And about one in three of those who had paid taxes before paid no taxes now. Revenues had increased after rates had been cut before. "We have paid back more money than we ever paid in," Will Rogers joked. Perhaps even more would come now. The tax law was the very kind of action Calvin, Jr., had described in his letter about "the first boy of the land" back in August 1923. If Coolidge was a loner, he was a loner who had forged a historic partnership, that with Mellon. If grief could yield a gift, the grief over Calvin had yielded one for Mellon and, perhaps, the country.

Content with his work, Coolidge in this period finally indulged in two purchases, one for himself, one for the country. He hired a sculptor, Bryant Baker, to go to Plymouth and make a bust of Colonel John. Baker was a distinguished artist and had sculpted both Norwegian King Olaf as a child and Great Britain's King Edward VII. Coolidge took the bust to his study, so that he could see John and not merely hear his voice on the phone. Coolidge's second move was to allow the federal government to buy up the great collection of Abraham Lincoln material, the Oldroyd Collection, for the $50,000 the ancient and distinguished owner, Captain Osborn Oldroyd, demanded. That debit was one the federal government could handle.

At 2:25 P.M. on February 25, 1926, the president of the Senate, Dawes, transmitted the legislation to the White House. On the morning of February 26, the moment finally came to sign the tax bill. By 10:10 A.M., the president was waiting, but some who were invited had not shown up yet: General Lord, ranking Democrats such as John Nance Garner of Texas, Secretary Mellon. Reporters noticed that Mellon, when he arrived, was beaming. When Senator Furnifold Simmons of North Carolina, the last to arrive, finally made it to the signing, he was in such a hurry that he failed to put out his cigar and held it in his hand as Coolidge signed. Cameras clicked and flashed. In an effort to be friendly, Reed Smoot, the legendary Republican Finance Committee chairman, reached over to grasp the hand of a Democrat, Senator Simmons, and grabbed the cigar itself. The stogie, by that time, was fortunately no longer lit, but was demolished in the course of the upheaval and interaction. That was kind of an inside joke in itself, since Senator Smoot had contested the cigar tax reduction.

"I note you are still doing those clear, grim, silent miracles; making Congress eat out of your hand, lie down and roll over and play dead dog, and also jump through hoops," William Allen White wrote to Coolidge that spring after the tax victory.

The other press men did not view it so broadly. But they found themselves reflecting on other details of the great signing. On that day Coolidge had seemed preoccupied, not so much with taxes as with debt negotiations and the Italians. On paper, at least, the tax cut cost the government $388 million, or, potentially, a year's surplus. Though Coolidge was now a Mellon convert, it would always make him nervous to forgo that much revenue, if only on paper. The U.S. flag by the president's desk obscured the politicians present from some angles. Cameramen asked the president for permission to remove the flag. But Coolidge, who normally obliged the press men, this time denied permission. The Stars and Stripes had to be part of the scene; they came before individual politicians.

The happiest person present at the scene of the signing had proved to be the normally dour Mellon. "He smiled continually," wrote a *New York Times* reporter in wonder. Mellon's smile was not that of a politician. It was the anticipatory smile of a scholar. The Treasury secretary was enjoying the unexpected opportunity to complete an experiment he had feared aborted. For so long Mellon had told everyone, including Coolidge, that the Mellon Plan could allow the national economy to move to greater heights. Now, finally, and on the greatest field of all, scientific taxation would see its test.

TWELVE

❦

THE FLOOD AND THE FLIER

Washington, D.C.

ONE OF THE FIRST visitors Coolidge received in Washington after his vacation in the summer of 1926 was the president of the Goodyear Tire & Rubber Company, P. W. Litchfield. Litchfield arrived, chief aeronautics engineer in tow, to seek Coolidge's support for Goodyear's new airship fleet. The company planned to build a dirigible of 6 million cubic feet, larger than past airships. Aviation, whether by dirigible or airplane, was now common in the Midwest. In fact, the damage done by flooding across the Midwest was being captured that month in arresting panorama shots of submerged houses taken from airplanes. Litchfield and his engineer, however, set their sights beyond the heartland: their dirigible would cross the Atlantic between New York and London. The New York–London Line, Litchfield told reporters, "should prove a successful commercial venture in oceanic travel." The 1925 accident of a navy airship, the *Shenandoah*, would not deter Goodyear. The new airship would complete its voyage in "two and one-half days, or not more than three," the rubber company reported. That was half the time of the old ocean liners from before the war. But planes might yet make it in two days.

The faster, the better, as far as Coolidge was concerned. The scientific taxation experiment of Mellon was under way, but the plan did not have forever to prove it could deliver. Any unpredicted event could stall the experiment in its crucial demonstration year. The growth and results from the tax experiment had to come fast, if the experiment were to see completion and prove it could benefit all. In a key way, aviation had the potential to help Coolidge and Mellon out. For one thing, flight fired the national imagination, and distracted people from their sorrows. "Well after I finish a long siege," Will Rogers would write, "I sorter begin to look up in the sky and see what is flying over." Second, aviation contributed to commerce itself, by enabling companies to work faster, mail to be delivered sooner, and connections to be made where there had been none before. Growth in turn helped the tax revenues flow.

That technology had such transformative power was something Coolidge had known since his afternoons at the depot of Ludlow or the period when street trolleys of the Connecticut River Valley had enthralled him and Alfred Pearce Dennis on their evening rides. Lately, it had been cars that had sped up commerce. Even as Mellon's tax experiment proceeded, trucks were replacing rail freight faster than anyone had suspected, and Coolidge hoped to profit from his own conviction that transport had more distance to run. That month, via his broker, R. L. Day, Coolidge had picked up 100 shares of Mack Trucks preferred stock at 108¾ dollars a share. Technology could not do everything forever, but it could help you through an impasse. If civil aviation, not the military, took the lead, all the better. In the private sphere, invention worked especially powerfully. Conversely, as Coolidge knew, the price was especially high where machines failed, where connections were not made, when technology came too late.

The price of being too late had become all too clear again to him just the spring before. Coolidge's father had begun to fade in January and February. One of John's legs had no longer worked. The Colonel had suffered some kind of a stroke. The telephone line to the bed no longer sufficed; Coolidge was ready to travel up when the doctors ordered. But the busy legislative season had kept his eyes on Congress in that period. Every deal Mellon cut with a foreign government to refinance its loans had to be approved by Congress; an especially generous one with Italy, whereby the debt was readjusted down to a fifth of the old level, had required forceful backing from Coolidge in January and February to win passage.

BORN ON THE FOURTH OF JULY.
Calvin Coolidge came into the world
on July 4, 1872, in the downstairs
bedroom of a small house adjacent to
his father's general store in Plymouth
Notch, Vermont. Coolidge wrote
of his fellow villagers: "They were a
hardy, self-contained people."

A FATHER'S WISDOM. From his
father, John Calvin Coolidge, Sr., the
president learned what he called the
"fundamental idea of both private
and public business." Over the course
of his life John Coolidge served as
merchant, town tax collector, general
store operator, notary, selectman,
sheriff, and member of both the
Vermont House of Representatives
and the State Senate. Wrote Coolidge:
"If there was any physical requirement
of country life which he could not
perform, I do not know what it was."

THE OUDEN. At Amherst College in Massachusetts, an institution founded for impoverished Protestant clergy, the Vermonter initially attracted little notice and failed, at first, to be admitted to one of the numerous fraternities. Senior year, however, his debate skills drew the attention of more popular students such as Dwight Morrow. Amherst alumni, including his future employers, began to notice Coolidge as well.

A SIMPLE RENTAL. The Coolidges' home at 21 Massasoit Street in Northampton, Massachusetts. Home ownership was the rage when the Coolidges married in 1905. Yet the Coolidges rented their home, half of a two-family house. Their linens were purchased secondhand from the Norwood Hotel.

LOOMING FIGURES. Senator Murray Crane, from Coolidge's own Western Massachusetts, helped Coolidge from his early days in Northampton politics. The reticent Crane became Coolidge's mentor. Senator Henry Cabot Lodge of Boston and Nahant, Massachusetts, treated Coolidge as a parvenu, even when Coolidge presided over the U.S. Senate as vice president.

A STRIKE TO END ALL STRIKES. In 1919, when Coolidge was serving as Massachusetts governor, the Boston police affiliated with the American Federation of Labor and went on strike. Many expected the new governor to negotiate with the strikers. Their pay was low and their station houses infested with vermin.

THE ALLY. Coolidge stood by Edwin Curtis, the Boston police commissioner, and supported his decision to discharge the striking policemen.

"THERE IS NO RIGHT TO STRIKE AGAINST THE PUBLIC SAFETY BY ANYBODY, ANYWHERE, ANY TIME." Coolidge at his desk during the 1919 Boston police strike. In standing up against the strikers, Coolidge upstaged President Woodrow Wilson, who was waffling on labor unrest. Coolidge's steely resolve during the strike calmed a nervous nation. "No doubt, it was the police strike of Boston that brought me into national prominence," Coolidge later wrote.

AN EDUCATED FIRST LADY. Coolidge and his wife, Grace, casting their ballots in the 1920 presidential election shortly after the passage of the Nineteenth Amendment, which gave women the right to vote. Grace, who trained to teach the deaf at the Clarke School after college, was the first first lady to have graduated from a coed university.

AN ELECTION TO END UNCERTAINTY. In a time of enormous budget deficits and high taxes, Warren Harding and Coolidge campaigned on the theme of "normalcy." After Harding's 1920 election, Congress passed a landmark budget law and tax cuts. When Harding died, Coolidge vowed to carry out Harding's policies "to perfection."

A NOTARY'S INAUGURATION. Upon hearing that Harding had died suddenly on a summer trip out west, Coolidge was sworn into office in the early hours of August 3, 1923. Coolidge's father, a notary public, administered the oath of office. The plainness of the village inaugural reinforced the Coolidge message: American democracy starts at the local level. Above is one of the many re-creations of the swearing in.

"I AM FOR ECONOMY. AFTER THAT I AM FOR MORE ECONOMY." From his first days in office, Coolidge met regularly with General Herbert Lord, the director of the Bureau of the Budget. In sustained sessions, they trimmed and cut the expenditures of the federal government. This was Coolidge's way of telling the country he would not relent until the war debts were reduced.

SURPRISINGLY LOQUACIOUS. Congress quickly learned that "Silent Cal" was not as taciturn as alleged. The title of this cartoon is "But when he does speak, he says a mouthful." The speech of December 1923 was the one in which he staked his presidency on tax cuts.

A SON'S SENSE OF OFFICE. Coolidge sent his younger son, Calvin, Jr., to work in a Massachusetts tobacco field over the summer. A fellow laborer told the boy, "If my father was president, I would not work in a tobacco field." Young Calvin responded, "If your father were my father, you would."

BEFORE A LOSS. Calvin Coolidge, Jr.; President Coolidge; the first lady; and John Coolidge on June 30, 1924. The day this picture was taken, Calvin, Jr., had developed a blister on his toe from playing tennis on the White House court. A week later the boy died of sepsis.

AN OUTSTANDING VICTORY. The swearing in of President Calvin Coolidge on March 4, 1925. Coolidge won an absolute majority of the popular vote although he faced two competitors, Democrat John W. Davis and Progressive Robert La Follette, a former Republican.

"I DON'T KNOW WHAT I WOULD DO WITHOUT HER." Grace, a kind extrovert, paved the way in Washington for the reserved Coolidge. Coolidge protected his wife jealously. In all matters, their friends counseled, Grace came first.

TECHNOLOGY IS KEY. Coolidge meeting with Thomas Edison in 1924. His reputation as a Victorian throwback notwithstanding, Coolidge avidly promoted and used new technologies, from the radio to cars to airplanes. Coolidge himself benefited politically from the radio, through which he often addressed the public. "Over the radio," said editor William Allen White, "he went straight to the popular heart."

THE AMHERST MEN. Dwight Morrow, an old Amherst friend, in September of 1925, when he was chair of the Special Aviation Board. Another Amherst acquaintance, Harlan Fiske Stone, became Coolidge's attorney general and then Supreme Court justice.

THE ADVISER. Coolidge with Treasury Secretary Andrew Mellon. Mellon wagered that what he called scientific taxation would yield greater budget surpluses and a stronger economy. Coolidge backed Mellon in his policy experiment. Observers joked that the two reserved men conversed in pauses.

ALOFT. President Coolidge speaks at a ceremony held in honor of Charles Lindbergh, after he completed his epic flight from America to France. Aviation was to Coolidge evidence of the country's future greatness and its ability to get around regulatory bottlenecks involving highways and railroads.

CONFLICT OVER A FLOOD. Members of Coolidge's cabinet gathered to discuss the administration's response to the disastrous Mississippi River Valley flood of 1927. Herbert Hoover, at center, advocated strong federal intervention and infrastructure spending.

"I DO NOT CHOOSE TO RUN FOR PRESIDENT IN NINETEEN TWENTY-EIGHT." With these historic words, Coolidge upended his party by refusing to run for office even though polls indicated he was a sure winner. This note and other copies were handed out to shocked reporters during Coolidge's 1927 stay in the Black Hills of South Dakota.

A DIFFICULT DECISION. Coolidge, ambivalent, at a ceremony naming him honorary chief of the Sioux Native Americans, days after his decision not to seek reelection. *Left to right*: Grace Coolidge, Calvin Coolidge, Rosebud Yellow Robe, Chief Chauncey Yellow Robe, and Henry Standing Bear. His policy of helping Indians to assimilate through education differed dramatically from his successors' treatment of Native Americans as a nation and a group.

A PRESIDENTIAL MONUMENT. Gutzon Borglum's model for his presidential colossus. Coolidge visited the site and endorsed Borglum's plan to sculpt past presidents into the Black Hills of South Dakota. Coolidge, however, was loath to endorse monuments to himself.

A TEST OF CHARACTER AND FEDERALISM. After the Mississippi flood, a flood struck the president's native Vermont. He had not gone to the Mississippi flood, and he did not go to this one, to demonstrate his commitment to the authority of a state government in an emergency. This image depicts Montpelier, the capital.

SAVE WORDS. The Coolidge administration went to great lengths to instill frugality in the federal government. In the spring of 1928, General Lord wrote to Coolidge to say that the placard above was placed on the desks of correspondence clerks of the Department of Agriculture's Bureau of Animal Industry "with a view to reducing the number and length of letters."

ANOTHER HISTORIC PARTNERSHIP. After working with Andrew Mellon to pass historic tax cuts, Coolidge teamed up with Secretary of State Frank Kellogg to write the Kellogg-Briand Pact against war. Critics called the treaty a swordless sheath, but Coolidge believed its emphasis on law would foster worldwide peace.

LIKE THE MEN OF OLD. The Republican Party repeatedly asked Coolidge to reconsider his decision not to run—in vain. Coolidge said that "the chances of having wise and faithful public service are increased by a change in the presidential office after a moderate length of time."

"—THRICE PRESENTED HIM A KINGLY CROWN, WHICH HE DID THRICE REFUSE"—Julius Caesar

WONDER BOY. Coolidge and Hoover on the day of Hoover's inauguration. Coolidge disliked Hoover and called him "Wonder Boy."

IN DUE TIME. Coolidge passed away on January 5, 1933. He was buried with his father, mother, and son Calvin at the small cemetery in Plymouth Notch. "In due time the good fortune of the United States to have had such a man as Calvin Coolidge in just the years he filled that office will be more clearly realized than it has yet been," *The Wall Street Journal* commented.

The week the doctors attending his father deemed it time to summon the president north, Plymouth had been, still, literally snowbound. Coolidge paced as Colonel Starling dictated the elaborate preparations for the trip up to the village to men in Massachusetts and Vermont over the phone: the Presidential Special would travel to Woodstock; there they would transfer to cars and then to sleighs for the final leg of the journey to Plymouth. Workers from both Woodstock and Ludlow engaged in a competition to clear the roads for cars. Some new to the task had been chagrined to discover that the last mile of the trip to Plymouth was "nearly perpendicular." By the time Coolidge and his wife reached Plymouth in their double sleigh, the men were already shoveling another path, to the cemetery.

The death of his father hit Coolidge harder than he had expected, and his father's affairs preoccupied him for months. He sorted through John's bankbooks and found that his deposit box at the bank contained a diamond ring and savings account books and bonds adding up to $43,601.25, an enormous amount in those days and a testimony to the thrift John had practiced. Neighbor Edward Blanchard, Walter Lynds, and others were left to oversee the Coolidge properties. Lynds had a secondhand boiler to process the sugar. Coolidge corresponded with them; he was now a landlord. But it was hard to go back with John gone. That summer the Coolidges had established the summer White House not in Plymouth with Aurora Pierce but in New York's Adirondacks. It had been a pleasant enough time, including fishing excursions arranged by Colonel Starling. A comfort to both Coolidges was that Mrs. Jaffray had finally departed the White House for good. Frank Stearns had arranged for a replacement, Ellen Riley of Ipswich, who had worked in Boston at R. H. Stearns. The papers reported that Miss Riley had been picked "because of her wide knowledge of New England food." Still, physical distance had not kept Coolidge from reviewing, link by link, that chain of events that had led up to John Coolidge's death; instead of mourning just Calvin, now he had to mourn them both.

Now, in Washington, Coolidge and Mellon had their hands full defending the tax cut. Coolidge had laid siege to Congress before; now they felt themselves to be the ones besieged, like Will Rogers. With each month that passed, lawmakers readied new plans to convert their revenues into deficits or to change the law so that the value of the experiment would never be visible. Muscle Shoals, the nitrate plant at the Wilson

Dam on the Tennessee River, remained in the federal government's hands; progressives such as Senator Norris of Nebraska, who had just ascended to the position of chairman of the Senate Judiciary Committee, might yet make Muscle Shoals into the basis of a chain of federal hydropower plants. In the halls of the Senate, the topic of Muscle Shoals would not die; its nickname was "The Alabama Ghost." Though Harding and Coolidge had fought off agricultural subsidy before, the farm senators now sought a new kind of intervention, a government office that managed prices and guaranteed farmers parity, which was defined as the same high price levels that had been the rule years before. The case that farmers deserved regulated high prices remained easy to make as long as the farmers had to pay the artificially high prices for their tools and goods that were ensured by the Coolidge-backed Republican tariff.

Other challenges kept popping up. Many Democrats were like Senator Robinson, and wanted to beat Coolidge and Mellon at their own game, cutting rates, but then using any extra revenue not for debt reduction or tax rebates but for new large programs. The loudest and most authoritative demand for costly programs came from infrastructure engineers, led by Herbert Hoover. Hoover stood by Coolidge and his agriculture secretary, William Jardine, in their hand-to-hand combat with the farming bloc. But in exchange the commerce secretary demanded much, including White House backing for an expensive system of dams and sluices and a new rerouting of the Colorado, Mississippi, and Columbia rivers, not to mention the Great Lakes. The military thought that any extra cash ought to be spent on new cruiser ships; the House Naval Committee was applying all its weight to get Coolidge to put more cruisers into the budget. Policymaking was likely to become tougher after the midterm. If the Republicans, the incumbent party this time, lost seats in the midterms, then their foothold would become weaker. If the progressives or labor parties gained, they too might interrupt the tax plan. There had been costly natural disasters, like the floods in the Midwest. Then there was the economic weather: Ford planned to shut down his factories to build a new model to replace the Model T; that might cause a recession all by itself and strengthen the progressives.

When aviation would be able to realize its potential was not yet clear. Nearly a decade before, the New York hotel owner Raymond Orteig had established the prize offering $25,000 to the first flier who traveled nonstop from the United States to Paris. Now airmen and navies were getting close to succeeding and figured they could hop the Atlantic in a mere day or day and a half. In September, the French fighting ace Captain René Fonck had set off from Roosevelt Field in New York for France. Coolidge, still at Paul Smith's Hotel in the Adirondacks for the summer, had wired Fonck and his American partner, Lieutenant Lawrence Curtin, to cheer them on in their "fine and courageous adventure." A gas tank leak in the end had prevented that crossing. Storms at sea had caused the next delay. Then, on September 21, Fonck's plane crashed at takeoff, cartwheeled on the runway of Roosevelt Field, and exploded into flames, killing two of Fonck's crew.

In October, eager to sustain the budget side of the experiment as always, Coolidge met with Lord six times and reduced a tariff on paintbrush handles by half, his second cut that year, the other a reduction in a duty on live bob quail. Coolidge planned a speech, but another event intervened: the aurora borealis interfered with the telegraph communication. The midwestern floodwaters receded; a visit from Queen Marie of Romania ate up days. Meanwhile, the progressives duly made the expected advances. Though he had missed the graduation of John at Mercersburg in 1924, Coolidge hoped to travel out to dedicate a new memorial chapel at Mercersburg. The bells of the chapel had been cast in Croydon, England, using copper from all over the world, including bits from Lord Nelson's flagship at Trafalgar, a tiny shaving from the Liberty Bell, and a copper wire from an airplane, PN-9, which had made the first flight to Hawaii.

Grace went, taking white roses; yet other roses were dropped from the sky by an airplane. But again, Coolidge was not there, owing to another crisis: too much bounty. The crop that year was so great that farmers feared the volume would drive down their prices enough to kill their farms. Coolidge arranged a credit for farmers; it was a compromise that placated the cotton men, reducing the pressure for the larger sin of passing systematic price management. That week there was good aviation news: a Marine Corps captain completed a cross-country flight from San Diego to Washington, the best record of flying hours for the navy without accident. Coolidge did take time for this, bringing the flier to the White House and awarding the trophy on the lawn.

The floodwaters of the Midwest subsided yet further, but by December the results of the election brought a new tide of trouble. In the House, Republicans retained their majority, but lost seats, including two to the new Farmer-Labor Party candidates who would press for some version of agricultural price setting or subsidy. In the Senate the blow was worse. Coolidge's old ally William Butler of Massachusetts lost his bid for election to the Senate seat he had been holding since the death of Lodge after 1924. Overall the Senate was now effectively tied, with Republicans holding forty-eight seats to the Democrats' forty-six. Dawes's vote became crucial.

Aware that money spoke louder than words, Coolidge and Mellon decided to demonstrate the value of their cuts by making Christmas come early that year, rebating some of the cash the cuts had generated. "Tax Refund, Coolidge Plan" read the headlines, announcing that they would redistribute $150 million of the surplus, a 10 or 12 percent cut in the tax bill people paid, if Congress backed the concept up with a resolution. Nearly every area of the economy was prospering; even the cotton surplus was of course prosperity, if only the mismatch of farmers to buyers could be sorted out. The Commerce Department's annual report, released that fall, would note that nearly every industry from mineral production to mail-order houses had seen significant increases since 1923, with electricity up to 179 compared with a 1919 base of 100. Farm prices were not down. Department store revenues were at 133 compared with those of 1919, though the chain stories, which emphasized price, were prevailing over service stores like RH Stearns. The United States' standard of living was higher than ever before.

The *Chicago Tribune*, reporting the tax giveback news, underscored that Coolidge in no way saw the election as a repudiation "of himself or his party." In the same pages the *Tribune* carried a story of yet another of that autumn's many aviation mishaps. Caught in a snowstorm, a mail plane had suffered engine failure over Bloomington, Illinois, on a trip between St. Louis and Chicago; the pilot had parachuted 13,000 feet and landed in a farm field. The pilot's name, the paper said, was Charles A. Lindbergh. It was not the first time he had bailed out; after engine failure in September he had parachuted down in Ottawa, Illinois, as well. Two weeks later a navy aviator, Lieutenant Edward Curtis, died in Norfolk at the navy base hospital after injuries received in a crash. In England, the Royal Air Force suffered three fatal crashes in a week.

Coolidge was eager for more evidence from his tax experiment, in part because he knew Mellon, seventy-one now, would not want to fight the tax wars forever. The wedding of Mellon's daughter, Ailsa, had taken place that past spring; the Coolidges had attended; indeed, they had had their portraits painted by the same artist who had rendered Ailsa the year of her marriage, Philip Alexius de László. The Treasury secretary now wanted to focus on a federal building project with the Fine Arts Committee that would give Washington a complex of edifices worthy of its rank as a world capital. If Washington were to be the world's creditor—and Mellon was ensuring that it would remain so—it must be more beautiful, like London, whose structures, such as the National Gallery, Mellon so admired. The new project was a set of buildings, which would be known collectively as the Federal Triangle. A well-known sculptor, not Bryant Baker but Gutzon Borglum, who was famous for carving heroic figures in stones in the landscape, was seeking out Mellon for an appropriation for a new project, giant profiles of presidents he would cut into the ancient granite of South Dakota. Mellon was also making other outlays, some personal. In 1926, while the federal government had purchased the Oldroyd Lincoln collection, Mellon had himself been busy purchasing paintings for himself and the National Gallery, a great Rembrandt, *A Young Man Seated at a Table*, and Rogier van der Weyden's *Portrait of a Lady*.

The talk of another term for Coolidge was already loud; however the party fared, however angry committees were at his reluctance to appropriate, Silent Cal's ways were enormously popular. To be sure, Grace was still homesick for her friend Therese Hills, her street in Northampton, and her son, John. She was at work on a patchwork coverlet for the enormous Lincoln Bed, which expressed her view about the amount of time they should stay in Washington: it would be forty-eight squares, the number of months Coolidge would serve in his first full term. There was also space for a dateline: "August 3, 1923–March 4, 1929." Still, the Coolidges were now as much at home in Washington as they would ever be. Their menagerie had only grown, to include more dogs, birds, and a raccoon, Rebecca. Without Mrs. Jaffray, Grace found the White House more comfortable and was plotting a renovation of the upstairs to take place during the summer of 1927. She liked Miss Riley, who took care of Rebecca and kept meticulous books for the president. With Miss Riley, Grace found with satisfaction, she could be a better host and could experiment. "Did you ever eat a green salad with tiny bits of fried bacon scattered over it just before serving with oil dressing?—Rather nice,"

Grace wrote to the housekeeper. Or, "Please have mint sauce for the lamb." Grace found she could also respond to the president more easily: "Dear Miss Riley, When the ham is carved tomorrow will you see that it is cut so that the President can get that little round piece which lies near the bone?—G.C."

Coolidge for his part also found pleasure in hosting, playing up the role of the Vermonter in Washington. Lynn Cady, the farmer who worked his father's acres, sent him a one-gallon can of maple syrup. "I have used some and find it very fine," the president had written back, enclosing a check for $5. "I think the House has ordered some but if you need a market for some let me know." Coolidge served the syrup at the congressional breakfasts he hosted, along with sausage. Through Cady and Lynds, who worked the limekiln lot, Coolidge continued to experience the difficulty of farming. He had asked Lynds to send him payments for whatever Lynds took off the limekiln lot, but those payments clearly could not be much. A reporter noted that Plymouth's age-old problem of isolation remained: "The sirup producer is in the same boat as the milk producer. Indeed he is the same fellow. He lives far back from ready transportation." The Vermont Maple Products Cooperative Exchange had been established years before, but distance, again, was a problem for some producers, including the limekiln lot, even when Plymouth was not snowbound. "It lays half way up the mountainside between Plymouth Church and the March sunset," the same reporter had noted.

Meanwhile, Coolidge and Lord scoured preliminary reports on the taxes, meeting sixteen times in November and December. When not with Lord, Coolidge busied himself planning and pushing back when pushed. The United States kept a contingent force in Nicaragua more or less constantly; Coolidge wanted to end that conflict and would send the former secretary of war, Henry Stimson, down to mediate. Regular vetoes had to be used sparingly, for overrides like the one he had experienced on the bonus bill hurt the authority of the administration. Coolidge could continue to use pocket vetoes at the end of sessions, killing bills by failing to sign them in the recess. Pocket vetoes were difficult to undo; they could not be overridden. Congress had to start anew with a new law in the next session. He used the pocket veto to kill a bill that introduced new pensions for widows of Civil War soldiers. Like so much pension legislation, it affected a tiny group, but established a principle that could be broadened to provide a benefit for millions. Coolidge, like Harding, found himself playing Scrooge.

In the budget message Coolidge sent to Congress on December 9, 1926, the president made aviation his cause, asking specifically that $3 million be spent to regulate the skies and promote aviation commerce. In aviation he saw profits where he did not see them in, say, shipping: none of the lines being operated by the government was self-sustaining, he warned. Most important, he made the case for his tax experiment. "With the experience of another year's test of the Revenue Act of 1926, and with a more accurate knowledge which the year will give," he said, the United States could set policy, but only then.

He'd asked for "another year's test," but as early as that Christmas Coolidge and Lord were receiving preliminary results of the tax experiment. The Treasury's surplus for the next fiscal year was already $218.3 million, or $74.4 million higher than it had been the previous year, before the 25 percent top rate. Mellon had saved so much, a billion dollars in fact, that for the 1927 fiscal year the national debt would be $19 billion, a third down from the $28 billion that had greeted Harding. The White House would have three large trees, which Grace promised to decorate herself with electric lights, tinsel, and candy canes. This year the Coolidges gave the White House staff gold coins. Grace hosted diplomatic dinners, to which not only the cabinet, including of course Mellon, but also old friends were invited: George Pratt from Amherst; Mortimer Schiff, whose shirts Morrow had received as hand-me-downs during college; Bruce Barton; General Lord; the Stearnses; and Evalyn McLean. On Christmas Eve Coolidge and Grace went to the living tree, which had itself taken root at Sherman Square; Coolidge himself touched the button and "under leaden skies that threatened to bring snow tomorrow, lights flashed."

Coolidge wondered when the outlook would brighten for flight. If only flight could be made safer. On December 22, the president received the Aeronautical Chamber of Commerce, a delegation of men representing two hundred companies in some part of the new industry, all arguing that aviation was the future of the U.S. economy. But in Great Britain the House of Commons was stirring over the appalling number of air deaths, eighty-three, that had taken place up to early December 1926. "We are constantly making experiments," Prime Minister Baldwin apologized, trying to suggest that the Royal Air Force might improve the following year. The very same day that Coolidge received the Chamber of Commerce men, three army aviators met their death when their planes collided over Rantoul, Illinois; a fourth died later. But Governor John Trumbull of Connecticut, whose daughter Coolidge's own son, John, was now seeing, was becoming a pilot. Senator Hiram Bingham of the same state had flown since the war. The more Coolidge thought about planes, the more enthusiastic he was. He had always argued that aviation had the potential to obviate, at least to some extent, destroyers or battleships, perhaps eventually allowing savings in outlays for the War Department. His conviction strengthened: the future was brighter for flight if commerce, not the War Department, drove the industry. Here, though, he encountered resistance. Years before, it had been Mitchell who pushed for military spending, a force in the air, so stridently that he had been court-martialed and mustered out of service; Dwight Morrow's board and a law he had signed afterward had pushed aviation away from the military and over to commerce. But now Coolidge confronted a tougher antagonist: Will Rogers. Rogers, like Mitchell, wanted more military spending on planes. "Mr. Coolidge on account of his economy plan has suggested they fly as high as they can on what little gas they have and then coast. In that way they get twice the amount of distance out of the same amount of gas," wrote Rogers.

Rogers was picking up on something: the administration itself was tired of its own saving policy. Lord might still be holding up that $3 billion budget as the target. "That $3 billion," Lord told the departments at the January budget meeting, was "still beckoning us on." But Lord and Coolidge, as hard as they were trying, knew they could not cut much more. "With a full treasury and revenues at flood it requires courage to continue along the lines we have been following," Coolidge confessed to the same crowd. Even after a record of ten meetings that December, and a record of sixty-three meetings for 1926, the debut year of the Mellon Plan, they were not sure they could do much more. The old Two Percent Club he had created to reward departments that saved was no longer feasible. Departments could not find 2 percent more to cut. Now Lord was running a One Percent Club. By selecting those who had served General Pershing in the war, the Budget Bureau had given the directors a certain protection from criticism: what military man would attack General Dawes or General Lord? But now that immunity was wearing off. The Naval Board and the army general staff were alleging that, Morrow Board or no, General Lord was jeopardizing national defense. The tax experiment was not yet ready to yield all its evidence. "We are waiting [for] a test of the producing ability of the revenue act of 1926," Coolidge clarified. The tax experiment and the flight experiment moved together in his mind. The Orteig Prize was in the news all the time now, trumping little bits of more mundane news, little stories like that of high water at Cairo, Illinois. More fliers were building or finding planes to compete for it. The radial air-cooled engine, high-lift airfoils, and lighter construction made easy flight likelier. The questions were whether the prize flight would be by monoplane or biplane, or whether it would be a Frenchman, American, or Englishman who would win the prize, not whether the prize would be won.

Meanwhile, though, Congress pressed Coolidge harder. Senator Carter Glass, seeking new cruisers, was especially eager to haul General Lord before a senate committee. "I don't think he is so hedged about by titled consequence that he can't come here," Glass said. In February, Glass's colleagues pushed on farms. Senator McNary and Representative Haugen were offering up yet another farm bill. This one created a government fund of $250 million to stabilize the price of five commodities: cotton, wheat, corn, rice, and swine. Though commodity prices were high, they still stood nowhere near where they had been in the war. Considering the farm legislation, Coolidge also tended to his own land, farming by letter, wire, or telephone. He worried that Cady, his tenant at the Notch, was not prepared for such surprises as drought or flood. "If you have a little dry weather, I am afraid your feed will be short for ten cows," he wrote Cady, advising him to consider letting another lot to graze the cattle. Coolidge went on, adding more instructions: "I should cut some spruce trees on the limekiln lot and draw them into the mill and have them so as to have some spruce lumber." The economics of it all did not necessarily add up. Cady was talking of an investment in an evaporator. That made sense only if Cady committed to continuing to farm, Coolidge noted. The president also included a quiet line of resignation: "If you should leave I should probably close up the farm."

On February 15, the Coolidges retreated to the *Mayflower* for dinner with Secretary of Agriculture Jardine and his wife and other agriculture department staffers. The Senate had already passed a version of the legislation. The House of Representatives had then passed the bill.

Sometimes the *Mayflower* made him feel like a captain, and sometimes, like a prisoner. Angering such a large constituency was not a pleasure, especially since there was one area where it was not wrong: the poor situation that the farmers endured was in part the result of Republican tariffs. The tariffs hurt not only foreigners, but also the international comity Coolidge so often sought to foster.

As if to rub it all in, the president of Cuba, whose entire economy was hurt by U.S. sugar tariffs, canceled his plan to attend a dinner at the White House scheduled for the day Coolidge vetoed the farm legislation, February 25. Gerardo Machado canceled on such short notice that the fresh raspberry sauce, birds, and butter to prepare the dinner had already been ordered, not to mention $100 worth of cigars. Miss Riley was able to recycle some but not all of the items purchased and regretfully alerted Coolidge that they had to write off $32.33 from her budget. A veto "will be the political finish of President Coolidge," *The New York Times* reported farm bloc politicians as warning. By vetoing, Coolidge might also hurt his party. The Republicans could not stand without the West, and many western senators wanted the legislation.

February was the month of George Washington's birthday. As plans for celebration this year were made, everyone was conscious that a few years hence, in 1932, the country would mark the two hundredth anniversary of the birth of the first president. Even Congress was already preparing to mark the occasion and had established a commission to plan it, which the president chaired. Washington would have understood; when Coolidge scrutinized Miss Riley's accounts, he was merely replicating the scrutiny Washington had applied to Mount Vernon's. The details of Washington's life—his work as a farmer and businessman, what he had done with his stock shares, how he had arranged his retirement—held Coolidge's attention now. As with Lincoln, Coolidge thought, one must guard against deifying Washington, making him an imaginary character: presidents failed, and that shouldn't be obscured by the superlatives. But of course Washington was one who, unlike Lincoln, had emphasized the authority of the states. A president had to respect the states. On February 22, Coolidge delivered a speech about Washington before both houses of Congress and the Supreme Court and greeted forty-two descendants of the first president, who lined up to meet him. Honoring presidents was a constant theme for both Coolidge and Mellon. The sculptor Gutzon Borglum had selected the presidents whose profiles he would chisel into the Black Hills: Washington, Jefferson, and Lincoln. In its scope, Borglum's ambition recalled the ambition of the transatlantic flight, or Hoover's waterways system: the Borglum figures would be 465 feet high. He had already selected the spot for the sculpture; Mount Rushmore, a great crag named after a New York attorney who had wandered through decades back. Accompanying the monument was to be an "entablature," on which would be "deeply graven an outline of the history of the United States."

Like many others, Borglum was seeking federal funds and sought to craft his project so that it would win Coolidge's acceptance. He and Senator Norbeck of South Dakota, one of the Republican senators who supported McNary-Haugen, estimated the cost at $500,000. But when he won an audience with the Treasury secretary that February, Borglum asked for only half that, saying that private donors or the state might pay the rest. Participation was key; that was federalism: "I want to get the people's teeth into the thing." Mellon agreed, but Norbeck was furious that Borglum had not gone for more. "You could have gotten it all," said Norbeck, feisty in his confidence that the administration was agonizing over turning down the farm bloc yet again. He wanted to get something out of all the exchanges. The first couple was planning to spend the summer somewhere out west; it would be an enormous boon to commerce in South Dakota if the Coolidges chose the Black Hills for the summer White House. But Borglum cleverly understood that the buy-in mattered more than the amount. "Before we know it Borglum will be working with his air drills and mastodonic outlines," the *Aberdeen Press* wrote at the good news.

Norbeck was not the only one taking advantage of Coolidge's vulnerability on farms to advance other issues. Herbert Hoover was pressing hard for a bill that would appropriate $125 million, a good share of the annual surplus, to help the states build a dam on the Colorado River. Many of the same senators and congressmen who wanted a farm subsidy also supported this law. Senator Gifford Pinchot, the old conservationist, championed Hoover's project with such superlatives it was hard to challenge him: "The boulder canyon dam will be incomparably the greatest of all dams." But others mounted a filibuster against the dam, again mostly to exact concessions in unrelated areas, such as loans for veterans or passage of the Muscle Shoals legislation, which had been waiting for resolution for nearly ten years. Nature was conspiring in a tragic way to bolster Hoover's case for outlays and water management: in California a great storm was driving ranchers from their homes; San Diego was virtually isolated, and water had flooded to heights over men's heads in the Mission Valley. As if California were not enough, a great northeast gale hit New Jersey and Long Island the same week Coolidge was formatting his final thoughts on farm legislation. The storm was so rough it tossed houses in Long Beach into the sea; on normally tranquil Staten Island, 1,500 had to flee their homes.

On February 25, Coolidge did veto McNary-Haugen, appending a thoughtful message of more than three thousand words—long but necessary to show the seriousness with which he took the petition. "The chief objection to the bill is that it would not benefit the farmer," he wrote. The bill would push up prices. That would make commodities expensive and decrease demand. "To expect to increase prices and then maintain them on a higher level by means of a plan which must of necessity increase production while decreasing consumption is to fly in the face of economic law as well established as any law of nature." The president also signed McFadden-Pepper, a bank law that could help farmers. Hopefully that would buy time as well.

The farm bloc blustered and roared. But somehow, especially because of approaches like that of Senator Norbeck of South Dakota, Coolidge reckoned that there were ways to mend rifts. His summer stay in New York had enabled him to face off with Governor Al Smith. A stay in South Dakota in the summer of 1927 would be a good way for Coolidge to begin to make it up with at least some members of the farm bloc, and Starling, the Secret Service man, began to think about whether the hills might really be the right choice for the summer White House. Beyond politics, Starling was thinking of the president's mood. Starling now assigned himself the job of cheering up Coolidge. The White House was making a move to a temporary house while repairs were made; the repairs would finish while the Coolidges were away for the summer. But where? The summer before, on vacation in New York State, Starling had taught Coolidge the rudiments of fishing; the trout of the Black Hills might be just the place to develop that skill or even make the transfer from worm fishing to fly fishing. Hoover was a master fly fisherman. The senators and state representatives lobbied hard for South Dakota; they pointed out that the Black Hills were known not only for trout but also for cool, mosquito-free nights. Starling traveled out and saw that

Dakotans, whatever their votes on agriculture in Congress, were more than eager to have the Coolidges. It would be a coup for the state to host the summer White House, a move that would bring commerce and launch a new industry, automobile tourism. The Harney Park Lodge, thirty miles from Rapid City and alluringly private, could be the president's summer home. The governors and senators guaranteed fine fishing. The hills themselves were what lured Grace, who loved long walks. It was decided: a summer in South Dakota it would be.

Beyond assenting to the travel plan, however, Coolidge gave no attention to the summer. His mind was on the results of the great tax experiment, which would come in June at the semiannual meeting of the Budget Bureau. Before any move to South Dakota he and Grace would have to move to a temporary home at Dupont Circle, the McKim, Mead & White mansion built for the R. W. Patterson family. They left the White House awaiting substantial renovations on the residential floor; Grace was creating a "sky parlor" up top where she could take the sun. They were weary of their own "megaphone" effect; when they whispered something, the world received it as a roar. Their fondness for animals yielded a perpetual parade of new gift pets. The mayor of Johannesburg, South Africa, sent the Coolidges a gift of two lion cubs. Exploiting the publicity opportunity in the gift, the White House let it be known that the animals would be named "Tax Reduction" and "Budget Bureau." But the animals themselves were too much for either Dupont Circle or the keepers at the White House; they went to the zoo.

To be at Dupont Circle was itself a kind of recognition of how far Calvin and Grace had come. In the old days Florence Harding had denied the Coolidges a house like the Patterson mansion; more important, the Coolidges had denied themselves such houses. Grace was no longer thinking of Washington in any case; she wanted to head to Northampton, where both her son and her mother, who was ill, waited. Yet Coolidge insisted that she stay; he needed her. Even their church was unsettled; Reverend Pierce would hold services that spring in the Metropolitan Theatre while the church building itself underwent repairs. Both Coolidges kept going by telling themselves that the weight of the work was temporary, as were the constraints. Their son John was dating Florence Trumbull now; they liked the Trumbulls and hosted their daughter Jean, Florence's sister, for a meal after the New Year. The Coolidges now joked about a return to private life, especially the use of public transport—warning that Grace "would soon be walking, riding in streetcars and taxicabs." The idea of walking on the street like a common citizen, Grace replied pointedly, held "no terrors" for her.

Coolidge diverted himself yet again by looking heavenward and following the Orteig Prize. One of the most likely winners was Commander Richard Evelyn Byrd, who had already flown from the North Pole to Spitzbergen, Norway. Another was the great French flying ace Charles Nungesser, who had served with Quentin Roosevelt. Yet a third was the midwestern mail pilot Charles Lindbergh. Byrd was a navy man; Lindbergh's employer, the Robertson Aircraft Corporation, was, by contrast, a private company, albeit one that maintained a contract with the U.S. Post Office. Lindbergh was opting for a monoplane; he placed his order for the plane with Ryan Airlines in California, buying the item on credit. He was spending March at the firm, watching the plane as it was built from two lengths of steel tubing. Lindbergh was already known for his bravery; the papers reported that he was a member of the "caterpillar club," made up of pilots who had repeatedly been forced to parachute from planes and so were said to have seen their lives "hang from a slip of silk."

Of course, Coolidge was not the only one in the administration who placed faith in the transformative power of new technology. On April 7, Hoover tested out a new medium. In Washington, before a kind of telephone camera, he spoke, and people in a New York Bell Laboratories auditorium both heard and saw him. A large public had seen the transmission of "human sight," as Hoover, momentarily awed, put it, and for the first time in history. Hoover, Coolidge noticed, was omnipresent in that period. One day the question was flood control, the next aviation or radio. Much of his advice was good, but he pressed in so; people murmured that Hoover was secretary of commerce and assistant secretary of everything else. Unhappy with Secretary Kellogg's management of China, an area Hoover knew very well, Hoover put forward his own views on how to deal with Chinese nationalists in Nanking and even permitted talk that he might take Kellogg's place at State. He thought he knew better how to deal with Chinese nationalists in Nanking. Coolidge fumed. Kellogg, his appointment after Charles Evans Hughes, was an old-time lawyer, not a China hand like Hoover; in fact, Kellogg had gone straight from the farm to reading law in Rochester, Minnesota, at age nineteen, skipping college. His experiences as a lawyer and senator had given him something Hoover lacked: long experience in judging timing in diplomacy and politics. Even if Kellogg were wrong and Hoover right, Coolidge's impulse was always to back up his man. There was no cabinet split over China, he told the press on April 15. He had never "considered that it was for one member of the Cabinet to have any very great weight in trying to indicate to another member of the cabinet how the latter member should conduct the affairs of his own Department." Just to close out the possibility, Coolidge became explicit: "While I am on that I might state again that Mr. Kellogg isn't going to resign. If he does resign, Mr. Hoover will not be appointed Secretary of State."

Coolidge meant the sharp words to end a controversy; instead, they triggered one. The sitting president was tangling with one of his likeliest successors. At a time when floods were spreading, Hoover's stock was moving up. The world's greatest engineer, it was presumed, must know what to do in the South, where there was more troubling news. The Mississippi had continued to swell since the high-water mark at New Year's at Cairo, and yet more water came. Three separate tornadoes had raged through the lower Mississippi Valley that March, killing forty-five people. The administration sent in the Red Cross. But the floodwaters continued to rise. A wall of water pushed down the river, covering an area where nearly a million people lived. After yet more rains, the levees from Cairo to Helena, Arkansas, were still holding, but a total of fourteen people had drowned in damage further south. In the Midwest, railroad service was paralyzed and eleven had died when waters sloshed across Kansas and Oklahoma. By April 15, the Mississippi waters had torn the great levees and thousands of acres were underwater; the Arkansas River hit 36.1 feet at Fort Smith, the papers reported, the highest level in nearly a century. Half a million people were expected to be forced out of their homes in coming days. Governors and mayors began to talk about the president coming down.

Almost overnight, between one budget meeting with Lord and the next, Coolidge was confronting an event to trump events, a real flood, not a figurative one. And it was fast becoming the greatest national emergency of his time in Washington.

This was the very sort of test George Washington had warned of, a test of federalism. A commander in chief might lead a nation in war. He might order destroyers around the Atlantic; he might dispatch troops to Nicaragua. But Coolidge did not deem it appropriate for a president to march south like a general into governors' territory to manage a flood rescue. The job of the executive branch in such situations was to coordinate, offer limited supplies, and encourage. But the job of the chief executive did not go further. It was wrong, on principle, for a president to intrude upon a governor; that was basic federalism. Rescue was work for the state governments. A number of governors and senators shared this view. Governor Austin Peay of Tennessee, a Democrat, took a position to the right of Coolidge on that: he turned down the Red Cross, too, because he "felt that the people should be expected to provide for themselves," as a Red Cross official had noted. Praise for Coolidge's position came from *The New York Times*: "Fortunately, there are still some things that can be done without the wisdom of Congress and the all-fathering Federal Government."

The decision not to go to the flood areas cost Coolidge: in the towns and refugee tents, families and whole towns were losing their livelihood and more; this was a photo that made the president look inhumane. The reality of the suffering in the South was far clearer than in prior disasters because of the aerial photos and the reports that rattled off the telegraph. But his resolve hardened. If he looked inhumane, so be it. The federal government had not often spent on large-scale rescues before; Grover Cleveland, a Democrat, had vetoed an appropriation for drought sufferers in Texas. Theodore Roosevelt had been cautious about sending cash to Louisiana during the yellow fever epidemic. The situation was similar to the ones Cleveland and Roosevelt had encountered. It would do another kind of damage to change precedent.

Instead the president did what he could do: send his best emissary, Hoover. On April 22, Coolidge appointed Hoover chairman of a relief mission to coordinate the rescue. The War Department would draw on surplus supplies and send 1,453 war tents, 16,207 pyramidal tents, and 11,102 cots to refugee centers; 27,405 blankets would come from the government as well. But much of the rest of the money, Coolidge said, would have to come from the private sector. "The Federal departments have no funds for relief," *The Washington Post* wrote, transmitting the Coolidge message painstakingly. As it turned out, $5 million would not be nearly enough; more levees were breaking, and seventy-five towns found themselves in the path of a wall of water. Many dozens, and then hundreds, were drowning, and in the end, the papers now reported, more than 3 million acres would be flooded.

Hoover slipped into the role as flood chief so naturally that it was as if the war had never ended, as if he were again rescuing Belgium. The commerce secretary popped up everywhere in the news: He talked railroads into transporting the displaced for free and carrying freight at a discount. He commandeered private outboard motors and built motorboats of plywood. He urged the people who were not yet flooded out, such as the population around the Bayou des Glaises levee, to evacuate early, then rescued by train the tens of thousands who had ignored his warning. He helped the Red Cross launch a fund drive; within a month the charity had already collected promises of more than $8 million, an enormous sum. Within weeks of Hoover leadership, several hundred thousand people were safely housed in new refugee camps—many planned, right down to the latrines, by Hoover and his team. Hoover asked governors of each state to name a dictator of resources—he used the word "dictator"—and the governors complied. Hoover managed the dysentery and the hunts for the missing along the floodwaters in their states hour by hour. He and the Red Cross sent the refugees to camps at Vicksburg, Delta, and Natchez. A hundred thousand blankets from army warehouses were shipped to warm the refugees. Not everyone in the South approved of all Hoover did. Later it would become clear that he had undercounted the dead significantly—there were hundreds—and that he failed to help the black populations of Greenville, Mississippi, and elsewhere.

Still, given the scale of it all, Hoover's feat amazed. At the end of April, the governors of four states invited Coolidge down to inspect the devastation. The Mississippi River was now swelling so that below Memphis it spread sixty miles. "A vast sheet of water as yellow as the China Sea at the mouth of the Yangtze," is how a writer for *National Geographic* would describe it. In some places, the water rose to fifty feet deep. A great majority of those displaced were poor and black. The national disaster made the case for federal management of water, whether on the Mississippi or on the Colorado, far more effectively than Hoover ever could.

Coolidge worked hard in the other areas that, to him, made sense for a president: raising charity money, for example. By endorsing the Red Cross and speaking publicly, he drove the appeal money from $5 million to $10 million a matter of weeks. As much as Hoover's work, the administration's ability to raise charity funds struck foreign governments.

The Times of London expressed its awe at the charitable response in the United States: "Hardly less bewildering than such catastrophes is the speed with which the American people rush to rescue, organize generous relief and make it seem as though such things"—the disasters—"could never have been." Coolidge sent thirty-six navy seaplanes to help Hoover in his work. He established and tested a policy position for the federal government: rescue, yes; reconstruction, no. Hoover issued a report that backed the president up, writing that it seemed to the Mississippi Flood Committee, which he chaired, that reconstruction work, resettlement and long-view construction "must be undertaken under the leadership of the states involved. . . . and therefore the federal and other national agencies should give support rather than attempt to direct." Hoover privately backed a greater role for Washington but was not ready to say so.

Others, however, were blunter. "I am not one of those who believe in rushing to Congress with every problem that arises," Franklin Roosevelt of New York said. But this flood was the kind of occasion "in which immediate action by Congress is imperative." Roosevelt and other Democrats began to pressure him for an extraordinary session of Congress to plan flood spending. Even outside the parties, the pressure was greater. The sculptor Gutzon Borglum was hawking a grand but impractical theory that water might be diverted to Texas. "Boulder Dam Bill to Pass," *The Washington Post* pronounced on May 7. It was becoming a foregone conclusion that flood management would be the biggest peacetime project; over a few years, the water experts were predicting, as much as $2 billion ought to be spent. General Edward Jadwin, the chief army engineer, was already sketching out what seemed to be a colossal infrastructure project. Some observers viewed the waterways question now as a test not of Coolidge's federalism but of his modernity: if Coolidge were to be a modern president, he would have to be part of the new waterways drive. After all, Hoover had upstaged Coolidge just as Coolidge had once upstaged Woodrow Wilson. Still, Coolidge refused to call the special session.

There were additional frustrations. That spring Coolidge had issued a call for the five parties to the Five-Power agreements arising from the Washington Naval Conference in 1921–1922 to meet in Geneva to seal a new treaty. The United States wanted to extend the old cruiser limitation to cover other craft. The conference was set to open in Geneva in June, with Great Britain and Japan present, both furiously disagreeing with the terms put forward by the United States. The hostility of Japan that Coolidge had anticipated during the debate over the immigration law had indeed materialized. France was, so far, declining to come. Italy was also not committing itself, allowing only that it would attend "in some manner." French Foreign Minister Aristide Briand was proposing a pact to outlaw war between France and the United States. Kellogg disliked the idea; he thought the Americans who led the peace treaty movement, such as Nicholas Murray Butler of Columbia, were "god damned fools." To ask a nation to agree to give up war as a means of policy was to limit its power in the most direct of ways. The idea seemed so off to Coolidge that at first he did not even want to think of it or consider rumors that his own secretary of state, Kellogg, was sympathetic to it. "I never heard of any such thing," Coolidge would tell his press conference of the prospect of consideration of such a pact by him and Kellogg when it came up.

By May, several pilots were ready to take Orteig's challenge: they included Charles Nungesser, the French ace, and Bert Acosta. Acosta had already warmed up by circling New York City for fifty-one hours and eleven minutes in his Wright-Bellanca WB-2 monoplane, *Columbia*, in the process covering more than the distance to Paris, 3,600 miles. "Acosta and Nungesser are the likeliest wave jumpers," wrote one columnist. The airports at Roosevelt and Curtis Field now thrummed with the vibrations of Orteig Prize competitors. Yet more calamities ensued, and Harry Guggenheim, the president of the large Daniel Guggenheim Foundation for the Promotion of Aeronautics, pledged $100,000 in prize money for fliers who managed safe flights of long distances. On May 8, after a disconcerting hangar fire and storms at sea had delayed him, Nungesser and his partner, Captain François Coli, departed Le Bourget outside Paris in their plane, *White Bird*, with a scheduled arrival in New York two days hence, or less. A crowd, many in evening dress, waved them off. Observers at Le Havre, and then observers on the Irish coast, told of seeing the plane, but on May 9, there was an ominous silence; the watchers on Newfoundland saw nothing; St. John's reported nothing but a brisk northeast wind.

Coolidge monitored the situation and instructed Mellon at Treasury to put "every available facility of the coast guard to work patrolling," *The Washington Post* reported. On May 10, fearing the gasoline might run out, the U.S. Navy sent out the naval tug *Wandank* to troll Nova

Scotia for the plane. There was a report that the plane had been spotted at Maine, where the *Kronprinzessin* had found refuge, and the Boston Navy Yard wired hopefully, "Nungesser plane passed Portland, Me., headed south, flying very fast." But the Maine sighting could not be confirmed. Coolidge signaled to the French that eighteen warships were ready to hunt for the *White Bird* should they request; Raymond Orteig offered a $5,000 prize for anyone who sighted Nungesser, but even after five destroyers patrolled the steamship lanes, nothing was found. All Coolidge could do then was wire his sympathies to French President Gaston Doumergue.

Yet days later, while the country was still in the haze of the Nungesser news, another flier was taking off: Lindbergh, from the American side. It was hard to imagine that he would dare to do so after so many deaths, and of such skilled pilots; at the airstrip on Long Island, they nicknamed the young pilot "the flying fool." Coolidge wired his best wishes. From his post at the temporary White House, and busy with steel strike troubles, Coolidge nonetheless followed this new flight too. In the silence, while the world awaited the Lindbergh news, more details of the pilot and his endeavor came out. The twenty-five-year-old mail pilot was the son of the late lawmaker Charles August Lindbergh, the isolationist who had represented Minnesota's Sixth District years before. He was a mailman who had found backers among private companies. He had supervised the construction of the monoplane, which represented the sum of all the knowledge that had been acquired in the past thirty years about flight. Its cowling and propeller spinners were made of soft aluminum. The blades were duralumin, an alloy. But there was also a bit of the familiar in the monoplane: the spars were made of spruce.

On May 21, a signal came from Paris. Lindbergh had indeed landed. Here, finally, was the flash of news Coolidge had hoped for. One could only begin to consider the results a feat like Lindbergh's would yield. If Harding, Coolidge, and Mellon had worked to bring back normalcy, they had sometimes wondered why they were doing so. "The more we learn of his accomplishment, in going from New York to Paris, the greater it seems to have been," the president wonderingly told his press conference. "That is something that grows on us the more we contemplate it." To pick Lindbergh up, Coolidge sent a battleship.

Queen Marie of Romania had visited, King George V of England had visited, Will Rogers had called; but now, at the temporary home on

Dupont Circle, the first couple prepared for the most important guest of Coolidge's presidency, Colonel Lindbergh, and his mother, Evangeline Lindbergh, starting June 10. To join them in hosting, Coolidge summoned his old friend, Dwight Morrow. Coolidge also began preparing a speech, to deliver at the Washington Monument.

The Lindbergh landing in Washington still proved bumpy. Mrs. Lindbergh did not materialize the day she was expected, June 10; it turned out that the hero's mother was in Baltimore. The White House sent a car to retrieve her. Once she was settled in her bedroom on Dupont Circle, she could watch the crowds that waited outside the white mansion. Lindbergh himself was not yet there, though that day he arrived in America; a convoy of two blimps, four destroyers, and planes accompanied Lindbergh up the Chesapeake. Mrs. Lindbergh dined with the Morrows and the Coolidges. Afterward, Morrow was left to entertain Mrs. Lindbergh. It was time for Coolidge's and Lord's own acrobatics, the semiannual budget meeting.

Inspired by the events of the past year, Lord had labored over his speech and developed an enormous, awkward metaphor involving water, ships, flight, and taxation. "Waves of new expenditure as a result of new legislation and continued legitimate growth and development of federal business have swept over the economy boat," he told the government departments. Treasury had cut the federal debt by $68 million in May alone, which meant the government was on track to eliminate the debt sooner than even Mellon had imagined. The surplus for the eleven months up to June 1, the real test, was larger than it had been the year before, when the new tax rates had become law. Indeed, Coolidge predicted that in the fiscal year that would close on June 30, there would be a $599 million surplus, compared with $378 million the preceding year. Mellon and Coolidge took pains to make the case that such revenues might not flow forever. Coolidge warned that tax cuts might not be made every year. Still, it was a glorious surplus, one they could use to pay down the debt. The virtuous circle could continue.

Back in their offices in the coming days, the Treasury men also discovered something else. Critics like James Couzens had always said Mellon's tax cuts were for the rich, and continued to depict Mellon himself as a tax cheat. Others had supported Couzens, including the humorist Will Rogers, suspecting Couzens was onto something: "He knew illuminum was light but he knew it wasent as light as its taxes," Rogers wrote in his trademark dialect spelling. But the new revenues undermined the argument that Mellon's laws benefited the rich. For a good share of the new revenue was coming from higher earners. By lowering rates on the wealthy, the Treasury had actually collected more from them. A greater portion of the income tax came from top earners than had at the beginning of the decade. In 1927, those earning over $50,000—a tremendous sum—would pay about 80 percent of the income taxes, whereas in 1920 those top earners had paid about half. "The income tax in this country," as Mellon wrote triumphantly to one of the Treasury's correspondents, "has become a class rather than a national tax." The municipal bond prices still reflected a premium, the difference between their value and the value of a bond that was taxed. But as Mellon's charts had predicted, the premium was smaller. The spread between yield of tax-advantaged municipal bonds and Liberty Bonds on the one hand and federal Treasury bonds on the other was narrower now that the income tax rate had come down. The era of "tax tuberculosis," as one lawmaker had called it, seemed to be ending. That meant money was flowing into companies as well as state or local governments. The Lindbergh superstar status might lighten the costs of the flood in a direct way: the post office broke its rule against putting living men on stamps and proposed Lindbergh Flood stamps, two cents each, reading "Hail Lindbergh," so that the aviator's fame might pay for relief.

It was all proving so close to what Mellon had hypothesized years before in *Taxation: The People's Business*. That the budget had not been cut to $3 billion did not matter because commerce had expanded so much. Mellon's experiment might not survive forever, but it had survived long enough to prove itself a success. People understood now that lowering taxes might often be the better move. Scientific taxation could not offset great spending splurges, but it could relieve some spending, bring down the debt, and foster prosperity. The administration's signal that the general direction of tax rates would be downward had helped for years, even before he and Mellon had perfected their law. Perhaps direction mattered as much as rate. In any case, the results were powerful. The commerce helped the country endure whatever events challenged it. As horrific as the flood had been, the South would surmount it. *The Wall Street Journal*, surveying the South, reminded readers that despite the losses in places such as Greenville, there were many areas where the effect could "scarcely be felt." The region seemed to be recovering.

Along with three hundred thousand others, a record, the Coolidges and the cabinet waited in the Saturday sun at the Washington Monument. Mellon stood beside Grace; Commander Byrd, who had nearly beaten Lindbergh to the Orteig Prize, was present, and so was Secretary of State Kellogg, who had dueled with Lindbergh's father in his day. Alice Longworth and Attorney General Sargent could be seen nearby. Coolidge introduced Mrs. Lindbergh, who remained seated, but the crowd began to call "stand up," and Grace, laughing, took her hand and pulled Mrs. Lindbergh up. She bowed, and the applause was deafening.

Lindbergh finally arrived, even at his height scarcely visible among the loud stripes and garish flower arrangements around the podium. It fell to the president to convey the meaning of this event, different from the others. Coolidge praised Lindbergh's daring, to be sure, but also the fact that Lindbergh was a man of service: "modest, congenial, a man of good moral habits and regular in his business transactions." For the large crowd and the millions more listening by radio, Coolidge traced the arc of Lindbergh's life, crediting his mother, "who dowered her son with her own modesty and charm." Coolidge also took care to emphasize the construction of the plane, "that over 100 separate companies furnished materials, parts or service" in the making of the *Spirit of St. Louis*. The flight was also an international event, an indirect way for all the nations involved to get past the failures of the still stalled Geneva Conference, and the French intransigence over French debts to the United States. "France had the opportunity to show clearly her good will for America," as Coolidge said. Lindbergh then joked for the crowd and told of the warmth with which the French people and government greeted him. Commerce and a monoplane had succeeded where a thousand diplomats were failing.

After that, everything felt easy; the Coolidges brought Lindbergh home again as if he were their own. On Sunday they even took him and his mother with them to church, fussing over them like family. When Lindbergh appeared ready to go in a white suit, Coolidge was surprised; a darker suit would be more appropriate; Lindbergh should change. Lindbergh "did not readily see the necessity for it," Ike Hoover, the usher, noted. But Coolidge insisted, and Lindbergh acquiesced. The Coolidges, for this short time, felt as though they had two sons. They even asked Lindbergh to inscribe a picture for John.

The Congregational Church was undergoing renovation, so the service was in a metropolitan theater. Reverend Pierce sermonized on the topic of speech, and how a person's character might be judged by his words. New parishioners flooded the theater to catch a glimpse of the aviator. Following church, the Coolidge and the Lindberghs found themselves alone again, on Dupont Circle. Coolidge invited only two people to join them and the Lindberghs for lunch: the young journalist Henry Cabot Lodge, the grandson of Henry Cabot Lodge, and his wife. Lodge, the junior man in the room, did not speak, but neither did Lindbergh or Coolidge, perhaps under the influence of the sermon. There was suddenly a duel of the silent. Coolidge finally asked Lindbergh how it was flying for Robertson as a contract mailman. The work was interesting, Lindbergh replied, but it got "tiresome, flying over the same mountains, the same rivers," all the time. Coolidge told Lindbergh that he ought to think of Coolidge on the *Mayflower*. "Same *Mayflower*, same Potomac, same bank, same everything, except the changes of the season." Days like this, however, made it the dreariness worth it. And later other little details of the Lindbergh visit came back to the Coolidges. Grace had queried Mrs. Lindbergh about whether she ever warned her son against danger. Mrs. Lindbergh told Grace that she did not, that to share her fear with him out of her own fear might scare him.

Everyone seemed to want something of Lindbergh. The facts about him were shared like treasure: That his plane had flown faster than the experts expected. That, during his days barnstorming, he had learned that another pilot wanted to test a parachute by simply jumping from 1,500 feet; Lindbergh had devised a sandbag dummy to make the test safe. Word was that someone had checked with the Bureau of Internal Revenue as to whether a prize like Lindbergh's might be subject to income tax. Embarrassed, Mellon's staff had to report that the Orteig Award was subject to the levy. "It's just something that can't be helped," said an anonymous bureau spokesman. "When we tax the money paid to a beauty contest winner, I don't see how we can pass up the Lindbergh Prize." Lindbergh owed $1,233.75 by the graduated code. Instantly, though, donors were there, offering to foot Lindy's bill. In a cable, a Dallas man, William E. Easterwood, Jr., offered to pay the amount so that "the kid can have every cent of the prize money."

Nor would the enthusiasm abate after Lindbergh departed Washington. Hoover was trying to lure him to the Department of Commerce. Lindbergh thought that instead he might embark on a new cross-country tour to promote aeronautics. The tour was to be subsidized by a charity, the Daniel Guggenheim Foundation for the Promotion of Aeronautics, and between flights Lindbergh could work on his autobiography. Lindbergh wanted to capture not only the flight but also his specific analysis of the industry: that planes were so dangerous because the military had crafted them first, and that the design had been for war, not safety; that U.S. civil aviation suffered the disadvantage of lacking much support in the past, but that this very absence might prove an advantage in the future. "Now that the public is realizing its value and is supporting it, commercial flying will grow rapidly," Lindbergh predicted.

As soon as the Lindberghs departed, the Coolidges began to plan out their summer. They would leave shortly, and John would join them later in the Black Hills. Coolidge wrote him a friendly letter, letting John know that "we were pleased you did well this year." John was heading up to summer school at Burlington, and Coolidge wanted him to stop at Plymouth to check up on their house and farm. It was not yet clear whether Coolidge himself would make it to Vermont at all that year.

Though the Coolidges could not know all the details, South Dakota that month was engaging in its wild preparations, not as large as those for Lindbergh in Washington but still, by Black Hills standards, fit for a king. The sculptor Borglum was laying wires and hiring men to display his presidential monument; his federal funding, after all, remained only a promise from Mellon that Coolidge and Lord might yet kill in one of their sessions. The town of Rapid City was readying an office for Coolidge at its high school; Coolidge's private secretary, Everett Sanders, would get his own place in the principal's room. A private telephone line from the school building to the lodge had gone in, and a telegraph wire from the school to Washington. The road from the presidential office at Rapid City to his lodge was rough, and state surveyors were in a quandary; they did not have time to survey and grade it before Coolidge's arrival. Grade the road without the surveyors, Governor William Bulow had ordered. The South Dakota prep work was also culinary. Seventy-five chickens were being nourished on a special diet of milk and fine grain, so that the fried chicken dinner to be made for the president and other guests at an agricultural picnic in mid-July would please the presidential palate. But it was to fishing that the Dakotans gave the most attention. In their enthusiastic promotions, they feared, they had created a trap for themselves. They had to deliver the fishing trip to end all trips. Yet Coolidge, unlike Dawes or Hoover, remained the most basic of fishermen, and the Dakota fish had earned fame for their wiliness. "We knew that he never would be able to catch one of our Black Hills trout," Governor Bulow later recalled. Colluding with gamesmen from all over the region, Bulow and his fish warden hatched a plan. As far away as Omaha, night crawlers had been fed on their own special diet, milk and oatmeal, so that worms twelve inches long would bait the presidential hook. At the state's Spearfish Hatchery swam thousands of ancient, fat trout, fish so domesticated they could hardly be likened to the wild trout of the stream. Some of them were fifteen years old. The warden's deputies netted hundreds of the hatchery fish and put them into trucks, then transported them by night to the president's pond. They also stretched a wire net at each end of Squaw Creek, where the president would fish, and unloaded the hatchery trout between nets. Squaw Creek would give the president the finest trout fishing ground in the world. "Those trout would fight and battle one another to see which one could grab the President's hook first," Governor Bulow predicted. To show their respect, the hosts even renamed the creek after Grace Coolidge.

The reason for the frenzy was something the Coolidges had not yet themselves fully taken in. Coolidge too had become a symbol—similar, in many minds, as improbable as it seemed, to Lindbergh. "Maybe we can get Cal to fly to the Black Hills," mused Rogers aloud in his column. Coolidge's achievements seemed to many worthy of emulation. Republicans looked likely to win the presidential election in 1928. When asked to rank which national issues mattered for the party, party members placed "continuation of Coolidge policies" ahead of "economy in government," They placed "economy in government" ahead of tax cuts or tariffs. If the policies of Coolidge continued long enough, Republicans believed, as with aviation, the remotest corners of the country, the tiniest village, could at last be reached.

Even at last Plymouth Notch. Late in July, the storekeeper Florence Cilley's ward Violet, one of the girls in the village, discovered something strange: a paper that had apparently fallen from the sky. She picked it up and found a greeting from Colonel Lindbergh, addressed to "The City of Plymouth." Lindbergh himself had dropped it from his monoplane as he toured, passing Plymouth on his way to Bellows Falls and Keene. The ribbon in the sky that landed on the ground of the village that the railroad had passed told of something more than flying. Commerce could do anything and touch any place now that it was, finally, aloft.

THIRTEEN

DECISION AT RUSHMORE

South Dakota

IT WAS ONE THING to hear tell of Gutzon Borglum, and another to hear him with your own ears. The roar of his jackhammers cut through the forests above the mining town of Keystone. The jackhammers were drilling holes into some of the oldest granite in the world, preparing to carve the faces of the country's great presidents out of a great wall of stone. The dynamite broke up the rock so that more work could proceed. If Borglum finished, Mount Rushmore would be the greatest monument ever constructed in America—the presidents chiseled from head to waist, the figures in the rock on a larger scale than the Statue of Liberty. The finished group, Borglum said, would be 465 feet tall, 150 feet taller than the lady with the lamp. In the images in the newspapers, Washington, Jefferson, and Lincoln held their heads together and overlooked the hills. The granite there was harder than the granite of Vermont. The weather was such that Borglum could work only a few months a year. The geologists estimated that a millennium could pass before the wind eroded even an inch from Jefferson's chin or Lincoln's brow. If Borglum could be sustained in the job, the undertaking would be completed and the presidential profiles would slice into eternity.

But only if Borglum stayed.

"Only if" was also the sentiment of many Americans about Coolidge that summer of 1927. They wanted Coolidge, the trusted pilot. Even with another Republican at the helm, the prosperity might stall. Fortunately, the president seemed willing to run again. If anything, this western trip to the Black Hills, where Borglum drilled, was proving that. The best test of any candidate's goodwill was how he chose to deal with his party's largest problem: in the Republicans' case, reconciling western farmers and eastern manufacturers. Reconciling in turn would be easy if he could win the hearts of the westerners. That was exactly what Coolidge had begun to do the moment his train, complete with Mrs. Coolidge, five canaries, two dogs, Rebecca the raccoon, Miss Riley, and dozens of aides, rolled out of Union Station. He may have irritated Boston and New York by situating the summer White House farther west than any preceding president had dared to.

"Never so far off," *The New York Times* commented acidly. But even in the first few hours of his ride, he found thousands of new fans. At Hammond, Indiana, a smoky steel town known for angry strikes, 50,000 people showed up to hear Coolidge lecture on the tame conservative topic of religious faith—and applauded. One of Coolidge's tasks was to highlight the fact that farms were doing somewhat better; commodity prices were up. Another was to show that while all Americans came from a farm, not all of them had to stay there. In Minnesota the president asked a man how the crops were. It turned out that the man was a car salesman. The president's error caused general amusement, but it also underscored his point. As the train crossed into South Dakota, "the state turned into a 400-mile cheering section," *Time* magazine reported. Five thousand supporters greeted the Coolidges in Huron; Mrs. Coolidge chatted up those who gathered near the train and was given peonies.

At Pierre, amid yet more crowds, the train halted, so that the governor, William Bulow, might show the president around the capital. This was an unexpectedly hot and noisy diversion on a day when Coolidge was hoping to get to the hills and his cool lodge retreat. Bulow, a Democrat, had plenty to say about the Grand Old Party policies, but at first he found Coolidge's famous silence disconcerting. The president's first question, when he finally asked one, sounded to Bulow like a trap: how did South Dakota enforce Prohibition?

"Pretty well, but not absolutely," Bulow finally replied, a response crafted to evade legal trouble but also to elicit more conversation. That did not come. But Bulow saw that Coolidge took in what he said. The crowds chattered and shouted around them. Sitting with Coolidge, Bulow found, one began to fall into Coolidge's rhythm. After more silence, Coolidge inquired about the population of Pierre. Thirty-five hundred, Bulow estimated. Well, said Coolidge, they must be about all out.

In Rapid City, the people in the next crowd craned their necks to catch a glimpse of the Coolidges disembarking. The first thing the Dakotans could see was the white paws of the collies as they climbed out of the railroad car. Then came the Coolidges themselves. Joining them was Senator Norbeck, who had boarded the train at the state line. In moments, the raindrops stopped, and the sun cut through the clouds. The cameras clicked, catching the light on the presidential pair. The crowd around them waved flags and offered gifts. Mrs. Coolidge was given Canterbury bells and roses. Upon inspection, the Dakotans decided that the easterners, the Coolidges, did not look so different from themselves. For all the talk about eastern banks, a place like Vermont was where many of them had come from. The granite here might be older than the granite of Vermont, but granite was granite. Here gold fever had come and gone; it had done the same in little Plymouth. Here farming was a challenge; that was even truer, of course, in Plymouth. The president, word already had it, planned to visit with relatives, Brewer cousins, who had settled in Fulton, South Dakota. Reconciliation came more easily than all had thought. The Coolidges and the Dakotans might have been eyeing one another for the first time. But they didn't merely meet. They recognized each other.

Looking around at the ungraded roads, the Coolidges saw that their visit was a crucial one for the South Dakota economy. With automobile tourism just beginning, it was important for a place like the Black Hills to get its bid in early. First, though, the state needed some attractions. Borglum's sculpture would be one. The ability to claim that the Black Hills had been the site of a presidential visit was another. If investors and tourists knew about South Dakota, then there would be money for the roads or electricity that South Dakota needed to host them. The Coolidge stay was an opportunity for Senator Norbeck to win federal support for South Dakota's state parks, including Harney Park, on whose acreage the game sat. Every gain tourism made meant that farming's troubles would matter less.

The Dakotans were relieved to see that the first couple understood that. Grace praised everything at the lodge, especially the foliage. Coolidge patronized the local tobacco shop, J. H. Roberts, in Rapid City. Miss Riley placed her orders with the Black Hills grocery. When Prudence Prim, the female collie, fell ill, the Coolidges sent her off to Fort Meade for care. Churches were important for tourists. The Coolidges made their way to the Congregational church in Hermosa, a simple clapboard structure, which, the photos showed, differed not so much from the Houses of God in Vermont. A twenty-year-old student preacher, Rolf Lium, happened to be preaching his first sermon on June 19. The eighty-four citizens of the town showed up, many in Model T's, to greet the Coolidges and attend church with them. Grace's strong soprano could be heard clearly on Sundays thereafter, and the ladies noted that the first lady knew her hymns.

Crucial for South Dakota's future was that the president display enthusiasm for trout fishing, the key attraction in the state's new tourism drive. Here Coolidge got off to a slow start, trying it out hastily one day in his business suit before departing in a hurry to his office in Rapid City. But soon after, he tried again, and the results made it to the table at the lodge. "Exactly what I like," he pronounced gratifyingly upon eating a breakfast of his first catch and touring the area. The next trips to Grace Coolidge Creek were more leisurely, and the papers reported each visit. "President fishes a second time," the headlines cheered. Even Grace, they were proud to announce, was trying fishing, along with the Secret Service man Jim Haley. By now Haley, like Starling, had been with the Coolidges for four years. Reporters noted that unlike the president, Grace baited her own hook.

From the Republican leaders' point of view, the Coolidge performance only improved from there. Coolidge obligingly donned big rubber waders, chaps, and other regional symbols, and equipped his staff with ten-gallon hats. He and Grace even allowed themselves to be filmed in western outfits. Coolidge received a spirited horse, Kit, as a birthday gift from the Boy Scouts of Custer and even mounted for a July 6 trek up a steep trail. This drove the western radical progressives crazy, so crazy that they turned vindictive. "The president of the United States has become a pitiful puppet of publicity," argued the editors of *The People's Business*, a progressive periodical. "The movie pictures' audiences roar with laughter as this bewildered little man teeters down the steps in vaudeville chaps and timidly grasps the reins of the gift horse which he fears to mount." The dress-up scenes also infuriated some stuffy Bostonians. After Coolidge had shown off a pair of western high boots, along with a neckerchief, the *Boston Transcript* could not contain itself: "We believe our own Mr. Frank W. Stearns with his accurate and discriminating tastes would not have allowed this to happen if he had been on the scene." But the Dakotans themselves were pleased by the Coolidges' willingness to ham it up. Their suspicion that a cooperative president would draw tourists was already proving correct. Within weeks of his arrival, thousands of Americans were heading up to the Black Hills for a glimpse of Coolidge. The Cleveland *Plain Dealer* noted, perhaps enviously, "Unconsciously Coolidge blazed a motorist trail."

To be available to his guest, Governor Bulow had decided to occupy a cabin on the state park property near Coolidge's lodge. In those first days Bulow also busied himself arranging other treats: a local mountain would be renamed Mount Coolidge. After the first couple settled in, however, the harried governor decided to take a break from presidential hosting for a day trip of genuine trout fishing, not the staged kind, at Davenport Dam. The dam lay above Sturgis, fifty miles from the game lodge. A knock came at the door. It was Starling, who wanted to know if the governor and Mrs. Bulow could come for dinner. Well, that would be complicated; Bulow did not know if he could make the fifty miles back in time for dinner.

But Starling was not asking. He was ordering. "Boy, when you get an invitation from the President of the United States, that is a command." At the dinner that night, Bulow came face-to-face with the harvest of his own scheming. There upon his plate lay a trout, not just any trout but one of the old hatchery liver-feds that he and the parks men had dumped into Coolidge's creek area. Bulow was already unsteady from the thought of spending an evening with the president; the park superintendent had given him two brandies to calm his nerves. But two brandies were not enough to handle the fish. As the president tucked in, the governor struck up a conversation with the fish: "Seems to me I've seen you before."

What was that? the president asked. The governor told the president he was just commenting that the dinner was trout. But for the brandy, Bulow might not have been able to eat the fish at all. "On the first bite I could taste the ground liver and horse meat upon which that trout had lived for years," he later recalled.

Once the dreaded fish course had passed, the mood lightened, as it had in the car. Bulow discovered in Coolidge a supple and friendly intelligence. Afterward, the president invited the governor to sit with him by the great lodge fire. Coolidge offered a cigar; the governor asked if he could chew tobacco. The men began to talk about South Dakota, and the governor was surprised by how much the president knew about the state. Bulow recalled a line that the poet Oliver Goldsmith had written about the breadth of knowledge of a village schoolmaster, "And still the wonder grew that one small head could carry all he knew." As the Bulows made their way in the dark around midnight to their cottage, the governor told his wife that though he was a Democrat, he might vote for Coolidge.

One mendicant still waited for attention: Borglum. Through reporters, the sculptor offered up to Coolidge tempting tidbits of news about the Rushmore project. The number of presidents to be immortalized had risen to four, to include Theodore Roosevelt. The explanatory words of U.S. history, what Borglum called "the entablature," would be graven into the rock so deeply that a reader might decipher the words from a great distance. The Chicago utilities magnate Samuel Insull had recently made a great loan to the Borglum project: a diesel-powered electric generating plant for its base camp. To ensure that he really received the appropriation that Mellon had agreed to in Washington, Borglum figured, Rushmore needed a presidential visit. He therefore wanted to offer Coolidge the chance to dedicate the site and to write the explanatory text. But Coolidge's visit was planned for only three weeks, and Coolidge was not responding. Desperate, Borglum found a new approach. In the third week of June, when General Leonard Wood, the old presidential hopeful, happened to be calling on Coolidge, discussing the Philippines, the guests at the state lodge heard a buzz overhead.

It was not Lindbergh but a pilot named Clyde Ice whom Borglum had hired to fly over the lodge. Ice dropped a wreath of flowers, weighed down by two moccasins, with a note reading "Greetings from Mount Rushmore to Mount Coolidge." The "Lindy approach" worked here too: Mrs. Coolidge wrote a thank-you note: "Your greeting from the air found glad welcome and we echo it back to you." Borglum got his coveted appointment and made his pitch for a presidential ascent of the mountain. The Coolidges were enjoying their stay; soon after, they thrilled the Dakotans by letting it be known they would stay beyond the planned three weeks. South Dakota swelled with pleasure; men recalled that the state had been the first to declare for Coolidge as a vice presidential candidate way back when, before the 1920 convention. Since then the state's convention law had been changed. But George Henry, a secretary to one of the state's U.S. senators, was now declaring Coolidge's conquest of South Dakota for 1928 completed. "Mr. Coolidge seems to have sold himself to the state, especially the western half of it," he told a reporter for *The Oregonian*. Two incidents, the press men noticed, did not fit into the idyllic presidential postcard. The first was the death of Prudence Prim, who, it emerged, had caught distemper.

The second came one day in late June, when the thermometer in Rapid City rose to 90 degrees, hardly what had been advertised by the Black Hills promoters who had sold the chief on the trip in the first place. When the president returned to the lodge for lunch, he found that Mrs. Coolidge was not yet back from a hike with Jim Haley. With the reporters watching, the chief executive planted himself on the porch to wait, like a sentry. Observers guessed that the great concern of Coolidge was that a rattler had got to his wife. At 2:15 P.M., an hour after the president's return, Grace's white sport skirt and sweater appeared before the lodge. Grace and Haley had lost their way in the Hills—not hard to do—and had been gone for five hours. From their posts around the property, the Coolidges' attendants could see Grace drinking from a glass of water and the president pacing. The first couple went inside. Within days the word was out: Jim Haley had been removed from the first lady's detail and sent far away from South Dakota. The new bodyguard was John Fitzgerald, also a Secret Service veteran.

Coolidge had misfired. This time, the notion of protecting the presidency from scandal truly was pretense. Indeed, the very press he so assiduously avoided now came to him because of his action. Coolidge sensed that most of the reporters in his pool were afraid to write a major feature about the event; they might, however, place the odd detail about the contretemps in other stories, or write short items. At a press conference the next day, June 28, he sought to throw them off the path: "You will find that at the end of your stay here that your work will be more satisfactory if you take up some particular thing and write a very good story about it." Haley's move was described to reporters as a change, not a demotion. No one was fooled.

Still, after several days, it seemed clear that the Haley event would not trigger a larger story. Grace was spotted shopping with her new Secret Service man, John Fitzgerald. A functioning summer White House moved in a rhythm all its own; one by one the visitors came and were heard out by the president. The U.S. marines in Nicaragua were attacked by the rebel lieutenant Augusto Sandino in the town of Ocotal. Sandino and his men charged yelling, "Viva Sandino!" and "Death to the Yankees!" In an intense battle, the marines finally flew five De Havilland bombers over the Sandino men. The Sandino men scattered. Peace would be harder to attain than many had hoped. Mexico would turn into Nicaragua if the administration and Congress did not act. The crisis in Mexico had driven the U.S. ambassador there to resign and write a furious report: the Plutarco Calles government was waging a Soviet-style war against churches and confiscating U.S.-owned properties.

Coolidge received James Sheffield, the departing ambassador, and began to formulate a response. He had Dwight Morrow in mind for Mexico, and wrote to ask him to succeed Sheffield as ambassador. Betty Morrow felt snubbed. For Coolidge to offer a post to his friend at this stage in his presidency seemed tardy, given the longevity of the friendship. Adding insult to injury, the post was not the one the Morrows had hoped for. Coolidge resembled a kind of malevolent Father Christmas, wrote Mrs. Morrow. "The blow has fallen," she wrote. "President Coolidge wrote to Dwight today asking him to be Ambassador to Mexico and Dwight is going to do it! 'No skates or sleds left in my bag!' says Santa Claus, 'but here's a silly little whistle!'" In her view a more dignified position, such as ambassador to the Court of St. James's, suited a J. P. Morgan partner better.

Lindbergh himself wondered about Mexico. "From what little I have seen at our border stops, I am afraid the post will be a difficult one," he said. Still, others, including Charles Dawes, saw the placing of Morrow in Mexico City as an example of Coolidge's wisdom. The United States needed Morrow in Mexico. Mexicans were taking U.S. property, and the leader, Calles, was confronting the difficult decision of whether to stay on for future years. In addition, Dawes told Morrow that he reckoned taking this job amounted to a brilliant career move: "The position in Mexico, to take which might ruin the ordinary diplomat of so-called 'high class,' will make you. You cannot afford to take an easier diplomatic position of higher rank." Within a year or two, Morrow's son Dwight would follow John Coolidge to Amherst. Both Morrow and Coolidge hoped that their sons would learn from someone like Garman. A job like the Mexico post was the very kind of service Garman had taught about decades before. "The President wants me very much to go to Mexico and I am going—that is to say I am going if you stick to your bargain and go with me," Morrow wrote to his wife. Morrow vowed above all to listen to the Mexicans and hear them out.

Coolidge was doing his listening, too, albeit of an easier variety. A large picnic of farmers from three states, a high point of the summer for the region, took place that month at a federal experimental farm in Ardmore. The president and Mrs. Coolidge were served chicken fried by farmers' wives, along with corn grown right at the station, topped off by ice cream. Governor Bulow, ready to star, sported a high beaver hat. Grace Coolidge dressed up: she wore her signature white dress but added a red blazer and red hat. This time the president, though, *The New York Times* reported, "had doffed his Western habiliments."

Before a large audience that included the Coolidges, Senator Norbeck and Governor Bulow debated the old tariff yet again. Did not Coolidge's veto of McNary-Haugen mean it was finally time to reduce tariffs? Bulow's remarks captured the attention of the *Springfield Republican*. The paper noted carefully Bulow's position: "If price fixing is taboo for farmers, it should be eliminated from industries." The reality, Bulow pointed out, was that farmers were the free marketeers here: reducing the tariff would merely be restoring supply and demand. "The price[s] of most things that a farmer has to buy are artificially fixed by reason of discriminatory tariff legislation." Soon after the debate, Bulow told reporters that the combination of President and Mrs. Coolidge was "unbeatable." The recent St. Paul conference of the McNary-Haugenites was "nothing but the reflex action of a chicken with its head cut off," *The Washington Post* columnist Carlisle Bargeron paraphrased Governor Bulow as adding.

As the days continued, the stream of visitors at the summer White House, Rapid City, and the lodge continued as well. The same day Hoover called about flood relief, Coolidge learned to his surprise that he had another guest. Senator Smoot of Utah, a great tariff advocate, awaited him at the game lodge. Coolidge left Hoover to his paperwork and rode out in his car to see Smoot, whose aim was to convince Coolidge to call a special session of Congress where he might push for flood relief and also tax legislation. Hoover was moving on, anyway; his destination was Bohemian Grove, an exclusive retreat of the powerful in California. The West was also the goal of other Republicans. If Coolidge had South Dakota sewn up, Oregon and California were still not certain; Nick Longworth had put Oregon and Hollywood on his itinerary.

Meanwhile, there were even more meetings for Coolidge, many of which reportedly concluded with the good prospects for the fall. "Mr. Coolidge will be re-nominated and reelected," declared the state's former agriculture secretary after his meeting. Summed up *The Washington Post*'s Bargeron: "There is little wonder that the President is enjoying his vacation."

On July 25, the White House postmen at the Rapid City High School opened the mail and found a letter calculated to break down the hardest of granite. It was from Borglum, designed to obliterate any further resistance to a Mount Rushmore ascent and detailing his plan for the text upon the entablature. "My Dear Mr. President," it opened, and after reports of his own travels Borglum came to his substance:

> *Before leaving I had in mind to call personally and ask you about the big inscription I am going to cut on the west wall of Rushmore. You know from my letters and descriptions there is to be a tablet space provided for an historic record of events founding and covering dates commemorated in the memorial. I am of course shaping this inscription and determining its character.*

Borglum went on to list sample dates of years that such texts would cover: 1776, of course, 1787, 1803, and so on. Borglum made much of 1907, as the year Roosevelt had "fulfilled the prophecy of Columbus by cutting the Isthmus of Panama to the world a way for world communication between eastern and western seas." That could have been predicted; Borglum had long been a very public Roosevelt fan and even wore his mustache like Teddy's. Finally, Borglum made his request: "My real thought is that the framing of the language of this tablet should be by you. Doane Robinson says you are the ablest master of phrase living. My own thought on this is expressed in my earnest wish that you be the one author of that tablet, it should be simple, brief, biblical in its simplicity." Borglum let Coolidge know that he would consider it a "colossal blunder" if such a project were *not* directed by the president. After all,

Borglum noted, by this trip, Coolidge had become "the first president who has included the real west in his home life." Borglum completed his plea with a man-to-man tip on fishing, suggesting that Coolidge and Colonel Starling try out Sand Creek, Wyoming. The whole pitch emphasized the aspirational: like Coolidge, even before him, Borglum was an avid Lindbergh fan. Lincoln was Borglum's hero—Borglum had even named his son Lincoln. The inscription work seemed perfect for Coolidge, modest yet important.

Coolidge did not say he would necessarily accept the work. Indeed, the Coolidges shared frustratingly few specifics about their plans, short- or long-term, with the correspondents in the press pool. Indeed, when reporters pressed Coolidge one too many times on the question of taking a trip to Yellowstone—the reporters liked the idea—Coolidge simply replied, "I like it well enough here." Grace chimed in, sassily, "If you think you'd like it out in the park, why don't you go out there?" To the press, the summer White House now truly felt official, and across the country, people were becoming accustomed to the idea of it too. *Black Hills Engineer*, the quarterly of the South Dakota State School of Mines, was preparing an entire "President Coolidge Number," which would detail the technicalities of the Coolidge visit, right down to the number of direct telephone lines laid from Rapid City to Chicago (three) or the number of planes (three) that could fit in the new hangar at Rapid City Airport built as part of the airmail delivery service for the chief. The Stearnses were not in the Black Hills, and neither was Clarence Barron. But such friends kept up with their various Coolidge projects. Barron was setting the stage for the Coolidge Fund at the Clarke School, dropping hints about the excellence of the institution in the press. Along with his Yellowstone travel literature, Coolidge scrutinized an invitation from President Machado of Cuba to attend the Pan-American Conference in Cuba in 1928; the president thought Cuba might be a trip worth making.

One Sunday the Coolidges hosted Guy and George Brewer, children of Milan Brewer, the brother of Coolidge's grandmother Sarah. Together the Brewers and the Coolidges attended the little church in Hermosa. After lunch, they sat on the porch at the lodge and exchanged reminiscences. Reporters had recently noticed that Coolidge was focusing on the world arms conference and that his telegraph was manned so that he might snap up news from negotiators in Lucerne. As the Coolidges worked, they thought about their son John, who would visit them in August, and his girlfriend, Florence Trumbull. Her father, John Trumbull, did not come to South Dakota but did travel to a governors' conference on Michigan's Mackinac Island; the conference was also attended by Governor John Weeks of Vermont. At the meeting Weeks declared his own decision not to run again, a bow to the old Mountain Rule of Vermont: "I am not a candidate to succeed myself because of the unwritten law of my state that a government official be satisfied with one term." At some point in this period there was also news of Mount Rushmore; Coolidge had agreed to go up it.

Early August brought yet another visitor to the lodge: Senator Arthur Capper, a member of the Agriculture Committee and a proponent of the Republican alternative to McNary-Haugen, cooperative marketing. On August 2, Coolidge and Capper headed into Rapid City. It was the fourth anniversary of Coolidge's ascent to the presidency. The press men found Coolidge downright chatty, holding forth on his record, a natural enough topic for an anniversary. The Coolidge years had enjoyed peace. Wages had moved up slightly. There had been a reduction of the national debt when he was in office, about $4 billion, Coolidge noted. In addition to military peace, there had been "a very marked time of peace in the industrial world," so different from what they'd all encountered back in the turbulence of 1919. The president spoke of past tax cuts. He conceded that the boot and shoe industries weren't faring well, but perfection was impossible. Closing, Coolidge mentioned casually that the reporters might want to come back later: "I may have a further statement to make." Anything he said would come too late for the financial markets. But not too late for California.

Coolidge, Capper, and Sanders returned for the second press conference. Capper later recalled that he had attended out of curiosity, just to see what a presidential press conference was like. Sanders, recalling it all later, remembered that at 11:40 A.M., Coolidge called in Everett Sanders for a moment. The president handed him a note and asked him to have Erwin Geisser, the confidential stenographer, prepare twenty copies on small slips. The slips were folded. At the conference itself, Coolidge asked a simple question: "Is everybody here?" He then handed the reporters the slips.

On the little papers were twelve words: "I do not choose to run for President in nineteen twenty eight." The reporters were aghast. They asked if Coolidge would comment. "No," came the reply. The newsmen stampeded for the telephones and telegraph; some ran down sidewalks or drove their cars to a faraway office rather than wait. For Coolidge's twelve, a full 50,000 words moved on the wire from the reporters in Rapid City. Within hours, and across the nation, Republicans likewise got the astonishing report.

The party could not believe what it heard, and moved into a frenzy of confirmation, seeking out sources around the globe. Scouted out in Baden-Baden, Germany, Bascom Slemp, the president's former secretary, speculated that Coolidge had meant that he would accept a nomination "if such nomination is the free expression of popular will." "Coolidge's Withdrawal Takes Whole Nation by Surprise," wrote *The Boston Globe*. Even Hoover was skeptical: tracked down by reporters at the Bohemian Grove refuge, he released his own statement: "I regret the suggestion in the President's statement." Grace's mother, Lemira Goodhue, repeated a version of a famous line of Will Rogers. "I know nothing of the President's policies except what I read in the papers." Rogers himself deemed Coolidge's statement "the best worded acceptance of a nomination ever uttered by a candidate."

With each day that passed, the confidence that Coolidge might yet run for a new term grew. The stock market made up its mind that Coolidge was just bluffing, or stalling for tactical reasons, as he had so visibly in 1920. The day after the announcement, August 3, prices of shares dropped wildly in the first moments of trading, and then rose. The *Globe* set its newspaperman semanticists to analyzing the meaning of the verb "choose." Reached in Newark, former senator Frelinghuysen of New Jersey, who had played golf with Harding in the old days, issued a careful statement: "I hope that the President will not continue in his determination not to run for the nomination in 1928." Governor Lowden of Illinois, one of Coolidge's old Republican rivals, was blunt: "I know of no man who has run away from the presidency." GOP Chairman Butler said he thought that Coolidge would still accept if he were nominated.

After all, Coolidge had often played coy before. It might be his way of timing his campaign. Coolidge was simply saying that if he ran, it would be on the people's vote, not his own. Others found continued hope for a third-term candidacy in the president's behavior. Coolidge seemed to have little idea about work after leaving office. "It hadn't occurred to me that I needed to think what I would be doing after the presidency," he confessed to reporters on August 5. This frank honesty suggested the announcement might be more feint than commitment to retirement. The first couple traveled to Deadwood to meet the Sioux. A Native American girl, Rosebud Robe, placed a feathered war bonnet on Coolidge's head; they named Coolidge "Leading Eagle." Coolidge posed with great solemnity. That itself was evidence of a candidacy: people might mock such photos, but it made the hosts, the constituents, happy. When the Coolidges drove to visit a former governor of South Dakota, the road was rough and Coolidge got out and joined the others in pushing the wagon. Perhaps, the press speculated, Coolidge wasn't talking elections because his mind was preoccupied with serious tasks. That month Nicola Sacco and Bartolomeo Vanzetti, the two men convicted of the murder of two men in Braintree, Massachusetts, were to go to their deaths. Some observers were warning that there would be riots again in Boston if Coolidge did not intervene. Forty-five thousand garment workers threatened to strike over the execution. The committee to defend the men was warning Charles Lindbergh that he would have to appeal to the president or face the consequence that his own achievement would be undone. "All goodwill in Europe for America created by your magnificent flight now destroyed by pending execution two radicals."

August 10 brought the long-awaited visit to Borglum. As much preparation as the Coolidge visit had demanded, his hosts had not readied the road up the mountain. The first car heading up got stuck, "and stayed stuck all day," as Howdy Peterson, one of the workmen on the site, later recalled. Coolidge gamely rode up, though not on the Boy Scouts' Kit, who was proving too feisty; Starling had fixed up a more cooperative horse, Mistletoe. Senator Simeon Fess accompanied him on his own steed. Rolf Lium, the young preacher from the Hermosa church, came up as well. Everyone was in a fine mood, especially Starling, the Secret Service man. Senator Norbeck, who had come to appreciate him, and who had already named a stream after Mrs. Coolidge and a mountain after the president, had told Starling he was naming a valley below the peak of Mount Rushmore "Starling Basin"—"in your honor." It was a Secret Service man's job to be unseen. The unexpected kindness overwhelmed Starling.

Borglum assigned to the president the job of handing over the steel bits with which Borglum would drill the first holes. The sculptor, always dramatic, had also arranged a salute to the president of twenty-one blasts, but the blasts came not from guns but rather from the dynamite blasting twenty-one tree stumps. When Coolidge rose to speak, reporters noted, the yellow tops of his cowboy boots and his sandy hair shone in the sunlight.

And now Coolidge did say all the things he had not at the press conference the week before, delivering an address of more than a thousand words. He found it natural, he said, that Borglum's art should begin with George Washington; Washington had formed people's aspirations, to make them not greater men but rather "into permanent institutions." Coolidge praised Jefferson, Lincoln, and also Roosevelt, who had "brought into closer relationship the east and the west." The monument itself, Coolidge said, ought to be a "national shrine": "money spent for such a purpose is certain of adequate returns in the nature of increased public welfare." This last line was what Borglum had been waiting for: Coolidge had confirmed that Rushmore would have federal support.

Over the moon at the assurance, Borglum expanded his vision. "I am getting old," he told the crowd, "but I may yet live long enough to put the bust of Coolidge alongside those of Washington, Jefferson, Lincoln and Roosevelt." He continued, "We want your connection with it shown in some other way than by just your presence! I want the name of Coolidge on that mountain!" Shortly thereafter, he disappeared. The crowd looked up: like a spider, a man was coming down the side of the mountain on a cable. The cable steadied and slowed. The man was Borglum. Suddenly, the sound of the drilling on Washington's visage was heard.

But the determined line of Coolidge's back as he quickly moved from Borglum also struck the crowd. There was something about the president's demeanor, the quick way he backed off and departed, that gave those who had been so curious about his future their answer. The Republican Party might want Coolidge to continue. Stearns might. Morrow might. But he would not. The statement of August 2 was real; he had meant it. It would stand. There would be no third term.

Some reasons for Coolidge's resolve were evident on that day. Coolidge, who had grown up among horses, had struggled to mount Kit. He had let others attach his spurs rather than lean down himself. This was a different man from what he had been five years before. The allergies and the breathing trouble that were his official complaints might not be his only illnesses. Having watched Harding and Wilson fail, not to mention numerous senators and congressmen, both Coolidges asked themselves whether Calvin might be next; there was little way of knowing whether a man's chest pains were fatal or even whether they were from the stomach or the heart. Everyone thought back to various bouts of indigestion in the case of Wilson or Harding that had proved to something more serious.

Beyond Coolidge's health were other concerns. Both Coolidges were tired of Washington. The tensions between them and the time away from Northampton were becoming too great. Starling, when he thought about it all, was coming to understand that. The incident at the lodge with Haley had stayed with them and those around them. Starling especially regretted it, since he had worked with Haley all these years; Haley had been with Starling since the days of the Hardings in Alaska. "Had I been there I might have staved off the president's wrath," he later thought. The tough decisions of the presidency were also wearing Coolidge down. Many alleged that he had the authority to intervene in the Sacco and Vanzetti case. Coolidge had long maintained that the federal government could not involve itself in the matter, but demands still poured in from around the world. The day before, a crowd of fifteen thousand had gathered in New York's Union Square to protest the execution. But, most of all, the decision not to run again was a decision about political power. "He realizes, as did Theodore Roosevelt in 1904," said Nicholas Murray Butler of Columbia, "that it is the essence of a matter that counts and not merely the form." A president was surrounded by yes-men; eventually, a president started to believe them and forget the work of those permanent institutions he had mentioned Washington forming. Even great presidents like the ones Borglum was sculpting forgot that the office mattered more than the man.

The wording that had confused his friends and the papers had not represented indecision. With the "I do not choose to run" statement, Coolidge was placing a kind of bookend at the end of his career, which he had begun with that other ambiguous statement: "I have not decided to study law." New Englanders relished their independence, which was why Coolidge had said, "I do not choose," emphasizing his own authority. Starling was seeing his initial analysis of the thirtieth president confirmed. "Nothing is more sacred to a New England Yankee than this privilege as an individual to make up his own mind," Starling thought.

Standing by this resolution not to run would be difficult. Another term represented a chance to clean up messes, big and small. Columnists were already criticizing Coolidge's legacy. The columnist Mark Sullivan wrote a biting piece criticizing his appointments, noting of appointments, "That was the kind of thing that Theodore Roosevelt, on the contrary, excelled in." Several days after the climb on Rushmore, and even before Sullivan's column was published, General Lord would arrive in South Dakota to meet with Coolidge. Calendar records showed that Lord and Coolidge were closing in on their two hundredth meeting. Yet their $3 billion goal seemed farther than it had a year before.

But once Coolidge chose, the choice would be final. If Coolidge sought to stop the spending, he had to set an example himself. And if he believed in the mechanisms he and Mellon had established, he had to let them run for themselves, and not hover over them. By tending too long to the commerce or freedom he had fostered, Coolidge might stunt that very commerce or freedom. If Coolidge believed, as George Washington had, he would retreat as Washington had, prove that the office really was one of "president," literally one who presided, not autocrat. Any remaining goodwill should be dedicated to a final, great project Coolidge had in mind for the end of the presidency. As for Mount Rushmore, Coolidge knew where he stood. Composing the inscription Borglum sought represented service. A colossal bust beside Roosevelt and Washington did not. There was a case for monuments to other presidents. But the best monument to his kind of presidency was no monument at all.

CHAPTER FOURTEEN

COOLIDGE AGONISTES

Washington, D.C.

LIKE A SHIP, NEW England hove into view. Boston, Amherst, Northampton, and Vermont all claimed the Coolidges' attention when they arrived back in Washington that September of 1927. It was if they had never gone to South Dakota. In Northampton, Grace's mother, Lemira Goodhue, waited on Massasoit Street. John was just a few miles across the Connecticut River from Northampton at Amherst College, starting his senior year. In Vermont, where the mills struggled to survive and agriculture remained weak, the cheese factory was still running in Plymouth, producing eight hundred pounds a week. The managers were hopefully making yet another of their infinite adjustments, selling not just in bulk but also in smaller three- or five-pound boxes, more convenient for the household. The president had missed the sesquicentennial of the Battle of Bennington that summer despite the entreaties of John Spargo, the curator of the museum near the enormous Bennington Battle Monument. Though the post office had issued 40 million special Green Mountain Boys stamps, Coolidge had not materialized. Vermonters were getting over the fact that their kinsman had forgone the opportunity to honor the colonists' victory over General Burgoyne for the pleasure of donning a Sioux headdress of feathers in Pine Ridge, South Dakota, and being initiated into the tribe by a direct descendant of Sitting Bull. But the Green Mountain State was ready to forgive, if only he came soon.

Coolidge did intend to return north, indeed, to make up whatever he could to Vermont, Grace, his son John, and others whom the presidency had forced him to neglect. But not right away. His main goal now, in the last eighteen months, was to serve effectively, to use what capital he had accumulated wisely. That intention applied to whatever literal capital, dollars, might flow his own way in coming months or years. Morrow and Barron were fund-raising for him. Instead of allocating that money to burnish his own memory or even that of Judge Forbes with a presidential archive, Coolidge was insisting the donor gifts go to the charity that meant the most to Grace, the Clarke School for the Deaf. The other kind of capital, the political kind, Coolidge intended to use to defend his established policies; a consistent legacy was a stronger legacy.

There was even one area where something more than defense work, new legislation, seemed warranted. That area was foreign policy. The French foreign minister, Aristide Briand, was seeking a bilateral treaty renouncing war between the United States and France. That idea did not seem satisfactory, but Coolidge might try something else. He was wary of a great treaty, which looked like an easy way to a fiasco; the memories of his recent failure in Geneva in disarmament, or Wilson's League of Nations downfall, were fresh. Still, Coolidge reckoned, he had banked enough capital for one more big project. His party and colleagues on the Hill, he figured, would be grateful that he had made his election decision early, leaving the Republicans time to find a new candidate. For them to reward him in his last year and a half with support for his legislative projects, whether budgets or a new law, was simple logic.

Unfortunately it was logic his colleagues did not see. From those very first hours back in Washington, indeed, Coolidge discerned that his fellow politicians and lawmakers interpreted the summer's events differently. Instead of gratefully accepting his decision about the 1928 race, the Republican Party still fixated upon him as the only possible candidate, pestering him relentlessly. And instead of granting him support for his policies, Congress was already treating him like a lame duck, someone who would find no partner for his plans. Indeed, with unexpected boldness, lawmakers were pressing for him to give ground in areas where he had drawn the line.

The pressure started with the loud demands to call a special session of Congress to discuss extra appropriations, an idea lawmakers knew Coolidge would deplore. The navy sought another fleet of ships; the army and merchant marine wanted more money to refurbish old ones. It seemed Coolidge's success at halting a great waterways program last spring had been only temporary. Now lawmakers were ready with an update of their law, which would cost hundreds of millions of dollars and rival the damage of the bonus legislation. Southern lawmakers had exploited his voyage to South Dakota to plot their own laws. "Coolidge Away, Mice Enjoy Play," as *The New York Times* put it. "Mr. Chief," as some southerners now called Hoover, was too sophisticated to publicly advocate for a giant new flood control system that his boss would dislike. If the government followed the recommendations of some of the engineers, it would spend $325 million, greater than the surplus most years and one of the largest single expenditures since World War I. But the commerce secretary was already quietly laying the groundwork for such a law.

What's more, the lawmakers' case for extensive flood spending was stronger now than it had been a few months before. The suggestions in the press of total recovery had been premature: now, in the fall, the Red Cross estimated 607,000 southerners still needed winter clothing. Hundreds of thousands of southerners were not yet resettled; the planters were finding themselves in difficulty because many blacks had seized the opportunity to head north forever Coolidge had developed his argument on the floods: states were a larger presence in the economy than the federal government; in peacetime, they spent more than the federal government, at least twice more. Next to business or the states, the federal government was a pygmy, and asking Washington to spend was to change its role. But he was finding less sympathy for that argument now, as well. One senator, Thaddeus Caraway of Arkansas, argued that Coolidge was being disingenuous in taking the position that the responsibility for the flood was not with Washington because the waters that came down the Mississippi covered 40,000 square miles and came from thirty-one states. Caraway also made it a point to praise the commerce secretary and contrast his performance to Coolidge's: "The South appreciates what Mr. Hoover has done." Caraway even framed his argument as a personal challenge to the Vermonter Coolidge: "I venture to say that if a similar disaster had affected New England that the president would have had no hesitation in calling an extra session," Caraway jeered. "Unfortunately he was unable to visualize the situation."

This time, even the normally friendly press was joining the attack on the president. *The New York Times* wrote, "The Administration viewpoint is that with no plans for flood control yet formulated there can be no approbation of public money for that purpose in the immediate future. As to the purposes of the Administration concerning Government relief for the distressed people in the flooded areas, no information was forthcoming." But Coolidge mostly stayed downstairs, pushing back when the calls for a special session came, denying that a consensus was forming on the matter. "As far as I can see there won't be any occasion for a special session of Congress," he told his press conference grimly on September 20.

The unexpected challenges were forcing Coolidge to consider how he allocated his own time, just as he had in those tense days in the summer of 1919, or in his first hours as president after Harding's death. The White House looked good after its renovations; the sky parlor up top especially pleased Grace, who retreated there with her birds and animals. But Coolidge was stuck downstairs at his desk. "I am having the usual experience with a good many members of the House and the Senate that are returning to Washington," he complained to his press conference on October 4. "They are all interested in some plan that calls for a considerable expenditure of public money."

This was a period when Americans were celebrating the nation's sesquicentennial. But what Coolidge noticed was how much time went to military or diplomatic meetings necessary because of World War I. The effects of earlier wars and incursions, dating all the way back to the Spanish-American War, claimed many hours. The reality was plain to see in the president's appointment book. In these first six weeks back from South Dakota, Coolidge attended exercises at the U.S. Army War College in Carlisle, Pennsylvania; worked to repair relations with Mexico by inaugurating a direct telephone line with President Calles; met with Wilhelm Heye, the chief of the German army; heard out an emissary from the Ras Tafari, the Ethiopian prince regent; endeavored to placate Japan by receiving a rear admiral from a Japanese training squadron; received his own secretary of war several times; and met with the former German minister of finance and the governor of the National Bank of Belgium to gain perspective on European debts.

The cost of past wars was also evident in the pages of accounts over which he and Lord labored. They would have reached their $3 billion goal, passed it even, long ago, if not for wars. Outlays that fiscal year for veterans' care and other payments to vets were about equivalent to all the payments made for civilian government together, and larger than any other single kind of payment by the federal government. If you totaled the veteran payments with the military costs and the amount paid in interest on debt mostly generated by wars, you could see that about three-fourths of the federal costs had to do with war in one way or another. And of course both the veterans and the military wanted more: he and Lord spent much time plotting to fend off military spending demands, whether an army request for airplanes to defend the Panama Canal or a navy demand for battleships. You could even argue that the war was damaging the political culture. Charles Forbes, Harding's original Veterans Bureau chief, was still in Leavenworth Prison for the fraud he had committed with federal moneys. All over Washington could be found the detritus of war-related scandal, such as the Teapot Dome decision relating to naval reserves; Albert Fall lay ill in room 765 of the Mayflower Hotel. War had left other kinds of messes, including legal trouble. It was hard to fight with Calles of Mexico over private property claims when Andy Mellon had not yet, even to this day, been able to clarify the status of alien property seized by the United States. It was all a waste, like the *Mount Vernon*, the army's name for the *Kronprinzessin*. The once glorious ship was now rotting in dry dock near Norfolk.

War even, still, affected seemingly removed areas like interest rates, although the effect featured multiple stages that one had to trace. Lower interest rates benefited Europe and its ability to pay wartime debts and therefore gain its own normalcy, or "normality," the word Mellon preferred. When U.S. rates were low relative to Europe's, European investments looked attractive, and Germany, Great Britain, France, or Italy could draw cash and gold and find it easier to pay off war debts. But lower interest rates in the United States were tenable only if U.S. conditions actually warranted such rates. And those conditions occurred only when commerce was strong and Washington was unobtrusive. "To get the government out of business," as Mellon had written a colleague, "whether it be in banks, utilities or monopolies, has become one of the most essential steps to a permanent fiscal restoration of Europe." A new war would instantly interrupt Mellon's virtuous circles, whether of interest rates or taxes. Coolidge was beginning to tell himself that commerce, low taxes, and even civil aviation might work in the short term but did not suffice in the long term. If war caused waste, men of law and law itself had to be used to stop it.

The men of law were already at work: in Mexico, Morrow was using all his formidable skill from his years as an attorney and at J. P. Morgan to isolate the commonalities between angry American property owners and the Calles government. Colonel Stimson was in Nicaragua, where he too might succeed at his brokering, winning an agreement for elections that fall. Stimson was disarming Nicaragua by buying up rifles from the rebels. Rather than intervene in national conflicts, the administration often found itself helping to arm or disarm one side or the other in a conflict. That seemed an acceptable proxy. Lawyering or brokering was also the great skill of Coolidge's secretary of state, Frank Kellogg, a skill Kellogg had begun to amass all the way back in the days when he had read the law and prosecuted great antitrust cases. One reason Coolidge liked Kellogg was that Kellogg was the old-fashioned kind of lawyer, like himself and Sargent and Lincoln: men who had read the law, and worked in the country before the city. Kellogg, who had gone straight from the farm to the law office in Rochester, Minnesota, without attending college, was turning seventy-one that December. Kellogg was older even than Sargent, just a year younger than Mellon. With Kellogg and Morrow, Coolidge planned to do some lawyerly diplomacy of his own by making a strategic trip to a Latin country; he would address the Sixth Pan-American Conference in Havana in January.

But when it came to a grander plan, that new law or treaty, Coolidge was stymied. His old rule had been that the United States intervened in nations when U.S. property or lives needed defending, but that did not seem to suffice. Aristide Briand's bilateral treaty between the United States and France was a trap that might destabilize instead of stabilize. As William Castle at the State Department explained to Paul Claudel, Briand's ambassador, what Briand sought would merely enable France to bully Germany with the confidence the United States would not intervene. Wrote Castle in his diary of Claudel, "I countered by asking him what effect he thought a treaty between the United States and Germany outlawing war would have on France. He admitted that would have a very exciting effect, that people would say that Germany was purchasing security from attack by the United States so that she could more readily attack her neighbors."

One of Coolidge's many visitors that September, the emissary from

Ethiopia, had brought a splendid gift from the prince regent: a heavy golden shield studded with thirty-two diamonds. The renovation of the summer had spiffed up the White House, but the shield outshone its surroundings. Even its red velvet casing was luxurious, so lush it too caught the eye. Along with the gift came a plea. Currently the United States had no representative in Addis Ababa. The prince regent hoped that the United States would send an ambassador. Ethiopia was asking for a U.S. presence because the United States "has no selfish political interest." This was an indirect way of telling Coolidge what he already knew: that the Ethiopians were concerned that the British and Italians were colluding against them. American companies had their own interest there: shortly the government of the prince regent would negotiate a contract with J. G. White, a New York company, to engineer a dam in Ethiopia. Ethiopia was trying to buy American rifles, and the State Department was trying to limit the number to 50,000.

Coolidge left the shield on his desk while he worked. If he could see his way to a multination treaty, there were several ways in which such an agreement could reduce the tensions in a place like Ethiopia. It could deter both Italy and Great Britain from pressing Ethiopia. If the language in the treaty left the country free to defend itself, it might not do so much damage. It might bring goodwill. It might represent economy. There were plenty of supporters for this kind of peace treaty. William Borah, the chairman of the Senate Foreign Relations Committee, had been pushing for the outlawry of war for years. And there was Briand, whose picture was on the cover of *Time* magazine that autumn. Borah of Idaho resembled Briand of Paris in style: both men lived to be contrary. To a party loyalist like Coolidge, the habit was disconcerting. Time spent demonstrating your independence was sometimes time squandered. Senator Watson of Indiana had been with Coolidge when the president made his sarcastic comment about Borah for once riding the same direction as his horse. Now Watson and others were watching to see what Coolidge might do. By supporting some kind of global accord denouncing war, Coolidge might coopt both posturers, not to mention numerous advocates of some form of global peace or accord across the country. If Coolidge could get a multilateral treaty he could himself accept and get the Senate to ratify it, he would unite the party Henry Cabot Lodge had so long before divided, rope in the independents for once, and succeed where Wilson had failed.

That autumn of 1927, Briand was playing hard to get. Both he and the British were frustrating Secretary Kellogg's effort to win the naval treaty at the Geneva Conference; in fact, irritatingly, Great Britain and France were colluding to exclude the United States by writing their own bilateral agreement. That in turn, Kellogg wrote sadly to Coolidge, meant that the United States would probably have to invest in a great program to build new ships. Congress seemed hardly in the mood to be lassoed—in fact lawmakers were openly mounting rebellion. They sought not only hundreds of millions for flood reconstruction but also nearly $300 million or $400 million in tax reductions, about a fourth more than Mellon deemed prudent. The leaders were John Nance Garner of Texas, the ranking minority member on the House Ways and Means Committee, and Senator Furnifold Simmons, who sat on the Finance Committee in the Senate. Their tax plan called for the repeal of a tax on cars, reductions in the middle brackets of the income tax, and a corporate tax cut. This was not quite scientific taxation, for it did not entirely emphasize cuts at the top and in Mellon's analysis was therefore less valuable. If the tax plan wasn't structured correctly, and if a certain share of its harvest wasn't used to reduce the government debt, the revenues might not flow in, and the evidence of their experiment would be muddied.

Like jealous parents, Coolidge and Mellon fussed over any outsider's demand for change. The U.S. Chamber of Commerce, which had long supported Coolidge, this time was backing the Democrats' tax plan. What was worse, the Chamber of Commerce was staking out a new position on deficits. "While no deficit is looked for should the rate reduction herein be made effective," it announced in early November, "it is obvious that in view of the excellent credit standing of the government and the low interest rates at which it can borrow money there would be no great cause for alarm even though a deficit should, through unexpected developments, arise in any year."

At the White House, Coolidge exploded. To give intellectual credence to the idea that a government could permit a deficit, he deemed folly. Intentionally lowering interest rates to ease European recovery was one thing. That was what the Federal Reserve, with Mellon's blessing, was doing. But a deficit of the federal government was a signal to the market that the United States was not a good investment. And countries that were not good investments lost control of their money; if the United

States looked as though it was heading toward insolvency, dollars and gold would go to Europe, whatever Coolidge, Mellon, and the Federal Reserve intended. The virtuous circle would be broken. *The Wall Street Journal*, politely paraphrasing Coolidge, said that the president reckoned that the Chamber's plan had been made "without knowledge of the budget law" and that the plan overall was "the most absurd thing he ever heard of." If now, in good times, high times, the government went into deficit, there would be no money left for the downturn that he suspected was coming.

Next came another shock. Even Mellon, who had been so faithful until now, betrayed impatience with the impulsive Coolidge thrift. In a report about case delays at the Board of Tax Appeals, his Treasury found that Coolidge's relentless budgeting policy represented the basis of the delays. At the salary level at Treasury, Mellon wrote, "it has been impossible to build up and retain an adequate personnel." A full fifty-two attorneys had resigned from the general counsel's office. A total of 4,727 professionals and technicians had left Treasury in the past seven years. Since it took years to build up an expert, the loss caused by that false economy, he estimated, was "incalculable." The departure of one man, a key expert in negotiations of a tax settlement with mining companies, had been caused by a dispute over a $300-a-year salary difference. That man's departure had cost the Treasury a full $100 million in revenues, he wrote pointedly in his note to Coolidge.

He had not felt so much alone since the vice presidency. John, at college, had just blithely agreed to serve for a third year on the "hop committee" that planned proms even though he knew Coolidge disapproved of too much socializing. Grace expressed concern about Coolidge's workload for the year ahead and, especially, Coolidge's health, but often kept her distance, retreating to her new sky parlor, or busying herself about Washington. The papers reported that Grace had paid a courtesy call at a tea room on Seventeenth Street opened by the new wife of Jim Haley, the Secret Service man Coolidge had transferred. The fact that he was now actively raising money for the Clarke School with Clarence Barron did not seem to compensate for the offenses of recent years.

Nor were others readily available. Coolidge's relationship with Vice President Dawes seemed destined never to recover from the poor start they had had in 1925. Many Republicans, including Borah, were plotting to move the party to the left; Borah had allowed he might back George Norris, who sought federal ownership of hydropower. The most obvious example of Coolidge's challenge with Congress in this period was the attendance record of his presidential breakfasts. Ike Hoover, the White House usher, noticed something about them: Congressmen would go to extraordinary lengths to find a reason not to come. Hoover even collected the RSVPs for one breakfast, as they represented such an amusing roster of excuses:

> Senator Heflin: regrets, sick.
> Senator Norris: unable to locate.
> Senator Pittman: regrets, sick.
> Senator Reed, of Missouri: regrets, sick friend.

The guests who did materialize found Coolidge too silent. "What did he have us here for?" they muttered on leaving. To the usher, such extraordinary lack of communication was evidence that Coolidge had become an impotent president. He could no longer negotiate, perhaps even no longer delegate or choose personnel well.

At the State Department Kellogg's deputies found much to criticize in both Kellogg and Coolidge: Kellogg they deemed overly moody, an aging Minnesotan who sometimes greeted his staff in the morning with a storm of rage. Kellogg's hands shook, they noticed; he was blind in one eye, and his uneven education—skipping high school and college for law school—meant his manner was not always smooth or diplomatic, a source of great irritation to the protocol-obsessed staff at the State Department. Kellogg's assistant secretary, William Castle, found Kellogg especially disconcerting. Castle, a former member of the Harvard faculty, was typical: he worked meticulously to complete the tasks Kellogg assigned but was already cultivating a relationship with Hoover. In the press, hostility was also mounting. The writer Sinclair Lewis was working on a novel mocking Coolidge, targeting the president and his admirers as the ultimate in empty-headedness and banality.

That fall there was yet another artist present at the White House, commissioned by Amherst, to paint the president's portrait, Ercole Cartotto, an Italian American. Concerned at the hostility, Grace overcame the distance between herself and Coolidge, albeit only momentarily, to beseech Cartotto not to paint Coolidge as a stereotype, a "fearsome man without a vestige of kindness." Cartotto told Grace he did see a grimness. Cartotto sketched every weekday; he observed Coolidge in meetings with General Lord and tried to capture the line that his mouth formed when he was going over the budget. Men misunderstood Coolidge, Cartotto explained to Grace after a few days. The painter was not willing to soften the president, despite what Grace said. "In New York, people think of the President so"—and Cartotto slumped down, to pantomime a weakling. Where the others saw weakness in Coolidge, he said, he saw strength. For Grace, he bared his teeth. "I show them tiger," he told Grace.

But not many others, even in Coolidge's entourage, saw the tiger. Coolidge sat for Cartotto, met with the dignitaries, and took morning and afternoon walks with Starling. It was to Starling that Coolidge tried to articulate his concerns. The Dow Jones Industrial Average that fall of 1927 hung just below 200, a third higher than its levels in 1926. As far as Coolidge was concerned, this was too high. He "feared the results" of the current policies, especially the ones the progressives had imposed. He also believed in principle that it would be worse to intervene at the Federal Reserve, at the Treasury, or in markets. It was an odd fix for Coolidge, Starling reckoned. "It was strange that he, the most popular man in the country, was the exact opposite in every way of what the public was taking for its model." On December 6, there was a Republican meeting at the White House, the kind of East Room event at which Coolidge could count on being cornered by Republican National Committee men and pressured to reconsider. Their pressure was likely to be so great that Coolidge lost courage and asked Sanders, his secretary, and Starling to go with him: "They're going to try to get me to run again, and I won't do it." He handed out a new text: "My statement stands. No one should be led to suppose that I have modified it. My decision will be respected. After I had been eliminated, the party began, and should continue the serious task of selection of another candidate from among the numbers of distinguished men available." The verb "had," Coolidge thought, ought to allay the political uncertainty.

Coolidge's own mind was on another kind of uncertainty, economic uncertainty. "He saw economic disaster ahead," Starling later recalled. But Coolidge also believed it was wrong to do anything about it. Living an exemplary life was proving more difficult than even he had imagined, and he grew crabby, exercising control in those few areas where he would allow himself. One day, as they walked together down the street, Coolidge held his silence, then finally said to Starling, "Well, they're going to elect that superman Hoover, and he's going to have some trouble. He's going to have to spend money." He went on, "But he won't spend enough. Then the Democrats will come in and they'll spend money like water. But they don't know anything about money." They would want Coolidge to come back again, but he wouldn't be available.

The issue he and Hoover were most likely to tangle about that winter was waterpower. Hoover, coy before, was now heating up. Hoover sought a victory that winter, and reasonably enough: a great program of hundreds of millions would give him something solid to campaign on in an election year. Compared with the progressives, who sought complete government ownership of waterpower, not to mention a law that ensured that Muscle Shoals would stay in government hands, Hoover suddenly looked like a moderate. The papers were picking up on Hoover's new energy. "A Water Power Battle Is at Hand," read a *New York Times* headline on October 30. "All Afraid of Hoover," read the *Los Angeles Times*. Coolidge for his part was girding to block the flood of spending. He had some time, but not much, to lay out his arguments; the opening of Congress was barely a month away.

No one—not Starling, Kellogg, Mellon, Hoover, or Coolidge himself—could have been prepared for what came next. On Wednesday, November 2, while Washington considered reports that Senator Norbeck of South Dakota might run for vice president, a rainstorm started in New England. All Thursday the rain continued while in Washington Coolidge saw the secretary of war and discussed Prohibition enforcement with delegates from a national crime conference. Reports came that squalls were tying up shipping.

By Thursday night, flooding had commenced all down the Connecticut Valley. At Pittsfield, the waters rose so fast that men used dynamite to blow up an old bridge and save a town from the flood. The three express trains that ran from Montreal to Boston were all ordered to hang back in Montreal until news came from Vermont. In the next days, more reports from Massachusetts filtered in. Holyoke was just about wiped out; at Springfield, the West Springfield Dike had broken, releasing floodwaters into West Springfield and Agawam and forcing thousands out of their homes. Young women from Smith College, where Morrow's daughter Anne studied, were performing relief work.

Hampshire County had even released its prisoners in Northampton to help strengthen the dike. John Coolidge, the president's son, had seen the Connecticut River's waters ride to historic highs at the Holyoke Dam.

But it was from Vermont that the worst shocks came, all over the next forty-eight hours: whole bridges, entire Main Streets, were wiped out; great long stretches of new railroad were washed away. Even paths normally safe from flooding were inundated; the engineer on the *Ambassador* stopped his train after feeling the tracks "soften" under him. At Winooski, an iron bridge across the river was carried up and then down into the waters. At Gaysville, the villagers put their belongings in the church, which was on higher ground. The next day the river pulled the church away. "We never saw it again, except as a mass of kindling," someone wrote. At Bennington, the water poured down Main Street, knocking out wires and darkening the town. The governor himself spent a restless night in the Pavilion Hotel in the capital; his wife described the waters "rushing and roaring like a big mad ocean." More dire was the fate of the state's lieutenant governor. At Barre, he was swept away when he attempted to leave his car and wade; his body was discovered only the next afternoon. The lieutenant governor's brother was forced to walk fifteen miles to attend the funeral.

The waters had swept away large parts of towns; at Waterbury, where the asylum was, 121 Holstein cows drowned. The damage in the state capital, Montpelier, amounted to $2 million, the equivalent of one-eighth of the annual state budget. At Burlington, the damage was not as bad, but the town was isolated, reachable only by a steamer that traveled on Lake Champlain over to Fort Kent. In Windsor, people had to be saved with boats. Plymouth was spared, but Ludlow was not. The waters rose up the steep banks to the Black River Academy. They swept away a historic steel bridge, the main railway to Rutland. And St. Johnsbury, where Coolidge had spent the brief time preparing for Amherst, saw a loss that would cost more than $10 million; three bridges were wiped out. On the night of Sunday, November 6, Governor John Weeks found a telephone booth to call the president and brief him. As he left the booth, he later recalled, the press men were there; one said, "Vermont has gone to hell! She can never come back."

Vermont seemed ruined, "smashed," as *The Boston Globe* put it. A blanket of snow now covered the icy floodwaters, slowing the recovery and rendering many roads treacherous. Though the state had not taken federal aid before, it might need that aid now—not just highway aid, which would probably come, but something greater. Vermont might fail without Coolidge's help. "This is the story that Vermont won't tell. But the people of the ruined valleys admit it to those they have seen, and wistfully they watch for those who love Vermont to read it between the lines without being told," said *The Boston Globe*. "The pitiable $75,000 that is appropriated by the Red Cross is less than Boston raised in the first week for the Mississippi." Vermont needed not $1 million but $10 million to rebuild the railroads and towns. "Is not Vermont worth as much as France to the United States?" the *Globe* reporter paraphrased a businessman as saying. "Calvin Coolidge is a Vermonter. Perhaps that boast of the state is now its chief liability," the reporter concluded.

It all amounted to retribution of biblical proportions. Senator Caraway's challenge had come to life. Coolidge had not gone down to Mississippi when the water had flowed over the levees. He had not called a special session of Congress for the southern floods. If the president was to demonstrate consistency, he could not go up to Vermont or call a special session now. If he went to Vermont now, he could not stand on principle in the great flood-funding debate. Without Coolidge, there would be no obstacle remaining to an enormous new flood program. Even as the president took in news from Vermont, southern states were pressing for a Coolidge endorsement of additional funding from the federal government to cover the cost of spillways in the new dam proposal. Hoover was letting them know that Coolidge might well give in. Only Coolidge could limit the federal flood spending, and only if he was consistent. "He can't do for his own, you see, more than he did for the others," one Vermonter explained to reporter Louis Lyons. If ever there was a test of living by example, this was it.

Coolidge stayed in Washington. Just as before, the federal rescue was to come through the supervision of the Red Cross. Coolidge himself would lead a fund-raising drive; a public relations campaign from the chief executive, just as in the case of the spring, seemed within bounds. He launched this modest plan with a group of Vermonters, including Porter Dale, the Vermont senator from Island Pond who had gone to his house when Harding had died. That was his limit, he explained on November 8, to his press conference group. First, he described the damage to the road leading to Plymouth. "A quarter mile stretch of the mountain slipped down into the road and cut off travel temporarily between the Union and where I live." Then he summarized the administration's position in a single sentence. "From anything I know about the section that was flooded in Vermont, there would be nothing that could be done there about flood control."

Vermont labored to right itself. Governor Weeks appointed his own disaster manager, Fred Howland, the president of the National Life Insurance Company. Howland had read law in the office of William Dillingham, the same office where Coolidge had once been offered a clerkship. The damage at some of the mills was enormous. Governor Trumbull, the father of John Coolidge's friend Florence, wired an offer of assistance, as did Governor Smith of New York. There were more reports of damage. At Winooski, the loss at the American Woolen Company was $1 million; New England Power suffered $1 million in damage at Bellows Falls. The Rutland Railway Light and Power was down $300,000. Governor Weeks created a Flood Survey Committee that carefully cataloged what had been discovered in November: 7,056 acres of farming land had been reported wiped out; 200 barns were gone; 1,704 head of cattle and 7,215 chickens were dead; and 2,535 cords of wood had been destroyed. Surveyors believed they had captured only three-quarters of the loss.

If Coolidge was to follow his spring protocol, he now had to dispatch Hoover. He did, but only after shipping Attorney General Sargent home to write a report of the whole fiasco. No matter the timing, the thought was painful: Hoover, not Coolidge, arrived on his own special train at Essex Junction, Hoover in the little caravan of cars, doing the inspecting. The Vermonters noticed that when Hoover's car got stuck, Hoover let the others push and sat in the car, an important man. They had Howland, their own relief manager, and turned snidely against Hoover. "Herbert Hoover came, and saw, and suggested, and left," as one Vermonter summed up the commerce secretary. An additional misfortune came out of the Hoover visit: Hoover's aide, Reuben Sleight, died in a plane crash near Montpelier.

The critics didn't let up. "Vermont villagers do not agree with the reported opinion of their distinguished neighbor, President Coolidge, that nothing much can be done about flood control in the valleys among the Green Mountains," wrote a columnist in the *St. Albans Daily Messenger.* "At Waterbury they don't hesitate to blame the force of their disaster to the power plant dam just below the river 'that plugged up the gorge,' they say. The power companies are looked at by the flooded villagers as very largely responsible for the horrors of last Thursday night." Armistice Day came, and Vermont dedicated the day to reconstruction, a move that won admiration across the country. "Every able-bodied man in President Coolidge's home state turned out for a day of toil, broken only by a two-minute pause at 11 a.m. for a silent tribute to the World war dead," the *Rockford Daily Republic* of Illinois wrote.

Coolidge made a personal contribution to the Red Cross Fund for Vermont but stopped at that and watched Vermont struggle from a distance. The state legislature determined that it had to have its own special session, a rarity in the history of Vermont, to enact emergency funding. But even getting to Montpelier was difficult.

Coolidge worked through Thanksgiving on the State of the Union address, retreating to the *Mayflower* to write and entertain Senator Curtis, who was running for president. Word came after Thanksgiving that the Vermont state legislature was ready to hold its extra session. After weeks of repair and the building of temporary bridges, the Vermont state government sent its own train, a legislative special, by Montpelier and Wells River Railway to Montpelier. Weeks opened with a reading from the Forty-sixth Psalm, "God is our refuge and our strength." The governor sought $8.5 million for repair, or half the state budget, and the lawmakers passed the bill. Grimly, the legislature also approved a $300,000 loan to the railroad. Some in Vermont deemed the spending enslavement. Whole generations would be paying back this money. But Vermont was also proud. In size, the bond issue was "the greatest work ever done in a single day by the Vermont legislature," the *St. Albans Daily Messenger* announced.

Hoover had turned his attention back to the South and the construction of flood legislation; he was traveling, phoning, and wiring, not always with Coolidge in the know. He was quietly telling southerners that there would be funding for spillways and other costs. Kansas City was selected as the city for the Republican convention the next year; Coolidge could read in the papers that the fight boiled down to Hoover and Dawes. Beating Coolidge to the punch, on December 6, just before the State of the Union, Hoover published the Commerce Department's general economic report, blaring prosperity: though the country's population had grown only 55 percent since the turn of the century, key fields such as mining were up 248 percent in dollars; railway service was up 199 percent.

Coolidge finally finished his State of the Union address. It mirrored his indecision over foreign policy. The United States had been unable to come to agreement with Great Britain, and the naval treaty of the past year had to be recognized as a casualty of that. On the Kellogg and Briand peace treaty question, he punted, carefully positioning the administration so as to be not far from and not close to endorsing a compact. The United States did not need a treaty, he wrote in the message, even if it was considering one: "Proposals for promoting the peace of the world will have careful consideration. But we are not a people who are always seeking for a sign. We know that peace comes from honesty and fair dealing, from moderation, and a generous regard for the rights of others. The heart of the Nation is more important than treaties." In other areas, he was his old clear, brief self. Farmers sought more help, but he signaled that he would block farm legislation: "It is impossible to provide by law an assured success for those who engage in farming." On the merchant marine and government entry into the ship business, he was equally frank: "Public operation is not a success." American Indians were seeking additional funding beyond what they had received; the most important thing Coolidge could do had already been done: the government had granted the Indians full citizenship in 1924.

The part that the entire South and Vermont were waiting for came toward the end, published in the paper under "Flood Control." Coolidge acknowledged the gravity of the Mississippi flood: "It is necessary to look upon this emergency as a national disaster." The federal government had carried some costs; the owners of land adjacent to dikes had paid only one-third of the costs necessary. Further federal assistance should be "confined" to the true flood area of the lower Mississippi. Last in the flood section came New England. Coolidge allowed that "a considerable sum of money will be available through the regular channels in the Department of Agriculture for reconstruction of highways." It might be necessary to grant special aid "for this purpose." But that was all.

It was the South that voiced its fury: "President Coolidge has demanded an impossibility of the Lower Mississippi Valley. These states cannot make any substantial contribution toward the adequate works for the control of floods," correspondent George Coad wrote in *The New York Times* of December 11. Because Hoover had hinted that more was promised, especially regarding the contentious spillways, the rage against Coolidge burned hot. The most one could do to excuse Coolidge was to presume ignorance: "A few persons entertain the hope that agitation might even win the President to the valley's view. These men think that Mr. Coolidge has been inadequately informed. If he understood the problem, he would see the flaws in his present reasoning."

As the holiday neared, disappointments mounted. Morrow had hosted Lindbergh in Mexico with great success, but the Coolidge combination of aviation and arms shipments was not always working as foreign policy. Stimson, operating in Nicaragua, had demonstrated great talent, but he and General Hilario Moncado, who was leading the Nicaraguan government, had not stopped General Sandino and his rebels; on the contrary, Sandino's men were refusing to turn in their guns for any price; their refusal to be bought by the Americans looked like character. After a visit from Stimson, it was clear that Coolidge might once again have to dispatch the marines; at the end of the year five marines would be killed and twenty-three wounded at Quilali with matériel stolen from a U.S.-owned gold mine by General Sandino. Dispatching Lindbergh, the plan for January, might not be enough to prevent civil war in Nicaragua. The idea of shipping arms through proxies to one party or the other in a national conflict was merely making the United States look sinister. That winter, in his funny spelling, Will Rogers would write a column that skewered the administration for the policy:

> Here we are the Nation that is always hollering for
> dissarmament, and Peace, and just because we are not smart enough
> to settle our differences by diplomacy (because we have none) why
> we are going to make it possible for somebody else to exterminate
> the faction that we don't like. Suppose they don't like Coolidge down
> there, and they would allow arms to be shipped into this Country to
> arm a revolution against our Government that is in Power. Boy,
> what a howl we would put up! But it's us doing it down their way
> now, so that's all right. Here is the humatarian nation of the world
> fixing so more people can get shot.

The State Department's behind-the-scenes foreign policy was not popular. It was Borah's simple outlawry of war that was popular.

That December, Grace's mother entered the Cooley Dickinson Hospital in Northampton with influenza; she improved, and then relapsed. Grace telephoned the doctors and would travel to Northampton early the next year with her own entourage, including Dr. Boone. John and her mother preoccupied Grace now. A weighty Vermont delegation called on Coolidge in Washington. Its members included Governor Weeks and both senators, not to mention Frank Partridge, the president of the Vermont Marble Company, to make the case for federal funds. But the Vermonters left the presidential meeting with no commitment for money from Coolidge. "The president's attitude was not revealed," the papers wrote. The president also received woolen wristlets as a Christmas gift from a grandmother, with a card: "These are to keep you warm when you come back to Vermont."

But Coolidge insisted on remaining in the Washington area for Christmas. After pressure from the papers, he also wrote out a Christmas greeting in his own hand for the nation. The new process of facsimile made it possible for the newspapers to share his lines:

> *Christmas is not a time or a season but a state of mind. To*
> *cherish peace and good will, to be plenteous in mercy, is to have the*
> *real spirit of Christmas. If we think on these things there will be born*
> *in us a Savior and over us all will shine a star sending its gleam of*
> *hope to the world.*

The words touched, but they did not console. Though Coolidge could and did light the national Christmas tree, Christmas was rougher in Vermont. The Christmas tree harvest waiting for delivery near Mount Holly had been ruined, the trees strewn across wrecked train tracks, hopelessly bent and waterlogged. Coolidge could not do for his own what he did not do for others, just as someone had commented to the newspaper reporters. He had stood on principle this last time. Doing so had cost him so much, and no one, not even Vermonters, understood.

FIFTEEN

꙳꙳꙳

THE SHIELD AND THE BOOK

Washington, D.C.

ONE SUNNY JANUARY DAY in 1928 the people of Cuba gathered at Havana harbor to mount the greatest welcome they had ever given a foreign leader. Thousands climbed onto the Morro Castle and the rooftops of buildings, craning their necks to get a glimpse of the battleship USS *Texas* as it moved into the harbor. Every balcony near the harbor was packed with cheering families. Overhead, six Cuban army planes circled to protect the *Texas* and her long convoy, which included three destroyers and the cruiser *Memphis*. Whistles shrieked; the *Texas* fired her sixteen-pounders in salute. Cannons at Fort La Cabaña saluted back.

The leader was Coolidge. This time, he was the traveler arriving in the port, not the host, as he had been when the troops with all their joys and troubles had returned to Boston in 1919. This time, the occasion was preventing future wars, rather than ending one that had just past, or those before. Coolidge's disembarkation point at Capitania del Puerto sat only a few hundred yards from where the great battleship *Maine* had sunk three decades before.

President Machado greeted the Coolidges royally at the palace. At the Pan-American Conference the next morning, leaders from twenty-one Latin American nations were also in attendance. In his speech at the conference, Coolidge spoke of respect, democracy, and law. There had to be, he said, an "exact footing of equality" among nations. He also advanced the principle of self-government for Latin American nations. Finally, he spoke against force. It was time to heed "the admonition to beat our swords into plowshares." The phrase resonated because just days before, Coolidge had ordered marines into Nicaragua.

Yet the Cubans ignored the Nicaraguan story. They were interested in every aspect of their guests: Grace's splendidly large red hat and Coolidge's coloring—they called him "Rubio," red-haired. They praised Charles Evans Hughes, Coolidge's former secretary of state. Hughes's bearded presence added dignity to the sessions at the conference. The Cubans commented on the gravitas of Hughes, Ambassador Morrow, and Secretary of State Kellogg as the three stood in the background on the *Texas* or on the stages in Havana. The reporters noticed that presidents Coolidge and Machado both wore horn-rimmed glasses when they read; the cartoon similarity between the statesmen seemed to confirm Coolidge's statements that there was a "footing of equality." The Associated Press cheered that "it was a spectacle such as this American President has never before participated in and recalled to mind the clamorous entry of Woodrow Wilson into Paris." Above all, Coolidge, Morrow, and Kellogg noticed one thing: the scale of the crowds. Noble Brandon Judah, the ambassador to Cuba, estimated sixty thousand in the streets alone. No one knew the exact total, but it was thought to be at least 200,000. The message was clear: Cubans, like the citizens of so many other nations, were not merely glad to undertake a common project with the United States. They were eager to do so. All they were waiting for was an invitation.

That invitation was something the Coolidge administration might provide, even now, in the difficult, beleaguered final year of the Coolidge presidency. Indeed, by the time Coolidge arrived in Havana, the plan had already been scripted by the secretary of state. Kellogg and then Coolidge had quietly made up their minds that the United States would indeed lead a great peace compact among nations after all. Soon—the State Department and White House would make public Coolidge's endorsement of such a grand move. In the meantime, over the coming weeks, Kellogg would lay the groundwork by wooing moody foreign leaders, starting with the grandiose Aristide Briand and following with the German, Japanese, and British leaders. Even as the major states were won, Kellogg would invite additional nations, such as Cuba, Ethiopia, and even Russia, to be signatories. Finally the administration would come to the most difficult part: winning the ratification by the Senate. This victory would not come easily: the crowds in European cities had also hung from the balconies to see Woodrow Wilson, yet the Senate had denied Wilson his League of Nations. Still, Kellogg was determined. Nineteen twenty-eight was the year of the presidential election. A successful campaign for a treaty and its result might matter more than any election. The peace treaty would be Coolidge's last legacy. It was Kellogg who had first seen how such a victory might be possible, even in a year when Congress was openly mounting a revolt.

The key to success or failure lay in Kellogg's or, for that matter, Coolidge's ability to surprise. And surprising others was an art both men had mastered. Originally country lawyers, Kellogg and Coolidge had made careers out of being underestimated, of stealing others' thunder, of delivering more than anyone expected. Now Coolidge's apparent weakness and indifference after the Geneva Treaty and the Vermont flood, like Kellogg's age and trembling hands, would throw their opponents off. Men always loved best those projects they thought were their own, and in the case of the peace treaty the idea belonged to both Borah and Briand as well. The pair were likely to go along as long as they perceived themselves as the leaders and Coolidge and Kellogg as secondary figures playing catch-up. The lame-duck president and his old codger of a secretary would prevail over the foreign statesmen, the garrulous senators, even their own staffs, by outfoxing them.

The treaty itself had crystallized in Kellogg's mind as the administration had tried to decide what to make of Briand's irritating bilateral plan. Briand had proposed that plan in the newspapers in April 1927, and for months after, Kellogg had made a show of ignoring him. But perhaps, Kellogg had begun to think, one could use Briand's document as a basis for a treaty among the great powers, a "universal undertaking not to resort to war." That "might make a more signal contribution to world peace by joining in an effort to obtain the adherence of all the principal powers of the world to a declaration renouncing war as an instrument of policy." Such a declaration, he wrote in one State Department paper, "could not but be an impressive example." With the word "example," Kellogg knew, he might lure not only Briand but also Coolidge.

THE SHIELD AND THE BOOK 409

At first Kellogg had not even been sure whether Coolidge would back him. Over the fall, Coolidge had more than once publicly shied away from a treaty, once by raising the question of whether it bound the United States in an unconstitutional fashion, and then again in the State of the Union address by asking if the country needed such a treaty. Still, a treaty about examples was an extension of Coolidge's general philosophy of living by example. Kellogg reckoned that Coolidge, now nearing the end of his career, would naturally be ready to return to the law, coming full circle to where he had begun so many years before in the Forbes Library. And even as far back as the Massachusetts Senate, Coolidge had counseled that in moments of confusion, the people and the lawmakers should turn their eyes back to the law. Observing a law in common had represented, he had said in that first great speech as president of the Senate, the "sublime revelation of man's relation to man," democracy in its truest form. As World War I ended, Coolidge, as Massachusetts lieutenant governor, had done everything to find political middle ground, to pull parties together to get through the siege. Now Coolidge would sacrifice in the same way for a war against wars, pulling all together, to beat, as Coolidge put it in the Havana speech, "swords into plowshares."

Over the course of the fall it had become evident that the Geneva naval conference truly was failing; Kellogg's case for a new peace treaty had become stronger. The flop meant that the naval arms race was back on, and that the United States would have to spend wildly to keep up: "I think there is a pretty strong feeling we should extend our building program," Kellogg had written to the president. Once again the sheer expense of war and its consequences daunted them both. In that period, half of the budget went to the Department of War, interest payments, and veterans' benefits. Anything that could reduce the pressure to spend on arms would be welcome at this point. But Kellogg had felt it best to keep the project quiet at first: even his own staff, he thought, must be kept partially in the dark. Gossips and snobs sat all over the State Department. If his men, or Coolidge's, did not know the extent or seriousness of the treaty campaign, so much the better.

It had been mid-December when the white-haired secretary had commenced his treaty campaign. On December 22, the same week the Vermont delegation had implored Coolidge for money, the secretary of state made his crucial first move, speaking in a closed session of the Senate Foreign Relations Committee. "Outlawry," the word for the concept, was practically a synonym for "Borah." To advance a related idea as his own, Kellogg knew, was to ensure that the proud Idaho senator would kill it. In the meeting Kellogg had therefore come at the topic obliquely, speaking of condemning war, and Franco-U.S. agreements, in the hopes that Senator Borah would take up the topic for himself. The plan had worked like a charm. "But Mr. Secretary," Borah had said, "the American counterproposal should be a pact to outlaw war between all nations of the world. We should point out that this is too important to confine only to this country and France." All of them, Borah had gone on, were frustrated with bilateral agreements such as the one Great Britain was writing with France on arms. Kellogg had held his tongue until Borah had polled the room and found support for a compact among nations. Indeed, the senators had rushed to push the treaty idea. "That's the best way to get rid of the damn thing," Senator George Moses of New Hampshire had thrown in enthusiastically. "Put the baby on their doorstep. Extend it to all nations."

At the White House, meanwhile, there had been subtle signs that the president was warming to the treaty project. The evidence was in the household budget. In December, Miss Riley, the housekeeper, noticed with concern that she would have to spend above her monthly allowance to meet the extra costs of unexpected diplomatic invitations. A surprise extra dinner for the governor-general of Canada, along with a few other cabinet and diplomatic dinners, had featured caviar, green turtle soup, and other extravagances not always on the table, including beef tenderloin and extra imported grapes. "We really did spend a lot," Miss Riley wrote apologetically to the president, a total of nearly $350 extra. But spending a little extra on coddling diplomats now might be an economy that would benefit the national household later.

Just after Christmas, Kellogg had finished his treaty draft. A call came in from the French—the Quai d'Orsay, too, was ready to talk about treaties. Kellogg, keen to get his text out before the French sent theirs, hurried over to the White House to win explicit approval of the project from Coolidge. The language was sufficiently general, Kellogg had explained, that it would not compromise the federal government's sovereignty. The president heard the secretary out on a few other basic questions. The scene felt familiar, two lawyers working through a document. The constitutionality question that Coolidge raised in his State of the Union address was covered now: the power to defend itself remained with the United States, and Coolidge might choose how he construed the concept of defense. When Kellogg was finished laying out what was promised and what was necessary for such a treaty, Coolidge looked up and asked simply, "We can do that, can we not?" Kellogg replied that he thought they could.

Kellogg had suggested a second policy to his president. Like Borah, the French would want to haggle, draw matters out, trade secret documents back and forth all year, as had happened during the purgatorial Geneva talks. Perhaps Briand had never intended that his proposal become reality. That was the guess of William Castle, who reported to Borah at the State Department. "It is more and more evident to me that Briand made his first suggestion for political reasons solely and that he has now got a bad case of cold feet," Castle would write.

Why not, Kellogg asked, go around the French statesman and simply publish the U.S. treaty offer in the next day's paper? After all, Briand had made his own offer nearly a year before, through the newspapers and through peace activists such as James Shotwell of Columbia University, whose plan featured not "outlawry" but language closer to Briand's, "denunciation of war as national policy." A direct approach to Coolidge by Shotwell to discuss denunciation and Shotwell's own interactions with Briand had elicited a terse rebuff in White House shorthand: "Pres advised no suggestion from French Govt has come to State Dept. Until such suggestion is made by French to Am Govt Pres sees no advantage in conferring with volunteers." Now the moment had come to give Briand some of his own medicine. "If this is to be carried through, it will need all the power of an informed public opinion," Kellogg told Coolidge. "Full publicity is the only way." All right then, Coolidge said. "Go ahead."

No one had known how Briand would react to Kellogg's draft, though the State Department staff had nursed its suspicions. Briand had "cold feet," Castle chuckled, and "they will be positively frozen when we drive him into the open and make him do something, or refuse to do something, which on paper at least is a step toward prevention of war." Just as Kellogg had predicted, papers the world over had published word of the United States' offer and Kellogg's description of it. Briand's first response was to insist that his Franco-U.S. agreement come early and be completed before any large compact among nations. Some of the French papers had backed Briand up, with the *Journal des Débats* writing, "The

State Department, for effect abroad, prefers to appear to be doing something rather than signing a formal document." Briand left the door open for more talks: progress, but nothing firm. And that was where matters stood when the Coolidges boarded the train with Will Rogers for the first leg of their Cuba trip.

Kellogg and Coolidge both knew that when the president returned to Washington after Cuba, domestic legislation, not international treaties, would command their attention. Indeed, the thought enervated Coolidge; Starling, his bodyguard, noticed his exhaustion in Miami. It was early in the legislative season, but the press was already amusing itself tracing the various Coolidge legislative humiliations. Coolidge had backed a minimalist merchant marine. The Senate passed an expansive outlay and rules that virtually guaranteed that expensive, money-losing ships would remain in government hands. Coolidge had opposed the refitting of German ships, which years back experts had deemed "worse than a waste of good money"; lawmakers wanted to spend at least $12 million to reconstruct the aging craft. Coolidge had asked that the legislature allocate a large share of the spending on floods to the states; in the legislation Congress was passing, the states would pay only one-fifth of the costs. Coolidge had rejected farm subsidy; the farmers were seeking another subsidy law. Moving Muscle Shoals out of government control seemed crucial to Coolidge; Senator Norris had yet more legislation ready to keep the dam and plant in the government's hands. Coolidge and Mellon had proposed a tax reduction of $225 million and warned anything above that would yield a deficit; the House voted for $289 million. Many thought that for Coolidge, the worst was yet to come.

Hoover was making himself visible everywhere, already boasting that he had 323 votes from convention delegates, though the GOP convention was many months away. Even at the colleges, the sentiment was shifting. Fifty-eight percent of Yale students now endorsed Hoover, despite several years previously having been so faithful to Coolidge that they had copied his smoking habits. Coolidge's diminished status meant diminished prospects for tax reform. But the weaker status also, Coolidge and Kellogg thought, might even facilitate Kellogg's maneuvering. To sell the treaty further, the secretary of state needed some kind of public statement of support from the sitting president, a line to cite to foreign ambassadors. But such a statement could not earn too much notice at this stage, or it would be debated, and Kellogg's pitch to foreign offices undermined. Coolidge dutifully dropped the comment about broadening the Briand treaty at his press conference at the end of January: "Our general position being that we would like to make treaties of that kind, thinking that it would be more advantageous if they were made with several great powers than to undertake such a treaty with one country alone." That gave Kellogg time to lock in the elusive Briand. Through Paul Claudel and others, Briand was quibbling over phrasing. Instead of opposing "war as an instrument of national policy," his own original words, the treaty, he now said, should be against "wars of aggression."

The press obediently ignored the president's treaty statement and Briand too. Instead the reporters focused on human interest stories. Grace was ill. After shaking hands with a thousand people at a February 1 reception, she collapsed. Again the doctors came; she was also taken to see Dr. Hugh Young of Johns Hopkins, who met her at the U.S. Naval Hospital at Twenty-third and E streets on February 8. Kidney trouble, the same malady that had stricken Florence Harding, now afflicted Grace Coolidge. Dr. Young met with Coolidge in his private study, so that few would notice, and diagrammed a picture of the kidney for the perturbed president. Grace did not improve quickly, and on February 13, the White House staff observed, Coolidge sat with his wife for almost the whole day. Grace's old friend from Massasoit Street, Therese Hills, also came down to spend time with her.

Coolidge's friends made his priority, the Clarke School, theirs. Perhaps in an effort to cheer up the first couple, Barron sent a lengthy update of his campaign drive to raise cash for the Clarke Fund. A New York committee that included Herbert Pratt believed it had raised at least $800,000 in the New York area alone before any public announcement. February 16 brought the annual Army-Navy Reception, a trial for Coolidge, since it gave the opportunity for the brass to trumpet the case for more battleships. Grace could not go downstairs; Coolidge determined to set a personal record and managed to shake hands with 2,360 guests in an hour and five minutes. He went back upstairs to report the number, the staff noticed. At least in that small way he might spare her.

By March, Kellogg was growing bolder. Rather than give in to Briand, Kellogg held his frozen feet to the fire, insisting that Briand stick to his own initial language of the year before, denouncing war as policy. Interestingly, Briand was giving in, and miraculously, by February, headlines such as "Briand Elated" could be found in the papers. Peace activists such as Professor Shotwell of Columbia and Salmon Levinson, a prominent lawyer in Chicago, were doing Kellogg's publicity work for him and getting the idea of an international treaty into the air.

Many erstwhile antagonists were proving similarly enthusiastic. Borah was on the march, publishing a commentary in *The New York Times*: "One Great Treaty to Outlaw All Wars." In the article, he clarified that in his view a breach by one country would release the other signers from their obligations. He was eager to ensure that the public knew such a treaty was his idea, and spelled that out explicitly for reporters. "Borah Gets Credit for French Treaty," one headline read. As if Borah were not enough, all the suffrage groups, Jane Addams of Hull-House, and Eleanor Roosevelt, the wife of Coolidge's 1920 opponent, were busy chatting up the topic. From Cleveland, a convention of ministers preached its approval. Kellogg's plot was working. Instead of dragging the administration's treaty back, the administration's critics were launching the treaty for him. The white-haired Minnesotan whom so many had written off seemed to have shed ten or twenty years; each morning he scurried along Seventeenth Street to the side door of the State, War, and Navy Building. Though his staff did not always understand where Kellogg was going or necessarily agree with him, the staffers enjoyed the advantage they now seemed to hold over Briand. Kellogg was proving limber enough to back Briand into a corner. "I do not think the French will agree," Castle at the State Department wrote of Kellogg's proposal of a multilateral treaty, "but I think they will have an awful time not to agree." Concluded Castle, "We have Monsieur Briand out on a limb and we might as well keep him there."

In Berlin at the Reichstag, Foreign Minister Gustav Stresemann was already attempting to paint Germany as the leader of antiwar projects such as the treaty. After all, Stresemann noted, "We are disarmed." Naturally enough, Germany was grateful that the United States had not succumbed to Briand and signed his Franco-U.S. pact, leaving Germany out. "It is a cause of satisfaction that the United States in this matter showed active interest in security problems," he said. The Germans got behind the project.

And just as Kellogg had suspected he would, Coolidge was becoming a treaty booster. The idea suited the old Coolidge rule of completing Harding's work: Harding had said in his inaugural address so far back, "Mankind needs a world wide benediction of understanding." The treaty fitted his and Harding's philosophy: ask much of nations and men, and they would rise to the level of your demand. Most unusually, the treaty also highlighted the value in this attitude. Not only did Kellogg support Coolidge but now Coolidge had another ally for the treaty in Dwight Morrow. When he did not confer with Kellogg, Coolidge was conferring with Morrow. For the first time, watching the men together, others could see a bond that had been heretofore invisible to most eyes. "The main difference between Morrow and Coolidge," the financier Bernard Baruch noted, "was that Morrow talked and loved to talk and was always charming in conversation." Coolidge, by contrast, was still true to stereotype on the outside, shy and silent. Yet he "had all the human qualities that Dwight had. This is undoubtedly the bond which held them most strongly."

One of the few outsiders to get a glimpse of Coolidge's thinking was the painter Cartotto. Finishing his portrait, Cartotto was coming to know a different Coolidge from what he had expected. The supposedly incurious Coolidge interrogated Cartotto on every aspect of his life. He asked about Cartotto's citizenship; Cartotto had been born in Italy but had worked long in the United States and was a naturalized citizen. Coolidge asked about government, religious institutions, and the U.S. military; Cartotto had served in the U.S. Army. The portrait work challenged Cartotto, and when Coolidge kept him over a weekend, the Coolidges sent flowers to Mrs. Cartotto. Meanwhile, Grace was recovering and even traveling to Northampton to visit her mother.

It had been less than a year since Coolidge had been attacked for not intervening in the execution of Sacco and Vanzetti. Progressives had deemed Coolidge as anti-immigrant as Gompers since his signing of the Johnson Act. But to call Coolidge anti-immigrant was wrong, Cartotto saw. The difference between Coolidge and some progressives was that Coolidge believed that immigrants should come only if the United States could absorb them and only if they were prepared to make an effort to assimilate. It was Coolidge's conviction, dating back to his days in Northampton at the Home Culture Club, that citizens must know their country and learn its language to become good citizens. Cartotto was particularly sensitive because his own English remained imperfect and because in the papers there had been complaints that foreigners were being chosen over Americans to paint official Washington portraits. One day a diplomat showed up during one of their sittings. The president introduced the man, who promptly asked the usual question: "Italian or American?" Coolidge answered for Cartotto: "Both." That saved Cartotto much embarrassment. Coolidge later explained his defense and his admiration of Cartotto to the artist: "You can serve this land better and more by bringing to it the best you inherited."

At the State Department, meanwhile, the surprised staff observed Kellogg moving into a frenzy of activity. When he was not negotiating with various countries, Kellogg was engaged in other diplomatic work, mostly emphasizing law over force. Often the president joined him. Coolidge and the State Department had, for instance, considered what might be the best gift of thanks to the Ethiopian prince regent for the gold shield. After conferring with Kellogg, Coolidge sent the Ras Tafari his own token: a leather-bound copy of the first volume of a new reference work, *Moore's International Law Digest*, part of a series by a foremost international jurist, John Bassett Moore. "To my great and good friend, H.I.H. Ras Taffari Makonen," wrote Coolidge in the flyleaf.

By April, the writer Sinclair Lewis had finished his book, which he titled *The Man Who Knew Coolidge*. This was an attack on middle-class culture generally, and Coolidge specifically. But Coolidge hardly cared. Kellogg was rounding up further signatories, including Great Britain. Great Britain was objecting that the treaty conflicted with the Locarno Treaty, whose signatories had bound themselves to go to war under certain conditions. Great Britain was insisting that it would sign nothing of which all its dominions were not part. Kellogg and Castle turned bad into good by offering that all Locarno signers, including the British dominions, become signatories as well. If there were conflicts among treaties, at least all nations would be subject to them. There was general agreement. That brought the number of the nations ready to sign to fifteen. Belatedly, the staff at the State Department was realizing that its chief might succeed with the treaty project and might even view it as something more than a diplomatic feint. "The funny thing," wrote Castle in his diary of the undersecretary of state Robert Olds and Kellogg, "is that Olds and the secretary seem to take it all with profound seriousness." On April 28, Kellogg, following his policy of speaking to the world through publicity rather than cables, gave a speech at the International Law Association. There was nothing in the treaty, he said, that "restricts or impairs in any way the right to self defense." Self-defense was a natural right. Kellogg now anticipated he would get many more signatories beyond the fifteen. It was gratifying to see that number, but other numbers in Coolidge's life were not pretty. Hoover went to Coolidge in May to let him know that he had four hundred delegates out of the possible thousand but would even now give up if Coolidge wanted him to. "If you have 400 delegates, you better keep them," Coolidge snapped and would not say anything more.

That spring of April 1928, Coolidge vetoed a number of bills: a costly new national defense act, two acts giving Indian tribes standing to sue in the Court of Claims, a law to build rural post roads, and a law to provide for the coordination of public health activities by the federal government. He also vetoed a bill extending new payments to veterans from the World War, though it seemed clear that the veto would be overridden. But some detected a weakening in Coolidge, and guessed he was giving up. The president signed a tax bill that cut rates where he would not have cut them first, on new cars. "I think it is a mistake from my point of view to repeal the automobile taxes," he told his press men. Federal subsidy of highways was "a new proposition," he grimly noted, But if the federal government was going to subsidize, then no tax was better suited to funding highways than this automobile tax. In another moment of apparent resignation, Coolidge signed flood legislation that represented one of the largest single outlays the federal government had made since the war. Gone was the principle of states paying their share that he had endorsed so often; the burden of this law fell upon Washington. The lawmakers had passed a bill subsidizing fisheries and civil service jobs for veterans, and, most symbolically, an expensive government plan to keep Muscle Shoals in federal hands. Coolidge appeared indifferent. "I haven't seen the Muscle Shoals bill and know but very little about it," he told the press group.

Once the recess came, however, the tiger pounced. He used the lethal pocket veto for Muscle Shoals, the fisheries, and civil service jobs for vets. Suddenly, instead of writing stories about Grace or Hoover, *The New York Times* committed space to trying to explain the obscurity of the pocket veto to readers: Coolidge "disapproves it by inaction" was how the paper finally captured it.

In the same period, Kellogg was hunting down further signatories, one by one. His bounty was already impressive: that spring, Italy, Japan, Germany, and Great Britain not only had indicated that they would sign but also were already reviewing drafts of the treaty. The text was a partial playback of Briand's own writing and, now giving in, Briand was flattered. On May 7, a day the Coolidge administration had wrestled with lawmakers over the flood funding, a remarkable event had taken place at Heidelberg University. Gustav Stresemann, the German foreign minister, and Jacob Schurman, the U.S. ambassador to Germany, had gone to the historic university to accept honorary degrees. Schurman, Kellogg's deputy, flattered Germany by elevating it in a speech above France: Germany and the United States, he told the students, were together "marching forward in a great and noble adventure in the cause of humane civilization." The students pounded the floor with their feet to express their approval. Again the French government protested, though this time the form the protest took was more pout than rant. "The picture drawn by Mr. Schurman of Germany with America leading France and the other nations on the road to peace hurts the French intensely," explained *The New York Times*.

The media interest yielded precisely what the State Department sought: Germany's eagerness made the other parties eager to sign Kellogg's treaty sooner. "Germany Accepts Our Anti-war Plan Would Sign at Once," read a headline two weeks later; "Turkey Sees Need for Balkan Peace"; "India Is Ready." All the peace activists in the United States were beginning to realize they might get a real treaty after all. Nicholas Murray Butler thought the idea had come from him: he recalled advising Briand to read Carl von Clausewitz, the Prussian military strategist. Clausewitz had written of war as an instrument of policy. The treaty renounced war as an instrument. Butler felt certain that Briand had taken Butler's advice and based his formulation on the recommended book. The treaty was not yet a success, but it already had many fathers.

"My inside information," Salmon Levinson, the old advocate of outlawry, wrote to an ally, "is that everybody, from the president on, is 18k fine on Outlawry. Oh, the miracle of it!" On Memorial Day, with Congress safely out of session, Coolidge finally made the great public pro-treaty declaration Kellogg would need to collect signatures. He chose to do so at Gettysburg, Lincoln's great battlefield. The treaty was so new, Coolidge told the crowd, but had already had an effect. During the eleven months since Briand had made his statement calling for a treaty to end the use of war as a policy, "this suggestion has been developed into one of the most impressive peace movements the world has ever seen." A nation could prevent bloody battles like Gettysburg; but to do so the country must "bend our every effort to prevent any recurrence of war."

Coolidge's main sentiment as summer approached was relief. He had made it through his last great legislative session after all; all he need do now was finish decently. At the semiannual meeting with Lord, Coolidge was able to state the case for the treaty indirectly, by pointing to the solidifying achievement that each additional month or year of peace represented. In July 1921, there had been 5.7 million Americans out of work; now that figure was 1.8 million. Manufacturing output was up by a third since that time. Iron and steel production had doubled. They might not complete many more tax cuts, but the revenue acts of 1921, 1924, 1926, and 1928 represented a strong record. The national debt of $28 billion, nearly all war costs, was finally down to $17.65 billion. As Coolidge would say of the debt, "It is one-third paid." For the first time since the Black Hills, there was even some contentment at home. Grace's illness had sobered Coolidge, and he now objected less when Grace traveled. She in turn was softening. Coolidge liked the way the household was running, right down to the housekeeping. The December splurge on diplomats notwithstanding, Miss Riley's books now showed that she had managed well that year. In 1926, the feeding of the White House had cost $11,667.10, versus $9,116.39 for 1927, a total saving of $2,550.71. "To Miss Riley," wrote Coolidge in pencil, "Very fine improvement."

The real trick now for Coolidge, the test of character, was to get through the election year without veering from his determined path of retirement and without losing his temper. Succeeding would not be easy, especially given the mounting evidence that Hoover, the activist, would subvert the Coolidge legacy. Even now there were Republicans eager to label Coolidge as a dark horse and announce his entry into the contest; Coolidge had to withstand the temptation that had lured Theodore Roosevelt to jump in at the last moment. To provide the president with distance, Starling had gone to extremes, establishing that year's summer White House at a fishing retreat called Cedar Lodge on the Brule River in northern Wisconsin, by Lake Superior. The retreat was advertised as dry, cool, and mosquito-free. The Coolidges were to depart in mid-June, thereby missing the Republican National Convention.

That attempt to divert themselves failed when Grace fell ill again, delaying departure and leaving them both stranded in Washington during the first days of the convention. Hoover was nominated while the Coolidges were still on the train and still within reach of those who would seek to report the Coolidge reaction. There was disappointment even once the Coolidges arrived in Wisconsin: it rained hard when dry warmth was necessary for Mrs. Coolidge's health. Even at the lodge, escaping Hoover's emanations proved difficult: Cedar Lodge was a fly-fishing lodge, which meant that Coolidge had to fish Hoover's way. There were other, smaller humiliations, too. Vermont's Mountain Rule of a single term for governors was a precedent that had inspired Coolidge, just as George Washington's decision not to run again had. The very summer before, Governor Weeks had made clear he would honor the Mountain Rule. But in the meantime, after Coolidge had decided to forgo his own chance, Governor Weeks had changed his mind: he was breaking the rule by running again. That July there was also troubling news from Mexico. The new president, General Álvaro Obregón, was assassinated. Mexico was still nowhere near normalcy and perhaps settling into dictatorship: as Morrow had feared, now President Calles might find a way to stay in office after all.

Grace began to recover after July 4, when the rain stopped. But Coolidge still found it difficult to contain his sour mood. The Hoovers traveled up to Brule River, but the president insisted on seeing only Hoover and Mrs. Hoover; all the others in the Hoover party had to stay on the mainland. Even Coolidge's staff revolted; they were friendly with George Akerson, Hoover's secretary. "Let's bring him over anyhow," said Starling. He would rather face Coolidge's rage than tell Akerson he could not come. John was there, and Mrs. Coolidge, now improved, joined him in chatting with Lou Hoover. But Coolidge was still surly. The press asked Coolidge for a comment. Once again, Coolidge exploded. "Let him talk," he said. "He is going to be president."

That very day, Coolidge recovered his poise and even fished with Hoover. The press, interviewing him afterward, tried to goad him into commenting on who was the better fisherman. Coolidge, frank, said of Hoover, "He is a more expert fisherman than I am." When the reporters asked if they could put that on the record, Coolidge said, "No." Cedar Lodge was, after all, affording the Coolidges a chance to relax; Grace was definitively better, tan even. Coolidge improved in his fishing: he joked with the reporters a few weeks later, "I haven't caught them all, but I have them pretty well intimidated." Here at Cedar Lodge, he was able to reflect on his work. Reporters in the pool asked what he made of the new tax legislation, which emphasized business tax cuts, and whether it, like the preceding Coolidge cuts, would draw extra revenue. "Well, no," Coolidge said. Corporation income would be the same, he thought. But there was a way to get more revenue. "There is another tax reduction that usually brings up the revenue, and that is one in relation to capital increases. That is, persons buy land or they buy securities and hold them. When the tax is very high they don't sell on account of feeling that if they sell they have got to give so much to the Government that they had better hold it," he added. Dilating on his beloved topic, the president went on, "And when taxes were reduced on that item of income it resulted in a considerable increase."

By now, however, it was increases in the treaty's signators, not tax revenue increases, that were taking Coolidge's attention. The pact was set for signature by the Great Powers in Paris. In mid-August, a crowd of 15,000 attendees of an American Legion conference greeted Coolidge at Marathon Park in Wausau, Wisconsin. The great memory in everyone's mind was the speed with which the war had begun; how a chain of treaties had yanked so many nations into a world war. It made sense therefore now to lay out a network for peace that worked the other way, as a check that pulled countries back when a conflict flared. Concluded the president, "Had an agreement of this kind been in existence in 1914, there is every reason to suppose that it would have saved the situation." The crowd roared its praise with shouts of "Atta boy, Cal!"

In that period Kellogg and Coolidge worked intensely, just as Mellon and Coolidge had once done. Kellogg traveled throughout Europe, laying the ground for treaty signature in Paris in August. Of course all the parties sought more changes now: a German diplomat confided in the U.S. chargé d'affaires that the German Foreign Office had emendations to offer but could not be seen to hold up the process, as the German public, which was pro-treaty, would be offended.

As the treaty came close to reality, the ghost of Henry Cabot Lodge returned via his grandson, the same one who had joined the Coolidges at their lunch for the Lindberghs. Lodge penned a hostile editorial on Kellogg-Briand for the *New York Herald Tribune*. He remarked, "The conception of renouncing war by government fiat is inherently absurd." Some of Kellogg's own colleagues were now the ones with the cold feet. Sounding like Briand now, Castle, the assistant secretary, was furiously anxious, writing in his diary, "They think they are remaking the world and actually it is nothing but a beautiful gesture while the Jugoslavs tear down the Italian consular flags and the Chinese fight." From Wisconsin, Coolidge monitored the project closely, concerned that his partner, Kellogg, would concede too much to the French or British. The British, for example, were seeking unrelated naval concessions and trying to hold the treaty hostage. Perhaps Paris would prove too seductive to Kellogg. "I have your wire relative to the British naval proposals," Coolidge wrote to Kellogg on August 3. "What I desire relative to have done in relation to these at present is nothing at all." Then Coolidge went on, "I do not especially like the meeting that is to be held in Paris. While it is ostensibly to sign the treaty, I cannot help wonder whether it will be for some other purpose not yet disclosed." Address nothing but the treaty, Coolidge warned. "I am very sorry that I agreed to go to Paris to sign the treaty," Kellogg, now back in the calmer United States, wired back. Last-minute complaints flew thick and fast to the State Department.

Yet on August 27, in the clock room at the Quai d'Orsay, the signing went off just as planned. Six foreign ministers—Mackenzie King of Canada, Gustav Stresemann of Germany, Edvard Beneš of Czechoslovakia, August Zaleski of Poland, Paul Hymans of Belgium, and Lord Cushendun of Great Britain—took turns using a golden pen brought by the French for the occasion. Observing it all was a crowd of proud Americans, including Dr. Hugh Young, the Johns Hopkins doctor who had treated Grace. Also present were leaders from other nations who would shortly sign the treaty as well; Italy, Japan, New Zealand. Even at that glorious moment, Kellogg proved himself a model of modesty. Briand, predictably, gave a formal sonorous speech about the treaty's "moral force," and claimed credit for its creation. When Briand finished, quiet cries for *l'Américain* ran through the crowd, which expected Kellogg to take his turn. But instead Briand moved forward, reading the treaty, and the diplomats went forward to sign, having some difficulty, especially Kellogg, with the heavy pen the French had provided. Once again, Kellogg had smoothed over a moment by subordinating his own interests. From America, Coolidge wired a congratulatory note to the French president, underscoring that the treaty "had its inception in the proposal submitted last year by the government of France." Almost instantly, additional nations signaled they would join the original group: Portugal, Romania, Austria, Brazil, and, gratifyingly, Cuba. The first part of Coolidge's commitment at Havana was complete.

There was more work to do. Kellogg and Coolidge had not even yet reached the ratification stage, the spot where Wilson had faltered. "I hope it will be well with the American Senate," a Hungarian correspondent, recalling Wilson, had joked as Kellogg had passed him in Paris. But Kellogg and Coolidge were a team now. At Union Station, Kellogg and his wife were there to greet the Coolidges when they returned to Washington for the final stretch of the treaty campaign, autumn and winter.

The other party there to greet the Coolidges at the station remained the challenge: Hoover. Coolidge's work that fall would suppress his own demon, his discontent over Hoover. Coolidge had promised to do the minimum to support Hoover, and he did. Hoover looked sure to win now on a platform of "continuation of Coolidge policies." Coolidge's frustration—not one that he could do anything about—remained that voters seemed to overlook the distinctions between his style and Hoover's. The difference even showed up in the way they ran their farms. Hoover saw his farm as a showcase for his own competence. Hoover's farm was his ranch twenty-four miles from Bakersfield. The ranch was six times as large as Coolidge's farm, subirrigated and electrified. Nine pumps pulled water from nine wells day and night. The Hoover farm was divided into thirty plots for ten different crops, some permanent, such as grapes and apricots, and some rotating, such as melons, peas, and cotton. Hoover spoke to his manager, Harvey Kilburn, who in turn managed a flexible workforce of between forty-five and three hundred workers, depending on the crops and seasons. For Hoover, farming was a business. For Coolidge, farming was an exercise in property rights and federalism.

Coolidge's farm was fewer than 300 acres even now, much of it not cultivated but woodland. He tended to each detail himself and not always efficiently. October 8, 1928, for example, found him writing to the tax authorities in the town of Northampton, "I wish you would be kind enough to mail my tax bill here to me in Washington." The tax bills in his files were simple documents: "home," "lime kiln lot," 10 cows worth $400 for the tax year 1927. When Coolidge wrote to local authorities, he enclosed a stamped envelope ready for return mail.

Coolidge's thoughts ran along the same frustrating lines as they had the year before. The downturn was coming. But bad policy, especially Hoover's spending policy, would make any downturn worse; the deficit Hoover ran might cause investors to lose confidence in the United States and gold to go to Europe. Then the recession would worsen. Yet it would be wrong to intervene. Coolidge's anxiety was only greater because the Dow Jones stock index had risen alarmingly since he had talked with Starling the year before. Indeed, the Dow had passed the 250 mark that October. His own instinct was to turn to insurance, the trusted alternate to investment in stocks. His son John had started with the railroad, which seemed on surer footing; he hoped John could stay there. Attorney General Sargent campaigned for Hoover in New England; in a speech Sargent even presented Hoover as the best insurance that prosperity would continue. Sargent described Hoover as a "hard-working, patient, understanding, sympathetic, courteous, serious-minded Christian gentleman."

Coolidge managed to hold his silence on the race as the election neared. But there was a commentator who made the case for Coolidge's policy on his behalf: Will Rogers. Rogers's way of saying that something was missing in the current presidential campaign was to turn to parody: with Coolidge absent, he announced a Rogers candidacy. Rogers told readers that he was campaigning on behalf of a group he called the Silent Majority—the name that Bruce Barton had given to describe Coolidge's following all those years before. "I am not the 'Greatest Administrator of All Time,' or 'the Greatest Executive a state ever had,'" wrote Rogers in *Life*. "But those other fellows want to live in the White House, and in order to get there, they will promise anything from perpetual motion to eternal salvation." Rogers's platform featured only one plank, minimalism: "If elected, I will resign."

Just before the election, Coolidge's court abandoned him. "I had the smallest cabinet meeting I think this morning on record," he told the press on Friday, November 2. "It started with 3 members but finished with four." When Hoover was elected, Rogers desisted, and Coolidge's own fears seemed to be fulfilled. Hoover captured a record number of votes, 21.5 million, with Al Smith of New York taking only 15 million. The hearty Smith won Massachusetts, a kind of backhanded compliment to Coolidge: if the state could not have Coolidge, it would have no Republican at all. But New York, Smith's own state, went for Hoover.

Coolidge's mood darkened after the election; this time, he was unable to overcome his loss or concern about the damage of future policies. It upset him that his budget seemed to be moving into deficit. "I have been keeping in very close touch with General Lord on the question of a possible deficit," he told the press men. His legacy might be damaged even before he left office. A second concern was the Dow Jones Average. The average had climbed impressively in one week following Hoover's election. It had risen 50 percent since the day Coolidge had announced he would not run again, an enormous amount. A crash was coming, he knew, and the higher the market went, the worse the disruption would be. The Federal Reserve was attempting to impose a new sense of caution by raising interest rates, but the market was not responding. In Coolidge's public statements, his entire goal was to steady the market, rather than crash it: on January 6, 1929, he would tell reporters that "the prospect for the immediate future seems to be as good as usual." But what was "usual"? The rise of the market was beyond anything he had experienced in his working life. At the very least, there might be bank crashes. Coolidge had always prepared for such events by banking at multiple institutions. At the time of his father's death, John, Coolidge, and Coolidge's son John had maintained deposits, all of a hundred or a few thousand each, in more than twenty local banks, from the Springfield Savings Bank of Springfield, Vermont, to the Nonotuck Savings Bank in Northampton or the Amherst Savings Bank.

Coolidge conferred with Charles Merrill, an Amherst man who had founded a firm to serve middle-class investors on Wall Street. He agreed with Merrill that there was cause for concern. Call money, the cash investors used to borrow, was now priced at 7 or 8 percent; stocks would yield less. Either interest rates had to come down or stock prices had to fall, the pair agreed. Merrill offered Coolidge a job at $100,000, but Coolidge demurred. He knew nothing about investment banking. Merrill countered that he wanted Coolidge for another purpose: to warn against speculation, to speak out so that investors made themselves less vulnerable to a coming crash. Still, Coolidge could not see entering an area where he knew so little. There was always the danger of disrupting the market unduly by speaking out: the presidency had a megaphone effect. Merrill decided to be his own spokesman and in the coming months signaled his concern by pulling out of the market.

Other glum events crowded the autumn. Clarence Barron, upon whom the fund drive for the Clarke School depended, died suddenly while taking a cure in Battle Creek, Michigan. Barron had already raised hundreds of thousands, but his death left uncertain whether the $2 million goal of the drive would be achieved. Grace in any case was still absenting herself from the White House, either visiting her mother in Northampton or spending time with John, who was planning his marriage to Florence Trumbull. It had been so many years since Coolidge had wooed Grace in letters. Now he began to do so again. "Everything seems to be going all right at the house," he wrote in one letter from Washington to Northampton, and let her know a fact that he thought would please her, that the White House staff had found some silver in packages that had been there since the days of the family of Franklin Pierce. He concluded with a veiled question: "I wonder if you have begun to think about coming home." In the next letter, Coolidge tried again: "I am looking forward to having you back next week, as indicated."

Grace and Coolidge were finally planning a holiday, on Sapelo Island off Georgia, but it was mostly the president who was doing the preparing. He tried to tempt her with travelogue: "A Mr. LaGerce came in to tell me about Sapeloe Island" (Coolidge spelled it as was common in those days, with an "e"). "The accent is on the second syllable," he wrote her carefully. "There are all kinds of fishes down there the which I am planning to catch." As Christmas neared, on December 20, he wrote, "My dear Grace: An opossum has just come from Georgia." December 21: "The opossum has been sent to the zoo." December 22: "I do not seem to have any letter from you."

That month even the treaty itself seemed, if only momentarily, to be in jeopardy. At the Senate, Dawes reviewed the votes and expressed his concern that one faction or another might still block ratification. Borah, key as the Senate Foreign Relations Committee chair, was spending his energy drawing publicity on two different topics: a naval limitation agreement with Great Britain and his own correspondence with President Calles of Mexico.

Hoover was making himself felt, engineering and establishing new spending categories, starting with the dam on the Colorado River. As soon as Congress came back, it honored its new president by passing the Colorado Dam legislation, the favorite of the president-elect. Coolidge's remaining work was to thank the numerous stakeholders in the project by signing the dam into law with their pens. Perhaps to distract himself from his irritation at having to sign, he played the politician's game with his signature. First, Coolidge picked up one pen and wrote, "Calvin." He picked up another and wrote, "Cool." With yet a third, he wrote "idge," and dotted the "i." Two pens went to the lawmakers who had sponsored the bill, Senator Hiram Johnson and Congressman Phil Swing of California, the third to a Hearst newspaperman who had followed the story. Yet Coolidge was not entirely able to sustain his restraint. Hoover planned a trip to Latin America and let Coolidge know he required a battleship for transport. Coolidge suggested that he take a cruiser: "It would not cost so much." Hoover did not relent. Finally Coolidge offered the battleship *Maryland* for the trip south and the *Utah* to bring Hoover home from Montevideo.

This was one of Coolidge's final swipes at Hoover. For as the holiday season came, Coolidge did find that he was able to look past Hoover, take pleasure in his own record, and look toward the treaty and the future. Gutzon Borglum's appropriation for Mount Rushmore would make it into law and included a role for Coolidge: the text, the law said, would be "indited by Calvin Coolidge." This small vanity he was still ready to permit himself. On November 28, a day Hoover was in Costa Rica, Frank Stearns celebrated his birthday. Coolidge knew that Stearns had always been sensitive that Coolidge had not relied upon him as Wilson had relied upon Colonel House. Now Coolidge gave Stearns *The Intimate Papers of Colonel House*. That was Coolidge's way of saying that Stearns's friendship had meant just as much to the thirtieth president as Colonel House's friendship had to the twenty-eighth. In December 1928, Coolidge might have been expected to cease his meetings with Lord; the Coolidges had many plans that month, including the trip to Sapelo Island. Yet Coolidge met with General Lord five times. Though the new tax law was not perfect scientific taxation, the rate cuts had not hurt revenue after all. "The yield from corporation taxes increased in marked degree," *The New York Times* noted. Coolidge and Mellon both wondered whether that was because interest rates had swung too low, but now the Federal Reserve branches were raising them. Then stock prices might come down. But even more important than the outcome was that the market be allowed to set the prices.

When Coolidge and Grace returned from their winter holiday, their mood was better, and Coolidge could see that popular opinion was likely to suppress any great opposition to ratification. At the State Department, some five hundred letters a day were flowing in, nearly all favoring the treaty. There was also personal good news coming to the Coolidges: the Clarke School Fund, thanks in good measure to Clarence Barron, was approaching $2 million. Their son, John, was working out the details of his life with Florence Trumbull. Dwight Morrow was himself thinking of running for office. In various ways, much of Coolidge's work might continue.

In January 1929, Coolidge and Lord arranged their own farewell party: the final budget meeting in Memorial Hall. To commemorate the work of cutting, they added something new to the ritual: a radio hookup so that the entire country could hear their budget meeting, the sixteenth, and know what he had been doing all these years. The budget success was owed not to a man but to a law, the Budget Act of 1921, Coolidge and Lord emphasized. "The results of economy which have meant so much to our own country and indirectly to the world, would not have been successful without the bureau of the budget," Coolidge said. This budget session was Lord's swan song, and he intended to sing it: his theme was how his hard work with the president saved the country from Congress's spending folly. "The pruning knife fell here and there and everywhere in the grim fight for a balanced budget. Proposed expenditures of doubtful immediate necessity went under the guillotine. As a result of this drastic action and an improvement in the revenue outlook, the budget for 1930 as submitted to Congress showed a possible surplus for the current year of $36,990,192." But, Lord went on, "while the flush of victory still mantled our cheeks unexpected and unheralded demands rudely wiped out our $37 million surplus and put in its place an apparent deficit of about the same amount." A deficit of that amount infuriated Coolidge and Lord, but not most others, to whom it seemed trivial. What mattered was that Coolidge and Lord were leaving the federal government smaller than they had found it.

Coolidge had prevailed through the sieges after all. Neither his wife nor his son, John, had forgiven him entirely; Grace's trips to Northampton and John's distance told him that. But he might win them back yet after the presidency. He could hope because he had already managed to reconcile with Vermont.

That reconciliation had taken place back in September 1928. The long-delayed moment had finally come to make a trip to his birthplace. Amid reports of another natural disaster, this time a gale in Florida, the president, the first lady, and Attorney General Sargent had boarded the Presidential Special to inspect Vermont's recovery work. The Coolidges had stopped in Northampton to visit Mrs. Goodhue; Mrs. Coolidge spent half an hour beside her mother at the hospital. They were likely to settle there; Coolidge could practice law, and Grace had the Clarke School. Next they had traveled north to Greenfield, Massachusetts, near the Turners Falls Dam, where the water had flowed over a year before.

That time John had not been with them; he was settling in as a boarder at the house of a professor of divinity at 233 Edwards Street in New Haven, Connecticut, and beginning work at the New York, New Haven and Hartford Railroad.

Soon the Presidential Special crossed the border into Vermont and met the people: at Brattleboro, Bellows Falls, Windsor, and nine other towns the crowds were there, waiting. Park Pollard, the cousin who had seconded the nomination for Al Smith at the Democratic Convention in Houston, climbed aboard. Later, the train pulled into Bethel and Montpelier, where the flood had been so disastrous, and picked up Governor Weeks. They saw White River Junction and Burlington, where they went to Green Mountain Cemetery to lay a wreath on the grave of Grace's father. Four thousand stood at Middlebury, where the streets had become rivers and the inhabitants and animals had fled to the hills. Shortly it was on to Rutland. All in all the Coolidges made twelve stops, and at each stop Vermonters watched the first couple's eyes take in their progress: the tracks were down, the trains were running. The most skilled railway men of Vermont were selected to man the train. The state had made itself whole. From Rutland, the Coolidges rode in a car to Plymouth Notch. The Coolidges stopped at the little cemetery below the village. They laid white roses on the graves of Colonel Coolidge, his mother, and their son. A fried chicken supper was provided to them by Aurora Pierce.

They slept in the old white house at Plymouth. In the morning, Coolidge had checked his cow stalls (there was enough hay for the winter but not enough oats, he told Mr. Cady) and studied the dairy business: his cows' milk went for $.0488 a quart, and the cows produced 75 quarts a day apiece. Everything came in for inspection: Coolidge pounded the sills and announced that they were ready for replacement. The *Times* reporter watched him, "a man of small stature dressed in a blue business suit and brown hat." Last of all, Coolidge, the *Times* reported, "drove some distance over the hills to the twenty-five acres of maple grove given to him by his grandfather." Leaving Grace in the car, the president walked the lot and "climbed over rock and fence," as the paper noted.

They had been ready to begin the return trip to Washington, but Vermont did not want to let them go. They stopped at Ludlow to see the Black River Academy, where the water had risen. At each station on the way down, cheers and applause greeted them. In Rutland, a former student of Grace, Charlotta Walker, gave the first lady a bouquet of flowers. At Bennington, the last stop before Massachusetts, five thousand waited at the rough blue marble structure for the first couple. It was about 7:00 P.M. when the Coolidges' train pulled up and the president and the first lady appeared on the rear coach platform. "Speech, speech!" the crowd cried. John Spargo, the director of the Bennington Museum, was finally getting the visit he had sought since the anniversary of the Battle of Bennington. The shouts, the crowd expected, would be in vain. The press had been warned there would be no newsworthy speech on that trip—perhaps no speech at all, or if anything, a line or two.

The president started off routinely. First he offered a simple thank-you to his fellow Vermonters for the two days of hospitality. Then he praised the railroads that were running, the highways open to traffic for "those who wish to travel by automobile." This was a kind of "Open for business" declaration from the president for which Vermont business leaders had so long waited; it was welcome, but standard and not different from what Coolidge had done for the Black Hills. Then Coolidge surprised them all by continuing. He was in fact going to give, as the *Springfield Republican* noted, "the only rear-end speech since he became chief magistrate." There were no microphones. The president spoke without notes. But then, he was telling old friends what they already knew.

"Vermont is a state I love," Coolidge said, and a reporter could hear the emotion in the voice. "I could not look upon the peaks of Ascutney, Killington, Mansfield and Equinox without being moved. It was here that I saw the first light of day; here that I received my bride. Here my dead lie buried, pillowed among the everlasting hills. I love Vermont because of her hills and valleys, her scenery and invigorating climate, but most of all I love her because of her indomitable people. They are a race of pioneers who almost impoverished themselves for a love of others. If ever the spirit of liberty should vanish from the rest of the Union, it could be restored by the generous store held by the people in this brave little state of Vermont."

The moment Coolidge finished, the reporters bent over their note-books. If what he had said was to be recorded, they would have to be the recorders. In fact the speech was reported with different wording, as each reporter heard it slightly differently. *Time* magazine wrote "impoverished" and "buried." Other papers transcribed "beggared." Some heard the word "Whittier," which was a mountain, but in New Hampshire.

Perhaps the president had erred? He loved the poet. Some reporters heard "Equinos," not "Equinox"; some thought Coolidge might have read a poem and reviewed the syllables to see if they scanned as verse. Across the state and, a day later, across the nation, the telegraph wires clattered again. "Vermont," "state I love," "pioneers," and "indomitable" were set in type over and over again. There were many ways to help a people, Coolidge had said. Vermont's way was to allow people to help themselves, as the reporter had noted during the flood. That had been the greatness of the speech. Later, Coolidge would select his own version for history. But all the versions were a reminder that all Americans had a little Vermont in them. Vermonters did not mind starting small if they could do something themselves. They preferred it. Small was not the way of Hoover, the man who would be succeeding him in the presidential office, but it was Coolidge's way. The trip to New England had given him a touch of the peace he might yet find.

At Sapelo, Coolidge had thought again about his treaty, even as he fished and hunted with Starling. The reasoning behind the treaty was not perfect, he knew. Coolidge wrote a note to Morrow to try to explain his choice. "By nature I am a barbarian. I should like to revert to savagery and spend all my time hunting and fishing. I have a strong opinion this feeling is shared very generally by many people. Probably none of us however are going to do what we should like to do most but are going to struggle on somewhat unsuccessfully trying to do what we think we ought to do." When the Coolidges returned from their holiday early in the year, the Senate was already opening debate on the treaty.

Kellogg, wisely, was insisting that the Senate vote on the treaty without qualification. Coolidge backed him up: "I do not think any reservations ought to be attached." For a full two days, Coolidge and Kellogg waited while Borah led the Senate as the members blasted their opinions to their heart's content, lecturing one another on the history of outlawry. Those who advocated the building of new battleships were soothed with the promise of legislation to fund new ships in coming years, but even those new ships could not offset the drama of the pact. Senators Thomas Walsh of Montana and William King of Utah spoke for a total of three hours. Senator J. Thomas Heflin of Alabama, the same senator whose absence the usher had noted at the Coolidge breakfast, spoke for the pact as well. Senator Carter Glass of Virginia denounced the treaty as idiocy. "I am not willing that anybody in Virginia shall think I am simple enough to suppose that it is worth a postage stamp in the direction of accomplishing permanent peace," he said—and signaled that he would vote "yes." Senator Hiram Johnson of California, one of Coolidge's erstwhile presidential opponents and a foe of the World Court, argued that this treaty would prove ineffectual without enforcement mechanisms. To capture the weakness he saw, Johnson quoted an old poem: "A helmless ship, a houseless street, a wordless book, a swordless sheath."

Yet while the senators yapped, whispered, shouted, and bloviated, as Harding would have said, it became clear that the lawmakers would not block the treaty. The opposition simply was not there. "I find myself more or less in a state of irritation," Dawes, who was presiding, wrote. Suddenly, the reporters recognized the game Coolidge had played, the extent to which he had been in control from the start. When the moment seemed ripe, Coolidge, who had been taking reports at the White House, alerted Dawes that he wanted a vote. This time, Dawes sprang to it. He promised to "steam up" the process. Names were called. Votes were counted. Glass, Johnson, and Borah had all voted "yes." The Kellogg-Briand Treaty had been ratified by a thundering margin, 85–1.

In this pact Coolidge won his final political victory. He had proved that he was far from isolated or weak. He had made a new partner of a cabinet member, this time Kellogg instead of Mellon, and with that partner had passed a law as ambitious as his tax legislation. He had demonstrated yet again his skills as an administrator, productively delegating to a crucial deputy, Kellogg, and thereby achieving a legislative victory far greater in scope than he could have won alone. He had outwitted fellow Republicans, shown he was ahead of them, and unified the Republican Party, pulling together the fabric of the party so many years after Lodge had first torn it. He also had unified the country in a way that neither party had managed since the Lodge-Wilson feud.

Already scholars and journalists were recasting the past to depict the country as a place that would always have supported such a treaty. The state legislature of Wisconsin, whose Senator John Blaine was the only member of the chamber to vote "no," was so furious that members promptly introduced resolutions to point out to Washington that Blaine's position did not reflect general sentiment in the state. Posthumously, Theodore Roosevelt, the Rough Rider, joined in service of Coolidge's treaty. At Oyster Bay that month, members of the Theodore Roosevelt

Pilgrimage Association read aloud from a 1910 text by Roosevelt: it was the duty of wise statesmen, Roosevelt had said, "to encourage and build up every movement which will tend to substitute some other agency for force in the settlement of international disputes." Coolidge had succeeded where both Wilson and Harding had failed in winning a great multilateral treaty that united not only a party or a nation but the world.

At the White House signing of the treaty resolution, the reporters crowded in. "Keep perfectly still," they said to Kellogg, who was shaking, and "Keep your hand steady"—difficult for him. Coolidge was tense, as at all signings, even telling a State Department employee who hovered too much to "go away" from the table. Castle of the State Department wrote that "the president's face looked like murder." But what he took for anger in Coolidge was exhaustion and determination. He was once again demonstrating service. The vast majority of the United States had wanted this treaty. Toward the end, Kellogg's office had received up to six hundred letters a day and the White House two hundred, of which, Coolidge had mentioned to reporters, "I haven't seen one that is in opposition." He had tired toward the end but had not flagged.

The determination this time regarded the law. The treaty had drawn the smaller nations. The Cuban senate had ratified the pact in a unanimous vote on December 12. So had Ethiopia, the country whose prince had sent the shield. But whether the treaty would protect those nations or make them vulnerable was not clear. The greatest threat to Ethiopia, the Italy of Benito Mussolini, had not yet ratified the agreement. The treaty might in future years merely provide fatal cover for dictatorships. Still the treaty had value as law, as precedent, as a model. If the United States leaned on law, the restless nations of the world might do the same. It took the United States away from its habit of arbitrary interventions like those he himself had been party to in Nicaragua, the kind of intervention that had been especially common since Theodore Roosevelt.

It was of New England again that the president thought. In the end what New England meant to him was upholding the law and sharing what he found in the Forbes Library even as he prepared to go back to it. Now he was exporting the law to the world, illuminating the way, just as in the Amherst motto itself: "Terras irradient," "Let them illuminate the earth." Every hour that remained in his presidency was an hour he could use to emphasize the primacy of law. Let the potentates send their golden shields. He would send back law books.

CODA: THE BLESSING

Northampton

SOON AFTER THE PRESIDENTIAL inauguration of 1929, William Allen White, the editor of *The Emporia Gazette* of Kansas, called at the White House. The Hoovers were just settling in; it had been only a month or two since the army trucks had backed up to the service door to collect the Coolidges' boxes for storage and to be shipped to Northampton. Yet a shift impressed White. "There is another atmosphere around there from the Coolidge atmosphere," he wrote in a letter to his friend Henry Haskell in London, thinking of the old Rough Rider. "It is the Roosevelt atmosphere, stepped down through a vast transformance, but still Rooseveltian, muffled but quite as vigorous. At the table Hoover lets the conversation die. Roosevelt never did. But at the desk, I fancy, Hoover gets more done than Roosevelt. And both are going in the same direction."

There were other changes. The new president publicly decommissioned the old Coolidge favorite, the *Mayflower*, in the name of a cause Coolidge could not assail: economy. Another outlay of the Coolidge White House, costing $15,000 a year, was also publicized by the Hoover administration: the White House stables. Hoover shut them down noisily. General Lord, Coolidge's old partner at the Budget Bureau, was leaving government. For the first time since 1920, June came and went without a semiannual budget meeting.

The Coolidges were bent on shutting out such details, and on leaving them behind. From the moment they boarded the train at Union Station, they could feel the pleasure of abandoning their roles as public figures, leaving behind that coat and tails, those formal dresses they had donned back when they arrived in March 1921. The Coolidges' relief at their changed status was so obvious that it lent itself to a cartoon: *The New Yorker* published a drawing of two middle-aged people walking across the snow toward the steps of the Massasoit Street house. As Grace said, their old house was like an old jacket, a relief after the constraints of Washington—"It fits us like a comfortable well-worn garment which has adjusted itself to our peculiarities."

Still, as much as he wished, Coolidge could not be deaf to the emanations from the capital city. And the fact remained that the course of the Coolidge retirement was not certain. Coolidge's health was proving uneven—he coughed or sneezed and had more trouble breathing than he expected, even when he rested. He tired even on days when he did little. His voice was weak. The only other living ex-president was William Howard Taft, now at the Supreme Court, and Taft was also not well. Coolidge felt lucky to have survived that killer, the presidency. Still, others noted he had no great plans. Will Rogers noted that Coolidge seemed underemployed and made a simple suggestion: "Put Cal to Work."

But what work? The most obvious job for Coolidge, the presidency of Amherst College, had recently been taken. Coolidge wanted to write, but it was not clear that his writings would be welcome. In the last days at the White House, Coolidge had received a letter from his old acquaintance Bruce Barton. Barton had made a suggestion in regard to the period after the presidency. "I should like to express the hope you will not write too much," he said. Barton told Coolidge that a bit of restraint on the part of former presidents served the office of the presidency best.

In Northampton, the Coolidges encountered small troubles. They might have liked to pull on the old well-worn garment Grace had described. But that garment, like their little house, no longer fitted. The crowds that appeared in the first days did not abate; dozens or even hundreds of people passed by their house when Coolidge sat on the porch. He had pulled himself out of Garman's river of life and wanted to watch it flow by, but even in Northampton, people would not let him. Coolidge thought he might divert the callers by keeping office hours on Main Street. There the sign invited visitors: "Coolidge and Hemenway, Law

Office: Walk In." Yet the reporters persisted, ignoring protocol and knocking on the door at Massasoit Street on a Sunday.

The assignments Coolidge did take struck others by their modesty. He had sent a clear signal to Wall Street that he would not serve there: he expected a crash, as he had grumbled to Starling on their White House walks, and also knew he would not like the policy changes that followed a crash, either. Coolidge simply was not sure that the federal government ought to regulate financial markets, or that ex-presidents should work in finance. "I have considerable doubt as to whether the national government can interpose to make it so," he had told the press pool once. After a while, Wall Street had heeded him: Coolidge held no Wall Street job.

The inventor of the flashlight, Conrad Hubert, had died in 1928 and had asked in his will that three-quarters of his fortune be given away by a committee made up of a Catholic, a Protestant, and a Jew. Governor Al Smith was selected as the Catholic; Julius Rosenwald, the founder of Sears, who also sat on a Mount Rushmore board, as the Jew; and Coolidge as the Protestant. The men would give away $4 million to start with and more later. They made the biggest bequests to the Boy Scouts, the Girl Scouts, and hospitals of varying denominations. In addition, Coolidge joined the board of New York Life Insurance Company, a company with which he had had his own policy for thirty-seven years. He liked everything about the board, even the idiosyncrasies of the compensation structure: a gold piece for each board trip and two nights' stay at the Vanderbilt Hotel on Park Avenue. But insurance seemed small beans for a former president. "It's really kinder hard to tell just what he is supposed to do," acknowledged Rogers in another column.

To be sure, there were many pleasant distractions that first year. John had predicted in a letter to Grace that life in Northampton would bring them all together: "I'll be so glad when you and father get back home. Then everything will seem natural again." And it was true. When the Coolidges stepped off the train, Grace later recalled, they realized that the office of the presidency was what had separated them. He was no longer "the President," as she had referred to him so often. He was suddenly Calvin again. And his being Calvin made her Grace. "As we turned and reentered the car I suddenly realized that I had come back to myself," she wrote later. The double harness of public office, which they had worn so long, from the first year of their marriage, was finally lifting off, as if by magic.

The Coolidges came together also through the pleasure of seeing their young people move forward. Dwight Morrow's daughter, Anne, married Charles Lindbergh. Florence Trumbull was planning her wedding with John; in a relaxed moment Florence remarked, good-naturedly, that when it came to the wedding date, "Lindy may beat us to it." Lindy did beat Florence and John to their wedding, marrying in May. But by September, it was time for the Coolidge-Trumbull wedding in Plainville, Connecticut. Six airplanes decorated the cake, which suited the mood of hope and, especially, the pilot father of the bride, Governor Trumbull. John had always enjoyed the mechanical, and the wedding was filmed with sound, a talkie. That was too much even for radio-friendly Coolidge, who, when he found a mike in the rug near him, ordered it taken away. John's best man was Stephen Brown, the friend with whom his father had sent him off to Amherst. Coolidge's doctor, Stephen's father, was there. Kenneth Welles, the minister from the Edwards Church who had confirmed John and Calvin, Jr., officiated.

Like Calvin and Grace before them, John and Florence started humbly: the rent on their New Haven apartment, the papers reported, was $78 a month, double the now-legendary $32 the Coolidges had paid for the Massasoit Street house, but still modest. Reporters were after Coolidge to know what the Coolidges' gift to their son would be. Coolidge quipped, "I do not choose to say." Grace gave her son and Florence a colonial furniture set for their bedroom. Coolidge gave a generous check to the young couple—an amount, the papers reported, in four figures.

But soon after the wedding the cloud of concern returned. Perhaps Coolidge's tight-lipped presence in the White House had tamed the markets. Since Coolidge had issued his "I do not choose" statement, the Dow Jones Industrial Average had gone wild, rising from around 180 to, currently, over 360. Now, around the time of John's wedding, came the first great crash. Coolidge issued no public statement. A president's words—even those of a president in retirement—had a megaphone effect. In the case of his own savings, Coolidge moved to hedge. He purchased shares in Standard Brands, a new company consolidating retail companies such as Fleischmann's Yeast and Chase & Sanborn, the coffee and tea company. Morrow's old firm, J. P. Morgan, brought Coolidge in on the initial public offering. Both investment houses and the *Wall Street Journal* editors had long deemed retail food companies "depression-proof." Food was something people had to buy, the reasoning went. Going long on yeast, a food product used to make beer, was a mischievous way to bet that Prohibition might not always hold.

The little joke soured as the market sank. In November 1929, the Dow dropped below 200, the level at which 1928 had started. Charles Merrill had been correct. There would indeed be a deficit shortly. Coolidge might have predicted Hoover's reaction to the crash; the president followed the prescriptions he had made as far back as the great labor conference of the early 1920s, from which Coolidge had been absent. Hoover was exhorting businesses to keep wages high so that workers could spend their money and keep the economy going. This was different from past policies. This idea—high wages in a downturn—came straight out of the newer texts but not Coolidge's. Coolidge believed that for markets to find their level, businesses had to choose their own wages and prices. Yet worse than any specific action Hoover took was the general alarm that Hoover struck, so different from the calming policy of Coolidge, Harding, or Mellon. "The cure for such storms is action," Hoover told the country in a speech on December 5. These new policies were strange to Coolidge, and his old friends were not there to defend the old ways: not Harding, of course; not the senior senator Philander Knox; not Clarence Barron; not Taft, who would die late that winter.

That fall brought other bad news. After her long illness, Mrs. Goodhue died. The week she was buried in Burlington also brought a large dip in the Dow. General Lord had left office to try to capture a small share of the boom after years of earning an army salary, but his career shift had not come at a propitious time. An unexpected professional challenge arose, this time involving Coolidge's most promising assignment: the short history to be engraved on the granite at Rushmore. Coolidge and Borglum had now been corresponding about the inditing of the entablature, or granite wall, for years. The letters, Borglum was promising, might be read miles away and would last for millennia. While Coolidge worked, Borglum delivered first-class publicity, dropping tidbits of information here and there to keep the country interested. Borglum let it be known, for example, that Coolidge in his inditing would touch on only eight events: the Declaration of Independence, the Constitution's framing, the Louisiana Purchase, the admission of Texas to the union, the Oregon boundary settlement, the admission of California to the union, the Civil War's end, and the completion of the Panama Canal, a choice that ought to have rung alarms for its Roosevelt-style emphasis on the frontier. Not all names would appear, perhaps not even Lincoln's, but Coolidge would be listed as the author. Gratifyingly, Borglum announced the first lines would be ready on July 4, 1930, Coolidge's birthday.

Such a task represented an opportunity for precision Coolidge relished. Here, Coolidge determined, he might have to forgo plain language for the sake of accuracy. If qualifications, commas, dashes, or other punctuation marks were necessary to get closer to the true meaning of a document, he would use them. The ambiguities of documents he would treat, such as the Declaration of Independence, commanded precious respect. At one point the Declaration's text suggested that the document's authority inhered in the states ("we, therefore, the representatives of the united States of America . . ."). But at another point, in the same sentence, the Declaration was put forward as emanating from citizens ("and by Authority of the good People of these Colonies"). So in writing about the Declaration, Coolidge might carefully skip the question of authority and describe the document as "the Declaration of Independence—the eternal right to seek happiness through self government." Coolidge penned his drafts carefully, intent on delivering language of legal precision, and shipped his words to Borglum.

Then came the shock. The papers were reporting that Coolidge's text was wrong. The text as printed described the people of the United States as declaring independence, when, some scholars argued, it had been the states that had done so. The second shock, of greater magnitude, came next: the language in the newspaper, attributed to him, was not the language that Coolidge had sent. Coolidge had indeed written, "The Declaration of Independence—the eternal right to happiness through self-government and the divine duty to defend that right at any sacrifice." Borglum had made the text read, "In the year of our Lord 1776 the people declared the eternal right to seek happiness—self-government—and the divine duty to defend that right at any sacrifice." Borglum's prose was clearer. But Borglum had committed the ultimate act of hubris. He had edited a former president, and one renowned for his craftsmanship at that.

Here was the sort of story of which newsmen only dreamed. "Borglum Shows Coolidge How," crowed one paper. "Every newspaper reporter in the land, smarting from the discipline of unfeeling copy desks, will sympathize with the man who didn't choose," cackled the editors of *The Plain*

Dealer in Cleveland. And every detail of Mount Rushmore—the task assigned Coolidge, the behavior of Borglum—was now rehearsed in the papers. Across the nation editors printed both versions, line for line, so that readers might compare and judge for themselves. Coolidge had written in his legalistic way, just as he had been thinking. There had been no mention in the Coolidge version of the people writing the Declaration. Coolidge, hyperaware of scholarly debate, had carefully omitted naming "the people" as authors. Borglum had rewritten, mentioning the people, and had also committed another offense: He had rendered Coolidge vulnerable to allegations that the former president and governor of the Commonwealth of Massachusetts was a sloppy constitutionalist.

Borglum, true to form, ignored the silence from Massachusetts and began chiseling the edited Coolidge words into stone. The politicians of South Dakota, chagrined at the result of such a long courtship, tried to make amends: Representative William Williamson told the Associated Press that Coolidge might write a version that Borglum could not edit. But the silent back of New England was now already turned for good. Borglum would proceed, but it would be without the thirtieth president.

Spring came, and the outlook failed to brighten. Though the Dow Jones Industrial Average was recouping some of its losses, the depression-proof stock to which J. P. Morgan had tipped Coolidge off was struggling; in April 1930, Coolidge sold his shares of Standard Brands, taking a $21,570 loss. One might have blamed some features of the downturn on Coolidge's own administration. Some commentators, including W. C. Durant, the founder of General Motors, accused Mellon of pushing the Fed into making interest rate increases, alleging they in turn caused the crash. Others argued that the Federal Reserve had been too easy. As *The Wall Street Journal* put it, "the board's fault was in leaning backwards in its desire not to penalize business by high commercial money rates." Yet other critics were warning that the Grand Old Party's pro-tariff policy had hurt the world economy and then the United States' own. Yet the Republicans, led by Senator Reed Smoot of Utah and Representative Willis Hawley of Oregon, were already in the midst of passing yet another tariff. A sugar tariff rate increase was included in the levy; there was even an increase in the tariff on maple syrup, aimed at advantaging New England and Coolidge's own Vermont over Canada. That year Coolidge's own former secretary, Everett Sanders, lobbied against protection on behalf of the Canadian maple syrup producers. Mexico and Cuba likewise were expressing distress at the tariff. "Observers say President Hoover committed a fatal mistake in signing the tariff measure, and it is further asserted that the tariff law may go far to undo here the great work of reconciliation effected by Ambassador Morrow," reported *The New York Times* on June 21, 1930, from Mexico City.

Yet now came two changes that did cheer the Coolidges. The first was their own concession to reality: the crowds would never go away. Massasoit Street, dear as it was, no longer suited them. In its place the Coolidges bought a house not far away on Hampton Terrace: the Beeches, a comfortable structure with several acres of grounds and a gate. The acreage at the Beeches provided enough room "for the doggies to run," as Coolidge told the press. There was also a brook. The Coolidges had discovered that while freedom was not possible, one could create the illusion of freedom on a private property, if it was large enough. Even their move, of course, earned disconcerting amounts of press; Elsa Comey, the prior owner, found that fifty cars an hour tried to enter her driveway once word of the famous purchase got out. The price was $45,000, a high amount for Northampton and a thousand times their monthly rent on Massasoit Street. Coolidge paid cash.

The second cause for cheer was a writing opportunity that made it possible to move beyond Borglum. McClure, a large syndicate, admired the brief autobiography he had published just after the presidency—indeed many admired the slim book. Now the syndicate invited Coolidge to publish a short daily column, 150 to 200 words. The pay was alluring, $3,000 a week, which alone raised his salary well above the $75,000 a year he had earned in the White House. And Coolidge might earn even more, 60 percent of any revenues from syndicating papers, of which there were hundreds across the nation. But the rules in the contract about the column were stiff: "It should be filed not later than three o'clock Eastern Standard Time. An hour earlier would be advantageous while Daylight Saving Time is in effect."

Coolidge had decided to ignore Barton and compete with Rogers. Indeed, he was eager to do so. His health was not improving, but he readied a secretary and took up the project at the end of June. He wrote out his first draft on trade, the area in which he had been most attacked, in pencil, and edited it in pencil, trying out sentences. "Largely because trade has declined we have set about finding fault with nearly everything," he wrote. Then he changed that: "Largely because of some decline in trade, we have set about finding fault with nearly everybody and everything." In such a column, he would be forced to reaffirm his positions, wrong or right, and take new ones. He would have to decide if and when to criticize the White House or others. But that was also the fun. In these columns he spoke to his Northampton church acquaintances, or Amherst alumni, or the townsmen of Rapid City, not to the salons of Massachusetts Avenue: "My countrymen, it is time to stop criticizing and quarreling and begin sympathizing and helping." The columns spoke so simply that some newspapers laughed at them. One magazine, the *Outlook and Independent*, made up a mocking ad:

> *Americans!*
> *Start the Day Right!*
> *Take Dr. Coolidge's Simple Faith Tablets*
> *And Smile at Hard Times*

But from the start Coolidge the columnist also addressed policy and how it might improve the increasingly alarming conditions of the country. The downturn was remarkable; jobs were scarce, but prices were also low. In his July 9 column, Coolidge turned to history—today Americans were distressed about price declines, but drops in prices were not always a bad thing. There had been price declines in the recessions of 1812 and between the 1870s and 1890s, yet "population and wealth increased greatly." That was Coolidge's suggestion that low prices might not be fatal. As Barton might have predicted, he found himself caught between the impulse to describe what he saw and to serve the nation or the party. On July 12, he sought to identify what had impeded recovery after the autumn crash. The answer, he concluded, was the uncertainty he had feared while still president. Now he made his opinion explicit: "Business can stand anything better than uncertainty." But Coolidge also suggested that uncertainty might now be passing. The new tariff was not perfect, but it was better to have it done than looming ahead. Oversubscription to a German loan had reduced uncertainty throughout Europe, and the recess of Congress, in Coolidge's view, reduced the possibility of counterproductive action over the summer. The country seemed to do better when Congress was on holiday; that had been the problem with Harding's perpetual extra sessions.

In those first weeks Coolidge allowed himself to complain that Congress was spending far more than he had predicted; Hoover was not stopping the flow of cash. The new annual budgets were going to be closer to $4 billion than the now-impossible target of $3 billion. On July 4, his birthday, Coolidge's column warned quietly, "The expenditure of money has been too large." He blamed senators, "whose work had been too much impaired by a petty spirit of factionalism and obstruction." He tried to encourage Washington to place parts of the government in the private sector when it could. "The post office ought to be self-supporting," he wrote on August 4, 1930.

What had been missing in his life since the presidency had been the old rhythm of meetings with Lord. Now Coolidge found a new rhythm with his column secretary, Herman Beaty. Coolidge arrived at the office at eight in the morning, ready to sort the mail and talk over topics of the day. Beaty, eager to beat his boss, tried to arrive a little earlier, only to find that Coolidge was onto him, and arrived earlier still. When they got closer to seven than eight, Coolidge called a draw and told Beaty, "Been here first twenty-odd years and I guess I'll have to keep on. You needn't come until 9."

The morning might begin when Coolidge reclined back in his chair, rested a foot on the half-open drawer of his desk, and prepared the cigar for insertion in the famous Coolidge paper cigar holder. Next, a conversation might ensue. Coolidge let Beaty choose the topic. Some days it was Nicaragua: Amherst might send experts to lecture him on Nicaragua; Coolidge told Beaty he had let them know he trusted the State Department more. There was a vacant New Jersey seat in the U.S. Senate that Morrow decided to run for; Coolidge, penned a praiseful introduction for a short biography of his friend. But Coolidge also worried aloud to Beaty about Morrow; the friend who had made his way in the wilds of Mexico might not make it in the snake pit that was the U.S. Senate. After the discussion, Coolidge sat down with his pencil and composed his short items, warning Beaty that his columns had to be short. If he spilled extra words, Coolidge said, that "might put them out," them being the editors at the syndicating papers.

Beaty was as keen an observer of men as Starling. He too noticed the paradox of Coolidge. At times the man seemed selfish. There were reports from Vermont that someone was taking wood from the lime-kiln lot, and to Beaty's astonishment, Coolidge flew into a rage, at once writing to his attorney, who happened to be Sargent, the former attorney general. Yet Coolidge was also capable of great magnanimity. Beaty one day discovered Coolidge wrapping up a hundred gold coins in a Christmas package, a gift for James Lucey. Coolidge's partner, Ralph Hemenway, also saw that generous streak. In Northampton one of the many local banks in which Coolidge had money, the Hampshire County Trust, closed after finding itself short $285,000. Hemenway was more deeply involved in the bank. As Hemenway contemplated the possibilities of ruin, a slip of paper was placed on his blotter. Hemenway looked at the document: it was a check from Coolidge for $5,000. He looked up to see Coolidge moving away and heard his colleague say quietly, "And as much more as you want."

Beaty and others could see considerable achievement when they looked at Coolidge's legal record. While president, Coolidge had appointed not only Harlan Stone to the Supreme Court but seventy-eight other federal judges. Days after Coolidge left office, the Supreme Court upheld the pocket veto, the president's ability to kill a bill during the congressional recess. That key power, now ensured, would enable a president to veto not only Indian land claims or the nationalization of Muscle Shoals but also other congressional spending programs. Hoover might not activate the Budget Bureau, but the Budget Law of 1921 remained on the books, a tool for other presidents; the pocket veto was another valuable device. Though Coolidge was no Murray Crane, he did count some successors in politics. One was Morrow, who did earn a seat in the Senate. Morrow won surprising support by taking a realistic position on Prohibition that others dared not take: repeal the Eighteenth Amendment so that the states might decide whether to be dry or wet. As a senator, he sat in an inconspicuous seat and listened. "A baby senator should be seen and not heard," he told others. One of Morrow's first acts as a lawmaker was to change the standard line in senators' correspondence: "I shall be glad to do all I possibly can for you." Now that read, in Coolidge-esque style, "I shall be glad to do all I properly can." Another Coolidge successor was Bruce Barton, who would eventually run for Congress. Garman and Morse would have been proud.

As Beaty noticed, Coolidge still tried to live by example. Gifts arrived often at the Main Street law office. Singed by the bonfire of the Harding scandals, Coolidge remained extremely careful not to accept anything inappropriate. Grace's health was better now, and one day a diamond bracelet arrived, the sort of thing that would have glowed against her olive skin. The owner had sent it to Coolidge for safekeeping. People did things like that with Coolidge, viewing him as if he were a bank.

"Coolidge treated the bracelet as if it were a scorpion," Beaty later recalled. The former president asked where the bracelet had come from, saw to it that the item was repacked, and shipped the package back to the sender with "ample witnesses."

Another story, told by Richard Scandrett, Morrow's brother-in-law, caught Coolidge demonstrating how to handle a contract. Scandrett described a meeting at the Vanderbilt involving a deal between *Collier's* and Coolidge. The magazine had asked him to write ten articles for the high sum of $2,000 each, but the magazine had published only six. Summoned by the ex-president to meet at the hotel, the editor knew what question would come, and it did: "I made a contract with you to write ten articles at $2,000 each and I wrote them and you published six, and you haven't published the other four." Yes, came the editor's reply, with the predictable response: the magazine had paid for all ten. "But if they aren't worth publishing," Coolidge said, "they oughtn't to be paid for," and he pulled out a check for $8,000. The move was deliberate, and deliberately Coolidge: somehow he had not pleased the other party. He gave the money back even though the contract did not say that he had to. The point, for him, was a simple one: it was important to show people that you cared about what they expected, so that they would want to do business with you again.

In his columns Coolidge asked readers whether the market's troubles would enlarge the government in a fashion that would prove irreversible once prosperity returned. Until then, the main work, in his view, was to endure bravely and ensure that the government not do too much damage. On August 20, he welcomed news of increases in sales of life insurance "when sales in so many other directions have been decreasing." Purchasing insurance, especially life insurance that paid pensions, annuities, would keep Americans independent: "It is a long step toward abolishing poverty." Here he was explaining the logic behind the New York Life directorship. Life insurance wasn't merely safe; it was the alternative to speculation, a protection during recessions.

But that fall of 1930, unemployment stayed high, and Coolidge's columns took on an edge. "When people are bewildered, they tend to become credulous," Coolidge reminded his readers on November 28.

That was the danger now, he said, as was expecting too much from Washington. "A large expenditure of public money to stimulate trade is a temporary expedient which begs the question," he added. "Many local governments are already taxing the people too much. Business does not need more burdens than less." "One of the hardest problems the Congress has to meet is the constant pressure of outside influences," Coolidge went on in his December 1 column. On December 3, he praised Hoover's message to Congress for its "sanity and restraint."

The same December, the Nobel Prize Committee awarded its prize in literature to Sinclair Lewis, the author who had published *The Man Who Knew Coolidge*. Now Coolidge came closer than he had since the days of the shabby *Delineator* articles to losing his temper in print. "Presentation of a Nobel prize to Sinclair Lewis has aroused considerable discussion," Coolidge wrote on December 15. "Whether his books will survive as literature remains to be seen," added Coolidge tartly. Then he defended the United States generally from Lewis, and himself in the process. "The world waits in our anteroom for our advice and assistance. The name Mr. Lewis gives us is unimportant. The record of our deeds will surpass all books."

In fact Coolidge wasn't merely criticizing the eminent writer for political reasons. He was competing with Lewis as an author, along with Will Rogers. Coolidge had long taken pride in his speeches. When Ercole Cartotto came to visit, they spoke about Cartotto's art. Then Coolidge gestured to the books on his wall, so lovingly assembled by Frank Stearns, and said, "Those are *my* works of art." But now Coolidge was enjoying this new career as a journalist, codifying the Coolidge philosophy, inditing after all. The great fact about the columns, whether they were homilies or critiques, was their popularity. The sixty papers that initially subscribed were joined later by others, even though the rates for Coolidge copy were higher than those to which they were accustomed. In 1930, Coolidge had liquidated his Standard Brands stock. On January 2, 1931, his account at J. P. Morgan had a cash balance of $137,099.38. In addition, his records show that his daily articles brought in much more money on top of the $3,000 that McClure paid. From the *Tokyo Japanese Advertiser* to the *Richmond Palladium* of Indiana to the *St. Louis Post-Dispatch* and the *New York Herald Tribune*, papers bought his column; the author's share of the syndicating revenues as of September 27, 1930, totaled $49,725.61. Coolidge's autobiography, written in a rush just as he left the presidency, was doing fine in print. Not every reader appreciated its spare language, but the short book would stand up well to the self-centered narratives other statesmen produced, especially those who relied on dictation and, in their vanity, failed to revise. In the autobiography, readers who for many months had been guessing finally learned what Coolidge had meant when he said, "I do not choose":

> It is difficult for men in high office to avoid the malady of self-delusion. They are always surrounded by worshipers. They are constantly, and for the most part sincerely, assured of their greatness.

In the book, curious readers could find more clues to the reasoning behind Coolidge's actions. His minister, Jason Noble Pierce, had come closest to guessing Coolidge's intentions. Coolidge believed, like Lord Acton, that power corrupted. As he wrote, "The chances of having wise and faithful public service are increased by a change in the presidential office after a moderate length of time." Aware of the quality of his prose, he proudly shared the details of his work habits with reporters. Dictation had been recommended to him, but in the end, he told them, he had written "longhand, alone."

For Coolidge all the writing—autobiography, long articles, and *McClure's* columns—was also a personal relief. The dignity of the presidency had required of the Coolidges that they restrain themselves in all areas, including the death of their son: they had had to mourn Calvin in a quiet manner. Now Coolidge could tell how the loss of Calvin had changed his life. "When he went, the glory of the presidency went with him," he wrote in his autobiography. Grace, too, was free to speak about Calvin freely, and she did. That alone made matters better. One night in the summer of 1929, she had woken up to pen a poem of her own:

> You, my son,
> Have shown me God,
> Your kiss upon my cheek
> Has made me feel the gentle touch
> Of Him who leads us on.
> The memory of your smile, when young,
> Reveals His face.

With Coolidge's encouragement, Grace also tried prose. As she waited in a hotel room in Springfield while Coolidge attended an Amherst trustees' meeting, she began to write about her life, using hotel stationery and interrupting her usual sewing: "I sewed and wrote in turn until I became rather more interested in the paper than in the cloth and by mid-night I had covered a surprising number of sheets." She showed Coolidge the writing, and "he approved of my efforts in even greater measure than I had thought possible," she later wrote. In fact, to her astonishment, "he established himself my manager without request and without commission" and got them published, encouraging even more work. The Clarke School had been a $2 million gift—the $2 million that Barron and Coolidge had raised had been money forgone for Coolidge's own papers. To Grace, this personal encouragement was worth more than $2 million. Coolidge was a different man from the one who had forbidden horseback riding and rotated her Secret Service agent to another post. The Clarke School was there, Grace's to enjoy and improve. The Coolidges were truly back together.

Yet as 1931 passed, the country flagged and the Coolidges flagged along with it. The increased spending by Washington had not ended the Depression, but strained the budget so that another part of the Coolidge legacy was threatened. At Treasury, Mellon had been willing to endure a deficit for one year or two, but a continued deficit, especially a large deficit, he would deem disastrous. To sustain the United States' credit and the gold standard, the secretary would balance the budget. If Hoover and Congress did not cut spending, he would raise taxes. Already that spring there was talk of "lowering exemptions"—the word "lowering" sounded benign, but in that instance, the shift represented an effective tax increase. In a February 1931 column, Coolidge, now feeling isolated, made the argument against increases: "A higher tax means real wages are lower. . . . Every home is burdened"—and at a difficult time. Still, Coolidge saw, the tax rates would go up, because spending was rising: "Unless the people resist vigorously and immediately, they will be overwhelmed." At the end of the year, the estimates of the deficit would be $2 billion. Mellon would abandon the Treasury and head for Great Britain as ambassador, but not before sanctioning an enormous tax increase. In one law, every step forward they had taken with the income tax was reversed. The new top rate would be in the 60s, higher than when Coolidge had become president.

To see his accomplishments so challenged by events and government policy was hard. In the spring of 1931, Coolidge, appalled at the budget demands of the military, mentioned one remaining friend, General Lord. Coolidge wrote in his column that "some years ago careful investigations were made by General Lord in an attempt to stabilize military measures." But within months, Lord, too, was gone; he died at the Woodley after a nervous breakdown and complications of influenza. As the summer neared, the column drew enormous profits. Coolidge earned $16,659 in syndication money for June alone. But he decided that month would be his last as a columnist; as with the presidency, he wanted his service captured in a round number, quitting column writing a year after he had started. "At times we can be thankful for what is behind us," he wrote at the end. The flower had wilted as fast as it had bloomed. On June 30, 1931, the day of his last column, the Dow Jones Industrial Average stood at 150, down from the 226 of June 30, 1930, when his column had started.

The House Agriculture Committee would soon begin to assail so-called speculators. Coolidge's old appointee at the Interstate Commerce Commission, Woodlock, was now back at *The Wall Street Journal*, asserting that speculators were traders and without traders there would be no trading. But with the stock market below 100 that fall of 1931, few were heeding him. Congress passed an amendment to the tax law that required all future presidents to pay income tax; this meant that any president who wanted to go back to the old tradition that Coolidge had honored would have to wage a noisy battle all the way up to the U.S. Supreme Court. In this period Coolidge still smoked heavily, and Grace noticed his breathing worsening. As so often in the past, she now helped by distracting him; she even bobbed her hair, which, reporters noted, made Coolidge smile.

With the fall of 1931 came another sudden blow. The rush of politics had taxed Dwight Morrow. One evening the new senator went to bed ill in Englewood and died in the night from a heart attack. Coolidge went stiff. To his wife, he wrote with an odd mixture of affection and formality: "My dear Grace, As I am going to the funeral of Senator Morrow I shall not be home before Thursday. With much love." Another invisible wire of communication, this time not with his father but with his friend, had snapped. A few months later, the Coolidges could tell themselves it was Morrow's fortune to die when he had. In March, the baby of Anne

Morrow and Charles Lindbergh was kidnapped from their estate. The Coolidges felt a kinship with their friends' daughter and son-in-law. For all the challenges that celebrity imposed on an ex-president, the challenges for a Lindbergh were even greater. In his autobiography Coolidge had made the argument that his son had lost his life because he had been president. It was certain that the Lindbergh baby had lost his life because of his father's fame.

To their own son, John, anxious at his railroad job, Coolidge now sent reassuring letters. "You are doing very well," he wrote on March 14, 1932. "A good many families have been raised on much less income than you have. . . . Today was your grandmother's birthday." And then, on April 11: "Dear John, you looked so badly when you were here that I feel worried about you. If anything is worrying you you should write me at once to tell me about it. Do not give any thoughts to your investments." It was hard to halt John's anxiety, for Coolidge shared it.

The Republican Party was also down. There was no way it could elude responsibility for the current trouble. Hoover would bear the blame for this period, and Democrats could now step in to lead the economic rescue. Franklin Roosevelt's popularity was becoming harder to ignore, even in Northampton, where a local author, Earle Looker, published a biographical sketch of the New York governor. In April, Roosevelt gave a speech that resonated with Americans across the nation. Over the radio, he spoke of "the Forgotten Man at the bottom of the economic pyramid," a little fellow who was not getting by in the downturn. Roosevelt's was not the "forgotten man" of the Sumner book that Morrow had sent to Coolidge so long before, the taxpayer Coolidge defended. Roosevelt's forgotten man was the poor man. Roosevelt believed it was this forgotten man who must be the focus now.

Over the summer of 1932, new events advantaged the Democrats, officially the bigger spending party, and damaged the Republicans, who were not, as Coolidge had predicted to Starling, ready to spend as much. The old soldiers who had come to Washington before came again, along with many more. Hoover eventually sent out troops to remove these forgotten men. As Coolidge noticed, Roosevelt never promised to sign the bonus himself. Instead, he waffled. But more than one in ten men, perhaps two in ten, were now out of work; Roosevelt's plan, a New Deal for America, sounded better every day.

At first Coolidge refused to be drawn into the election. He was busy making improvements in Plymouth, adding new rooms and electricity to the old homestead. He was particular about the details, and Grace wisely did not intrude. "As I told John, it is his wing, and I am letting him flap it," she wrote to Maude Trumbull, Florence's mother. Coolidge was already in correspondence with the agriculture department of the state of Vermont about improving his land. He mentioned to Grace that "the children," John and Florence, might come for a holiday to Plymouth; that would be economical. Coolidge also received a historian who was interested in writing Coolidge's biography, Claude Fuess of the boarding school Phillips Andover. The former president relaxed enough to give Fuess a thoughtful interview, to frame history, including an ironic comparison of himself and his old nemesis Lodge. Lodge had been accused of being inconsistent, he reminded Fuess, but it was important to recall that Lodge had served in Washington for decades. Given the duration of his tenure, it was no surprise that his positions had shifted over time. "Now my career was meteoric, and I didn't have time to alter my views. That was one difference between Senator Lodge and me. There were others."

But again, humor no longer seemed called for. As support for Franklin Roosevelt grew, the calls from the Republican Party began to come to the Beeches. Hoover the rescuer was bungling the rescue so badly. The party needed a president who was not Hoover to speak up for the party: that meant Coolidge. Fortunately for the Republican National Committee, its chairman was Everett Sanders, whom Coolidge trusted so much; Sanders could make the contact. Opening a letter in Plymouth to find a query about a visit from Sanders, Coolidge sent back a typically gracious response: DELIGHTED STOP MY CAR WILL MEET YOU IN LUDLOW OR RUTLAND ANY TIME YOU SAY. Sanders noted that that was Coolidge's indirect New England way of telling him how to come. Sanders had mentioned Ludlow; Coolidge was telling him that Rutland made more sense.

At the house, Sanders noticed that Coolidge looked pale and thinner than before. He pressed Coolidge nonetheless, and Coolidge wrote a pro-Hoover article for Sanders and the GOP as a favor. That article, in turn, provoked requests for speeches. The thought of it all wearied Coolidge. Had he not said everything there was to say? On the bottom of a letter that he wrote later to Sanders to try to convey his reluctance, he added something: "What subjects can I discuss?" But Sanders and the GOP would not release Coolidge; Roosevelt was charging forward, and if Hoover could not stop him, perhaps Coolidge could. The states were not able to feed the hungry, not this year. Roosevelt talked of a New Deal, of implementing across the land the kind of social programs he had supported in New York. That was attracting more and more voters. The national head of publicity for the party wrote to beg for an appearance by Coolidge: "We are willing to send recording machinery to his house and put it up in his bedroom or anywhere else he will have it and let him speak 15 minutes into it." Coolidge did not take the publicists up on the bedroom offer. But he did give in and agree to speak, and properly, in New York. "Well, I am a regular Republican," he had once told Congressman Bertrand Snell, another Amherst man; "I am willing to go up or down with my party." Now, by volunteering, he was proving that that was still true.

At Madison Square Garden, a crowd of tens of thousands greeted him. Tired but decided, he opened with a lengthy defense of Hoover and warned against switching horses in the middle of a race. But Coolidge also got to a more philosophical point. Roosevelt might mention the forgotten man, but he could not claim to be the only one who would serve him. "The charge is made that the Republican Party and its candidates do not have any solicitude for the general welfare of the common run of people." But the GOP had done its part for the forgotten man: "Always the end has been to improve the wellbeing of the ordinary run of people." Roosevelt attacked the rich, but his attack seemed odd, coming as it did from a wealthy man. Coolidge defended Hoover, noting it was important to remember that Hoover came from a common background: "He was not born to the enjoyment of generations of inherited wealth." Finally, Coolidge tried to provoke Roosevelt a bit. Roosevelt had been silent on whether he supported the soldiers' bonus; let him take a position, Coolidge said, and not waffle. He closed his speech with a reminder of Grover Cleveland. Cleveland, Americans would remember, had not spent federal money in a depression; on the contrary, he had tightened up. Again he pushed, suggesting that the Democratic Party was no longer the responsible party it had once been. Cleveland had stood on sound and conservative principles. Indeed, "he was so sound on most economic questions that his party deserted him."

Coolidge's remarks went over so well that what he had feared indeed happened: the voracious party demanded yet more. UNABLE TO MAKE

SPEECH, Coolidge telegraphed back, sounding like his father. Yet come November, right before the election, he did address the nation again, that time by radio from Northampton. He tried to articulate his concern that the election had become a spending contest, the sort Republicans always lost.

"When the American people make a major decision like the election of a President," he said, "they do not offer themselves to the highest bidder but seek to determine conscientiously what justice and true patriotism require them to do." Now he could see that his morose prediction to Starling, the Secret Service man, had proved more than true. Hoover had spent more money than he should have; he had spent like a Democrat. But that spending hadn't been enough to ensure even Hoover's own reelection.

After Roosevelt triumphed in November, Coolidge's first thought was to hunt down Sanders, the unfortunate campaign manager, and console him: "Since we did not win, the natural reaction will be to begin to blame each other for the defeat." "I feel sure that you will find nothing but gratitude and praise for the work you did."

Coolidge suspected what would happen next. At the Vanderbilt Hotel for a meeting, he also saw Henry Stoddard, an editor at the New York *Evening Mail*. Coolidge was concerned that economy—savings—might not occur under Roosevelt, whatever the candidate had promised in that regard over the year. There was another problem: the Democrats would pursue action for action's sake, continuing where Hoover had started. "The Democrats will probably set aside the Hoover measures and try some of their own. That only means more experimenting with legislation." Harding's great inaugural address about the damage of experimentation seemed gone from memory. Though Coolidge could not know the details, he did know that Roosevelt stood for something like the opposite: "bold, persistent experimentation."

That the country had moved so far from "normalcy" to "experimentation" seemed strange to him. "I have been out of touch so long with political activities I feel that I no longer fit in with these times," he told Stoddard. Then he and his secretary rode with Stoddard to Grand Central to catch the Springfield Express back to New England. Coolidge did not really like to be away from home now. That month from New York he would write to Grace, "I have thought of you all the time since I left home."

Others shared Coolidge's sense of isolation. So many habits of the 1920s—the affection for the individual, the enthusiasm for the reproduction of colonial furniture, the attention to New England, suddenly seemed outdated. Even Robert Frost, who had felt himself unassailable, now sensed that he was wrong for what he called "these times." "Mr. Frost does not understand our time and will make no effort to understand it," the critic Isidor Schneider wrote in *The Nation*. He accused Frost of replying to contemporary ideas "with know-nothing arrogance." Schneider mocked Frost's denial of social reality: "Me for the hills where I don't have to choose."

At Christmastime, Coolidge, too, headed for the hills. The cause was another funeral, that of William Stickney, his father's old mentor and business partner from Ludlow. Stickney was the governor who had made his father an honorary colonel. "In other periods of depression it has always been possible to see some things which were solid and upon which you could base hope," Coolidge told Charles Andrews, an Amherst classmate who happened to visit with his wife at the Beeches on New Year's Day. "But as I look about I now see nothing to give ground for hope—nothing of man."

On Thursday, January 5, the newspapers greeted Americans with stories of the incoming administration. Roosevelt would go to Muscle Shoals with George Norris, a sure signal that the new president would back government control of waterpower in the South. Roosevelt had already suggested an extra session of Congress if the short session before inauguration did not yield the legislation he sought. Now it seemed that Roosevelt would take greater license than other presidents. "Plan Free Hand for Roosevelt," read the headline on page one of *The Wall Street Journal*. A second headline read: "Power Like Wilson's." Coolidge went to the office but did not feel well; around ten his secretary, Harry Ross, drove him home. The pair saw Grace, who was heading out to do errands. Coolidge talked a bit about his partridge shooting. He and Harry also discussed a jigsaw puzzle he had received at the New Year as a gift—a picture of George Washington with his own name, Calvin Coolidge, in the background. Then Coolidge conferred with the gardener, Robert Smith, before going upstairs.

Around lunchtime, Grace went up and called. But this time there was no reply. When she found him in his dressing room, he was already gone. He had been shaving, just as he had been the first time she saw him that day through the window on Round Hill. He had removed his jacket. She could see from where Coolidge lay on the floor that it had all come over him suddenly. The heart attack he had always feared had come. He had once described his father as ready for death, ready to be with Victoria, with Carrie, with Sarah and Calvin Galusha. Grace took consolation from the thought that now Calvin, too, was home with their son.

The stock market closed. Amherst halted studies for a day and sent Dwight Morrow, Jr., and Lucius Eastman, sons of Coolidge's classmates, to the funeral. The flags came down to half-mast. Congress recessed.

Sleeping cars arrived from Washington. Coolidge's was a simple funeral, astonishingly simple for a former president. There was no eulogy, no address; there were just two hymns, as Al Smith, who came with the rest of the throng, noticed. One hymn was an especially familiar one, heard also at Harding's funeral train, "Lead, Kindly Light." Bernard Baruch, the great financier, shared a pew with Henry Long, the loyal secretary who had stood by Coolidge at the State House by Boston Common during the tough strike days of 1919. Both President Hoover and the first lady attended, as did Lou Hoover's successor, Eleanor Roosevelt; Frank Stearns and Judge Hammond were there, along with Charles Andrews and James Lucey. Even in the duration of the event, Coolidge made himself present: the service lasted only twenty-two minutes.

The Coolidge family and a few others motored up to Plymouth to bury him. At the cemetery where they had buried so many others, now he was finally buried. Grace asked the young minister to read a version of a poem by the Australian poet Robert Richardson:

> *Warm summer sun,*
> *Shine kindly here;*
> *Warm southern wind,*
> *Blow softly here;*
> *Green sod above*
> *Lie light, lie light.*
> *Good-night, dear heart,*
> *Good-night, good-night.*

Later Governor Smith, who himself had often persevered after setbacks, expressed the judgment that Coolidge's greatest feat had been to restore the dignity and prestige of the presidency when it had reached "the lowest ebb in our history." Coolidge was, he said, "in the class of presidents who were distinguished for character more than for heroic achievements."

Eminent men wonder about their final years. The ideal retirement coincides with the period when the world most appreciates the retiree's achievements. This coincidence was not given to Coolidge. But that did not mean his work was not complete, ready as a kind of blessing for another era. The paper that understood that right away was Clarence Barron's business daily, *The Wall Street Journal*, which published a short obituary. This might not be the moment, wrote the paper's editors in the "Review and Outlook" section. However, "in due time, the good fortune of the United States to have had such a man as Calvin Coolidge in just the years he filled that office will be more clearly realized than it has yet been."

Among the receipts, speech drafts, bankbooks, and letters that Grace, John, and the men at the Forbes Library would sift through was the presidential correspondence about the limekiln lot. In 1926, around the time of Colonel John's last illness, Coolidge's neighbor Walter Lynds had inquired about sugaring on the limekiln lot and perhaps taking wood out. Coolidge's response had been businesslike: "I am perfectly willing that you should take the limekiln sugar lot and draw out any wood that is down and pay such price as you think the whole thing is worth." But he had then thought again and taken a different tone in another letter to Walter: "I want to thank you for making syrup last year and sending it to me and also for the can you sent me this year. I do not imagine you found the lime kiln lot very profitable and I do not wish you to pay me any money for it. I am therefore returning you the check." Coolidge wanted to give Lynds something, just as he always wanted to give the country something. What he didn't realize was that he already had.

ACKNOWLEDGMENTS

THIS BOOK ABOUT OBLIGATIONS itself owes much to many. The first words of thanks are due to my agents, Sarah Chalfant, Scott Moyers, Adam Eaglin, and Andrew Wylie, who saw value in this project before anyone else did. Deep thanks also go to Tim Duggan, my editor at HarperCollins, who stood by this book through several drafts. Tim's insights have greatly strengthened *Coolidge*, as they did the manuscript of the preceding book, *The Forgotten Man*. Emily Cunningham oversaw this mammoth project with Tim.

Many colleagues from journalism have proved friends of this book. John Batchelor and Lee Mason have given much airtime to Cal and to me, including wonderful opportunities to cohost their stunning show on WABC. At Bloomberg, where my column appears, the following editors have been exceedingly helpful and have shown an interest in history: James Greiff, David Shipley, Katy Roberts, Tim Lavin, and Matt Winkler. Staffer Leslie Fox knows how to cheer projects forward. Cal Thomas, a relation of Calvin Coolidge, has been unstinting in his loyalty to this project.

Most of this volume was written during my time as a senior fellow at the Council on Foreign Relations. I am particularly grateful to President Richard Haass, James Lindsay, Janine Hill, and Amy Baker, all of whom helped with this project from start to finish. To Ms. Baker goes credit for much of the "operations" work. Benn Steil and Jagdish Bhagwati, my colleagues at CFR, inspired me with their work and served as sounding boards. CFR's library helped me track down old and obscure volumes. Suzanne Helm and Betsy Gude were strong allies.

The generosity of Paul Singer helped make this book possible.

Thank you also to Paul Singer's colleagues, Anne Dickerson and Margaret Hoover, for their support, insight, and cheer. Much can be learned from Ms. Hoover's *American Individualism*, a strong defense of her great-grandfather's values. Coolidge did not appreciate every aspect of his successor.

The Alice and Thomas Tisch Foundation allowed me to carry out the extensive research for this biography. This project would not have been possible without their aid, and I am grateful for it. The Ewing Marion Kauffman Foundation funded several projects undertaken by me at the Council on Foreign Relations. This portrait of a most entrepreneurial lawmaker was written in Kauffman's spirit. A grant from the National Endowment for the Humanities supported the earliest stages of this project, the book blog. Special thanks are due to Bruce Cole for his interest. At New York University's Stern School of Business, where I teach, Richard Sylla, Lawrence White, and Thomas Cooley have proved thoughtful. Thank you, NYU, for the opportunity to try out many Coolidge ideas and to learn from you. Robert James and Cathy Paglia James did much to support a graphic project produced in tandem with this, *The Forgotten Man, Graphic* (with Paul Rivoche as coauthor). Ken Weinstein's Hudson Institute and Larry Mone's Manhattan Institute were supporters.

At the Bush Library and Institute, Stacy Cinatl, Michael Meece, Matthew Denhart, Michael McMahan, and ambassadors James Glassman and Mark Langdale provided support. Mr. Denhart demonstrated great talent as an editor. Alan Lowe and Anita McBride kindly hosted me in the spring of 2012 at their wonderful first ladies event. I owe a special debt to President George W. Bush and Mrs. Laura Bush for their interest in this project. Readers extraordinaire, the former first couple have no idea of the extent to which they inspire. As someone asked, "Where's that book?"

I am indebted to the community of Coolidge scholars that has enthusiastically supported my research. Everyone at the Calvin Coolidge Memorial Foundation helped with tracking down Coolidge's letters and fact-checking the book. That institution, perhaps more than any other, has kept Coolidge's legacy alive through the decades. I am particularly grateful to my colleagues on the board or advisory boards of the Calvin Coolidge Memorial Foundation: Jay Barrett, Cyndy Bittinger, Andrew Kostanecki, Barbara O'Connell, Joan Randall, David Shribman, and Stephen Woods. To Mr. Barrett, many thanks for the insights, especially in regard to migration from Vermont. James Ottaway, Jr., was a friend, as was Mary Ottaway; the Ottaways opened their home and their sugar shack to this project. A particular thank-you to director David Serra and Kate Bradley. My gratitude goes to the talented Mimi Baird, whose literary insights and joie de vivre inspire.

The Coolidge family today comports itself with the same dignity and grace as in the days of the president and his father. Christopher Jeter and Jennifer Harville offered the special knowledge of Coolidge that only descendants could share. Mr. Jeter helped me trace the owners of the limekiln lot and the many branches of the Coolidge family tree. To visit the farmhouse and see Colonel Coolidge's papers enriched this book. Thank you to Kathy Lynds for her family's review.

Robert Kirby offered so much advice that it is impossible to enumerate all he has done. His deep knowledge of Coolidge has greatly enriched this book. Jerry Wallace, the author of *Calvin Coolidge: Our First Radio President*, knows the archival record on Coolidge better than anyone else. Many budget-related materials were pointed out by him. David Serra has proved a valuable friend. Milton Valera of the National Notary Association offered insights on the role of the notary and organized the publication of a volume on Coolidge titled *Why Coolidge Matters: How Civility in Politics Can Bring a Nation Together*. William Jenney of the President Calvin Coolidge State Historic Site is a living source on Coolidge's early life. No one else knows as much about Coolidge's childhood and youth as Mr. Jenney does. David Pietrusza, an authority on the 1920s and Coolidge both, helped me navigate the period and offered important insights on Coolidge's life. Joseph Thorndike of *Tax Notes* explained the federal tax policies of the 1920s. Thank you, Joe, too, for your work on the Coolidge blog. Geoffrey Norman taught me much about Coolidge and the Green Mountain State.

It has been my good fortune that the archivists charged with preserving the documents relating to Coolidge's life are an exceptionally devoted group. Julie Bartlett Nelson of the Calvin Coolidge Presidential Library and Museum at the Forbes Library in Northampton, Massachusetts, opened her collection to me and served as a guide to the other archives of New England. Peter Nelson of the Amherst College Archives and Special Collections graciously hunted down the records of Coolidge's undergraduate years as well as his letters home. Paul Carnahan of the Vermont Historical Society in Barre helped make sense of the records of Oliver Coolidge. Thank you too to Naomi Allen and Elizabeth Carroll-Horrocks of the State Library of Massachusetts, who unearthed important records from Coolidge's years as governor. Timothy Sprattler of the Phillips Academy (Andover) Archive uncovered some materials that an early biographer of Coolidge, Claude M. Fuess, had used. Sigrid Pohl Perry of the Northwestern University Special Collection helped find materials on Charles Dawes. I am indebted too to the staff at the Library of Congress and the Holy Cross College Archives and Special Collections.

It would not have been possible to go through all the materials necessary for this volume without the support of a number of researchers. Joanne Dooley found many of the primary sources for this volume. Her meticulousness and nose for archival findings improved this book. Her encouragement and editing, whether emanating from Canada, France, or the Commonwealth of Massachusetts, will not be forgotten. It was Joanne who carried the president's unpublished press conferences for digitization; may visitors to the Forbes Library enjoy them in the future. Susan Strange photographed Coolidge's White House appointment books. Allison White helped analyze many primary sources. Erica Libby provided quality work. Helena Rice and Marjorie Strong looked through materials at the Vermont Historical Society. Fred Burwell and Heather Hoff of Beloit College sent the materials from the papers of Irving Maurer. Ruth Mandel assisted with finding images.

Friends in the background who have supported this project include: Roger Kimball, who published a Coolidge essay and hosted a conference; Lawrence Mone and Diana Furchtgott-Roth of Manhattan Institute; and Walter Russell Mead, a professor at Bard College. Thomas Smith sponsored lectures on Coolidge; though Coolidge did not know Friedrich Hayek, he would have understood him. James Piereson provided wise counsel. Chris Demuth at Hudson Institute always knows best.

A number of readers have given generously of their time: Mimi Baird, Gene Smiley, and Hendrik Booraem. Rik will shortly publish a new book on the youth of Gerald Ford. The senior reader of *Coolidge* was Jerry Wallace, who has had much to say about and done much to improve the book at every stage. Andrew Kostanecki and Gerry Jones read as well. John Bennett raced through the manuscript at breakneck speed yet somehow managed to work thoroughly and helpfully. Theo Lipsky read much of this manuscript and improved it. Two friends have shaped the narrative of this book. The first is the storied editor Robert Asahina, now of the Bush Institute's 4% Growth Project. The second is Nikolai Krylov of the Council on Foreign Relations. Mr. Krylov's narrative vision would be a gift to any author, and his historical insights, particularly concerning the Kellogg-Briand Pact and tax policy, illuminated *Coolidge*'s path.

Eli Lipsky, Theo Lipsky, Flora Lipsky, and Helen Lipsky have listened and helped enormously. Eli, Theo, Flora, and Helen provided the environment that made this book possible. Beatrice Barran did much as well. Jane Dowd and Noah Shlaes supported this project, as did Jared Shlaes and Nancy DeGrazia. My debt to Seth Lipsky is incalculable.

A NOTE ON SOURCES

The thirtieth president remained obscure for so long because of a love story and two principles. The love story is the story of his love for his wife, Grace Anna Goodhue Coolidge. The principles were humility and federalism.

A woman of great empathy, Grace accompanied Coolidge at every stage in a tense and difficult career, often serving as a bridge between her terse, preoccupied husband and the world. Coolidge was enormously grateful. "For almost a quarter of a century she has borne with my infirmities and I have rejoiced in her graces," he wrote in his autobiography. In the Coolidges' day there were no large presidential libraries; it was up to friends and supporters to subsidize the presidents' projects after their presidencies, to fund repositories for that share of their papers that did not go to the Library of Congress or state archives. Coolidge did turn to his friends for postpresidential charity: Frank Stearns, his old Boston patron; Dwight Morrow; and Clarence Barron, the newspaper publisher. Over time the men raised $2 million, a significant sum. But at Coolidge's behest, this money went not to the maintenance of his own papers but to fund the institution most important to Grace, the Clarke School for the Deaf in Northampton, Massachusetts, where she had been teaching when the pair first met. In this way the president, who accurately suspected that he might not live long, ensured that his wife had a large and meaningful endeavor that would benefit many and fill her decades.

The principles mattered as well. The idea that his life's papers might be displayed grandly offended Coolidge as the kind of "self-aggrandizement" he condemned in others. Coolidge approved of the National Archives and even backed a $1 million appropriation toward a structure to house the archives. But the modern concept of a large, federally funded presidential library he would have deemed inappropriate; if the public should pay for a presidential library, it should pay at the town or state level. State and town governments or private philanthropies were, in Coolidge's opinion, the proper custodians of citizens' materials, even of citizen-presidents. Coolidge did give specifically presidential papers to the Library of Congress. Perhaps the most important materials at the Library of Congress are Coolidge's appointment books, a day-by-day account of his presidency. I collaborated with a researcher to photograph these in their entirety; their contents offer a window into Coolidge's relationship with his cabinet and some insight into his priorities as president. The Library of Congress also houses the papers of Edward T. Clark, Coolidge's secretary; Everett Sanders, his secretary after Clark; and Joel T. Boone, his White House physician. Boone kept a detailed diary in which he recorded his interactions with the Coolidge family, and he drafted an unpublished memoir in which he discussed his service to the Coolidges. Boone's papers offer a firsthand look into the personal relationships within the Coolidge White House.

But it was Judge Forbes's Library of Northampton, an institution founded by a local judge in the spirit of Andrew Carnegie and a monument to self-improvement, that Coolidge deemed the proper repository for his nonpresidential papers: letters, records from his time in state and town government, and personal documents. So it was to Northampton that the trucks rolled when he left the White House.

Even in Coolidge's day, the Forbes Library received insufficient funds for the support of the Coolidge materials. To its credit, the library, now home to the Calvin Coolidge Presidential Library and Museum, has maintained those papers well. Thanks to the talent of its current archivist, Julie Bartlett Nelson, and her predecessors, the collection is beautifully preserved. The Forbes Library has materials from his life before and after the presidency, including documents related to his law practice and time as a Massachusetts politician. The Forbes Library also has the transcripts of Coolidge's unpublished White House press conferences. I have worked with the Forbes Library to digitize these transcripts. A visit to the library affords much pleasure. In addition to the extensive collection of documents there, the Forbes Library also displays some of Coolidge's personal items, including his electric exercise horse. One of the valuable assets at the Forbes Library is the finding aid to the Coolidge files, edited by Lawrence E. Wikander, and arranged and microfilmed under a grant of the perspicacious Earhart Foundation.

Many of the Coolidge materials are dispersed elsewhere. The Vermont Historical Society in Barre, Vermont, houses materials from Coolidge's ancestors as well as some of his own childhood writings. The legal documents regarding Oliver Coolidge's incarceration, as well as his letters, are also in the Barre files. The Historical Society also holds the remarkable papers of Ellen Riley, the Coolidges' housekeeper at the White House, including her detailed diary.

Plymouth Notch, Vermont, is home to two important institutions devoted to Coolidge. The Calvin Coolidge Memorial Foundation, of which I am a trustee, offers a wealth of significant materials, particularly relating to Coolidge's childhood and adolescence. Its shelves also contain Grace Coolidge's letters to her fraternity (sorority) sisters of Pi Beta Phi. Years before, this foundation issued a wonderful and still valuable series of publications called *The Real Calvin Coolidge* that combined scholarly essays along with reprinted version of original documents related to Coolidge. The second institution is the President Calvin Coolidge State Historic Site, an open-air museum devoted to Coolidge. The medal Coolidge won for his essay on America's roots is in the state's collection, as is the shield given him by the Abyssinian regent. Plymouth Notch is the primary address for Coolidge pilgrims. Visitors to the Notch may inspect Coolidge's father's store, the house in which Coolidge grew up, and furnishings the Coolidges themselves had used. Some materials of Coolidge's, most interestingly the diaries and town government records of his father, John Coolidge, are in the possession of Coolidge descendants. The Town Clerk's Office of Plymouth, Vermont, has the land records that trace the Coolidge property lineage, including that of the limekiln lot. Any research into Coolidge's life must start in Plymouth Notch.

Boston is home to several significant collections related to Coolidge, particularly to his time as a Massachusetts politician. The Massachusetts State Archives store the records of Coolidge's legislative initiatives and voting during his tenure as state representative and senator. The Boston Public Library's Boston Police Strike Documents of 1919 Special Collection is the primary resource for study of that event. Finally, the Massachusetts Historical Society's Winthrop Murray Crane Collection has some of Crane's correspondence with Coolidge.

The Amherst College Archives and Special Collections offers materials from Coolidge's undergraduate days, including the papers of the professor he so esteemed, Charles Garman. The Dwight W. Morrow Papers there have letters between Morrow and Coolidge. The Holy Cross College Archives and Special Collections house the papers of Coolidge's close friend and political ally, Frank Waterman Stearns, including some of his correspondence with Coolidge. The Northwestern University Library Special Collections Department has the papers of Charles G. Dawes, Coolidge's flamboyant vice president. The Smith College Archives in Northampton, Massachusetts, house the papers of Elizabeth Cutter Morrow, the wife of Dwight Morrow, which shed some light on her relationship with Grace. The Houghton Library at Harvard College stores the diaries of William R. Castle, a state department official. Castle wrote extensive entries several times a week that described the development of Coolidge's foreign policy as seen from within the State Department and related some of the Washington gossip of the time. Beloit College has the diaries of Irving Maurer, the minister at the Coolidges' Edwards Church in Northampton and later a president of Beloit College in Wisconsin. Harding and Coolidge's speeches to the Business Organization of Government as well as the addresses of Coolidge's budget director, General Lord, are key to grasping the two administrations' commitment to budget cutting.

There are a number of excellent published volumes of Coolidge's letters as well as the personal accounts of people who knew him. The gold standard of Coolidge editing remains Edward Connery Lathem's volume of correspondence between Coolidge and his father, titled *Your Son, Calvin Coolidge: A Selection of Letters from Calvin Coolidge to His Father.* Lathem also pulled together a remarkable collection of eulogies and remembrances of Coolidge, titled *Meet Calvin Coolidge: The Man Behind the Myth*, written by those close to him as well as prominent figures from the period. In addition, Lathem published a collection from Coolidge's syndicated newspaper column, written after his presidency, titled *Calvin Coolidge Says.*

The best biography of Calvin Coolidge was written by Calvin Coolidge himself. *The Autobiography of Calvin Coolidge*, published in 1929, is a slim volume that nonetheless sketches a remarkably lucid account of his life and is a starting point for understanding the man. Claude M. Fuess's biography, *Calvin Coolidge: The Man from Vermont*, one of the earliest ones, remains among the best and is particularly useful, as the author interviewed many of Coolidge's acquaintances. Fuess's history of Amherst College, although not devoted specifically to Coolidge, is also magisterial and important to understanding how that institution shaped Coolidge as a young man. The same holds for his remarkable volume covering Amherst's service in World War I. Those interested in Coolidge's continuing relationship with Amherst will likely find the story of Alexander Meiklejohn's conflict with the college of interest. Adam R. Nelson provides a strong account in *Education and Democracy: The Meaning of Alexander Meiklejohn, 1872–1964*. Douglas C. Wilson's essay, "The Story in the Meiklejohn Files," reprinted in a volume he edited called *Passages of Time: Narratives in the History of Amherst College*, is a briefer but still thorough description.

Hendrik Booraem V's *The Provincial: Calvin Coolidge and His World, 1885–1895*, an excellent volume, is the best source on Coolidge's childhood. *Calvin Coolidge Meets Charles Edward Garman* by John Waterhouse is a surprising account of Coolidge's intellectual maturation as a college student. Susan Lewis Well's *Calvin Coolidge at Home in Northampton* describes the Coolidges' life in that city, with accounts of their neighbors and everyday affairs that are unique to that volume. John L. Blair's 1971 dissertation, *The Governorship of Calvin Coolidge, 1919–1921*, is the best work on that period of Coolidge's life. It is also an excellent source on Coolidge's role in the 1919 Boston Police strike. Some Boston police material from the period, including the invaluable Volume 56 of the Boston police records and the Annual Reports of the Boston police commissioner, have been digitized by the Boston Public Library and are available online. *The Life of Calvin Coolidge* by Horace Green, published in 1924, is particularly interesting because it reproduces Coolidge's own letters in which he inquires about his ancestors and genealogy. Another early biography is Michael E. Hennessy's *Calvin Coolidge*, published in 1924. Readers interested in the Massachusetts of Coolidge's era will find that author's *Four Decades of Massachusetts Politics, 1890–1935*, very useful. Especially instructive and containing much detail is Margaret

Jane Fischer's excellent *Calvin Coolidge, Jr.*, published by the Calvin Coolidge Memorial Foundation in 1981. Thomas B. Silver's historiographical work on how Coolidge has been viewed by succeeding generations, titled *Coolidge and the Historians*, is useful for understanding how the scholarship on Coolidge has evolved. Silver was the president of the *Claremont Review of Books*, which published a number of excellent essays on Coolidge and the 1920s.

Most of what has been written about Coolidge has, of course, been devoted to his years as president. In *The Tormented President: Calvin Coolidge, Death, and Clinical Depression* Robert Gilbert offers an idiosyncratic but compelling account of Coolidge's presidency. Scholars will find Arthur Fleser's excellent study of Coolidge's speeches, *A Rhetorical Study of the Speaking of Calvin Coolidge*, of interest. John L. Blair's essay, "A Time for Parting: The Negro During the Coolidge Years," published in the December 1962 issue of *Journal of American Studies*, is one of the few pieces of scholarship devoted to the Coolidge administration's relationship with the African-American community. Jerry Wallace's *Calvin Coolidge: Our First Radio President* describes a side of Coolidge few biographers address: his early adoption of technology. Wallace's insightful account of Coolidge's trips to Kansas City illuminates the complex issue of veterans' conditions and demands in the interwar period. Those particularly interested in the question of the veterans' bonus should read "War, Taxes, and Income Redistribution in the Twenties: The 1924 Veterans' Bonus and the Defeat of the Mellon Plan" by Anne Alstott and Benjamin Novick (Yale Law School, Public Law Working Paper No. 109). Although not devoted to Coolidge in particular, John M. Barry's *Rising Tide: The Great Mississippi Flood of 1927 and How It Changed America* is an important account of that natural disaster and Coolidge's reaction to it. *"The Troubled Roar of the Waters": Vermont in Flood and Recovery, 1927–1931*, by Deborah Pickman Clifford and Nicholas Clifford is a lucid history of the Vermont flood of 1927, a disaster that struck Coolidge's native state during his presidency. Readers looking for economic data from the Coolidge years should look to *The Historical Statistics of the United States*, which is available in several editions. *The First Measured Century*, by Theodore Caplow, Louis Hicks, and Ben Wattenberg, is less detailed but also useful.

My friend David Pietrusza has brought Coolidge back to life with his volumes about the president; concurrent to this book will be published a documentary biography of the president by Pietrusza. Donald McCoy's *Calvin Coolidge: The Quiet President*, published in 1967, offers a strong narrative of Coolidge's life. Among the bibliographies, McCoy's is the strongest. William Allen White published two biographies of Coolidge: *Calvin Coolidge: The Man Who Is President* in 1925 and a longer work titled *A Puritan in Babylon: The Story of Calvin Coolidge* in 1938. Though the latter volume is very well written and engaging, it is in places unreliable. Two complete biographies of Coolidge published more recently, *Coolidge: An American Enigma* by Robert Sobel and *Calvin Coolidge* by David Greenberg, are also both fine works. *Coolidge*, one of Sobel's last volumes, was where many encountered the president's economic side first. It is regrettable that Sobel, a master of that quirky subgenre, the economic biography, did not live on to enjoy the appreciation that greeted this telling volume.

No study of Coolidge would be complete without a review of the writings about his wife, one of the greatest first ladies, Grace Goodhue Coolidge. Her autobiography, edited by Lawrence Wikander and Robert Ferrell, offers perhaps our best window into Coolidge as a husband and father. Grace's own life story is compelling, and her autobiography tells it well. Ishbel Ross's *Grace Coolidge and Her Era* and Cynthia Bittinger's *Grace Coolidge: Sudden Star* are the two most authoritative biographies of the first lady. Robert H. Ferrell's *Grace Coolidge: The People's Lady in Silent Cal's White House* is also a useful source. Ferrell's work generally is impeccable.

There are also a number of excellent biographies of Coolidge's friends and associates. Harold Nicolson's biography of Dwight Morrow, Alpheus Thomas Mason's biography of Harlan Fiske Stone, and Merlo J. Pusey's biography of Charles Evans Hughes are particularly useful in their description of that period as a whole. Robert K. Murray's *The Harding Era: Warren G. Harding and His Administration* is thus far the best volume on Harding's presidency, but Jim Grant's forthcoming book promises to usurp that title. George Nash's monumental multivolume biography of Herbert Hoover, Coolidge's commerce secretary and successor as president, titled *The Life of Herbert Hoover*, is essential reading for those seeking to understand Coolidge's cabinet and the Republican Party of that period. *The Memoirs of Herbert Hoover*, particularly the sections devoted to his years in the cabinet, is also of interest. Researchers will find important material from that period of Hoover's life both at the Herbert Hoover Presidential Library in West Branch, Iowa, and at the Hoover Institution at Stanford University. *Secrets of the White House*, published in 1927 and written by Elizabeth Jaffray, who had been the White House housekeeper since the Taft era, is an unusual but wonderful volume, a rare bottom-up view of the White House household.

The worst consequence of Coolidge's ambivalence in regard to his legacy is that many Coolidge papers are simply missing, especially correspondence with fellow cabinet members, family letters that came to him, or, for example, notes of employees at key moments in government. Coolidge's secretary, Edward Clark, reported that Coolidge caused material to be destroyed. In a letter, Clark wrote, "Mr. Coolidge's desire was to destroy everything in the so-called personal files and there would have been nothing preserved if I had not taken some things out on my responsibility." His wife, Grace, also told an archivist at the Library of Congress that Coolidge had had many of his White House papers destroyed. Julie Bartlett Nelson, an archivist at the Forbes Library, estimates that those losses, though large, may not have been intentional. My own conclusion, having hunted for Coolidge documents over the years, is that Franklin Roosevelt, Herbert Hoover, and Congress displayed some wisdom when they envisioned the central repositories that are today's presidential libraries. Government-funded libraries can provide great value, even for those suspicious generally of government funding. The George W. Bush Center, where I work, will house a federally funded presidential library supported by the National Archives in a spectacular building worthy of Judge Forbes and funded by private donors. The Center, like the Franklin Delano Roosevelt Library and the George Bush Library and Museum at Texas A&M, proves that public and private can upon occasion work marvelously together.

But knowledge nowadays also comes by other means, some of which Coolidge, a great student of serendipitous innovation, would have much appreciated. As this book was being written, an increasing number of primary sources became easily accessible online. Searchable archives of newspapers and magazines online allow us to read history written as it happened. Where once a researcher encountered four primary sources for a document, now he encounters hundreds. The online archives of *The New York Times*, *The Washington Post*, *The Boston Globe*, *The Wall Street Journal*, and *Time* are therefore invaluable. Online archives of regional papers such as the *Springfield Republican* and *Hampshire Gazette*, although often more difficult to use, are no less important. Other resources, such as Ancestry.com, which are in part user-generated, provide insights impossible to find elsewhere. Families have kindly shared what small information they have in the hunt for Oliver Coolidge. Some readers have supplied information by sending it to SilentCal.com, a website that was funded generously by the National Endowment for the Humanities. Wonderful start-ups such as Kai Verborg's quirky Coolidge Blog (http:// kaiology.wordpress.com) also supply insights into Coolidge. It is somehow not surprising that Coolidge's most faithful blogger lives outside the United States.

On the website of the Internet Archive (www.archive.org), an independent nonprofit digital library, readers will find videos of Coolidge that were not available just five years ago. On the website of the Library of Congress, one can browse through hundreds of photographs once available only to those who journeyed to Washington. In this uncoordinated fashion, driven by numerous institutions and guided by many hands, Coolidge finds his own way back to us.

NOTES

Introduction: The Curse

1 To no one had this: Details of Oliver Coolidge's time in Woodstock
Common Jail, as well as his correspondence, are in the Oliver Coolidge
papers within the Coolidge Family Papers at the Vermont Historical
Society in Barre, Vt.

1 "your promis that you would": Letter from Oliver Coolidge to Calvin
Coolidge, April 29, 1849, Document 215, Folder 10, "Coolidge, Calvin
G., Correspondence, 1845–1849," Coolidge Family Papers, Vermont
Historical Society, Barre, Vt. The full sentence in this letter reads, "If
you know also that being involved lest I should be destitute of a home
for myself & family I deeded you my farm and had your promis that you
would redeem at any time when I wished by having pay for what I owed
you this promis was made by both you and your wife." The lengthy
letter goes on for pages. It continues, "Calvin, who has led you estray
[astray] I have been told by mummy that it is your wife if that is the
case I fear you will both fall into the ditch together for we read if the
blind lead the blind that will both fall together. There is one thing I will
mention hear [here] that I long to say respecting your not letting me
have the farm again after you had settled with me you said the reason
you did not deed back the farm you wanted to keep it in the family you
have got it in your family and there for it appears as if it has been a curse
to the family."

2 "no more courts, nor collectors": Marion L. Starkey, *A Little Rebellion*
(New York: Alfred A. Knopf, 1955), 15.

2 That year spring: Spring came late in 1849, as documented on p. 9 of the
1853 appendix to Zadock Thompson, *History of Vermont: Natural, Civil
and Statistical* (Burlington, Vt.: Zadock Thompson, 1853).

3 "my health is not good": Oliver Coolidge to Sally Billings, May 10, 1849,
Oliver Coolidge Papers, Coolidge Family Papers, Vermont Historical
Society, Barre, Vt.

3 "But if still": The poem of Oliver Coolidge, stored in the Coolidge
Family Papers, Vermont Historical Society, Barre, is written in the
idiosyncratic spelling of the period ("an") and labeled by the author:
"April the 28th 1849, Composed & written in woodstock jail by Oliver
Coolidge for his brother Calvin."

4 Angry veterans roamed: The cost of living in Massachusetts increased
by 99 percent between 1910 and 1920, according to the Massachusetts
Commission on the Necessaries of Life, cited in *Report of the Special
Commission on Teachers' Salaries, State of Massachusetts* (Boston: Wright &
Potter, 1920), 23.

5 "Nothing in this world": Although often attributed to Coolidge, that
quotation appeared as early as 1910 in the *Locomotive Engineers Journal*,
attributed to "anonymous." "Pearls of Wisdom from Many Lips,"
Locomotive Engineers' Monthly Journal 44, no. 12 (December 1910): 1030.

5 The others told Calvin, Jr.: Calvin, Jr.'s, response in the tobacco field
to the young men who told him they would quit if their father became
president is quoted in various places and with slight variations. "You
would if your father were my father" is how E. Whiting cites it in
Edward Elwell Whiting, *President Coolidge: A Contemporary Estimate*
(Boston: Atlantic Monthly Press, 1923), 10. This author went with
Christopher Coolidge Jeter, "Growing Up a Coolidge," Calvin Coolidge
Memorial Foundation, 1998.

6 a parody of *A Christmas Carol*: The Coolidge parody appeared in the
London Sunday Chronicle and was cited in an American paper. "Wilson
Call on Coolidge: Dickens Christmas Carol Modernized," *The Atlanta
Constitution*, December 22, 1927.

6 lynchings themselves became less frequent: Scholars have long relied
on lists of lynchings created by the NAACP, the *Chicago Tribune*, and
Tuskegee University. More recent scholarship has used newspaper
accounts from southern states to attempt to more accurately estimate
the number of lynchings. *Historical Statistics of the United States: Earliest
Times to the Present* (Cambridge, Mass.: Cambridge University Press,
2006) has two series estimating lynchings, Ec254 and Ec251. Both show
an overall decline in lynching over the course of the 1920s. Stewart E.
Tolnay and E. M. Beck, *A Festival of Violence: An Analysis of Southern
Lynchings, 1882–1930* (Urbana: University of Illinois Press, 1995),
provides a thorough analysis of lynching rates and the phenomenon
itself.

6 When in 1929 the thirtieth: To chart the size of government, as measured by government spending, this book used HS 47 of the Census Department, Federal Government, Receipts and Outlays, U.S. Census Bureau, *Statistical Abstract, 2003*. In 1923, the spending of the federal government was $3.140 billion; in 1929, it was $3.127 billion. See http://www.census.gov/statab/hist/HS-47.pdf.

7 "the most insignificant office": On December 19, 1793, Adams wrote, "But my country has in its wisdom contrived for me the most insignificant office that ever the invention of man contrived or his imagination conceived. And as I can do neither good nor evil, I must be borne away by others, and meet the common fate." Quoted in *Works of John Adams, Second President of the United States: With a Life of the Author, Notes and Illustrations*, ed. Charles Francis Adams (Boston: Little, Brown and Co., 1856), vol. 1.

9 "Men do not make laws": This line comes from "Have Faith in Massachusetts," Coolidge's inaugural speech as president of the Massachusetts General Court in January 1914. This speech, like many of Coolidge's, can be found on the Calvin Coolidge Memorial Foundation website.

10 "Nobody": Edward Connery Lathem, ed., *Meet Calvin Coolidge: The Man Behind the Myth* (Brattleboro, Vt.: Stephen Greene Press, 1960), 148.

10 "it sometimes seems as if": Bruce Barton, "Concerning Calvin Coolidge," *Collier's*, November 22, 1919, p. 28.

10 "if they would go along": Coolidge's paraphrase of Garman is in Calvin Coolidge, *The Autobiography of Calvin Coolidge* (New York: Cosmopolitan Books, 1929), 100.

10 "I never knew": Calvin Coolidge to Ada Taintor, Calvin Coolidge to Lynn Cady, January 26, 1920, Calvin Coolidge Presidential Library and Museum, Forbes Library, Northampton, Mass.

10 Late December 1925: Calvin Coolidge to town clerk of Wallingford, December 28, 1925. "My great grandfather lived for a time in Wallingford before going to the West," he wrote. "I wish you would look at your records and see when he was first taxed there and when last." Calvin Coolidge Presidential Library and Museum, Forbes Library, Northampton, Mass.

11 She replanted the spruce: Grace Coolidge to Therese Hills, August–September 1924, Hills Collection, box 17, MS 17-6, Calvin Coolidge Presidential Library and Museum, Forbes Library, Northampton, Mass.

11 "nice sugar": The full text of John Coolidge's letter to a customer is reprinted in the St. Johnsbury *Caledonian Record*, April 4, 1924, p. 4.

12 "importance of the obvious": Amherst man Bruce Barton reports Coolidge declaring this toward the end of his life in Lathem, ed., *Meet Calvin Coolidge*, 185.

Chapter 1: Snowbound

13 Each year eight hundred: That was Coolidge's estimate of the yield of the lot, found in Calvin Coolidge. *The Autobiography of Calvin Coolidge* (New York: Cosmopolitan Book Corporation, 1929), 26.

14 Young Arabian: The poster that C. G. Coolidge produced to advertise Young Arabian is republished in Jane Curtis, Will Curtis, and Frank Lieberman, *Return to These Hills* (Plymouth, Vt.: Curtis-Lieberman Books, 1985), 31.

14 the 1842 church: The $31 fee paid for the pew in the Plymouth Notch church is reported in Barbara Chiolino, Barbara Mahon, and Eliza Ward, *Recollections and Stories of Plymouth, Vermont* (Plymouth, Vt.: Five Corners Publications, 1992), 82.

15 Granite too had been found: Albert David Hagar and Elkanah Billings, *Report on the Economical Geography, Physical Geography and Scenery of Vermont* (Claremont, N.H.: Claremont Manufacturing, 1862), 12.

15 "Scripture Cake": The recipe for Scripture Cake can be found in document 215, 4, Coolidge Family Papers, Vermont Historical Society, Barre, Vt.

16 "Snow-Bound": John Greenleaf Whittier, *Snow-Bound, a Winter Idyl*, 1866. The original title had a hyphen.

16 They belonged to no one else: This is a paraphrase of some of Coolidge's own descriptions of Vermonters, uttered at various points. For example, Coolidge said, "They belong to themselves, live within their income and fear no man." "His Old Neighbors Hail 'Cal' Coolidge," *The New York Times*, July 16, 1920.

17 "onerous and perplexing": "Jonas Galusha, The Fifth Governor of Vermont," address by Reverend Pliny H. White, in *Addresses Delivered Before the Vermont Historical Society, 16 April 1866* (Montpelier, Vt.: E. P. Walton, Printer, 1866), 6.

17 In the Vermont records: Ibid., 30. Reverend White wrote, "There is still extant in the secretary of State's office an account of Jonas Galusha against the State, to the amount of £10, 4s. 6d. for executing the sentence of the Supreme Court upon Abel Geer, by cutting off his right ear and branding him upon the forehead with the letter C."

17 "more money is spent": Quoted in Prentiss Cutler Dodge, *Encyclopedia, Vermont Biography* (Burlington, Vt.: Ullery Publishing Company, 1912), 31.

17 Another Coolidge cousin, Carlos Coolidge: Coolidge was governor from 1848 to 1850. An example of debtor legislation was "An act to establish courts of insolvency and provide for the equal distribution of the effects of insolvent debtors." *Vermont Phoenix*, December 27, 1850, 11.

19 Vermont, after all, had been: The constitution of Vermont, adopted in 1777—before Vermont joined the United States as the fourteenth state—says, "No person born in this country, or brought from over

sea, ought to be holden by law, to serve any person as a servant, slave or apprentice, after arriving to the age of twenty-one years, unless bound by the person's own consent, after arriving to such age, or bound by law for the payment of debts, damages, fines, costs, or the like."

19 Another John Coolidge: The grave of John T. Coolidge, MD, and his wartime service are documented at www.vermontcivilwar.org.

20 "I hope you will end": Victoria Coolidge to John C. Coolidge, October 20 [ca. 1868–1876], box 217, 34, Coolidge Family Papers, Vermont Historical Society, Barre, Vt.

21 "the use and yeald": Plymouth Land Records, quoted in *Your Son, Calvin Coolidge: A Selection of Letters from Calvin Coolidge to His Father,* ed. Edward Connery Lathem (Montpelier, Vt.: Vermont Historical Society, 1968), 77. The text reads, "Know all men by these presents that we Calvin G Coolidge & Sarah A. Coolidge both of Plymouth in the County of Windsor & State of Vermont for & in consideration of the natural love & affection which we bear & have unto our Grandson John C. Coolidge Jr. have and by these do give grant convey & confirm unto the said John C. Coolidge Jr. the full use & yeald of a certain piece or parcel of land hereinafter described during the full life time of the said John C. Coolidge Jr. to come into possession of said premises at the age of 21 years . . . after the deceas of the said John C. Coolidge Jr. the said premises are to become the absolute property of the children of the said John C. Coolidge Jr. their heirs and assigns forever."

21 *The Green Mountain Boys*: President Coolidge recalled his reading list in his autobiography.

21 Calvin, at age ten: The "Tumbling Blocks" quilt top that Calvin made and the soapstone bed warmer his family used are on display at the President Calvin Coolidge State Historic Site in Plymouth Notch, Vt.

21 "more sap": John Coolidge is quoted in Edward Elwell Whiting, *President Coolidge: A Contemporary Estimate* (Boston: Atlantic Monthly Press, 1923), 10.

21 She stayed home: The diary of Victoria Moor Coolidge, a possession of Christopher Jeter and Jenny Harville, provides the best detail.

23 "he did not wish": Coolidge, *Autobiography*, 22.

23 "Is the school house": The results of the survey and many other details of Coolidge's childhood and youth can be found in Hendrik Booraem, *The Provincial: Calvin Coolidge and His World, 1885–1895* (Lewisburg, Pa.: Bucknell University Press, 1994).

23 "From scenes like these": Coolidge slightly misquoted this line from Robert Burns's poem "The Cotter's Saturday Night" when he sought to describe life in Plymouth on a later visit; see "His Old Neighbors Hail 'Cal' Coolidge." Burns wrote "grandeur," Coolidge said "greatness."

24 "Many years before": This story is one of several of Coolidge's school essays and papers held at the Vermont Historical Society in Box 391, 29 of the Coolidge Family Papers.

25 The boy put his wages: All these details are outlined in Booraem, *The Provincial*.

25 "I rec. your letter": The letters from Calvin in the Black River Academy period can be found at the Vermont Historical Society in Barre, as can his diary, which reports his sister's death.

26 "I remember one night": Quoted in Claude Fuess, *Calvin Coolidge* (Boston: Little, Brown, 1940), 33.

27 $7.20 a term: The receipt of $7.20 for the fall term of 1888 is in the files of the Coolidge Memorial Site at Plymouth Notch, Vt.

27 updated with brick and an addition: Information on the jail is available at John Cotton Dana Library and Research Library and Archives, Woodstock History Center, Woodstock, Vt.

27 among "thieves and ruffians": This is detailed in Booraem, *The Provincial*, 103.

28 "a Democrat couldn't": William Allen White, *A Puritan in Babylon: The Story of Calvin Coolidge* (New York: Macmillan, 1938), 26.

29 He and the nearby farmers: Booraem, *The Provincial*, covers the story and the farmers; the discussion of the cheese factory is in chapter 8.

Chapter 2: The Ouden

32 The Fairbanks family: Many of the details of Coolidge's time in St. Johnsbury are in Richard Beck, *A Proud Tradition, a Bright Future: A Sesquicentennial History of St. Johnsbury Academy* (St. Johnsbury, Vt.: St. Johnsbury Academy, 1992), 33–39. The archive of *The Caledonian*, the local newspaper, also carries some material.

33 From its beginning: Claude Fuess, *Amherst: The Story of a New England College* (Boston: Little, Brown, and Company, 1935), 55.

33 Charles Garman: John Almon Waterhouse, *Calvin Coolidge Meets Charles Edward Garman* (Rutland, Vt.: Academy Books, 1984), 8.

33 "while I lookt stedfastly": Wayne A. Wiegand, "The 'Amherst Method': The Origins of the Dewey Decimal Classification Scheme," *Libraries & Culture* 33, no. 2 (Spring 1998): 176.

35 weighed only 119.5 pounds: Physical Education and Hygiene Department Records, Amherst College Archives and Special Collections, Amherst College Library, Amherst, Mass.

35 the average wage earner: Robert A. Margo, "Hourly and Weekly Earnings in Selected Industries and for Lower Skilled Labor: 1890–1926," in *Historical Statistics of the United States, Earliest Times to the Present: Millennial Edition*, ed. Susan B. Carter, Scott Sigmund Gartner, Michael R. Haines, Alan L. Olmstead, Richard Sutch, and Gavin Wright (New York: Cambridge University Press, 2006), series Ba4319.

36 he would receive a salary: Adam R. Nelson, *Education and Democracy: The Meaning of Alexander Meiklejohn, 1872–1964* (Madison: University of Wisconsin Press, 2001), 33.

36 "I am in a pleasant place": Calvin Coolidge to John C. Coolidge, October 15, 1891, in *Your Son, Calvin Coolidge: A Selection of Letters from Calvin Coolidge to His Father,* ed. Edward Connery Lathem (Montpelier, Vt.: Vermont Historical Society, 1968), 25. Coolidge's letters to his father are dispersed among several archives, but nearly all are to be found together in Lathem's meticulously edited volume.

36 "This term is almost done": Calvin Coolidge to Sarah Almeda Coolidge, November 23, 1891, Miscellaneous Manuscripts Collection, Archives and Special Collections, Amherst College Library, Amherst, Mass.

37 His stepmother kindly: Calvin Coolidge to Carrie Coolidge, January 10, 1892, in Lathem, ed., *Your Son, Calvin Coolidge,* 30.

38 What money Morrow took: Harold Nicolson, *Dwight Morrow* (London: Constable & Co., 1935), 214.

39 "The class in Greek": Quoted in Claude M. Fuess, *Calvin Coolidge: The Man from Vermont* (Boston: Little, Brown and Company, 1940), 56. Copies of *The Olio,* the Amherst yearbook, can be viewed at the Amherst College Archives and Special Collections.

40 Cleveland had vetoed: Cleveland vetoed 414 bills, of which 110 were pocket vetoes, in his first term. A chart displaying all the presidential vetoes of Coolidge's lifetime can be found in *Presidential Vetoes: 1789– 1988,* ed. Walter J. Stewart and Gregory Harness, S. Pub. 102-12, U.S. Government Printing Office, 1992.

41 "[of] the thirty-three professors": The poll of Amherst professors is reported in "Professors for Cleveland," *The New York Times,* October 24, 1892.

42 arrived from County Kerry: The 1900 Census gives James Lucey's arrival date as 1880 and lists his trade as shoemaker.

42 The Beta Theta Pi brothers: The explicit rejection of Coolidge by Morrow for the fraternity is documented in a letter from Lucius Eastman to Coolidge's biographer Claude Fuess: "We decided in junior year that we should add a member to our delegation, selecting a man who had developed and shown ability. We offered a bid to Percy Deering, Coolidge's roommate. Deering refused the bid unless we could take Coolidge with him. Dwight as well as others, but with much more emphasis absolutely refused this suggestion and we didn't take Deering in primarily because Dwight and some of the rest of the Delegation were unwilling to take Coolidge." Lucius Eastman to Claude Fuess, January 27, 1933, Claude Fuess Collection, Calvin Coolidge Presidential Library and Museum, Forbes Library, Northampton, Mass.

45 "New England taught that doctrine": "Proceedings in Detail," *The New York Times,* February 2, 1892, 2.

47 Fairbanks Scales: A good source on Fairbanks Scales is Allen Rice Yale, Jr., *Ingenious and Enterprising Mechanics: A Case Study of Industrialization in Rural Vermont, 1815–1900*, PhD dissertation, University of Connecticut, 1995.

50 "fruitless victory": Anson D. Morse, *Parties and Party Leaders* (Boston: Marshall Jones Company, 1923), 123.

51 "I understand the trustees": This letter is quoted in a detailed description of the controversies at Amherst in Hendrik Booraem, *The Provincial: Calvin Coolidge and His World, 1885–1895* (Lewisburg, Pa.: Bucknell University Press, 1994), 180.

52 *Tess of the d'Urbervilles: Tess* was first published in England in the early 1890s. It sold well but was deemed controversial in the United States.

52 "a devil of him first": *Letters, Lectures, and Address of Charles Edward Garman: A Memorial Volume*, ed. Eliza Miner Garman (Boston and New York: Houghton Mifflin Company, 1909), 305.

52 "But why should not": Ibid., 343.

53 "I have been thinking": April 26, 1894, letter from Coolidge to his father in Lathem, ed., *Your Son, Calvin Coolidge*, 56.

54 "a man of power": Coolidge's paraphrase of Garman is in Calvin Coolidge, *The Autobiography of Calvin Coolidge* (New York: Cosmopolitan Book Corporation, 1929), 100.

55 "One should never trouble": Coolidge's lines to Dwight Morrow about promotion are quoted in Nicolson, *Dwight Morrow*, 91.

55 "Margaret's Mist": The text of the story is available at the Calvin Coolidge Presidential Library and Museum, Forbes Library, Northampton, Mass.

55 "the black water closing": "Margaret's Mist" is quoted in Arthur Fleser, *A Rhetorical Study of the Speaking of Calvin Coolidge* (Lewiston, N.Y.: Edwin Mellen Press, 1990), 13.

57 lightning had struck: "The barns of JC Coolidge of Plymouth were struck by lightning and burned a few days ago." "Condensed State News," *St. Albans Messenger*, August 25, 1892.

58 Yet the speech: *Amherst Student*, June 25, 1895, 266–268. The text of the Grove Oration is available at www.calvin-coolidge.org/html/grove_oration.html. Many other speeches by Coolidge are also available at the Calvin Coolidge Memorial Foundation, www.calvin-coolidge.org.

58 His grade point average: Lathem, ed., *Your Son, Calvin Coolidge*, 72.

58 His graduation was noted: "Amherst College Notes," *Caledonian*, June 28, 1895.

Chapter 3: Determination

60 Each piece of slate: Many details about the library can be found on its excellent website, www.forbeslibrary.org, as well as in Lawrence

Wikander, *Disposed to Learn: The First Seventy-five Years of the Forbes Library* (Northampton, Mass.: Trustees of Forbes Library, 1972).

60   Tuition at Harvard Law School: *The Law School of Harvard University, Announcements, 1895–96* (Cambridge, Mass.: Harvard University, 1895), 10.

60   But in the end it just hadn't sat: Dwight Morrow to James Sheffield, June 1, 1920, series 1, box 13, folder 30, Dwight Morrow Papers, Amherst College Archives and Special Collections, Amherst College Library, Amherst, Mass. In that letter to John Sheffield, Morrow wrote, "When he graduated from Amherst in 1895 he [Coolidge] did not have enough money to go to a law school."

61   Charles Forbes: J. L. Harrison to John M. Greene, enclosing biographical sketch of Charles Edward Forbes by C. A. Cutter, December 3, 1917, Origins Collection, series 2, folder 5, Smith College Archives, Smith College, Northampton, Mass.

62   The Boston and Maine Railroad: The Boston and Maine opened North Station in 1894. Details of Massachusetts's growth and connections can be found in *Massachusetts: A Guide to Its Places and People*, a Federal Writers' Project of the Works Progress Administration of Massachusetts (Boston: Houghton Mifflin, 1937), 635.

64   Daniel Shays's men: During Shays's Rebellion more than a thousand farmers converged on the Court of Common Pleas in Northampton. David P. Szatmary, *Shays' Rebellion: The Making of an Agrarian Insurrection* (Amherst: University of Massachusetts Press, 1980), 58.

64   Coolidge boarded at 162 King Street: Susan Lewis Well, *Calvin Coolidge at Home in Northampton* (Northampton, Mass.: Calvin Coolidge Presidential Library and Museum, Forbes Library, 2008), 5. Well's volume is an excellent source on Coolidge's years in Northampton.

64   his college hairstyle: Calvin Coolidge, *The Autobiography of Calvin Coolidge* (New York: Cosmopolitan Book Corporation, 1929), 73.

65   "a strong sentiment": Theodore Roosevelt, *Theodore Roosevelt: An Autobiography* (New York: Macmillan, 1913), 208.

66   Dwight Morrow was languishing: Harold Nicolson, *Dwight Morrow* (London: Constable & Co., 1935), 44.

66   "I had noted": Claude M. Fuess, *Calvin Coolidge: The Man from Vermont* (Boston: Little, Brown and Company, 1940), 74.

67   Hammond and Field filed: Lyndall Gordon, *Lives like Loaded Guns: Emily Dickinson and Her Family's Feuds* (New York: Viking, 2012), 292.

67   Marsh had used college funds: Stanley King, *A History of the Endowment of Amherst College* (Amherst, Mass.: Amherst College, 1950), 107.

68   At the Democratic National Convention: In the summer of 1896 the papers carried the details of Bryan's address; for example, see "Fourth Ballot," *The New York Times*, July 11, 1896.

68 They asked Coolidge: Coolidge's brief visit home and the gold debate are mentioned in Fuess, *Calvin Coolidge*, 82.

69 he had qualified: Coolidge, *The Autobiography of Calvin Coolidge*, 78.

72 represented the New York, New Haven and Hartford: A list of Hammond and Field clients is supplied in Charles F. Warner, *Northampton of Today: Depicted by Pen and Camera* (Northampton, Mass.: Picturesque Publishing, 1902), p. 81.

73 Dennis, like most people: Alfred Pearce Dennis, "The Man Who Became President," in *Meet Calvin Coolidge: The Man Behind the Myth*, ed. Edward Connery Lathem (Brattleboro, Vt.: Stephen Greene Press, 1960), 17.

73 seventy cents: Alfred Pearce Dennis, *Gods and Little Fishes* (Indianapolis, Ind.: Bobbs-Merrill Company, 1924). That volume provides an especially precise picture of Coolidge as a young lawyer at the county seat.

73 "to a chance": Dennis, "The Man Who Became President," in Lathem, ed., *Meet Calvin Coolidge*, 18.

74 Winthrop Murray Crane: Carolyn W. Johnson, *Winthrop Murray Crane: A Study in Republican Leadership, 1892–1920* (Northampton, Mass.: Smith College, 1967).

76 "My dear Miss Deering": Deering correspondence supplied by Jim Cooke, Coolidge impersonator, correspondence of September 16, 2012.

77 not like the Carpenters' Union: the details of this and other local trade unions are listed in *Northampton-Easthampton Directory* (Northampton, Mass.: Price & Lee, 1902), 252.

77 "leaving the parties": This line of President Cleveland is contained in his letter to President Roosevelt of October 4, 1902, reprinted in *Theodore Roosevelt and His Time as Shown in His Letters*, ed. Joseph Bucklin Bishop (New York: Scribner's, 1920), 204.

79 listed on page 267: *Northampton Directory*, 267. A trove of such directories can be found in genealogy databases, including Ancestry. com.

80 "My dear Miss Goodhue": Calvin Coolidge to Grace Goodhue Coolidge, June 6, 1904, Box 392, 1, Coolidge Family Papers, Vermont Historical Society, Barre, Vt. The courtship correspondence is located here.

83 "too poor to be": Details and quotations from Barton can be found in Richard Fried's excellent *The Man Everybody Knew: Bruce Barton and the Making of Modern America* (Chicago: Ivan R. Dee, 2005).

84 Andrew Carnegie, its great donor: Philip Butcher, *George W. Cable: The Northampton Years* (New York: Columbia University Press, 1959), 203.

85 That October, Wilbur Wright: T. A. Heppenheimer, *First Flight: The Wright Brothers and the Invention of the Airplane* (Hoboken, N.J.: John Wiley & Sons, 2003), 244.

85 Mrs. Goodhue had long since: Grace Coolidge, *Grace Coolidge: An Autobiography*, ed. Robert H. Ferrell and Lawrence E. Wikander (Worland, Wyo.: High Plains Publishing, 1992), 20.

86 "Come to see": Ishbel Ross, *Grace Coolidge and Her Era: The Story of a President's Wife* (Plymouth, Vt.: Calvin Coolidge Memorial Foundation, 1988), 16–17.

86 They would buy bread: Ibid., 18.

87 The Coolidges brought a counterpane: Robert H. Ferrell, *Grace Coolidge: The People's Lady in Silent Cal's White House* (Lawrence: University of Kansas Press, 2008), 26.

87 in a dress: Ross, *Grace Coolidge and Her Era*, 21.

Chapter 4: The Roosevelt Way

88 Within a few weeks: More information about the school committee election is in John J. Kennedy, "His Only Defeat," *The Real Calvin Coolidge* 2 (1986).

89 "Only the fact that the President": "From the Montreal Gazette: As Canada Politely Puts It," *The New York Times*, October 14, 1905, p. 8.

90 "Might give me time": Claude M. Fuess, *Calvin Coolidge: The Man from Vermont* (Boston: Little, Brown and Company, 1940), 90.

90 Lunch in the enormous dining room: Susan Lewis Well, *Calvin Coolidge at Home in Northampton* (Northampton, Mass.: Calvin Coolidge Presidential Library and Museum, Forbes Library, 2008), 39.

91 "A man is not really": Lendol Calder, *Financing the American Dream* (Princeton, N.J.: Princeton University Press, 2001), 64.

92 Among the books were: A number of authors have written about Coolidge's book collection, including William Allen White, *A Puritan in Babylon: The Story of Calvin Coolidge* (New York: Macmillan Company, 1938), 64.

92 From Northampton, Calvin and Grace traveled: Grace Coolidge, *Grace Coolidge: An Autobiography*, ed. Lawrence E. Wikander and Robert H. Ferrell (Worland, Wyo.: High Plains Publishing, 1992), 38.

93 "Little John is as strong": Calvin Coolidge to John C. Coolidge, September 11, 1906, in *Your Son, Calvin Coolidge: A Selection of Letters from Calvin Coolidge to His Father*, ed. Edward Connery Lathem (Montpelier, Vt.: Vermont Historical Society, 1968), 105.

94 "The frost may be": The text of Coolidge's speech was printed in the October 27, 1906, edition of *The Hampshire Gazette*.

94 felt no shame: Much later, speaking with Bertrand Snell, a Republican member of Congress, Coolidge would say, "I am a regular Republican. I am willing to go up or down with my party." Snell's memory of the chat is in Edward Connery Lathem, ed., *Meet Calvin Coolidge: The Man Behind the Myth* (Brattleboro, Vt.: Stephen Greene Press, 1960), 110.

95   A few weeks later: Robert Sobel, *Coolidge: An American Enigma* (Washington, D.C.: Regnery Publishing, 1998), 56.

95   "the hub of the solar system.": Oliver Wendell Holmes, *The Autocrat of the Breakfast Table* (New York: Thomas Y. Crowell, Publishers, 1900), 124.

96   "Dear John, This will introduce": Edward Elwell Whiting, *President Coolidge: A Contemporary Estimate* (Boston: Atlantic Monthly Press, 1923), 74.

97   the state constitution stipulated: *Manual for the Use of the General Court, 1907* (Boston: Wright & Potter, 1907), 495.

97   the Ways and Means Committee: Fred Wilbur Powell, *The Recent Movement for State Budget Reform, 1911–1917*, thesis, Columbia University, 1918; reprinted in *Municipal Research*, New York, no. 91 (November 1917), 47.

97   Coolidge went before: "Tariff Petition Forwarded," *Springfield Republican*, February 13, 1907, 11.

98   –11 degrees: The temperature was recorded at Amherst by the Massachusetts Agricultural Experiment Station, vols. 205–288, 1906–1912.

100   Among Brandeis's disciples: Claude M. Fuess, *Joseph B. Eastman: Servant of the People* (New York: Columbia University Press, 1952), 55.

100   Much later, his papers: *The Curse of Bigness* was published in 1934, but the ideas were present in Brandeis's arguments from the turn of the century.

101   The Hepburn Act might be deterring: The case that it was the legislation that hurt the prospects for cross-country rail business is made in Edwin J. Clapp, *Transportation* (New York: Alexander Hamilton Institute, 1918), 197–199.

101   From 1905 to 1907: Ibid., 199.

101   "The railroad campaign": Ibid.

101   The speaker replied: Whiting, *President Coolidge: A Contemporary Estimate*, 78.

104   The Northampton team pointed out: "Taxation of Colleges," *Springfield Daily Republican*, February 28, 1908, 7.

107   The 1910 Census: There were approximately 223,000 Irish-born immigrants and 85,000 Italians in 1910. Coolidge's progress and the changing electorate are tracked meticulously in John L. Blair, *The Governorship of Calvin Coolidge, 1919–1921*, PhD dissertation, University of Chicago, 1971.

109   "square deal": The speech referred to is the New Nationalism Speech, delivered August 31, 1910, in Kansas. One version of the full text can be found at www.teachingamericanhistory.org/library/index. asp?document=501.

110   "sitting in the seats": Grace Coolidge's account of the trip in a letter to Carrie Coolidge, December 11, 1910, reprinted in Lathem, ed., *Your Son, Calvin Coolidge*, 116.

111   He represented both Amherst and Springfield: Blair, *The Governorship of Calvin Coolidge, 1919–1921*, vol. 1, 6, 7, and 44.

111   "It was as good as a show": This line from a newspaperman is quoted in White, *Puritan in Babylon*, 149.

112   Edward Filene, the merchant: Kim McQuaid, "An American Owenite: Edward A. Filene and the Parameters of Industrial Reform, 1890–1937," *American Journal of Economics and Sociology* 35, no. 1 (January 1976): 80.

113   "the same towering ambitions": John Dean, *Warren G. Harding* (New York: Times Books, 2004), 29.

113   "We cannot permanently": Stephen Stagner, "The Recall of Judicial Decisions and the Due Process Debate," *American Journal of Legal History* 24, no. 3 (July 1980): 257.

113   Coolidge lined up with eighteen other: "Test on People's Primary Comes in the Senate Today," *Boston Journal*, March 11, 1912, 1.

114   Workers at the American Woolen Company: This contemporary account of the strike that discusses the role immigrants played in it is representative of much of what was written in the mainstream press at the time. W. Jett. Lauck, "The Lesson from Lawrence," *North American Review* 195, no. 678 (May 1912): 665–672.

114   the IWW collected $5,250: Bruce Watson, *Bread and Roses: Mills, Migrants, and the Struggle for the American Dream* (New York: Viking, 2005), 203.

116   The premier flyer: The text of "A Contract with the People," the 1912 Progressive Party Platform, can be found at http://www.pbs.org/wgbh/americanexperience/features/primary-resources/tr-progressive/.

120   Harlan Stone was now: Alpheus Thomas Mason, *Harlan Fiske Stone: Pillar of the Law* (New York: Viking Press, 1956), 83.

124   "Inauguration is over": Lathem, ed., *Your Son, Calvin Coolidge*, 126.

Chapter 5: War

125   The evening star: This story is told in several places. One is "Account of Eliot Wadsworth," *Boston Evening Transcript*, August 6, 1914.

126   The price and provenance of marble: "Governor Lays Cornerstone," *Springfield Union*, August 7, 1914.

126   "The production of our plant": E. H. Broadwell, letter to the editor, *Springfield Republican*, August 6, 1914.

127   Senator Lodge: Karl Schriftgiesser, *The Gentleman from Massachusetts: Henry Cabot Lodge* (Boston: Atlantic Monthly Press/Little, Brown and Company, 1944), 260.

127   The crowning achievement: "Coolidge Kills Stock Tax Bill," *The Boston Journal*, July 2, 1914.

129 he addressed a crowd of three hundred farmers: "Farmers Gather," *Springfield Union*, August 13, 1914, 9.

132 "The yeas have it": Alpheus Thomas Mason, *Brandeis: A Free Man's Life* (New York: Viking, 1946), 174.

133 At Amherst, President Meiklejohn: Claude M. Fuess, ed., *The Amherst Memorial Volume: A Record of the Contribution Made by Amherst College and Amherst Men in the World War, 1914–1918* (Amherst, Mass.: Amherst College Press, 1926), 3.

133 The Aluminum Company of America: Charles C. Carr, *Alcoa: An American Enterprise* (New York: Rinehart and Co., 1952), 150.

134 "murder on the high seas": Stefan Lorant, *The Life and Times of Theodore Roosevelt* (Garden City, N.Y.: Doubleday, 1959), 603.

135 the legislature of 1915 had enacted: Michael E. Hennessy, *Twenty-five Years of Massachusetts Politics: From Russell to McCall, 1890–1915* (Boston: Practical Politics, 1917), 376.

137 Coolidge had lost Ham's town: Frank Waterman Stearns to Dwight Morrow, October 7, 1915, series 1, box 43, folder 23, Dwight Morrow Papers, Amherst College Archives and Special Collections, Amherst College Library, Amherst, Mass.

138 "an eloquent listener": "Bay State Grooming Coolidge," *Baltimore Sun*, December 14, 1919, gives a typical description: "He is a most eloquent listener, waits until you have said your say. . . ."

138 the staff at the Bureau of Internal Revenue: Shelley Davis, *IRS Historical Fact Book: A Chronology* (Washington, D.C.: Department of the Treasury, Internal Revenue Service, 1993), 89.

143 There was violence: Stephen Puleo, *The Boston Italians: A Story of Pride, Perseverance, and Paesani, from the Years of the Great Immigration to the Present Day* (Boston: Beacon Press, 2007), 107.

143 "I had formed": William McAdoo, *The Crowded Years: The Reminiscences of William G. McAdoo* (Boston: Houghton Mifflin, 1931), 382.

145 "While Washington was yet dumb": Speech delivered at the Tremont Temple, November 3, 1917, in Calvin Coolidge, *Have Faith in Massachusetts: A Collection of Speeches and Messages* (Boston: Houghton Mifflin, 1919), 88. The speech is available at http://www.calvin-coolidge.org/html/tremont_temple_-_november_3__1.html.

146 Later he figured: Frank Waterman Stearns to Dwight Morrow, February 7, 1919, series 1, box 43, folder 23, Dwight Morrow Papers, Amherst College Archives and Special Collections, Amherst College Library, Amherst, Mass.

146 "It was 2:30": Calvin Coolidge to John C. Coolidge, November 6, 1918, in *Your Son, Calvin Coolidge: A Selection of Letters from Calvin Coolidge to His Father*, ed. Edward Connery Lathem (Montpelier, Vt.: Vermont Historical Society, 1968), 142.

147 "treason": "Calls Opposition to War Treason," *The New York Times*, January 2, 1918.

148 "We have reached": Clement's speech is in the archives of the state of Vermont at Vermont-archives.org.

148 At dinner with Clarence Barron: Clarence Barron, *They Told Barron: Conversations and Revelations of an American Pepys in Wall Street*, ed. Arthur Pound and Samuel Taylor Moore (New York: Harper and Brothers, 1930), 17.

148 because of the revolution in Russia: "Kronstadt in Flames," *The New York Times*, June 18, 1919.

149 The Yankee Division alone: Harry A. Benwell, *History of the Yankee Division* (Boston: Cornhill Company, 1919), 5.

149 Coolidge had issued a proclamation: "Coolidge and Peters Differ Regarding Holiday for Wilson," *The Boston Globe*, February 22, 1919.

149 "a great leader of the world": William Allen White reported this in *A Puritan in Babylon: The Story of Calvin Coolidge* (New York: Macmillan, 1938), 144.

150 On April 3: *Fourteenth Annual Report of the Police Commissioner for the City of Boston: Year Ending November 30, 1919* (Boston: Wright & Potter Printing Co., State Printers, 1920), 34.

150 Amid the din: "Yankee Troops Welcomed to New England," *Springfield Republican*, April 5, 1919.

150 "I welcome you": Ibid.

Chapter 6: The Strike

151 Boston Police Union Number 16,807: A good short account of the story of Union 16,807 can be found in *The Police Chief* 73, no. 5 (May 2006), published online at policechiefmagazine.org.

151 "A police officer cannot consistently": Police Commissioner O'Meara is quoted in Claude M. Fuess, *Calvin Coolidge: The Man from Vermont* (Boston: Little, Brown, 1940), 206.

152 De Valera had appeared: "Eamon De Valera Pleads Irish Cause at Fenway Park," *The Boston Globe*, June 30, 1919.

152 "I am tired": "Ole Hanson Quits," *The New York Times*, August 29, 1919.

153 The cost of food: The National Bureau of Economic Research website provides data series on this period, including Index of 58 Foods, Retail, series ao4184. That index shows that prices rose from a level of 60 in 1913 to 112 in 1919. http://www.nber.org/databases/macrohistory/rectdata/04/a04184.dat.

154 Blind and Cripples' Union: "Hearing on Bills to Help Cripples: Deitrick Wants State to Supply Employment," *The Boston Globe*, October 22, 1919, 3.

154 The policemen had selected as union president: McInnes's work and life are described in "Police Union Head Has Fine Record," *The Boston Globe*, September 8, 1919.

154 there were not yet stoplights: The installation of some of the first lights is described in "Globe Is Mushroomed into Street," *The Springfield Republican*, August 1, 1921, 3.

155 "Governor in about 9:30": The summer 1919 diary entries of Coolidge's secretary, Henry Follansbee Long, are reprinted in Robert Gilbert, *The Tormented President: Calvin Coolidge, Death, and Clinical Depression* (Westport, Conn.: Praeger, 2003), 85.

155 Their destination was the old burial ground: Judge Field described the details of this trip in remarks he gave before the Hampshire County Bar after Coolidge's death. At least one author has suggested that the visit to Watertown was related to Coolidge's agony over the police strike, but Field gives no evidence of that. The text of Field's remarks is at the Calvin Coolidge Presidential Library and Museum, at the Forbes Library, in Northampton, Mass.

155 "I think you might find him some comfort": This line comes in a June 23, 1918, letter from Coolidge to his father in *Your Son, Calvin Coolidge: A Selection of Letters from Calvin Coolidge to His Father*, ed. Edward Connery Lathem (Montpelier, Vt.: Vermont Historical Society, 1968), 139.

155 "Governor getting tired": These details come from a letter describing Coolidge's summer calendar from Henry Follansbee Long to Coolidge's biographer, Claude Fuess. Henry F. Long to Claude M. Fuess, August 4, 1938, Fuess Collection, Calvin Coolidge Presidential Library and Museum, Forbes Library, Northampton, Mass.

156 The matter of jurisdiction was complicated: Coolidge lays out the subtleties in his autobiography, *The Autobiography of Calvin Coolidge* (New York: Cosmopolitan Book Corporation, 1929), 130.

156 More than a thousand police: Fifteen hundred policemen were involved; more than 1,100 walked out. This material, and more detail on the strike, can be found in Richard Lyons, "The Boston Police Strike of 1919," *New England Quarterly* 20, no. 2 (June 1947): 147–168.

156 The president of the R. H. Stearns Department Store: Many details about the Boston Police strike can be found in *Boston Police Records* 56 (January 1, 1919–December 31, 1919), Boston Public Library, Boston, Mass.

157 "Bay State Orations": Fuess, *Calvin Coolidge*, 235–236.

157 "Here was presented": "A Night of Terror and Riot," *Hampshire Gazette*, September 10, 1919.

158 At around 2:00 P.M. Wednesday, at the State Armory in West Newton, an alarm rang: Massachusetts State Guard, 11th Infantry Regiment, "A" Company, *Dates, Data and Ditties: Tour of Duty, "A" Company, 11th*

Regiment Infantry, Massachusetts State Guard, During the Strike of the Boston Police, Nineteen Hundred and Nineteen (Boston: The Company, 1920), 11. This short memoir of "A" Company gives many details on the guard side of the strike.

158 "nawsty": Ibid.

159 "As viewed here": "Troops in Boston; Washington Concerned," *The Christian Science Monitor*, September 12, 1919.

159 "The president suggests the advisability": Wilson's opinion, laid out by adviser James Tumulty, is republished in "President Orders Halt in Police Row," *The Washington Post*, September 11, 1919.

160 "Nothing doing": *Hampshire Gazette*, September 11, 1919.

161 "The police are all on strike": Jessie Woodrow Wilson Sayre to Woodrow Wilson, September 10, 1919, in *The Papers of Woodrow Wilson*, vol. 63, September–November 5, 1919, ed. Arthur S. Link and J. E. Little (Princeton, N.J.: Princeton University Press, 1990), 168.

161 Fifty-three officers: "Fatal Riot in Boston," *The Washington Post*, September 11, 1919, 1.

161 "The crowd laughed and hooted": "Rioting Is Renewed in Boston," *Hampshire Gazette*, September 11, 1919. This is an evening paper, but it was apparently reporting events on September 10.

161 a young man was killed: "State Guards Fire," *The Boston Globe*, September 11, 1919, 1.

163 The damage of the night of September 9: "$200,000 Loss by Lawless Mob," *The Boston Globe*, September 11, 1919.

166 All day long: The picture of Boston on September 11, 1919, is sketched in "One More Killing, but Rioting Is Stopped, Governor Takes Over Command in Boston: Henry Grote Is Shot Dead . . . No Action by Central Labor Union," *The Boston Globe*, September 12, 1919.

166 in case the sailors mutinied: "War Department Ready," *New York Tribune*, September 12, 1919.

167 "it has gone by": This letter from Storrow is quoted in Henry Greenleaf Pearson, *Son of New England: James Jackson Storrow, 1864–1926* (Boston: Thomas Todd Company, 1932), 233.

167 "The action of the police": *Daily Hampshire Gazette*, September 12, 1919. The *Gazette* was then an evening paper.

168 coming down on the Boston police: Wilson's turn is described by Admiral Cary Travers Grayson, his doctor, in a September 11 entry in his diary in Link and Little, eds., *The Papers of Woodrow Wilson*, vol. 63, September–November 5, 1919, 169.

168 "The American Federation of Labor": The *Wall Street Journal* editors wrote, "A policeman is a trustee of the lives and fortunes of other men. He should not at any time find himself penalized by the acceptance of his trust. This however is a secondary question, whatever ransom a successful police union might exact. No such union is tolerable under

a government of law. The American Federation of Labor is depriving the Law of its right hand and Mr. Wilson, by temporizing with the unionized, while he talks valiantly to Boston is hoisting the flag of surrender." "No Police Union Permissible," *The Wall Street Journal*, September 13, 1919.

169 *Boston Labor World*: Editorial, *Boston Labor World*, September 13, 1919, p. 8. At the time this book was written, that periodical was not available in digital form; this material was retrieved from microfiche at the Boston Public Library.

169 "Deeply appreciate": John L. Blair, *The Governorship of Calvin Coolidge, 1919–1921*, PhD dissertation, University of Chicago, 1971, vol. 2, p. 406.

170 "If the authorities give": "Gompers Appeals for Boston Police," *The New York Times*, September 14, 1919.

171 "REPLYING TO YOUR TELEGRAM": Blair, *The Governorship of Calvin Coolidge, 1919–1921*, vol. 2, pp. 407–408. The telegram is reprinted here with all the punctuation words; elsewhere, those are omitted.

171 The event was also a welcome home: "Coolidge, McCall, and Edwards Speak at Westfield's 250th Anniversary," *The Springfield Republican*, September 4, 1919.

172 "Shall we throw": Calvin Coolidge, *Have Faith in Massachusetts* (Boston: Houghton Mifflin, 1919), 207.

Chapter 7: The Reign of Law

173 "all that noble band": The responses of Reverend Cortland Myers, Reverend Edward Cummings, and Reverend Frank Haggard are described in "Dr. Alexander Mann Condemns Police," *The Boston Globe*, September 15, 1919.

173 Even the Catholic priests: The responses of Father Patterson and Father Burns appear in "South Boston Priests Condemn," *The Boston Globe*, September 15, 1919.

174 William Jennings Bryan spoke out: "Boston Riots Made William Jennings Bryan Wonder," *The Boston Globe*, September 17, 1919, 4.

174 "I knew you would": This letter to Elmer Slayton Newton is quoted in Robert Sobel, *Coolidge: An American Enigma* (Washington, D.C.: Regnery, 1998), 145.

175 That, Stearns hoped: R. H. Stearns Co. advertisement, *The Boston Globe*, September 15, 1919, 16.

175 Truman later recalled: This famous quote and the circumstances of Truman's business enterprise are described on the Harry S. Truman Library website at http://www.trumanlibrary.org/lifetimes/home.html.

175 "I want to say": Francis Russell, *A City in Terror: 1919, the Boston Police Strike* (New York: Viking Press, 1976), 200.

175 The horse, whose name: "Pals Meet on Tremont Street: 'Duffy' Police Horse Gives His Old Master a Joyful Greeting," *The Boston Globe*, September 17, 1919.

177 The laws ranged: Governor Coolidge to Herman Hormel, 6 Beacon Street, October 8, 1919, in Letters of Gov. Coolidge Compiled under the Direction of Claude Fuess, Calvin Coolidge Memorial Library, Forbes Library, Northampton, Mass.

177 "complete intellectual bankruptcy": Harold Nicolson, *Dwight Morrow* (London: Constable & Co., 1935), 242.

177 America would be "Russianized": "Blame Wilson for Labor's 'Insolence,'" *The Boston Globe*, September 22, 1919.

178 "quite remarkable": Calvin Coolidge to his father, postmarked September 22, 1919, in *Your Son, Calvin Coolidge: A Selection of Letters from Calvin Coolidge to His Father*, ed. Edward Connery Lathem (Montpelier, Vt.: Vermont Historical Society, 1968), 149.

178 Grace came to Boston: Ibid.

179 To Stearns, Morrow summed up: Cited in Nicolson, *Dwight Morrow*, 243.

180 "This was a service": Calvin Coolidge to John C. Coolidge, September 26, 1919, in Lathem, ed., *Your Son, Calvin Coolidge*, 150.

180 "You are to blame": Quoted in "Long Criticises Elevated Bill," *The Boston Globe*, October 3, 1919.

180 That hurt, because: On p. 30 of his autobiography, Coolidge makes his long-standing regret on that point clear: "I have always felt that I should have called out the State Guard as soon as the police left their posts."

181 Employers would give a lot: David Brody, *Labor in Crisis: The Steel Strike of 1919* (Philadelphia: Lippincott, 1965), 123.

181 "We have a petticoat government!": Donald Young, *American Roulette: The History and Dilemma of the Vice Presidency* (New York: Holt, Rinehart and Winston, 1965), 134.

181 "a strike against the American public": Governor Lowden is quoted saying this about a coal strike in "Governors Back the President," *The New York Times*, October 27, 1919, 1.

182 "It is a great event": Calvin Coolidge to John C. Coolidge, October 25, 1919, in Lathem, ed., *Your Son, Calvin Coolidge*, 154.

182 "We are facing": Quoted in "Law's Supremacy," *The Christian Science Monitor*, October 28, 1919.

182 "When this campaign is over": "Coolidge Hits at Trafficking with Disorder," *The Springfield Republican*, November 2, 1919, 2.

183 Long took the labor hotbed: John L. Blair, *The Governorship of Calvin Coolidge, 1919–1921*, PhD dissertation, University of Chicago, 1971, vol. 1, p. 220.

183 even in Suffolk County: Ibid., 231.

183 "victory for law and order": The full text of the telegram reads, "Hon. Calvin Coolidge, Boston, Mass. I congratulate you upon your election as a victory for law and order. When that is the issue all Americans must stand together. Woodrow Wilson." "Congratulations to Coolidge by Wilson," *The Boston Globe*, November 6, 1919.

183 Governor James Goodrich of Indiana: Ibid.

184 It featured Coolidge at the helm: Arthur Fleser, *A Rhetorical Study of the Speaking of Calvin Coolidge* (Lewiston, N.Y.: Edwin Mellen Press, 1990), 20.

184 "Catholics, Protestants and Hebrews": "Governor Names New State Boards," *The Boston Globe*, November 25, 1919.

184 "He shut himself away": "Baxter Derides Coolidge Boom," *The Boston Globe*, November 27, 1919.

185 On November 23: "Washington Is Stirred by the Hoax Perpetrated Here," *The Atlanta Constitution*, November 25, 1919. Mention of "Nearer, My God" is in "False Report of Death," *The Atlanta Constitution*, November 24, 1919.

186 "It sometimes seems": Barton's relationship with Coolidge is discussed in Kerry W. Buckley, "A President for the 'Great Silent Majority': Bruce Barton's Construction of Calvin Coolidge," *The New England Quarterly* 76, no. 4 (December 2003), 593–626.

186 "an army of pompous phrases": William G. McAdoo, *The Crowded Years: The Reminiscences of William G. McAdoo* (Boston: Houghton Mifflin, 1931), 389.

187 Lodge was recognizing Calvin Coolidge: Claude M. Fuess, *Calvin Coolidge: The Man from Vermont* (Boston: Little, Brown and Company, 1940), 241–242.

187 Coolidge wrote back: "Coolidge Won't Run for Vice President: Letters Declining Candidacy Are Made Public at Boston," *Columbus Ledger*, December 31, 1919.

187 "For present attainment": "For Present Attainment, for Future Hope; Gov. Coolidge Proclaims Thanksgiving," *The Boston Globe*, November 15, 1919 (display advertisement).

Chapter 8: Normalcy

189 "I have not been": "Coolidge Says He Is Not a Candidate," *The Boston Globe*, January 26, 1920.

189 "it took some time": John S. Merrill, "Politics and Politicians," *The Boston Globe*, February 1, 1920.

190 In February, John McInnes resigned: "McInnes Resigns," *The Boston Globe*, February 23, 1920.

190 Jobs remained scarce: "Hoover Out for Republican Nomination," *The New York Times*, March 31, 1920.

190 "relations between capital and labor": This quote and other positions of General Wood are laid out in a letter to voters, "How Wood Stands on Current Issues," *The New York Times*, February 25, 1920.

190 "250,000 useless jobs": "Johnson Demands Cut in Living Cost," *The New York Times*, February 16, 1920.

191 a budget law that would give more authority: Wilson vetoed the bill. "President Vetoes Bill as Unconstitutional," *The New York Times*, June 5, 1920.

191 "living in a fool's paradise": "W. P. G. Harding Dies," *The New York Times*, April 8, 1930.

191 "as bad as it was": "Wilson Wants Use of Secret Service in Profiteer Hunt," *The New York Times*, August 13, 1919.

191 "Isn't it a strange thing": This comment by Coolidge is cited by Bruce Barton in "The President Shouldn't Know Too Much," *The Real Calvin Coolidge* 2 (1986), 20.

192 "caused by tariffs": "A great and primary lesson for the United States is in a thorough understanding that this war was caused by tariffs." Clarence Barron, *The Audacious War* (Boston and New York: Houghton Mifflin), 173.

192 "Throughout these volumes": Harold Nicolson, *Dwight Morrow* (London: Constable & Co., 1935), 244.

192 "on the whole sound": Coolidge letter to Dwight Morrow of March 10, 1920, in Morrow Collection, Amherst College, Amherst, Mass.

192 "My observation": This quote appears and the correspondence between Coolidge and Morrow is described in Nicolson, *Dwight Morrow*, 244.

193 "the present is one": " 'Thrift Only Hope,' Gillett Declares," *The New York Times*, February 15, 1920.

193 The federal war debt: A good source for federal debt figures from 1900 is the U.S. Treasury, http://www.treasurydirect.gov/govt/reports/pd/histdebt/histdebt_histo3.htm.

193 "strike of capital": "Strike by Capital Predicted by Bache," *The New York Times*, June 30, 1920.

193 "the liquifaction of frozen loans": George F. Babbitt, " 'Round the Town," *The Boston Globe*, May 23, 1920.

194 a college student named Whittaker Chambers: Sam Tanenhaus, *Whittaker Chambers: A Biography* (New York: Random House, 1998).

195 he had just returned: *The Vermont Tribune*, May 13, 1922, reported that Governor Coolidge had been in Plymouth a few days before. The illness of Carrie Coolidge is also discussed in *Your Son, Calvin Coolidge: A Selection of Letters from Calvin Coolidge to His Father*, ed. Edward Connery Lathem (Montpelier, Vt.: Vermont Historical Society, 1968), 158.

195 "punishing those who charge": Quoted in "Wilson Target of G.O.P. Chiefs," *The Boston Globe*, May 15, 1920, 1.

195 "the false economics": This Harding line, slightly awkward, is reported ibid.

195 "If I lived in Massachusetts": Claude M. Fuess, *Calvin Coolidge: The Man from Vermont* (Boston: Little, Brown and Company, 1940), 249.

195 "America's present need": Frederick E. Schortemeier, *Rededicating America: Life and Recent Speeches of Warren G. Harding* (Indianapolis, Ind.: Bobbs-Merrill Company, 1920), 223–224.

196 Overall, the Missouri Lowden: "Lowden Money Paid to Delegates," *The New York Times*, June 2, 1920.

197 Lowden, it emerged: William T. Hutchinson, *Lowden of Illinois: The Life of Frank O. Lowden* (Chicago: University of Chicago Press, 1957), vol. 2, 440.

197 "Your letter of the 6th inst.": Quoted in Lathem, ed., *Your Son, Calvin Coolidge*, 163.

198 "Gov. Coolidge's friends": "Bay State Picks Delegates," *The Boston Globe*, April 27, 1920.

198 "About his cradle": Calvin Coolidge, "Lincoln Day Proclamation, January 30, 1919," in *Have Faith in Massachusetts* (Boston: Houghton Mifflin, 1919), 166.

199 "bosh": H. L. Mencken, *A Mencken Chrestomathy: His Own Selection of His Choicest Writing* (New York: Vintage, 1982), 409.

199 Lodge then presided: Karl Schriftgiesser, *The Gentleman from Massachusetts: Henry Cabot Lodge* (Boston: Atlantic Monthly Press/Little, Brown, and Company, 1944), 354.

200 there was even a photo: Nicolson, *Dwight Morrow*, 246.

200 "the smoke filled room": Raymond Clapper, the United Press reporter, is credited with the phrase in Stephen L. Vaughn, ed., *Encyclopedia of American Journalism* (New York: Routledge, 2008).

201 "whose name traveled": Quoted in Lathem, ed., *Your Son, Calvin Coolidge*, 167.

201 "He never at any time": James E. Watson, *As I Knew Them: Memoirs of James E. Watson, Former United States Senator from Indiana* (Indianapolis, Ind.: Bobbs-Merrill Company, 1936), 226.

201 It was as though: James Morgan, "Senator Harding's Nomination, Sweeping Old Guard Triumph," *The Boston Globe*, June 14, 1920.

202 "Some humble delegates": George Wharton Pepper, *Philadelphia Lawyer: An Autobiography* (Philadelphia: J. B. Lippincott, 1944), 136.

202 "Those who were at Chicago": Frank Stearns to Calvin Coolidge, March 21, 1921, Stearns Collection, Amherst College.

202 "Many of us feel however": Quoted in Nicolson, *Dwight Morrow*, 246.

203 "I have noticed": "Elks Make Harding a 'Surprise' Visit," *The New York Times*, July 21, 1920.

203 Coolidge would soon begin: *Omaha World Herald*, September 13, 1920.

203 Cox set out: John A. Morello, *Selling the President, 1920: Albert D. Lasker, Advertising, and the Election of Warren G. Harding* (Westport, Conn.: Praeger, 2001), 79.

203 "A good clean": "Gompers Glad Cox Was Named," *The New York Times*, July 7, 1920.

203 "Why the sneer": "Acceptance Speech of Governor Cox," *The Miami Herald*, August 8, 1920, p. 1.

203 "Have you harvested the fruits": The announcement in Vanzetti's pocket is reprinted in *The Letters of Sacco and Vanzetti*, ed. Gardner Jackson (New York, Penguin, 2007), 244.

204 Charles Ponzi: The response of Coolidge, while still governor, to market manipulation foreshadows his responses later as president. Coolidge believed that the states, rather than the federal government, should handle such troubles. See "Coolidge for Curb as Ponzi Sequel," *The New York Times*, August 19, 1920.

205 "I find the underlying thing": "Harding Men Aim to Shift League as Chief Issue," *The New York Times*, August 11, 1920.

205 "Women's ingrain silk stockings": *Boston Herald* advertisement, September 6, 1920.

205 The paper roasted Harding: The editors of another paper, *The Wyoming State Tribune*, reprinted part of *The Daily Star*'s erroneous editorial in "A Real Boomerang," July 19, 1920, 4.

205 Coolidge went to Portland: The text of his Portland speech is quoted and discussed in many papers, including "Coolidge's Criticism of League Cheered at Portland Rally," *Boston Herald*, September 9, 1920, 1.

206 "The first half": "Sees Only Straddle by Republicans," *The New York Times*, September 12, 1920.

206 "Judge nothing can prevent": Quoted in Robert K. Murray, *The Harding Era: Warren G. Harding and His Administration* (Minneapolis: University of Minnesota Press, 1969), 62.

207 "financial orgy": "Harding Demands Federal Economy," *The New York Times*, September 19, 1920.

207 One ticker: Beverly Gage, *The Day Wall Street Exploded: A Story of America in Its First Age of Terror* (New York: Oxford University Press, 2009), 36.

208 "You will make": Quoted in Morello, *Selling the President, 1920*, 92.

208 "Had he been": Calvin Coolidge to John C. Coolidge, October 8, 1920, in Latham, ed., *Your Son, Calvin Coolidge*, 169.

208 "I came to bury": William Allen White, *A Puritan in Babylon: The Story of Calvin Coolidge* (New York: Macmillan, 1938), 219.

208 The Germans, for example: Harold Jefferson Coolidge and Robert Howard Lord, *Archibald Cary Coolidge: Life and Letters* (Boston: Houghton Mifflin Company, 1932), 242.

209 "in this time": "Coolidge Agrees to Sit in Cabinet at Harding's Wish," *The New York Times*, December 17, 1920.

210 "oblivious to rank": Calvin Coolidge, *The Price of Freedom: Speeches and Addresses* (New York: C. Scribner's Sons, 1924), 13.

210 "The universal demand": 1924 Republican Party Platform, American Presidency Project at University of California/Santa Barbara.

211 "The finance success": "Harding's Cabinet All That Could Be Desired," *The Wall Street Journal*, March 1, 1921, 1.

213 "Mr. Coolidge, a medium-sized man": Henry Fountain Ashurst, *A Many-Colored Toga*, ed. George F. Sparks (Tucson: University of Arizona Press, 1962), 137.

213 "I take up": Coolidge, *The Price of Freedom*, p. 34.

213 "By Calvin Coolidge Jr.": "My Impressions," *Boston Sunday Advertiser*, March 5, 1921.

214 "Owing to mechanical device": "President Pledges to Restore Ideals of Our Fathers," *The Washington Post*, March 5, 1921.

214 Someone suggested to Coolidge: Robert H. Ferrell, *The Strange Deaths of President Harding* (Columbia: University of Missouri Press, 1998), 109.

215 "He could smoke": Watson, *As I Knew Them*, 226.

215 Mellon would have to take his oath: The fact that Mellon was sworn in first is reported in "Mellon Takes Oath and Begins Work," *The Boston Globe*, March 5, 1921; the fact that the oath was deemed invalid is reported in David Cannadine, *Mellon: An American Life* (New York: Knopf, 2006), 272.

Chapter 9: "A Most Insignificant Office"

216 The coat and tails lay: The specific suite number is available in Cynthia D. Bittinger, *Grace Coolidge: Sudden Star*, Presidential Wives Series (New York: Nova History Publications, 2005), 43.

216 These were the overalls: The comparison of dress clothing to overalls in Coolidge's service as vice president is made in Edward Lowry, *Washington Close-ups: Intimate Views of Some Public Figures* (New York: Republic Books, 1930), 24.

216 "to distinctly subordinate": The quote on the intent to keep Union Station low can be found in "Building Height Limitation Staff Report of the Committee on the District of Columbia, U.S. House of Representatives," April 1, 1976, p. 2.

216 "Imagine five hundred or more women": Quoted in William McAdoo, *Crowded Years: The Reminiscences of William G. McAdoo* (Boston: Houghton Mifflin, 1931), 263.

217 "putting all celebration aside": Warren G. Harding, telegram to Edward B. McLean, Evalyn Walsh McLean Papers, Manuscript Division, Library of Congress, Washington, D.C.

217 Three long tables: Evalyn Walsh McLean describes the dinner in detail, as well as Coolidge's stomachache, in Evalyn Walsh McLean, *Father Struck It Rich* (Fort Collins, Colo.: First Light Publishing, 1996), 192.

217 "Let 'em look in": Robert K. Murray, *The Harding Era: Warren G. Harding and His Administration* (Minneapolis: University of Minnesota Press, 1969), 113.

217 the tails of six quadrupeds: A photo featuring Mrs. Harding's furs in the inaugural can be found in the Library of Congress American Memory Collection, National Photo Company Collection, no. 12443, 2.

217 Edward McLean's efforts: A wonderful account of Washington from the point of view of the McLeans, including the story of the *Enquirer*'s endorsement, can be found in McLean, *Father Struck It Rich*, 184.

218 Grace won the general over: Much material on Grace's time, including this discussion with Pershing, can be found in Ishbel Ross, *Grace Coolidge and Her Era* (Plymouth, Vt.: Calvin Coolidge Memorial Foundation, 1988).

218 the lack of formality: Coolidge described his experience of the inauguration in his autobiography. Calvin Coolidge, *The Autobiography of Calvin Coolidge* (New York: Cosmopolitan Book Corporation, 1929), 156–158.

219 "So the fellow": Quoted in Ben Yagoda, *Will Rogers: A Biography* (New York: Knopf, 1993), 189.

220 Washingtonians noted approvingly: A good sketch of Grace, including this quote and others, can be found in Ross, *Grace Coolidge and Her Era*.

220 That Grace deemed unfair: Robert Ferrell, *Grace Coolidge: The People's Lady in Silent Cal's White House* (Lawrence: University Press of Kansas, 2008), 52.

220 "This way": Grace Coolidge, *Grace Coolidge: An Autobiography*, ed. Lawrence E. Wikander and Robert H. Ferrell (Worland, Wyo.: High Plains Publishing, 1992), 59.

220 In a letter to Foster Stearns: Ross, *Grace Coolidge and Her Era*, 66.

221 "You lose": This anecdote is retold often, and the fact that Grace herself retold it is reported in Ross, *Grace Coolidge and Her Era*, 162.

222 Harry Daugherty was there: Good photos of the cabinet can be found at the Library of Congress, Prints and Records Division.

222 the board of the Federal Reserve: The Federal Reserve System as created by the 1913 Federal Reserve Act differed from the modern system in that the Treasury secretary and the comptroller of the currency sat on the Fed board. A good short history of the Fed, Roger T. Johnson, "Historical Beginnings . . . The Federal Reserve," is at http://www.bos .frb.org/about/pubs/begin.pdf.

222 no "stallion dollar": Lowry, *Washington Close-ups*, 179.

223 "The Senate would do": Coolidge, *The Autobiography of Calvin Coolidge*, 162.

224 Grace and Calvin, Jr., popped corn: Margaret Jane Fischer, *Calvin Coolidge, Jr., 1908–1924* (Plymouth Notch, Vt.: Calvin Coolidge Memorial Foundation, 1981), 14.

225 Beside his bed was a table: The *Michigan Library Bulletin* of September 1923 contains an article on the vice president's reading material. Included on Coolidge's reading list are the Bible, fifteen volumes on the tariff, several volumes on the U.S. Constitution, Bridgeman's *New England*, and *A Prophet of Universal Peace*, a biography of Whitelaw Reid. See "What Coolidge Reads," *The Michigan Library Bulletin* 14, no. 4 (1923), 12.

226 "Fellow workers": Charles G. Dawes, *The First Year of the Budget of the United States* (New York: Harper and Brothers, 1923), 5–6.

226 Harding backed up: An example of Harding's economy by executive order was his December 1921 order that employees at the Panama Canal be charged for their own rent and fuel. "Orders Panama Economy," *The New York Times*, December 18, 1921.

227 Mrs. Harding, called "the Duchess": Alice Roosevelt Longworth mentioned the nickname in her interview with Michael Teague in Alice Roosevelt Longworth and Michael Teague, *Mrs. L.: Conversations with Alice Roosevelt Longworth* (Garden City, N.Y.: Doubleday, 1981), 170.

227 "the general atmosphere": Ibid., 170.

227 golf cabinet: References to the "golf cabinet" are in articles such as "Two Members of Harding Golf Cabinet Are Being Voted On," *Fort Worth Star-Telegram*, June 19, 1922.

227 poker cabinet: The papers politely avoided writing about the poker cabinet during Harding's tenure, but staff members and presidential historians have noted its existence, as in James W. Davis, *American Presidency* (Westport, Conn.: Praeger Press, 1995), 199.

227 The poker cabinet averaged: Irwin Hood Hoover, *Forty-two Years in the White House* (Boston: Houghton Mifflin, 1934), 250.

228 Norris deemed this slipup: The story is told in Donald R. McCoy, *Calvin Coolidge: The Quiet President* (New York: Macmillan, 1967), 135, and also in the Senate biography of Coolidge, "Calvin Coolidge, 29th Vice President," http://www.jcp.senate.gov/artandhistory/history/common/generic/VP_Calvin_Coolidge.htm.

229 "One of his favorite": George W. Pepper, *Philadelphia Lawyer: An Autobiography* (New York: Lippincott, 1944), 149.

229 The articles were remarkably: Calvin Coolidge, "Enemies of the Republic," *The Delineator*, June 1921.

230 "I am not qualified to discuss educational matters": Coolidge letter to Dwight Morrow, May 16, 1914, Coolidge correspondence, Dwight W. Morrow Collection, Amherst College Archive, Amherst, Mass.

230 "It tends to bring about": "A Teapot Tempest," editorial, *The Anaconda Standard*, May 30, 1921.

231 "Only the most polished finesse": The *Los Angeles Times* wrote of "scenes of disorder and near violence never paralleled within the memory of the oldest senator." "Bonus Bill Is Beaten: McCumber and Reed Are Near Battle While Coolidge Stands Powerless," *Los Angeles Times*, July 16, 1921.

231 "I love every stick": Quoted in Cynthia D. Bittinger, *Grace Coolidge: Sudden Star*, Presidential Wives Series (New York: Nova History Publications, 2005), 44.

231 That summer Coolidge: "Coolidge Appoints Neighbor's Son," *Springfield Republican*, July 16, 1921; and "Other Half Knows Little of Life on Coolidge Side," *The Advocate*, March 30, 1929. Thomas Plummer returned to civilian life after several years at West Point.

232 "liked it because": Coolidge's church habits are detailed in Jason Noble Pierce, "Coolidge's Past Got Invitations to Dinner at the White House," *Baltimore Afro-American*, February 18, 1933.

232 Grace became a fan: Ross, *Grace Coolidge and Her Era*, 149.

233 President Harding changed the policy: "Resolutions of League," *Good Government*, vol. 37–39 (1921).

233 On top of his note: Calvin Coolidge to Frank W. Stearns, September 28, 1921, Stearns Family Papers, College of the Holy Cross, Worcester, Mass.

235 Kinsley asked Coolidge: Earle S. Kinsley, *Recollections of Vermonters in State and National Affairs* (Rutland, Vt.: privately printed, 1946), 117.

235 "he can differentiate": Frank W. Stearns to Calvin Coolidge, December 29, 1921, Stearns Family Papers, College of the Holy Cross, Worcester, Mass.

236 "Secretary Mellon is a businessman": "Dawes Waves Brooms in Wrath," *The Washington Post*, February 4, 1922.

236 On February 16: Frank W. Stearns, telegram to Calvin Coolidge, February 16, 1922, Stearns Family Papers, College of the Holy Cross, Worcester, Mass.

237 When Coolidge discussed: Barron transcribed his interviews in his notebooks in the voice of the person he interviewed. This quotation in regard to Coolidge's question can be found in the August 25, 1921, entry in Clarence Barron, *They Told Barron: Conversations and Revelations of an American Pepys in Wall Street*, ed. Arthur Pound and Samuel Taylor Moore (New York: Harper and Brothers, 1930), 247. Barron's accessible writings offer wonderful insights into the workings of the financial world.

237 "were very much pleased": Frank W. Stearns to Calvin Coolidge, January 20, 1922, Stearns Family Papers, College of the Holy Cross, Worcester, Mass.

237 "I came away": Frank W. Stearns to Calvin Coolidge, March 16, 1922, Stearns Family Papers, College of the Holy Cross, Worcester, Mass.

237 "It makes me": Ibid.

237 "Your letters all received": This angry letter from 1922 to Stearns from Coolidge is cited in Claude M. Fuess, *Calvin Coolidge: The Man from Vermont* (Westport, Conn.: Greenwood Press, 1976), 303.

239 Clarence Barron commented: Barron reckoned that in 1917 3 million barrels of the Mexican Petroleum Company's oil went to New England and 3 million to Standard Oil of New Jersey, whereas only 4 million went to South America. Clarence Walker Barron, *The Mexican Problem* (New York: Houghton Mifflin, 1917), 92.

241 I have heard from: Douglas Wilson, *Passages of Time: Narratives in the History of Amherst College* (Amherst, Mass: Amherst College Press, 2007), 148.

241 "He does not understand": Quoted in Douglas C. Wilson, "The Story in the Meiklejohn Files II: Finals Showdown," ibid.,122.

241 Meiklejohn was establishing: The details of the classes were laid out a year later in "Crisis at Amherst," *Springfield Republican*, June 14, 1923.

241 the strike was taking: "Strikes Halt Trend of Business Upward," *The New York Times*, July 17, 1922.

241 On September 1: "Daugherty Obtains Order," *The New York Times*, September 2, 1922.

241 "pet": "Judge Is Daugherty 'Pet,' Says Gompers," *The New York Times*, September 12, 1922.

242 But Harding vetoed: A good guide to all presidential vetoes can be found in "Summary of Bills Vetoed, 1789–Present," www.senate.gov/reference/Legislation/Vetoes/vetoCounts.htm.

242 Lodge bitterly tore: Karl Schriftgiesser, *The Gentleman from Massachusetts: Henry Cabot Lodge* (Boston: Atlantic Monthly Press/Little, Brown and Company, 1944), 357.

242 "I wish they would": Ibid., 359.

243 Grace, who had become: "Dance Giving Is Popular in Society in Washington," *The Oregonian*, December 17, 1922.

243 As Harding thought over: Mrs. Harding's illness is described at length in Carl Sferrazza Anthony, *Florence Harding: The First Lady, the Jazz Age, and the Death of America's Most Scandalous President* (New York: William Morrow, 1998).

243 "The commissioner of pensions": Harding's veto statement, which included the mention of the billions, is reprinted in "Harding Veto Halts Big Pension Outlay Under Bursum Bill," *The New York Times*, January 4, 1923.

244 "The simple fact": James E. Watson, *As I Knew Them: Memoirs of James E. Watson, Former United States Senator from Indiana* (Indianapolis, Ind.: Bobbs-Merrill Company, 1936), 226.

245 "From the present viewpoint": Quoted in New England Historical Society's spring conference talk by Cynthia D. Bittinger, the author of *Grace Coolidge: Sudden Star.*

246 "It was William Harding": This quotation and analysis of the Federal Reserve under Harding are in "Men in Wall Street's Eye: Introducing Mr. Daniel Richard Crissinger," *Barron's,* February 5, 1923.

246 Daniel Crissinger: In 1923, W. P. G. Harding assumed the post of president of the Federal Reserve Bank of Boston. Crissinger was appointed and confirmed over the winter of 1922–1923. The editors of *Barron's* tried to imagine what Harding would say if he were explaining the Crissinger appointment to the top job at the Federal Reserve, concluding, "The financiers want W.P.G. Harding renamed, while the agricultural bloc in the Senate promise no end of trouble for me in the event I reappoint him." "Men in Wall Street's Eye: Introducing Mr. Daniel Richard Crissinger," *Barron's,* February 5, 1923.

246 Mellon was not pleased: David Cannadine, *Mellon: An American Life* (New York: Knopf, 2006), 282.

247 "Not in rewards": "Mrs. Calvin Coolidge," *Rockford Morning Star,* July 29, 1923.

247 "by thinking, they meant": This quotation comes from Robert Frost to Louis Untermeyer, August 12, 1924, in *The Letters of Robert Frost to Louis Untermeyer,* ed. Louis Untermeyer (New York: Holt, Rinehart and Winston, 1963), 170.

248 The event took place: Harold Nicolson, *Dwight Morrow* (London: Constable & Co., 1935), 267.

248 Meiklejohn indeed did not go quietly: "Meiklejohn Resigns Amherst Headship," *The New York Times,* June 20, 1923. The trustees offered Meiklejohn a chair after a year of leave.

248 Three out of twenty-nine: Details of the fight are laid out in Nicolson, *Dwight Morrow.*

249 Coolidge counseled postponement: "It is interesting to note that in the multiplicity of his vacation engagements to deliver addresses, he has found time to attend a meeting of the People's Institute, to deliver an address at the fiftieth anniversary celebration of a little village savings bank, to be interviewed as to the advisability of the city's erecting a new city hall—Mr. Coolidge advised waiting. . . ." "Personalities," *Barron's,* May 28, 1923.

250 The reporters visited: "Coolidge Sure of Harding's Recovery," *Springfield Daily Republican,* August 1, 1923.

251 "Harding Gains": "Harding Gains," *The New York Times,* August 2, 1923.

Chapter 10: The Budget

254 The meetings took place: The dates and times of Coolidge's meetings with General Lord and other officials are in his appointment books, Calvin Coolidge Papers, series 4, box 4, 289–291, Manuscript Division, Library of Congress, Washington, D.C.

254 "necessary": "Necessary" appears beside General Lord's name in the presidential appointment book of August 13, 1923. Calvin Coolidge Papers, series 4, box 4:, 289–91, Manuscript Division, Library of Congress, Washington, D.C. According to that book, Coolidge's first four White House meetings with Lord took place on August 13 ("necessary") and September 14, 21, and 28.

255 "I am going to try": Calvin Coolidge to Frank Stearns, quoted in Robert Ferrell, *The Presidency of Calvin Coolidge* (Lawrence: University Press of Kansas, 1998), 24.

255 "practical affairs of his day": Carl Schurz, *Abraham Lincoln: An Essay, with an Introduction by Calvin Coolidge* (Boston: Houghton Mifflin, 1920), iv.

256 "I don't know what I would do without her": Calvin Coolidge to John C. Coolidge, June 6, 1921, in *Your Son, Calvin Coolidge: A Selection of Letters from Calvin Coolidge to His Father*, ed. Edward Connery Lathem (Montpelier, Vt.: Vermont Historical Society, 1968), 181.

256 "close the ranks": Quoted in Claude Fuess, *Calvin Coolidge: The Man from Vermont* (Boston: Little, Brown, 1940), 321.

256 Coolidge received Samuel Gompers: Samuel Gompers, memorandum, August 6, 1923, in *The Samuel Gompers Papers*, ed. Peter J. Albert and Grace Palladino, vol. 12, *The Last Years, 1922–1924* (Urbana: University of Illinois Press, 2010), 296–299.

256 "a good talk": S. Parker Gilbert to Andrew Mellon, August 4, 1923, box 27, cables 1923, Central Files of the Office of the Secretary of the Treasury, National Archives and Record Administration II, College Park, Md.

257 "She is very nice": Quoted in Ishbel Ross, *Grace Coolidge and Her Era: The Story of a President's Wife* (Plymouth, Vt.: Calvin Coolidge Memorial Foundation, 1988), 84.

258 "Forget it": Mellon told Senator George W. Pepper that Coolidge said this. George W. Pepper, *In the Senate* (New York: Ayer, 1974), 93.

258 "I would like": Quoted in Cynthia D. Bittinger, *Grace Coolidge: Sudden Star*, Presidential Wives Series (New York: Nova History Publications, 2005), 58.

258 "Good Morning, Colonel Starling": Quoted in Edmund W. Starling with Thomas Sugrue, *Starling of the White House: The Story of the Man Whose Secret Service Detail Guarded Five Presidents from Woodrow Wilson to Franklin D. Roosevelt* (New York: Simon and Schuster, 1946), 204.

258 "I want you yourself": Quoted in William Allen White, *A Puritan in Babylon: The Story of Calvin Coolidge* (New York: Macmillan Company, 1938), 247.

259 "We are going": President Calvin Coolidge's Unpublished Press Conferences, August 21, 1923, vol. 1, p. 00002, Calvin Coolidge Presidential Library and Museum, Forbes Library, Northampton, Mass.

259 In the morning light: Richard C. Garvey, "The Night the President Met the Burglar," *Los Angeles Times*, August 6, 1983. Later the burglar did pay back Coolidge's $32 loan.

259 "Just now it occurred": Quoted in Bittinger, *Grace Coolidge*, 54.

260 The Coolidges took: Elizabeth Jaffray, *Secrets of the White House* (New York: Cosmopolitan Book Corporation, 1927), 100–101.

260 Coolidge walked around quietly: Starling, *Starling of the White House*, 207.

261 Coolidge, more relaxed: George Wharton Pepper, *Philadelphia Lawyer: An Autobiography* (Philadelphia: J. B. Lippincott, 1944), 196.

261 You sit right here: The remarkable Fox News motion picture footage of Coolidge's first cabinet meeting, including Coolidge's gesture to Mellon, is in the National Archives, 88843. National Archives and Records Administration—ARC Identifier 88843/Local Identifier AAS-AAS–112.

262 on September 15: "Reductions of $40,000,000 to $50,000,000 Are Agreed To; Cut in Veterans Bureau," *The New York Times*, September 16, 1923.

263 Allen Treadway: "Seeks Legislation on Hard Coal Costs: Massachusetts Representative Asks Coolidge to Call Session," *The New York Times*, September 21, 1923.

263 "get rid of Daugherty": Claudius O. Johnson, *Borah of Idaho* (New York: Longmans, Green, and Co., 1936), 288.

263 "if he makes good": "Borah Sees Coolidge as Logical Nominee," *The New York Times*, August 12, 1923.

263 Middlebury College: "Middlebury Sends Tree to Coolidge," *The New York Times*, December 13, 1923.

263 with electric lights: The National Park Service has documented the history of White House trees, from this tree at the Ellipse to its successor at Sherman Square, at www.nps.gov/whho/historyculture/history-of-the-national-christmas-trees.htm.

265 "what the traffic will bear": Andrew Mellon, *Taxation: The People's Business*, (New York: Macmillan, 1924), 16.

266 "fruitfulness": Coolidge's Thanksgiving Proclamation of 1923, University of California/Santa Barbara Presidential Project.

266 Bursum, the great: "Lawmakers Express Views on Tax Cuts," *The New York Times*, November 17, 1923.

267 the Italian ambassador: These appointments, along with many others with foreign dignitaries, are listed in the president's appointment book.

267 David Lloyd George: "Coolidge Very Glad Lloyd George Came," *The New York Times*, October 28, 1923.

268 Ashurst noted: Henry Fountain Ashurst, *A Many-Colored Toga*, ed. George F. Sparks (Tucson: University of Arizona Press, 1962), 205.

270 "The president of the United States": Jaffray, *Secrets of the White House*, 98.

270 Mrs. Coolidge sent: Ibid., 100.

271 "It really was": James E. Watson, *As I Knew Them: Memoirs of James E. Watson, Former United States Senator from Indiana* (Indianapolis, Ind.: Bobbs-Merrill Company, 1936), 236.

271 A packed House of Representatives: "House Applauds Message," *The New York Times*, December 7, 1923.

272 Coolidge had taken the time to write out: "Coolidge's Views on Taxation in His Own Handwriting," *The Springfield Republican*, December 7, 1923.

272 League of Nations—topic closed: The full text of the president's remarkable First Annual Message of December 6, 1923, is at www.presidency.ucsb.edu/ws/index.php?pid=29564.

275 "In no sense": Quoted in Bittinger, *Grace Coolidge*, 110.

276 "I have to furnish": Starling, *Starling of the White House*, 212.

276 "I told 'em to scrap it": Edward G. Lowry, *Washington Close-ups: Intimate Views of Some Public Figures* (Boston: Houghton Mifflin, 1921), 159.

277 "abnormally high": Mellon, *Taxation: The People's Business*, 178.

278 "a new kind of meeting": *Addresses of the President of the United States and the Director of the Bureau of the Budget at the Sixth Regular Meeting of the Business Organization of the Government at Memorial Continental Hall, January 21, 1924* (Washington, D.C.: U.S. Government Printing Office, 1924), 1.

278 "We have you beaten": "Longworth Defies Backers of Bonus to Delay Tax Vote: 'We Have You Beaten' He Tells Soldiers Who Demand Priority; GOP Leaders Sure of Program as Set," *The Washington Post*, January 9, 1924.

279 Joseph Robinson: "Democrats Draft Own Plan to Slash Small Taxes More," *The New York Times*. January 6, 1924.

279 but Woodrow Wilson: "Robinson for Tax Cut: Says Father of Reduction Is Not Mellon, but Wilson," *The New York Times*, January 6, 1924.

280 "No, don't do that": Merlo J. Pusey, *Charles Evans Hughes* (New York: Columbia University Press, 1964), 2: 565.

280 "He greatly delayed": Herbert Hoover, *The Memoirs of Herbert Hoover: The Cabinet and the Presidency, 1920–1933* (New York: Macmillan, 1952), 54.

283 "Well, Doctor," he said: Milton F. Heller, *The Presidents' Doctor: An Insider's View of Three First Families* (New York: Vantage Press, 2000), 87.

283 "She was his queen": "She was his queen and he wanted to give her everything and do anything for her," Lillian Rogers Parks, *My Thirty Years Backstairs at the White House* (New York: Fleet Publishing Corp., 1961), 183.

283 Coolidge loved the cap: The story is told by Wilson Brown, a navy aide, in *Meet Calvin Coolidge: The Man Behind the Myth*, ed. Edward Connery Lathem (Brattleboro, Vt.: Stephen Greene Press, 1960), 107.

283 "Aye, aye, sir.": Typescript of Joel T. Boone's unpublished memoir, XXI–101, Container 46, Joel T. Boone Papers, Manuscript Division, Library of Congress, Washington, D.C.

284 "You tell ol' man Davis": Starling, *Starling of the White House*, 209.

284 Stone replaced him: Athan G. Theoharis and John Stuart Cox, *The Boss: J. Edgar Hoover and the Great American Inquisition* (Philadelphia: Temple University Press, 1988), 84.

285 "Please have an analysis": Calvin Coolidge to Andrew Mellon, April 24, 1924, series 1, box 21, Calvin Coolidge Papers, Manuscript Division, Library of Congress, Washington, D.C.

286 "I need to find": Calvin Coolidge to Frederick Allis, May 9, 1924, Box 4 Folder 20, Coolidge Collection, Amherst College.

286 the Senate sustained: Coolidge's veto was sustained by the Senate 53–28 on May 13, 1924. A record of all the vetoes and congressional responses can be found in "Presidential Vetoes, 1789–1988," S. Pub. 102-12, available at online reference pages of the U.S. Senate, at senate.gov/reference.

287 the house voted 306 to 58: "Huge Votes for Exclusion," *The New York Times*, May 16, 1924, 1.

287 "get out in the open": "Mrs. Coolidge Submits to Treatment," *Daily Hampshire Gazette*, May 22, 1924.

288 His position now: Calvin Coolidge, *The Mind of the President as Revealed by Himself in His Own Words: President Coolidge's Views on Public Questions Selected and Arranged by Subjects*, ed. C. Bascom Slemp (Garden City, N.Y.: Doubleday, Page & Co., 1926), 222.

289 *The Wall Street Journal* : "A Tax Bill for Veto," *The Wall Street Journal*, May 23, 1924.

289 "hazing the president": "To put it shortly, the Senate has spent some valuable months in what can only be described as hazing the President. In the point of view of even the Republican members of his party Mr. Coolidge was the accident of an accident. . . . Mr. Coolidge is not a vindictive man, but he is too sound and competent a politician not to have a good memory." "Hazing the President," *The Wall Street Journal*, May 17, 1924.

290 2,517 clerks would have to be hired: "General Davis said the war department was adding 2,517 clerks." "Asks $131,943,138 to Meet Bonus Cost," *The New York Times*, May 31, 1924.

291 by a ratio of 250 to one: "Coolidge Beats Lodge in Poll on the Bonus," *The New York Times*, May 26, 1924.

291 The big powers like Hearst and Ford: "Mr. Hearst wants to support Coolidge if he can. He was in favor of Mellon's tax bill." Hearst General Manager Frederick Dumaine, taken down by Clarence Barron on June 24, 1924, and published in Clarence Barron, *They Told Barron: Conversations and Revelations of an American Pepys in Wall Street*, ed. Arthur Pound and Samuel Taylor Moore (New York: Harper and Brothers, 1930), 254.

291 "Who Made Coolidge?": The text of the editorial, which won the 1924 Pulitzer Prize, is in the *Boston Herald*, May 18, 1924, p. 12.

292 "without reasons": "Text of the President's Statement Criticizing Provisions of Tax Law," *The New York Times*, June 3, 1924.

292 "The postal service": The text of President Coolidge's veto message is in "President Warns Congress," *The New York Times*, June 8, 1924.

293 Hoover, however, fought: Hoover, *The Memoirs of Herbert Hoover: The Cabinet and the Presidency, 1920–1933*, 56.

294 "Just then it seemed": Charles G. Dawes, *Notes as Vice President, 1928–1929* (Boston: Little, Brown, and Company, 1935), 18.

295 "Pandemonium Breaks Loose": *Daily Register Gazette*, July 2, 1924.

296 On June 30, John and Calvin: Typescript of Joel T. Boone's unpublished memoir, XXI–200, Container 46, Joel T. Boone Papers, Manuscript Division, Library of Congress, Washington, D.C.

296 "We are often told": *Addresses of the President of the United States and the Director of the Bureau of the Budget at the Seventh Regular Meeting of the Business Organization of the Government at Memorial Continental Hall, June 30, 1924* (Washington, D.C.: U.S. Government Printing Office, 1924), 1.

296 "Our item of expense": The text on pencils was written by his assistant director, R. O. Kloeber. The full text reads, "The bureau has given special attention to economy in this direction. Only one pencil at a time is now issued to any one and he is expected to turn in the unused portion of the last one received. The results justify the practice. Our item of expense for pencils is materially less." *Third Annual Report of the Director of the Bureau of the Budget to the President of the United States, July 1, 1924* (Washington, D.C.: U.S. Government Printing Office, 1924), 217.

297 In the box, Calvin, Jr., smiled: Margaret Jane Fischer, *Calvin Coolidge, Jr.* (Plymouth Notch, Vt.: Calvin Coolidge Memorial Foundation, 1981), 19.

297 "Mac, Mac, Mac": "M'Adoo Brings Up Reserves," *The New York Times*, July 3, 1924.

298 Calvin, Jr., also had a fever.: XXI–200, 201 Joel T. Boone papers. Library of Congress, Washington, D.C. Dr. Boone's papers convey much material about the Coolidges and their health.

299 CALVIN STILL CRITICALLY ILL: Telegram to Mrs. R. B. Hills, Box 18, Folder 15, Forbes Library. The telegram was sent on July 5 at 1:49 P.M.

300 CALVINS CONDITION STILL CRITICAL: Telegram to Mrs. R. B. Hills, sent at 8:30 A.M. July 7, 1924.

300 the tank exploded: XXI–207, Joel T. Boone papers, Library of Congress, Washington, D.C.

300 which Colonel Coolidge also heard: That Colonel Coolidge did listen to the announcement on the radio is referred to in a letter in Leonard Bates, *Senator Thomas J. Walsh of Montana* (Champaign: University of Illinois Press, 1999), 245.

300 A low moan: The reaction of the Democratic National Convention to the news of the death of Calvin, Jr., is described in a remarkable unsigned editorial in *The New York Times*: "Their sorrows are his, as he frequently testifies, but in an especial sense his are also theirs." "The President's Son," *The New York Times*, July 9, 1924, p. 18.

Chapter 11: The Siege and the Spruce

301 the spruce from the old limekiln lot: The transplanting of the tree from the limekiln lot to the White House grounds, its location, and the fact that she thought of creating a plaque for it are all described by Grace in an undated letter marked "Monday" to Therese Hills, August–September 1924, Hills Collection, Box 17 MS 17–6, Forbes Library. She wrote that one could see the tree "from the president's room." The fate of the tree could not be discovered by the author; Grace Coolidge planted many symbolic and commemorative trees over the course of her life in Washington.

302 "When I look out": Claude Fuess quotes Scandrett as saying this in Claude M. Fuess, *Calvin Coolidge: The Man from Vermont* (Westport, Conn.: Greenwood Press, 1976), 351.

302 Had Coolidge not: Coolidge supplies this logic in his autobiography.

302 "It is hard to see": Calvin Coolidge, "What It Means to Be a Boy Scout," in *Foundations of the Republic: Speeches and Addresses* (New York: Scribner, 1926), 68.

303 he ordered others: In 1953, Grace wrote to John, "Father ordered his stone and Calvin's at the time of your brother's death and had a blank place left for the date of his own death. He also had a piece of matching granite reserved . . . for my grave," quoted in Cynthia D. Bittinger, *Grace Coolidge: Sudden Star*, Presidential Wives Series (New York: Nova History Publications, 2005).

303 "if he had lived," Fuess, *Calvin Coolidge*, 351.

304 "economic thumbscrews": Nancy C. Unger, *Fighting Bob La Follette: The Righteous Reformer* (Chapel Hill: University of North Carolina Press, 2000), 300.

304 "inexpressible disgust": Quoted ibid., 292.

305 Young Robert La Follette: Adam R. Nelson, *Education and Democracy: The Meaning of Alexander Meiklejohn, 1872–1964* (Madison: University of Wisconsin Press, 2001), 137.

305 "but in the making": Unger, *Fighting Bob La Follette*, 293.

306 a funny, rueful poem: John Coolidge's poem is posted on the wall of the cheese factory site in Plymouth Notch today.

306 "If there had been no war": This insightful statement is quoted in "Coolidge Upholds Farm Cooperation," *The New York Times*, January 6, 1925.

307 "Made for and used": "Coolidge Gives Ford Bucket," *Springfield Republican*, August 21, 1924.

307 "My father had it": Quoted in Ishbel Ross, *Grace Coolidge and Her Era: the Story of a President's Wife* (Plymouth, Vt.: Calvin Coolidge Memorial Foundation, 1988), 132. The story of the gift of the sap bucket was carried in many papers, including "Coolidge Gift of Sap Bucket," *Register Gazette*, August 19, 1924.

308 Coolidge's great-grandparents: "Site of Kin's Graves," *San Diego Union*, June 1, 1928. Coolidge paid for new headstones for Israel and Sally Brewer and corresponded at length in regard to the headstones; he paid for perpetual care of Lot 48, where the Brewers lay, as well. Records of Hampden town cemetery, folders 1–3, personal files 73, Forbes Library.

309 "My hearing ain't as good": Charles G. Dawes, *Notes as Vice President, 1928–1929* (Boston: Little, Brown, and Company, 1935), 24.

309 The White House did not often: Ross, *Grace Coolidge and Her Era*, 133.

309 The Coolidges were still: Calvin Coolidge, *The Autobiography of Calvin Coolidge* (New York: Cosmopolitan Book Corporation, 1929), 208.

313 "My dear John": Calvin Coolidge to John Coolidge, September 24, 1924, Calvin Coolidge Presidential Library and Museum, Forbes Library, Northampton, Mass.

313 several thousand druggists: Coolidge's speech to the National Association of Retail Druggists was reported in "Coolidge Pledges Economy at Home and Peace Abroad," *The New York Times*, September 25, 1924. The full text is in "President Pledges Aids," *The Washington Post*, September 25, 1924.

313 The Coolidge-Dawes Caravan: "Coolidge Caravan Starts on Long Tour," *The New York Times*, September 10, 1924.

313 "I was amazed": This letter is quoted in Alvin Felzenberg, "Calvin Coolidge and Race," 1988, Calvin Coolidge Memorial Foundation website. The controversy is also described in many newspaper articles, for example, "Coolidge to Defense of Negro Candidate," *The Plain Dealer* (Topeka, Kansas), August 15, 1924.

314 "I want you to know": Calvin Coolidge, "Discriminating Benevolence," in *Foundations of the Republic*, 172.

315 "really consists of": Harvey O'Connor, *Mellon's Millions: The Biography of a Fortune; the Life and Times of Andrew W. Mellon* (New York: John Day Company, 1933), 173.

316 "I know you count": Evalyn Walsh McLean, *Father Struck It Rich* (Boston: Little, Brown, and Company, 1936), 214.

317 "Colonel, whenever a boy": Edmund W. Starling with Thomas Sugrue, *Starling of the White House: The Story of the Man Whose Secret Service Detail Guarded Five Presidents from Woodrow Wilson to Franklin D. Roosevelt* (New York: Simon and Schuster, 1946), 224.

317 "I cannot for a moment": Henry Cabot Lodge to Calvin Coolidge, 29 October 1924, Calvin Coolidge Presidential Library and Museum, Forbes Library, Northampton, Mass.

318 A *Literary Digest* poll: "Coolidge Certain of Election," *Seattle Daily Times*, October 31, 1924.

320 "What makes these things": Will Rogers's insightful commentary runs throughout the Coolidge presidency. "America's Return to Wall Street," in *Will Rogers' Weekly Columns*, ed. James M. Smallwood and Steven K. Gragert (Claremore, Okla.: Will Rogers Memorial Museums, 2009), vol. 1, 298.

320 two-thirds of the Senate: Until 1975, ending a filibuster required a two-thirds vote of the Senate.

321 Unexpectedly, Dawes refused: "Dawes May Remain Away from Cabinet," Associated Press story, published in *Rockford Register Gazette*, November 26, 1924. "General Dawes Will Not Sit in Cabinet," *Boston Herald*, November 26, 1924.

321 "Coolidge knew nothing": "Coolidge knew nothing of this or Jess Smith or Daugherty while Coolidge was vice president," Dumaine, quoted by Barron in Clarence Barron, *They Told Barron: Conversations and Revelations of an American Pepys in Wall Street*, ed. Arthur Pound and Samuel Taylor Moore (New York: Harper and Brothers, 1930), 254.

321 "Only out of production": "An Income Tax Reflection," *The Wall Street Journal*, December 10, 1924.

322 The Supreme Court was deciding: "Supreme Court Gets Mal Daugherty Case," *The New York Times*, December 6, 1924.

322 "The Harding administration scandals were so vivid": Ira R. T. Smith, *"Dear Mr. President . . ."; The Story of Fifty Years in the White House Mail Room* (New York: Julian Messner, 1949), 131.

323 Post office bags: Those details were carried in the pages of a new magazine, *Time*, on February 25, 1925.

323 "The chief business": The full text of Coolidge's January 17, 1925, address to the American Society of Newspaper Editors can be found at the American Presidency Project of University of California/Santa Barbara, www.presidency.ucsb.edu.

324 Coolidge had already prepped: Alpheus Thomas Mason, *Harlan Fiske Stone: Pillar of the Law* (New York: Viking Press, 1956), 179.

324 "A Senator, acting": "Thank God for a MAN!" *The Washington Post*, January 29, 1925, p. 6.

325 Indeed, the vice president–elect: "Dawes Runs Short of Inaugural Tickets, Has Only 18 for Clamoring Host of Friends," *The New York Times*, February 13, 1925.

325 "Whatever is decided on": Charles G. Dawes to Calvin Coolidge, February 14, 1925, Series 1, Box 6:33, Charles G. Dawes Papers, Special Collections, Northwestern University Library, Evanston, Illinois.

325 "For both of them": Starling, *Starling of the White House*, 210.

326 "The main thing I want": Calvin Coolidge to John Calvin Coolidge, Sr., February 12, 1925, in *Your Son, Calvin Coolidge: A Selection of Letters from Calvin Coolidge to His Father*, ed. Edward Connery Lathem (Montpelier, Vt.: Vermont Historical Society, 1968), 199.

327 Instead of rising: The length of Dawes's speech differs slightly depending on the source; this count comes from "Vice President Causes a Stir," *The New York Times* (March 5 1924).

328 "Well, you're such a great": Starling, *Starling of the White House*, 229.

329 "The great senatorial": Robert C. Byrd, *The Senate, 1789–1989*, ed. Mary Sharon Hall (Washington, D.C.: U.S. Government Printing Office, 1988), vol. 1, 443.

330 "Economy reaches everywhere": "Full Text of President Coolidge's Message," *The Boston Globe*, December 3, 1924.

330 On April 24, 1925: "Tax Receipts Gain," *The New York Times*, April 24, 1925.

330 "cheeseparing": Coolidge frequently referred to cheese; one mention of "cheeseparing" appears, for example, in President Calvin Coolidge's Unpublished Press Conferences, November 19, 1926, vol. 7, p. 01159, Calvin Coolidge Presidential Library and Museum, Forbes Library, Northampton, Mass.

331 "seven barrels of spoiled": *Addresses of the President of the United States and the Director of the Bureau of the Budget at the Ninth Regular Meeting of the Business Organization of the Government at Memorial Continental Hall, June 22, 1925* (Washington, D.C.: U.S. Government Printing Office, 1925), 16.

332 The new recess appointee: Claude M. Fuess, *Joseph B. Eastman: Servant of the People* (New York: Columbia University Press, 1952), 161.

333 "I want my son John": Calvin Coolidge to William Jesse Newlin, May 27, 1925, Calvin Coolidge Presidential Library and Museum, Forbes Library, Northampton, Mass.

333 "Your letter went to Washington": The letters from this period, the harshest in Coolidge's relationship with John, are housed in the Coolidge Family Papers, Vermont Historical Society, Barre, Vt.

334 "Some bull!": Quoted in Starling, *Starling of the White House*, 234. Coolidge's visit with Barron is also detailed there.

335 "My Dear Mr. Morrow": Quoted in Harold Nicolson, *Dwight Morrow* (London: Constable & Co, 1935), 297.

336 "Whether one traces": The text of Coolidge's American Legion Speech of October 6, 1925, is at www.presidency.ucsb.edu/ws/index .php?pid=438#axzz1zz7FM400.

336 the papers noted: The Coolidge anniversary is noted, for example, in "Coolidge Is on Way," *Greensboro Record*, October 5, 1925, p. 2.

336 "Particularly do we want": "Colored Congregationalists Thank Coolidge," *Kansas City Advocate*, November 6, 1925, p. 1.

336 "Two years afterward": "Silence," *The Afro-American*, October 17, 1925, p. 9.

336 When the framers: Calvin Coolidge, "Government and Business," in *Foundations of the Republic*, 318.

336 The president and his cabinet secretary: Their plan included $193,575,000 in income tax cuts, $20 million in estate tax cuts, $12 million in cuts on cigars, and $9 million in cuts on auto taxes. *The New York Times*, "Tax Bill Is Finished," November 24 1925.

337 Mellon and Hoover both: "Coolidge Lights Up Tree to Inaugurate: Cabinet Members See Ceremony Marking Most Prosperous Yuletide," *The New York Times*, December 25, 1925.

338 "I would like to have": Calvin Coolidge to John Calvin Coolidge, Sr., January 20, 1926, in Lathem, ed., *Your Son, Calvin Coolidge*, 222.

338 "Pay your debts": Quoted in "Puts New Tax Cuts Up to $338,000,000," *The New York Times*, January 3, 1926.

340 "I note you are still": William Allen White to Calvin Coolidge, received April 9, 1926, Calvin Coolidge Personal Presidential Files, Forbes Library, Northampton, Mass.

340 it would always made him nervous: After signing the law, Coolidge warned that there would be no more tax cuts. "The Week Reviewed," *Barron's*, March 1, 1926.

Chapter 12: The Flood and the Flier

341 One of the first visitors: "New York–London Line of Dirigibles Planned," *The New York Times*, September 22, 1926.

342 Mack Trucks preferred stock: Coolidge's purchase of Mack Trucks shares and some of the documents for other investments can be found in Coolidge Family Papers, doc. 392, Vermont Historical Society, Barre, Vt.

343 and then to sleighs: Edmund Starling gives a detailed account of the trip to Plymouth and John Coolidge's death in Edmund W. Starling with Thomas Sugrue, *Starling of the White House: The Story of the Man Whose*

Secret Service Detail Guarded Five Presidents from Woodrow Wilson to Franklin D. Roosevelt (New York: Simon and Schuster, 1946), 238.

343 "nearly perpendicular": "The last mile of the journey is nearly perpendicular." "Roads for President: Woodstock to Plymouth Rote Broken Out—Col. Coolidge Sinks into State of Coma," *The Boston Globe*, March 18, 1926.

343 adding up to $43,601.35: William W. Stickney wrote to Coolidge on March 22, just days after John Coolidge's death, with this report. Coolidge Family Papers, doc. 392, Vermont Historical Society, Barre, Vt.

343 Ellen Riley of Ipswich: "Interview with William Jenney of the Calvin Coolidge Homestead Site," *The Day*, May 17, 1995. Also, "To Keep House for Coolidges: Miss Ellen Riley of Ipswich Given Post," *Boston Herald*, July 2, 1926.

343 "because of her wide knowledge": St. Petersburg, Florida, *Evening Independent*, July 2, 1926.

344 demand for costly programs: Herbert Hoover, *The Memoirs of Herbert Hoover: The Cabinet and the Presidency, 1920–1933* (New York: Macmillan, 1952), 114–115. Hoover wrote that "President Coolidge was not very enthusiastic over some of these ideas [about water development projects], because they would be costly."

345 bob quail: "The Presidency," *Time*, October 25, 1926, reported the tariff reduction on paintbrushes and live bob quail.

345 yet other roses: "The Presidency," *Time*, October 25, 1926.

347 There was also space: White says he was told of the bedspread by Frank Buxton, the *Boston Herald* journalist who won the Pulitzer Prize for "Who Made Coolidge?" William Allen White, *A Puritan in Babylon: The Story of Calvin Coolidge* (New York: Macmillan Company, 1938).

347 "Did you ever eat": Ellen Riley White House Papers, MSA 632, Vermont Historical Society, Barre, Vt.

348 "I have used some": Calvin Coolidge to Lynn Cady, April 19, 1926, Calvin Coolidge Presidential Library and Museum, Forbes Library, Northampton, Mass.

348 "The sirup producer": The reporter Louis M. Lyons wrote of the transport problems of the syrup and milk men: "He has the most sought after delicacies, sweet sirup, sweet cream. But his difficulties and limitations for merchandising are such that it is hard to figure his profits." "Sugaring Off," *The Boston Globe*, March 28, 1926.

348 Coolidge could continue: *Presidential Vetoes, 1789–1988* (Washington, D.C.: U.S. Government Printing Office, 1992), 231. Coolidge pocket-vetoed two pieces of legislation in the spring of 1927.

349 "With the experience": "Text of the President's Budget Message," *The New York Times*, December 9, 1926.

349 "under leaden skies": "Coolidge Lights Great Yule Tree," *The New York Times*, December 25, 1926.

351 "We are waiting [for] a test": *Addresses of the President of the United States and the Director of the Bureau of the Budget at the Twelfth Regular Meeting of the Business Organization of the Government at Memorial Continental Hall, January 29, 1927* (Washington, D.C.: U.S. Government Printing Office, 1927), 7.

351 The radial air-cooled engine: Charles Lindbergh, *We* (New York: G. P. Putnam's Sons, 1927), 198.

351 "I don't think": "Senate Committee Flouts President," *The New York Times,* January 18, 1927.

351 "If you have": Calvin Coolidge to Lynn Cady, February 16, 1927, Personal Presidential Files (microfiche), Calvin Coolidge Presidential Library and Museum, Forbes Library, Northampton, Mass.

351 "If you should leave": Ibid.

352 Miss Riley was able: "Ordered for dinner for President of Cuba and Unable to Cancel or Return," February 25, 1927, Ellen Riley White House Papers, MSA 632, Vermont Historical Society, Barre, Vt.

352 "will be the political finish": The *Times* wrote, "Farm bloc adherents insist that if a veto comes from the White House it will be the political finish of President Coolidge and put an end to all talk of another term for him." "Veto by the President Generally Expected," *The New York Times,* February 18, 1927.

353 "You could have gotten": Rex Alan Smith, *The Carving of Mount Rushmore* (New York: Abbeville Press, 1985), 173. Smith's account of the Rushmore story is colorful and readable.

354 "The chief objection": Coolidge's veto response to the 1927 McNary-Haugen legislation is reported in "Fears for All Industry: President Says Measure Threatens the Basis of Prosperity, Price Fixing Is Condemned," *The New York Times,* February 26, 1927.

354 The president also signed: "Coolidge Signs Branch Bank Bill," *The New York Times,* February 26, 1927.

356 The idea of walking: Ishbel Ross, *Grace Coolidge and Her Era: the Story of a President's Wife* (Plymouth, Vt.: Calvin Coolidge Memorial Foundation, 1988), 217.

356 Hoover put forward: "Mr. Hoover has been spoken of frequently as a probability for the office of secretary of state," a columnist noted. "Capital Mystified on Hoover's Status with the President," *The New York Times,* April 17, 1927.

357 "considered that it was": President Calvin Coolidge's Unpublished Press Conferences, April 15, 1927, vol. 8, p. 01208, Calvin Coolidge Presidential Library and Museum, Forbes Library, Northampton, Mass.

359 "A vast sheet of water": Frederick Simplich, "The Great Mississippi Flood of 1927," *National Geographic* 52, no. 3 (September 1927): 268.

362 the spars were made of spruce: Charles A. Lindbergh, *The Spirit of St. Louis* (New York: Scribner, 2003), 536.

362 "The more we learn": President Calvin Coolidge's Unpublished
Press Conferences, May 24, 1927, vol. 8, p. 01351, Calvin Coolidge
Presidential Library and Museum, Forbes Library, Northampton, Mass.

363 Once she was settled: Irwin Hood Hoover, *Forty-two Years in the White
House* (Boston: Houghton Mifflin, 1934), 158.

363 Indeed, Coolidge predicted: *Addresses of the President of the United States
and the Director of the Bureau of the Budget at the Thirteenth Regular
Meeting of the Business Organization of the Government at Memorial
Continental Hall, June 10, 1927, Washington, D.C.* (Washington, D.C.:
U.S. Government Printing Office, 1927), 2.

363 "He knew illuminum was light": This line about James Couzens
appeared in "Rogers Tells City," *Omaha News World*, January 30, 1927.

364 The spread between: Evidence that taxes mattered more than patriotism
for bond buyers can be found in Sung Won Kang and Hugh Rockoff,
"Capitalizing Patriotism: The Liberty Loans of World War I," National
Bureau of Economic Research, 2006 Working Paper.

364 The era of "tax tuberculosis": "Tax Tuberculosis," *The New York Times*,
January 30, 1921, p. 22.

365 "modest, congenial": A wonderful audio clip of this speech and
Lindbergh's response can be found at http://historymatters.gmu
.edu/d/5133/.

366 "Same *Mayflower*, same Potomac": William J. Miller, *Henry Cabot Lodge*
(New York: Heinemann, 1967), 75. This biography of the senator's
grandson contains several Coolidge anecdotes.

366 Lindbergh owed $1,233.75: "Lindbergh's Prizes Taxed," *The New York
Times*, May 23, 1927. National newspapers such as *The New York Times*,
The Washington Post, and *The Wall Street Journal* covered Lindbergh
and other aviators extensively and are therefore useful sources on the
subject.

367 Coolidge wanted him: Calvin Coolidge to John Coolidge, June 27,
1927, Box 392:17, Coolidge Family Papers, Vermont Historical Society,
Barre, Vt.

368 "We knew that he": William J. Bulow, "In the Black Hills," in *Meet
Calvin Coolidge: The Man Behind the Myth*, ed. Edward Connery Lathem
(Brattleboro, Vt.: Stephen Greene Press, 1960), 120.

Chapter 13: Decision at Rushmore

371 "Never so far off": "Summer White House Was Never So Far Off," *The
New York Times*, June 5, 1927.

371 "Pretty well": William J. Bulow, "In the Black Hills," in *Meet Calvin
Coolidge: The Man Behind the Myth*, ed. Edward Connery Lathem
(Brattleboro, Vt.: Stephen Greene Press, 1960), 118.

373 Coolidge patronized the local tobacco shop: President Coolidge
Number, *Black Hills Engineer* 15, no. 4 (November 1927), endpapers.

373 Miss Riley placed her orders: Ellen Riley White House Papers, MSA 632, Vermont Historical Society, Barre, Vt.

374 "Boy, when you get": Quoted in Bulow, "In the Black Hills," 119.

374 "Seems to me I've seen you before": Rex Alan Smith, *The Carving of Mount Rushmore* (New York: Abbeville Press, 1985), 147.

374 "On the first bite": Bulow, "In the Black Hills," 121.

375 "Greetings from Mount Rushmore": John Taliaferro, *Great White Fathers: The Story of the Obsessive Quest to Create Mount Rushmore* (New York: Public Affairs, 2002), 226.

376 the great concern: Edmund W. Starling, *Starling of the White House* (New York: Simon and Schuster, 1946), 252.

376 "You will find": President Calvin Coolidge's Unpublished Press Conferences, June 28, 1927, vol. 8, p. 01389, Calvin Coolidge Presidential Library and Museum, Forbes Library, Northampton, Mass.

376 No one was fooled: Paul F. Boller, Jr., *Presidential Wives*, 2nd ed. (New York: Oxford University Press, 1998), 269.

377 "The blow has fallen": Quoted in Harold Nicolson, *Dwight Morrow* (London: Constable & Co., 1935), 307.

377 Still, others: Charles G. Dawes, *Notes as Vice President, 1928–1929* (Boston: Little, Brown, and Company, 1935), 7.

378 The recent St. Paul conference: Carlisle Bargeron paraphrased Bulow in "Hoover Will Visit Coolidge to Talk Over Flood Relief," *The Washington Post* (July 17, 1928).

379 "My Dear Mr. President": Gutzon Borglum to Calvin Coolidge, July 22, 1927, Calvin Coolidge Presidential Library and Museum, Forbes Library, Northampton, Mass.

380 "I like it well enough": President Calvin Coolidge's Unpublished Press Conferences, July 29, 1927, vol. 9, p. 01422, Calvin Coolidge Presidential Library and Museum, Forbes Library, Northampton, Mass.

381 "I am not a candidate": Deborah Pickman Clifford and Nicholas R. Clifford, *"The Troubled Roar of the Waters": Vermont in Flood and Recovery, 1927–1931* (Durham: University of New Hampshire Press, 2007), 129–130.

382 For Coolidge's twelve: John T. Lambert, "The Presidential News Service," President Coolidge Number, *Black Hills Engineer* 15, no. 4 (November 1927): 266.

382 "if such nomination": "Slemp Sees No Change," *The New York Times*, August 4, 1927.

382 "It hadn't occurred to me": Press conference of August 5, 1927, Unpublished Press Conferences, Calvin Coolidge Memorial Collection, Forbes Library, Northampton, Mass.

383 A Native American girl: John A. Stanley, "Preparing the Presidential Home in the State Park," President Coolidge Number, *Black Hills Engineer* 15, no. 4 (November 1927): 229.

383 The first car: Smith, *The Carving of Mount Rushmore*, 151.

383 "in your honor": Starling recounts his conversation with Norbeck in *Starling of the White House*.

384 "I may yet live long enough": Smith, *The Carving of Mount Rushmore*, 153.

384 But the determined line: A video of this scene exists at Critical Past (Pathé News) and may be ordered for classrooms. See also Starling, *Starling of the White House*, 251.

385 Everyone thought back: That Coolidge himself was worried about his heart is evidenced in the fact that he insisted that his attending physicians take his pulse twice a day. Milton F. Heller, Jr., *The Presidents' Doctor: An Insider's View of Three First Families* (New York, Vantage, 2000), 78.

385 "Had I been there": Starling, *Starling of the White House*, 253.

385 "He realizes": "Party Here Is Amazed," *The New York Times*, August 3, 1927.

385 "Nothing is more sacred": Starling, *Starling of the White House*, 259.

Chapter 14: Coolidge Agonistes

389 "The South appreciates": "Coolidge Refusal of Extra Sessions Roils Democrats," *The Washington Post*, September 16, 1927.

390 "I am having the usual experience": Unpublished press conferences of President Coolidge, Calvin Coolidge Memorial Library, vol. 9, p. 01485, press conference of October 4, 1927.

391 Outlays that fiscal year: M. Slade Kendrick with Mark Wehle, "A Century and a Half of Fiscal Expenditures," National Bureau of Economic Research, 1955, 77.

392 "I countered by asking him": Alfred L. Castle, *Diplomatic Realism: William R. Castle, Jr., and American Foreign Policy, 1919–1953* (Honolulu: Samuel N. and Mary Castle Foundation, 1998), 34.

393 a heavy golden shield: The shield is now in the collection of the Vermont Division for Historic Preservation, President Calvin Coolidge State Historic Site, Plymouth, Vt.

393 "has no selfish political interest": "Abyssinian Envoy Visits U.S. President," *Chicago Defender*, October 1, 1927, p. 3.

395 "the most absurd thing": "Coolidge on C. of C. Plan," *The Wall Street Journal*, November 26, 1927, p. 2.

395 That man's departure had cost: Andrew Mellon to Calvin Coolidge, December 3, 1927, series 1, box 21, Calvin Coolidge Papers, Manuscript Division, Library of Congress, Washington, D.C.

395 John, at college: "John Coolidge on Class Hop Committee, 3d Time," *Boston Herald*, November 1, 1927.

395   The papers reported that Grace: The story of the tea room call is in "Today in Washington by Rodney Deutscher," *The Greensboro Record*, October 26, 1927, p. 4.

395   The fact that he was now: Calvin Coolidge to Clarence Barron, October 21, 1927, Calvin Coolidge Presidential Library and Museum, Forbes Library, Northampton, Mass.

396   Hoover even collected the RSVPs: Irwin Hood Hoover, *Forty-two Years in the White House* (Boston: Houghton Mifflin, 1934), 127.

396   The writer Sinclair Lewis: Lewis wrote *The Man Who Knew Coolidge* over the fall and winter of 1927–1928. D. J. Dooley, *The Art of Sinclair Lewis* (Lincoln: University of Nebraska Press, 1967), 142.

396   That fall there was yet another: Reports differ on when Cartotto's painting was made, but the painter himself dates it to 1927. Ercole Cartotto, "The Man in the Portraits," in *Meet Calvin Coolidge: The Man Behind the Myth*, ed. Edward Connery Lathem (Brattleboro, Vt.: Stephen Greene Press, 1960), 128–130.

397   "feared the results": This telling discussion between Starling and Coolidge is reported in Edmund W. Starling with Thomas Sugrue, *Starling of the White House: The Story of the Man Whose Secret Service Detail Guarded Five Presidents from Woodrow Wilson to Franklin D. Roosevelt* (New York: Simon and Schuster, 1946), 263.

397   "They're going to try": Ibid.

399   But it was from Vermont: The best volume on the Vermont flood is Deborah Pickman Clifford and Nicholas R. Clifford, *"The Troubled Roar of the Waters": Vermont in Flood and Recovery, 1927–1931* (Durham: University of New Hampshire Press, 2007).

400   "He can't do for his own": "Vermont Folk Too Proud," *The Boston Globe*, November 13, 1927.

402   "the greatest work ever done": "Special Session Now Only History," *St. Albans Messenger*, December 1, 1927.

403   "Proposals for promoting": Coolidge's Fifth Annual Message to Congress, December 6, 1927, American Presidency Project, University of California/Santa Barbara.

404   "Here we are the Nation": Rogers spelled and punctuated in his own fashion. "Will on Mexican Relations," in *Will Rogers' Weekly Articles*, ed. James M. Smallwood and Steven K. Gragert (Stillwater: Oklahoma State University Press, 1981), vol. 4, column 223.

Chapter 15: The Shield and the Book

408   "universal undertaking": Robert H. Ferrell, *Peace in Their Time*, 107.

409   half of the budget: *Statistical Abstract of the United States*, 72nd ed. (Washington, D.C.: U.S. Department of Commerce, 1951), 306. Total expenditures of the federal government are listed as $3.182 billion for the period 1926–1930. Of that, $405 million went to the Department of

Army and Air Force, $340 million to the Department of the Navy, $244 million to veterans' pensions, $738 million to interest on the public debt, and $37 million to Indians, leaving $1.4 million for "all other."

410 "But Mr. Secretary": Marian Cecilia McKenna, *Borah* (Ann Arbor: University of Michigan Press, 1961), 244.

410 "That's the best way": Quoted ibid., 244.

411 "We can do that": Quoted in David Bryn-Jones, *Frank B. Kellogg: A Biography* (New York: G. P. Putnam's Sons, 1937), 232.

411 Kellogg had suggested: The White House and State Department's deliberations about Briand's proposal are detailed in Robert H. Ferrell, *Peace in Their Time: The Origins of the Kellogg-Briand Pact* (New Haven, Conn.: Yale University Press, 1952); Bryn-Jones, *Frank B. Kellogg*; and Alfred Castle, *Diplomatic Realism: William R. Castle, Jr., and American Foreign Policy, 1919–1953* (Honolulu: University of Hawai'i Press, 1998).

411 "If this is to be": The whole exchange is in Bryn-Jones, *Frank B. Kellogg*, 232–233.

412 "worse than a waste": "Ship Board Proposal a Waste," *The Wall Street Journal*, March 17, 1923.

413 "Our general position": Quoted in *The Talkative President: The Off-the-Record Press Conferences of Calvin Coolidge*, ed. Robert Ferrell and Howard Quint (Amherst: University of Massachusetts Press, 1964), 215. See also President Calvin Coolidge's Unpublished Press Conferences, January 31, 1928, vol. 10, p. 01588, Calvin Coolidge Presidential Library and Museum, Forbes Library, Northampton, Massachusetts.

413 He went back upstairs: Robert H. Ferrell, *Grace Coolidge: The People's Lady in Silent Cal's White House* (Lawrence: University of Kansas Press, 2008), 114–115.

414 "Briand Elated": "Briand Elated at Plan's Success," *Los Angeles Times*, February 2, 1928.

414 "We are disarmed": "Kellogg Hailed by Stresemann," *Los Angeles Times*, January 31, 1928.

415 "The main difference": Bernard M. Baruch, "So Different," in *Meet Calvin Coolidge: The Man Behind the Myth*, ed. Edward Connery Lathem (Brattleboro, Vt.: Stephen Greene Press, 1960), 135.

415 The portrait work challenged Cartotto: Ercole Cartotto, "The Man in the Portraits," in Lathem, ed., *Meet Calvin Coolidge*, 128–129.

415 Grace was recovering: Grace Coolidge's visits to Northampton were extensively covered in the *Springfield Republican* in the spring of 1928.

416 After conferring with Kellogg: Frank B. Kellogg to Calvin Coolidge, February 20, 1928, Calvin Coolidge Papers, Manuscript Division, Library of Congress, Washington, D.C.

417 "If you have 400 delegates": Herbert Hoover, *The Memoirs of Herbert Hoover: The Cabinet and the Presidency, 1920–1933* (New York: Macmillan, 1952), 193.

417   The president signed a tax bill: The 1928 tax law cut corporate taxes and
a 3 percent manufacturers' tax on autos. The act cut the tax on theater
admissions as well. It did not, however, cut the marginal rates on the
income tax as other rate cuts had. Therefore the act did not represent
"scientific taxation" to the extent that preceding legislation did. The
total estimated cost of the 1928 tax cut in revenue was higher than
Treasury's recommendation.

417   "I think it is a mistake": Coolidge criticized the repeal of auto taxes in an
April 27, 1928, press conference. He went on, "We had already repealed
40 per cent of them. We might reasonably look to that source of revenue
for the expenses which the Federal government is incurring in road
construction. Road construction by the federal government, of course, is
a new proposition. Ferrell and Quint, eds., *The Talkative President*, 111.

418   "My inside information": Quoted in Ferrell, *Peace in Their Time*, 176.

419   "It is one-third paid": *Addresses of the President of the United States and
the Director of the Bureau of the Budget at the Fifteenth Regular Meeting of
the Business Organization of the Government, June 11, 1928* (Washington,
D.C.: U.S. Government Printing Office, 1928), 3.

419   "To Miss Riley": Ellen Riley White House Papers, MSA 632, Vermont
Historical Society, Barre, Vt.

420   "Let's bring him over": Edmund W. Starling with Thomas Sugrue,
*Starling of the White House: The Story of the Man Whose Secret Ser-
vice Detail Guarded Five Presidents from Woodrow Wilson to Franklin D.
Roosevelt* (New York: Simon and Schuster, 1946), 268.

420   "Let him talk": Ibid.

421   "Well, no": President Calvin Coolidge's Unpublished Press Conferences,
August 7, 1928, vol. 11, p. 01696, Calvin Coolidge Presidential Library
and Museum, Forbes Library, Northampton, Mass.

421   "Had an agreement": The speech Coolidge delivered on August 15,
1928, in Wausau, Wis., was carried in many papers, including the *San
Diego Union*: "Calvin Coolidge Firm," August 16, 1928, 1.

421   "The conception of renouncing": Lodge's editorial is detailed in
William J. Miller, *Henry Cabot Lodge: A Biography* (New York:
Heinemann, 1967), 83.

422   quiet cries for *l'Américain*: This and other details of the signing can be
found in Ferrell, *Peace in Their Time*, 218.

423   "I hope it will be": "This is a matter entirely up to the Senate," Kellogg
replied. Quoted ibid., 213.

423   "continuation of Coolidge policies": "Hoover Appeals to Bay State Vote
to Stand by Party," *The New York Times*, October 16, 1928.

423   Hoover saw his farm: Details of the Hoover farm can be found in
"Hoover as a Farmer Makes Ends Meet: Engineering Methods Applied
to His California Acres Produce Ten Major Crops a Year," *The New York
Times*, August 26, 1928.

423 "I wish you would": Calvin Coolidge to Collector of Taxes, City Hall, Northampton, October 8, 1928, in Calvin Coolidge Presidential Library and Museum, Forbes Library, Northampton, Mass.

423 The tax bills in his files: Tax Inventory to Be Filed with Listers, Tax Year 1927, Personal Presidential File 1, Calvin Coolidge Presidential Library and Museum, Forbes Library, Northampton, Mass.

424 "I had the smallest": President Calvin Coolidge's Unpublished Press Conferences, November 2, 1928, vol. 11, p. 01746, Calvin Coolidge Presidential Library and Museum, Forbes Library, Northampton, Mass.

425 "the prospect for": President Calvin Coolidge's Unpublished Press Conferences, January 8, 1929, vol. 11, p. 01783, Calvin Coolidge Presidential Library and Museum, Forbes Library, Northampton, Mass.

425 more than twenty local banks: Coolidge's investments and his father's can be found in Document 392, Coolidge Family Papers, Vermont Historical Society, Barre, Vt.

425 He agreed with Merrill: Charles Merrill's visit to the White House and Coolidge's concurrence are detailed in Edwin J. Perkins, *Wall Street to Main Street: Charles Merrill and Middle-Class Investors* (Cambridge, Mass.: Cambridge University Press, 1999), 103.

426 First, Coolidge picked up: The pen story is told in "The Presidency," *Time*, December 31, 1928.

427 "It would not cost": Hoover, *The Memoirs of Herbert Hoover: The Cabinet and the Presidency 1920–1933*, 211.

428 final budget meeting: "Coolidge Demands Further Economies to Aid Prosperity," *The New York Times*, January 29, 1929.

428 "The results of economy": "Thrift Plea Renewed," *Los Angeles Times*, January 29, 1929.

429 "a man of small stature": Coolidge's clothing and other details from the Vermont trip are given in "Coolidge in Speech Extols Vermont," *The New York Times*, September 22, 1928. The story also reported his visit to the sugar lot.

430 "Speech, speech!": Reported in "Coolidge Praises People of Native State in Most Fervent Talk of His Career," *Springfield Republican*, September 22, 1928.

430 "Vermont is a state I love": Many versions of this speech exist, including ones autographed and approved by Coolidge months after the speech was given. The version in the text is that reported by *Time* magazine on October 1, 1928. Other versions, reported elsewhere, used different wording.

431 "I do not think": President Calvin Coolidge's Unpublished Press Conferences, November 23, 1928, vol. 11, p. 01759, Calvin Coolidge Presidential Library and Museum, Forbes Library, Northampton, Mass.

431 Senator Carter Glass: Ferrell, *Peace in Their Time*, 251.

432 To capture the weakness: Michael A. Weatherson and Hal W. Bochin, *Hiram Johnson: Political Revivalist* (Lanham, Md.: University Press of America, 1995), 153.

432 Suddenly, the reporters recognized: That Coolidge had planned it all along is evident in an article by Wickham Steed, a British editor. In a review of Coolidge's autobiography published in *Time and Tide*, a U.K. magazine, Steed wrote that in the autumn of 1927, he called on Coolidge and found the president already immersed in the subject of the Kellogg-Briand Pact. He concluded: "But for his perspicacious and persistent action, it is doubtful what is known as the Paris Peace Pact would ever have been concluded. It is doubtful whether Mr. Kellogg would ever have taken action." Wickham Steed, "A Great American," series 1, box 43, folder 28, Dwight Morrow Papers. Amherst College Archives and Special Collections, Amherst College Library, Amherst, Mass.

433 "Keep perfectly still": Ferrell, *Peace in Their Time*, 254.

433 Castle of the State Department: Diary of Castle, January 17, 1928, Houghton Library, Harvard College Library.

433 It took the United States away: Robert Ferrell, *The Presidency of Calvin Coolidge* (Lawrence: University Press of Kansas, 1998), 142. The document discusses a memo from Kellogg in which he warns ambassadors against an expansive interpretation of the Monroe Doctrine; the doctrine, he wrote, "is not a lance it; is a shield."

Coda: The Blessing

434 "There is another": *Selected Letters of William Allen White, 1899–1943*, ed. Walter Johnson (New York: H. Holt and Company, 1947), 292.

434 Hoover shut them down: Seven saddle horses were ordered to the army remount service, and the stable attendants to the cavalry. "White House Stables Closed by Hoover in Interests of Economy," *Springfield Republican*, March 26, 1929.

435 "It fits us": "Mrs. Coolidge Glorifies Return to Cottage Life," *Lodi* (California) *Sentinel*, January 14, 1930.

435 The only other living ex-president: William Howard Taft fell ill the following winter and died in 1930.

435 "Put Cal to Work": "Put Cal to Work," in *Will Rogers' Weekly Articles*, ed. James M. Smallwood and Steven K. Gragert (Stillwater: Oklahoma State University Press, 1981), vol. 4, column 441.

435 "I should like to express": Bruce Barton to President Coolidge, February 17, 1929, Calvin Coolidge Personal Files, Forbes Library, Northampton, Mass.

436 Yet the reporters persisted: Lathem, ed., *Meet Calvin Coolidge*, 167.

436 "I have considerable doubt": Quoted in *The Talkative President: The Off-the-Record Press Conferences of Calvin Coolidge*, ed. Robert Ferrell and Howard Quint (Amherst: University of Massachusetts Press, 1964), 134.

436 "It's really kinder": Smallwood and Gragert, eds., *Will Rogers' Weekly Articles*, vol. 4, column 330.

436 John had predicted: John's thoughts about the Coolidges' future are cited in Cynthia Bittinger, *Grace Coolidge: Sudden Star*, Presidential Wives Series (New York: Nova History Publications, 2005), 99.

437 "Lindy may beat us to it": Quoted in "Miss Trumbull Plans: Fiancee of John Coolidge Says Lindbergh 'May Beat Us to It,'" *Boston Herald*, February 27, 1929.

437 Six airplanes: "Planes Adorn John Coolidge Wedding Cake," *Dallas Morning News*, September 23, 1929, 1.

437 That was too much: "Daylight Time Fools Sargent; 'Mike' in House Angers Coolidge," *Boston Herald*, September 24, 1929.

437 the rent: The rent is reported in "Notables at Wedding," Associated Press, reprinted in *The Repository* (Canton, Ohio), September 23, 1929.

437 Coolidge gave: That the amount was "four figures" is mentioned in "Florence and John Take a Motor Trip," *Rockford Daily Gazette*, September 24, 1929.

437 He purchased shares: Coolidge's financial documents, including the purchase and sale of Standard Brands shares, are stored in the Vermont Historical Society, Barre, Vt.

437 "depression-proof": The *Journal*'s comment in its entirety reads, "Important interests are optimistic on the long pull prospects of Standard Brands, because the company is in a 'depression-proof' industry." "Abreast of the Market," *The Wall Street Journal*, November 28, 1929. One letter in January 1931 shows that Coolidge suffered a $21,570 loss on 3,000 shares of Standard Brands that he bought in September 1929 and sold in April 1930.

438 Coolidge and Borglum had now been: Their correspondence is now in the Calvin Coolidge Presidential Library and Museum, Forbes Library, Northampton, Mass.

440 But the silent back: Rex Alan Smith, *The Carving of Mount Rushmore* (New York: Abbeville Press, 1985), 283.

440 Some commentators, including: "Mr. Durant's Invective," *The Wall Street Journal*, April 25, 1930.

441 fifty cars an hour: Susan Lewis Well, "Calvin Coolidge: At Home in Northampton," 64. Well describes the move in detail.

441 Coolidge paid cash: "Coolidge Buys a $45,000 Estate," *The New York Times*, April 2, 1930.

441 "It should be filed": The details of Coolidge's column are laid out in the introduction of *Calvin Coolidge Says: Dispatches Written by Former-President Coolidge and Syndicated to Newspapers in 1930–1931*, ed. Edward Connery Lathem (Plymouth, Vt.: Calvin Coolidge Memorial Foundation, 1972).

443 "Been here first twenty-odd years": Herman Beaty, "A Secretary's View," in *Meet Calvin Coolidge: The Man Behind the Myth*, ed. Edward Connery Lathem (Brattleboro, Vt.: Stephen Greene Press, 1960), 175.

443 "might put them out": Ibid., 176.

444 "And as much more": Ralph W. Hemenway, "His Law Partner Looks Back," in Lathem, ed., *Meet Calvin Coolidge*, 171.

444 Days after Coolidge left office: *Okanogan Indians et al. v. United States* was the test case of the pocket veto. A good account of it can be found in *Time*, March 25, 1929.

445 "Coolidge treated the bracelet": Beaty, "A Secretary's View," in Lathem, ed., *Meet Calvin Coolidge*.

445 Another story: This account appears in "Remembering Calvin Coolidge," a memoir dictated by Scandrett and recorded by Richard Polenberg for the Cornell Oral History Program, *Vermont History XI* (1972): 194.

446 "Those are *my* works of art": Ercole Cartotto, "The Man in the Portraits," in Lathem, ed., *Meet Calvin Coolidge*, 130.

446 In addition, his records show: Calvin Coolidge Financial Records, box 392, 20 and 26, Coolidge Family Papers, Vermont Historical Society, Barre, Vt.

447 "You, my son": Cyndy Bittinger transcribed Grace's poem of July 1929 and added some details about it in a one-page essay on the Calvin Coolidge Memorial Foundation website, "Grace Anna Goodhue Coolidge and Her Poetry," www.calvin-coolidge.org/html/poetry.html. See also Grace Goodhue Coolidge, *Grace Coolidge: An Autobiography*, ed. Robert H. Ferrell and Lawrence E. Wikander (Plymouth, Vt.: Calvin Coolidge Memorial Foundation, 1992), 115.

448 "I sewed and wrote": Quoted in Ishbel Ross, *Grace Coolidge and Her Era: The Story of a President's Wife* (Plymouth, Vt.: Calvin Coolidge Memorial Foundation 1988), 273.

448 "he established himself": Grace Coolidge Round Robin Letters, Calvin Coolidge Memorial Foundation, Plymouth, Vt.

450 "You are doing very well": The letters to John are in the Coolidge Family Papers, Vermont Historical Society, Barre, Vt.

451 "Now my career": Claude M. Fuess, *Calvin Coolidge: The Man from Vermont* (Boston: Little, Brown, 1940), 494.

451 "That was one difference": Ibid.

451 "What subjects can I discuss?": This postscript to a September 21 letter is quoted by Sanders in his memoir in Lathem, ed., *Meet Calvin Coolidge*.

452 "We are willing": Henry J. Allen, in charge of publicity for the Republican National Committee, quoted in Lathem, ed., *Meet Calvin Coolidge*, 204.

452 "UNABLE TO MAKE SPEECH": Everett Sanders, "A Final Effort," in Lathem, ed., *Meet Calvin Coolidge*, 206.

453 "I have thought of you": Calvin Coolidge to Grace Coolidge, December 8, 1932, Document 392, Folder 12, Coolidge Family Papers, Vermont Historial Society, Barre, Vt.

454 "Me for the hills": James G. Hepburn, ed., *Robert Frost: An Introduction* (New York: Holt, Rinehart and Winston, 1961), 60.

454 "But as I look about": Charles Andrews remembered this line of Coolidge's in Lathem, ed., *Meet Calvin Coolidge*, 216.

454 He and Harry also: Many details of this last morning can be read in "Found by Mrs. Coolidge," *The New York Times*, January 6, 1933.

455 One hymn was: William Allen White, *A Puritan in Babylon: The Story of Calvin Coolidge* (New York: Macmillan, 1938), 442. White mentions "Lead Kindly Light." Colonel Starling recalls hearing "Lead Kindly Light" outside Harding's funeral train in Edmund W. Starling, *Starling of the White House* (New York: Simon and Schuster, 1946), 201.

455 Eleanor Roosevelt: The guests who attended are listed in many news stories, such as the Associated Press's "Coolidge Buried in Native Vermont," printed in the Canton, Ohio, *Repository*, January 8, 1933.

455 the service lasted: "The Death of Coolidge," *Time*, January 16, 1933.

456 "the lowest ebb": Alfred E. Smith, "A Shining Public Example," in Lathem, ed., *Meet Calvin Coolidge*, 220.

456 Clarence Barron's business daily: The short obituary is "Calvin Coolidge," *The Wall Street Journal*, January 6, 1933, 6.

456 "I am perfectly willing": Calvin Coolidge to Walter Lynds, January 12, 1926, Calvin Coolidge Presidential Library and Museum, Forbes Library, Northampton, Mass.

456 "I want to thank you": Calvin Coolidge to Walter Lynds, May 6, 1927, Calvin Coolidge Presidential Library and Museum, Forbes Library, Northampton, Mass.

SELECTED BIBLIOGRAPHY

BOOKS AND DISSERTATIONS

Abels, Jules. *In the Time of Silent Cal*. New York: Putnam, 1969.

Abrams, Richard M. *Conservatism in a Progressive Era: Massachusetts Politics, 1900–1912*. Cambridge, Mass.: Harvard University Press, 1964.

Adams, Samuel Hopkins. *Incredible Era*. New York: Octagon Books, 1979.

Addresses of the President of the United States and the Director of the Bureau of the Budget at the Regular Meetings of the Business Organization of the Government. Washington, D.C.: U.S. Government Printing Office, 1921–1928.

Aldrich, Lewis Cass, and Frank R. Holmes, eds. *History of Windsor County, Vermont: With Illustrations and Biographical Sketches of Some of Its Prominent Men and Pioneers*. Syracuse, N.Y.: D. Mason & Co., 1891.

Anderson, Benjamin M. *Economics and the Public Welfare: A Financial and Economic History of the United States, 1914–1946*. New York: D. Van Nostrand, 1949.

Bagby, Wesley M. *The Road to Normalcy: The Presidential Campaign and Election of 1920*. Baltimore: Johns Hopkins Press, 1962.

Barron, Clarence. *They Told Barron: Conversations and Revelations of an American Pepys in Wall Street*. Ed. Arthur Pound and Samuel Taylor Moore. New York: Harper and Brothers, 1930.

Beck, Richard. *A Proud Tradition, a Bright Future: A Sesquicentennial History of St. Johnsbury Academy*. St. Johnsbury, Vt.: St. Johnsbury Academy, 1992.

Benson, Susan Porter. *Counter Cultures: Saleswomen, Managers, and Customers in American Department Stores, 1890–1940*. Urbana: University of Illinois Press, 1986.

Benwell, Harry A. *History of the Yankee Division*. Boston: Cornhill Company, 1919.

Berg, A. Scott. *Lindbergh*. New York: G. P. Putnam's Sons, 1998.

Bernays, Edward L. *Biography of an Idea: Memoirs of Public Relations Counsel Edward L. Bernays*. New York: Simon and Schuster, 1965.

Bittinger, Cynthia D. *Grace Coolidge: Sudden Star*. Presidential Wives Series. New York: Nova History Publications, 2005.

Blair, John L. *The Governorship of Calvin Coolidge, 1919–1921*. PhD diss., University of Chicago, 1971.

Boller, Paul F., Jr., *Presidential Wives*, 2nd ed. New York: Oxford University Press, 1998.

Booraem, Hendrik. *The Provincial: Calvin Coolidge and His World, 1885–1895*. Lewisburg, Pa.: Bucknell University Press, 1994.

Bradley, James. *The Imperial Cruise: A Secret History of Empire and War*. New York: Little, Brown, 2009.

Bridgman, A. M., ed. *A Souvenir of Massachusetts Legislators 1915*, vol. 24. Stoughton, Mass.: Pequa Press Co., 1915.

Bryant, Blanche Brown, and Gertrude Elaine Baker. *Genealogical Records of the Founders and Early Settlers of Plymouth, Vermont*. DeLand, Fla.: E. O. Painter Printing Co., 1967.

Bryn-Jones, David. *Frank B. Kellogg: A Biography*. New York: G. P. Putnam's Sons, 1937.

Burrill, Ellen Mudge. *The State House: Boston, Massachusetts*. Boston: Wright and Potter Printing Company, 1921.

Butcher, Phillip. *George W. Cable: The Northampton Years*. New York: Columbia University Press, 1959.

Carr, Charles C. *Alcoa: An American Enterprise*. New York: Rinehart and Co., 1952.

Castle, Alfred. *Diplomatic Realism: William R. Castle, Jr., and American Foreign Policy, 1919–1953*. Honolulu: Samuel N. and Mary Castle Foundation, 1998.

Chamberlin, Joseph Edgar. *The Boston Transcript; A History of Its First Hundred Years*. Boston: Houghton Mifflin, 1930.

City of Northampton. *The Meadow City's Quarter-Millennial Book: A Memorial of the Celebration of the Two Hundred and Fiftieth Anniversary of the Settlement of the Town of Northampton: Massachusetts. June 5th, 6th and 7th, 1904*.

Clapp, Edwin J. *Transportation*. New York: Alexander Hamilton Institute, 1918.

Clark, Christopher. *Social Change in America: From the Revolution through the Civil War*. Chicago: Ivan R. Dee, 2006.

Clifford, Deborah Pickman, and Nicholas R. Clifford. *"The Troubled Roar of the Waters": Vermont in Flood and Recovery, 1927–1931*. Durham: University of New Hampshire Press, 2007.

Committee of the President's Conference on Unemployment. *Business Cycles and Unemployment: Report and Recommendations of a Committee of the President's Conference on Unemployment Including an Investigation Made Under the Auspices of the National Bureau of Economic Research*. New York: McGraw-Hill Book Company, 1923.

Conant, Edward. *Conant's Vermont*. Rutland, Vt.: Tuttle Company, 1890.

Conklin, Geoff, ed. *The New Republic Anthology: 1915–1935.* New York: Dodge Publishing, 1936.

Coolidge, Calvin. *The Autobiography of Calvin Coolidge.* New York: Cosmopolitan Book Corporation, 1929.

Coolidge, Calvin. *Have Faith in Massachusetts: A Collection of Speeches and Messages.* Boston: Houghton Mifflin, 1919.

———. *Calvin Coolidge Says: Dispatches Written by Former-President Coolidge and Syndicated to Newspapers in 1930–1931.* Ed. Edward Connery Lathem. Plymouth, Vt.: Calvin Coolidge Memorial Foundation, 1972.

———. *Foundations of the Republic: Speeches and Addresses.* New York: Scribner, 1926.

———. Introduction to *Abraham Lincoln: An Essay* by Carl Schurz. Boston: Houghton Mifflin, 1920.

———. *Messages to the General Court, Official Addresses, Proclamations and State Papers of His Excellency Governor Calvin Coolidge for the Years Nineteen Hundred and Nineteen and Nineteen Hundred and Twenty.* Ed. Henry F. Long. Boston: Commonwealth of Massachusetts, 1920.

———. *The Mind of the President as Revealed by Himself in His Own Words. President Coolidge's Views on Public Questions Selected and Arranged by Subjects.* Ed. C. Bascom Slemp. Garden City, N.Y.: Doubleday, Page & Co., 1926.

———. *The Price of Freedom: Speeches and Addresses.* New York: C. Scribner's Sons, 1924.

———. *Your Son, Calvin Coolidge: A Selection of Letters from Calvin Coolidge to His Father.* Ed. Edward Connery Lathem. Montpelier, Vt.: Vermont Historical Society, 1968.

Coolidge, Emma Downing. *Descendants of John and Mary Coolidge of Watertown, Massachusetts, 1630.* Boston: Wright & Potter Printing Company, 1930.

Coolidge, Grace Goodhue. *Grace Coolidge: An Autobiography.* Ed. Robert H. Ferrell and Lawrence E. Wikander. Worland, Wyo.: High Plains Publishing Company, 1992.

Coolidge, Harold Jefferson, and Robert Howard Lord. *Archibald Cary Coolidge: Life and Letters.* Boston: Houghton Mifflin Company, 1932.

Coolidge, Henry D., and James W. Kimball. *Manual for the Use of the General Court Containing the Rules of the Two Branches.* Boston: Wright & Potter Printing Company, 1913.

Cordery, Stacy A. *Alice: Alice Roosevelt Longworth, from White House Princess to Washington Power Broker.* New York: Penguin Group, 2007.

Curtis, Jane, Will Curtis, and Frank Lieberman. *Return to These Hills: The Vermont Years of Calvin Coolidge.* Woodstock, Vt.: Curtis-Lieberman Books, 1985.

Cutter, William Richard, and William Frederick Adams, eds. *Genealogical and Personal Memoirs Relating to the Families of the State of Massachusetts.* New York: Lewis Historical Publishing Company, 1910.

Dana, Henry Swan. *History of Woodstock, Vermont.* Boston: Houghton Mifflin and Company, 1889.

Davidson, Roger H., Susan Webb Hammond, and Raymond W. Smock, eds. *Masters of the House: Congressional Leadership over Two Centuries*. Boulder, Colo.: Westview Press/HarperCollins, 1998.

Davis, Shelley. *IRS Historical Fact Book: A Chronology*. Washington D.C.: Department of the Treasury, Internal Revenue Service, 1993.

Dawes, Charles G. *The First Year of the Budget of the United States*. New York: Harper & Brothers, 1923.

———. *Notes as Vice President: 1928–1929*. Boston: Little, Brown, 1935.

Day, Clarence. *In the Green Mountain Country*. New Haven, Conn.: Yale University Press, 1934.

Dean, John Wesley. *Warren G. Harding*. New York: Times Books, 2004.

Dennis, Alfred Pearce. *Gods and Little Fishes*. Indianapolis, Ind.: Bobbs-Merrill Company, 1924.

Dickinson, Emily. *The Letters of Emily Dickinson*. Ed. Thomas Herbert Johnson and Theodora Ward. Cambridge, Mass.: Belknap Press of Harvard University Press, 1958.

Doheny, David A. *David Finley: Quiet Force for America's Arts*. Washington, D.C.: National Trust for Historic Preservation, 2006.

Erskine, John. *The Memory of Certain Persons*. Philadelphia: J. B. Lippincott Company, 1947.

Fairbanks, Edward Taylor. *The Wrought Brim: Twelve Discourses Given in the South Church, St. Johnsbury, Vermont*. St. Johnsbury, Vt.: Press of the Caledonian Company, 1902.

Faulkner, Harold Underwood. *From Versailles to the New Deal: A Chronicle of the Harding-Coolidge-Hoover Era*. Chronicles of America Series, vol. 51. New Haven, Conn.: Yale University Press, 1950.

Felzenberg, Alvin Stephen. *The Leaders We Deserved (and a Few We Didn't): Rethinking the Presidential Rating Game*. New York: Basic Books, 2008.

Ferrell, Robert H. *Grace Coolidge: The People's Lady in Silent Cal's White House*. Lawrence: University of Kansas Press, 2008.

———. *Peace in Their Time: The Origins of the Kellogg-Briand Pact*. New Haven, Conn.: Yale University Press, 1952.

———. *The Presidency of Calvin Coolidge*. American Presidency Series. Lawrence: University Press of Kansas, 1998.

———. *The Strange Deaths of President Harding*. Columbia: University of Missouri Press, 1998.

Ferrell, Robert H., and Howard Quint, eds. *The Talkative President: The Off-the-Record Press Conferences of Calvin Coolidge*. Amherst: University of Massachusetts Press, 1964.

Fischer, Margaret Jane. *Calvin Coolidge, Jr., 1908–1924*. Plymouth Notch, Vt.: Calvin Coolidge Memorial Foundation, 1981.

Fleser, Arthur F. *A Rhetorical Study of the Speaking of Calvin Coolidge*. Lewiston, N.Y.: Edwin Mellen Press, 1990.

Flink, James J. *The Automobile Age*. Cambridge, Mass.: MIT Press, 1988.

Fourteenth Annual Report of the Police Commissioner for the City of Boston, Year Ending November 30, 1919. Boston: Wright & Potter Printing Co., 1920.

Fourth Annual Report of the Police Commissioner for the City of Boston, Year Ending November 30, 1909. Boston: Wright & Potter Printing Co., 1910.

Fried, Richard M. *The Man Everybody Knew: Bruce Barton and the Making of Modern America.* Chicago: Ivan R. Dee, 2005.

Frost, Robert, and Elinor Frost. *Family Letters of Robert and Elinor Frost.* Ed. Arnold E. Grade. Albany, N.Y.: State University of New York Press, 1972.

Fuess, Claude Moore, ed. *The Amherst Memorial Volume: A Record of the Contribution Made by Amherst College and Amherst Men in the World War, 1914–1918.* Amherst, Mass.: Amherst College Press, 1926.

———. *Amherst: The Story of a New England College.* Boston: Little, Brown, 1935.

———. *Calvin Coolidge: The Man from Vermont.* Boston: Little, Brown, 1940.

———. *Joseph B. Eastman: Servant of the People.* New York: Columbia University Press, 1952.

Gage, Beverly. *The Day Wall Street Exploded: A Story of America in Its First Age of Terror.* New York: Oxford University Press, 2009.

Garman, Charles Edward. *Letters, Lectures and Addresses of Charles Edward Garman: A Memorial Volume.* Ed. Eliza Miner Garman. Boston and New York: Houghton Mifflin, 1909.

Gawalt, Gerard W. *The Promise of Power: The Emergence of the Legal Profession in Massachusetts, 1760–1840.* Westport, Conn.: Greenwood Press, 1979.

Gilbert, Robert E. *The Tormented President: Calvin Coolidge, Death, and Clinical Depression.* Westport, Conn.: Praeger Publishers, 2003.

Gordon, Lyndall. *Lives like Loaded Guns: Emily Dickinson and Her Family's Feuds.* New York: Viking, 2012.

Green, Horace. *The Life of Calvin Coolidge.* New York: Duffield & Company, 1924.

Greenberg, David. *Calvin Coolidge.* New York: Times Books, 2007.

Greene, J. R. *A Bibliography of Pamphlets Relating to Calvin Coolidge, 1910–1988.* Northampton, Mass.: Forbes Library, 1989.

Gulick, Luther H. *Evolution of the Budget in Massachusetts.* New York: Macmillan, 1920.

Gullan, Harold I. *First Fathers: The Men Who Inspired Our Presidents.* Hoboken, N.J.: John Wiley & Sons, 2004.

Hanson, Ole. *Americanism Versus Bolshevism.* Garden City, N.Y.: Doubleday, Page & Co., 1920.

Harness, Gregory. *Presidential Vetoes, 1789–1988.* Washington, D.C.: U.S. Government Printing Office, 1992.

Harris, Seymour Edwin. *Economics of Harvard.* New York: McGraw-Hill, 1970.

Hatfield, Mark O., with the Senate Historical Office. *Vice-presidents of the United States, 1789–1993.* Senate Document 104–26, 1997.

Hawley, Ellis Wayne. *The Great War and the Search for a Modern Order: A History of the American People and Their Institutions, 1917–1933,* 2nd ed. New York: St. Martin's Press, 1992.

————, ed. *Herbert Hoover as Secretary of Commerce: Studies in New Era Thought and Practice.* Iowa City: University of Iowa Press, 1981.

Haynes, John Earl, ed. *Calvin Coolidge and the Coolidge Era: Essays on the History of the 1920s.* Washington, D.C.: Library of Congress, 1998.

Heller, Milton F. *The Presidents' Doctor: An Insider's View of Three First Families.* New York: Vantage Press, 2000.

Hennessy, Michael E. *Calvin Coolidge: From a Green Mountain to the White House.* New York: G. P. Putnam's Sons, 1924.

————. *Twenty-five Years of Massachusetts Politics: From Russell to McCall, 1890–1915.* Boston: Practical Politics, 1917.

Herman, Gerald. *The Pivotal Conflict: A Comprehensive Chronology of the First World War, 1914–1919.* New York: Greenwood Press, 1992.

Hillquit, Morris, Samuel Gompers, and Max J. Hayes. *The Double Edge of Labor's Sword: Discussion and Testimony on Socialism and Trade-Unionism Before the Commission on Industrial Relations.* Chicago: Socialist Party, National Office, 1914.

Holbrook, Stewart Hall. *Ethan Allen.* New York: Macmillan Company, 1940.

Hoover, Herbert. *The Memoirs of Herbert Hoover: Years of Adventure, 1874–1920.* New York: Macmillan Company, 1951.

Hoover, Herbert. *The Memoirs of Herbert Hoover: The Cabinet and the President, 1920–1933.* New York: Macmillan Company, 1952.

Hoover, Irwin Hood. *Forty-two Years in the White House.* Boston: Houghton Mifflin, 1934.

Hounshell, David A. *From the American System to Mass Production, 1800–1932: The Development of Manufacturing Technology in the United States.* Baltimore: Johns Hopkins University Press, 1984.

Howe, Mark De Wolfe. *Holmes-Laski Letters: The Correspondence of Mr. Justice Holmes and Harold J. Laski,* vol. 1, 1916–1935. New York: Atheneum, 1963.

Hutchinson, William T. *Lowden of Illinois: The Life of Frank O. Lowden.* Chicago: University of Chicago Press, 1957.

Jaffray, Elizabeth. *Secrets of the White House.* New York: Cosmopolitan Book Corporation, 1927.

Johnson, Carolyn W. *Winthrop Murray Crane: A Study in Republican Leadership, 1892–1920.* Northampton, Mass.: Smith College, 1967.

Kessner, Thomas. *The Flight of the Century: Charles Lindbergh and the Rise of American Aviation.* New York: Oxford University Press, 2010.

King, Stanley. *A History of the Endowment of Amherst College.* Amherst, Mass.: Amherst College, 1950.

Kinsley, Earle S. *Recollections of Vermonters in State and National Affairs.* Rutland, Vt.: privately printed, 1946.

Kull, Andrew. *New England Cemeteries: A Collector's Guide.* Brattleboro, Vt.: Stephen Greene Press, 1975.

Lathem, Edward Connery, ed. *Meet Calvin Coolidge: The Man Behind the Myth.* Brattleboro, Vt.: Stephen Greene Press, 1960.

Leach, William R. *Land of Desire: Merchants, Power and the Rise of a New American Culture*. New York: Pantheon Books, 1993.

Le Duc, Thomas. *Piety and Intellect at Amherst College, 1865–1912*. New York: Columbia University Press, 1946.

Lindbergh, Charles A. *The Spirit of St. Louis*. New York: Scribner, 2003.

———. *We*. New York: G. P. Putnam's Sons, 1927.

Longworth, Alice Roosevelt, and Michael Teague. *Mrs. L.: Conversations with Alice Roosevelt Longworth*. Garden City, N.Y.: Doubleday, 1981.

Lorant, Stefan. *The Life and Times of Theodore Roosevelt*. Garden City, N.Y.: Doubleday, 1959.

Lovestone, Jay. *The Coolidge Program: Capitalist Democracy & Prosperity Exposed*. New York: Workers Library, 1927.

Lowry, Edward. *Washington Close-ups: Intimate Views of Some Public Figures*. Boston: Houghton Mifflin, 1921.

Marchand, Roland. *Advertising the American Dream: Making Way for Modernity, 1920–1940*. Berkeley: University of California Press, 1985.

Martin, Christopher T. *Edward Filene and the Promise of Industrial Democracy*. PhD diss., University of Rochester, 2002.

Mason, Alpheus Thomas. *Brandeis: A Free Man's Life*. New York: Viking Press, 1946.

———. *Harlan Fiske Stone: Pillar of the Law*. New York: Viking Press, 1956.

May, Lary. *Screening Out the Past: The Birth of Mass Culture and the Motion Picture Industry*. Oxford, England: Oxford University Press, 1980.

McAdoo, William Gibbs. *Crowded Years: The Reminiscences of William G. McAdoo*. Boston: Houghton Mifflin, 1931.

McCartney, Laton. *The Teapot Domes: How Big Oil Bought the Harding White House and Tried to Steal the Country*. New York: Random House: 2008.

McCoy, Donald R. *Calvin Coolidge: The Quiet President*. New York: Macmillan Company, 1967.

McKenna, Marian Cecilia. *Borah*. Ann Arbor: University of Michigan Press, 1961.

McLean, Evalyn Walsh. *Father Struck It Rich*. Boston: Little, Brown, 1936.

Mertins, Louis. *Robert Frost: Life and Talks-Walking*. Norman: University of Oklahoma Press, 1965.

Moran, Philip R., ed. *Calvin Coolidge, 1872–1933: Chronology, Documents, Bibliographical Aids*. Dobbs Ferry, N.Y.: Oceana Publications, 1970.

Morello, John A. *Selling the President, 1920: Albert D. Lasker, Advertising, and the Election of Warren G. Harding*. Westport, Conn.: Praeger, 2001.

Morse, Anson D. *Parties and Party Leaders*. Boston, Mass.: Marshall Jones Company, 1923.

Mott, Frank Luther. *Golden Multitudes: The Story of Best Sellers in the United States*. New York: Macmillan Company, 1947.

Murray, Robert K. *The Harding Era: Warren G. Harding and His Administration*. Minneapolis: University of Minnesota Press, 1969.

———. *Red Scare: A Study in National Hysteria, 1919–1920*. Minneapolis: University of Minnesota Press, 1956.

Nedwick, Robert S. *Nedwick's Season of Frost: An Interrupted Biography of Robert Frost.* Ed. William A. Sutton. Albany: State University of New York Press, 1976.

Nelson, Adam R. *Education and Democracy: The Meaning of Alexander Meiklejohn, 1872–1964.* Madison: University of Wisconsin Press, 2001.

Nicolson, Harold. *Dwight Morrow.* London: Constable & Co., 1935.

O'Brien, Ruth. *Workers' Paradox: The Republican Origins of New Deal Labor Policy, 1886–1935.* Chapel Hill: University of North Carolina Press, 1998.

O'Brien, William Francis, ed. *Two Peacemakers in Paris.* College Station: Texas A&M, 1978.

O'Connor, Harvey. *Mellon's Millions: The Biography of a Fortune; the Life and Times of Andrew W. Mellon.* New York: John Day Company, 1933.

Olson, James Stuart. *Historical Dictionary of the 1920s: From World War I to the New Deal, 1919–1933.* New York: Greenwood Press, 1988.

Papke, David Ray. *The Pullman Case: The Clash of Labor and Capital in Industrial America.* Lawrence: University Press of Kansas, 1999.

Pearson, Henry Greenleaf. *Son of New England: James Jackson Storrow, 1864–1926.* Boston: Thomas Todd, 1932.

Pepper, George Wharton. *Philadelphia Lawyer: An Autobiography.* Philadelphia: J. B. Lippincott, 1944.

Perry, Eugene H. *A Socrates for All Seasons: Alexander Meiklejohn and Deliberative Democracy.* Bloomington, Ind.: iUniverse, 2011.

Pietrusza, David. *1920: The Year of the Six Presidents.* New York: Carroll and Graf, 2010.

Powell, Fred Wilbur. *The Recent Movement for State Budget Reform, 1911–1917.* New York: Columbia University, 1918.

Pringle, Henry F. *Theodore Roosevelt: A Biography.* New York: Harcourt Brace, 1931.

Pritchard, William H. *Frost: A Literary Life Reconsidered.* New York: Oxford University Press, 1984.

Puleo, Stephen. *The Boston Italians: A Story of Pride, Perseverance, and Paesani, from the Years of the Great Immigration to the Present Day.* Boston: Beacon Press, 2007.

Richards, Leonard L. *Shays's Rebellion: The American Revolution's Final Battle.* Philadelphia: University of Pennsylvania Press, 2002.

Roberts, Kenneth Lewis. *Concentrated New England: A Sketch of Calvin Coolidge.* Indianapolis, Ind.: Bobbs-Merrill Company, 1924.

Robinson, Ray. *American Original: A Life of Will Rogers.* New York: Oxford University Press, 1996.

Roosevelt, Franklin D. *F.D.R., His Personal Letters; Early Years.* Ed. Elliott Roosevelt. New York: Duell, Sloan and Pearce, 1947.

Roosevelt, Theodore. *Theodore Roosevelt: An Autobiography.* New York: Macmillan, 1913.

Ross, Ishbel. *Grace Coolidge and Her Era: The Story of a President's Wife.* Plymouth, Vt.: Calvin Coolidge Memorial Foundation, 1988.

Rossiter, William Sidney, ed. *Days and Ways in Old Boston.* Boston: R. H. Stearns and Company, 1915.

Russell, Francis. *A City in Terror: 1919, the Boston Police Strike*. New York: Viking Press, 1976.

———. *A City in Terror: Calvin Coolidge and the 1919 Boston Police Strike*. Boston: Beacon Press, 2005.

Savage, Edward H. *Police Records and Recollections, or, Boston by Daylight and Gaslight*. Boston: Joseph P. Dale and Co., 1873.

Sawyer, Roland D. *Cal Coolidge, President*. Boston: Four Seas Company, 1924.

Schortemeier, Frederick E. *Rededicating America: Life and Recent Speeches of Warren G. Harding*. Indianapolis, Ind.: Bobbs-Merrill Company, 1920.

Schriftgiesser, Karl. *The Gentleman from Massachusetts: Henry Cabot Lodge*. Boston: Atlantic Monthly Press/Little, Brown, 1944.

Secretary of the Commonwealth of Massachusetts. *Number of Assessed Polls, Registered Voters and Persons Who Voted in Each Voting Precinct at the State, City and Town Elections*. Boston: Wright & Potter Printing Co., 1918.

Seelye, John. *Memory's Nation: The Place of Plymouth Rock*. Chapel Hill: University of North Carolina Press, 1998.

Silver, Thomas B. *Coolidge and the Historians*. Durham, N.C.: Carolina Academic Press for the Claremont Institute, 1982.

Slade, William. *Vermont State Papers: Being a Collection of Records and Documents, Connected with the Assumption and Establishment of Government by the People of Vermont, from the Year 1779 to 1786, Inclusive*. Middlebury, Vt.: J. W. Copeland, 1823.

Slater, Joseph. *Public Workers: Government Employee Unions, the Law and the State, 1900–1962*. Ithaca, N.Y.: Cornell University Press, 2004.

Smith, Ira R. T., with Joe Alex Morris. *"Dear Mr. President . . .": The Story of Fifty Years in the White House Mail Room*. New York: Julian Messner, 1949.

Smith, Rex Alan. *The Carving of Mount Rushmore*. New York: Abbeville Press, 1985.

Smulyan, Susan. *Selling Radio: The Commercialization of American Broadcasting, 1920–1934*. Washington, D.C.: Smithsonian Institution Press, 1994.

Sobel, Robert. *Coolidge: An American Enigma*. Washington, D.C.: Regnery, 1998.

Sparks, George, ed. *A Many Colored Toga: The Diary of Henry Fountain Ashurst*. Tucson: University of Arizona, 1962.

Stanlis, Peter J. *Robert Frost: The Poet as Philosopher*. Wilmington, Del.: ISI Books, 2007.

Starbuck, Dane. *The Goodriches: An American Family*. Indianapolis, Ind.: Liberty Fund, 2001.

Starling, Edmund W. *Starling of the White House: The Story of the Man Whose Secret Service Detail Guarded Five Presidents from Woodrow Wilson to Franklin D. Roosevelt*. New York: Simon and Schuster, 1946.

Stearn, Gerald Emanuel. *Gompers*. Englewood Cliffs, N.J.: Prentice-Hall, 1971.

Sterling, Bryan B., and Frances M. *Will Rogers' World: America's Foremost Political Humorist Comments on the Twenties and Thirties—and Eighties and Nineties*. New York: M. Evans and Company, 1989.

Taft, William Howard. *Popular Government: Its Essence, Its Permanence and Its Perils.* New Haven, Conn.: Yale University Press, 1913.

Tager, Jack. *Boston Riots: Three Centuries of Social Violence.* Boston: Northeastern University Press, 2001.

Taliaferro, John. *Great White Fathers: The Story of the Obsessive Quest to Create Mount Rushmore.* New York: Public Affairs, 2002.

The Minimum Wage: A Failing Experiment. Together with Some Sidelights on the Massachusetts Experience. Boston: Executive Committee of Merchants and Manufacturers of Massachusetts, 1916.

The Tercentenary History Committee (Town of Northampton). *The Northampton Book: Chapters from 300 Years in the Life of a New England Town, 1654–1954.* Northampton, Mass.: Northampton Tercentenary Committee, 1956.

Theoharis, Athan G., and John Stuart Cox. *The Boss: J. Edgar Hoover and the Great American Inquisition.* Philadelphia: Temple University Press, 1988.

Thompson, Lawrence Roger. *Robert Frost: The Early Years, 1874–1915.* New York: Holt, Rinehart and Winston, 1966.

Unger, Nancy C. *Fighting Bob La Follette: The Righteous Reformer.* Chapel Hill: University of North Carolina Press, 2000.

U.S. Department of Commerce. *Historical Statistics of the United States: Colonial Times to 1970.* Washington, D.C.: U.S. Government Printing Office, 1975.

Vermont Legislative Directory. *Vermont Legislative History.* Montpelier, Vt.: Capital Press, 1910.

Wallace, Jerry L. *Calvin Coolidge: Our First Radio President.* Plymouth, Vt.: Calvin Coolidge Memorial Foundation, 2008.

Warner, Charles F., and Frederick Knab (artist). *Northampton of Today: Depicted by Pen and Camera.* Northampton, Mass.: Picturesque Publishing Company, 1902.

Washburn, R. M. *Calvin Coolidge: His First Biography.* Boston: Small, Maynard and Company, 1923.

Waterhouse, John Almon. *Calvin Coolidge Meets Charles Edward Garman.* Rutland, Vt.: Academy Books, 1984.

Watson, Bruce. *Bread and Roses: Mills, Migrants, and the Struggle for the American Dream.* New York: Viking, 2005.

———. *Sacco and Vanzetti: The Men, the Murders, and the Judgment of Mankind.* New York: Penguin Group, 2007.

Watson, James E. *As I Knew Them: Memoirs of James E. Watson, Former United States Senator from Indiana.* Indianapolis, Ind.: Bobbs-Merrill Company, 1936.

Wayman, Dorothy G. *David I. Walsh: Citizen-Patriot.* Milwaukee, Wis.: Bruce Publishing Co., 1952.

Weatherson, Michael A., and Hal W. Bochin. *Hiram Johnson: Political Revivalist.* Lanham, Md.: University Press of America, 1995.

Webb, Kenneth. *From Plymouth Notch to President: The Farm Boyhood of Calvin Coolidge.* Taftsville, Vt.: Countryman Press, 1978.

Well, Susan Lewis. *Calvin Coolidge at Home in Northampton.* Northampton, Mass.: Calvin Coolidge Presidential Library and Museum, Forbes Library, 2008.

Welter, Rush. *Bennington, Vermont: An Industrial History.* New York: Columbia University, 1959.

White, William Allen. *Calvin Coolidge: The Man Who Is President.* New York: Macmillan Company, 1925.

———. *A Puritan in Babylon: The Story of Calvin Coolidge.* New York: Macmillan Company, 1938.

———. *Selected Letters of William Allen White, 1899–1943.* Ed. Walter Johnson. New York: H. Holt and Company, 1947.

Whiting, Edward Elwell. *President Coolidge: A Contemporary Estimate.* Boston: Atlantic Monthly Press, 1923.

Wikander, Lawrence E. *Disposed to Learn: The First Seventy-five Years of Forbes Library.* Northampton, Mass.: Trustees of Forbes Library, 1972.

Wilbur, Ruth E., and C. Keith Wilbur. *Bid Us God Speed: The History of the Edwards Church of Northampton, Massachusetts, 1883–1983.* Canaan, N.H.: Phoenix Publishing, 1983.

Wilson, Douglas, *Passages of Time: Narratives in the History of Amherst College.* Amherst, Mass.: Amherst College Press, 2007.

Wilson, Woodrow. *The Papers of Woodrow Wilson,* vol. 63, September–November 5, 1919. Ed. Arthur S. Link and J. E. Little. Princeton, N.J.: Princeton University Press, 1990.

Wooddy, Carroll H. *The Growth of the Federal Government, 1915–1932.* New York: McGraw-Hill, 1934.

Woods, Robert Archey. *The Preparation of Calvin Coolidge: An Interpretation.* Boston: Houghton Mifflin Company, 1924.

Yagoda, Ben. *Will Rogers: A Biography.* New York: Knopf, 1993.

Yale, Allen Rice, Jr. *Ingenious and Enterprising Mechanics: A Case Study of Industrialization in Rural Vermont, 1815–1900.* PhD diss., University of Connecticut, 1995.

SPECIAL DOCUMENTS AND ARTICLES

Blair, John. "Calvin Coolidge and the Advent of Radio Politics." *Vermont History Journal* 44, no. 1 (1976): 28–37.

Boston Police Commissioner's records, January 1, 1919, to December 31, 1919. Boston Public Library, http://bpl.bibliocommons.com/item/show/3279360042_police_records.

Buckley, Kerry W. "A President for the 'Great Silent Majority': Bruce Barton's Construction of Calvin Coolidge." *The New England Quarterly* 76, no. 4 (December 2003): 593–626.

"Dates, Data and Ditties: Tour of Duty, 'A' Company, 11th Regiment Infantry Massachusetts State Guard During the Strike of the Boston Police." Boston, 1920.

Lauck, Jett. "The Lesson from Lawrence." *North American Review* 195, no. 678 (May 1912): 665–672.

McQuaid, Kim. "An American Owenite: Edward A. Filene and the Parameters of Industrial Reform, 1890–1937." *American Journal of Economics and Sociology* 35, no. 1 (January 1976): 80.

"Pearls of Wisdom from Many Lips." *Locomotive Engineers' Monthly Journal* 44, no. 12 (1910): 1030.

Pollitt, Brian H. "The Cuban Sugar Economy and the Great Depression." *Bulletin of Latin American Research* 3, no. 2 (1984): 3–28.

"President Coolidge Number." *Black Hills Engineer* 15, no. 4, 1927.

The Real Calvin Coolidge, vols. 1–18. Presidential Library, Calvin Coolidge Memorial Foundation, Plymouth Notch, Vt.

Shugerman, Jed Handelsman. "The Floodgates of Strict Liability: Bursting Reservoirs and the Adoption of Fletcher V. Rylands in the Gilded Age." *The Yale Law Journal* 110, no. 2 (2000): 333–378.

Simplich, Frederick. "The Great Mississippi Flood of 1927." *National Geographic* 52, no. 3 (September 1927): 268.

Stagner, Stephen. "The Recall of Judicial Decisions and the Due Process Debate." *American Journal of Legal History* 24, no. 3 (July 1980): 257.

Walton, Jill M. "Northampton Local Monuments: Testaments to an Enduring Historical Legacy." *Historical Journal of Massachusetts* 33, no. 1 (2005): 57–84.

Wiegand, Wayne A. "The 'Amherst Method': The Origins of the Dewey Decimal Classification Scheme." *Libraries & Culture* 33, no. 2 (1998): 175–194.

ARCHIVES

Amherst College. Catalogs. Amherst College Archives and Special Collections, Amherst, Mass.

Boone, Joel T. Papers. Library of Congress, Washington, D.C.

Castle, William R. Diaries, Houghton Library, Harvard University.

Clark, Edward Tracy. Papers. Library of Congress, Washington, D.C.

Coolidge Family Papers Addendum. Vermont Historical Society, Montpelier, Vt.

Coolidge Family Papers. Vermont Historical Society, Montpelier, Vt.

Coolidge, Calvin. Papers. Library of Congress, Washington D.C.

Coolidge, Calvin. Papers. Forbes Library, Northampton, Mass.

Coolidge, Calvin, Unpublished Press Conferences, Calvin Coolidge Memorial Collection, Forbes Library, Northampton, Mass.

Coolidge, Carlos. "Inaugural Address of Carlos Coolidge as It Appears in the Journal of the Senate October Session 1848." Burlington, Vt., October 19, 1848.

———. "Inaugural Address of Carlos Coolidge as It Appears in the Journal of the Senate October Session 1849." Burlington, Vt., October 13, 1849.

Coolidge, Grace. Round Robin Letters, 1923–1969. Special Collections, Calvin Coolidge Memorial Foundation, Plymouth Notch, Vt.

Dawes, Charles G. Papers, Special Collections, Northwestern University Library, Evanston, Ill.

Fuess, Claude, Collection. Calvin Coolidge Presidential Library and Museum, Forbes Library, Northampton, Mass.

———. Materials for a Biography of Frank Waterman Stearns. Amherst College Archives and Special Collections, Amherst, Mass.

Garman Family Papers. Amherst College Archives and Special Collections, Amherst, Mass.

Hall, Jozy Dell, ed. "White House Days: An Extraction from the Washington Post from Aug. 3, 1923–March 5, 1929." Washington, D.C., January 1931 (typed manuscript).

Harvard University. The Law School of Harvard University, Announcements, 1895–96. Cambridge, Mass.

Judah, Brandon Noble. "Diary of My Stay in Cuba." Library of Congress, Washington, D.C.

Maurer, Irving. Diaries. Beloit College Archives, Beloit, Mich.

Meteorological Observations at the Hatch Experiment Station, Massachusetts Agricultural College. Bulletin No. 21. Amherst, Mass., September 1890.

Meteorological Observations at the Hatch Experiment Station, Massachusetts Agricultural College. Bulletin No. 289–384. Amherst, Mass., 1913–1920.

Morrow, Dwight W. Papers. Amherst College Archives and Special Collections, Amherst, Mass.

Office of the Treasury. Central Files. National Archives and Record Administration II, College Park, Md.

Riley, Ellen. White House Papers. Vermont Historical Society, Barre, Vt.

Sanders, Everett. Papers. Library of Congress, Washington, D.C.

Stearns Family Papers. Holy Cross College Special Collections. Holy Cross College, Worcester, Mass.

Stearns, Frank W. Papers. Phillips Academy Archive, Andover, Mass.

INDEX

⌣~⌣~⌣

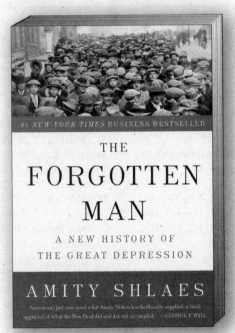